GATEWAY TO THE GREAT BOOKS

GATEWAY
TO THE
GREAT BOOKS

Gateway
to the
Great Books

ROBERT M. HUTCHINS, MORTIMER J. ADLER
Editors in Chief

CLIFTON FADIMAN
Associate Editor

7

MAN AND

SOCIETY

Encyclopædia Britannica, Inc.

WILLIAM BENTON
Publisher

Chicago, London, Toronto, Geneva, Sydney

Portrait illustrations are by Fred Steffen

Contents
of Volume 7

Sir Francis Bacon [1]

1561–1626

The world to which Bacon addresses himself in these essays—indeed, in all of his essays—is both a greater and a smaller thing than the world that Henry Adams, for example, talks about. It is smaller in so far as it lacks both a future and a past, having only a present. Yet it is greater, too, in that its present has a permanence which the passage of three hundred years has very little modified. For the subject of these essays is superior to history, being the world as it exists at any time—the world that has young men and old, parents and children, marriage and single life, great place, seditions and troubles, custom and education, followers and friends, usury (or interest), and riches—the world, in short, that does not move or change. It is the world we have always with us, being human; and to know it is to recognize ourselves.

Not that in any sense it is the best world possible; it is merely the best one going, and the worst, since it is the only one there is. Bacon is serene about this, as any man may be whose philosopher in worldly matters is Machiavelli. Perhaps a better world can be conceived. In terms of these essays, it might combine the virtues of youth and age, just as it might be altogether free of civil strife, or cause men to act according to their knowledge rather than from habit. But none of those things happens to be true, Bacon reminds us, in the world that confronts us, of which we are obliged to make, he says, the best use we can.

Nor is there after all any lack of motion in such a world, lest we think it tame or dull. The motion is made by men as they move through it—as they rise, for instance, in the hierarchy of its stations.

---

[1] For a biography of Sir Francis Bacon, see Vol. 5, pp. 90–92, in this set.

1

Bacon, who did just that, is concerned to counsel those who do it after him, and to save them also from falling as he fell. Both things can happen in his world, which stands still while men attempt to master it, and waits too while one collects the truth about it in these brief and brilliant essays.

Of Youth
and Age

A man that is young in years may be old in hours, if he have lost no time. But that happeneth rarely. Generally, youth is like the first cogitations, not so wise as the second. For there is a youth in thoughts, as well as in ages. And yet the invention of young men is more lively than that of old; and imaginations stream into their minds better, and as it were more divinely. Natures that have much heat and great and violent desires and perturbations are not ripe for action till they have passed the meridian of their years; as it was with Julius Caesar, and Septimius Severus. Of the latter of whom it is said, *Juventutem egit erroribus, imo furoribus, plenam* [He spent a youth full of errors, even of madness]. And yet he was the ablest emperor, almost, of all the list. But reposed natures may do well in youth. As it is seen in Augustus Caesar, Cosmus Duke of Florence, Gaston de Fois, and others. On the other side, heat and vivacity in age is an excellent composition for business.

Young men are fitter to invent than to judge; fitter for execution than for counsel; and fitter for new projects than for settled business. For the experience of age, in things that fall within the compass of it, directeth them; but in new things, abuseth them. The errors of young men are the ruin of business; but the errors of aged men amount but to this, that more might have been done, or sooner. Young men, in the conduct and manage of actions, embrace more than they can hold; stir more than they can quiet; fly to the end, without consideration of the means and degrees; pursue some few principles which they have chanced upon absurdly; care not to innovate, which draws unknown inconveniences; use extreme remedies at first; and that which doubleth all errors, will not acknowledge or retract them; like an unready horse, that will neither stop nor turn. Men of age object too much, consult too long, adventure too little, repent too soon, and seldom drive business home to the full period, but content

3

themselves with a mediocrity of success. Certainly it is good to compound employments of both; for that will be good for the present, because the virtues of either age may correct the defects of both; and good for succession, that young men may be learners, while men in age are actors; and, lastly, good for extern accidents, because authority followeth old men, and favour and popularity youth. But for the moral part, perhaps youth will have the pre-eminence, as age hath for the politic.

A certain rabbin, upon the text, "Your young men shall see visions, and your old men shall dream dreams," inferreth that young men are admitted nearer to God than old, because vision is a clearer revelation than a dream. And certainly, the more a man drinketh of the world, the more it intoxicateth: and age doth profit rather in the powers of understanding, than in the virtues of the will and affections. There be some have an over-early ripeness in their years, which fadeth betimes. These are, first, such as have brittle wits, the edge whereof is soon turned; such as was Hermogenes the rhetorician, whose books are exceeding subtle; who afterwards waxed stupid. A second sort is of those that have some natural dispositions which have better grace in youth than in age; such as is a fluent and luxuriant speech; which becomes youth well, but not age: so Tully saith of Hortensius, *Idem manebat, neque idem decebat* [He continued in the same manner, even when it no longer became him]. The third is of such as take too high a strain at the first, and are magnanimous more than tract of years can uphold. As was Scipio Africanus, of whom Livy saith in effect, *Ultima primis cedebant* [His last days were not equal to his first].

Of Parents
and Children

The joys of parents are secret; and so are their griefs and fears. They cannot utter the one; nor they will not utter the other. Children sweeten labours; but they make misfortunes more bitter. They increase the cares of life; but they mitigate the remembrance of death. The perpetuity by generation is common to beasts; but memory, merit, and noble works are proper to men. And surely a man shall see the noblest works and foundations have proceeded from childless men; which have sought to express the images of their minds, where those of their bodies have failed. So the care of posterity is most in them that have no posterity. They that are the first raisers of their houses are most indulgent towards their children; beholding them as the continuance not only of their kind but of their work; and so both children and creatures.

The difference in affection of parents towards their several children is many times unequal; and sometimes unworthy; especially in the mother; as Solomon saith, "A wise son rejoiceth the father, but an ungracious son shames the mother." A man shall see, where there is a house full of children, one or two of the eldest respected, and the youngest made wantons; but in the midst some that are as it were forgotten, who many times nevertheless prove the best. The illiberality of parents in allowance towards their children is an harmful error; makes them base; acquaints them with shifts; makes them sort with mean company; and makes them surfeit more when they come to plenty. And therefore the proof is best, when men keep their authority towards their children, but not their purse. Men have a foolish manner (both parents and schoolmasters and servants) in creating and breeding an emulation between brothers during childhood, which many times sorteth to discord when they are men, and disturbeth families. The Italians make little difference between children and nephews or near kinsfolk; but so they be of the lump, they care not

5

though they pass not through their own body. And, to say truth, in nature it is much a like matter; insomuch that we see a nephew sometimes resembleth an uncle or a kinsman more than his own parents; as the blood happens. Let parents choose betimes the vocations and courses they mean their children should take; for then they are most flexible; and let them not too much apply themselves to the disposition of their children, as thinking they will take best to that which they have most mind to. It is true, that if the affection or aptness of the children be extraordinary, then it is good not to cross it; but generally the precept is good, *optimum elige, suave et facile illud faciet consuetudo* [choose the best; habit will make it pleasant and easy]. Younger brothers are commonly fortunate, but seldom or never where the elder are disinherited.

Of Marriage
and Single Life

H e that hath wife and children hath given hostages to fortune; for they are impediments to great enterprises, either of virtue or mischief. Certainly the best works, and of greatest merit for the public, have proceeded from the unmarried or childless men; which both in affection and means have married and endowed the public. Yet it were great reason that those that have children should have greatest care of future times; unto which they know they must transmit their dearest pledges. Some there are, who though they lead a single life, yet their thoughts do end with themselves, and account future times impertinences. Nay, there are some other that account wife and children but as bills of charges. Nay more, there are some foolish, rich, covetous men that take a pride in having no children, because they may be thought so much the richer. For perhaps they have heard some talk, "Such an one is a great rich man," and another except to it, "Yea, but he hath a great charge of children"; as if it were an abatement to his riches. But the most ordinary cause of a single life is liberty, especially in certain self-pleasing and humorous minds, which are so sensible of every restraint, as they will go near to think their girdles and garters to be bonds and shackles. Unmarried men are best friends, best masters, best servants; but not always best subjects; for they are light to run away; and almost all fugitives are of that condition.

A single life doth well with churchmen; for charity will hardly water the ground where it must first fill a pool. It is indifferent for judges and magistrates; for if they be facile and corrupt, you shall have a servant five times worse than a wife. For soldiers, I find the generals commonly in their hortatives put men in mind of their wives and children; and I think the despising of marriage amongst the Turks maketh the vulgar soldier more base. Certainly wife and children are a kind of discipline of

7

humanity; and single men, though they may be many times more charitable, because their means are less exhaust, yet, on the other side, they are more cruel and hardhearted (good to make severe inquisitors), because their tenderness is not so oft called upon.

Grave natures, led by custom, and therefore constant, are commonly loving husbands; as was said of Ulysses, *vetulam suam praetulit immortalitati* [he preferred his aged wife to immortality]. Chaste women are often proud and forward, as presuming upon the merit of their chastity. It is one of the best bonds both of chastity and obedience in the wife if she think her husband wise; which she will never do if she find him jealous. Wives are young men's mistresses; companions for middle age; and old men's nurses. So as a man may have a quarrel to marry when he will. But yet he was reputed one of the wise men that made answer to the question, when a man should marry?—"A young man not yet, an elder man not at all." It is often seen that bad husbands have very good wives; whether it be that it raiseth the price of their husband's kindness when it comes; or that the wives take a pride in their patience. But this never fails if the bad husbands were of their own choosing, against their friends' consent; for then they will be sure to make good their own folly.

Of Great Place

Men in great place are thrice servants: servants of the sovereign or state; servants of fame; and servants of business. So as they have no freedom; neither in their persons, nor in their actions, nor in their times. It is a strange desire, to seek power and to lose liberty: or to seek power over others and to lose power over a man's self. The rising unto place is laborious; and by pains men come to greater pains; and it is sometimes base; and by indignities men come to dignities. The standing is slippery, and the regress is either a downfall, or at least an eclipse, which is a melancholy thing. *Cum non sis qui fueris, non esse cur velis vivere* [When you are not what you were, there is no reason for you to wish to live longer]. Nay, retire men cannot when they would, neither will they when it were reason; but are impatient of privateness, even in age and sickness, which require the shadow; like old townsmen, that will be still sitting at their street door, though thereby they offer age to scorn. Certainly great persons had need to borrow other men's opinions, to think themselves happy; for if they judge by their own feeling, they cannot find it: but if they think with themselves what other men think of them, and that other men would fain be as they are, then they are happy as it were by report; when perhaps they find the contrary within. For they are the first that find their own griefs, though they be the last that find their own faults.

Certainly men in great fortunes are strangers to themselves, and while they are in the puzzle of business they have no time to tend their health either of body or mind. *Illi mors gravis incubat, qui notus nimis omnibus, ignotus moritur sibi* [Death lies heavily upon him who, too well-known to all, dies unknown to himself]. In place there is licence to do good and evil; whereof the latter is a curse: for in evil the best condition is not to will; the second not to can. But power to do good is the true and lawful end of aspiring. For good thoughts (though God accept them) yet towards men are little better than good dreams, except they be put in act;

9

and that cannot be without power and place, as the vantage and commanding ground. Merit and good works is the end of man's motion; and conscience of the same is the accomplishment of man's rest. For if a man can be partaker of God's theatre, he shall likewise be partaker of God's rest. *Et conversus Deus, ut aspiceret opera quae fecerunt manus suae, vidit quod omnia essent bona nimis* [And God turned to consider the works of his own hands, and he saw that they were all exceedingly good]; and then the sabbath.

In the discharge of thy place set before thee the best examples; for imitation is a globe of precepts. And after a time set before thee thine own example; and examine thyself strictly whether thou didst not best at first. Neglect not also the examples of those that have carried themselves ill in the same place; not to set off thyself by taxing their memory, but to direct thyself what to avoid. Reform therefore, without bravery or scandal of former times and persons; but yet set it down to thyself as well to create good precedents as to follow them. Reduce things to the first institution, and observe wherein and how they have degenerate; but yet ask counsel of both times; of the ancient time, what is best; and of the latter time, what is fittest. Seek to make thy course regular, that men may know beforehand what they may expect; but be not too positive and peremptory; and express thyself well when thou digressest from thy rule. Preserve the right of thy place; but stir not questions of jurisdiction: and rather assume thy right in silence and *de facto*, than voice it with claims and challenges. Preserve likewise the rights of inferior places; and think it more honour to direct in chief than to be busy in all. Embrace and invite helps and advices touching the execution of thy place; and do not drive away such as bring thee information, as meddlers; but accept of them in good part.

The vices of authority are chiefly four: delays, corruption, roughness, and facility. For delays; give easy access; keep times appointed; go through with that which is in hand, and interlace not business but of necessity. For corruption; do not only bind thine own hands or thy servants' hands from taking, but bind the hands of suitors also from offering. For integrity used doth the one; but integrity professed, and with a manifest detestation of bribery, doth the other. And avoid not only the fault, but the suspicion. Whosoever is found variable, and changeth manifestly without manifest cause, giveth suspicion of corruption. Therefore always when thou changest thine opinion or course, profess it plainly, and declare it, together with the reasons that move thee to change; and do not think to steal it. A servant or a favourite, if he be inward, and no other apparent cause of esteem, is commonly thought but a byway to close corruption. For roughness; it is a needless cause of discontent: severity breedeth fear, but roughness breedeth hate. Even reproofs from authority ought to be grave, and not taunting. As for facility; it is worse than bribery. For bribes come but now and then; but if importunity or idle respects lead a man, he shall never be without. As Solomon saith, "To respect persons is not good; for such a man will transgress for a piece of bread." It is most true that was anciently spoken, "A place showeth the man." And it showeth some to the better, and some to the worse. *Omnium consensu capax imperii, nisi imperasset* [Had he not been emperor, all would have agreed that he was worthy of holding supreme power], saith Tacitus of Galba; but of Vespasian he saith, *Solus imperantium, Vespasianus mutatus in melius* [Vespasian alone was changed for the better by the possession of power], though the one was meant of sufficiency, the other of manners and affection. It is an assured sign of a worthy and generous spirit, whom honour amends. For honour is, or should be, the place of virtue; and as in nature things move violently to their place and calmly in their place, so virtue in ambition is violent, in authority settled and calm. All rising to great place is by a winding stair; and if there be factions, it is good to side a man's self whilst he is in the rising, and to balance himself when he is placed. Use the memory of thy predecessor fairly and tenderly; for if thou dost not, it is a debt will sure be paid when thou art gone. If thou have colleagues, respect them, and rather call them when they look not for it, than exclude them when they have reason to look to be called. Be not too sensible or too remembering of thy place in conversation and private answers to suitors; but let it rather be said, "When he sits in place he is another man."

Of Seditions
and Troubles

Shepherds of people had need know the calendars of tempests in state; which are commonly greatest when things grow to equality; as natural tempests are greatest about the *Equinoctia*. And as there are certain hollow blasts of wind and secret swellings of seas before a tempest, so are there in states:

> *Ille etiam caecos instare tumultus*
> *Saepe monet, fraudesque et operta tumescere bella.*

[Often a violent commotion gives warning of dark disturbances, of deception and secret war ready to burst forth.—Virgil.]

Libels and licentious discourses against the state, when they are frequent and open; and in like sort, false news often running up and down to the disadvantage of the state, and hastily embraced; are amongst the signs of troubles. Virgil giving the pedigree of Fame, saith "she was sister to the Giants":

> *Illam Terra parens, ira irritata Deorum,*
> *Extremam (ut perhibent) Coeo Enceladoque sororem*
> *Progenuit.*

[Mother Earth, in wrath at the anger of the gods, brought forth that youngest sister (as they assert) of Coeus and Enceladus.]

As if fames were the relics of seditions past; but they are no less indeed the preludes of seditions to come. Howsoever he noteth it right, that seditious tumults and seditious fames differ no more but as brother and sister, masculine and feminine; especially if it come to that, that the best actions of a state, and the most plausible, and which ought to give greatest contentment, are taken in ill sense, and traduced: for that shows the envy great, as Tacitus saith, *conflata magna invidia, seu bene seu male gesta premunt* [when great ill will is kindled against the government, both

12

good and evil actions are oppressive]. Neither doth it follow, that because these fames are a sign of troubles, that the suppressing of them with too much severity should be a remedy of troubles. For the despising of them many times checks them best; and the going about to stop them doth but make a wonder long-lived. Also that kind of obedience which Tacitus speaketh of, is to be held suspected: *Erant in officio, sed tamen qui mallent mandata imperantium interpretari, quam exequi* [There are those in office who prefer interpreting commands to executing them]; disputing, excusing, cavilling upon mandates and directions, is a kind of shaking off the yoke, and assay of disobedience; especially if in those disputings they which are for the direction speak fearfully and tenderly, and those that are against it audaciously.

Also, as Machiavel noteth well, when princes, that ought to be common parents, make themselves as a party, and lean to a side, it is as a boat that is overthrown by uneven weight on the one side; as was well seen in the time of Henry the Third of France; for first himself entered league for the extirpation of the Protestants; and presently after the same league was turned upon himself. For when the authority of princes is made but an accessary to a cause, and that there be other bands that tie faster than the band of sovereignty, kings begin to be put almost out of possession.

Also, when discords, and quarrels, and factions are carried openly and audaciously, it is a sign the reverence of government is lost. For the motions of the greatest persons in a government ought to be as the motions of the planets under *primum mobile;* (according to the old opinion) which is, that every of them is carried swiftly by the highest motion, and softly in their own motion. And therefore, when great ones in their own particular motion move violently, and, as Tacitus expresseth it well, *liberius quam ut imperantium meminissent* [more unrestrained than they would be if they were mindful of government], it is a sign the orbs are out of frame. For reverence is that wherewith princes are girt from God; who threateneth the dissolving thereof; *Solvam cingula regum* [I will loose the girdles of kings].

So when any of the four pillars of government are mainly shaken or weakened (which are Religion, Justice, Counsel, and Treasure), men had need to pray for fair weather. But let us pass from this part of predictions (concerning which, nevertheless, more light may be taken from that which followeth); and let us speak first of the Materials of seditions; then of the Motives of them; and thirdly of the Remedies.

Concerning the Materials of seditions. It is a thing well to be considered; for the surest way to prevent seditions (if the times do bear it)

is to take away the matter of them. For if there be fuel prepared, it is
hard to tell whence the spark shall come that shall set it on fire. The
matter of seditions is of two kinds; much poverty and much discontentment. It is certain, so many overthrown estates, so many votes for troubles.
Lucan noteth well the state of Rome before the civil war,

> *Hinc usura vorax, rapidumque in tempore foenus,*
> *Hinc concussa fides, et multis utile bellum.*
> [Hence ravenous usury, and short-term interest
> Hence shaken credit, and war which is advantageous to many.]

This same *multis utile bellum* is an assured and infallible sign of a state
disposed to seditions and troubles. And if this poverty and broken estate
in the better sort be joined with a want and necessity in the mean people,
the danger is imminent and great. For the rebellions of the belly are the
worst. As for discontentments, they are in the politic body like to humours
in the natural, which are apt to gather a preternatural heat and to inflame. And let no prince measure the danger of them by this, whether
they be just or unjust: for that were to imagine people to be too reasonable; who do often spurn at their own good: nor yet by this, whether the
griefs whereupon they rise be in fact great or small: for they are the most
dangerous discontentments where the fear is greater than the feeling:
Dolendi modus, timendi non item [Pain has a limit, but fear has none].
Besides, in great oppressions, the same things that provoke the patience,
do withal mate the courage; but in fears it is not so. Neither let any
prince or state be secure concerning discontentments, because they have
been often, or have been long, and yet no peril hath ensued: for as it is
true that every vapour or fume doth not turn into a storm; so it is nevertheless true that storms, though they blow over divers times, yet may fall
at last; and, as the Spanish proverb noteth well, "The cord breaketh at the
last by the weakest pull."

The Causes and Motives of seditions are innovation in religion; taxes;
alteration of laws and customs; breaking of privileges; general oppression;
advancement of unworthy persons; strangers; dearths; disbanded soldiers;
factions grown desperate; and whatsoever, in offending people, joineth
and knitteth them in a common cause.

For the Remedies; there may be some general preservatives, whereof
we will speak: as for the just cure, it must answer to the particular disease;
and so be left to counsel rather than rule.

The first remedy or prevention is to remove by all means possible that
material cause of sedition whereof we spake; which is, want and poverty

in the estate. To which purpose serveth the opening and well-balancing of trade; the cherishing of manufactures; the banishing of idleness; the repressing of waste and excess by sumptuary laws; the improvement and husbanding of the soil; the regulating of prices of things vendible; the moderating of taxes and tributes, and the like. Generally, it is to be foreseen that the population of a kingdom (especially if it be not mown down by wars) do not exceed the stock of the kingdom which should maintain them. Neither is the population to be reckoned only by number; for a smaller number that spend more and earn less, do wear out an estate sooner than a greater number that live lower and gather more. Therefore the multiplying of nobility and other degrees of quality in an over proportion to the common people doth speedily bring a state of necessity; and so doth likewise an overgrown clergy; for they bring nothing to the stock; and in like manner, when more are bred scholars than preferments can take off.

It is likewise to be remembered, that forasmuch as the increase of any estate must be upon the foreigner (for whatsoever is somewhere gotten is somewhere lost), there be but three things which one nation selleth unto another; the commodity as nature yieldeth it; the manufacture; and the vecture, or carriage. So that if these three wheels go, wealth will flow as in a spring tide. And it cometh many times to pass that *materiam superabit opus;* that the work and carriage is more worth than the material, and enricheth a state more; as is notably seen in the Low-Countrymen, who have the best mines above ground in the world.

Above all things, good policy is to be used that the treasure and monies in a state be not gathered into few hands. For otherwise a state may have a great stock, and yet starve. And money is like muck, not good except it be spread. This is done chiefly by suppressing, or at the least keeping a strait hand upon the devouring trades of usury, ingrossing, great pasturages, and the like.

For removing discontentments, or at least the danger of them, there is in every state (as we know) two portions of subjects: the noblesse and the commonalty. When one of these is discontent, the danger is not great; for common people are of slow motion, if they be not excited by the greater sort; and the greater sort are of small strength, except the multitude be apt and ready to move of themselves. Then is the danger, when the greater sort do but wait for the troubling of the waters amongst the meaner, that then they may declare themselves. The poets feign that the rest of the gods would have bound Jupiter; which he hearing of, by the counsel of Pallas, sent for Briareus, with his hundred hands, to come in to his aid. An emblem, no doubt, to show how safe it is for monarchs to make sure of the good will of common people.

To give moderate liberty for griefs and discontentments to evaporate (so it be without too great insolency or bravery), is a safe way. For he that turneth the humours back, and maketh the wound bleed inwards, endangereth malign ulcers and pernicious imposthumations.

The part of Epimetheus might well become Prometheus, in the case of discontentments; for there is not a better provision against them. Epimetheus, when griefs and evils flew abroad, at last shut the lid, and kept hope in the bottom of the vessel. Certainly, the politic and artificial nourishing and entertaining of hopes, and carrying men from hopes to hopes, is one of the best antidotes against the poison of discontentments. And it is a certain sign of a wise government and proceeding, when it can hold men's hearts by hopes, when it cannot by satisfaction; and when it can handle things in such manner, as no evil shall appear so peremptory but that it hath some outlet of hope: which is the less hard to do, because both particular persons and factions are apt enough to flatter themselves, or at least to brave that they believe not.

Also the foresight and prevention, that there be no likely or fit head whereunto discontented persons may resort, and under whom they may join, is a known, but an excellent point of caution. I understand a fit head to be one that hath greatness and reputation; that hath confidence with the discontented party, and upon whom they turn their eyes; and that is thought discontented in his own particular: which kind of persons are either to be won and reconciled to the state, and that in a fast and true manner; or to be fronted with some other of the same party, that may oppose them, and so divide the reputation. Generally, the dividing and breaking of all factions and combinations that are adverse to the state, and setting them at distance, or at least distrust, among themselves, is not one of the worst remedies. For it is a desperate case, if those that hold with the proceeding of the state be full of discord and faction, and those that are against it be entire and united.

I have noted that some witty and sharp speeches which have fallen from princes have given fire to seditions. Caesar did himself infinite hurt in that speech, *Sylla nescivit literas, non potuit dictare* [Sylla was not a scholar, he was unable to dictate]: for it did utterly cut off that hope which men had entertained, that he would at one time or other give over his dictatorship. Galba undid himself by that speech, *legi a se militem, non emi* [that he had levied his soldiers, not bought them]: for it put the soldiers out of hope of the donative. Probus likewise, by that speech,

Si vixero, non opus erit amplius Romano imperio militibus [If I live, there will be no more work for soldiers in the Roman Empire]: a speech of great despair for the soldiers. And many the like. Surely princes had need, in tender matters and ticklish times, to beware what they say; especially in these short speeches, which fly abroad like darts, and are thought to be shot out of their secret intentions. For as for large discourses, they are flat things, and not so much noted.

Lastly, let princes, against all events, not be without some great person, one or rather more, of military valour, near unto them, for the repressing of seditions in their beginnings. For without that, there useth to be more trepidation in court upon the first breaking out of troubles than were fit. And the state runneth the danger of that which Tacitus saith; *Atque is habitus animorum fuit, ut pessimum facinus auderent pauci, plures vellent, omnes paterentur* [And such was their state of mind that a few were ready to attempt mischief, more to wish it, and all to permit it]. But let such military persons be assured, and well reputed of, rather than factious and popular; holding also good correspondence with the other great men in the state; or else the remedy is worse than the disease.

Of Custom
and Education

Men's thoughts are much according to their inclination; their discourse and speeches according to their learning and infused opinions; but their deeds are after as they have been accustomed. And therefore as Machiavel well noteth (though in an evil-favoured instance), there is no trusting to the force of nature nor to the bravery of words, except it be corroborate by custom. His instance is, that for the achieving of a desperate conspiracy, a man should not rest upon the fierceness of any man's nature, or his resolute undertakings; but take such an one as hath had his hands formerly in blood. But Machiavel knew not a friar Clement, nor a Ravillac, nor a Jaureguy, nor a Baltazar Gerard; yet his rule holdeth still, that nature, nor the engagement of words, are not so forcible as custom. Only superstition is now so well advanced, that men of the first blood are as firm as butchers by occupation; and votary resolution is made equipollent to custom even in matter of blood. In other things the predominancy of custom is everywhere visible; insomuch as a man would wonder to hear men profess, protest, engage, give great words, and then do just as they have done before; as if they were dead images, and engines moved only by the wheels of custom.

We see also the reign or tyranny of custom, what it is. The Indians (I mean the sect of their wise men) lay themselves quietly upon a stack of wood, and so sacrifice themselves by fire. Nay the wives strive to be burned with the corpses of their husbands. The lads of Sparta, of ancient time, were wont to be scourged upon the altar of Diana, without so much as queching [flinching]. I remember, in the beginning of Queen Elizabeth's time of England, an Irish rebel condemned put up a petition to the Deputy that he might be hanged in a withe, and not in an halter; because it had been so used with former rebels. There be monks in Russia, for penance, that will sit a whole night in a vessel of water, till they be engaged with hard ice. Many examples may be put of the force of custom, both upon mind and body. Therefore, since custom is the principal magistrate of man's life, let men by all means endeavour to obtain good customs. Certainly custom is most perfect when it beginneth in young years: this we call education; which is, in effect, but an early custom. So we see, in languages the tongue is more pliant to all expressions and sounds, the joints are more supple to all feats of activity and motions, in youth than afterwards. For it is true that late learners cannot so well take the ply; except it be in some minds that have not suffered themselves to fix, but have kept themselves open and prepared to receive continual amendment, which is exceeding rare. But if the force of custom simple and separate be great, the force of custom copulate and conjoined and collegiate is far greater. For there example teacheth, company comforteth, emulation quickeneth, glory raiseth: so as in such places the force of custom is in his exaltation. Certainly the great multiplication of virtues upon human nature resteth upon societies well ordained and disciplined. For commonwealths and good governments do nourish virtue grown, but do not much mend the seeds. But the misery is that the most effectual means are now applied to the ends least to be desired.

Of Followers
and Friends

Costly followers are not to be liked; lest while a man maketh his train longer, he make his wings shorter. I reckon to be costly, not them alone which charge the purse, but which are wearisome and importune in suits. Ordinary followers ought to challenge no higher conditions than countenance, recommendation, and protection from wrongs. Factious followers are worse to be liked, which follow not upon affection to him with whom they range themselves, but upon discontentment conceived against some other; whereupon commonly ensueth that ill intelligence that we many times see between great personages. Likewise glorious followers, who make themselves as trumpets of the commendation of those they follow, are full of inconvenience; for they taint business through want of secrecy; and they export honour from a man, and make him a return in envy. There is a kind of followers likewise which are dangerous, being indeed espials; which inquire the secrets of the house, and bear tales of them to others. Yet such men, many times, are in great favour; for they are officious, and commonly exchange tales. The following by certain estates of men, answerable to that which a great person himself professeth (as of soldiers to him that hath been employed in the wars, and the like), hath ever been a thing civil, and well taken even in monarchies; so it be without too much pomp or popularity. But the most honourable kind of following is to be followed as one that apprehendeth to advance virtue and desert in all sorts of persons. And yet, where there is no eminent odds in sufficiency, it is better to take with the more passable, than with the more able. And besides, to speak truth, in base times active men are of more use than virtuous. It is true that in government it is good to use men of one rank equally: for to countenance some extraordinarily, is to make them insolent, and the rest discontent; because they may claim a due. But contrariwise, in favour, to use men with much difference and election is good; for it maketh the persons preferred more thankful, and the rest more officious: because all is of favour.

It is good discretion not to make too much of any man at the first; because one cannot hold out that proportion. To be governed (as we call it) by one, is not safe; for it shows softness, and gives a freedom to scandal and disreputation; for those that would not censure or speak ill of a man immediately, will talk more boldly of those that are so great with them, and thereby wound their honour. Yet to be distracted with many is worse; for it makes men to be of the last impression, and full of change. To take advice of some few friends is ever honourable; for lookers-on many times see more than gamesters; and the vale best discovereth the hill. There is little friendship in the world, and least of all between equals, which was wont to be magnified. That that is, is between superior and inferior, whose fortunes may comprehend the one the other.

Of Usury

Many have made witty invectives against Usury. They say
that it is a pity the devil should have God's part, which is the tithe. That
the usurer is the greatest sabbath-breaker, because his plough goeth every
Sunday. That the usurer is the drone that Virgil speaketh of:

> Ignavum fucos pecus a praesepibus arcent.
> [They prohibit the drones, a slothful swarm, access to the beehives.]

That the usurer breaketh the first law that was made for mankind after
the fall, which was, in sudore vultus tui comedes panem tuum [in the
sweat of thy face shalt thou eat bread], not in sudore vultus alieni [in the
sweat of another]. That usurers should have orange-tawny bonnets, because they do judaize. That it is against nature for money to beget money;
and the like. I say this only, that usury is a concessum propter duritiem
cordis [thing permitted through hardness of heart]; for since there must
be borrowing and lending, and men are so hard of heart as they will not
lend freely, usury must be permitted. Some others have made suspicious
and cunning propositions of banks, discovery of men's estates, and other
inventions. But few have spoken of usury usefully. It is good to set before
us the incommodities and commodities of usury, that the good may be
either weighed out or culled out; and warily to provide, that while we
make forth to that which is better, we meet not with that which is worse.

The discommodities of usury are, first, that it makes fewer merchants.
For were it not for this lazy trade of usury, money would not lie still, but
would in great part be employed upon merchandising; which is the vena
porta [gate vein] of wealth in a state. The second, that it makes poor
merchants. For as a farmer cannot husband his ground so well if he sit at
a great rent; so the merchant cannot drive his trade so well, if he sit at
great usury. The third is incident to the other two; and that is the decay
of customs of kings or states, which ebb or flow with merchandising. The

fourth, that it bringeth the treasure of a realm or state into a few hands. For the usurer being at certainties, and others at uncertainties, at the end of the game most of the money will be in the box; and ever a state flourisheth when wealth is most equally spread. The fifth, that it beats down the price of land; for the employment of money is chiefly either merchandising or purchasing; and usury waylays both. The sixth, that it doth dull and damp all industries, improvements, and new inventions, wherein money would be stirring, if it were not for this slug. The last, that it is the canker and ruin of many men's estates; which in process of time breeds a public poverty.

On the other side, the commodities of usury are, first, that howsoever usury in some respect hindereth merchandising, yet in some other it advanceth it; for it is certain that the greatest part of trade is driven by young merchants, upon borrowing at interest; so as if the usurer either call in or keep back his money, there will ensue presently a great stand of trade. The second is that were it not for this easy borrowing upon interest, men's necessities would draw upon them a most sudden undoing; in that they would be forced to sell their means (be it lands or goods) far under foot; and so, whereas usury doth but gnaw upon them, bad markets would swallow them quite up. As for mortgaging or pawning, it will little mend the matter: for either men will not take pawns without use; or if they do, they will look precisely for the forfeiture. I remember a cruel monied man in the country that would say, "The devil take this usury, it keep us from forfeitures of mortgages and bonds." The third and last is that it is a vanity to conceive that there would be ordinary borrowing without profit; and it is impossible to conceive the number of inconveniences that will ensue, if borrowing be cramped. Therefore to speak of the abolishing of usury is idle. All states have ever had it, in one kind or rate, or other. So as that opinion must be sent to Utopia.

To speak now of the reformation and reiglement of usury; how the discommodities of it may be best avoided, and the commodities retained. It appears by the balance of commodities and discommodities of usury, two things are to be reconciled. The one, that the tooth of usury be grinded, that it bite not too much; the other, that there be left open a means to invite monied men to lend to the merchants, for the continuing and quickening of trade. This cannot be done, except you introduce two several sorts of usury, a less and a greater. For if you reduce usury to one low rate, it will ease the common borrower, but the merchant will be to seek for money. And it is to be noted, that the trade of merchandise, being the most lucrative, may bear usury at a good rate: other contracts not so.

To serve both intentions, the way would be briefly thus. That there be two rates of usury; the one free, and general for all; the other under licence only, to certain persons and in certain places of merchandising. First therefore, let usury in general be reduced to five in the hundred; and let that rate be proclaimed to be free and current; and let the state shut itself out to take any penalty for the same. This will preserve borrowing from any general stop or dryness. This will ease infinite borrowers in the country. This will, in good part, raise the price of land, because land purchased at sixteen years' purchase will yield six in the hundred, and somewhat more; whereas this rate of interest yields but five. This by like reason will encourage and edge industrious and profitable improvements; because many will rather venture in that kind than take five in the hundred, especially having been used to greater profit. Secondly, let there be certain persons licensed to lend to known merchants upon usury at a higher rate; and let it be with the cautions following. Let the rate be, even with the merchant himself, somewhat more easy than that he used formerly to pay; for by that means all borrowers shall have some ease by this reformation, be he merchant, or whosoever. Let it be no bank or common stock, but every man be master of his own money. Not that I altogether mislike banks, but they will hardly be brooked, in regard of certain suspicions. Let the state be answered some small matter for the licence, and the rest left to the lender; for if the abatement be but small, it will no whit discourage the lender. For he, for example, that took before ten or nine in the hundred, will sooner descend to eight in the hundred, than give over his trade of usury, and go from certain gains to gains of hazard. Let these licensed lenders be in number indefinite, but restrained to certain principal cities and towns of merchandising; for then they will be hardly able to colour other men's monies in the country: so as the licence of nine will not suck away the current rate of five; for no man will lend his monies far off, nor put them into unknown hands.

If it be objected that this doth in a sort authorize usury, which before was in some places but permissive; the answer is, that it is better to mitigate usury by declaration, than to suffer it to rage by connivance.

Of Riches

I cannot call Riches better than the baggage of virtue. The Roman word is better, *impedimenta*. For as the baggage is to an army, so is riches to virtue. It cannot be spared nor left behind, but it hindereth the march; yea and the care of it sometimes loseth or disturbeth the victory. Of great riches there is no real use, except it be in the distribution; the rest is but conceit. So saith Solomon, "Where much is, there are many to consume it; and what hath the owner but the sight of it with his eyes?" The personal fruition in any man cannot reach to feel great riches: there is a custody of them; or a power of dole and donative of them; or a fame of them; but no solid use to the owner. Do you not see what feigned prices are set upon little stones and rarities? And what works of ostentation are undertaken, because there might seem to be some use of great riches? But then you will say, they may be of use to buy men out of dangers or troubles. As Solomon saith, "Riches are as a strong hold, in the imagination of the rich man." But this is excellently expressed, that it is in imagination, and not always in fact. For certainly great riches have sold more men than they have bought out. Seek not proud riches, but such as thou mayest get justly, use soberly, distribute cheerfully, and leave contentedly. Yet have no abstract nor friarly contempt of them. But distinguish, as Cicero saith well of Rabirius Posthumus, *In studio rei amplificandae apparebat, non avaritiae praedam, sed instrumentum bonitati quaeri* [In his efforts to increase his substance, it was evident that he did not seek a prey for avarice but an instrument for doing good]. Hearken also to Solomon, and beware of hasty gathering of riches; *Qui festinat ad divitias, non erit insons* [He who makes haste to acquire riches shall not be innocent].

The poets feign that when Plutus (which is Riches) is sent from Jupiter, he limps and goes slowly; but when he is sent from Pluto, he runs and is swift of foot. Meaning that riches gotten by good means and just labour pace slowly; but when they come by the death of others (as by the course of inheritance, testaments, and the like), they come tumbling upon a

25

man. But it might be applied likewise to Pluto, taking him for the devil. For when riches come from the devil (as by fraud and oppression and unjust means), they come upon speed. The ways to enrich are many, and most of them foul. Parsimony is one of the best, and yet is not innocent; for it withholdeth men from works of liberality and charity. The improvement of the ground is the most natural obtaining of riches; for it is our great mother's blessing, the earth's; but it is slow. And yet where men of great wealth do stoop to husbandry, it multiplieth riches exceedingly. I knew a nobleman in England that had the greatest audits of any man in my time; a great grazier, a great sheep-master, a great timber man, a great collier, a great corn-master, a great lead-man, and so of iron, and a number of the like points of husbandry. So as the earth seemed a sea to him, in respect of the perpetual importation.

It was truly observed by one, that himself came very hardly to a little riches, and very easily to great riches. For when a man's stock is come to that, that he can expect the prime of markets, and overcome those bargains which for their greatness are few men's money, and be partner in the industries of younger men, he cannot but increase mainly.

The gains of ordinary trades and vocations are honest; and furthered by two things chiefly; by diligence, and by a good name for good and fair dealing. But the gains of bargains are of a more doubtful nature; when men shall wait upon others' necessity, broke by servants and instruments to draw them on, put off others cunningly that would be better chapmen, and the like practices, which are crafty and naught. As for the chopping of bargains, when a man buys not to hold but to sell over again, that commonly grindeth double, both upon the seller and upon the buyer. Sharings do greatly enrich, if the hands be well chosen that are trusted. Usury is the certainest means of gain, though one of the worst; as that whereby a man doth eat his bread *in sudore vultus alieni* [in the sweat of another's face]; and besides, doth plough upon Sundays. But yet certain though it be, it hath flaws; for that the scriveners and brokers do value unsound men to serve their own turn. The fortune in being the first in an invention or in a privilege doth cause sometimes a wonderful overgrowth in riches; as it was with the first sugar man in the Canaries. Therefore if a man can play the true logician, to have as well judgment as invention, he may do great matters; especially if the times be fit. He that resteth upon gains certain shall hardly grow to great riches; and he that puts all upon adventures doth oftentimes break and come to poverty: it is good therefore to guard adventures with certainties that may uphold losses. Monopolies, and coemption of wares for resale, where they are not restrained, are great means to enrich; especially if the party have intelligence what things are like to come into request, and so store himself beforehand. Riches gotten by service, though it be of the best rise, yet when they are gotten by flattery, feeding humours, and other servile conditions, they may be placed amongst the worst. As for fishing for testaments and executorships (as Tacitus saith of Seneca, *testamenta et orbos tamquam indagine capi* [he took executorships and guardianships as with a net]), it is yet worse; by how much men submit themselves to meaner persons than in service.

Believe not much them that seem to despise riches; for they despise them that despair of them; and none worse when they come to them. Be not penny-wise; riches have wings, and sometimes they fly away of themselves, sometimes they must be sent flying to bring in more. Men leave their riches either to their kindred, or to the public; and moderate portions prosper best in both. A great state left to an heir, is as a lure to all the birds of prey round about to seize on him, if he be not the better stablished in years and judgment. Likewise glorious gifts and foundations are like sacrifices without salt; and but the painted sepulchres of alms, which soon will putrefy and corrupt inwardly. Therefore measure not thine advancements by quantity, but frame them by measure, and defer not charities till death; for certainly, if a man weigh it rightly, he that doth so is rather liberal of another man's than of his own.

The foregoing essays
are from a collection of Bacon's essays
entitled ESSAYS: CIVIL AND MORAL.

Jonathan Swift

1667–1745

Jonathan Swift was born in Dublin, of English parents, on November 30, 1667. The generosity of his examiners gave him a degree at Trinity College. He crossed to England and in 1689 became secretary to Sir William Temple at Moor Park. Except for an interval as a clergyman near Belfast, Swift remained at Moor Park until Sir William died in 1699.

There Swift became tutor and friend to Esther Johnson, a child who would grow up to be the "Stella" of his *Journal to Stella*. There, too, he wrote *The Battle of the Books* and *A Tale of a Tub*. After Temple's death, Swift found a clerical post at Laracor, near Dublin. He took a D.D. in 1701. That same year, at Swift's invitation, Stella and a woman companion settled in Laracor.

Swift spent much time in London. He was friendly with Pope, Steele, and Addison. In 1708 he published the "Isaac Bickerstaff" letters, a hoax on a notorious London astrologer. Swift had been a Whig in politics. But when the Whigs fell from office, he became the intimate of the new Tory ministers, Oxford and Bolingbroke. As their principal writer, he got hold of considerable power, which he enjoyed.

Queen Anne appointed him Dean of St. Patrick's, Dublin. He was hardly welcomed when he took office in 1713. A little later the Queen

---

*Notes from the artist: "Portrait of Swift in clerical garb . . .
the background is a scene from his A Tale of a Tub,
a brilliant satire on, among other things, the clergy."*

Jonathan
Swift

died, and the Tory ministry fell. Swift supported Oxford and even
offered to share his imprisonment. Then he retired to his Dublin
cathedral. His relations with Stella were complicated by the devotion of Esther Vanhomrigh, the daughter of a Dublin merchant, who
appears as the "Vanessa" of his writings.

He is said to have spent "a third of his income on charities." In
1724 his *Drapier Letters,* an attack on an unjust coinage system, put
all Ireland in a rage. Two years later, the anonymous *Gulliver's
Travels* was published. By 1742 his mental condition was such that
guardians were appointed. He died on October 19, 1745, and was
buried beside Stella, his "violent friend," in the crypt of St. Patrick's.

Taine speaks of Swift's "exaggerated and terrible pride" that "made
the haughtiness of the most powerful ministers and most mighty
lords bow beneath his arrogance." It was one aspect of his force of
personality. This force was condensed, in all Swift's work, by the
pressure of his necessity to fit human life into an unchanging
frame of reason. So we have the massive, rolling onset of his prose.
Its clarity, exactness, and power make it a fit instrument for its purpose. It has great social leverage. We think of Swift as the greatest
satirist in English.

One of the signs of a good writer is that we can intersect his work
at many angles. We can find more than one level of meaning in it.
This is true even in such a simple case as Swift's *Resolutions when
I Come to Be Old.* On the surface, it is just what the title suggests:
a man writing a memorandum to himself in the form of a list of
axioms intended to govern a wise old age. Would they, in fact, do
that? We are inclined to think that they might, at least in the social
sense.

Then we notice that all but one of the axioms begin with *not.* The
exception is a check on the rest. The author is laying down acts and
types of behavior to be avoided, not things to be done. Ricardo
Quintana points out that the situations mentioned are "the stock
ones of social comedy." But is it not possible that Swift and the
authors of the social comedies had both observed the same types of
behavior in a more or less standardized society? And is it not true
that Swift here catches certain traits of old men in any civilized
society?

In *An Essay on Modern Education,* we observe once more that

Swift is concerned, not with the needs or wishes of the individual, but with those of an aristocratic society which he must be taught to serve. As an old friend of the philosopher George Berkeley and his wife, Swift was often persuaded to read to Mrs. Berkeley from her favorite book, Robert Boyle's *Meditations*. He wrote a parody, *A Meditation upon a Broomstick*, and read it out to her as if it were one of Boyle's. Only Swift could have conceived the broomstick as a comic symbol of man and then stood it on its head.

Swift, Berkeley, and Edmund Burke were all outraged by the British misgovernment of Ireland in the eighteenth century. *A Modest Proposal* is one fruit of that outrage. We are told that there are tens of thousands of unwanted babies in Ireland. They cannot be provided for. Very well, says Swift. Let us sell them and eat them. The argument is faultless and masterly. It is delivered in the enlightened tone of a man who proposes a new kind of stock-raising for the benefit of the country. There is nothing at all wrong with it except that it is inhuman. But is it more inhuman than allowing these same children to starve to death? Irony, satire, humor, reason gone mad—Swift brings all these to bear on a problem that still troubles the human race.

Resolutions
when
I Come to Be Old

Not to marry a young woman.

Not to keep young company, unless they really desire it.

Not to be peevish, or morose, or suspicious.

Not to scorn present ways, or wits, or fashions, or men, or war, etc.

Not to be fond of children.

Not to tell the same story over and over to the same people.

Not to be covetous.

Not to neglect decency, or cleanliness, for fear of falling into nastiness.

Not to be over-severe with young people, but give allowances for their youthful follies and weaknesses.

Not to be influenced by or give ear to knavish tattling servants, or others.

Not to be too free of advice, nor trouble any but those that desire it.

To desire some good friends to inform me which of these resolutions I break or neglect, and wherein; and reform accordingly.

Not to talk much, nor of myself.

Not to boast of my former beauty, or strength, or favour with ladies, etc.

Not to hearken to flatteries, nor conceive I can be beloved by a young woman; *et eos qui haereditatem captant, odisse ac vitare* [and to hate and avoid those who seek a legacy].

Not to be positive or opinionative.

Not to set up for observing all these rules, for fear I should observe none.

An Essay
on Modern Education

From frequently reflecting upon the course and method of educating youth in this and a neighbouring kingdom, with the general success and consequence thereof, I am come to this determination, that education is always the worse in proportion to the wealth of and grandeur of the parents; nor do I doubt in the least that if the whole world were now under the dominion of one monarch (provided I might be allowed to choose where he should fix the seat of his empire) the only son and heir of that monarch would be the worst educated mortal that ever was born since the creation; and I doubt [fear] the same proportion will hold through all degrees and titles, from an emperor downwards to the common gentry.

I do not say that this hath been always the case, for in better times it was directly otherwise, and a scholar may fill half his Greek and Roman shelves with authors of the noblest birth, as well as highest virtue; nor do I tax all nations at present with this defect, for I know there are some to be excepted, and particularly Scotland, under all the disadvantages of its climate and soil, if that happiness be not rather owing even to those very disadvantages. What is then to be done if this reflection must fix on two countries, which will be most ready to take offense, and which of all others it will be least prudent or safe to offend?

But there is one circumstance yet more dangerous and lamentable: For if, according to the *postulatum* already laid down, the higher quality any youth is of, he is in greater likelihood to be worse educated, it behoves me to dread and keep far from the verge of *scandalum magnatum*.

Retracting therefore that hazardous *postulatum*, I shall venture no further at present than to say that perhaps some additional care in educating the sons of nobility and principal gentry might not be ill em-

33

ployed. If this be not delivered with softness enough, I must for the future be silent.

In the mean time, let me ask only two questions, which relate to England. I ask first how it comes about that for above sixty years past the chief conduct of affairs hath been generally placed in the hands of new men, with very few exceptions? The noblest blood of England having been shed in the Great Rebellion, many great families became extinct, or supported only by minors. When the king was restored, very few of those lords remained who began or at least had improved their education under the happy reign of King James or King Charles I, of which lords the two principal were the Marquis of Ormond and the Earl of Southampton. The minors have, or had, during the Rebellion and usurpation, either received too much tincture of bad principles from those fanatic times or, coming to age at the Restoration, fell into the vices of that dissolute reign.

I date from this era the corrupt method of education among us, and the consequence thereof, in the necessity the crown lay under of introducing new men into the chief conduct of public affairs, or to the office of what we now call prime ministers, men of art, knowledge, application, and insinuation, merely for want of a supply among the nobility. They were generally (though not always) of good birth, sometimes younger brothers, at other times such who, although inheriting good estates, yet happened to be well educated and provided with learning; such under that King were Hyde, Bridgeman, Clifford, Osborn, Godolphin, Ashley-Cooper; few or none under the short reign of King James II. Under King William: Somers, Montagu, Churchill, Vernon, Boyle, and many others. Under the Queen: Harley, St. John, Harcourt, Trevor, who indeed were persons of the best private families but unadorned with titles. So in the following reign, Mr. Robert Walpole was for many years prime minister, in which post he still happily continues. His brother Horace is ambassador extraordinary to France. Mr. Addison and Mr. Craggs, without the least allowance to support them, have been secretaries of state.

If the facts have been thus for above sixty years past (whereof I could with a little further recollection produce many more instances), I would ask again how it hath happened that in a nation plentifully abounding with nobility so great share in the most competent parts of public management hath been for so long a period chiefly entrusted to commoners, unless some omissions or defects of the highest import may be charged upon those to whom the care of educating our noble youth hath been committed? For if there be any difference between human creatures in the point of natural parts, as we usually call them, it should seem that the advantage lies on the side of children born from noble and wealthy parents, the same traditional sloth and luxury which render their body weak and effeminate perhaps refining and giving a freer motion to the spirits beyond what can be expected from the gross, robust issue of meaner mortals. Add to this the peculiar advantages which all young noblemen possess by the privileges of their birth, such as a free access to courts, and a universal deference paid to their persons.

But as my Lord Bacon charged it for a fault on princes that they are impatient to compass ends without giving themselves the trouble of consulting or executing the means, so perhaps it may be the disposition of young nobles, either from the indulgence of parents, tutors, and governors or their own inactivity, that they expect the accomplishments of a good education without the least expense of time or study to acquire them.

What I said last I am ready to retract, for the case is infinitely worse; and the very maxims set up to direct modern education are enough to destroy all the seeds of knowledge, honour, wisdom, and virtue among us. The current opinion prevails that the study of Greek and Latin is loss of time; that public schools by mingling the sons of noblemen with those of the vulgar engage the former in bad company; that whipping breaks the spirits of lads well born; that universities make young men pedants; that to dance, fence, speak French, and know how to behave yourself among great persons of both sexes comprehends the whole duty of a gentleman.

I cannot but think this wise system of education hath been much cultivated among us by those worthies of the Army who during the last war, returning from Flanders at the close of each campaign, became the dictators of behaviour, dress, and politeness to all those youngsters who frequent chocolate-coffee-gaming-houses, drawing-rooms, operas, levees, and assemblies; where a colonel by his pay, perquisites, and plunder was qualified to outshine many peers of the realm; and by the influence of an exotic habit and demeanor, added to other foreign accomplishments, gave the law to the whole town, and was copied as the standard pattern of whatever was refined in dress, equipage, conversation, or diversions.

I remember in those times an admired original of that vocation sitting in a coffee-house near two gentlemen, whereof one was of the clergy, who were engaged in some discourse that savoured of learning; this officer thought fit to interpose, and professing to deliver the sentiments of his fraternity, as well as his own (and probably did so of too many among them), turning to the clergyman, spoke in the following manner, "D——n me, Doctor, say what you will, the army is the only school for gentlemen. Do you think my Lord Marlborough beat the French with Greek and Latin? D——n me, a scholar when he comes into good company, what is he but an ass? D——n me, I would be glad by G-d to see any of your scholars with his nouns, and his verbs, and his philosophy, and trigonometry, what a figure he would make at a siege or blockade, or rencountering—D——n me," etc. After which he proceeded with a volley of military terms less significant, sounding worse, and harder to be understood than any that were ever coined by the commentators upon Aristotle. I would not here be thought to charge the soldiery with ignorance and contempt of learning, without allowing exceptions, of which I have known many; but, however, the worse example, especially in a great majority, will certainly prevail.

I have heard that the late Earl of Oxford, in the time of his ministry, never passed by White's Chocolate-House (the common rendezvous of infamous sharpers and noble cullies) without bestowing a curse upon that famous academy as the bane of half the English nobility. I have likewise been told another passage concerning that great minister, which, because it gives a humorous idea of one principal ingredient in modern education, take as follows. Le-Sack, the famous French dancing-master, in great admiration, asked a friend whether it were true that Mr. Harley was made an earl and Lord Treasurer? And finding it confirmed, said, "Well, I wonder what the devil the Queen could see in him, for I attended him two years, and he was the greatest dunce that ever I taught."

Another hindrance to good education, and I think the greatest of any, is that pernicious custom in rich and noble families of entertaining French tutors in their houses. These wretched pedagogues are enjoined by the father to take special care that the boy shall be perfect in his French; by the mother that master must not walk till he is hot, nor be suffered to play with other boys, nor be wet in his feet, nor daub his clothes, and to see that dancing-master attends constantly and does his duty; she further insists that the child be not kept too long poring on his book, because he is subject to sore eyes and of a weakly constitution.

By these methods, the young gentleman is in every article as fully accomplished at eight years old as at eight and twenty, age adding only to the growth of his person and his vice; so that if you should look at him in his boyhood through the magnifying end of a perspective, and in his manhood through the other, it would be impossible to spy any difference: the same airs, the same strut, the same cock of his hat, and posture of his sword (as far as the change of fashions will allow), the same understanding, the same compass of knowledge, with the very same absurdity, impudence, and impertinence of tongue.

He is taught from the nursery that he must inherit a great estate, and hath no need to mind his book, which is a lesson he never forgets to the end of his life. His chief solace is to steal down and play at span-farthing with the page, or young blackamoor, or little favourite footboy, one of which is his principal confident and bosom friend.

There is one young lord in this town who, by an unexampled piece of good fortune, was miraculously snatched out of the gulf of ignorance, confined to a public school for a due term of years, well whipped when he deserved it, clad no better than his comrades and always their playfellow on the same foot, had no precedence in the school but what was given him by his merit and lost it whenever he was negligent. It is well known how many mutinies were bred at this unprecedented treatment, what complaints among his relations, and other great ones of both sexes; that his stockings with silver clocks were ravished from him; that he wore his own hair; that his dress was undistinguished; that he was not fit to appear at a ball or assembly, nor suffered to go to either: And it was with the utmost difficulty that he became qualified for his present removal, where he may probably be farther persecuted, and possibly with success, if the firmness of a very worthy governor and his own good dispositions will not preserve him. I confess I cannot but wish he may go on in the way he began, because I have a curiosity to know by so singular an experiment whether truth, honour, justice, temperance, courage, and good sense, acquired by a school and college education, may not produce a very tolerable lad, although he should happen to fail in one or two of those accomplishments which in the general vogue are held so important to the finishing of a gentleman.

It is true, I have known an academical education to have been exploded in public assemblies, and have heard more than one or two persons of high rank declare they could learn nothing more at Oxford and Cambridge than to drink ale and smoke tobacco; wherein I firmly believed them, and could have added some hundred examples from my own observation in one of those universities; but they all were of young heirs sent thither only for form, either from schools where they were not suffered by their careful parents to stay above three months in the year, or from under the management of French family-tutors, who yet often attended them to their college to prevent all possibility of their improvement. But I never yet knew any one person of quality who followed his studies at the university, and carried away his just proportion of learning, that was not ready upon all occasions to celebrate and defend that course of education, and to prove a patron of learned men.

There is one circumstance in a learned education which ought to have much weight, even with those who have no learning at all. The books read at school and colleges are full of incitements to virtue and discouragements from vice, drawn from the wisest reasons, the strongest motives, and the most influencing examples. Thus, young minds are filled early with an inclination to good and an abhorrence of evil, both which increase in them according to the advances they make in literature; and, although they may be, and too often are, drawn by the temptations of youth, and the opportunities of a large fortune, into some irregularities when they come forward into the great world, it is ever with reluctance and compunction of mind, because their bias to virtue still continues. They may stray sometimes out of infirmity or compliance, but they will soon return to the right road and keep it always in view. I speak only of those excesses which are too much the attendants of youth and warmer blood, for, as to the points of honour, truth, justice, and other noble gifts of the mind wherein the temperature of the body hath no concern, they are seldom or ever known to be wild.

I have engaged myself very unwarily in too copious a subject for so short a paper. The present scope I would aim at is to prove that some proportion of human knowledge appears requisite to those who, by their birth or fortune, are called to the making of laws and, in a subordinate way, to the execution of them; and that such knowledge is not to be obtained without a miracle under the frequent, corrupt, and sottish methods of educating those who are born to wealth or titles. For I would have it remembered that I do by no means confine these remarks to young persons of noble birth, the same errors running through all families where there is wealth enough to afford that their sons (at least the eldest) may be good for nothing. Why should my son be a scholar when it is not intended that he should live by his learning? By this rule, if what is commonly said be true, that money answers all things, why should my son be honest, temperate, just, or charitable, since he hath no intention to depend upon any of these qualities for a maintenance?

When all is done, perhaps upon the whole the matter is not so bad as I would make it; and God, who works good out of evil, acting only by the ordinary cause and rule of nature, permits this continual circulation of human things for His own unsearchable ends. The father grows rich by avarice, injustice, oppression; he is a tyrant in the neighbourhood over slaves and beggars, whom he calls his tenants. Why should he desire to have qualities infused into his son which himself never possessed, or knew, or found the want of in the acquisition of his wealth? The son bred in sloth and idleness becomes a spendthrift, a cully, a profligate, and goes out of the world a beggar, as his father came in. Thus the former is punished for his own sins, as well as for those of the latter. The dunghill, having raised a huge mushroom of short duration, is now spread to enrich other men's lands. It is indeed of worse consequence where noble families are gone to decay, because their titles and privileges outlive their estates; and politicians tell us that nothing is more dangerous to the public than a numerous nobility without merit or fortune. But even here, God hath likewise prescribed some remedy in the order of nature, so many great families coming to an end by the sloth, luxury, and abandoned lusts, which enervated their breed through every succession, producing gradually a more effeminate race, wholly unfit for propagation.

A Meditation
upon a Broomstick

This single stick, which you now behold ingloriously lying in that neglected corner, I once knew in a flourishing state in a forest. It was full of sap, full of leaves, and full of boughs. But now in vain does the busy art of man pretend to vie with nature by tying that withered bundle of twigs to its sapless trunk. 'Tis now at best but the reverse of what it was, a tree turned upside down, the branches on the earth, and the root in the air. 'Tis now handled by every dirty wench, condemned to do her drudgery, and, by a capricious kind of fate, destined to make other things clean, and be nasty itself. At length, worn to the stumps in the service of the maids, 'tis either thrown out-of-doors or condemned to the last use of kindling a fire. When I beheld this, I sighed and said within myself, Surely mortal man is a broomstick; nature sent him into the world strong and lusty in a thriving condition, wearing his own hair on his head, the proper branches of this reasoning vegetable, till the axe of intemperance has lopped off his green boughs and left him a withered trunk. He then flies to art and puts on a periwig, valuing himself upon an unnatural bundle of hairs, all covered with powder that never grew on his head; but now should this our broomstick pretend to enter the scene, proud of those birchen spoils it never bore, and all covered with dust, though the sweepings of the finest lady's chamber, we should be apt to ridicule and despise its vanity. Partial judges that we are of our own excellencies and other men's defaults!

But a broomstick, perhaps you will say, is an emblem of a tree standing on its head; and pray what is man but a topsy-turvy creature, his animal faculties perpetually mounted on his rational, his head where his heels should be, groveling on the earth! And yet, with all his faults, he sets up to be a universal reformer and corrector of abuses, a remover of grievances, rakes into every slut's corner of nature, bringing hidden corruptions to the light, and raises a mighty dust where there was none before, sharing deeply all the while in the very same pollutions he pretends to sweep away. His last days are spent in slavery to women, and generally the least deserving; till worn to the stumps, like his brother Bezom, he is either kicked out-of-doors or made use of to kindle flames for others to warm themselves by.

A Modest Proposal
for
Preventing the Children of Ireland from Being a Burden to Their Parents or Country

It is a melancholy object to those who walk through this great town or travel in the country when they see the streets, the roads and cabin-doors crowded with beggars of the female sex, followed by three, four, or six children, all in rags, and importuning every passenger for an alms. These mothers, instead of being able to work for their honest livelihood, are forced to employ all their time in strolling to beg sustenance for their helpless infants, who, as they grow up, either turn thieves for want of work, or leave their dear native country, to fight for the pretender in Spain, or sell themselves to the Barbadoes.

I think it is agreed by all parties that this prodigious number of children in the arms, or on the backs, or at the heels of their mothers, and frequently of their fathers, is in the present deplorable state of the kingdom a very great additional grievance; and therefore whoever could find out a fair, cheap and easy method of making these children sound and useful members of the Commonwealth would deserve so well of the public as to have his statue set up for a preserver of the nation.

But my intention is very far from being confined to provide only for the children of professed beggars; it is of a much greater extent, and shall take in the whole number of infants at a certain age who are born of parents in effect as little able to support them as those who demand our charity in the streets.

As to my own part, having turned my thoughts, for many years, upon this important subject, and maturely weighed the several schemes of other projectors, I have always found them grossly mistaken in their computation. It is true, a child just dropt from its dam may be supported by her milk for a solar year with little other nourishment, at most not above the value of two shillings, which the mother may certainly get, or the value in scraps, by her lawful occupation of begging; and it is exactly at one year old that I propose to provide for them in such a manner as, instead of being a charge upon their parents or the parish, or wanting food and raiment for the rest of their lives, they shall, on the contrary, contribute to the feeding and partly to the clothing of many thousands.

There is likewise another great advantage in my scheme, that it will prevent those voluntary abortions, and that horrid practice of women murdering their bastard children, alas! too frequent among us, sacrificing the poor innocent babes, I doubt, more to avoid the expense than the shame, which would move tears and pity in the most savage and inhuman breast.

The number of souls in this kingdom being usually reckoned one million and a half, of these I calculate there may be about two hundred thousand couple whose wives are breeders; from which number I subtract thirty thousand couples who are able to maintain their own children, although I apprehend there cannot be so many under the present distresses of the kingdom; but this being granted, there will remain a hundred and seventy thousand breeders. I again subtract fifty thousand, for those women who miscarry, or whose children die by accident or disease within the year. There only remain a hundred and twenty thousand children of poor parents annually born. The question therefore is how this number shall be reared and provided for. Which, as I have already said, under the present situation of affairs is utterly impossible by all the methods hitherto proposed, for we can neither employ them in handicraft or agriculture: we neither build houses (I mean in the country) nor cultivate land. They can very seldom pick up a livelihood by stealing till they arrive at six years old, except where they are of towardly parts; although, I confess, they learn the rudiments much earlier; during which time they can however be properly looked upon only as probationers, as I have been informed by a principal gentleman in the county of Cavan, who protested to me that he never knew above one or two instances under the age of six, even in a part of the kingdom so renowned for the quickest proficiency in that art.

I am assured by our merchants that a boy or a girl before twelve years old is no saleable commodity, and even when they come to this age, they will not yield above three pounds, or three pounds and half a crown at most, on the exchange; which cannot turn to account either to the parents or kingdom, the charge of nutriment and rags having been at least four times that value.

I shall now therefore humbly propose my own thoughts, which I hope will not be liable to the least objection.

I have been assured by a very knowing American of my acquaintance in London that a young healthy child well nursed is at a year old a most delicious nourishing and wholesome food, whether stewed, roasted, baked, or boiled; and I make no doubt that it will equally serve in a fricassee or a ragout.

I do therefore humbly offer it to public consideration, that of the hundred and twenty thousand children already computed, twenty thousand may be reserved for breed, whereof only one-fourth part to be males; which is more than we allow to sheep, black cattle, or swine, and my reason is that these children are seldom the fruits of marriage, a circumstance not much regarded by our savages; therefore, one male will be sufficient to serve four females. That the remaining hundred thousand may at a year old be offered in sale to the persons of quality and fortune, through the kingdom, always advising the mother to let them suck plentifully in the last month so as to render them plump and fat for a good table. A child will make two dishes at an entertainment for friends, and when the family dines alone, the fore or hind quarter will make a reasonable dish, and seasoned with a little pepper or salt will be very good boiled on the fourth day, especially in winter.

I have reckoned upon a medium that a child just born will weigh 12 pounds, and in a solar year, if tolerably nursed, increase to 28 pounds.

I grant this food will be somewhat dear, and therefore very proper for landlords, who, as they have already devoured most of the parents, seem to have the best title to the children.

Infant's flesh will be in season throughout the year, but more plentiful in March, and a little before and after; for we are told by a grave author, an eminent French physician, that fish being a prolific diet, there are more children born in Roman Catholic countries about nine months after Lent than at any other season; therefore reckoning a year after Lent, the markets will be more glutted than usual, because the number of popish infants is at least three to one in this kingdom, and therefore it will have one other collateral advantage, by lessening the number of papists among us.

I have already computed the charge of nursing a beggar's child (in which list I reckon all cottagers, labourers, and four-fifths of the farmers) to be about two shillings per annum, rags included; and I believe no gentleman would repine to give ten shillings for the carcass of a good fat child, which, as I have said, will make four dishes of excellent nutritive meat, when he hath only some particular friend, or his own family to dine with him. Thus the squire will learn to be a good landlord, and grow popular among his tenants, the mother will have eight shillings neat profit, and be fit for work till she produces another child.

Those who are more thrifty (as I must confess the times require) may flay the carcass; the skin of which, artificially dressed, will make admirable gloves for ladies, and summer boots for fine gentlemen.

As to our city of Dublin, shambles may be appointed for this purpose, in the most convenient parts of it, and butchers we may be assured will not be wanting; although I rather recommend buying the children alive, and dressing them hot from the knife, as we do roasting pigs.

A very worthy person, a true lover of his country, and whose virtues I highly esteem, was lately pleased, in discoursing on this matter, to offer a refinement upon my scheme. He said that many gentlemen of this kingdom having of late destroyed their deer, he conceived that the want of venison might be well supplied by the bodies of young lads and maidens, not exceeding fourteen years of age, nor under twelve, so great a number of both sexes in every country being now ready to starve for want of work and service: and these to be disposed of by their parents if alive, or otherwise by their nearest relations. But with due deference to so excellent a friend, and so deserving a patriot, I cannot be altogether in his sentiments; for as to the males, my American acquaintance assured me from frequent experience that their flesh was generally tough and lean, like that of our schoolboys, by continual exercise, and their taste disagreeable, and to fatten them would not answer the charge. Then as to the females, it would, I think with humble submission, be a loss to the public, because they soon would become breeders themselves. And besides it is not improbable that some scrupulous people might be apt to censure such a practice (although indeed very unjustly) as a little bordering upon cruelty, which, I confess, hath always been with me the strongest objection against any project, how soever well intended.

But in order to justify my friend, he confessed that this expedient was put into his head by the famous Sallmanaazor, a native of the island Formosa, who came from thence to London, above twenty years ago, and in conversation told my friend that in his country when any young person happened to be put to death, the executioner sold the carcass to persons of quality, as a prime dainty, and that, in his time, the body of a plump girl of fifteen, who was crucified for an attempt to poison the Emperor, was sold to His Imperial Majesty's prime minister of state, and other great mandarins of the court, in joints from the gibbet, at four hundred crowns. Neither indeed can I deny that if the same use were made of several plump young girls in this town, who, without one single groat to their fortunes, cannot stir abroad without a chair, and appear at a playhouse and assemblies in foreign fineries, which they never will pay for, the kingdom would not be the worse.

Some persons of a desponding spirit are in great concern about that vast number of poor people who are aged, diseased, or maimed, and I have been desired to employ my thoughts on what course may be taken to ease the nation of so grievous an encumbrance. But I am not in the least pain upon that matter, because it is very well known that they are every day dying, and rotting, by cold and famine, and filth, and vermin, as fast as can be reasonably expected. And as to the younger labourers, they are now in almost as hopeful a condition. They cannot get work, and consequently pine away for want of nourishment to a degree that if at any time they are accidentally hired to common labour, they have not strength to perform it, and thus the country and themselves are happily delivered from the evils to come.

I have too long digressed, and therefore shall return to my subject. I think the advantages by the proposal which I have made are obvious and many, as well as of the highest importance.

For first, as I have already observed, it would greatly lessen the number of papists, with whom we are yearly overrun, being the principal breeders of the nation, as well as our most dangerous enemies, and who stay at home on purpose with a design to deliver the kingdom to the pretender, hoping to take their advantage by the absence of so many good Protestants, who have chosen rather to leave their country than stay at home and pay tithes against their conscience to an Episcopal curate.

Secondly, the poorer tenants will have something valuable of their own which by law may be made liable to distress, and help to pay their landlord's rent, their corn and cattle being already seized, and money a thing unknown.

Thirdly, whereas the maintenance of a hundred thousand children, from two years old and upwards, cannot be computed at less than ten shillings a piece per annum, the nation's stock will be thereby increased fifty thousand pounds per annum, besides the profit of a new dish, introduced to the tables of all gentlemen of fortune in the kingdom who have any refinement in taste, and the money will circulate among ourselves, the goods being entirely of our own growth and manufacture.

Fourthly, the constant breeders, besides the gain of eight shillings sterling per annum, by the sale of their children, will be rid of the charge of maintaining them after the first year.

Fifthly, this food would likewise bring great custom to taverns, where the vintners will certainly be so prudent as to procure the best receipts for dressing it to perfection; and consequently have their houses frequented by all the fine gentlemen, who justly value themselves upon their knowledge in good eating; and a skilful cook, who understands how to oblige his guests, will contrive to make it as expensive as they please.

Sixthly, this would be a great inducement to marriage, which all wise nations have either encouraged by rewards or enforced by laws and penalties. It would increase the care and tenderness of mothers towards their children, when they were sure of a settlement for life to the poor babes, provided in some sort by the public to their annual profit instead of expense; we should soon see an honest emulation among the married women which of them could bring the fattest child to the market. Men would become as fond of their wives during the time of their pregnancy as they are now of their mares in foal, their cows in calf, or sows when they are ready to farrow, nor offer to beat or kick them (as is too frequent a practice) for fear of a miscarriage.

Many other advantages might be enumerated. For instance, the addition of some thousand carcasses in our exportation of barreled beef, the propagation of swine's flesh, and improvement in the art of making good bacon, so much wanted among us by the great destruction of pigs, too frequent at our tables, which are no way comparable in taste or magnificence to a well-grown, fat yearling child, which roasted whole will make a considerable figure at a Lord Mayor's feast or any other public entertainment. But this, and many others, I omit, being studious of brevity.

Supposing that one thousand families in this city would be constant customers for infant's flesh, besides others who might have it at merry meetings, particularly at weddings and christenings, I compute that Dublin would take off annually about twenty thousand carcasses, and the rest of the kingdom (where probably they will be sold somewhat cheaper) the remaining eighty thousand.

I can think of no one objection that will possibly be raised against this proposal, unless it should be urged that the number of people will be thereby much lessened in the kingdom. This I freely own, and 'twas indeed one principal design in offering it to the world. I desire the reader will observe that I calculate my remedy for this one individual kingdom of Ireland, and for no other that ever was, is, or, I think, ever can be upon earth. Therefore let no man talk to me of other expedients: of taxing our absentees at five shillings a pound; of using neither clothes nor household furniture except what is of our own growth and manufacture; of utterly rejecting the materials and instruments that promote foreign luxury; of curing the expensiveness of pride, vanity, idleness, and gaming in our women; of introducing a vein of parsimony, prudence, and temperance; of learning to love our country, wherein we differ even from Laplanders, and the inhabitants of Topinamboo; of quitting our animosities and factions, nor act any longer like the Jews, who were murdering one another at the very moment their city was taken; of being a little cautious not to sell our country and consciences for nothing; of teaching landlords to have at least one degree of mercy towards their tenants. Lastly, of putting a spirit of honesty, industry, and skill into our shopkeepers, who, if a resolution could now be taken to buy only our native goods, would immediately unite to cheat and exact upon us in the price, the measure, and the goodness, nor could ever yet be brought to make one fair proposal of just dealing, though often and earnestly invited to it.

Therefore I repeat, let no man talk to me of these and the like expedients till he hath at least some glimpse of hope that there will ever be some hearty and sincere attempt to put them in practice.

But as to myself, having been wearied out for many years with offering vain, idle, visionary thoughts, and at length utterly despairing of success, I fortunately fell upon this proposal, which, as it is wholly new, so it hath something solid and real, of no expense and little trouble, full in our own power, and whereby we can incur no danger in disobliging England. For this kind of commodity will not bear exportation, the flesh being of too tender a consistence to admit a long continuance in salt, although perhaps I could name a country which would be glad to eat up our whole nation without it.

After all, I am not so violently bent upon my own opinion as to reject any offer, proposed by wise men, which shall be found equally innocent, cheap, easy, and effectual. But before something of that kind shall be advanced in contradiction to my scheme, and offering a better, I desire the author or authors will be pleased maturely to consider two points: first, as things now stand, how they will be able to find food and raiment for a hundred thousand useless mouths and backs. And secondly, there being a round million of creatures in human figure throughout this kingdom whose whole subsistence put into a common stock would leave them in debt two millions of pounds sterling, adding those who are beggars by profession to the bulk of farmers, cottagers, and labourers, with their wives and children, who are beggars in effect; I desire those politicians who dislike my overture, and may perhaps be so bold to attempt an answer, that they will first ask the parents of these mortals whether they would not at this day think it a great happiness to have been sold for food at a year old in the manner I prescribe, and thereby have avoided such a perpetual scene of misfortunes as they have since gone through, by the oppression of landlords, the impossibility of paying rent without money or trade, the want of common sustenance, with neither house nor clothes to cover them from the inclemencies of the weather, and the most inevitable prospect of entailing the like or greater miseries upon their breed for ever.

I profess in the sincerity of my heart that I have not the least personal interest in endeavouring to promote this necessary work, having no other motive than the public good of my country, by advancing our trade, providing for infants, relieving the poor, and giving some pleasure to the rich. I have no children by which I can propose to get a single penny, the youngest being nine years old, and my wife past child-bearing.

David Hume [1]

1711–1776

The essay form, in which Hume gracefully expresses his ideas here, had its beginning as far back as Plutarch and Montaigne. It is usually a short, informal, often personal bit of writing, on some non-technical subject of general interest. Reading a good essay is like sitting around the fireplace while a master conversationalist, at his best, explains and defends his extraordinary views on an ordinary subject. Happily, these essays, except for the last, are also contributions to economic theory.

The first essay is provocative enough for anyone. For centuries it had been assumed, without question, that luxuries and the refinements of life are vices which produce effeminacy and loss of martial courage. The civilized man's taste for fine foods, wines, apparel, and the like, had been compared unfavorably with the rough manners and sterling virtues of the barbarian. Is not this absurd, Hume asks. "No gratification, however sensual, can of itself be esteemed vicious," he claims. It becomes so only when it leads a man to neglect his duty to his family and friends. There is nothing abominable, after all, in pleasure or its refinements. They give men something to live and fight for. The French and English, devoted to the arts and to the art of fine living, are as courageous as they come. They have great wealth and highly developed industries too. Is there any answer to this commonsensical argument?

In the second essay, Hume tells us that money is a great stimulator of industry and of refined tastes and luxuries. Yet it does not follow that the more a nation has, the better off it is. A nation never suffers internally from a shortage of money or gold. If it had only half as

---

[1] For a biography of David Hume, see Vol. 5, pp. 99–101, in this set.

much, its commodities would cost half as much; if it had twice as much, they would cost twice as much. Money is a mere symbol of the exchange value of commodities. In a very simple economy, goods are bartered and money is not needed. Yet such an economy remains simple and rude: wants are primitive and undiversified; industry does not develop; the arts are neglected.

"The quantity of gold and silver is in itself altogether indifferent," according to Hume, for the wealth of a nation consists of its men and commodities, and depends on how well the commodities are marketed and how widely money is circulated. Although the increase of gold and money does not by itself increase wealth, it spurs the industry of the people. As a result, goods are produced more cheaply and prices do not rise proportionately. Moreover, prices and wages do not rise at once. There is a lag, and this also benefits the economy, for it stimulates demand.

A very perceptive and logical essay, you will admit, but has not Hume forgotten that gold is not a mere symbol but also a commodity, the price of which may vary?

Of the Balance of Trade seeks to deflate another very widespread conviction, namely, that an unfavorable balance of trade will eventually ruin a country, draining off its gold to other nations. Hume argues, against the free traders here, that if a country loses gold in trade, the domestic cost of labor and commodities will decline. Sales abroad will then increase, and gold will flow back into the country. The trade balance will cease to be unfavorable. A correction in the opposite direction will occur when the trade balance is favorable. In the same way, water always maintains the same level. Parliaments can pass laws to maintain a favorable trade balance, but they will be found ineffective or harmful. Is this always so?

Most of us nowadays would agree with Hume that the best taxes are those levied on luxuries, and that taxes on commodities are far better than poll taxes. We would tend to approve the reasons he gives. But we may not be so sure that eighteenth-century artisans could easily absorb moderate taxes without increasing their wages.

In Hume's last essay, we might question whether fact is really more entertaining, as well as more profitable, than fiction. And are we like children if we do not read history? How can a study of history be so profitable if history never repeats itself? Could Hume answer that *types* of situations recur, and that human nature, at any rate, is always the same?

Of Refinement
in the Arts

L uxury is a word of uncertain signification, and may be taken in a good as well as in a bad sense. In general, it means great refinement in the gratification of the senses; and any degree of it may be innocent or blameable, according to the age, or country, or condition of the person. The bounds between the virtue and the vice cannot here be exactly fixed more than in other moral subjects. To imagine that the gratifying of any sense, or the indulging of any delicacy in meat, drink, or apparel, is of itself a vice can never enter into a head that is not disordered by the frenzies of enthusiasm. I have, indeed, heard of a monk abroad, who, because the windows of his cell opened upon a noble prospect, made a covenant with his eyes never to turn that way, or receive so sensual a gratification. And such is the crime of drinking champagne or burgundy preferably to small beer or porter. These indulgences are only vices when they are pursued at the expense of some virtue, as liberality or charity; in like manner as they are follies when for them a man ruins his fortune, and reduces himself to want and beggary. Where they entrench upon no virtue, but leave ample subject whence to provide for friends, family, and every proper object of generosity or compassion, they are entirely innocent, and have in every age been acknowledged such by almost all moralists. To be entirely occupied with the luxury of the table, for instance, without any relish for the pleasures of ambition, study, or conversation, is a mark of stupidity, and is incompatible with any vigour of temper or genius. To confine one's expense entirely to such a gratification, without regard to friends or family, is an indication of a heart destitute of humanity or benevolence. But if a man reserve time sufficient for all laudable pursuits, and money sufficient for all generous purposes, he is free from every shadow of blame or reproach.

Since luxury may be considered either as innocent or blameable, one

may be surprised at those preposterous opinions which have been entertained concerning it; while men of libertine principles bestow praises
even on vicious luxury, and represent it as highly advantageous to society;
and on the other hand, men of severe morals blame even the most innocent luxury, and represent it as the source of all the corruptions, disorders,
and factions incident to civil government. We shall here endeavour to
correct both these extremes, by proving, first, that the ages of refinement
are both the happiest and most virtuous; secondly, that wherever luxury
ceases to be innocent, it also ceases to be beneficial; and when carried a
degree too far, is a quality pernicious, though perhaps not the most
pernicious, to political society.

To prove the first point, we need but consider the effects of refinement
both on private and on public life. Human happiness, according to the
most received notions, seems to consist in three ingredients: action,
pleasure, and indolence. And though these ingredients ought to be mixed
in different proportions, according to the particular disposition of the
person, yet no one ingredient can be entirely wanting, without destroying,
in some measure, the relish of the whole composition. Indolence or repose,
indeed, seems not of itself to contribute much to our enjoyment; but, like
sleep, is requisite as an indulgence to the weakness of human nature,
which cannot support an uninterrupted course of business or pleasure.
That quick march of the spirits which takes a man from himself, and
chiefly gives satisfaction, does in the end exhaust the mind, and requires
some intervals of repose, which, though agreeable for a moment, yet, if
prolonged, beget a languor and lethargy that destroys all enjoyment.
Education, custom, and example have a mighty influence in turning the
mind to any of these pursuits; and it must be owned that where they
promote a relish for action and pleasure, they are so far favourable to
human happiness. In times when industry and the arts flourish, men are
kept in perpetual occupation, and enjoy, as their reward, the occupation
itself, as well as those pleasures which are the fruit of their labour. The
mind acquires new vigour; enlarges its powers and faculties; and by an
assiduity in honest industry, both satisfies its natural appetites and
prevents the growth of unnatural ones, which commonly spring up when
nourished by ease and idleness. Banish those arts from society, you deprive men both of action and of pleasure; and leaving nothing but
indolence in their place, you even destroy the relish of indolence, which
never is agreeable but when it succeeds to labour, and recruits the spirits
exhausted by too much application and fatigue.

Another advantage of industry and of refinements in the mechanical arts is that they commonly produce some refinements in the liberal; nor can one be carried to perfection without being accompanied, in some degree, with the other. The same age which produces great philosophers and politicians, renowned generals and poets usually abounds with skilful weavers, and ship-carpenters. We cannot reasonably expect that a piece of woollen cloth will be brought to perfection in a nation which is ignorant of astronomy, or where ethics are neglected. The spirit of the age affects all the arts; and the minds of men, being once roused from their lethargy, and put into a fermentation, turn themselves on all sides, and carry improvements into every art and science. Profound ignorance is totally banished, and men enjoy the privilege of rational creatures to think as well as to act, to cultivate the pleasures of the mind as well as those of the body.

The more these refined arts advance, the more sociable men become: nor is it possible that when enriched with science, and possessed of a fund of conversation, they should be contented to remain in solitude, or live with their fellow-citizens in that distant manner which is peculiar to ignorant and barbarous nations. They flock into cities; love to receive and communicate knowledge; to show their wit or their breeding; their taste in conversation or living, in clothes or furniture. Curiosity allures the wise; vanity the foolish; and pleasure both. Particular clubs and societies are everywhere formed: both sexes meet in an easy and sociable manner; and the tempers of men, as well as their behaviour, refine apace. So that besides the improvements which they receive from knowledge and the liberal arts, it is impossible but they must feel an increase of humanity from the very habit of conversing together, and contribute to each other's pleasure and entertainment. Thus industry, knowledge, and humanity are linked together by an indissoluble chain, and are found, from experience as well as reason, to be peculiar to the more polished, and, what are commonly denominated, the more luxurious ages.

Nor are these advantages attended with disadvantages that bear any proportion to them. The more men refine upon pleasure, the less they indulge in excess of any kind; because nothing is more destructive to true pleasure than such excesses. One may safely affirm that the Tartars are oftener guilty of beastly gluttony, when they feast on their dead horses, than European courtiers with all their refinements of cookery. And if libertine love, or even infidelity to the marriage-bed, be more frequent in polite ages, when it is often regarded only as a piece of gallantry, drunkenness, on the other hand, is much less common: a vice more odious, and more pernicious both to mind and body. And in this matter I would appeal not only to an Ovid or a Petronius but to a Seneca or a Cato. We know that Caesar, during Catiline's conspiracy, being necessitated to put into Cato's hands a *billet-doux* which discovered an intrigue with Servilia, Cato's own sister, that stern philosopher threw it back to him with indignation; and in the bitterness of his wrath, gave him the appellation of drunkard, as a term more opprobrious than that with which he could more justly have reproached him.

But industry, knowledge, and humanity are not advantageous in private life alone: they diffuse their beneficial influence on the public, and render the government as great and flourishing as they make individuals happy and prosperous. The increase and consumption of all the commodities which serve to the ornament and pleasure of life are advantageous to society; because at the same time that they multiply those innocent gratifications to individuals, they are a kind of storehouse of labour, which, in the exigencies of state, may be turned to public service. In a nation where there is no demand for such superfluities, men sink into indolence, lose all enjoyment of life, and are useless to the public, which cannot maintain or support its fleets and armies from the industry of such slothful members.

The bounds of all the European kingdoms are, at present, nearly the same they were two hundred years ago: But what a difference is there in the power and grandeur of those kingdoms? Which can be ascribed to nothing but the increase of art and industry. When Charles VIII of France invaded Italy, he carried with him about 20,000 men: Yet this armament so exhausted the nation, as we learn from Guicciardini, that for some years it was not able to make so great an effort. The late king of France, in time of war, kept in pay above 400,000 men; though from Mazarin's death to his own, he was engaged in a course of wars that lasted near thirty years.

This industry is much promoted by the knowledge inseparable from ages of art and refinement; as, on the other hand, this knowledge enables the public to make the best advantage of the industry of its subjects. Laws, order, police, discipline: these can never be carried to any degree of perfection before human reason has refined itself by exercise, and by an application to the more vulgar arts, at least, of commerce and manufacture. Can we expect that a government will be well modelled by a people who know not how to make a spinning-wheel, or to employ a loom to advantage? Not to mention that all ignorant ages are infested with superstition, which throws the government off its bias, and disturbs men in the pursuit of their interest and happiness.

Knowledge in the arts of government naturally begets mildness and moderation, by instructing men in the advantages of humane maxims above rigour and severity, which drive subjects into rebellion, and make the return to submission impracticable, by cutting off all hopes of pardon. When the tempers of men are softened as well as their knowledge improved, this humanity appears still more conspicuous, and is the chief characteristic which distinguishes a civilized age from times of barbarity and ignorance. Factions are then less inveterate, revolutions less tragical, authority less severe and seditions less frequent. Even foreign wars abate of their cruelty; and after the field of battle, where honour and interest steel men against compassion as well as fear, the combatants divest themselves of the brute, and resume the man.

Nor need we fear that men, by losing their ferocity, will lose their martial spirit, or become less undaunted and vigorous in defence of their country or their liberty. The arts have no such effect in enervating either the mind or body. On the contrary, industry, their inseparable attendant, adds new force to both. And if anger, which is said to be the whetstone of courage, loses somewhat of its asperity by politeness and refinement, a sense of honour, which is a stronger, more constant, and more governable principle, acquires fresh vigour by that elevation of genius which arises from knowledge and a good education. Add to this that courage can neither have any duration nor be of any use when not accompanied with discipline and martial skill, which are seldom found among a barbarous people. The ancients remarked that Datames was the only barbarian that ever knew the art of war. And Pyrrhus, seeing the Romans marshal their army with some art and skill, said with surprise, "These barbarians have nothing barbarous in their discipline!" It is observable that, as the old Romans, by applying themselves solely to war, were almost the only uncivilized people that ever possessed military discipline so the modern Italians are the only civilized people, among Europeans, that ever wanted courage and a martial spirit. Those who would ascribe this effeminacy of the Italians to their luxury, or politeness, or application to the arts need but consider the French and English, whose bravery is as uncontestable as their love for the arts, and their assiduity in commerce. The Italian historians give us a more satisfactory reason for this degeneracy of their countrymen. They show us how the sword was dropped at once by all the Italian sovereigns; while the Venetian aristocracy was jealous of its subjects, the Florentine democracy applied itself entirely to commerce; Rome was governed by priests, and Naples by women. War then became the business of soldiers of fortune, who spared one another, and to the astonishment of the world, could engage a whole day in what they called a battle, and return at night to their camp, without the least bloodshed.

What has chiefly induced severe moralists to declaim against refinement in the arts is the example of ancient Rome, which joining to its poverty and rusticity, virtue and public spirit, rose to such a surprising height of grandeur and liberty; but having learned from its conquered provinces the Asiatic luxury, fell into every kind of corruption; whence arose sedition and civil wars, attended at last with the total loss of liberty. All the Latin classics, whom we peruse in our infancy, are full of these sentiments, and universally ascribe the ruin of their state to the arts and riches imported from the East: insomuch that Sallust represents a taste for painting as a vice no less than lewdness and drinking. And so popular were these sentiments, during the later ages of the republic, that this author abounds in praises of the old rigid Roman virtue, though himself the most egregious instance of modern luxury and corruption; speaks contemptuously of the Grecian eloquence, though the most elegant writer in the world; nay, employs preposterous digressions and declamations to this purpose, though a model of taste and correctness.

But it would be easy to prove that these writers mistook the cause of the disorders in the Roman state, and ascribed to luxury and the arts what really proceeded from an ill-modelled government, and the unlimited extent of conquests. Refinement on the pleasures and conveniences of life has no natural tendency to beget venality and corruption. The value which all men put upon any particular pleasure depends on comparison and experience; nor is a porter less greedy of money, which he spends on bacon and brandy, than a courtier, who purchases champagne and ortolans. Riches are valuable at all times, and to all men, because they always purchase pleasures, such as men are accustomed to, and desire: Nor can anything restrain or regulate the love of money, but a sense of honour and virtue; which, if it be not nearly equal at all times, will naturally abound most in ages of knowledge and refinement.

Of all European kingdoms, Poland seems the most defective in the arts of war as well as peace, mechanical as well as liberal; yet it is there that venality and corruption do most prevail. The nobles seem to have preserved their crown elective for no other purpose than regularly to sell it to the highest bidder. This is almost the only species of commerce with which that people are acquainted.

The liberties of England, so far from decaying since the improvements in the arts, have never flourished so much as during that period. And though corruption may seem to increase of late years, this is chiefly to be ascribed to our established liberty, when our princes have found the impossibility of governing without parliaments, or of terrifying parliaments by the phantom of prerogative. Not to mention that this corruption or venality prevails much more among the electors than the elected; and therefore cannot justly be ascribed to any refinements in luxury.

If we consider the matter in a proper light, we shall find that a progress in the arts is rather favourable to liberty, and has a natural tendency to preserve, if not produce, a free government. In rude unpolished nations, where the arts are neglected, all labour is bestowed on the cultivation of the ground; and the whole society is divided into two classes: proprietors of land, and their vassals or tenants. The latter are necessarily dependent, and fitted for slavery and subjection; especially where they possess no riches, and are not valued for their knowledge in agriculture, as must always be the case where the arts are neglected. The former naturally erect themselves into petty tyrants; and must either submit to an absolute master, for the sake of peace and order, or if they will preserve their independency, like the ancient barons, they must fall into feuds and contests among themselves, and throw the whole society into such confusion as is perhaps worse than the most despotic government. But where luxury nourishes commerce and industry, the peasants, by a proper cultivation of the land, become rich and independent; while the tradesmen and merchants acquire a share of the property, and draw authority and consideration to that middling rank of men who are the best and firmest basis of public liberty. These submit not to slavery, like the peasants, from poverty and meanness of spirit; and having no hopes of tyrannizing over others, like the barons, they are not tempted, for the sake of that gratification, to submit to the tyranny of their sovereign. They covet equal laws, which may secure their property, and preserve them from monarchical, as well as aristocratical, tyranny.

The lower house is the support of our popular government; and all the world acknowledges that it owed its chief influence and consideration to the increase of commerce, which threw such a balance of property into the hands of the commons. How inconsistent then is it to blame so violently a refinement in the arts, and to represent it as the bane of liberty and public spirit!

To declaim against present times, and magnify the virtue of remote ancestors, is a propensity almost inherent in human nature: And as the sentiments and opinions of civilized ages alone are transmitted to posterity, hence it is that we meet with so many severe judgments pronounced against luxury, and even science; and hence it is that at present we give so ready an assent to them. But the fallacy is easily perceived by comparing different nations that are contemporaries, where we both judge more impartially and can better set in opposition those manners with which we are sufficiently acquainted. Treachery and cruelty, the most pernicious and most odious of all vices, seem peculiar to uncivilized ages; and by the refined Greeks and Romans were ascribed to all the barbarous nations which surrounded them. They might justly, therefore, have presumed that their own ancestors, so highly celebrated, possessed no greater virtue, and were as much inferior to their posterity in honour and humanity as in taste and science. An ancient Frank or Saxon may be highly extolled: But I believe every man would think his life or fortune much less secure in the hands of a Moor or Tartar, than in those of a French or English gentleman, the rank of men the most civilized in the most civilized nations.

We come now to the second position which we propose to illustrate, to wit, that as innocent luxury, or a refinement in the arts and conveniences of life, is advantageous to the public, so wherever luxury ceases to be innocent, it also ceases to be beneficial; and when carried a degree farther, begins to be a quality pernicious, though, perhaps, not the most pernicious, to political society.

Let us consider what we call vicious luxury. No gratification, however sensual, can of itself be esteemed vicious. A gratification is only vicious when it engrosses all a man's expense, and leaves no ability for such acts of duty and generosity as are required by his situation and fortune. Suppose that he correct the vice, and employ part of his expense in the education of his children, in the support of his friends, and in relieving the poor: would any prejudice result to society? On the contrary, the same consumption would arise; and that labour which, at present, is employed only in producing a slender gratification to one man would relieve the necessitous, and bestow satisfaction on hundreds. The same care and toil that raise a dish of peas at Christmas would give bread to a whole family during six months. To say that without a vicious luxury the labour would not have been employed at all is only to say that there is some other defect in human nature, such as indolence, selfishness, inattention to others, for which luxury, in some measure, provides a remedy; as one poison may be an antidote to another. But virtue, like wholesome food, is better than poisons, however corrected.

Suppose the same number of men that are present in Great Britain, with the same soil and climate; I ask, is it not possible for them to be happier, by the most perfect way of life that can be imagined, and by the greatest reformation that Omnipotence itself could work in their temper and disposition? To assert that they cannot appears evidently ridiculous. As the land is able to maintain more than all its present inhabitants, they could never, in such a Utopian state, feel any other ills than those which arise from bodily sickness; and these are not the half of human miseries. All other ills spring from some vice, either in ourselves or others; and even many of our diseases proceed from the same origin. Remove the vices, and the ills follow. You must only take care to remove all the vices. If you remove part, you may render the matter worse. By banishing vicious luxury, without curing sloth and an indifference to others, you only diminish industry in the state, and add nothing to men's charity or their generosity. Let us, therefore, rest contented with asserting that two opposite vices in a state may be more advantageous than either of them alone; but let us never pronounce vice in itself advantageous. Is it not very inconsistent for an author to assert in one page that moral distinctions are inventions of politicians for public interest, and in the next page maintain that vice is advantageous to the public? And indeed it seems upon any system of morality little less than a contradiction in terms to talk of a vice which is in general beneficial to society.[1]

I thought this reasoning necessary in order to give some light to a philosophical question which has been much disputed in England. I call it a philosophical question, not a political one. For whatever may be the consequence of such a miraculous transformation of mankind as would endow them with every species of virtue, and free them from every species of vice, this concerns not the magistrate, who aims only at possibilities. He cannot cure every vice by substituting a virtue in its place. Very often he can only cure one vice by another; and in that case, he ought to prefer what is least pernicious to society. Luxury, when excessive, is the source of many ills; but is in general preferable to sloth and idleness, which would commonly succeed in its place, and are more hurtful both to private persons and to the public. When sloth reigns, a mean

---

1. Prodigality is not to be confounded with a refinement in the arts. It even appears that that vice is much less frequent in the cultivated ages. Industry and gain beget this frugality among the lower and middle ranks of men, and in all the busy professions. Men of high rank, indeed, it may be pretended, are more allured by the pleasures, which become more frequent. But idleness is the great source of prodigality at all times; and there are pleasures and vanities in every age, which allure men equally when they are unacquainted with better enjoyments. Not to mention that the high interest paid in rude times quickly consumes the fortunes of the landed gentry, and multiplies their necessities.

uncultivated way of life prevails among individuals, without society, without enjoyment. And if the sovereign, in such a situation, demands the service of his subjects, the labour of the state suffices only to furnish the necessaries of life to the labourers, and can afford nothing to those who are employed in the public service.

Of Money

Money is not, properly speaking, one of the subjects of commerce; but only the instrument which men have agreed upon to facilitate the exchange of one commodity for another. It is none of the wheels of trade: It is the oil which renders the motion of the wheels more smooth and easy. If we consider any one kingdom by itself, it is evident that the greater or less plenty of money is of no consequence; since the prices of commodities are always proportioned to the plenty of money, and a crown in Harry VII's time served the same purpose as a pound does at present. It is only the public which draws any advantage from the greater plenty of money; and that only in its wars and negotiations with foreign states. And this is the reason why all rich and trading countries from Carthage to Great Britain and Holland have employed mercenary troops, which they hired from their poorer neighbours. Were they to make use of their native subjects, they would find less advantage from their superior riches, and from their great plenty of gold and silver, since the pay of all their servants must rise in proportion to the public opulence. Our small army of 20,000 men is maintained at as great expense as a French army twice as numerous. The English fleet, during the late war, required as much money to support it as all the Roman legions which kept the whole world in subjection during the time of the emperors.[1]

The greater number of people and their greater industry are serviceable in all cases; at home and abroad, in private and in public. But the greater

---

1. A private soldier in the Roman infantry had a denarius a day, somewhat less than eightpence. The Roman emperors had commonly 25 legions in pay, which, allowing 5,000 men to a legion, makes 125,000. Tacit., *Ann.* lib. iv, 5. It is true, there were also auxiliaries to the legions; but their numbers are uncertain, as well as their pay. To consider only the legionaries, the pay of the private men could not exceed 1,600,000 pounds. Now, the parliament in the last war commonly allowed for the fleet 2,500,000. We have therefore 900,000 over for the officers and other expenses of the Roman legions. There seem to have been but few officers in the Roman armies, in comparison of what are employed in all our modern troops, except some Swiss corps. And these officers had very small pay: a centurion, for in-

plenty of money is very limited in its use, and may even sometimes be a loss to a nation in its commerce with foreigners.

There seems to be a happy concurrence of causes in human affairs which checks the growth of trade and riches, and hinders them from being confined entirely to one people; as might naturally at first be dreaded from the advantages of an established commerce. Where one nation has gotten the start of another in trade, it is very difficult for the latter to regain the ground it has lost; because of the superior industry and skill of the former, and the greater stocks of which its merchants are possessed, and which enable them to trade on so much smaller profits. But these advantages are compensated, in some measure, by the low price of labour in every nation which has not an extensive commerce, and does not much abound in gold and silver. Manufactures therefore gradually shift their places, leaving those countries and provinces which they have already enriched, and flying to others, whither they are allured by the cheapness of provisions and labour; till they have enriched these also, and are again banished by the same causes. And, in general, we may observe that the dearness of everything, from plenty of money, is a disadvantage which attends an established commerce, and sets bounds to it in every country, by enabling the poorer states to undersell the richer in all foreign markets.

This has made me entertain a doubt concerning the benefit of banks and paper credit, which are so generally esteemed advantageous to every nation. That provisions and labour should become dear by the increase of trade and money is, in many respects, an inconvenience; but an inconvenience that is unavoidable, and the effect of that public wealth and prosperity which are the end of all our wishes. It is compensated by the advantages which we reap from the possession of these precious metals, and the weight which they give the nation in all foreign wars and negotiations. But there appears no reason for increasing that inconvenience by a counterfeit money, which foreigners will not accept of in any payment, and which any great disorder in the state will reduce to nothing. There are, it is true, many people in every rich state, who, having large sums of money, would prefer paper with good security, as being of more easy

---

stance, only double a common soldier. And as the soldiers from their pay (Tacit., *Ann.* lib. i, 17) bought their own clothes, arms, tents, and baggage, this must also diminish considerably the other charges of the army. So little expensive was that mighty government, and so easy was its yoke over the world. And, indeed, this is the more natural conclusion from the foregoing calculations. For money, after the conquest of Egypt, seems to have been nearly in as great plenty at Rome as it is at present in the richest of the European kingdoms.

transport and more safe custody. If the public provide not a bank, private bankers will take advantage of this circumstance; as the goldsmiths formerly did in London, or as the bankers do at present in Dublin: And therefore it is better, it may be thought, that a public company should enjoy the benefit of that paper credit which always will have place in every opulent kingdom. But to endeavour artificially to increase such a credit can never be the interest of any trading nation; but must lay them under disadvantages, by increasing money beyond its natural proportion to labour and commodities, and thereby heightening their price to the merchant and manufacturer. And in this view, it must be allowed that no bank could be more advantageous than such a one as locked up all the money it received, and never augmented the circulating coin, as is usual, by returning part of its treasure into commerce. A public bank, by this expedient, might cut off much of the dealings of private bankers and money-jobbers; and though the state bore the charge of salaries to the directors and tellers of this bank (for, according to the preceding supposition, it would have no profit from its dealings), the national advantage, resulting from the low price of labour and the destruction of paper credit, would be a sufficient compensation. Not to mention that so large a sum, lying ready at command, would be a convenience in times of great public danger and distress; and what part of it was used might be replaced at leisure, when peace and tranquility was restored to the nation.

But of this subject of paper credit we shall treat more largely hereafter. And I shall finish this essay on money by proposing and explaining two observations, which may, perhaps, serve to employ the thoughts of our speculative politicians.

It was a shrewd observation of Anacharsis the Scythian, who had never seen money in his own country, that gold and silver seemed to him of no use to the Greeks, but to assist them in numeration and arithmetic. It is indeed evident that money is nothing but the representation of labour and commodities, and serves only as a method of rating or estimating them. Where coin is in greater plenty; as a greater quantity of it is required to represent the same quantity of goods; it can have no effect, either good or bad, taking a nation within itself; any more than it would make an alteration on a merchant's books, if instead of the Arabian method of notation, which requires few characters, he should make use of the Roman, which requires a great many. Nay, the greater quantity of money, like the Roman characters, is rather inconvenient, and requires greater trouble both to keep and transport it. But notwithstanding this conclusion, which must be allowed just, it is certain that since the discovery of the mines in America, industry has increased in all the nations of Europe, except in the possessors of those mines; and this may justly be ascribed, among other reasons, to the increase of gold and silver. Accordingly we find that in every kingdom into which money begins to flow in greater abundance than formerly, everything takes a new face: labour and industry gain life; the merchant becomes more enterprising, the manufacturer more diligent and skilful, and even the farmer follows his plough with greater alacrity and attention. This is not easily to be accounted for, if we consider only the influence which a greater abundance of coin has in the kingdom itself, by heightening the price of commodities, and obliging every one to pay a great number of these little yellow or white pieces for everything he purchases. And as to foreign trade, it appears that great plenty of money is rather disadvantageous, by raising the price of every kind of labour.

To account, then, for this phenomenon, we must consider that though the high price of commodities be a necessary consequence of the increase of gold and silver, yet it follows not immediately upon that increase; but some time is required before the money circulates through the whole state, and makes its effect be felt on all ranks of people. At first, no alteration is perceived; by degrees the price rises, first of one commodity, then of another; till the whole at last reaches a just proportion with the new quantity of specie which is in the kingdom. In my opinion, it is only in this interval or intermediate situation, between the acquisition of money and rise of prices, that the increasing quantity of gold and silver is favourable to industry. When any quantity of money is imported into a nation, it is not at first dispersed into many hands; but is confined to the coffers of a few persons, who immediately seek to employ it to advantage. Here are a set of manufacturers or merchants, we shall suppose, who have received returns of gold and silver for goods which they sent to Cadiz. They are thereby enabled to employ more workmen than formerly, who never dream of demanding higher wages, but are glad of employment from such good paymasters. If workmen become scarce, the manufacturer gives higher wages, but at first requires an increase of labour; and this is willingly submitted to by the artisan, who can now eat and drink better to compensate his additional toil and fatigue. He carries his money to market, where he finds everything at the same price as formerly, but returns with greater quantity and of better kinds, for the use of his family. The farmer and gardener, finding that all their commodities are taken off, apply themselves with alacrity to the raising more; and at the same time can afford to take better and more cloths from their tradesmen, whose price is the same as formerly, and their industry only whetted by so much new gain. It is easy to trace the money in its progress through the whole commonwealth, where we shall find that it must first quicken the diligence of every individual before it increase the price of labour.

And that the specie may increase to a considerable pitch, before it have this latter effect, appears, among other instances, from the frequent operations of the French king on the money; where it was always found that the augmenting of the numerary value did not produce a proportional rise of the prices, at least for some time. In the last year of Louis XIV money was raised three-sevenths, but prices augmented only one. Corn in France is now sold at the same price, or for the same number of livres, it was in 1683; though silver was then at 30 livres the mark, and is now at 50.[2] Not to mention the great addition of gold and silver, which may have come into that kingdom since the former period.

From the whole of this reasoning we may conclude that it is of no manner of consequence, with regard to the domestic happiness of a state, whether money be in a greater or less quantity. The good policy of the magistrate consists only in keeping it, if possible, still increasing; because, by that means, he keeps alive a spirit of industry in the nation, and increases the stock of labour, in which consists all real power and riches. A nation whose money decreases is actually, at that time, weaker and more miserable than another nation which possesses no more money, but is on the increasing hand. This will be easily accounted for, if we consider that

2. These facts I give upon the authority of M. du Tot in his *Reflections politiques,* an author of reputation. Though I must confess that the facts which he advances on other occasions are often so suspicious as to make his authority less in this matter. However, the general observation that the augmenting of the money in France does not at first proportionably augment the prices is certainly just.

By the by, this seems to be one of the best reasons which can be given for a gradual and universal increase of the denomination of money, though it has been entirely overlooked in all those volumes which have been written on that question by Melon, du Tot, and Paris de Verney. Were all our money, for instance, recoined, and a penny's worth of silver taken from every shilling, the new shilling would probably purchase everything that could have been bought by the old; the prices of everything would thereby be insensibly diminished; foreign trade enlivened; and domestic industry, by the circulation of a great number of pounds and shillings, would receive some increase and encouragement. In executing such a project, it would be better to make the new shilling pass for 24 halfpence, in order to preserve the illusion, and make it be taken for the same. And as a recoinage of our silver begins to be requisite, by the continual wearing of our shillings and sixpences, it may be doubtful whether we ought to imitate the example in King William's reign, when the clipt money was raised to the old standard.

the alterations in the quantity of money, either on one side or the other, are not immediately attended with proportionable alterations in the price of commodities. There is always an interval before matters be adjusted to their new situation; and this interval is as pernicious to industry when gold and silver are diminishing as it is advantageous when these metals are increasing. The workman has not the same employment from the manufacturer and merchant, though he pays the same price for everything in the market. The farmer cannot dispose of his corn and cattle, though he must pay the same rent to his landlord. The poverty, and beggary, and sloth which must ensue are easily forseen.

The second observation which I proposed to make with regard to money may be explained after the following manner. There are some kingdoms, and many provinces in Europe (and all of them were once in the same condition), where money is so scarce that the landlord can get none at all from his tenants; but is obliged to take his rent in kind, and either to consume it himself or transport it to places where he may find a market. In those countries, the prince can levy few or no taxes, but in the same manner: And as he will receive small benefit from impositions so paid, it is evident that such a kingdom has little force even at home; and cannot maintain fleets and armies to the same extent as if every part of it abounded in gold and silver. There is surely a greater disproportion between the force of Germany at present and what it was three centuries ago [3] than there is in its industry, people, and manufactures. The Austrian dominions in the empire are in general well peopled and well cultivated, and are of great extent; but have not a proportionable weight in the balance of Europe; proceeding, as is commonly supposed, from the scarcity of money. How do all these facts agree with that principle of reason that the quantity of gold and silver is in itself altogether indifferent? According to that principle wherever a sovereign has numbers of subjects, and these have plenty of commodities, he should of course be great and powerful, and they rich and happy, independent of the greater or lesser abundance of the precious metals. These admit of divisions and subdivisions to a great extent; and where the pieces might become so small as to be in danger of being lost, it is easy to mix the gold or silver with a baser metal, as is practised in some countries of Europe, and by that means raise the pieces to a bulk more sensible and convenient. They still serve the same purposes of exchange, whatever their number may be, or whatever colour they may be supposed to have.

---

3. The Italians gave to the Emperor Maximilian the nickname of Poccidanari. None of the enterprises of that prince ever succeeded, for want of money.

To these difficulties I answer that the effect, here supposed to flow from scarcity of money, really arises from the manners and customs of the people; and that we mistake, as is too usual, a collateral effect for a cause. The contradiction is only apparent; but it requires some thought and reflection to discover the principles by which we can reconcile reason to experience.

It seems a maxim almost self-evident that the prices of everything depend on the proportion between commodities and money, and that any considerable alteration on either has the same effect, either of heightening or lowering the price. Increase the commodities, they become cheaper; increase the money, they rise in their value. As, on the other hand, a diminution of the former, and that of the latter, have contrary tendencies.

It is also evident that the prices do not so much depend on the absolute quantity of commodities and that of money which are in a nation as on that of the commodities which come or may come to market and of the money which circulates. If the coin be locked up in chests, it is the same thing with regard to prices as if it were annihilated; if the commodities be hoarded in magazines and granaries, a like effect follows. As the money and commodities in these cases never meet, they cannot affect each other. Were we, at any time, to form conjectures concerning the price of provisions, the corn which the farmer must reserve for seed and for the maintenance of himself and family ought never to enter into the estimation. It is only the overplus, compared to the demand, that determines the value.

To apply these principles, we must consider that in the first and more uncultivated ages of any state, ere fancy has confounded her wants with those of nature, men, content with the produce of their own fields, or with those rude improvements which they themselves can work upon them, have little occasion for exchange, or least for money, which, by agreement, is the common measure of exchange. The wool of the farmer's own flock, spun in his own family, and wrought by a neighbouring weaver, who receives his payment in corn or wool, suffices for furniture and clothing. The carpenter, the smith, the mason, the tailor are retained by wages of a like nature; and the landlord himself, dwelling in the neighbourhood, is content to receive his rent in the commodities raised by the farmer. The greater part of these he consumes at home, in rustic hospitality; the rest, perhaps, he disposes of for money to the neighbouring town, whence he draws the few materials of his expense and luxury.

But after men begin to refine on all these enjoyments, and live not always at home, nor are content with what can be raised in their neighbourhood, there is more exchange and commerce of all kinds, and more money enters into that exchange. The tradesmen will not be paid in corn, because they want something more than barely to eat. The farmer goes beyond his own parish for the commodities he purchases, and cannot always carry his commodities to the merchant who supplies him. The landlord lives in the capital, or in a foreign country; and demands his rent in gold and silver, which can easily be transported to him. Great undertakers, and manufacturers, and merchants arise in every commodity; and these can conveniently deal in nothing but in specie. And consequently, in this situation of society, the coin enters into many more contracts, and by that means is much more employed than in the former.

The necessary effect is that, provided the money increase not in the nation, everything must become much cheaper in times of industry and refinement than in rude, uncultivated ages. It is the proportion between the circulating money and the commodities in the market which determines the prices. Goods that are consumed at home, or exchanged with other goods in the neighbourhood, never come to market; they affect not in the least the current specie; with regard to it they are as if totally annihilated; and consequently this method of using them sinks the proportion on the side of the commodities, and increases the prices. But after money enters into all contracts and sales, and is everywhere the measure of exchange, the same national cash has a much greater task to perform; all commodities are then in the market; the sphere of circulation is enlarged; it is the same case as if that individual sum were to serve a larger kingdom; and therefore, the proportion being here lessened on the side of the money, everything must become cheaper, and the prices gradually fall.

By the most exact computations that have been formed all over Europe, after making allowance for the alteration in the numerary value or the denomination, it is found that the prices of all things have only risen three or, at most, four times since the discovery of the West Indies. But will any one assert that there is not much more than four times the coin in Europe that was in the fifteenth century, and the centuries preceding it? The Spaniards and Portuguese from their mines, the English, French, and Dutch by their African trade, and by their interlopers in the West Indies, bring home about six millions a year, of which not above a third goes to the East Indies. This sum alone, in ten years, would probably double the ancient stock of money in Europe. And no other satisfactory reason can be given why all prices have not risen to a much more exorbitant height, except that which is derived from a change of customs and manners. Besides that more commodities are produced by additional industry, the same commodities come more to market, after men depart from their ancient simplicity of manners. And though this increase has not been equal to that of money, it has, however, been considerable, and has preserved the proportion between coin and commodities nearer the ancient standard.

Were the question proposed, Which of these methods of living in the people, the simple or refined, is the most advantageous to the state or public? I should, without much scruple, prefer the latter, in a view to politics at least; and should produce this as an additional reason for the ecouragement of trade and manufactures.

While men live in the ancient simple manner, and supply all their necessaries from domestic industry or from the neighbourhood, the sovereign can levy no taxes in money from a considerable part of his subjects; and if he will impose on them any burdens, he must take payment in commodities, with which alone they abound; a method attended with such great and obvious inconveniencies that they need not here be insisted on. All the money he can pretend to raise must be from his principal cities, where alone it circulates; and these, it is evident, cannot afford him so much as the whole state could, did gold and silver circulate throughout the whole. But besides this obvious diminution of the revenue, there is another cause of the poverty of the public in such a situation. Not only the sovereign receives less money, but the same money goes not so far as in times of industry and general commerce. Everything is dearer where the gold and silver are supposed equal; and that because fewer commodities come to market, and the whole coin bears a higher proportion to what is to be purchased by it; whence alone the prices of everything are fixed and determined.

Here then we may learn the fallacy of the remark, often to be met with in historians, and even in common conversation, that any particular state is weak, though fertile, populous, and well cultivated, merely because it wants money. It appears that the want of money can never injure any state within itself: for men and commodities are the real strength of any community. It is the simple manner of living which here hurts the public, by confining the gold and silver to few hands, and preventing its universal diffusion and circulation. On the contrary, industry and refinements of all kinds incorporate it with the whole state, however small its quantity may be: they digest it into every vein, so to speak; and make it enter into every transaction and contract. No hand is entirely empty of it. And as the prices of everything fall by that means, the sovereign has a double advantage: he may draw money by his taxes from every part of the state; and what he receives goes farther in every purchase and payment.

We may infer, from a comparison of prices, that money is not more plentiful in China, than it was in Europe three centuries ago: But what immense power is that empire possessed of, if we may judge by the civil and military establishment maintained by it? Polybius tells us that provisions were so cheap in Italy during his time that in some places the stated price for a meal at the inns was a *semis* a head, little more than a farthing! Yet the Roman power had even then subdued the whole known world. About a century before that period, the Carthaginian ambassador said, by way of raillery, that no people lived more sociably among themselves than the Romans; for that in every entertainment which, as foreign ministers, they received, they still observed the same plate at every table. The absolute quantity of the precious metals is a matter of great indifference. There are only two circumstances of any importance, namely, their gradual increase, and their thorough concoction and circulation through the state; and the influence of both these circumstances has here been explained.

Of the Balance of Trade

It is very usual, in nations ignorant of the nature of commerce, to prohibit the exportation of commodities, and to preserve among themselves whatever they think valuable and useful. They do not consider that in this prohibition they act directly contrary to their intention; and that the more is exported of any commodity, the more will be raised at home, of which they themselves will always have the first offer.

It is well known to the learned that the ancient laws of Athens rendered the exportation of figs criminal; that being supposed a species of fruit so excellent in Attica that the Athenians deemed it too delicious for the palate of any foreigner. And in this ridiculous prohibition they were so much in earnest that informers were thence called sycophants among them, from two Greek words which signify figs and discoverer. There are proofs in many old acts of parliament of the same ignorance in the nature of commerce, particularly in the reign of Edward III. And to this day, in France, the exportation of corn is almost always prohibited; in order, as they say, to prevent famines; though it is evident that nothing contributes more to the frequent famines which so much distress that fertile country.

The same jealous fear, with regard to money, has also prevailed among several nations; and it required both reason and experience to convince any people that these prohibitions serve to no other purpose than to raise the exchange against them, and produce a still greater exportation.

These errors, one may say, are gross and palpable: But there still prevails, even in nations well acquainted with commerce, a strong jealousy with regard to the balance of trade, and a fear that all their gold and silver may be leaving them. This seems to me, almost in every case, a groundless apprehension; and I should as soon dread that all our springs and rivers should be exhausted as that money should abandon a kingdom where there are people and industry. Let us carefully preserve these latter advantages; and we need never be apprehensive of losing the former.

It is easy to observe that all calculations concerning the balance of trade are founded on very uncertain facts and suppositions. The custom-house books are allowed to be an insufficient ground of reasoning; nor is the rate of exchange much better; unless we consider it with all nations, and know also the proportions of the several sums remitted; which one may safely pronounce impossible. Every man who has ever reasoned on this subject has always proved his theory, whatever it was, by facts and calculations, and by an enumeration of all the commodities sent to all foreign kingdoms.

The writings of Mr. Gee struck the nation with a universal panic when they saw it plainly demonstrated, by a detail of particulars, that the balance was against them for so considerable a sum as must leave them without a single shilling in five or six years. But luckily, twenty years have since elapsed, with an expensive foreign war; yet is it commonly supposed that money is still more plentiful among us than in any former period.

Nothing can be more entertaining on this head than Dr. Swift, an author so quick in discerning the mistakes and absurdities of others. He says, in his short view of the state of Ireland, that the whole cash of that kingdom formerly amounted but to 500,000 pounds; that out of this the Irish remitted every year a neat million to England, and had scarcely any other source from which they could compensate themselves, and little other foreign trade than the importation of French wines, for which they paid ready money. The consequence of this situation, which must be owned to be disadvantageous, was that in a course of three years the current money of Ireland, from 500,000 pounds was reduced to less than two. And at present, I suppose, in a course of 30 years it is absolutely nothing. Yet I know not how that opinion of the advance of riches in Ireland, which gave the Doctor so much indignation, seems still to continue, and gain ground with everybody.

In short, this apprehension of the wrong balance of trade appears of such a nature that it discovers itself wherever one is out of humour with the ministry, or is in low spirits; and as it can never be refuted by a particular detail of all the exports which counterbalance the imports, it may here be proper to form a general argument that they may prove the impossibility of this event as long as we preserve our people and our industry.

Suppose four-fifths of all the money in Great Britain to be annihilated in one night, and the nation reduced to the same condition, with regard to specie, as in the reigns of the Harrys and Edwards, what would be the consequence? Must not the price of all labour and commodities sink in proportion, and everything be sold as cheap as they were in those ages? What nation could then dispute with us in any foreign market, or pretend to navigate or to sell manufactures at the same price, which to us would afford sufficient profit? In how little time, therefore, must this bring back the money which we had lost, and raise us to the level of all the neighbouring nations? Where, after we have arrived, we immediately lose the advantage of the cheapness of labour and commodities; and the farther flowing in of money is stopped by our fulness and repletion.

Again, suppose that all the money of Great Britain were multiplied fivefold in a night, must not the contrary effect follow? Must not all labour and commodities rise to such an exorbitant height that no neighbouring nations could afford to buy from us; while their commodities, on the other hand, became comparatively so cheap that, in spite of all the laws which could be formed, they would be run in upon us, and our money flow out; till we fall to a level with foreigners, and lose that great superiority of riches, which had laid us under such disadvantages?

Now, it is evident, that the same causes which would correct these exorbitant inequalities, were they to happen miraculously, must prevent their happening in the common course of nature, and must forever, in all neighbouring nations, preserve money nearly proportionable to the art and industry of each nation. All water, wherever it communicates, remains always at a level. Ask naturalists the reason; they tell you that were it to be raised in any one place, the superior gravity of that part not being balanced must depress it, till it meet a counterpoise; and that the same cause, which redresses the inequality when it happens, must forever prevent it, without some violent external operation.[1]

Can one imagine that it had ever been possible, by any laws, or even by any art or industry, to have kept all the money in Spain which the galleons have brought from the Indies? Or that all commodities could be sold in France for a tenth of the price which they would yield on the other side of the Pyrenees, without finding their way thither, and drain-

---

1. There is another cause, though more limited in its operation, which checks the wrong balance of trade, to every particular nation to which the kingdom trades. When we import more goods than we export, the exchange turns against us, and this becomes a new encouragement to export; as much as the charge of carriage and insurance of the money which becomes due would amount to. For the exchange can never rise but a little higher than that sum.

ing from that immense treasure? What other reason, indeed, is there why all nations, at present, gain in their trade with Spain and Portugal, but because it is impossible to heap up money, more than any fluid, beyond its proper level? The sovereigns of these countries have shown that they wanted not inclination to keep their gold and silver to themselves had it been in any degree practicable.

But as any body of water may be raised above the level of the surrounding element, if the former has no communication with the latter, so in money, if the communication be cut off, by any material or physical impediment (for all laws alone are ineffectual), there may, in such a case, be a very great inequality of money. Thus the immense distance of China, together with the monopolies of our India companies, obstructing the communication, preserve in Europe the gold and silver, especially the latter, in much greater plenty than they are found in that kingdom. But, notwithstanding this great obstruction, the force of the causes abovementioned is still evident. The skill and ingenuity of Europe in general surpasses perhaps that of China, with regard to manual arts and manufactures; yet are we never able to trade thither without great disadvantage. And were it not for the continual recruits which we receive from America, money would soon sink in Europe, and rise in China, till it came nearly to a level in both places. Nor can any reasonable man doubt but that industrious nation, were they as near us as Poland or Barbary, would drain us of the overplus of our specie, and draw to themselves a larger share of the West Indian treasures. We need not have recourse to a physical attraction, in order to explain the necessity of this operation. There is a moral attraction, arising from the interests and passions of men, which is full as potent and infallible.

How is the balance kept in the provinces of every kingdom among themselves but by the force of this principle, which makes it impossible for money to lose its level, and either to rise or sink beyond the proportion of the labour and commodities which are in each province? Did not long experience make people easy on this head, what a fund of gloomy reflections might calculations afford to a melancholy Yorkshireman, while he computed and magnified the sums drawn to London by taxes, absentees, commodities, and found on comparison the opposite articles so much inferior? And no doubt, had the Heptarchy subsisted in England, the legislature of each state had been continually alarmed by the fear of a wrong balance; and as it is probable that the mutual hatred of these states would have been extremely violent on account of their close neighbourhood, they would have loaded and oppressed all commerce, by a jealous and superfluous caution. Since the union has removed the barriers between Scotland and England, which of these nations gains from the other by this free commerce? Or if the former kingdom has received any increase of riches, can it reasonably be accounted for by anything but the increase of its art and industry? It was a common apprehension in England before the union, as we learn from L'Abbe du Bos, that Scotland would soon drain them of their treasure were an open trade allowed; and on the other side the Tweed a contrary apprehension prevailed: With what justice in both, time has shown.

What happens in small portions of mankind must take place in greater. The provinces of the Roman empire, no doubt, kept their balance with each other, and with Italy, independent of the legislature; as much as the several counties of Great Britain, or the several parishes of each county. And any man who travels over Europe at this day may see, by the prices of commodities, that money, in spite of the absurd jealousy of princes and states, has brought itself nearly to a level; and that the difference between one kingdom and another is not greater in this respect than it is often between different provinces of the same kingdom. Men naturally flock to capital cities, seaports, and navigable rivers. There we find more men, more industry, more commodities, and consequently more money; but still the latter difference holds proportion with the former, and the level is preserved.[2]

Our jealousy and our hatred of France are without bounds; and the former sentiment, at least, must be acknowledged reasonable and well grounded. These passions have occasioned innumerable barriers and obstructions upon commerce, where we are accused of being commonly the aggressors. But what have we gained by the bargain? We lost the French market for our woollen manufactures, and transferred the commerce of wine to Spain and Portugal, where we buy worse liquor at a higher price. There are few Englishmen who would not think their coun-

---

2. It must carefully be remarked, that throughout this discourse, wherever I speak of the level of money, I mean always its proportional level to the commodities, labour, industry, and skill, which is in the several states. And I assert, that where these advantages are double, triple, quadruple, to what they are in the neighbouring states, the money infallibly will also be double, triple, quadruple. The only circumstance that can obstruct the exactness of these proportions, is the expense of transporting the commodities from one place to another; and this expense is sometimes unequal. Thus the corn, cattle, cheese, butter, of Derbyshire, cannot draw the money of London, so much as the manufactures of London draw the money of Derbyshire. But this objection is only a seeming one: For so far as the transport of commodities is expensive, so far is the communication between the places obstructed and imperfect.

try absolutely ruined were French wines sold in England so cheap and in such abundance as to supplant, in some measure, all ale, and home-brewed liquors: But would we lay aside prejudice, it would not be difficult to prove that nothing could be more innocent, perhaps advantageous. Each new acre of vineyard planted in France, in order to supply England with wine, would make it requisite for the French to take the produce of an English acre, sown in wheat or barley, in order to subsist themselves; and it is evident that we should thereby get command of the better commodity.

There are many edicts of the French king prohibiting the planting of new vineyards, and ordering all those which are lately planted to be grubbed up: so sensible are they, in that country, of the superior value of corn above every other product.

Mareschal Vauban complains often, and with reason, of the absurd duties which load the entry of those wines of Languedoc, Guienne, and other southern provinces that are imported into Britanny and Normandy. He entertained no doubt but these latter provinces could preserve their balance, notwithstanding the open commerce which he recommends. And it is evident that a few leagues more navigation to England would make no difference; or if it did, that it must operate alike on the commodities of both kingdoms.

There is indeed one expedient by which it is possible to sink, and another by which we may raise money beyond its natural level in any kingdom; but these cases, when examined, will be found to resolve into our general theory, and to bring additional authority to it.

I scarcely know any method of sinking money below its level but those institutions of banks, funds, and paper credit, which are so much practised in this kingdom. These render paper equivalent to money, circulate it throughout the whole state, make it supply the place of gold and silver, raise proportionably the price of labour and commodities, and by that means either banish a great part of those precious metals, or prevent their farther increase. What can be more short-sighted than our reasonings on this head? We fancy because an individual would be much richer were his stock of money doubled than the same good effect would follow were the money of every one increased; not considering that this would raise as much the price of every commodity, and reduce every man, in time, to the same condition as before. It is only in our public negotiations and transactions with foreigners that a greater stock of money is advantageous; and as our paper is there absolutely insignificant, we feel, by its means, all the ill effects arising from a great abundance of money, without reaping any of the advantages.[3]

Suppose that there are 12 millions of paper, which circulate in the kingdom as money (for we are not to imagine that all our enormous funds are employed in that shape), and suppose the real cash of the kingdom to be 18 millions: Here is a state which is found by experience to be able to hold a stock of 30 millions. I say, if it be able to hold it, it must of necessity have acquired it in gold and silver had we not obstructed the entrance of these metals by this new invention of paper. Whence would it have acquired that sum? From all the kingdoms of the world. But why? Because if you remove these 12 millions, money in this state is below its level compared with our neighbours; and we must immediately draw from all of them till we be full and saturate, so to speak, and can hold no more. By our present politics, we are as careful to stuff the nation with this fine commodity of bank-bills and chequer-notes as if we were afraid of being overburdened with the precious metals.

It is not to be doubted but the great plenty of bullion in France is, in a great measure, owing to the want of paper credit. The French have no banks: merchants bills do not there circulate as with us: Usury or lending on interest is not directly permitted; so that many have large sums in their coffers: great quantities of plate are used in private houses; and all the churches are full of it. By this means, provisions and labour still remain cheaper among them than in nations that are not half so rich in gold and silver. The advantages of this situation, in point of trade as well as in great public emergencies, are too evident to be disputed.

The same fashion a few years ago prevailed in Genoa, which still has place in England and Holland, of using services of china-ware instead of plate; but the senate, foreseeing the consequence, prohibited the use of that brittle commodity beyond a certain extent; while the use of silver-plate was left unlimited. And I suppose, in their late distresses, they felt the good effect of this ordinance. Our tax on plate is, perhaps, in this view, somewhat impolitic.

Before the introduction of paper money into our colonies, they had gold and silver sufficient for their circulation. Since the introduction of that commodity, the least inconveniency that has followed is the total banish-

---

3. We observed . . . [previously] that money when increasing gives encouragement to industry during the interval between the increase of money and rise of the prices. A good effect of this nature may follow too from paper credit; but it is dangerous to precipitate matters, at the risk of losing all by the failing of that credit, as must happen upon any violent shock in public affairs.

ment of the precious metals. And after the abolition of paper, can it be doubted but money will return, while these colonies possess manufactures and commodities, the only thing valuable in commerce, and for whose sake alone all men desire money.

What pity Lycurgus did not think of paper credit, when he wanted to banish gold and silver from Sparta! It would have served his purpose better than the lumps of iron he made use of as money; and would also have prevented more effectually all commerce with strangers, as being of so much less real and intrinsic value.

It must, however, be confessed that as all these questions of trade and money are extremely complicated, there are certain lights in which this subject may be placed so as to represent the advantages of paper credit and banks to be superior to their disadvantages. That they banish specie and bullion from a state is undoubtedly true; and whoever looks no farther than this circumstance does well to condemn them; but specie and bullion are not of so great consequence as not to admit of a compensation, and even an overbalance from the increase of industry and of credit, which may be promoted by the right use of paper money. It is well known of what advantage it is to a merchant to be able to discount his bills upon occasion; and everything that facilitates this species of traffic is favourable to the general commerce of a state. But private bankers are enabled to give such credit by the credit they receive from the depositing of money in their shops; and the bank of England in the same manner, from the liberty it has to issue its notes in all payments. There was an invention of this kind, which was fallen upon some years ago by the banks of Edinburgh; and which, as it is one of the most ingenious ideas that has been executed in commerce, has also been thought advantageous to Scotland. It is there called a Bank-Credit; and is of this nature: A man goes to the bank and finds surety to the amount, we shall suppose, of a thousand pounds. This money, or any part of it, he has the liberty of drawing out whenever he pleases, and he pays only the ordinary interest for it, while it is in his hands. He may, when he pleases, repay any sum so small as twenty pounds, and the interest is discounted from the very day of the repayment. The advantages resulting from this contrivance are manifold. As a man may find surety nearly to the amount of his substance, and his bank-credit is equivalent to ready money, a merchant does hereby in a manner coin his houses, his household furniture, the goods in his warehouse, the foreign debts due to him, his ships at sea; and can, upon occasion, employ them in all payments, as if they were the current money of the country. If a man borrow a thousand pounds from a private hand, besides that it is not always to be found when required, he pays interest for it, whether he be using it or not: His bank-credit costs him nothing except during the very moment in which it is of service to him: and this circumstance is of equal advantage as if he had borrowed money at much lower interest. Merchants, likewise from this invention, acquire a great facility in supporting each other's credit, which is a considerable security against bankruptcies. A man, when his own bank-credit is exhausted, goes to any of his neighbours who is not in the same condition; and he gets the money, which he replaces at his convenience.

After this practice had taken place during some years at Edinburgh, several companies of merchants at Glasgow carried the matter farther. They associated themselves into different banks, and issued notes so low as ten shillings, which they used in all payments for goods, manufactures, tradesmen's labour of all kinds; and these notes, from the established credit of the companies, passed as money in all payments throughout the country. By this means, a stock of five thousand pounds was able to perform the same operations as if it were six or seven; and merchants were thereby enabled to trade to a greater extent, and to require less profit in all their transactions. But whatever other advantages result from these inventions, it must still be allowed that besides giving too great facility to credit, which is dangerous, they banish the precious metals: and nothing can be a more evident proof of it than a comparison of the past and present condition of Scotland in that particular. It was found, upon the recoinage made after the union, that there was near a million of specie in that country: But notwithstanding the great increase of riches, commerce, and manufactures of all kinds, it is thought that even where there is no extraordinary drain made by England, the current specie will not now amount to a third of that sum.

But as our projects of paper credit are almost the only expedient by which we can sink money below its level, so, in my opinion, the only expedient by which we can raise money above it is a practice which we should all exclaim against as destructive, namely, the gathering of large sums into a public treasure, locking them up, and absolutely preventing their circulation. The fluid not communicating with the neighbouring element may, by such an artifice, be raised to what height we please. To prove this, we need only return to our first supposition, of annihilating the half or any part of our cash, where we found that the immediate consequence of such an event would be the attraction of an equal sum from all the neighbouring kingdoms. Nor does there seem to be any necessary bounds set, by the nature of things, to this practice of hoarding. A small city, like Geneva, continuing this policy for ages, might engross nine-tenths of the money of Europe. There seems, indeed, in the nature of man, an invincible obstacle to that immense growth of riches. A weak state, with an enormous treasure, will soon become a prey to some of its poorer but more powerful neighbours. A great state would dissipate its wealth in dangerous and ill-concerted projects; and probably destroy, with it, what is much more valuable, the industry, morals, and numbers of its people. The fluid, in this case, raised to too great a height, bursts and destroys the vessel that contains it; and mixing itself with the surrounding element, soon falls to its proper level.

So little are we commonly acquainted with this principle that though all historians agree in relating uniformly so recent an event as the immense treasure amassed by Harry VII (which they make amount to 2,700,000 pounds), we rather reject their concurring testimony than admit of a fact which agrees so ill with our inveterate prejudices. It is indeed probable that this sum might be three-fourths of all the money in England. But where is the difficulty in conceiving that such a sum might be amassed in twenty years by a cunning, rapacious, frugal, and almost absolute monarch? Nor is it probable that the diminution of circulating money was ever sensibly felt by the people, or ever did them any prejudice. The sinking of the prices of all commodities would immediately replace it, by giving England the advantage in its commerce with the neighbouring kingdoms.

Have we not an instance in the small republic of Athens with its allies, who, in about fifty years, between the Median and Peloponnesian wars, amassed a sum not much inferior to that of Harry VII? For all the Greek historians and orators agree that the Athenians collected in the citadel more than 10,000 talents, which they afterwards dissipated in their own ruin, in rash and imprudent enterprises. But when this money was set a running, and began to communicate with the surrounding fluid, what was the consequence? Did it remain in the state? No. For we find, by the memorable census mentioned by Demosthenes and Polybius, that, in about fifty years afterwards, the whole value of the republic, comprehending lands, houses, commodities, slaves, and money, was less than 6,000 talents.

What an ambitious high-spirited people was this, to collect and keep in their treasury, with a view to conquests, a sum, which it was every day in the power of the citizens, by a single vote, to distribute among themselves, and which would have gone near to triple the riches of every individual! For we must observe that the numbers and private riches of the Athenians are said, by ancient writers, to have been no greater at the beginning of the Peloponnesian War than at the beginning of the Macedonian.

Money was little more plentiful in Greece during the age of Philip and Perseus than in England during that of Harry VII: Yet these two monarchs in thirty years collected from the small kingdom of Macedon, a larger treasure than that of the English monarch. Paulus Aemilius brought to Rome about 1,700,000 pounds sterling. Pliny says, 2,400,000. And that was but a part of the Macedonian treasure. The rest was dissipated by the resistance and flight of Perseus.

We may learn from Stanian that the canton of Berne had 300,000 pounds lent at interest, and had above six times as much in their treasury. Here then is a sum hoarded of 1,800,000 pounds sterling, which is at least quadruple what should naturally circulate in such a petty state; and yet no one who travels in the Pais de Vaux, or any part of that canton, observes any want of money more than could be supposed in a country of that extent, soil, and situation. On the contrary, there are scarce any inland provinces in the continent of France or Germany where the inhabitants are at this time so opulent, though that canton has vastly increased its treasure since 1714, the time when Stanian wrote his judicious account of Switzerland.[4]

The account given by Appian of the treasure of the Ptolemies is so prodigious that one cannot admit of it; and so much the less because the historian says that the other successors of Alexander were also frugal, and had many of them treasures not much inferior. For this saving humour of the neighbouring princes must necessarily have checked the frugality of the Egyptian monarchs, according to the foregoing theory. The sum he mentions is 740,000 talents, or 191,166,666 pounds 13 shillings and 4 pence, according to Dr. Arbuthnot's computation. And yet Appian says that he extracted his account from the public records; and he was himself a native of Alexandria.

From these principles we may learn what judgment we ought to form of those numberless bars, obstructions, and imposts which all nations of Europe, and none more than England, have put upon trade; from an exorbitant desire of amassing money, which never will heap up beyond its level, while it circulates; or from an ill grounded apprehension of losing their specie, which never will sink below it. Could anything scatter our

---

4. The poverty which Stanian speaks of is only to be seen in the most mountainous cantons, where there is no commodity to bring money. And even there the people are not poorer than in the diocese of Saltsburgh on the one hand, or Savoy on the other.

riches, it would be such impolitic contrivances. But this general ill effect, however, results from them, that they deprive neighbouring nations of that free communication and exchange which the Author of the world has intended, by giving them soils, climates, and geniuses, so different from each other.

Our modern politics embrace the only method of banishing money, the using of paper credit; they reject the only method of amassing it, the practice of hoarding; and they adopt a hundred contrivances, which serve to no purpose but to check industry, and rob ourselves and our neighbours of the common benefits of art and nature.

All taxes, however, upon foreign commodities are not to be regarded as prejudicial or useless, but those only which are founded on the jealousy above-mentioned. A tax on German linen encourages home manufactures, and thereby multiplies our people and industry. A tax on brandy increases the sale of rum, and supports our southern colonies. And as it is necessary that imposts should be levied for the support of government, it may be thought more convenient to lay them on foreign commodities, which can easily be intercepted at the port, and subjected to the impost. We ought, however, always to remember the maxim of Dr. Swift that in the arithmetic of the customs, two and two make not four, but often make only one. It can scarcely be doubted, but if the duties on wine were lowered to a third, they would yield much more to the government than at present: Our people might thereby afford to drink commonly a better and more wholesome liquor; and no prejudice would ensue to the balance of trade, of which we are so jealous. The manufacture of ale beyond the agriculture is but inconsiderable, and gives employment to few hands. The transport of wine and corn would not be much inferior.

But are there not frequent instances, you will say, of states and kingdoms which were formerly rich and opulent and are now poor and beggarly? Has not the money left them with which they formerly abounded? I answer, if they lose their trade, industry, and people, they cannot expect to keep their gold and silver: for these precious metals will hold proportion to the former advantages. When Lisbon and Amsterdam got the East-India trade from Venice and Genoa, they also got the profits and money which arose from it. Where the seat of government is transferred, where expensive armies are maintained at a distance, where great funds are possessed by foreigners, there naturally follows from these causes a diminution of the specie. But these, we may observe, are violent and forcible methods of carrying away money, and are in time commonly attended with the transport of people and industry. But where these remain, and the drain is not continued, the money always finds its way back again, by a hundred canals, of which we have no notion or suspicion. What immense treasures have been spent, by so many nations, in Flanders, since the revolution, in the course of three long wars! More money perhaps than the half of what is at present in Europe. But what has now become of it? Is it in the narrow compass of the Austrian provinces? No, surely: It has most of it returned to the several countries whence it came, and has followed that art and industry by which at first it was acquired. For above a thousand years, the money of Europe has been flowing to Rome, by an open and sensible current; but it has been emptied by many secret and insensible canals: and the want of industry and commerce renders at present the papal dominions the poorest territory in all Italy.

In short, a government has great reason to preserve with care its people and its manufactures. Its money it may safely trust to the course of human affairs, without fear or jealousy. Or if it ever give attention to this latter circumstance, it ought only to be so far as it affects the former.

Of Taxes

There is a prevailing maxim, among some reasoners, that every new tax creates a new ability in the subject to bear it, and that each increase of public burdens increases proportionably the industry of the people. This maxim is of such a nature as is most likely to be abused; and is so much the more dangerous as its truth cannot be altogether denied: but it must be owned, when kept within certain bounds, to have some foundation in reason and experience.

When a tax is laid upon commodities which are consumed by the common people, the necessary consequence may seem to be either that the poor must retrench something from their way of living or raise their wages, so as to make the burden of the tax fall entirely upon the rich. But there is a third consequence which often follows upon taxes, namely, that the poor increase their industry, perform more work, and live as well as before, without demanding more for their labour. Where taxes are moderate, are laid on gradually, and affect not the necessaries of life, this consequence naturally follows; and it is certain that such difficulties often serve to excite the industry of a people, and render them more opulent and laborious than others who enjoy the greatest advantages. For we may observe, as a parallel instance, that the most commercial nations have not always possessed the greatest extent of fertile land; but, on the contrary, that they have laboured under many natural disadvantages. Tyre, Athens, Carthage, Rhodes, Genoa, Venice, Holland are strong examples to this purpose. And in all history, we find only three instances of large and fertile countries which have possessed much trade: the Netherlands, England, and France. The two former seem to have been allured by the advantages of their maritime situation, and the necessity they lay under of frequenting foreign ports in order to procure what their own climate refused them. And as to France, trade has come late into that kingdom, and seems to have been the effect of reflection and observation in an ingenious and enterprising people, who remarked the riches acquired by such of the neighbouring nations as cultivated navigation and commerce.

The places mentioned by Cicero as possessed of the greatest commerce in his time are Alexandria, Colchus, Tyre, Sidon, Andros, Cyprus, Pamphylia, Lycia, Rhodes, Chios, Byzantium, Lesbos, Smyrna, Miletum, Coos. All these, except Alexandria, were either small islands or narrow territories. And that city owed its trade entirely to the happiness of its situation.

Since therefore some natural necessities or disadvantages may be thought favourable to industry, why may not artificial burdens have the same effect? Sir William Temple, we may observe, ascribes the industry of the Dutch entirely to necessity, proceeding from their natural disadvantages; and illustrates his doctrine by a striking comparison with Ireland, "where," says he, "by the largeness and plenty of the soil, and scarcity of people, all things necessary to life are so cheap that an industrious man, by two days labour, may gain enough to feed him the rest of the week. Which I take to be a very plain ground of the laziness attributed to the people. For men naturally prefer ease before labour, and will not take pains if they can live idle; though when, by necessity, they have been inured to it, they cannot leave it, being grown a custom necessary to their health, and to their very entertainment. Nor perhaps is the change harder from constant ease to labour than from constant labour to ease." After which the author proceeds to confirm his doctrine, by enumerating, as above, the places where trade has most flourished, in ancient and modern times, and which are commonly observed to be such narrow confined territories as beget a necessity for industry.[1]

The best taxes are such as are levied upon consumptions, especially those of luxury, because such taxes are least felt by the people. They

---

1. 'Tis always observed, in years of scarcity, if it be not extreme, that the poor labour more, and really live better than in years of great plenty, when they indulge themselves in idleness and riot. I have been told, by a considerable manufacturer, that in the year 1740, when bread and provisions of all kinds were very dear, his workmen not only made a shift to live but paid debts which they had contracted in former years that were much more favourable and abundant.

This doctrine, therefore, with regard to taxes, may be admitted in some degree: But beware of the abuse. Exorbitant taxes, like extreme necessity, destroy industry, by producing despair; and even before they reach this pitch, they raise the wages of the labourer and manufacturer, and heighten the price of all commodities. An attentive disinterested legislature will observe the point when the emolument ceases, and the prejudice begins: But as the contrary character is much more common, 'tis to be feared that taxes all over Europe are multiplying to such a degree as will entirely crush all art and industry; tho', perhaps, their first increase, together with other circumstances, might have contributed to the growth of these advantages.

seem, in some measure, voluntary, since a man may choose how far he will use the commodity which is taxed; they are paid gradually, and insensibly; they naturally produce sobriety and frugality, if judiciously imposed; and being confounded with the natural price of the commodity, they are scarcely perceived by the consumers. Their only disadvantage is that they are expensive in the levying.

Taxes upon possessions are levied without expense, but have every other disadvantage. Most states, however, are obliged to have recourse to them, in order to supply the deficiencies of the other.

But the most pernicious of all taxes are the arbitrary. They are commonly converted, by their management, into punishments on industry; and also, by their unavoidable inequality are more grievous than by the real burden which they impose. It is surprising, therefore, to see them have place among any civilized people.

In general, all poll-taxes, even when not arbitrary, which they commonly are, may be esteemed dangerous: because it is so easy for the sovereign to add a little more, and a little more, to the sum demanded, that these taxes are apt to become altogether oppressive and intolerable. On the other hand, a duty upon commodities checks itself; and a prince will soon find that an increase of the impost is no increase of his revenue. It is not easy, therefore, for a people to be altogether ruined by such taxes.

Historians inform us that one of the chief causes of the destruction of the Roman state was the alteration which Constantine introduced into the finances, by substituting a universal poll-tax in lieu of almost all the tithes, customs, and excises which formerly composed the revenue of the empire. The people, in all the provinces, were so grinded and oppressed by the publicans that they were glad to take refuge under the conquering arms of the barbarians, whose dominion, as they had fewer necessities and less art, was found preferable to the refined tyranny of the Romans.

It is an opinion, zealously promoted by some political writers, that since all taxes, as they pretend, fall ultimately upon land, it were better to lay them originally there, and abolish every duty upon consumptions. But it is denied that all taxes fall ultimately upon land. If a duty be laid upon any commodity consumed by an artisan, he has two obvious expedients for paying it: he may retrench somewhat of his expense, or he may increase his labour. Both these resources are more easy and natural than that of heightening his wages. We see that in years of scarcity, the weaver either consumes less or labours more or employs both these expedients of frugality and industry, by which he is enabled to reach the end of the year. It is but just that he should subject himself to the same hardships, if they deserve the name, for the sake of the public, which gives him protection. By what contrivance can he raise the price of his labour? The manufacturer who employs him will not give him more: neither can he, because the merchant, who exports the cloth, cannot raise its price, being limited by the price which it yields in foreign markets. Every man, to be sure, is desirous of pushing off from himself the burden of any tax which is imposed, and of laying it upon others: but as every man has the same inclination, and is upon the defensive, no set of men can be supposed to prevail altogether in this contest. And why the landed gentleman should be the victim of the whole, and should not be able to defend himself as well as others are, I cannot readily imagine. All tradesmen, indeed, would willingly prey upon him, and divide him among them, if they could: but this inclination they always have, though no taxes were levied; and the same methods by which he guards against the imposition of tradesmen before taxes will serve him afterwards, and make them share the burden with him. They must be very heavy taxes, indeed, and very injudiciously levied, which the artisan will not, of himself, be enabled to pay, by superior industry and frugality, without raising the price of his labour.

I shall conclude this subject with observing that we have, with regard to taxes, an instance of what frequently happens in political institutions, that the consequences of things are diametrically opposite to what we should expect on the first appearance. It is regarded as a fundamental maxim of the Turkish government that the Grand Signior, though absolute master of the lives and fortunes of each individual, has no authority to impose a new tax; and every Ottoman prince who has made such an attempt either has been obliged to retract or has found the fatal effects of his perseverance. One would imagine that this prejudice or established opinion were the firmest barrier in the world against oppression; yet it is certain that its effect is quite contrary. The emperor, having no regular method of increasing his revenue, must allow all the bashaws and governors to oppress and abuse the subjects: and these he squeezes after their return from their government. Whereas, if he could impose a new tax, like our European princes, his interest would so far be united with that of his people that he would immediately feel the bad effects of these disorderly levies of money, and would find that a pound raised by a general imposition would have less pernicious effects than a shilling taken in so unequal and arbitrary a manner.

Of the Study
of History

There is nothing which I would recommend more earnestly to my female readers than the study of history as an occupation, of all others, the best suited both to their sex and education, much more instructive than their ordinary books of amusement, and more entertaining than those serious compositions which are usually to be found in their closets. Among other important truths which they may learn from history they may be informed of two particulars, the knowledge of which may contribute very much to their quiet and repose: that our sex, as well as theirs, are far from being such perfect creatures as they are apt to imagine, and that Love is not the only passion which governs the male world, but is often overcome by avarice, ambition, vanity, and a thousand other passions. Whether they be the false representations of mankind in those two particulars which endear romances and novels so much to the fair sex, I know not; but must confess that I am sorry to see them have such an aversion to matter of fact, and such an appetite for falsehood. I remember I was once desired by a young beauty, for whom I had some passion, to send her some novels and romances for her amusement in the country; but was not so ungenerous as to take the advantage which such a course of reading might have given me, being resolved not to make use of poisoned arms against her. I therefore sent her Plutarch's *Lives*, assuring her, at the same time, that there was not a word of truth in them from beginning to end. She perused them very attentively, 'till she came to the lives of Alexander and Caesar, whose names she had heard of by accident; and then returned me the book, with many reproaches for deceiving her.

I may indeed be told that the fair sex have no such aversion to history as I have represented, provided it be secret history, and contain some memorable transaction proper to excite their curiosity. But as I do not find that truth, which is the basis of history, is at all regarded in those anecdotes, I cannot admit of this as a proof of their passion for that study. However this may be, I see not why the same curiosity might not receive a more proper direction, and lead them to desire accounts of those who lived in past ages, as well as of their contemporaries. What is it to Cleora whether Fulvia entertains a secret commerce of love with Philander or not? Has she not equal reason to be pleased when she is informed (what is whispered about among historians) that Cato's sister had an intrigue with Caesar, and palmed her son, Marcus Brutus, upon her husband for his own, tho' in reality he was her gallant's? And are not the loves of Messalina or Julia as proper subjects of discourse as any intrigue that this city has produced of late years?

But I know not whence it comes that I have been thus seduced into a kind of raillery against the ladies: unless, perhaps, it proceed from the same cause which makes the person who is the favourite of the company be often the object of their good-natured jests and pleasantries. We are pleased to address ourselves after any manner to one who is agreeable to us; and, at the same time, presume that nothing will be taken amiss by a person who is secure of the good opinion and affections of every one present. I shall now proceed to handle my subject more seriously, and shall point out the many advantages which flow from the study of history, and show how well suited it is to every one, but particularly to those who are debarred the severer studies, by the tenderness of their complexion, and the weakness of their education. The advantages found in history seem to be of three kinds, as it amuses the fancy, as it improves the understanding, and as it strengthens virtue.

In reality, what more agreeable entertainment to the mind than to be transported into the remotest ages of the world, and to observe human society, in its infancy, making the first faint essays towards the arts and sciences. To see the policy of government, and the civility of conversation, refining by degrees, and everything which is ornamental to human life advancing towards its perfection. To remark the rise, progress, declension, and final extinction of the most flourishing empires: the virtues which contributed to their greatness, and the vices which drew on their ruin. In short, to see all human race, from the beginning of time, pass, as it were, in review before us; appearing in their true colours, without any of those disguises which, during their lifetime, so much perplexed the judgment of the beholders. What spectacle can be imagined so magnificent, so various, so interesting? What amusement, either of the senses or imagination, can be compared with it? Shall those trifling pastimes which engross so much of our time be preferred as more satisfactory, and more fit to engage our attention? How perverse must that taste be which is capable of so wrong a choice of pleasures?

But history is a most improving part of knowledge, as well as an agreeable amusement; and a great part of what we commonly call erudition, and value so highly, is nothing but an acquaintance with historical facts. An extensive knowledge of this kind belongs to men of letters; but I must think it an unpardonable ignorance in persons of whatever sex or condition not to be acquainted with the history of their own country, together with the histories of ancient Greece and Rome. A woman may behave herself with good manners, and have even some vivacity in her turn of wit; but where her mind is so unfurnished, 'tis impossible her conversation can afford any entertainment to men of sense and reflection.

I must add that history is not only a valuable part of knowledge but opens the door to many other parts, and affords materials to most of the sciences. And indeed, if we consider the shortness of human life, and our limited knowledge, even of what passes in our own time, we must be sensible that we should be forever children in understanding were it not for this invention, which extends our experience to all past ages, and to the most distant nations; making them contribute as much to our improvement in wisdom as if they had actually lain under our observation. A man acquainted with history may, in some respect, be said to have lived from the beginning of the world, and to have been making continual additions to his stock of knowledge in every century.

There is also an advantage in that experience which is acquired by history above what is learned by the practice of the world, that it brings us acquainted with human affairs, without diminishing in the least from the most delicate sentiments of virtue. And, to tell the truth, I know not any study or occupation so unexceptionable as history in this particular. Poets can paint virtue in the most charming colours; but, as they address themselves entirely to the passions, they often become advocates for vice. Even philosophers are apt to bewilder themselves in the subtility of their speculations; and we have seen some go as far as to deny the reality of all moral distinctions. But I think it a remark worthy the attention of the speculative that the historians have been, almost without exception, the true friends of virtue, and have always represented it in its proper colours, however they may have erred in their judgments of particular persons. Machiavel himself discovers a true sentiment of virtue in his history of Florence. When he talks as a politician, in his general reasonings, he considers poisoning, assassination and perjury as lawful arts of power; but when he speaks as a historian, in his particular narrations, he shows so keen an indignation against vice, and so warm an approbation of virtue, in many passages, that I could not forbear applying to him that remark of Horace, that if you chase away nature, tho' with ever so great indignity, she will always return upon you. Nor is this combination of historians in favour of virtue at all difficult to be accounted for. When a man of business enters into life and action, he is more apt to consider the characters of men as they have relation to his interest than as they stand in themselves; and has his judgment warped on every occasion by the violence of his passion. When a philosopher contemplates characters and manners in his closet, the general abstract view of the objects leaves the mind so cold and unmoved that the sentiments of nature have no room to play, and he scarce feels the difference between vice and virtue. History keeps in a just medium betwixt these extremes, and places the objects in their true point of view. The writers of history, as well as the readers, are sufficiently interested in the characters and events to have a lively sentiment of blame or praise; and, at the same time, have no particular interest or concern to pervert their judgment.

---

*The foregoing essays are from a collection
of Hume's essays entitled*
ESSAYS MORAL, POLITICAL AND LITERARY.

Plutarch

c. 46–120

The Greek biographer and philosopher Plutarch was born in Chaeronea in Boeotia. Little is known of his life, and not all of that is strictly reliable. He studied in Athens under Ammonius Saccas, the founder of Neoplatonism, and later lectured on philosophy in Rome. It is reported that the emperor Trajan gave him consular rank and that later the emperor Hadrian made him procurator of Greece. It is known, in any case, that he returned to his native Boeotia, where he officiated as a priest of Apollo at Delphi, and it was there that he died. A letter to his wife on the death of their only daughter has been preserved. Plutarch consoles her for her loss in tender and high-minded words and speaks of the four sons who remain to them and need their care.

The fame of Plutarch rests largely on his *Parallel Lives*,[1] in which he recounted the lives and fortunes of forty-six Greek and Roman statesmen and military leaders. Each Roman hero is paired with a Greek hero who is parallel to him in merits and in the odds he faced. He makes a close comparison of the abilities and moral excellence of the Greek hero with his Roman counterpart, which was a useful thing for a Greek to do at this time, when Greek influence was often resented in Rome. Those who wish to investigate will find that the Greeks come off very well in the comparison.

The influence of the *Parallel Lives* has been immense, but it would be difficult to trace because it is so often taken for granted. It was read for pleasure and instruction by most eminent writers and by statesmen when they were literate, and some learned all they knew about Plato and Aristotle from the absorbing biographies of Plu-

---

[1] See *Great Books of the Western World*, Vol. 14.

tarch. Platonic ideas of the virtues and nobility proper to princes and generals were thus painlessly infused. As a girl Queen Elizabeth I read North's new English translation of the *Lives* with delight. Shakespeare took history, plots, and characters from North's translation, as in *Julius Caesar, Coriolanus,* and *Antony and Cleopatra,* and in the last play adopted some passages, including one long one, almost without a change. The *Lives* has not only proved a rich source for literature but also for the history of the classic world.

The essay that follows is from Plutarch's *Moralia,* which consists of about sixty essays dealing with a great variety of topics, mostly ethical. The treatment of even abstract subjects is concrete and pictorial: we are given one episode after another to illustrate the point. The frequent quotations from Greek dramatists, and from poems which are otherwise irretrievably lost, are an added attraction.

The essay which you are to read, like the others, is packed with anecdotes. If this seems surprising to you, try to think of a better way of putting across ethical ideas. Suppose you were going to maintain that lack of anger is a worse fault than truculence, or too much anger. You could give your reasons, but to convince your listener you would be obliged to give instances and illustrations or anecdotes. Anecdotes, Plutarch said, throw a sudden light on a man's character, rendering his "natural dispositions more plain than the famous battles won, wherein are slain ten thousand men." Montaigne and Francis Bacon were greatly influenced by the anecdotal style of Plutarch's essays. The essay form itself owes a great deal to his example.

Plutarch's essay *Of Bashfulness* is an ingenious development of Aristotle's theory that the virtues are means between extremes— between passions which are both vicious. In the *Nicomachean Ethics,* Aristotle points out that both shamelessness and bashfulness

Notes from the artist: "The portrait of Plutarch is done in the manner of a Greek vase, the background incorporating other elements of Greek design. The head in the foreground is that of Pericles, subject of one of Plutarch's Parallel Lives."

PLVTARCH

are disapproved, and yet the modest man is praised. This is because
the bashful man "is ashamed of everything," and the shameless man
"is not ashamed of anything." In between these extremes is the
modest man, who is ashamed on the proper occasions, for the right
reasons, and in an appropriate degree.

Out of this abstract analysis comes all Plutarch's rich elaboration.
He is particularly concerned to show the evils that flow from bashfulness. If you have always regarded too little shame as a worse
fault than too much, you may well change your mind before you
have finished this essay. You may even discover that you are a little
inclined toward bashfulness yourself. Consider some of the marks
of bashfulness given by Plutarch. Do you lend money to a friend
who importunes you, though you yourself are short and know that
you will be embarrassed later? Do you invite a man to your party
when he brings up the subject, though you know he will spoil things
for other guests? Is it hard to say No? Or, when seriously ill, do you
send for the best doctor available in town, or do you call in a doctor
friend who would otherwise be offended? And what do you say
when your friend reads you his poem which is wretched, and waits
for your praise?

More important than anything else—are you developing your
talents and prospects sufficiently, or do you hate to push yourself
forward and to be conspicuous? "Too much anxiety and timidity
lest we may do wrong," Plutarch says, "is also to be avoided; because many men have become cowards and been deterred from
generous undertakings." Fear of malice and envy, as well as the
dangers and difficulties, holds them back.

In reading this essay you will find a number of names you do not
know but do not be disturbed. You can find most of them in the
Index of the *Lives* and the rest in a classical dictionary.

Of Bashfulness

Some plants there are, in their own nature wild and barren, and hurtful to seed and garden sets, which yet among able husbandmen pass for infallible signs of a rich and promising soil. In like manner, some passions of the mind not good in themselves yet serve as first shoots and promises of a disposition which is naturally good, and also capable of much improvement by cultivation. Among these I rank bashfulness, the subject of our present discourse; no ill sign indeed, but the cause and occasion of a great deal of harm. For the bashful oftentimes run into the same enormities as the most hardened and impudent, with this difference only, that the former feel a regret for such miscarriages, but the latter take a pleasure and satisfaction therein. The shameless person is without sense of grief for his baseness, and the bashful is in distress at the very appearance of it. For bashfulness is only modesty in the excess, and is aptly enough named *dusopia* [the being put out of countenance], since the face is in some sense confused and dejected with the mind. For as that grief which casts down the eyes is termed dejection, so that kind of modesty which cannot look another in the face is called bashfulness. The orator, speaking of a shameless fellow, said he carried harlots, not virgins, in his eyes; on the other hand, the sheepishly bashful betrays no less the effeminacy and softness of his mind in his looks, palliating his weakness, which exposes him to the mercy of impudence, with the specious name of modesty. Cato indeed was wont to say of young persons, he had a greater opinion of such as were subject to color than of those that looked pale; teaching us thereby to look with greater apprehension on the heinousness of an action than on the reprimand which might follow, and to be more afraid of the suspicion of doing an ill thing than of the danger of it. However, too much anxiety and timidity lest we may do wrong is also to be avoided; because many men have become cowards and been deterred from generous undertakings, no less for fear of calumny and detraction than by the danger or difficulty of such attempts.

While therefore we must not suffer the weakness in the one case to pass unnoticed, neither must we abet or countenance invincible impudence in the other, such as is reported of Anaxarchus,

> Whose doglike carriage and effrontery,
> Despising infamy, outfaced disgrace.

A convenient mien between both is rather to be endeavored after, by repressing the over impudent, and animating the too meek temper. But as this kind of cure is difficult, so is the restraining such excesses not without danger; for as a gardener, in stubbing up some wild or useless bushes, makes at them carelessly with his spade, or burns them off the ground, but in dressing a vine, or grafting an apple, or pruning an olive, carries his hand with the greatest wariness and deliberation, that he may not unluckily injure the tree; so a philosopher, in removing envy, that useless and untractable plant, or covetousness or immoderate love of pleasure from the mind of youth, may cut deep safely, and make a large scar; but if he be to apply his discourse to some more sensible or delicate part, such as the restraining excess of bashfulness, it lies upon him to be very careful not to cut off or eradicate modesty with the contrary vice. For nurses who too often wipe away the dirt from their infants are apt to tear their flesh and put them to pain. And in like manner we must not so far extirpate all bashfulness in youth as to leave them careless or impudent; but as those that pull down private houses adjoining to the temples of the Gods prop up such parts as are contiguous to them, so in undermining bashfulness, due regard is to be had to adjacent modesty, good nature, and humanity. And yet these are the very qualities by which bashfulness insinuates itself and becomes fixed in a man, flattering him that he is good-natured, courteous, and civil, and has common sense, and that he is not obstinate and inexorable. The Stoics, therefore, in their discourses of modesty, distinguish all along betwixt that and bashfulness, leaving not so much as ambiguity of terms for a pretense to the vice. However, asking their good leave, we shall make bold to use such words indifferently in either sense; or rather we shall follow the example of Homer, whose authority we have for it, that

> Much harm ofttimes from modesty befalls,
> Much good ofttimes.[1]

---

1. *The Iliad*, Book XXIV, 44 [Cf. *Great Books of the Western World*, Vol. 4, p. 171 (Ed.).]

And it was not done amiss of him to make mention of the hurtfulness of it first, because modesty becomes profitable only through reason, which cuts off what is superfluous and leaves a just mean behind.

In the first place, therefore, the bashful man must be persuaded and satisfied that that distemper of the mind is prejudicial to him, and that nothing which is so can be eligible. And withal, he must be cautious how he suffers himself to be cajoled and led by the nose with the titles of courteous or sociable, in exchange for those of grave, great, and just; nor like Pegasus in Euripides, who, when Bellerophon mounted him,

> With trembling stooped more than his lord desired,

must he debase himself and yield to all who make their addresses to him, for fear of appearing hard and ungentle.

It is recorded of Bocchoris, king of Egypt, a man of a very cruel nature, that the goddess Isis sent a kind of a serpent (called aspis), which winding itself about his head cast a shadow over him from above, and was a means to him of determining causes according to equity. But bashfulness, on the contrary, happening upon remiss and spiritless tempers, suffers them not to express their dislike of anything or to argue against it, but perverts many times the sentence of arbitrators, and stops the mouths of skillful pleaders, forcing them often to act and speak contrary to their conviction. And the most reckless man will always tyrannize and domineer over such a one, forcing his bashfulness by his own strength of impudence. Upon this account it is that bashfulness, like a low piece of soft ground, can make no resistance and decline no encounter, but is exposed to the meanest actions and vilest passions. But, above all, this is the worst guardian of raw and inexperienced youth. For, as Brutus said, he seems to have had but an ill education that has not learned to deny any thing. And no better overseer is it of the marriage bed or the woman's apartment; as the repentant lady in Sophocles accuses the spark that had debauched her,

> Thy tongue, thy flattering tongue prevailed.

So this vice, happening upon a disposition inclinable to debauchery, prepares and opens the way, and leaves all things easy and accessible to such as are ready to prefer their wicked designs. Presents and treats are irresistible baits for common mercenary creatures; but importunity, befriended with bashfulness on their side, has sometimes undone the modestest women. I omit what inconveniences this kind of modesty occasions, when it obliges men to lend their money to such whose credit is blown upon in the world, or to give bail for those they dare not trust; we do this, it is true, with an ill will, and in our heart reflect upon that old saying, Be bail, and pay for it, yet cannot make use of it in our practice.

How many this fault has ruined, it is no easy thing to recount. Creon in the play gave a very good lesson for others to follow, when he told Medea,

'Tis better now to brave thy direst hate,
Than curse a foolish easiness too late.[2]

Yet afterwards, being wrought upon through his bashfulness to grant her but one day longer, he ruined himself and family by it. For the same reason, some, suspecting designs against them of murder or poisoning, have neglected to provide for their safety. Thus Dion could not be ignorant of the treachery of Callippus, yet thought it unfit to entertain such thoughts of his pretended friend and guest, and so perished. So again, Antipater, the son of Cassander, having entertained Demetrius at supper, and being engaged by him for the next night, because he was unwilling to distrust one who had trusted him, went, and had his throat cut after supper. Polysperchon had promised Cassander for a hundred talents to murder Hercules, the son of Alexander by Barsine. Upon this he invites him to sup; but the young man, having some suspicion of the thing, pretends himself indisposed. Polysperchon coming to him said: "Sir, above all things endeavor after your father's courteous behavior and obliging way to his friends, unless haply you look on us with suspicion as if we were compassing your health." The young man out of mere modesty was prevailed upon to go, and was strangled as he sat at meat. It is not therefore (as some will have us believe) insignificant or ridiculous, but on the contrary very wise advice, which Hesiod gives,

Welcome a friend, but never call thy foe.

Be not bashful and mealy-mouthed in refusing him that you are satisfied has a pique against you; but never reject him that seemeth to put his trust in you. For if you invite, you must expect to be invited again; and sometime or other your entertainment will be repaid you, if bashfulness have once softened or turned the edge of that diffidence which ought to be your guard.

To the end therefore that we may get the better of this disease, which is the cause of so many evils, we must make our first attempts (as our cus-

2. Euripides, *Medea*, 290. [Cf. *Great Books of the Western World*, Vol. 5, p. 214 (Ed.).]

tom is in other things) upon matters of no great difficulty. As, if one drink to you after you have taken what is sufficient, be not so foolishly modest to do violence to your nature, but rather venture to pass the glass. Another, it may be, would tempt you to play at dice while drinking; be not over-persuaded into a compliance, for fear of being the subject of his drollery, but reply with Xenophanes, when Lasus of Hermione called him coward because he refused to play at dice: "Yes," said he, "I confess myself the greatest coward in the world, for I dare not do an ill thing." Again, you light upon an impertinent talker, that sticks upon you like a burr; don't be bashful, but break off the discourse, and pursue your business. These evasions and repulses, whereby our resolution and assurance are exercised in matters of less moment, will accustom us to it by degrees in greater occasions. And here it will be but seasonable to give you a passage, as it is recorded of Demosthenes. The Athenians having one time been moved to send succors to Harpalus, and themselves to engage in a war against Alexander, it happened that Philoxenus, Alexander's admiral, unexpectedly arrived on their coast; and the people being so astonished as to be speechless for very fear, Demosthenes cried out: "How would they endure the sun who are not able to look against a lamp! Or how would you comport yourself in weightier concerns, while your prince or the people had an awe over you, if you cannot refuse a glass of wine when an acquaintance offers it, or turn off an impertinent babbler, but suffer the eternal trifler to walk over you without telling him, 'Another time, good sir, at present I am in haste.'"

Besides all this, the exercising such a resolution is of great use in praising others. If one of my friend's harpers play lewdly, or a comedian he has hired at a great rate murder a piece of Menander in the acting, although the vulgar clap their hands and admire, I think it no moroseness or ill breeding to sit silently all the while, without servilely joining in the common applauses contrary to my judgment. For if you scruple to deal openly with him in these cases, what will you do, should he repeat to you an insipid composition of his own, or submit to your revisal a ridiculous oration? You will applaud, of course, and enter yourself into the list of common parasites and flatterers! But how then can you direct him impartially in the greatest administrations of his life? How be free with him where he fails in any duties of his trust or marriage, or neglects the offices incumbent on him as a member of the community? I must confess, I cannot by any means approve of the reply Pericles made to a friend who besought him to give false evidence, and that too upon oath, when he thus answered: "As far as the altar I am wholly at your service." Methinks he went too far. But he that has long before accustomed himself not to commend any thing against his judgment, or applaud an ill voice, or seem pleased with indecent scurrilities will never suffer things to come to that issue; nor will anyone be so bold as to solicit him in this manner: "Swear on my side, give false evidence, or bring in an unjust verdict."

After the same manner we may learn to refuse such as come to borrow considerable sums of us, if we have used to deny in little matters where refusal is easy. As Archelaus, king of Macedon, sat at supper, one of his retinue, a fellow who thought there was nothing so honest as to receive, begged of him a golden cup. But the king commanded a waiter to give it immediately to Euripides: "For you, sir," said he, "are fit indeed to ask anything, but to receive nothing; and he deserves to receive, though he lacks the confidence to ask." Thus wisely did he make his judgment, and not bashful timidity, his guide in bestowing favors. Yet we oftentimes, when the honesty, nearness, and necessities of our friends and relations are not motives sufficient to prevail with us to their relief, can give profusely to impudence and importunity, not out of any willingness to bestow our money so ill, but merely for want of confidence and resolution to deny. This was the case of Antigonus the elder. Being wearied out with the importunity of Bias, "Give," said he to his servants, "one talent to Bias and necessity." Yet at other times he was as expert at encountering such addresses as any prince, and dismissed them with as remarkable answers. Thus a certain Cynic one day begging of him a groat, he made answer, "That is not for a prince to give." And the poor man replying, "Then bestow a talent," he reparteed briskly, "Nor that for a Cynic or for a dog to receive." Diogenes went about begging to all the statues in the Ceramicus; and his answer to some that wondered at his fancy in it was he was practicing how to bear a repulse. But indeed it chiefly lies upon us to exercise ourselves in smaller matters to refuse an unreasonable request, that we may not be at loss how to refuse on occasions of greater magnitude. For no one, as Demosthenes says, who has spent all the money that he had in unnecessary expenses will have plenty of money that he has not for his necessary expenses. And our disgrace is increased manyfold, if we want what is necessary or decent, and abound in trifles and fopperies.

Yet bashfulness is not only a bad steward of our estate, but even in weightier concerns it refuses to hearken to the wholesome advice of right reason. Thus, in a dangerous fit of sickness, we send not to the ablest physician, for fear of giving offense to another of our acquaintance. Or, in taking tutors and governors for our children, we make choice of such as obtrude themselves upon us, not such as are better qualified for that service.

Or, in our lawsuits, we regard not to obtain counsel learned in the law, because we must gratify the son of some friend or relation, and give him an opportunity to show himself in the world. Nay, lastly, you shall find some that bear the name of philosophers, who call themselves Epicureans or Stoics, not out of choice, or upon the least conviction, but merely to oblige their friends or acquaintance, who have taken advantage of their modesty. Since then the case is so with us, we ought to prepare and exercise ourselves in things that we daily meet with and of course, not so much as indulging that foolish weakness in the choice of a barber or fuller, or in lodging in a paltry inn when better accommodation is to be had, to oblige the landlord who has cringed to us. But if it be merely to break ourselves of such follies, in those cases still we should make use of the best, though the difference be but inconsiderable: as the Pythagoreans were strict in observing not to cross their right knee with the left, or to use an even number with an odd, though all things else were indifferent. We must observe also, when we celebrate a sacrifice or keep a wedding or make a public entertainment, to deny ourselves so far as not to invite any that have been extremely complacent to us or that put themselves upon us, before those who are known for their good humor or whose conversation is like to prove beneficial. For he that has accustomed himself thus far will hardly be caught and surprised, nay, rather he shall not so much as be tempted, in greater instances.

And thus much may suffice concerning exercising ourselves. My first use of what has been said is to observe that all passions and distempers of the mind are still accompanied with those very evils which by their means we hoped to avoid. Thus disgrace pursues ambition; pain and indisposition, sensuality; softness and effeminacy are fretted with troubles; contentiousness, with disappointment and defeats. But this is nowhere more conspicuous than in bashfulness, which, endeavoring to avoid the smoke of reproach, throws itself into the fire. Such men, wanting confidence to withstand those that unreasonably importune them, afterwards feel shame before those who justly accuse them, and for fear of a slight private rebuke incur more public disgrace. For example, not having the heart to deny a friend that comes to borrow, in short time they are reduced to the same extremity themselves, and exposed openly. Some again, after promising to help friends in a lawsuit, are ashamed to face the opposite party, and are forced to hide their heads and run away. Many have been so unreasonably weak in this particular as to accept of disadvantageous proposals of marriage for a daughter or sister, and upon second thoughts have been forced to bring themselves off with an arrant lie.

One made this observation of the people of Asia, that they were all slaves to one man, merely because they could not pronounce that syllable No; but he spake only in raillery. But now the bashful man, though he be not able to say one word, has but to raise his brows or nod downward, as if he minded not, and he may decline many ungrateful and unreasonable offices. Euripides was wont to say, "Silence is an answer to a wise man"; but we seem to have greater occasion for it in our dealings with fools and unreasonable persons, for men of breeding and sense will be satisfied with reason and fair words. Upon this account we should be always provided with some notable sayings and choice apothegms of famous and excellent men, to repeat to the bashful—such as that of Phocion to Antipater, "You cannot have me for both a friend and a flatterer"; and that of his to the Athenians, when they called upon him to come in for his share to defray the expenses of a festival, "I am ashamed," said he, pointing to Callicles his creditor, "to contribute towards your follies, without paying this man his due." For, as Thucydides says, "It is an ill thing to be ashamed of one's poverty, but much worse not to make use of lawful endeavors to avoid it." [3] But he that is so foolishly good-natured that he cannot answer one that comes to borrow,

> My friend, no silver white have I in all my caves,

but gives him a promise to be better provided,

> The wretch has made himself a slave to shame,
> And drags a tiresome, though an unforged chain.

Persaeus, being about to accommodate a friend with a sum of money, paid it publicly in the market, and made the conditions before a banker, remembering, it may be, that of Hesiod,

> Seem not thy brother's honesty to doubt;
> Yet, smiling, call a witness to his hand.

But when his friend marveled and asked, "How now, so formally and according to law?" "Yea," quoth he, "because I would receive my money again as a friend, and not have to trouble the law to recover it." For many out of bashfulness, not taking care to have good security at first, have been forced afterwards to break with their friends, and to have recourse to law for their money.

Again, Plato writing to Dionysius, by Helicon of Cyzicus, gives the bearer a good character for honesty and moderation, but withal in the

---

3. *The Peloponnesian War*, Book II, 400 [Cf. *Great Books of the Western World*, Vol. 6, p. 397 (Ed.).]

postscript tells him, "Yet this I write of a man, who, as such, is by nature an animal subject to change." Xenocrates, though a man of rigid morals, was prevailed upon by this kind of modesty to recommend to Polysperchon a person, as it proved in the end, not so honest as he was reputed. For when the Macedonian in compliment bade him call for whatever he wanted, he presently desired a talent of silver. Polysperchon ordered it accordingly to be paid him, but dispatched away letters immediately to Xenocrates, advising him for the future to be better acquainted with those he recommended. Now all this came to pass through Xenocrates's ignorance of his man; but we oftentimes give testimonials and squander away our money to advance such as we are very well satisfied have no qualification or desert to recommend them, and this too with the forfeiture of our reputation, and without the pleasure that men have who are profuse upon whores and flatterers, but all the while in an agony, and struggling with that impudence which does violence to our reason. Whereas, if at any time, that verse can here be properly used,

I know the dreadful consequence, and fear,[4]

when such persons are at a man to forswear himself, or to give a wrong sentence, or to vote for an unjust bill, or lastly to be bound for one that will never be able to pay the debt.

All passions of the mind have repentance still pursuing them closely, but it overtakes this of bashfulness in the very act. For we give with regret, and we are in confusion while we bear false witness; our reputation is questioned when we engage for others, and when we fail we are condemned by all men. From this imperfection also it proceeds that many things are imposed upon us not in our power to perform, as to recommend such a man to court, or to carry up an address to the governor, because we dare not, or at least we will not, confess that we are unknown to the prince or that another has more of his ear. Lysander, on the other hand, when he was in disgrace at court, but yet for his great services was thought to preserve something of his former esteem with Agesilaus, made no scruple to dismiss suitors, directing them to such as were more powerful with the king. For it is no disgrace not to be able to do everything; but to undertake or pretend to what you are not made for is not only shameful but extremely troublesome and vexatious.

But to proceed to another head, we must perform all reasonable and good offices to those that deserve them, not forced thereto by fear of

---

4. Euripides, *Medea*, 1078. [Cf. *Great Books of the Western World*, Vol. 5, p. 221 (Ed.).]

shame, but cheerfully and readily. But where anything prejudicial or un-handsome is required of us, we ought to remember the story that is re-lated of Zeno. Meeting a young man of his acquaintance that slunk away under a wall, as if he would not be seen, and having learned from him that he withdrew from a friend that importuned him to perjure himself, "What," replied he, "you novice! is that fellow not afraid or ashamed to re-quire of thee what is unreasonable and unjust, and darest thou not stand against him in that which is just and honest?" For he that first started that doctrine, that knavery is the best defense against a knave, was but an ill teacher, advising us to keep off wickedness by imitating it. But for such as presume upon our modesty, to keep them off with their own weapons, and not gratify their unreasonable impudence with an easy compliance, is but just and good, and the duty of every wise man.

Neither is it a hard matter to put off some mean and ordinary people, which will be apt to prove troublesome to you in that nature. Some shift them off with a jest or a smart repartee; as Theocritus, being asked in the bath to lend his strigil [scraper] by two persons, whereof one was a stran-ger to him, and the other a notorious thief, made answer: "You, sir, I know not well enough, and you I know too well." And Lysimache, the priestess of Minerva Polias in Athens, when the muleteers that brought the provi-sion for the festival desired her to let them drink, replied, "No; for I fear it may grow into a custom." So again, when a captain's son, a young flutter-ing bully but a great coward, petitioned Antigonus for promotion, the lat-ter answered: "Sir, it is my way to reward my soldiers for their valor, not their parentage."

But if he that is importunate with us prove a man of great honor or in-terest (and such persons are not easily answered with excuses, when they come for our vote in the senate or judicial cases), at such a time perhaps it will be neither easy nor necessary to behave ourselves to them as Cato did towards Catulus. Catulus, a person of the highest rank among the Romans, and at that time censor, once waited on Cato, who was then quaestor and still a young man, on behalf of a friend whom Cato had fined; and when he had used a great deal of importunity to no purpose, yet would not be denied, Cato grew out of patience, and told him, "It would be an unseemly sight to have the censor dragged hence by my offi-cers." Catulus at this went away, out of countenance and very angry. But consider whether the answers of Agesilaus and Themistocles have not in them much more of candor and equity. Agesilaus, being bidden by his own father to give sentence contrary to law, replied: "I have been always taught by you to be observant of the laws, and I shall endeavor to obey you at this time, by doing nothing contrary to them." And Themistocles, when Simonides tempted him to commit a piece of injustice, said: "You would be no good poet, should you break the laws of verse; and should I judge against the law, I should make no better magistrate."

For it is not because of blunders in metre in lyric songs, as Plato observes, that cities and friends are set at variance to their utter ruin and destruction, but because of their blunders with regard to law and justice. Yet there are a sort of men that can be very curious and critical in their verses and letters and lyric measures, and yet would persuade others to neglect that justice and honesty which all men ought to observe in offices, in passing judgments, and in all actions. But these men are to be dealt with after the following manner. An orator perhaps presses you to show him favor in a cause to be heard before you, or a demagogue importunes you when you are a senator: tell him you are ready to please him, on condition that he make a solecism in the beginning of his oration, or be guilty of some barbarous expression in his narration. These terms, for shame, he will not accept; for some we see so superstitiously accurate as not to allow of two vowels meeting one another. Again, you are moved by a person of quality to something of ill reputation: bid him come over the market place at full noon dancing, or making buffoonlike grimaces; if he refuse, question him once more whether he think it a more heinous offense to make a solecism or a grimace than to break a law or to perjure one's self, or to show more favor to a rascal than to an honest man. Nicostratus the Argive, when Archidamus promised him a vast sum of money and his choice of the Spartan ladies in marriage if he would deliver up the town Cromnum into his hands, returned him this answer: He could no longer believe him descended from Hercules, he said, because Hercules traversed the world to destroy wicked men, but Archidamus made it his business to debauch those that were good. In like manner, if one that stands upon his quality or reputation presses us to do anything dishonorable, we must tell him freely he acts not as becomes a person of his character in the world.

But if it be a man of no quality that shall importune you, you may inquire of the covetous man whether he would lend you a considerable sum without any other security than your word; desire the proud man to give you the higher seat; or the ambitious, to quit his pretensions to some honor that lies fair for him. For, to deal plainly, it is a shameful thing that these men should continue so stiff, so resolute, and so unmoved in their vicious habits, while we, who profess ourselves lovers of justice and honesty, have too little command of ourselves not to give up and betray basely the cause of virtue. If they that would practice upon our modesty do this out of desire of glory or power, why should we contract disgrace or infamy to our-selves to advance the authority or set off the reputation of others—like those who bestow the reward wrongfully in public games, or betray their trust in collecting the poll, who confer indeed garlands and honors upon other men, but at the same time forfeit their own reputation and good word? But suppose it be matter of interest only that puts them upon it; why should it not appear an unreasonable piece of service for us to forego our reputation and conscience to no other purpose than to satisfy another man's avarice or make his coffers the heavier? After all, these I am afraid are the grand motives with most men in such cases, and they are even conscious that they are guilty; as men that are challenged and compelled to take too large a glass raise a hundred scruples and make as many gri-maces before they drink.

This weakness of the mind may be compared to a constitution of body that can endure neither heat nor cold. For let them be praised by those that thus impudently set upon them, and they are at once mollified and broken by the flattery; but let them be blamed or so much as suspected by the same men after their suit has been refused, and they are ready to die for woe and fear. We ought therefore to prepare and fortify ourselves against both extremes, so as to be made a prey neither to such as pretend to frighten nor to such as would cajole us. Thucydides is of opinion, since there is a necessary connection between envy and great undertakings, that he takes the wisest counsel who incurs envy by aiming the highest.[5] But we who esteem it less difficult to avoid the envy of all men than to escape the censure of those we live among ought to order things so as rather to grapple with the unjust hatred of evil men than to deserve their just accusation after we have served their base ends. We ought to go armed against that false and counterfeit praise such men are apt to fling upon us, not suffering ourselves like swine to be scratched and tickled by them, till, having got the advantage of us, they use us after their own pleasure. For they that reach out their ears to flatterers differ very little from such as stand fair and quiet to be tripped up, excepting that the for-mer catch the more disgraceful fall. These put up with the affronts and forbear the correction of wicked men, to get the reputation of good-natured or merciful; or else are drawn into needless and perilous quarrels at the instance of flatterers, who bear them in hand all the while for the only men of judgment, the only men not to be caught with flattery, and

---

5. *The Peloponnesian War,* II, 64. [See *Great Books of the Western World,* Vol. 6, pp. 403–404 (Ed.).]

call them the only men who have mouths and voices. Bion used to compare these men to pitchers: "Take them," said he, "by the ears, and you may move them as you please." Thus Alexinus, the sophist, was reporting many scandalous things in the lyceum of Stilpo the Megarian; but when one present informed him that Stilpo always spake very honorably of him, "Why truly," says he, "he is one of the most obliging and best of men." But now Menedemus, when it was told him that Alexinus often praised him, replied: "That may be, but I always talk against him; for he must be bad who either praises a bad man or is blamed by an honest one." So wary was he of being caught by such baits, agreeably to that precept of Hercules in Antisthenes, who cautioned his sons not to be thankful to such as were used to praise them, thereby meaning no more than that they should be so far from being wheedled thereby as not even to return their flatteries. That of Pindar was very apposite, and enough to be said in such a case: when one told him, "I cry you up among all men, and speak to your advantage on all occasions"; "And I," replied he, "am always very thankful in that I take care you shall not tell a lie."

I shall conclude with one general rule, of sovereign use against all the passions and diseases of the mind, but particularly beneficial to such as labor under the present distemper, bashfulness. And it is this: whenever they have given way to this weakness, let them store up carefully such failings in their memory, and taking therein deep and lively impressions of what remorse and disquiet they occasioned, bestow much time in reflecting upon them and keeping them fresh. For as travelers that have got a dangerous fall against such a stone, or sailors shipwrecked upon a particular promontory, keeping the image of their misfortune continually before them, appear fearful and apprehensive not only of the same but even the like dangers; so they that keep in mind the disgraceful and prejudicial effects of bashfulness will soon be enabled to restrain themselves in like cases, and will not easily slip again on any occasion.

"Of Bashfulness" is from a collection of Plutarch's essays entitled MORALIA.

Robert Louis Stevenson[1]

1850–1894

This thoroughly delightful essay has depth and insight too. It pays honor to the wistful dreams and incantations of youth and to the spark of youth and poetry that remains in grown men. It derides Zola and the realists for pretending that the meaning of life lies in humdrum, vulgar, conventional circumstance, and for suppressing joy. "For to miss the joy," Stevenson says, "is to miss all. In the joy of the actors lies the sense of any action . . . hence the haunting and truly spectral unreality of realistic books." But if the motive force of human striving is joy and hidden symbols, would not the true realist be the romancer?

Stevenson knows how to pack a great deal of romance into a gaunt realistic setting. The rugged seacoast, the scattering of houses and scraggy vegetation, a few Dickens-like characters furnish the background of the boys' doings. For those who can see, it also has its enchantments. Stevenson shows us how a mood of mixed fear and exultation was mirrored in the sea: ". . . the coil of equinoctial tempests; . . . the boats with their reefed lugsails scudding for the harbour mouth, where danger lay. . . ." The cold eye of the realists, watching the boys at their round of amusements, would see nothing wonderful. They played golf, they went fishing, swam in the sea, and gazed from an eminence at the surrounding country and the steeples of nearby towns. Commonplace pleasures? Yes, when viewed objectively.

The greatest joy which they had was quite different. It would appear to a casual observer to be the last word in silliness. Stevenson tells how the boys made a ritual of hiding bull's-eye lanterns under

---

[1] For a biography of Stevenson, see Vol. 2, pp. 284–286, in this set.

their top-coats and huddling together in secret discussions at night. So concealed, the lanterns served no purpose, or so it seemed, except to convey a preposterous sense of mystery. Zola, Stevenson says, would have missed the inner meaning and would have turned out a masterly picture of "shallowness and dullness."

Stevenson's own interpretation of the strange ritual is rich but oblique, and he leaves a great deal to you, the reader. Why does the boy exult and sing over the knowledge that, in the dark night unknown to anyone, he carries under his top-coat a hidden flame? Does the flame symbolize a secret strength, a magical power? And could the boys, in their secret nighttime conversations, have been concerned with anything as important as "the possibilities of existence?"

More than one key will sometimes fit the same lock. Each reader has his hidden lantern and is likely to see this thing according to his own light.

The Lantern–Bearers

These boys congregated every autumn about a certain easterly fisher-village, where they tasted in a high degree the glory of existence. The place was created seemingly on purpose for the diversion of young gentlemen. A street or two of houses, mostly red and many of them tiled; a number of fine trees clustered about the manse and the kirkyard, and turning the chief street into a shady alley; many little gardens more than usually bright with flowers; nets a-drying, and fisherwives scolding in the backward parts; a smell of fish, a genial smell of seaweed; whiffs of blowing sand at the street-corners; shops with golf-balls and bottled lollipops; another shop with penny pickwicks (that remarkable cigar) and the *London Journal*, dear to me for its startling pictures, and a few novels, dear for their suggestive names: such, as well as memory serves me, were the ingredients of the town. These you are to conceive posted on a spit between two sandy bays, and sparsely flanked with villas—enough for the boys to lodge in with their subsidiary parents, not enough (not yet enough) to cocknify the scene: a haven in the rocks in front; in front of that, a file of gray islets; to the left, endless links and sand wreaths, a wilderness of hiding-holes, alive with popping rabbits and soaring gulls; to the right, a range of seaward crags, one rugged brow beyond another, the ruins of a mighty and ancient fortress on the brink of one; coves between—now charmed into sunshine quiet, now whistling with wind and clamorous with bursting surges; the dens and sheltered hollows redolent of thyme and southernwood, the air at the cliff's edge brisk and clean and pungent of the sea—in front of all, the Bass Rock, tilted seaward like a doubtful bather, the surf ringing it with white, the solan geese hanging round its summit like a great and glittering smoke. This choice piece of seaboard was sacred, besides, to the wrecker; and the Bass, in the eye of fancy, still flew the colours of King James; and in the ear of fancy the arches of Tantallon still rang with horseshoe iron, and echoed to the commands of Bell-the-Cat.

There was nothing to mar your days, if you were a boy summering in that part, but the embarrassment of pleasure. You might golf if you wanted; but I seem to have been better employed. You might secrete yourself in the Lady's Walk, a certain sunless dingle of elders, all mossed over by the damp as green as grass, and dotted here and there by the streamside with roofless walls, the cold homes of anchorites. To fit themselves for life, and with a special eye to acquire the art of smoking, it was even common for the boys to harbour there; and you might have seen a single penny pickwick, honestly shared in lengths with a blunt knife, bestrew the glen with these apprentices. Again, you might join our fishing parties, where we sat perched as thick as solan geese, a covey of little anglers, boy and girl, angling over each other's heads, to the much entanglement of lines and loss of podleys and consequent shrill recrimination—shrill as the geese themselves. Indeed, had that been all, you might have done this often; but though fishing be a fine pastime, the podley is scarce to be regarded as a dainty for the table; and it was a point of honour that a boy should eat all that he had taken. Or again, you might climb the Law, where the whale's jaw-bone stood landmark in the buzzing wind, and behold the face of many counties, and the smoke and spires of many towns, and the sails of distant ships. You might bathe, now in the flaws of fine weather, that we pathetically call our summer, now in a gale of wind, with the sand scourging your bare hide, your clothes thrashing abroad from underneath their guardian stone, the froth of the great breakers casting you headlong ere it had drowned your knees. Or you might explore the tidal rocks, above all in the ebb of springs, when the very roots of the hills were for the nonce discovered; following my leader from one group to another, groping in slippery tangle for the wreck of ships, wading in pools after the abominable creatures of the sea, and ever with an eye cast backward on the march of the tide and the menaced line of your retreat. And then you might go Crusoeing, a word that covers all extempore eating in the open air: digging perhaps a house under the margin of the links, kindling a fire of the sea-ware, and cooking apples there— if they were truly apples, for I sometimes suppose the merchant must have played us off with some inferior and quite local fruit, capable of resolving, in the neighbourhood of fire, into mere sand and smoke and iodine; or perhaps pushing to Tantallon, you might lunch on sandwiches and visions in the grassy court, while the wind hummed in the crumbling turrets; or clambering along the coast, eat geans (the worst, I must suppose, in Christendom) from an adventurous gean tree that had taken root under a cliff, where it was shaken with an ague of east wind, and silvered after gales with salt, and grew so foreign among its bleak surroundings that to eat of its produce was an adventure in itself.

There are mingled some dismal memories with so many that were joyous. Of the fisherwife, for instance, who had cut her throat at Canty Bay; and of how I ran with the other children to the top of the Quadrant, and beheld a posse of silent people escorting a cart, and on the cart, bound in a chair, her throat bandaged, and the bandage all bloody—horror!—the fisherwife herself, who continued thenceforth to hag-ride my thoughts, and even to-day (as I recall the scene) darkens daylight. She was lodged in the little old jail in the chief street; but whether or no she died there, with a wise terror of the worst, I never inquired. She had been tippling; it was but a dingy tragedy; and it seems strange and hard that, after all these years, the poor crazy sinner should be still pilloried on her cart in the scrap-book of my memory. Nor shall I readily forget a certain house in the Quadrant where a visitor died, and a dark old woman continued to dwell alone with the dead body; nor how this old woman conceived a hatred to myself and one of my cousins, and in the dread hour of the dusk, as we were clambering on the garden-walls, opened a window in that house of mortality and cursed us in a shrill voice and with a marrowy choice of language. It was a pair of very colourless urchins that fled down the lane from this remarkable experience! But I recall with a more doubtful sentiment, compounded out of fear and exultation, the coil of equinoctial tempests; trumpeting squalls, scouring flaws of rain; the boats with their reefed lugsails scudding for the harbour mouth, where danger lay, for it was hard to make when the wind had any east in it; the wives clustered with blowing shawls at the pier-head, where (if fate was against them) they might see boat and husband and sons—their whole wealth and their whole family—engulfed under their eyes; and (what I saw but once) a troop of neighbours forcing such an unfortunate homeward, and she squalling and battling in their midst, a figure scarcely human, a tragic maenad.

These are things that I recall with interest; but what my memory dwells upon the most, I have been all this while withholding. It was a sport peculiar to the place, and indeed to a week or so of our two months' holiday there. Maybe it still flourishes in its native spot; for boys and their pastimes are swayed by periodic forces inscrutable to man; so that tops and marbles reappear in their due season, regular like the sun and moon; and the harmless art of knucklebones has seen the fall of the Roman Empire and the rise of the United States. It may still flourish in its native spot, but nowhere else, I am persuaded; for I tried myself to introduce it on Tweed-side, and was defeated lamentably; its charm being quite local, like a country wine that cannot be exported.

The idle manner of it was this:

Toward the end of September, when school-time was drawing near and the nights were already black, we would begin to sally from our respective villas, each equipped with a tin bull's-eye lantern. The thing was so well known that it had worn a rut in the commerce of Great Britain; and the grocers, about the due time, began to garnish their windows with our par-ticular brand of luminary. We wore them buckled to the waist upon a cricket belt, and over them, such was the rigour of the game, a buttoned top-coat. They smelled noisomely of blistered tin; they never burned aright, though they would always burn our fingers; their use was naught; the pleasure of them merely fanciful; and yet a boy with a bull's-eye un-der his top-coat asked for nothing more. The fishermen used lanterns about their boats, and it was from them, I suppose, that we had got the hint; but theirs were not bull's-eyes, nor did we ever play at being fisher-men. The police carried them at their belts, and we had plainly copied them in that; yet we did not pretend to be policemen. Burglars, indeed, we may have had some haunting thoughts of; and we had certainly an eye to past ages when lanterns were more common, and to certain story-books in which we had found them to figure very largely. But take it for all in all, the pleasure of the thing was substantive; and to be a boy with a bull's-eye under his top-coat was good enough for us.

When two of these asses met, there would be an anxious "Have you got your lantern?" and a gratified "Yes!" That was the shibboleth, and very needful too; for, as it was the rule to keep our glory contained, none could recognize a lantern-bearer, unless (like the polecat) by the smell. Four or five would sometimes climb into the belly of a ten-man lugger, with nothing but the thwarts above them—for the cabin was usually locked—or choose out some hollow of the links where the wind might whistle over-head. There the coats would be unbuttoned and the bull's-eyes discov-ered; and in the chequering glimmer, under the huge windy hall of the night, and cheered by a rich steam of toasting tinware, these fortunate young gentlemen would crouch together in the cold sand of the links or on the scaly bilges of the fishing-boat, and delight themselves with inap-propriate talk. Woe is me that I may not give some specimens—some of their foresights of life, or deep inquiries into the rudiments of man and nature, these were so fiery and so innocent, they were so richly silly, so romantically young. But the talk, at any rate, was but a condiment; and these gatherings themselves only accidents in the career of the lantern-bearer. The essence of this bliss was to walk by yourself in the black night; the slide shut, the top-coat buttoned; not a ray escaping, whether to conduct your footsteps or to make your glory public: a mere pillar of darkness in the dark; and all the while, deep down in the privacy of your fool's heart, to know you had a bull's-eye at your belt, and to exult and sing over the knowledge.

It is said that a poet has died young in the breast of the most stolid. It may be contended, rather, that this (somewhat minor) bard in almost every case survives, and is the spice of life to his possessor. Justice is not done to the versatility and the unplumbed childishness of man's imagination. His life from without may seem but a rude mound of mud; there will be some golden chamber at the heart of it, in which he dwells delighted; and for as dark as his pathway seems to the observer, he will have some kind of a bull's-eye at his belt.

It would be hard to pick out a career more cheerless than that of Dancer, the miser, as he figures in the "Old Bailey Reports," a prey to the most sordid persecutions, the butt of his neighbourhood, betrayed by his hired man, his house beleaguered by the impish schoolboy, and he himself grinding and fuming and impotently fleeing to the law against these pin-pricks. You marvel at first that any one should willingly prolong a life so destitute of charm and dignity; and then you call to memory that had he chosen, had he ceased to be a miser, he could have been freed at once from these trials, and might have built himself a castle and gone escorted by a squadron. For the love of more recondite joys, which we cannot estimate, which, it may be, we should envy, the man had willingly foregone both comfort and consideration. "His mind to him a kingdom was"; and sure enough, digging into that mind, which seems at first a dust-heap, we unearth some priceless jewels. For Dancer must have had the love of power and the disdain of using it, a noble character in itself; disdain of many pleasures, a chief part of what is commonly called wisdom; disdain of the inevitable end, that finest trait of mankind; scorn of men's opinions, another element of virtue; and at the back of all, a conscience just like yours and mine, whining like a cur, swindling like a thimblerigger, but still pointing (there or thereabout) to some conventional standard. Here were a cabinet portrait to which Hawthorne perhaps had done justice; and yet not Hawthorne either, for he was mildly minded, and it lay not in him to create for us that throb of the miser's pulse, his fretful energy of gusto, his vast arms of ambition clutching in he knows not what: insatiable, insane, a god with a muck-rake. Thus, at least, looking in the bosom of the miser, consideration detects the poet in the full tide of life, with more, indeed, of the poetic fire than usually goes to epics; and tracing that mean man about his cold hearth, and to and fro in his discomfortable house, spies within him a blazing bonfire of delight. And so with others who do not live by bread alone but by some cherished and perhaps fantastic pleasure; who are meat salesmen to the external eye, and possibly to themselves are Shakespeares, Napoleons, or Beethovens; who have not one virtue to rub against another in the field of active life, and yet perhaps, in the life of contemplation, sit with the saints. We see them on the street, and we can count their buttons; but heaven knows in what they pride themselves! Heaven knows where they have set their treasure!

There is one fable that touches very near the quick of life: the fable of the monk who passed into the woods, heard a bird break into song, hearkened for a trill or two, and found himself on his return a stranger at his convent gates; for he had been absent fifty years, and of all his comrades there survived but one to recognize him. It is not only in the woods that this enchanter carols, though perhaps he is native there. He sings in the more doleful places. The miser hears him and chuckles, and the days are moments. With no more apparatus than an ill-smelling lantern, I have evoked him on the naked links. All life that is not merely mechanical is spun out of two strands: seeking for that bird and hearing him. And it is just this that makes life so hard to value, and the delight of each so incommunicable. And it is just a knowledge of this, and a remembrance of those fortunate hours in which the bird has sung to us, that fills us with such wonder when we turn the pages of the realist. There, to be sure, we find a picture of life in so far as it consists of mud and of old iron, cheap desires and cheap fears, that which we are ashamed to remember and that which we are careless whether we forget; but of the note of that time-devouring nightingale we hear no news.

The case of these writers of romance is most obscure. They have been boys and youths; they have lingered outside the window of the beloved, who was then most probably writing to some one else; they have sat before a sheet of paper, and felt themselves mere continents of congested poetry, not one line of which would flow; they have walked alone in the woods; they have walked in cities under the countless lamps; they have been to sea; they have hated; they have feared; they have longed to knife a man, and maybe done it; the wild taste of life has stung their palate.

Or, if you deny them all the rest, one pleasure at least they have tasted to the full—their books are there to prove it—the keen pleasure of successful literary composition. And yet they fill the globe with volumes whose cleverness inspires me with despairing admiration, and whose consistent falsity to all I care to call existence, with despairing wrath. If I had no better hope than to continue to revolve among the dreary and petty businesses, and to be moved by the paltry hopes and fears with which they surround and animate their heroes, I declare I would die now. But there has never an hour of mine gone quite so dully yet; if it were spent waiting at a railway junction, I would have some scattering thoughts, I could count some grains of memory, compared to which the whole of one of these romances seems but dross.

These writers would retort (if I take them properly) that this was very true; that it was the same with themselves and other persons of (what they call) the artistic temperament; that in this we were exceptional, and should apparently be ashamed of ourselves; but that our works must deal exclusively with (what they call) the average man, who was a prodigious dull fellow, and quite dead to all but the paltriest considerations. I accept the issue. We can only know others by ourselves. The artistic temperament (a plague on the expression!) does not make us different from our fellow-men, or it would make us incapable of writing novels; and the average man (a murrain on the word!) is just like you and me, or he would not be average. It was Whitman who stamped a kind of Birmingham sacredness upon the latter phrase; but Whitman knew very well, and showed very nobly, that the average man was full of joys and full of a poetry of his own. And this harping on life's dullness and man's meanness is a loud profession of incompetence; it is one of two things: the cry of the blind eye, *I cannot see,* or the complaint of the dumb tongue, *I cannot utter.* To draw a life without delights is to prove I have not realized it. To picture a man without some sort of poetry—well, it goes near to prove my case, for it shows an author may have little enough. To see Dancer only as a dirty, old, small-minded, impotently fuming man, in a dirty house, besieged by Harrow boys, and probably beset by small attorneys, is to show myself as keen an observer as . . . the Harrow boys. But these young gentlemen (with a more becoming modesty) were content to pluck Dancer by the coat-tails; they did not suppose they had surprised his secret or could put him living in a book: and it is there my error would have lain. Or say that in the same romance—I continue to call these books romances, in the hope of giving pain—say that in the same romance, which now begins really to take shape, I should leave to speak of Dancer,

and follow instead the Harrow boys; and say that I came on some such
business as that of my lantern-bearers on the links; and described the boys
as very cold, spat upon by flurries of rain, and drearily surrounded, all of
which they were; and their talk as silly and indecent, which it certainly
was. I might upon these lines, and had I Zola's genius, turn out, in a page
or so, a gem of literary art, render the lantern-light with the touches of a
master, and lay on the indecency with the ungrudging hand of love; and
when all was done, what a triumph would my picture be of shallowness
and dullness! How it would have missed the point! How it would have
belied the boys! To the ear of the stenographer, the talk is merely silly and
indecent; but ask the boys themselves, and they are discussing (as it is
highly proper they should) the possibilities of existence. To the eye of the
observer they are wet and cold and drearily surrounded; but ask themselves, and they are in the heaven of a recondite pleasure, the ground of
which is an ill-smelling lantern.

For, to repeat, the ground of a man's joy is often hard to hit. It may
hinge at times upon a mere accessory, like the lantern; it may reside,
like Dancer's, in the mysterious inwards of psychology. It may consist with
perpetual failure, and find exercise in the continued chase. It has so little
bond with externals (such as the observer scribbles in his note-book)
that it may even touch them not; and the man's true life, for which he
consents to live, lies altogether in the field of fancy. The clergyman, in his
spare hours, may be winning battles, the farmer sailing ships, the banker
reaping triumph in the arts: all leading another life, plying another trade
from that they chose, like the poet's housebuilder, who, after all is cased in
stone,

> By his fireside, as impotent fancy prompts,
> Rebuilds it to his liking.

In such a case the poetry runs underground. The observer (poor soul, with
his documents!) is all abroad. For to look at the man is but to court deception. We shall see the trunk from which he draws his nourishment;
but he himself is above and abroad in the green dome of foliage, hummed
through by winds and nested in by nightingales. And the true realism
were that of the poets, to climb up after him like a squirrel, and catch
some glimpse of the heaven for which he lives. And the true realism, always and everywhere, is that of the poets: to find out where joy resides,
and give it a voice far beyond singing.

For to miss the joy is to miss all. In the joy of the actors lies the sense of any action. That is the explanation, that the excuse. To one who has not the secret of the lanterns, the scene upon the links is meaningless. And hence the haunting and truly spectral unreality of realistic books. Hence, when we read the English realists, the incredulous wonder with which we observe the hero's constancy under the submerging tide of dullness, and how he bears up with his jibbing sweetheart, and endures the chatter of idiot girls, and stands by his whole unfeatured wilderness of an existence, instead of seeking relief in drink or foreign travel. Hence in the French, in that meat market of middle-aged sensuality, the disgusted surprise with which we see the hero drift sidelong, and practically quite un-tempted, into every description of misconduct and dishonour. In each, we miss the personal poetry, the enchanted atmosphere, that rainbow work of fancy that clothes what is naked and seems to ennoble what is base; in each, life falls dead like dough, instead of soaring away like a balloon into the colours of the sunset; each is true, each inconceivable; for no man lives in the external truth, among salts and acids, but in the warm, phantasma-goric chamber of his brain, with the painted windows and the storied walls.

Of this falsity we have had a recent example from a man who knows far better—Tolstoy's *Powers of Darkness*. Here is a piece full of force and truth, yet quite untrue. For before Mikita was led into so dire a situation he was tempted, and temptations are beautiful at least in part; and a work which dwells on the ugliness of crime, and gives no hint of any loveliness in the temptation, sins against the modesty of life, and even when a Tol-stoy writes it, sinks to melodrama. The peasants are not understood; they saw their life in fairer colours; even the deaf girl was clothed in poetry for Mikita, or he had never fallen. And so, once again, even an Old Bailey melodrama, without some brightness of poetry and lustre of existence, falls into the inconceivable and ranks with fairy tales.

In nobler books we are moved with something like the emotions of life; and this emotion is very variously provoked. We are so moved when Le-vine labours in the field, when André sinks beyond emotion, when Rich-ard Feverel and Lucy Desborough meet beside the river, when Antony, "not cowardly, puts off his helmet," when Kent has infinite pity on the dy-ing Lear, when, in Dostoevsky's *Despised and Rejected*, the uncom-plaining hero drains his cup of suffering and virtue. These are notes that please the great heart of man. Not only love, and the fields, and the bright face of danger but sacrifice and death and unmerited suffering humbly supported touch in us the vein of the poetic. We love to think of them, we long to try them, we are humbly hopeful that we may prove heroes also.

We have heard, perhaps, too much of lesser matters. Here is the door, here is the open air. *Itur in antiquam silvam* [The way leads to an ancient wood].

"The Lantern-Bearers" is from a collection of Stevenson's essays entitled ACROSS THE PLAINS.

John Ruskin

1819–1900

John Ruskin, critic of art and of society, was born in London in 1819, the only child of Scottish parents, who were first cousins. His father was a prosperous wine merchant with a taste for art and literature, his mother a handsome, devoted woman with a stern Calvinist sense of duty. Their son's childhood was strictly supervised. Ruskin never owned a toy, was ignorant of all games, could neither dance nor ride to his dying day. On the other hand, he was a bookworm when he was five, by seven had begun to write a work of his own which grew to four volumes, and by the age of twenty had written a large body of poetry, drama, and romance, very little of which survives. He had also traveled almost everywhere in the civilized world and had acquired an exhaustive aesthetic education. Regarded by his parents as a prodigy, he was saved only by his own fine nature from being a prig.

Following his graduation in 1842 from Oxford, Ruskin began a career as an art critic that lasted for twenty years. He wrote *Modern Painters* in five volumes; the first volume, published in 1843, contained the famous defense of J. M. W. Turner, whose reputation Ruskin created. Two other works of this period were *The Seven Lamps of Architecture,* in which he laid down the principle that the

---

Notes from the artist: "A landscape of fantasy surrounds the portrait of Ruskin. A wild olive plant, a bird, and a flower recall some of the subjects of Ruskin's works. Hidden among the foliage at the right is a profile of Michelangelo, suggesting Ruskin's writings on art; while below, at left, is J. A. M. Whistler, who sued for libel after Ruskin attacked his painting."

art of a people is an expression of their life, and *The Stones of Venice,* which gave the city a special fame it has never lost.

After 1860 Ruskin turned from the study of art to social criticism. He had been stirred by the social injustice of the age and was henceforth to write endless articles and give countless lectures on the subject. None of these was as substantial as his works on art. Yet they were more forceful, so that he became famous as a social essayist. Among the collections of his pieces were *Unto This Last* (1862) and *Sesame and Lilies* (1865), where he laid out a scheme for society that was frankly utopian.

From 1869 to 1884 he was professor of art at Oxford, though he never ceased his social comment; indeed, art and social criticism had become one for him. In 1878 he suffered the first of a series of mental breakdowns which caused him increasing distress and made heavy work impossible. He also gave away to friends, charities, and various social objects the very large fortune which he had inherited from his father, as well as the considerable income from the sale of his books. The latter is said to have amounted to £4,000 a year—in modern money, perhaps $50,000. The last ten years of his life were spent in the care of friends, virtually in retirement. He died in 1900, probably the most celebrated figure in social criticism of his time.

The essays of Ruskin, as those of Emerson, tend to be inspired sermons; they exhort to honesty, achievement, truth, and to justice and a social conscience. But whereas Emerson remained serene and confident, Ruskin could sometimes denounce wholesale, as in the present essay, all the new gods and the distinctive progress of his age. Yet his wit was never caustic and unforgiving like Carlyle's, and there was more poetic sadness and nostalgia than wrath in his condemnation of the friends and life around him.

We are astounded to read the list of the things he denounces, for they are now mostly regarded as essentials of the good life. They include modern science; technology (which reduces the hours of labor while increasing its product); rapid transportation; and the kind of equality of individuals which goes along with democratic institutions. What can Ruskin be thinking of? What does he want to take the place of these modern innovations? He wants "admiration, hope, and love" to flourish. But admiration requires recognition of superiority and is supposedly inconsistent with equality, and love and hope do not go with factories and materialistic science. To live again as we should, we must free our civilization from the contempt of "the Middle Ages and of their chivalry."

But let us be sympathetic; that is the way to understanding. Is it not true that the greatest love stories are laid in medieval times or share something of its atmosphere? Is it not true, as Carlyle claimed, that machines are the death of heroes—of the heroic spirit and devotion? Was it not a long time before romance could adapt itself to industrial life? We must remember also that when Ruskin wrote, industry was still new and raw. It had covered the beautiful English countryside with smoke and ugly chimneys and factories. The workers, deprived of a plot of land to work, and even of clean air, worked long hours for a pittance and lived in dingy squalor. Money there was in the factory system, of course, but it was siphoned into the hands of a few who cared nothing for beauty nor for simple human worth.

We have now tried to be fair, but when all has been said in defense of Ruskin's medievalism—and there is a great deal more that could be added—we may still be unconvinced. Have not the Middle Ages been overrated? Was this period especially favorable to admiration, hope, and love? The enormously high mortality rate, spreading heartbreak with a prodigal hand, was a cruel reversal of both hope and love. And how much can we admire the knights and their tournaments, whose work was mostly destruction?

We will want to ask ourselves, also, how far the "progress" which Ruskin deplored could have been arrested, even if this was what was needed. Perhaps what he should have demanded was a reform, not a termination, of industrial civilization. From this point of view we can learn a great deal from Ruskin.

An Idealist's Arraignment
of the Age

For lo, the winter is past,
The rain is over and gone,
The flowers appear on the earth,
The time of the singing of birds is come,
Arise, oh my fair one, my dove,
And come.

My Friends,

It has been asked of me, very justly, why I have hitherto written to you of things you were little likely to care for, in words which it was difficult for you to understand. I have no fear but that you will one day understand all my poor words—the saddest of them perhaps too well. But I have great fear that you may never come to understand these written above, which are part of a king's love-song, in one sweet May, of many long since gone. I fear that for you the wild winter's rain may never pass, the flowers never appear on the earth; that for you no bird may ever sing; for you no perfect love arise and fulfil your life in peace. "And why not for us as for others?" Will you answer me so, and take my fear for you as an insult? Nay, it is no insult; nor am I happier than you. For me the birds do not sing, nor ever will. But they would for you, if you cared to have it so. When I told you that you would never understand that love-song, I meant only that you would not desire to understand it.

Are you again indignant with me? Do you think, though you should labour and grieve and be trodden down in dishonour all your days, at least you can keep that one joy of love and that one honour of home? Had you, indeed, kept that, you had kept all. But no men yet, in the history of the race, have lost it so piteously. In many a country and many an age, women have been compelled to labour for their husbands' wealth or bread; but never until now were they so homeless as to say, like the poor Samaritan, "I have no husband." Women of every country and people have sustained without complaint the labour of fellowship; for the women of the latter days in England it has been reserved to claim the privilege of isolation.

This, then, is the end of your universal education and civilization, and contempt of the ignorance of the Middle Ages and of their chivalry. Not only do you declare yourselves too indolent to labour for daughters and wives, and too poor to support them, but you have made the neglected and distracted creatures hold it for an honour to be independent of you and shriek for some hold of the mattock for themselves. Believe it or not, as you may, there has not been so low a level of thought reached by any race since they grew to be male and female out of star-fish or chickweed or whatever else they have been made from by natural selection—according to modern science.

That modern science, also, economic and of other kinds, has reached its climax at last. For it seems to be the appointed function of the nineteenth century to exhibit in all things the elect pattern of perfect folly, for a warning to the farthest future. Thus the statement of principle which I quoted to you in my last letter, from the circular of the Emigration Society, that it is over-production which is the cause of distress, is accurately the most foolish thing, not only hitherto ever said by men, but which it is possible for men ever to say, respecting their own business. It is a kind of opposite pole (or negative acme of mortal stupidity) to Newton's discovery of gravitation as an acme of mortal wisdom: as no wise being on earth will ever be able to make such another wise discovery, so no foolish being on earth will ever be capable of saying such another foolish thing through all the ages.

And the same crisis has been exactly reached by our natural science and by our art. It has several times chanced to me, since I began these papers, to have the exact thing shown or brought to me that I wanted for illustration, just in time; and it happened that, on the very day on which I published my last letter, I had to go to the Kensington Museum, and there I saw the most perfectly and roundly ill-done thing which, as yet, in my whole life, I ever saw produced by art. It had a tablet in front of it, bearing this inscription:

Statue in black and white marble, a Newfoundland Dog standing on a Serpent, which rests on a marble cushion, the pedestal ornamented with *pietra dura* fruits in relief.—*English. Present Century*. No. 1.

It was so very right for me, the Kensington people having been good enough to number it "1," the thing itself being almost incredible in its oneness; and, indeed, such a punctual accent over the iota of miscreation, so absolutely and exquisitely miscreant, that I am not myself capable of conceiving a number two or three, or any rivalship or association with it whatsoever. The extremity of its unvirtue consisted, observe, mainly in the quantity of instruction which was abused in it. It showed that the persons who produced it had seen everything, and practised everything; and misunderstood everything they saw, and misapplied everything they did. They had seen Roman work and Florentine work and Byzantine work and Gothic work; and misunderstanding of everything had passed through them as the mud does through earthworms, and here at last was their worm-cast of a production.

But the second chance that came to me that day was more significant still. From the Kensington Museum I went to an afternoon tea, at a house where I was sure to meet some nice people. And among the first I met was an old friend who had been hearing some lectures on botany at the Kensington Museum, and been delighted by them. She is the kind of person who gets good out of everything, and she was quite right in being delighted; besides that, as I found by her account of them, the lectures were really interesting and pleasantly given. She had expected botany to be dull, and had not found it so, and "had learned so much." On hearing this I proceeded naturally to inquire what; for my idea of her was that before she went to the lectures at all she had known more botany than she was likely to learn by them. So she told me that she had learned first of all that there "were seven sorts of leaves." Now, I have always a great suspicion of the number seven; because when I wrote *The Seven Lamps of Architecture*, it required all the ingenuity I was master of to prevent them from becoming eight, or even nine, on my hands. So I thought to myself that it would be very charming if there were only seven sorts of leaves; but that, perhaps, if one looked the woods and forests of the world carefully through, it was just possible that one might discover as many as eight sorts; and then where would my friend's new knowledge of botany be? So I said, "That was very pretty; but what more?" Then my friend told me that she had no idea, before, that petals were leaves. On which I thought to myself that it would not have been any great harm to her if she had remained under her old impression that petals were petals. But I said, "That was very pretty, too; and what more?" So then my friend told me that the lecturer said "the object of his lectures would be entirely accomplished if he could convince his hearers that there was no such thing as a flower." Now, in that sentence you have the most perfect and admirable summary given you of the general temper and purposes of modern science. It gives lectures on botany, of which the object is to show that there is no such thing as a flower; on humanity, to show that there is no such thing as a man; and on theology, to show there is no such thing as a God. No such thing as a man, but only a mechanism; no such thing as a God, but only a series of forces. The two faiths are essentially one: if you feel yourself to be only a machine, constructed to be a regulator of minor machinery, you will put your statue of such science on your Holborn Viaduct, and necessarily recognize only major machinery as regulating you.

I must explain the real meaning to you, however, of that saying of the botanical lecturer, for it has a wide bearing. Some fifty years ago the poet Goethe discovered that all the parts of plants had a kind of common nature and would change into each other. Now, this was a true discovery and a notable one; and you will find that, in fact, all plants are composed of essentially two parts—the leaf and root; one loving the light, the other darkness; one liking to be clean, the other to be dirty; one liking to grow for the most part up, the other for the most part down; and each having faculties and purposes of its own. But the pure one, which loves the light, has, above all things, the purpose of being married to another leaf, and having child-leaves and children's children of leaves, to make the earth fair forever. And when the leaves marry, they put on wedding-robes and are more glorious than Solomon in all his glory, and they have feasts of honey; and we call them "Flowers."

In a certain sense, therefore, you see the botanical lecturer was quite right. There are no such things as flowers—there are only leaves. Nay, farther than this, there may be a dignity in the less happy but unwithering leaf, which is, in some sort, better than the brief lily of its bloom—which the great poets always knew well, Chaucer before Goethe, and the writer of the *First Psalm* before Chaucer. The botanical lecturer was, in a deeper sense than he knew, right.

But in the deepest sense of all, the botanical lecturer was, to the extremity of wrongness, wrong; for leaf and root and fruit exist, all of them, only that there may be flowers. He disregarded the life and passion of the creature, which were its essence. Had he looked for these, he would have recognized that in the thought of Nature herself there is in a plant nothing else but its flowers.

Now, in exactly the sense that modern science declares there is no such thing as a flower, it has declared there is no such thing as a man but only a transitional form of ascidians and apes. It may or may not be true —it is not of the smallest consequence whether it be or not. The real fact is that, seen with human eyes, there is nothing else but Man; that all animals and beings beside him are only made that they may change into him; that the world truly exists only in the presence of Man, acts only in the passion of Man. The essence of light is in his eyes, the centre of force in his soul, the pertinence of action in his deeds. And all true science —which my Savoyard guide rightly scorned me when he thought I had not—all true science is *savoir vivre*. But all your modern science is the contrary of that. It is *savoir mourir*. And of its very discoveries, such as they are, it cannot make use.

That telegraphic signalling was a discovery; and conceivably, some day, may be a useful one. And there was some excuse for your being a little proud when, about last sixth of April (Coeur de Lion's death-day, and Albrecht Dürer's), you knotted a copper wire all the way to Bombay, and flashed a message along it and back. But what was the message, and what the answer? Is India the better for what you said to her? Are you the better for what she replied? If not, you have only wasted an all-round-the-world's length of copper wire—which is, indeed, about the sum of your doing. If you had had, perchance, two words of common sense to say, though you had taken wearisome time and trouble to send them— though you had written them slowly in gold, and sealed them with a hundred seals, and sent a squadron of ships of the line to carry the scroll; and the squadron had fought its way round the Cape of Good Hope, through a year of storms, with loss of all its ships but one—the two words of common sense would have been worth the carriage, and more. But you have not anything like so much as that to say, either to India or to any other place.

You think it a great triumph to make the sun draw brown landscapes for you. That was also a discovery, and some day may be useful. But the sun had drawn landscapes before for you, not in brown, but in green and blue and all imaginable colors, here in England. Not one of you ever looked at them then; not one of you cares for the loss of them now, when you have shut the sun out with smoke, so that he can draw nothing more except brown blots through a hole in a box. There was a rocky valley between Buxton and Bakewell, once upon a time, divine as the Vale of

Tempe; you might have seen the gods there morning and evening—Apollo and all the sweet Muses of the Light—walking in fair procession on the lawns of it and to and fro among the pinnacles of its crags. You cared neither for gods nor grass, but for cash (which you did not know the way to get); you thought you could get it by what the *Times* calls "Railroad Enterprise." You enterprised a railroad through the valley—you blasted its rocks away, heaped thousands of tons of shale into its lovely stream. The valley is gone, and the gods with it; and now every fool in Buxton can be at Bakewell in half an hour, and every fool in Bakewell at Buxton; which you think a lucrative process of exchange—you fools everywhere.

To talk at a distance, when you have nothing to say though you were ever so near; to go fast from this place to that, with nothing to do either at one or the other—these are powers certainly. Much more, power of increased production, if you indeed had got it, would be something to boast of. But are you so entirely sure that you *have* got it—that the mortal disease of plenty and afflictive affluence of good things are all you have to dread?

Observe. A man and a woman, with their children, properly trained, are able easily to cultivate as much ground as will feed them, to build as much wall and roof as will lodge them, and to spin and weave as much cloth as will clothe them. They can all be perfectly happy and healthy in doing this. Supposing that they invent machinery which will build, plough, thresh, cook, and weave, and that they have none of these things any more to do, but may read, or play croquet or cricket, all day long, I believe myself that they will neither be so good nor so happy as without the machines. But I waive my belief in this matter for the time. I will assume that they become more refined and moral persons, and that idleness is in future to be the mother of all good. But observe, I repeat, the power of your machine is only in enabling them to be idle. It will not enable them to live better than they did before, nor to live in greater numbers. Get your heads quite clear on this matter. Out of so much ground only so much living is to be got, with or without machinery. You may set a million of steam-ploughs to work on an acre, if you like—out of that acre only a given number of grains of corn will grow, scratch or scorch it as you will. So that the question is not at all whether, by having more machines, more of you can live. No machines will increase the possibilities of life. They only increase the possibilities of idleness. Suppose, for instance, you could get the oxen in your plough driven by a goblin, who would ask for no pay, not even a cream bowl (you have nearly managed to get it driven by an iron goblin, as it is), well, your furrow will take no more seeds than if you had held the stilts yourself. But instead of holding them you sit, I presume, on a bank beside the field, under an eglantine—watch the goblin at his work, and read poetry. Meantime, your wife in the house has also got a goblin to weave and wash for her. And she is lying on the sofa, reading poetry.

Now, as I said, I don't believe you would be happier so, but I am willing to believe it; only, since you are already such brave mechanists, show me at least one or two places where you *are* happier. Let me see one small example of approach to this seraphic condition. I can show you examples, millions of them, of happy people made happy by their own industry. Farm after farm I can show you in Bavaria, Switzerland, the Tyrol, and such other places, where men and women are perfectly happy and good, without any iron servants. Show me, therefore, some English family, with its fiery familiar, happier than these. Or bring me— for I am not inconvincible by any kind of evidence—bring me the testimony of an English family or two to their increased felicity. Or if you cannot do so much as that, can you convince even themselves of it? They are perhaps happy, if only they knew how happy they were. Virgil thought so, long ago, of simple rustics; but you hear at present your steam-propelled rustics are crying out that they are anything else than happy, and that they regard their boasted progress "in the light of a monstrous Sham." I must tell you one little thing, however, which greatly perplexes my imagination of the relieved ploughman sitting under his rose-bower, reading poetry. I have told it you before, indeed, but I forget where. There was really a great festivity, and expression of satisfaction in the new order of things, down in Cumberland, a little while ago; some first of May, I think it was, a country festival such as the old heathens, who had no iron servants, used to keep with piping and dancing. So I thought, from the liberated country people—their work all done for them by goblins—we should have some extraordinary piping and dancing. But there was no dancing at all, and they could not even provide their own piping. They had their goblin to pipe for them. They walked in procession after their steam-plough, and their steam-plough whistled to them occasionally in the most melodious manner it could. Which seemed to me, indeed, a return to more than Arcadian simplicity; for in old Arcadia plough-boys truly whistled as they went, for want of thought, whereas here was verily a large company walking without thought but not having any more even the capacity of doing their own whistling.

But next, as to the inside of the house. Before you got your power-looms a woman could always make herself a chemise and petticoat of bright and pretty appearance. I have seen a Bavarian peasant-woman at church in Munich looking a much grander creature, and more beautifully dressed, than any of the crossed and embroidered angels in Hesse's high-art frescoes (which happened to be just above her, so that I could look from one to the other). Well, here you are, in England, served by household demons, with five hundred fingers at least, weaving, for one that used to weave in the days of Minerva. You ought to be able to show me five hundred dresses for one that used to be; tidiness ought to have become five-hundred-fold tidier; tapestry should be increased into *cinquecento*-fold iridescence of tapestry. Not only your peasant-girl ought to be lying on the sofa, reading poetry, but she ought to have in her wardrobe five hundred petticoats instead of one. Is that, indeed, your issue? or are you only on a curiously crooked way to it?

It is just possible, indeed, that you may not have been allowed to get the use of the goblin's work—that other people may have got the use of it, and you none; because, perhaps, you have not been able to evoke goblins wholly for your own personal service, but have been borrowing goblins from the capitalist and paying interest, in the "position of William," on ghostly self-going planes. But suppose you had laid by capital enough, yourselves, to hire all the demons in the world—nay, all that are inside of it—are you quite sure you know what you might best set them to work at, and what "useful things" you should command them to make for you? I told you, last month, that no economist going (whether by steam or ghost) knew what are useful things and what are not. Very few of you know, yourselves, except by bitter experience of the want of them. And no demons, either of iron or spirit, can ever make them.

There are three material things, not only useful, but essential to life. No one "knows how to live" till he has got them.

These are pure air, water, and earth.

There are three immaterial things, not only useful, but essential to life. No one knows how to live till he has got them also.

These are admiration, hope, and love.

Admiration—the power of discerning and taking delight in what is beautiful in visible form and lovely in human character; and, necessarily, striving to produce what is beautiful in form and to become what is lovely in character.

Hope—the recognition, by true foresight, of better things to be reached hereafter, whether by ourselves or others; necessarily issuing in the straightforward and undisappointable effort to advance, according to our proper power, the gaining of them.

Love—both of family and neighbour, faithful and satisfied.

These are the six chiefly useful things to be got by political economy, when it *has* become a science. I will briefly tell you what modern political economy—the great *savoir mourir*—is doing with them.

The first three, I said, are pure air, water, and earth.

Heaven gives you the main elements of these. You can destroy them at your pleasure, or increase, almost without limit, the available quantities of them.

You can vitiate the air by your manner of life and of death to any extent. You might easily vitiate it so as to bring such a pestilence on the globe as would end all of you. You or your fellows, German and French, are at present vitiating it to the best of your power in every direction—chiefly at this moment with corpses and animal and vegetable ruin in war, changing men, horses, and garden-stuff into noxious gas. But everywhere, and all day long, you are vitiating it with foul chemical exhalations; and the horrible nests, which you call towns, are little more than laboratories for the distillation into heaven of venomous smokes and smells, mixed with effluvia from decaying animal matter and infectious miasmata from purulent disease. On the other hand, your power of purifying the air, by dealing properly and swiftly with all substances in corruption, by absolutely forbidding noxious manufactures, and by planting in all soils the trees which cleanse and invigorate earth and atmosphere, is literally infinite. You might make every breath of air you draw, food.

Secondly, your power over the rain and river-waters of the earth is infinite. You can bring rain where you will, by planting wisely and tending carefully; drought where you will, by ravage of woods and neglect of the soil. You might have the rivers of England as pure as the crystal of the rock; beautiful in falls, in lakes, in living pools; so full of fish that you might take them out with your hands instead of nets. Or you may do always as you have done now—turn every river of England into a common sewer, so that you cannot so much as baptize an English baby but with filth, unless you hold its face out in the rain; and even *that* falls dirty.

Then for the third, earth, meant to be nourishing for you and blossoming. You have learned about it that there is no such thing as a flower; and as far as your scientific hands and scientific brains, inventive of explosive and deathful instead of blossoming and life-giving dust, can contrive, you have turned the Mother Earth, Demeter, into the Avenger-Earth, Tisiphone—with the voice of your brother's blood crying out of it in one wild harmony round all its murderous sphere.

That is what you have done for the three material useful things.

Then for the three immaterial useful things. For admiration, you have learned contempt and conceit. There is no lovely thing ever yet done by man that you care for or can understand; but you are persuaded you are able to do much finer things yourselves. You gather and exhibit together, as if equally instructive, what is infinitely bad with what is infinitely good. You do not know which is which; you instinctively prefer the bad, and do more of it. You instinctively hate the good, and destroy it.

Then, secondly, for hope. You have not so much spirit of it in you as to begin any plan which will not pay for ten years; nor so much intelligence of it in you (either politicians or workmen) as to be able to form one clear idea of what you would like your country to become.

Then, thirdly, for love. You were ordered by the Founder of your religion to love your neighbour as yourselves. You have founded an entire science of political economy on what you have stated to be the constant instinct of man—the desire to defraud his neighbour. And you have driven your women mad, so that they ask no more for love nor for fellowship with you; but stand against you, and ask for "Justice."

Are there any of you who are tired of all this? Any of you, landlords or tenants? Employers or workmen? Are there any landlords, any masters, who would like better to be served by men than by iron devils? Any tenants, any workmen, who can be true to their leaders and to each other? Who can vow to work and to live faithfully, for the sake of the joy of their homes?

Will any such give the tenth of what they have and of what they earn, not to emigrate with, but to stay in England with, and do what is in their hands and hearts to make her a happy England?

I am not rich (as people now estimate riches), and great part of what I have is already engaged in maintaining art-workmen, or for other objects more or less of public utility. The tenth of whatever is left to me, estimated as accurately as I can (you shall see the accounts), I will make over to you in perpetuity, with the best security that English law can give, on Christmas Day of this year, with engagement to add the tithe of whatever I earn afterwards. Who else will help, with little or much? The object of such fund being to begin, and gradually—no matter how slowly—to increase, the buying and securing of land in England, which shall not be built upon, but cultivated by Englishmen with their own hands and such help of force as they can find in wind and wave. I do not care with how many or how few this thing is begun, nor on what inconsiderable scale— if it be but in two or three poor men's gardens. So much, at least, I can buy, myself, and give them. If no help come, I have done and said what I could, and there will be an end. If any help come to me, it is to be on the following conditions:

We will try to make some small piece of English ground beautiful, peaceful, and fruitful. We will have no steam-engines upon it, and no railroads; we will have no untended or unthought-of creatures on it; none wretched but the sick; none idle but the dead. We will have no liberty upon it, but instant obedience to known law and appointed persons; no equality upon it, but recognition of every betterness that we can find, and reprobation of every worseness. When we want to go anywhere, we will go there quietly and safely, not at forty miles an hour in the risk of our lives; when we want to carry anything anywhere, we will carry it either on the backs of beasts or on our own, or in carts or boats. We will have plenty of flowers and vegetables in our gardens, plenty of corn and grass in our fields—and few bricks. We will have some music and poetry; the children shall learn to dance to it and sing it; perhaps some of the old people, in time, may also. We will have some art, moreover; we will at least try if, like the Greeks, we can't make some pots. The Greeks used to paint pictures of gods on their pots. We, probably, cannot do as much; but we may put some pictures of insects on them, and reptiles—butterflies and frogs, if nothing better. There was an excellent old potter in France who used to put frogs and vipers into his dishes, to the admiration of mankind; we can surely put something nicer than that. Little by little, some higher art and imagination may manifest themselves among us, and feeble rays of science may dawn for us—botany, though too dull to dispute the existence of flowers; and history, though too simple to question the nativity of men; nay, even perhaps an uncalculating and uncovetous wisdom, as of rude Magi presenting, at such nativity, gifts of gold and frankincense.

Faithfully yours,

JOHN RUSKIN

"An Idealist's Arraignment of the Age"
is Letter V
in Ruskin's FORS CLAVIGERA.

William James

1842–1910

William James was born in New York City on January 11, 1842.
His father, Henry James, Sr., was heir to a fortune which made him
independent and enabled him to live as a student and a man of the
world. There were five children, the future novelist Henry James
being the second. Despite its size, the James family was constantly
traveling. As a result the children received their early education
mostly from schools and private tutors in England, France, Switzerland, and Germany.

William James was slow in discovering his vocation. He studied
painting with Hunt in Newport, attended the scientific school and
then medical school at Harvard, accompanied the Agassiz expedition to Brazil, and pursued the study of psychology in Germany,
before he became, in 1872, instructor of anatomy and physiology at
Harvard. Two years later he began teaching psychology and set up
the first laboratory in America in experimental psychology. From
then until he completed his *Principles of Psychology* [1] his energies
were mainly devoted to this subject.

Yet James had always been interested in the problems of philosophy. From 1890, when his great work on psychology was first
published, until his death he devoted himself almost entirely to philosophy. Besides his teaching at Harvard, where he was appointed
professor of philosophy, he gave many lectures and became a highly
popular speaker, in demand from coast to coast. The first volume
of his lectures appeared in 1897 under the title of *The Will to
Believe and Other Essays in Popular Philosophy*.[2] In 1901–02 he
delivered the Gifford Lectures on natural religion at the University

[1] See *Great Books of the Western World*, Vol. 53.
[2] See Vol. 10, pp. 39–57, in this set for the title essay.

of Edinburgh; these were published as *The Varieties of Religious Experience*. He developed his own philosophy of pragmatism in a book of that title published in 1907 and met the criticism of it in *The Meaning of Truth* (1909) and *A Pluralistic Universe* (1909). These works are written in a nontechnical and vigorous style. He was engaged in giving a more technical analysis and expression to his philosophy when he died, August 26, 1910.

The three essays presented here were first given as lectures. In them James gives an analysis and defense of individualism. The essay *On a Certain Blindness in Human Beings* he describes as "providing the perception on which my whole individualistic philosophy is based." He takes the position that each individual is of unique value and the source of what he calls "vital significance." Realization of this can lead to great personal joy and exhilaration. James gives high praise to the essay by Stevenson entitled *The Lantern-Bearers*,[3] which expresses this insight.

If the individual is a source of unique value, it becomes a central problem of education to find ways of recognizing and releasing the energies of the individual. This is the main topic considered in *The Energies of Men*. Convinced that most men use only a small part of their powers, James asks how they may be brought to the top of their abilities. Among the "energy-releasing" agents, he considers the excitement of the unusual stimulus, the example of others or rivalry with them, the demands of duty, or the challenge of a new task. He notes that ascetic exercises aimed at disciplining the will may serve the same purpose, as may also the opposition of new and different ideas.

James constantly opposes anything that prevents the appreciation of individual worth. The opinion that man is merely the creature of

---

[3] See Vol. 7, pp. 112–121, in this set.

Notes from the artist: "William James in his later years. Woven into his beard are drawings of his mother and father, as well as figures from James's own sketchbook. The quotation is taken from his collected letters, while on his coat is a facsimile of the title page of Pragmatism."

Wm. James

Ideals ought to aim at the transformation of reality — no less!

PRAGMATISM
A NEW NAME FOR SOME
OLD WAYS OF THINKING

POPULAR LECTURES ON PHILOSOPHY BY
WILLIAM JAMES

his environment is, to James, among the worst offenders in this respect. In *Great Men and Their Environment* he attacks *this* opinion as it is expressed in what is known as Social Darwinism. James maintains that this is a wholly erroneous and misleading extension of the Darwinian theory of evolution.

In these essays James does more than merely pose the problem of individualism. He also explores some of its more important possibilities and does this in a way that merits comparison with such a classic statement as that of John Stuart Mill in his essay *On Liberty.*[4]

---

[4] See *Great Books of the Western World,* Vol. 43, pp. 267–323.

On a Certain Blindness in Human Beings

Our judgments concerning the worth of things, big or little, depend on the *feelings* the things arouse in us. Where we judge a thing to be precious in consequence of the *idea* we frame of it, this is only because the idea is itself associated already with a feeling. If we were radically feelingless, and if ideas were the only things our mind could entertain, we should lose all our likes and dislikes at a stroke, and be unable to point to any one situation or experience in life more valuable or significant than any other.

Now the blindness in human beings, of which this discourse will treat, is the blindness with which we all are afflicted in regard to the feelings of creatures and people different from ourselves.

We are practical beings, each of us with limited functions and duties to perform. Each is bound to feel intensely the importance of his own duties and the significance of the situations that call these forth. But this feeling is in each of us a vital secret, for sympathy with which we vainly look to others. The others are too much absorbed in their own vital secrets to take an interest in ours. Hence the stupidity and injustice of our opinions, so far as they deal with the significance of alien lives. Hence the falsity of our judgments, so far as they presume to decide in an absolute way on the value of other persons' conditions or ideals.

Take our dogs and ourselves, connected as we are by a tie more intimate than most ties in this world; and yet, outside of that tie of friendly fondness, how insensible, each of us, to all that makes life significant for the other!—we to the rapture of bones under hedges, or smells of trees and lampposts, they to the delights of literature and art. As you sit reading the most moving romance you ever fell upon, what sort of a judge is your fox terrier of your behavior? With all his good will toward you, the nature of your conduct is absolutely excluded from his comprehension. To sit there like a senseless statue when you might be taking him to walk and throwing sticks for him to catch! What queer disease is this that comes over you every day, of holding things and staring at them like that for hours together, paralyzed of motion and vacant of all conscious life? The African savages came nearer the truth; but they, too, missed it when they gathered wonderingly round one of our American travelers who, in the interior, had just come into possession of a stray copy of the *New York Commercial Advertiser* and was devouring it column by column. When he got through, they offered him a high price for the mysterious object; and, being asked for what they wanted it, they said: "For an eye medicine"—that being the only reason they could conceive of for the protracted bath which he had given his eyes upon its surface.

The spectator's judgment is sure to miss the root of the matter, and to possess no truth. The subject judged knows a part of the world of reality which the judging spectator fails to see, knows more while the spectator knows less; and, wherever there is conflict of opinion and difference of vision, we are bound to believe that the truer side is the side that feels the more, and not the side that feels the less.

Let me take a personal example of the kind that befalls each one of us daily:

Some years ago, while journeying in the mountains of North Carolina, I passed by a large number of "coves," as they call them there, or heads of small valleys between the hills, which had been newly cleared and planted. The impression on my mind was one of unmitigated squalor. The settler had in every case cut down the more manageable trees, and left their charred stumps standing. The larger trees he had girdled and killed in order that their foliage should not cast a shade. He had then built a log cabin, plastering its chinks with clay, and had set up a tall zigzag rail fence around the scene of his havoc to keep the pigs and cattle out. Finally, he had irregularly planted the intervals between the stumps and trees with Indian corn, which grew among the chips; and there he dwelt with his wife and babes—an ax, a gun, a few utensils, and some pigs and chickens feeding in the woods being the sum total of his possessions.

The forest had been destroyed; and what had "improved" it out of existence was hideous, a sort of ulcer, without a single element of artificial grace to make up for the loss of Nature's beauty. Ugly, indeed, seemed the life of the squatter, scudding, as the sailors say, under bare poles, beginning again away back where our first ancestors started, and by hardly a single item the better off for all the achievements of the intervening generations.

"Talk about going back to nature!" I said to myself, oppressed by the dreariness, as I drove by. Talk of a country life for one's old age and for one's children! Never thus, with nothing but the bare ground and one's bare hands to fight the battle! Never, without the best spoils of culture woven in! The beauties and commodities gained by the centuries are sacred. They are our heritage and birthright. No modern person ought to be willing to live a day in such a state of rudimentariness and denudation.

Then I said to the mountaineer who was driving me, "What sort of people are they who have to make these new clearings?" "All of us," he replied. "Why, we ain't happy here unless we are getting one of these coves under cultivation." I instantly felt that I had been losing the whole inward significance of the situation. Because to me the clearings spoke of naught but denudation, I thought that to those whose sturdy arms and obedient axes had made them they could tell no other story. But, when *they* looked on the hideous stumps, what they thought of was personal victory. The chips, the girdled trees, and the vile split rails spoke of honest sweat, persistent toil and final reward. The cabin was a warrant of safety for self and wife and babes. In short, the clearing, which to me was a mere ugly picture on the retina, was to them a symbol redolent with moral memories and sang a very paean of duty, struggle, and success.

I had been as blind to the peculiar ideality of their conditions as they certainly would also have been to the ideality of mine had they had a peep at my strange indoor academic ways of life at Cambridge.

Wherever a process of life communicates an eagerness to him who lives it, there the life becomes genuinely significant. Sometimes the eagerness is more knit up with the motor activities, sometimes with the perceptions, sometimes with the imagination, sometimes with reflective thought. But, wherever it is found, there is the zest, the tingle, the excitement of reality; and there *is* "importance" in the only real and positive sense in which importance ever anywhere can be.

Robert Louis Stevenson has illustrated this by a case, drawn from the sphere of the imagination, in an essay which I really think deserves to become immortal, both for the truth of its matter and the excellence of its form.

Toward the end of September [Stevenson writes], when school-time was drawing near and the nights were already black, we would begin to sally from our respective villas, each equipped with a tin bull's-eye lantern. The thing was so well known that it had worn a rut in the commerce of Great Britain; and the grocers, about the due time, began to garnish their windows with our particular brand of luminary. We wore them buckled to the waist upon a cricket belt, and over them, such was the rigour of the game, a buttoned top-coat. They smelled noisomely of blistered tin; they never burned aright, though they would always burn our fingers; their use was naught; the pleasure of them merely fanciful; and yet a boy with a bull's-eye under his top-coat asked for nothing more. The fishermen used lanterns about their boats, and it was from them, I suppose, that we had got the hint; but theirs were not bull's-eyes, nor did we ever play at being fishermen. The police carried them at their belts, and we had plainly copied them in that; yet we did not pretend to be policemen. Burglars, indeed, we may have had some haunting thought of; and we had certainly an eye to past ages when lanterns were more common, and to certain story-books in which we had found them to figure very largely. But take it for all in all, the pleasure of the thing was substantive; and to be a boy with a bull's-eye under his top-coat was good enough for us.

When two of these asses met, there would be an anxious "Have you got your lantern?" and a gratified "Yes!" That was the shibboleth, and very needful too; for, as it was the rule to keep our glory contained, none could recognize a lantern-bearer, unless (like the polecat) by the smell. Four or five would sometimes climb into the belly of a ten-man lugger, with nothing but the thwarts above them—for the cabin was usually locked—or choose out some hollow of the links where the wind might whistle overhead. Then the coats would be unbuttoned, and the bull's-eyes discovered; and in the chequering glimmer, under the huge, windy hall of the night, and cheered by a rich steam of toasting tinware, these fortunate young gentlemen would crouch together in the cold sand of the links, or on the scaly bilges of the fishing-boat, and delight themselves with inappropriate talk. Woe is me that I may not give some specimens. . . . But the talk, at any rate, was but a condiment; and these gatherings themselves only accidents in the career of the lantern-bearer. The essence of this bliss was to walk by yourself in the black night; the slide shut, the top-coat buttoned; not a ray escaping, whether to conduct your footsteps or to make your glory public: a mere pillar of darkness in the dark; and all the while, deep down in the privacy of your fool's heart, to know you had a bull's-eye at your belt, and to exult and sing over the knowledge.

It is said that a poet has died young in the breast of the most stolid. It may be contended, rather, that this (somewhat minor) bard in almost every case survives, and is the spice of life to his possessor. Justice is not done to the versatility and the unplumbed childishness of man's imagination. His life from without may seem but a rude mound of mud; there will be some golden chamber at the heart of it, in which he dwells delighted; and for as dark as his pathway seems to the observer, he will have some kind of bull's-eye at his belt.

. . . There is one fable that touches very near the quick of life: the fable of the monk who passed into the woods, heard a bird break into song, hearkened for a trill or two, and found himself on his return a stranger at his convent gates; for he had been absent fifty years, and of all his comrades there survived but one to recognize him. It is not only in the woods that this enchanter carols, though perhaps he is native there. He sings in the most doleful places. The miser hears him and chuckles, and the days are moments. With no more apparatus than an ill-smelling lantern, I have evoked him on the naked links. All life that is not merely mechanical is spun out of two strands: seeking for that bird and hearing him. And it is just this that makes life so hard to value, and the delight of each so incommunicable. And it is just a knowledge of this, and a remembrance of those fortunate hours in which the bird has sung to us, that fills us with such wonder when we turn to the pages of the realist. There, to be sure, we find a picture of life in so far as it consists of mud and of old iron, cheap desires and cheap fears, that which we are ashamed to remember and that which we are careless whether we forget; but of the note of that time-devouring nightingale we hear no news.

. . . Say that I came [in such a realistic romance] on some such business as that of my lantern-bearers on the links; and described the boys as very cold, spat upon by flurries of rain, and drearily surrounded, all of which they were; and their talk as silly and indecent, which it certainly was. . . . To the eye of the observer they are wet and cold and drearily surrounded; but ask themselves, and they are in the heaven of a recondite pleasure, the ground of which is an ill-smelling lantern.

For, to repeat, the ground of a man's joy is often hard to hit. It may hinge at times upon a mere accessory, like the lantern; it may reside . . . in the mysterious inwards of psychology. . . . It has so little bond with externals . . . that it may even touch them not; and the man's true life, for which he consents to live, lies altogether in the field of fancy. . . . In such a case the poetry runs underground. The observer (poor soul, with his documents!) is all abroad. For to look at the man is but to court deception. We shall see the trunk from which he draws his nourishment; but he himself is above and abroad in the green dome of foliage, hummed through by winds and nested in by nightingales. And the true realism were that of the poets, to climb up after him like a squirrel, and catch some glimpse of the heaven for which he lives. And the true realism, always and everywhere, is that of the poets: to find out where joy resides, and give it a voice far beyond singing.

For to miss the joy is to miss all. In the joy of the actors lies the sense of any action. That is the explanation, that the excuse. To one who has not the secret of the lanterns, the scene upon the links is meaningless. And hence the haunting and truly spectral unreality of realistic books. . . . In each, we miss the personal poetry, the enchanted atmosphere, that rainbow work of fancy that clothes what is naked and seems to ennoble what is base; in each, life falls dead like dough, instead of soaring away like a balloon into the colours of the sunset; each is true, each inconceivable; for no man lives in the external truth, among salts and acids, but in the warm, phantasmagoric chamber of his brain, with the painted windows and the storied wall.[1]

These paragraphs are the best thing I know in all Stevenson. "To miss the joy is to miss all." Indeed, it is. Yet we are but finite, and each one of us has some single specialized vocation of his own. And it seems as if energy in the service of its particular duties might be got only by hardening the heart toward everything unlike them. Our deadness toward all but one particular kind of joy would thus be the price we inevitably have to pay for being practical creatures. Only in some pitiful dreamer, some philosopher, poet, or romancer, or when the common practical man becomes a lover, does the hard externality give way, and a gleam of insight into the ejective world, as Clifford called it, the vast world of inner life beyond us, so different from that of outer seeming, illuminate our mind. Then the whole scheme of our customary values gets confounded, then our self is riven and its narrow interests fly to pieces, then a new center and a new perspective must be found. The change is well described by my colleague, Josiah Royce:

What, then, is our neighbor? Thou hast regarded his thought, his feeling, as somehow different from thine. Thou hast said, "A pain in him is not like a pain in me, but something far easier to bear." He seems to thee a little less living than thou; his life is dim, it is cold, it is a pale fire beside thy own burning desires. . . . So, dimly and by instinct hast thou lived with thy neighbor, and hast known him not, being blind. Thou hast made [of him] a thing, no Self at all. Have done with this illusion, and simply try to learn the truth. Pain is pain, joy is joy, everywhere, even as in thee. In all the songs of the forest birds; in all the cries of the wounded and dying, struggling in the captor's power; in the boundless

---

1. *The Lantern-Bearers.* [See Vol. 7, pp. 112–121, in this set (Ed.).]

sea where the myriads of water creatures strive and die; amid all the countless hordes of savage men; in all sickness and sorrow; in all exultation and hope, everywhere, from the lowest to the noblest, the same conscious, burning, willful life is found, endlessly manifold as the forms of the living creatures, unquenchable as the fires of the sun, real as these impulses that even now throb in thine own little selfish heart. Lift up thy eyes, behold that life, and then turn away, and forget it as thou canst; but, if thou hast *known* that, thou hast begun to know thy duty.

This higher vision of an inner significance in what, until then, we had realized only in the dead external way often comes over a person suddenly; and, when it does so, it makes an epoch in his history. As Emerson says, there is a depth in those moments that constrains us to ascribe more reality to them than to all other experiences. The passion of love will shake one like an explosion, or some act will awaken a remorseful compunction that hangs like a cloud over all one's later day.

This mystic sense of hidden meaning starts upon us often from non-human natural things. I take this passage from *Obermann*, a French novel that had some vogue in its day:

Paris, March 7.—It was dark and rather cold. I was gloomy, and walked because I had nothing to do. I passed by some flowers placed breast-high upon a wall. A jonquil in bloom was there. It is the strongest expression of desire: it was the first perfume of the year. I felt all the happiness destined for man. This unutterable harmony of souls, the phantom of the ideal world, arose in me complete. I never felt anything so great or so instantaneous. I know not what shape, what analogy, what secret of relation it was that made me see in this flower a limitless beauty . . . I shall never enclose in a conception this power, this immensity that nothing will express; this form that nothing will contain; this ideal of a better world which one feels, but which it would seem that nature has not made.

Wordsworth and Shelley are similarly full of this sense of a limitless significance in natural things. In Wordsworth it was a somewhat austere and moral significance—a "lonely cheer."

> To every natural form, rock, fruit, or flower,
> Even the loose stones that cover the highway,
> I gave a moral life: I saw them feel,
> Or linked them to some feeling: the great mass
> Lay bedded in some quickening soul, and all
> That I beheld respired with inward meaning.[2]

---

2. *The Prelude,* Book III.

"Authentic tidings of invisible things!" Just what this hidden presence in nature was, which Wordsworth so rapturously felt, and in the light of which he lived, tramping the hills for days together, the poet never could explain logically or in articulate conceptions. Yet to the reader who may himself have had gleaming moments of a similar sort, the verses in which Wordsworth simply proclaims the fact of them come with a heart-satisfying authority:

> Magnificent
> The morning rose, in memorable pomp,
> Glorious as e'er I had beheld. In front
> The sea lay laughing at a distance; near,
> The solid mountains shone, bright as the clouds,
> Grain-tinctured, drenched in empyrean light;
> And in the meadows and the lower grounds
> Was all the sweetness of a common dawn—
> Dews, vapours, and the melody of birds,
> And labourers going forth to till the fields.
>
> Ah! need I say, dear Friend, that to the brim
> My heart was full; I made no vows, but vows
> Were then made for me; bond unknown to me
> Was given, that I should be, else sinning greatly,
> A dedicated Spirit. On I walked
> In thankful blessedness, which yet survives.[3]

As Wordsworth walked, filled with his strange inner joy, responsive thus to the secret life of nature round about him, his rural neighbors, tightly and narrowly intent upon their own affairs, their crops and lambs and fences, must have thought him a very insignificant and foolish personage. It surely never occurred to any one of them to wonder what was going on inside of *him* or what it might be worth. And yet that inner life of his carried the burden of a significance that has fed the souls of others, and fills them to this day with inner joy.

Richard Jefferies has written a remarkable autobiographic document entitled *The Story of My Heart*. It tells in many pages of the rapture with which in youth the sense of the life of nature filled him. On a certain hilltop he says:

> I was utterly alone with the sun and the earth. Lying down on the grass, I spoke in my soul to the earth, the sun, the air, and the distant sea, far beyond sight. . . . With all the intensity of feeling which exalted me, all the intense communion I held with the earth, the sun and

---
3. *The Prelude*, Book IV.

sky, the stars hidden by the light, with the ocean—in no manner can the thrilling depth of these feelings be written—with these I prayed as if they were the keys of an instrument. . . . The great sun, burning with light, the strong earth—dear earth—the warm sky, the pure air, the thought of ocean, the inexpressible beauty of all filled me with a rapture, an ecstasy, an inflatus. With this inflatus, too, I prayed. . . . The prayer, this soul-emotion, was in itself not for an object: it was a passion. I hid my face in the grass. I was wholly prostrated, I lost myself in the wrestle, I was rapt and carried away. . . . Had any shepherd accidentally seen me lying on the turf he would only have thought I was resting a few minutes. I made no outward show. Who could have imagined the whirlwind of passion that was going on in me as I reclined there!

Surely, a worthless hour of life when measured by the usual standards of commercial value. Yet in what other *kind* of value can the preciousness of any hour, made precious by any standard, consist if it consist not in feelings of excited significance like these, engendered in someone by what the hour contains?

Yet so blind and dead does the clamor of our own practical interests make us to all other things that it seems almost as if it were necessary to become worthless as a practical being if one is to hope to attain to any breadth of insight into the impersonal world of worths as such, to have any perception of life's meaning on a large objective scale. Only your mystic, your dreamer, or your insolvent tramp or loafer can afford so sympathetic an occupation, an occupation which will change the usual standards of human value in the twinkling of an eye, giving to foolishness a place ahead of power, and laying low in a minute the distinctions which it takes a hard-working conventional man a lifetime to build up. You may be a prophet at this rate; but you cannot be a worldly success.

Walt Whitman, for instance, is accounted by many of us a contemporary prophet. He abolishes the usual human distinctions, brings all conventionalisms into solution, and loves and celebrates hardly any human attributes save those elementary ones common to all members of the race. For this he becomes a sort of ideal tramp, a rider on omnibus tops and ferryboats, and, considered either practically or academically, a worthless, unproductive being. His verses are but ejaculations—things mostly without subject or verb, a succession of interjections on an immense scale. He felt the human crowd as rapturously as Wordsworth felt the mountains, felt it as an overpoweringly significant presence, simply to absorb one's mind in which should be business sufficient and worthy to fill the days of a serious man. As he crosses Brooklyn ferry, this is what he feels:

Flood-tide below me! I watch you face to face;
Clouds of the west! sun there half an hour high! I see you also face to face.
Crowds of men and women attired in the usual costumes! how curious you are to me!
On the ferryboats, the hundreds and hundreds that cross, returning home, are more curious to me than you suppose;
And you that shall cross from shore to shore years hence are more to me, and more in my meditations, than you might suppose.

. . . .

Others will enter the gates of the ferry, and cross from shore to shore;
Others will watch the run of the flood-tide;
Others will see the shipping of Manhattan north and west, and the heights of Brooklyn to the south and east;
Others will see the islands large and small;
Fifty years hence, others will see them as they cross, the sun half an hour high;
A hundred years hence, or ever so many hundred years hence, others will see them,
Will enjoy the sunset, the pouring in of the flood-tide, the falling back to the sea of the ebb-tide.
It avails not, neither time or place—distance avails not;

. . . .

Just as you feel when you look on the river and sky, so I felt;
Just as any of you is one of a living crowd, I was one of a crowd;
Just as you are refreshed by the gladness of the river and the bright flow, I was refreshed;
Just as you stand and lean on the rail, yet hurry with the swift current, I stood, yet was hurried;
Just as you look on the numberless masts of ships, and the thick-stemmed pipes of steamboats, I looked.
I too many and many a time crossed the river, the sun half an hour high;
I watched the Twelfth-month sea-gulls—I saw them high in the air, floating with motionless wings, oscillating their bodies,
I saw how the glistening yellow lit up parts of their bodies, and left the rest in strong shadow,
I saw the slow-wheeling circles, and the gradual edging toward the south.

. . . .

Saw the white sails of schooners and sloops—saw the ships at anchor,
The sailors at work in the rigging, or out astride the spars,

. . . .

The scallop-edged waves in the twilight, the ladled cups, the frolicsome crests and glistening,

The stretch afar growing dimmer and dimmer, the gray walls of the granite
storehouses by the docks,

. . . .

On the neighboring shore, the fires from the foundry chimneys burning
high . . . into the night,
Casting their flicker of black . . . into the clefts of streets.
These, and all else, were to me the same as they are to you; [4]

And so on, through the rest of a divinely beautiful poem. And, if you
wish to see what this hoary loafer considered the most worthy way of
profiting by life's heaven-sent opportunities, read the delicious volume of
his letters to a young car conductor who had become his friend:

NEW YORK, *Oct.* 9, 1868

DEAR PETE—It is splendid here this forenoon—bright and cool. I was
out early taking a short walk by the river only two squares from where I
live. . . . Shall I tell you about [my life] just to fill up? I generally
spend the forenoon in my room writing, etc., then take a bath, fix up,
and go out about twelve and loaf somewhere or call on someone down
town or on business, or perhaps, if it is very pleasant and I feel like it,
ride a trip with some driver friend on Broadway, from 23rd Street to
Bowling Green, three miles each way. (Every day I find I have plenty to
do, every hour is occupied with something.) You know it is a never
ending amusement and study and recreation for me to ride a couple of
hours on a pleasant afternoon on a Broadway stage in this way. You see
everything as you pass, a sort of living, endless panorama—shops and
splendid buildings and great windows: on the broad sidewalks crowds of
women richly dressed continually passing, altogether different, superior
in style and looks from any to be seen anywhere else—in fact a perfect
stream of people—men, too, dressed in high style, and plenty of foreigners—and then in the streets the thick crowd of carriages, stages, carts,
hotel and private coaches, and in fact all sorts of vehicles and many
first-class teams, mile after mile, and the splendor of such a great street
and so many tall, ornamental, noble buildings, many of them of white
marble, and the gaiety and motion on every side: you will not wonder
how much attraction all this is on a fine day to a great loafer like me,
who enjoys so much seeing the busy world move by him and exhibiting
itself for his amusement while he takes it easy and just looks on and observes.

Truly a futile way of passing the time, some of you may say, and not
altogether creditable to a grownup man. And yet, from the deepest
point of view, who knows the more of truth and who knows the less—

---

4. *Crossing Brooklyn Ferry.*

Whitman on his omnibus top, full of the inner joy with which the spectacle inspires him, or you, full of the disdain which the futility of his occupation excites?

When your ordinary Brooklynite or New Yorker, leading a life replete with too much luxury, or tired and careworn about his personal affairs, crosses the ferry or goes up Broadway, *his* fancy does not thus soar away "into the colours of the sunset," as did Whitman's, nor does he inwardly realize at all the indisputable fact that this world never did anywhere or at any time contain more of essential divinity, or of eternal meaning, than is embodied in the fields of vision over which his eyes so carelessly pass. There is life; and there, a step away, is death. There is the only kind of beauty there ever was. There is the old human struggle and its fruits together. There is the text and the sermon, the real and the ideal in one. But to the jaded and unquickened eye it is all dead and common, pure vulgarism, flatness, and disgust. "Hech! it is a sad sight!" says Carlyle, walking at night with someone who appeals to him to note the splendor of the stars. And that very repetition of the scene to new generations of men in *secula seculorum* [for ever and ever], that eternal recurrence of the common order, which so fills a Whitman with mystic satisfaction, is to a Schopenhauer, with the emotional anesthesia, the feeling of "awful inner emptiness" from out of which he views it all, the chief ingredient of the tedium it instills. What is life on the largest scale, he asks, but the same recurrent inanities, the same dog barking, the same fly buzzing forevermore? Yet of the kind of fiber of which such inanities consist is the material woven of all the excitements, joys, and meanings that ever were, or ever shall be, in this world.

To be rapt with satisfied attention, like Whitman, to the mere spectacle of the world's presence is one way, and the most fundamental way, of confessing one's sense of its unfathomable significance and importance. But how can one attain to the feeling of the vital significance of an experience if one have it not to begin with? There is no receipt which one can follow. Being a secret and a mystery, it often comes in mysteriously unexpected ways. It blossoms sometimes from out of the very grave wherein we imagined that our happiness was buried. Benvenuto Cellini, after a life all in the outer sunshine, made of adventures and artistic excitements, suddenly finds himself cast into a dungeon in the Castle of San Angelo. The place is horrible. Rats and wet and mold possess it. His leg is broken and his teeth fall out, apparently with scurvy. But his thoughts turn to God as they have never turned before. He gets a Bible, which he reads during the one hour in the twenty-four in which a wandering ray of daylight penetrates his cavern. He has religious visions. He sings psalms to himself and composes hymns. And thinking, on the last day of July, of the festivities customary on the morrow in Rome, he says to himself: "All these past years I celebrated this holiday with the vanities of the world: from this year henceforward I will do it with the divinity of God. And then I said to myself, 'Oh, how much more happy I am for this present life of mine than for all those things remembered!'"

But the great understander of these mysterious ebbs and flows is Tolstoy. They throb all through his novels. In his *War and Peace*, the hero, Pierre, is supposed to be the richest man in the Russian Empire. During the French invasion he is taken prisoner and dragged through much of the retreat. Cold, vermin, hunger, and every form of misery assail him, the result being a revelation to him of the real scale of life's values.

> Here only, and for the first time, he appreciated, because he was deprived of it, the happiness of eating when he was hungry, of drinking when he was thirsty, of sleeping when he was sleepy, and of talking when he felt the desire to exchange some words. . . . Later in life he always recurred with joy to this month of captivity, and never failed to speak with enthusiasm of the powerful and ineffaceable sensations, and especially of the moral calm which he had experienced at this epoch. When at daybreak, on the morrow of his imprisonment, he saw [I abridge here Tolstoy's description] the mountains with their wooded slopes disappearing in the grayish mist; when he felt the cool breeze caress him; when he saw the light drive away the vapors, and the sun rise majestically behind the clouds and cupolas, and the crosses, the dew, the distance, the river, sparkle in the splendid, cheerful rays—his heart overflowed with emotion. This emotion kept continually with him and increased a hundredfold as the difficulties of his situation grew graver. . . . He learned that man is meant for happiness and that this happiness is in him, in the satisfaction of the daily needs of existence, and that unhappiness is the fatal result not of our need but of our abundance. . . . When calm reigned in the camp, and the embers paled and little by little went out, the full moon had reached the zenith. The woods and the fields round about lay clearly visible; and, beyond the inundation of light which filled them, the view plunged into the limitless horizon. Then Pierre cast his eyes upon the firmament, filled at that hour with myriads of stars. "All that is mine," he thought. "All that is in me, is me! And that is what they think they have taken prisoner! That is what they have shut up in a cabin!" So he smiled and turned in to sleep among his comrades.[5]

The occasion and the experience, then, are nothing. It all depends on

---

5. See *Great Books of the Western World*, Vol. 51, pp. 577–582 *passim* [Ed.].

the capacity of the soul to be grasped, to have its life currents absorbed by what is given. "Crossing a bare common," says Emerson, "in snow puddles, at twilight, under a clouded sky, without having in my thoughts any occurrence of special good fortune, I have enjoyed a perfect exhilaration. I am glad to the brink of fear."

Life is always worth living if one have such responsive sensibilities. But we of the highly educated classes (so called) have most of us got far, far away from Nature. We are trained to seek the choice, the rare, the exquisite exclusively, and to overlook the common. We are stuffed with abstract conceptions and glib with verbalities and verbosities; and in the culture of these higher functions the peculiar sources of joy connected with our simpler functions often dry up, and we grow stone-blind and insensible to life's more elementary and general goods and joys.

The remedy under such conditions is to descend to a more profound and primitive level. To be imprisoned or shipwrecked or forced into the army would permanently show the good of life to many an overeducated pessimist. Living in the open air and on the ground, the lopsided beam of the balance slowly rises to the level line; and the oversensibilities and insensibilities even themselves out. The good of all the artificial schemes and fevers fades and pales; and that of seeing, smelling, tasting, sleeping, and daring and doing with one's body grows and grows. The savages and children of Nature, to whom we deem ourselves so much superior, certainly are alive where we are often dead, along these lines; and, could they write as glibly as we do, they would read us impressive lectures on our impatience for improvement and on our blindness to the fundamental static goods of life. "Ah! my brother," said a chieftain to his white guest, "thou wilt never know the happiness of both thinking of nothing and doing nothing. This, next to sleep, is the most enchanting of all things. Thus we were before our birth, and thus we shall be after death. Thy people . . . when they have finished reaping one field, they begin to plow another; and, if the day were not enough, I have seen them plow by moonlight. What is their life to ours—the life that is naught to them? Blind that they are, they lose it all! But we live in the present."

The intense interest that life can assume when brought down to the nonthinking level, the level of pure sensorial perception, has been beautifully described by a man who can write, Mr. W. H. Hudson, in his volume *Idle Days in Patagonia*.

> I spent the greater part of one winter [says this admirable author] at a point on the Rio Negro seventy or eighty miles from the sea.

. . . It was my custom to go out every morning on horse-back with my gun and, followed by one dog, to ride away from the valley; and no sooner would I climb the terrace and plunge into the gray, universal thicket than I would find myself as completely alone as if five hundred instead of only five miles separated me from the valley and river. So wild and solitary and remote seemed that gray waste, stretching away into infinitude, a waste untrodden by man, and where the wild animals are so few that they have made no discoverable path in the wilderness of thorns. . . . Not once nor twice nor thrice, but day after day I returned to this solitude, going to it in the morning as if to attend a festival, and leaving it only when hunger and thirst and the westering sun compelled me. And yet I had no object in going—no motive which could be put into words; for, although I carried a gun, there was nothing to shoot—the shooting was all left behind in the valley. . . . Sometimes I would pass a whole day without seeing one mammal, and perhaps not more than a dozen birds of any size. The weather at that time was cheerless, generally with a gray film of cloud spread over the sky, and a bleak wind, often cold enough to make my bridle-hand quite numb. . . . At a slow pace, which would have seemed intolerable under other circumstances, I would ride about for hours together at a stretch. On arriving at a hill, I would slowly ride to its summit, and stand there to survey the prospect. On every side it stretched away in great undulations, wild and irregular. How gray it all was! Hardly less so near at hand than on the haze-wrapped horizon where the hills were dim and the outline obscured by distance. Descending from my outlook, I would take up my aimless wanderings again, and visit other elevations to gaze on the same landscape from another point; and so on for hours. And at noon I would dismount, and sit or lie on my folded poncho for an hour or longer. One day in these rambles I discovered a small grove composed of twenty or thirty trees, growing at a convenient distance apart, that had evidently been resorted to by a herd of deer or other wild animals. This grove was on a hill differing in shape from other hills in its neighbourhood; and, after a time, I made a point of finding and using it as a resting-place every day at noon. I did not ask myself why I made choice of that one spot, sometimes going out of my way to sit there, instead of sitting down under any one of the millions of trees and bushes on any other hillside. I thought nothing about it, but acted unconsciously. Only afterwards it seemed to me that, after having rested there once, each time I wished to rest again, the wish came associated with the image of that particular clump of trees, with polished stems and clean bed of sand beneath; and in a short time I formed a habit of returning, animal-like, to repose at that same spot.

It was, perhaps, a mistake to say that I would sit down and rest, since I was never tired; and yet, without being tired, that noonday pause, during which I sat for an hour without moving, was strangely grateful. All day there would be no sound, not even the rustling of a leaf. One day, while *listening* to the silence, it occurred to my mind to wonder what the effect would be if I were to shout aloud. This seemed at the time a horrible suggestion which almost made me shudder. But during those solitary days it was a rare thing for any thought to cross my mind. In the state of mind I was in, thought had become impossible. My state was one of *suspense and watchfulness;* yet I had no expectation of meeting an adventure, and felt as free from apprehension as I feel now while sitting in a room in London. The state seemed familiar rather than strange, and accompanied by a strong feeling of elation; and I did not know that something had come between me and my intellect until I returned to my former self—to thinking and the old insipid existence [again].

I had undoubtedly *gone back;* and that state of intense watchfulness or alertness, rather, with suspension of the higher intellectual faculties, represented the mental state of the pure savage. He thinks little, reasons little, having a surer guide in his [mere sensory perceptions]. He is in perfect harmony with nature, and is nearly on a level, mentally, with the wild animals he preys on, and which in their turn sometimes prey on him.

For the spectator, such hours as Mr. Hudson writes of form a mere tale of emptiness, in which nothing happens, nothing is gained, and there is nothing to describe. They are meaningless and vacant tracts of time. To him who feels their inner secret, they tingle with an importance that unutterably vouches for itself. I am sorry for the boy or girl, or man or woman, who has never been touched by the spell of this mysterious sensorial life, with its irrationality, if so you like to call it, but its vigilance and its supreme felicity. The holidays of life are its most vitally significant portions, because they are, or at least should be, covered with just this kind of magically irresponsible spell.

And now what is the result of all these considerations and quotations? It is negative in one sense, but positive in another. It absolutely forbids us to be forward in pronouncing on the meaninglessness of forms of existence other than our own; and it commands us to tolerate, respect, and indulge those whom we see harmlessly interested and happy in their own ways, however unintelligible these may be to us. Hands off: neither the whole of truth nor the whole of good is revealed to any single observer, although each observer gains a partial superiority of insight from the peculiar position in which he stands. Even prisons and sickrooms have their special revelations. It is enough to ask of each of us that he should be faithful to his own opportunities and make the most of his own blessings, without presuming to regulate the rest of the vast field.

The Energies of Men

Everyone knows what it is to start a piece of work, either intellectual or muscular, feeling stale—or *oold*, as an Adirondack guide once put it to me. And everybody knows what it is to "warm up" to his job. The process of warming up gets particularly striking in the phenomenon known as "second wind." On usual occasions we make a practice of stopping an occupation as soon as we meet the first effective layer (so to call it) of fatigue. We have then walked, played, or worked "enough," so we desist. That amount of fatigue is an efficacious obstruction on this side of which our usual life is cast. But if an unusual necessity forces us to press onward, a surprising thing occurs. The fatigue gets worse up to a certain critical point, when gradually or suddenly it passes away, and we are fresher than before. We have evidently tapped a level of new energy, masked until then by the fatigue obstacle usually obeyed. There may be layer after layer of this experience. A third and a fourth "wind" may supervene. Mental activity shows the phenomenon as well as physical, and in exceptional cases we may find, beyond the very extremity of fatigue distress, amounts of ease and power that we never dreamed ourselves to own—sources of strength habitually not taxed at all, because habitually we never push through the obstruction, never pass those early critical points.

For many years I have mused on the phenomenon of second wind, trying to find a physiological theory. It is evident that our organism has stored-up reserves of energy that are ordinarily not called upon, but that may be called upon: deeper and deeper strata of combustible or explosible material, discontinuously arranged, but ready for use by anyone who probes so deep, and repairing themselves by rest as well as do the superficial strata. Most of us continue living unnecessarily near our surface. Our energy budget is like our nutritive budget. Physiologists say that a man is in "nutritive equilibrium" when day after day he neither gains nor loses weight. But the odd thing is that this condition may obtain on astonishingly different amounts of food. Take a man in nutritive equilibrium, and systematically increase or lessen his rations. In the first case he will begin to gain weight, in the second case to lose it. The change will be the greatest on the first day, less on the second, less still on the third, and so on, till he has gained all that he will gain, or lost all that he will lose, on that altered diet. He is now in nutritive equilibrium again, but with a new weight; and this neither lessens nor increases because his various combustion processes have adjusted themselves to the changed dietary. He gets rid, in one way or another, of just as much N,C,H, etc., as he takes in per diem.

Just so one can be in what I might call "efficiency equilibrium" (neither gaining nor losing power when once the equilibrium is reached) on astonishingly different quantities of work, no matter in what direction the work may be measured. It may be physical work, intellectual work, moral work, or spiritual work.

Of course there are limits: the trees don't grow into the sky. But the plain fact remains that men the world over possess amounts of resource which only very exceptional individuals push to their extremes of use. But the very same individual, pushing his energies to their extreme, may in a vast number of cases keep the pace up day after day, and find no "reaction" of a bad sort, so long as decent hygienic conditions are preserved. His more active rate of energizing does not wreck him; for the organism adapts itself and, as the rate of waste augments, augments correspondingly the rate of repair.

I say the *rate* and not the *time* of repair. The busiest man needs no more hours of rest than the idler. Some years ago Professor Patrick, of the Iowa State University, kept three young men awake for four days and nights. When his observations on them were finished, the subjects were permitted to sleep themselves out. All awoke from this sleep completely refreshed, but the one who took the longest to restore himself from his long vigil only slept one-third more time than was regular with him.

If my reader will put together these two conceptions, first, that few men live at their maximum of energy, and second, that anyone may be in vital equilibrium at very different rates of energizing, he will find, I think, that a very pretty practical problem of national economy, as well as of individual ethics, opens upon his view. In rough terms, we may say that a man who energizes below his normal maximum fails by just so much to profit by his chance at life; and that a nation filled with such men is inferior to a nation run at higher pressure. The problem is, then, how can men be trained up to their most useful pitch of energy? And how can nations make such training most accessible to all their sons and daughters. This, after all, is only the general problem of education, formulated in slightly different terms.

"Rough" terms, I said just now, because the words "energy" and "maximum" may easily suggest only *quantity* to the reader's mind, whereas in measuring the human energies of which I speak, qualities as well as quantities have to be taken into account. Everyone feels that his total *power* rises when he passes to a higher qualitative level of life.

Writing is higher than walking, thinking is higher than writing, deciding higher than thinking, deciding "no" higher than deciding "yes"—at least the man who passes from one of these activities to another will usually say that each later one involves a greater element of *inner work* than the earlier ones, even though the total heat given out or the foot-pounds expended by the organism may be less. Just how to conceive this inner work physiologically is as yet impossible, but psychologically we all know what the word means. We need a particular spur or effort to start us upon inner work; it tires us to sustain it; and when long sustained, we know how easily we lapse. When I speak of "energizing," and its rates and levels and sources, I mean therefore our inner as well as our outer work.

Let no one think, then, that our problem of individual and national economy is solely that of the maximum of pounds raisable against gravity, the maximum of locomotion, or of agitation of any sort, that human beings can accomplish. That might signify little more than hurrying and jumping about in unco-ordinated ways; whereas inner work, though it so often reinforces outer work, quite as often means its arrest. To relax, to say to ourselves (with the "new thoughters"), "Peace! be still!" is sometimes a great achievement of inner work. When I speak of human energizing in general, the reader must therefore understand that sum total of activities, some outer and some inner, some muscular, some emotional, some moral, some spiritual, of whose waxing and waning in himself he is at all times so well aware. How to keep it at an appreciable maximum? How not to let the level lapse? That is the great problem. But the work of men and women is of innumerable kinds, each kind being, as we say, carried on by a particular faculty; so the great problem splits into two subproblems thus:

1. What are the limits of human faculty in various directions?

2. By what diversity of means, in the differing types of human beings, may the faculties be stimulated to their best results?

Read in one way, these two questions sound both trivial and familiar:

there is a sense in which we have all asked them ever since we were born. Yet *as a methodical program of scientific inquiry*, I doubt whether they have ever been seriously taken up. If answered fully, almost the whole of mental science and of the science of conduct would find a place under them. I propose, in what follows, to press them on the reader's attention in an informal way.

The first point to agree upon in this enterprise is that *as a rule men habitually use only a small part of the powers which they actually possess and which they might use under appropriate conditions.*

Everyone is familiar with the phenomenon of feeling more or less alive on different days. Everyone knows on any given day that there are energies slumbering in him which the incitements of that day do not call forth, but which he might display if these were greater. Most of us feel as if a sort of cloud weighed upon us, keeping us below our highest notch of clearness in discernment, sureness in reasoning, or firmness in deciding. Compared with what we ought to be, we are only half awake. Our fires are damped, our drafts are checked. We are making use of only a small part of our possible mental and physical resources. In some persons this sense of being cut off from their rightful resources is extreme, and we then get the formidable neurasthenic and psychasthenic conditions, with life grown into one tissue of impossibilities, that so many medical books describe.

Stating the thing broadly, the human individual thus lives usually far within his limits; he possesses powers of various sorts which he habitually fails to use. He energizes below his *maximum*, and he behaves below his *optimum*. In elementary faculty, in co-ordination, in power of *inhibition* and control, in every conceivable way, his life is contracted like the field of vision of an hysteric subject—but with less excuse, for the poor hysteric is diseased, while in the rest of us it is only an inveterate *habit*—the habit of inferiority to our full self—that is bad.

Admit so much, then, and admit also that the charge of being inferior to their full self is far truer of some men than of others; then the practical question ensues: *to what do the better men owe their escape? And, in the fluctuations which all men feel in their own degree of energizing, to what are the improvements due when they occur?*

In general terms the answer is plain:

Either some unusual stimulus fills them with emotional excitement, or some unusual idea of necessity induces them to make an extra effort of will. *Excitements, ideas, and efforts,* in a word, are what carry us over the dam.

In those "hyperesthetic" conditions which chronic invalidism so often brings in its train, the dam has changed its normal place. The slightest functional exercise gives a distress which the patient yields to and stops. In such cases of "habit neurosis" a new range of power often comes in consequence of the "bullying treatment," of efforts which the doctor obliges the patient, much against his will, to make. First comes the very extremity of distress, then follows unexpected relief. There seems no doubt that *we are each and all of us to some extent victims of habit neurosis.* We have to admit the wider potential range and the habitually narrow actual use. We live subject to arrest by degrees of fatigue which we have come only from habit to obey. Most of us may learn to push the barrier farther off, and to live in perfect comfort on much higher levels of power.

Country people and city people, as a class, illustrate this difference. The rapid rate of life, the number of decisions in an hour, the many things to keep account of, in a busy city-man's or woman's life, seem monstrous to a country brother. He doesn't see how we live at all. A day in New York or Chicago fills him with terror. The danger and noise make it appear like a permanent earthquake. But *settle* him there, and in a year or two he will have caught the pulse beat. He will vibrate to the city's rhythms; and if he only succeeds in his avocation, whatever that may be, he will find a joy in all the hurry and the tension, he will keep the pace as well as any of us, and get as much out of himself in any week as he ever did in ten weeks in the country.

The stimuli of those who successfully respond and undergo the transformation here are duty, the example of others, and crowd pressure and contagion. The transformation, moreover, is a chronic one: the new level of energy becomes permanent. The duties of new offices of trust are constantly producing this effect on human beings appointed to them. The physiologists call a stimulus "dynamogenic" when it increases the muscular contractions of men to whom it is applied; but appeals can be dynamogenic morally as well as muscularly. We are witnessing here in America today the dynamogenic effect of a very exalted political office upon the energies of an individual who had already manifested a healthy amount of energy before the office came.

Humbler examples show perhaps still better what chronic effects duty's appeal may produce in chosen individuals. John Stuart Mill somewhere says that women excel men in the power of keeping up sustained moral excitement. Every case of illness nursed by wife or mother is a proof of this; and where can one find greater examples of sustained endurance than in those thousands of poor homes where the woman successfully holds the family together and keeps it going by taking all the thought and doing all the work—nursing, teaching, cooking, washing, sewing, scrubbing, saving, helping neighbors, "choring" outside—where does the catalogue end? If she does a bit of scolding now and then who can blame her? But often she does just the reverse— keeping the children clean and the man good tempered, and soothing and smoothing the whole neighborhood into finer shape.

Eighty years ago a certain Montyon left to the Académie Française a sum of money to be given in small prizes to the best examples of "virtue" of the year. The academy's committees, with great good sense, have shown a partiality to virtues simple and chronic, rather than to her spasmodic and dramatic flights; and the exemplary housewives reported on have been wonderful and admirable enough. In Paul Bourget's report for this year we find numerous cases, of which this is a type: Jeanne Chaix, eldest of six children; mother insane; father chronically ill. Jeanne, with no money but her wages at a pasteboard-box factory, directs the household, brings up the children, and successfully maintains the family of eight, which thus subsists, morally as well as materially, by the sole force of her valiant will. In some of these French cases charity to outsiders is added to the inner family burden; or helpless relatives, young or old, are adopted, as if the strength were inexhaustible and ample for every appeal. Details are too long to quote here; but human nature, responding to the call of duty, appears nowhere sublimer than in the person of these humble heroines of family life.

Turning from more chronic to acuter proofs of human nature's reserves of power, we find that the stimuli that carry us over the usually effective dam are most often the classic emotional ones: love, anger, crowd contagion or despair. Despair lames most people, but it wakes others fully up. Every siege or shipwreck or polar expedition brings out some hero who keeps the whole company in heart. Last year there was a terrible colliery explosion at Courrières in France. Two hundred corpses, if I remember rightly, were exhumed. After twenty days of excavation, the rescuers heard a voice. *"Me voici* [Here I am]," said the first man unearthed. He proved to be a collier named Nemy, who had taken command of thirteen others in the darkness, disciplined them and cheered them, and brought them out alive. Hardly any of them could see or speak or walk when brought into the day. Five days later, a different type of vital endurance was unexpectedly unburied in the person of one Berton who, isolated from any but dead companions, had been able to sleep away most of his time.

A new position of responsibility will usually show a man to be a far stronger creature than was supposed. Cromwell's and Grant's careers are the stock examples of how war will wake a man up. I owe to Professor C. E. Norton, my colleague, the permission to print part of a private letter from Colonel Baird-Smith written shortly after the six weeks' siege of Delhi, in 1857, for the victorious issue of which that excellent officer was chiefly to be thanked. He writes as follows:

. . . My poor wife had some reason to think that war and disease between them had left very little of a husband to take under nursing when she got him again. An attack of camp-scurvy had filled my mouth with sores, shaken every joint in my body, and covered me all over with sores and livid spots, so that I was marvellously unlovely to look upon. A smart knock on the ankle-joint from the splinter of a shell that burst in my face, in itself a mere *bagatelle* of a wound, had been of necessity neglected under the pressing and incessant calls upon me, and had grown worse and worse until the whole foot below the ankle became a black mass and seemed to threaten mortification. I insisted, however, on being allowed to use it till the place was taken, mortification or no; and though the pain was sometimes horrible, I carried my point and kept up to the last. On the day after the assault I had an unlucky fall on some bad ground, and it was an open question for a day or two whether I hadn't broken my arm at the elbow. Fortunately it turned out to be only a severe sprain, but I am still conscious of the wrench it gave me. To crown the whole pleasant catalogue, I was worn to a shadow by a constant diarrhoea, and consumed as much opium as would have done credit to my father-in-law (Thomas De Quincey). However, thank God, I have a good share of Tapleyism in me and come out strong under difficulties. I think I may confidently say that no man ever saw me out of heart, or ever heard one croaking word from me even when our prospects were gloomiest. We were sadly scourged by the cholera, and it was almost appalling to me to find that out of twenty-seven officers present, I could only muster fifteen for the operations of the attack. However, it was done, and after it was done came the collapse. Don't be horrified when I tell you that for the whole of the actual siege, and in truth for some little time before, I almost lived on brandy. Appetite for food I had none, but I forced myself to eat just sufficient to sustain life, and I had an incessant craving for brandy as the strongest stimulant I could get. Strange to say, I was quite unconscious of its affecting me in the slightest degree. *The excitement of the work was so great that no lesser one seemed to have any chance against it, and I certainly never found my intellect clearer or my nerves stronger in my life.* It was only my wretched body that was weak, and the moment the real work was done by our becoming complete masters of Delhi, I broke down without delay and discovered that if I wished to live I must continue no longer the system that had kept me up until the crisis was passed. With it passed away as if in a moment all desire to stimulate, and a perfect loathing of my late staff of life took possession of me.

Such experiences show how profound is the alteration in the manner in which, under excitement, our organism will sometimes perform its physiological work. The processes of repair become different when the reserves have to be used, and for weeks and months the deeper use may go on.

Morbid cases, here as elsewhere, lay the normal machinery bare. In the first number of Dr. Morton Prince's *Journal of Abnormal Psychology,* Dr. Janet has discussed five cases of morbid impulse, with an explanation that is precious for my present point of view. One is a girl who eats, eats, eats, all day. Another walks, walks, walks, and gets her food from an automobile that escorts her. Another is a dipsomaniac. A fourth pulls out her hair. A fifth wounds her flesh and burns her skin. Hitherto such freaks of impulse have received Greek names (as bulimia, dromomania, etc.) and been scientifically disposed of as "episodic syndromata of hereditary degeneration." But it turns out that Janet's cases are all what he calls psychasthenics, or victims of a chronic sense of weakness, torpor, lethargy, fatigue, insufficiency, impossibility, unreality and powerlessness of will; and that in each and all of them the particular activity pursued, deleterious though it be, has the temporary result of raising the sense of vitality and making the patient feel alive again. These things reanimate: they would reanimate *us,* but it happens that in each patient the particular freak activity chosen is the only thing that does reanimate; and therein lies the morbid state. The way to treat such persons is to discover to them more usual and useful ways of throwing their stores of vital energy into gear.

Colonel Baird-Smith, needing to draw on altogether extraordinary stores of energy, found that brandy and opium were ways of throwing them into gear.

Such cases are humanly typical. We are all to some degree oppressed, unfree. We don't come to our own. It is there, but we don't get at it. The threshold must be made to shift. Then many of us find that an eccentric activity—a "spree," say—relieves. There is no doubt that to some men sprees and excesses of almost any kind are medicinal, temporarily at any rate, in spite of what the moralists and doctors say.

But when the normal tasks and stimulations of life don't put a man's deeper levels of energy on tap, and he requires distinctly deleterious excitements, his constitution verges on the abnormal. The normal opener of deeper and deeper levels of energy is the will. The difficulty is to use it, to make the effort which the word volition implies. But if we *do* make it (or if a god, though he were only the god Chance, makes it through us), it will act dynamogenically on us for a month. It is notorious that a single successful effort of moral volition, such as saying "no" to some habitual temptation, or performing some courageous act, will launch a man on a higher level of energy for days and weeks, will give him a new range of power. "In the act of uncorking a whiskey bottle which I had brought home to get drunk upon," said a man to me, "I suddenly found myself running out into the garden, where I smashed it on the ground. I felt so happy and uplifted after this act that for two months I wasn't tempted to touch a drop."

The emotions and excitements due to usual situations are the usual inciters of the will. But these act discontinuously; and in the intervals the shallower levels of life tend to close in and shut us off. Accordingly the best practical knowers of the human soul have invented the thing known as methodical ascetic discipline to keep the deeper levels constantly in reach. Beginning with easy tasks, passing to harder ones, and exercising day by day, it is, I believe, admitted that disciples of asceticism can reach very high levels of freedom and power of will.

Ignatius Loyola's spiritual exercises must have produced this result in innumerable devotees. But the most venerable ascetic system, and the one whose results have the most voluminous experimental corroboration is undoubtedly the Yoga system in Hindustan. From time immemorial, by Hatha Yoga, Raja Yoga, Karma Yoga, or whatever code of practice it might be, Hindu aspirants to perfection have trained themselves, month in and out, for years. The result claimed, and certainly in many cases accorded by impartial judges, is strength of character, personal power, unshakability of soul. In an article in the *Philosophical Review*, from which I am largely copying here, I have quoted at great length the experience with Hatha Yoga of a very gifted European friend of mine who, by persistently carrying out for several months its methods of fasting from food and sleep, its exercises in breathing and thought concentration, and its fantastic posture gymnastics, seems to have succeeded in waking up deeper and deeper levels of will and moral and intellectual power in himself, and to have escaped from a decidedly menacing brain condition of the "circular" type, from which he had suffered for years.

Judging by my friend's letters, of which the last I have is written fourteen months after the Yoga training began, there can be no doubt of his relative regeneration. He has undergone material trials with indifference, traveled third-class on Mediterranean steamers, and fourth-class on African trains, living with the poorest Arabs and sharing their unaccustomed food, all with equanimity. His devotion to certain interests has been put to heavy strain, and nothing is more remarkable to me than the changed moral tone with which he reports the situation. A profound modification has unquestionably occurred in the running of his mental machinery. The gearing has changed, and his will is available otherwise than it was.

My friend is a man of very peculiar temperament. Few of us would have had the will to start upon the yoga training, which, once started, seemed to conjure the further will power needed out of itself. And not all of those who could launch themselves would have reached the same results. The Hindus themselves admit that in some men the results may come without call or bell. My friend writes to me: "You are quite right in thinking that religious crises, love crises, indignation crises may awaken in a very short time powers similar to those reached by years of patient Yoga practice."

Probably most medical men would treat this individual's case as one of what it is fashionable now to call by the name of "self-suggestion," or "expectant attention"—as if those phrases were explanatory, or meant more than the fact that certain men can be influenced, while others cannot be influenced, by certain sorts of ideas. This leads me to say a word about ideas considered as dynamogenic agents, or stimuli for unlocking what would otherwise be unused reservoirs of individual power.

One thing that ideas do is to contradict other ideas and keep us from believing them. An idea that thus negates a first idea may itself in turn be negated by a third idea, and the first idea may thus regain its natural influence over our belief and determine our behavior. Our philosophic and religious development proceeds thus by credulities, negations, and the negating of negations.

But whether for arousing or for stopping belief, ideas may fail to be efficacious, just as a wire at one time alive with electricity may at another time be dead. Here our insight into causes fails us, and we can only note results in general terms. In general, whether a given idea shall be a live idea depends more on the person into whose mind it is injected than on the idea itself. Which is the suggestive idea for this person, and which for that one? Mr. Fletcher's disciples regenerate themselves by the idea (and the fact) that they are chewing, and rechewing, and super-chewing their food. Dr. Dewey's pupils regenerate themselves by going without their breakfast—a fact, but also an ascetic idea. Not everyone can use these ideas with the same success.

But apart from such individually varying susceptibilities, there are common lines along which men simply as men tend to be inflammable by ideas. As certain objects naturally awaken love, anger, or cupidity, so certain ideas naturally awaken the energies of loyalty, courage, endurance, or devotion. When these ideas are effective in an individual's life, their effect is often very great indeed. They may transfigure it, unlocking innumerable powers which, but for the idea, would never have come into play. "Fatherland," "the Flag," "the Union," "Holy Church," "the Monroe Doctrine," "Truth," "Science," "Liberty," Garibaldi's phrase "Rome or Death," etc., are so many examples of energy-releasing ideas. The social nature of such phrases is an essential factor of their dynamic power. They are forces of detent in situations in which no other force produces equivalent effects, and each is a force of detent only in a specific group of men.

The memory that an oath or vow has been made will nerve one to abstinences and efforts otherwise impossible; witness the "pledge" in the history of the temperance movement. A mere promise to his sweetheart will clean up a youth's life all over—at any rate for a time. For such effects an educated susceptibility is required. The idea of one's "honor," for example, unlocks energy only in those of us who have had the education of a "gentleman," so called.

That delightful being Prince Pueckler-Muskau writes to his wife from England that he has invented "a sort of artificial resolution respecting things that are difficult of performance. My device," he continues, "is this: *I give my word of honor most solemnly to myself* to do or to leave undone this or that. I am of course extremely cautious in the use of this expedient, but when once the word is given, even though I afterwards think I have been precipitate or mistaken, I hold it to be perfectly irrevocable, whatever inconveniences I foresee likely to result. If I were capable of breaking my word after such mature consideration, I should lose all respect for myself—and what man of sense would not prefer death to such an alternative? . . . When the mysterious formula is pronounced, no alteration in my own view, nothing short of physical impossibilities, must, for the welfare of my soul, alter my will. . . . I find something very satisfactory in the thought that man has the power of framing such props and weapons out of the most trivial materials, indeed out of nothing, merely by the force of his will, which thereby truly deserves the name of omnipotent."

Conversions, whether they be political, scientific, philosophic, or religious, form another way in which bound energies are let loose. They unify us, and put a stop to ancient mental interferences. The result is freedom, and often a great enlargement of power. A belief that thus settles upon an individual always acts as a challenge to his will. But, for the particular challenge to operate, he must be the right challeng*ee*. In religious conversions we have so fine an adjustment that the idea may be in the mind of the challengee for years before it exerts its effects; and why it should do so then is often so far from obvious that the event is taken for a miracle of grace, and not a natural occurrence. Whatever it is, it may be a high-water mark of energy, in which "noes," once impossible, are easy, and in which a new range of "yeses" gains the right of way.

We are just now witnessing a very copious unlocking of energies by ideas in the persons of those converts to "New Thought," "Christian Science," "Metaphysical Healing," or other forms of spiritual philosophy, who are so numerous among us today. The ideas here are healthy minded and optimistic; and it is quite obvious that a wave of religious activity, analogous in some respects to the spread of early Christianity, Buddhism, and Mohammedanism, is passing over our American world. The common feature of these optimistic faiths is that they all tend to the suppression of what Mr. Horace Fletcher calls "fearthought." Fearthought he defines as the "self-suggestion of inferiority"; so that one may say that these systems all operate by the suggestion of power. And the power, small or great, comes in various shapes to the individual—power, as he will tell you, not to "mind" things that used to vex him, power to concentrate his mind, good cheer, good temper—in short, to put it mildly, a firmer, more elastic moral tone.

The most genuinely saintly person I have ever known is a friend of mine now suffering from cancer of the breast—I hope that she may pardon my citing her here as an example of what ideas can do. Her ideas have kept her a practically well woman for months after she should have given up and gone to bed. They have annulled all pain and weakness and given her a cheerful active life, unusually beneficent to others to whom she has afforded help. Her doctors, acquiescing in results they could not understand, have had the good sense to let her go her own way.

How far the mind-cure movement is destined to extend its influence, or what intellectual modifications it may yet undergo, no one can foretell. It is essentially a religious movement, and to academically nurtured minds its utterances are tasteless and often grotesque enough. It also incurs the natural enmity of medical politicians, and of the whole trades-union wing of that profession. But no unprejudiced observer can fail to recognize its importance as a social phenomenon today, and the higher medical minds are already trying to interpret it fairly, and make its power available for their own therapeutic ends.

Dr. Thomas Hyslop, of the great West Riding Asylum in England, said last year to the British Medical Association that the best sleep-producing agent which his practice had revealed to him was *prayer*. I say this, he added (I am sorry here that I must quote from memory), purely as a medical man. The exercise of prayer, in those who habitually exert it, must be regarded by us doctors as the most adequate and normal of all the pacifiers of the mind and calmers of the nerves.

But in few of us are functions not tied up by the exercise of other functions. Relatively few medical men and scientific men, I fancy, can pray. Few can carry on any living commerce with "God." Yet many of us are well aware of how much freer and abler our lives would be were such important forms of energizing not sealed up by the critical atmosphere in which we have been reared. There are in every-one potential forms of activity that actually are shunted out from use. Part of the imperfect vitality under which we labor can thus be easily explained. One part of our mind dams up—even *damns* up!—the other parts.

Conscience makes cowards of us all. Social conventions prevent us from telling the truth after the fashion of the heroes and heroines of Bernard Shaw. We all know persons who are models of excellence, but who belong to the extreme philistine type of mind. So deadly is their intellectual respectability that we can't converse about certain subjects at all, can't let our minds play over them, can't even mention them in their presence. I have numbered among my dearest friends persons thus inhibited intellectually, with whom I would gladly have been able to talk freely about certain interests of mine, certain authors, say, as Bernard Shaw, Chesterton, Edward Carpenter, H. G. Wells, but it wouldn't do, it made them too uncomfortable, they wouldn't play, I had to be silent. An intellect thus tied down by literality and decorum makes on one the same sort of impression that an able-bodied man would who should habituate himself to do his work with only one of his fingers, locking up the rest of his organism and leaving it unused.

I trust that by this time I have said enough to convince the reader both of the truth and of the importance of my thesis. The two questions, first, that of the possible extent of our powers; and, second, that of the various avenues of approach to them, the various keys for unlocking them in diverse individuals, dominate the whole problem of individual and national education. We need a topography of the limits of human power, similar to the chart which oculists use of the field of human vision. We need also a study of the various types of human being with reference to the different ways in which their energy reserves may be appealed to and set loose. Biographies and individual experiences of every kind may be drawn upon for evidence here.

Great Men
and Their Environment

A remarkable parallel, which I think has never been noticed, obtains between the facts of social evolution on the one hand and of zoological evolution as expounded by Mr. Darwin on the other.

It will be best to prepare the ground for my thesis by a few very general remarks on the method of getting at scientific truth. It is a common platitude that a complete acquaintance with any one thing, however small, would require a knowledge of the entire universe. Not a sparrow falls to the ground but some of the remote conditions of his fall are to be found in the Milky Way, in our federal constitution, or in the early history of Europe. That is to say, alter the Milky Way, alter the federal Constitution, alter the facts of our barbarian ancestry, and the universe would so far be a different universe from what it now is. One fact involved in the difference might be that the particular little street boy who threw the stone which brought down the sparrow might not find himself opposite the sparrow at that particular moment; or, finding himself there, he might not be in that particular serene and disengaged mood of mind which expressed itself in throwing the stone. But, true as all this is, it would be very foolish for anyone who was inquiring the cause of the sparrow's fall to overlook the boy as too personal, proximate, and so to speak anthropomorphic an agent, and to say that the true cause is the federal Constitution, the westward migration of the Celtic race, or the structure of the Milky Way. If we proceeded on that method, we might say with perfect legitimacy that a friend of ours who had slipped on the ice upon his doorstep and cracked his skull some months after dining with thirteen at the table died because of that ominous feast. I know, in fact, one such instance; and I might, if I chose, contend with perfect logical propriety that the slip on the ice was no real accident. "There are no accidents," I might say, "for science. The whole history of the

171

world converged to produce that slip. If anything had been left out, the slip would not have occurred just there and then. To say it would is to deny the relations of cause and effect throughout the universe. The real cause of the death was not the slip, *but the conditions which engendered the slip*—and among them his having sat at a table, six months previous, one among thirteen. *That* is truly the reason why he died within the year."

It will soon be seen whose arguments I am, in form, reproducing here. I would fain lay down the truth without polemics or recrimination. But unfortunately we never fully grasp the import of any true statement until we have a clear notion of what the opposite untrue statement would be. The error is needed to set off the truth, much as a dark background is required for exhibiting the brightness of a picture. And the error which I am going to use as a foil to set off what seems to me the truth of my own statements is contained in the philosophy of Mr. Herbert Spencer and his disciples. Our problem is, What are the causes that make communities change from generation to generation—that make the England of Queen Anne so different from the England of Elizabeth, the Harvard College of today so different from that of thirty years ago?

I shall reply to this problem, The difference is due to the accumulated influences of individuals, of their examples, their initiatives, and their decisions. The Spencerian school replies, The changes are irrespective of persons, and independent of individual control. They are due to the environment, to the circumstances, the physical geography, the ancestral conditions, the increasing experience of outer relations; to everything, in fact, except the Grants and the Bismarcks, the Joneses and the Smiths.

Now, I say that these theorizers are guilty of precisely the same fallacy as he who should ascribe the death of his friend to the dinner with thirteen, or the fall of the sparrow to the Milky Way. Like the dog in the fable, who drops his real bone to snatch at its image, they drop the real causes to snatch at others, which from no possible human point of view are available or attainable. Their fallacy is a practical one. Let us see where it lies. Although I believe in free will myself, I will waive that belief in this discussion, and assume with the Spencerians the predestination of all human actions. On that assumption I gladly allow that were the intelligence investigating the man's or the sparrow's death omniscient and omnipresent, able to take in the whole of time and space at a single glance, there would not be the slightest objection to the Milky Way or the fatal feast being invoked among the sought-for causes. Such a divine intelligence would see instantaneously all the infinite lines of convergence towards a given result, and it would, moreover, see impartially: it would see the fatal feast to be as much a condition of the sparrow's death as of the man's; it would see the boy with the stone to be as much a condition of the man's fall as of the sparrow's.

The human mind, however, is constituted on an entirely different plan. It has no such power of universal intuition. Its finiteness obliges it to see but two or three things at a time. If it wishes to take wider sweeps it has to use "general ideas," as they are called, and in so doing to drop all concrete truths. Thus, in the present case, if we as men wish to feel the connection between the Milky Way and the boy and the dinner and the sparrow and the man's death, we can do so only by falling back on the enormous emptiness of what is called an abstract proposition. We must say, All things in the world are fatally predetermined, and hang together in the adamantine fixity of a system of natural law. But in the vagueness of this vast proposition we have lost all the concrete facts and links; and in all practical matters the concrete links are the only things of importance. The human mind is essentially partial. It can be efficient at all only by *picking out* what to attend to, and ignoring everything else— by narrowing its point of view. Otherwise, what little strength it has is dispersed, and it loses its way altogether. Man always wants his curiosity gratified for a particular purpose. If, in the case of the sparrow, the purpose is punishment, it would be idiotic to wander off from the cats, boys, and other possible agencies close by in the street to survey the early Celts and the Milky Way: the boy would meanwhile escape. And if, in the case of the unfortunate man, we lose ourselves in contemplation of the thirteen-at-table mystery, and fail to notice the ice on the step and cover it with ashes, some other poor fellow, who never dined out in his life, may slip on it in coming to the door, and fall and break his head too.

It is, then, a necessity laid upon us as human beings to limit our view. In mathematics we know how this method of ignoring and neglecting quantities lying outside of a certain range has been adopted in the differential calculus. The calculator throws out all the "infinitesimals" of the quantities he is considering. He treats them (under certain rules) as if they did not exist. In themselves they exist perfectly all the while; but they are as if they did not exist for the purposes of his calculation. Just so an astronomer, in dealing with the tidal movements of the ocean, takes no account of the waves made by the wind, or by the pressure of all the steamers which day and night are moving their thousands of tons upon its surface. Just so the marksman, in sighting his rifle, allows for the motion of the wind, but not for the equally real motion of the earth and solar system. Just so a businessman's punctuality may overlook an error of five minutes, while a physicist, measuring the velocity of light, must count each thousandth of a second.

There are, in short, *different cycles of operation* in nature; different departments, so to speak, relatively independent of one another, so that what goes on at any moment in one may be compatible with almost any condition of things at the same time in the next. The mold on the biscuit in the storeroom of a man-of-war vegetates in absolute indifference to the nationality of the flag, the direction of the voyage, the weather, and the human dramas that may go on on board; and a mycologist may study it in complete abstraction from all these larger details. Only by so studying it, in fact, is there any chance of the mental concentration by which alone he may hope to learn something of its nature. On the other hand, the captain who in maneuvering the vessel through a naval fight should think it necessary to bring the moldy biscuit into his calculations would very likely lose the battle by reason of the excessive "thoroughness" of his mind.

The causes which operate in these incommensurable cycles are connected with one another only *if we take the whole universe into account.* For all lesser points of view it is lawful—nay, more, it is for human wisdom necessary—to regard them as disconnected and irrelevant to one another.

And this brings us nearer to our special topic. If we look at an animal or a human being distinguished from the rest of his kind by the possession of some extraordinary peculiarity, good or bad, we shall be able to discriminate between the causes which originally *produced* the peculiarity in him and the causes that *maintain* it after it is produced; and we shall see, if the peculiarity be one that he was born with, that these two sets of causes belong to two such irrelevant cycles. It was the triumphant originality of Darwin to see this, and to act accordingly. Separating the causes of production under the title of "tendencies to spontaneous variation," and relegating them to a physiological cycle which he forthwith agreed to ignore altogether,[1] he confined his attention to the causes of preservation, and under the names of natural selection and sexual selec-

---

1. Darwin's theory of pangenesis is, it is true, an attempt to account (among other things) for variation. But it occupies its own separate place, and its author no more invokes the environment when he talks of the adhesions of gemmules than he invokes these adhesions when he talks of the relations of the whole animal to the environment. *Divide et impera* [Divide and conquer]!

tion studied them exclusively as functions of the cycle of the environment.

Pre-Darwinian philosophers had also tried to establish the doctrine of descent with modification; but they all committed the blunder of clumping the two cycles of causation into one. What preserves an animal with his peculiarity, if it be a useful one, they saw to be the nature of the environment to which the peculiarity was adjusted. The giraffe with his peculiar neck is preserved by the fact that there are in his environment tall trees whose leaves he can digest. But these philosophers went further, and said that the presence of the trees not only maintained an animal with a long neck to browse upon their branches but also produced him. They *made* his neck long by the constant striving they aroused in him to reach up to them. The environment, in short, was supposed by these writers to mold the animal by a kind of direct pressure, very much as a seal presses the wax into harmony with itself. Numerous instances were given of the way in which this goes on under our eyes. The exercise of the forge makes the right arm strong, the palm grows callous to the oar, the mountain air distends the chest, the chased fox grows cunning and the chased bird shy, the arctic cold stimulates the animal combustion, and so forth. Now these changes, of which many more examples might be adduced, are at present distinguished by the special name of *adaptive* changes. Their peculiarity is that that very feature in the environment to which the animal's nature grows adjusted itself produces the adjustment. The "inner relation," to use Mr. Spencer's phrase, "corresponds" with its own efficient cause.

Darwin's first achievement was to show the utter insignificance in amount of these changes produced by direct adaptation, the immensely greater mass of changes being produced by internal molecular accidents, of which we know nothing. His next achievement was to define the true problem with which we have to deal when we study the effects of the visible environment on the animal. That problem is simply this: Is the environment more likely to *preserve or to destroy him* on account of this or that peculiarity with which he may be born? In giving the name "of accidental variations" to those peculiarities with which an animal is born, Darwin does not for a moment mean to suggest that they are not the fixed outcome of natural law. If the total system of the universe be taken into account, the causes of these variations and the visible environment which preserves or destroys them undoubtedly do, in some remote and roundabout way, hang together. What Darwin means is that, since that environment is a perfectly known thing, and its relations to the organism in the way of destruction or preservation are tangible and distinct, it would utterly confuse our finite understandings and frustrate our hopes of science to mix in with it facts from such a disparate and incommensurable cycle as that in which the variations are produced. This last cycle is that of occurrences before the animal is born. It is the cycle of influences upon ova and embryos; in which lie the causes that tip them and tilt them towards masculinity or femininity, towards strength or weakness, towards health or disease, and towards divergence from the parent type. What are the causes there?

In the first place, they are molecular and invisible—inaccessible, therefore, to direct observation of any kind. Secondly, their operations are compatible with any social, political, and physical conditions of environment. The same parents, living in the same environing conditions, may at one birth produce a genius, at the next an idiot or a monster. The visible external conditions are therefore not direct determinants of this cycle; and the more we consider the matter, the more we are forced to believe that two children of the same parents are made to differ from each other by causes as disproportionate to their ultimate effects as is the famous pebble on the Rocky Mountain crest, which separates two raindrops, to the Gulf of St. Lawrence and the Pacific Ocean toward which it makes them severally flow.

The great mechanical distinction between transitive forces and discharging forces is nowhere illustrated on such a scale as in physiology. Almost all causes there are forces of *detent*, which operate by simply unlocking energy already stored up. They are upsetters of unstable equilibria, and the resultant effect depends infinitely more on the nature of the materials upset than on that of the particular stimulus which joggles them down. Galvanic work, equal to unity, done on a frog's nerve will discharge from the muscle to which the nerve belongs mechanical work equal to seventy thousand; and exactly the same muscular effect will emerge if other irritants than galvanism are employed. The irritant has merely started or provoked something which then went on of itself—as a match may start a fire which consumes a whole town. And qualitatively as well as quantitatively the effect may be absolutely incommensurable with the cause. We find this condition of things in all organic matter. Chemists are distracted by the difficulties which the instability of albuminoid compounds opposes to their study. Two specimens, treated in what outwardly seem scrupulously identical conditions, behave in quite different ways. You know about the invisible factors of fermentation, and how the fate of a jar of milk—whether it turn into a sour clot or a mass of kumiss—depends on whether the lactic acid ferment or the alcoholic is introduced first and gets ahead of the other in starting the process. Now, when the result is the tendency of an ovum, itself invisible to the naked eye, to tip towards this direction or that in its further evolution—to bring forth a genius or a dunce, even as the raindrop passes east or west of the pebble—is it not obvious that the deflecting cause must lie in a region so recondite and minute, must be such a ferment of a ferment, an infinitesimal of so high an order that surmise itself may never succeed even in attempting to frame an image of it?

Such being the case, was not Darwin right to turn his back upon that region altogether, and to keep his own problem carefully free from all entanglement with matters such as these? The success of his work is a sufficiently affirmative reply.

And this brings us at last to the heart of our subject. The causes of production of great men lie in a sphere wholly inaccessible to the social philosopher. He must simply accept geniuses as data, just as Darwin accepts his spontaneous variations. For him, as for Darwin, the only problem is, these data being given, how does the environment affect them, and how do they affect the environment? Now, I affirm that the relation of the visible environment to the great man is in the main exactly what it is to the "variation" in the Darwinian philosophy. It chiefly adopts or rejects, preserves or destroys, in short *selects* him.[2] And whenever it adopts and preserves the great man, it becomes modified by his influence in an entirely original and peculiar way. He acts as a ferment, and changes its constitution, just as the advent of a new zoological species changes the faunal and floral equilibrium of the region in which it appears. We all recollect Mr. Darwin's famous statement of the influence of cats on the growth of clover in their neighborhood. We all have read of the effects of the European rabbit in New Zealand, and we have many of us taken part in the controversy about the English sparrow here— whether he kills most cankerworms, or drives away most native birds. Just so the great man, whether he be an importation from without like Clive in India or Agassiz here, or whether he spring from the soil like Mohammed or Franklin, brings about a rearrangement, on a large or a small scale, of the pre-existing social relations.

2. It is true that it remodels him, also, to some degree, by its educative influence, and that this constitutes a considerable difference between the social case and the zoological case. I neglect this aspect of the relation here, for the other is the more important. At the end of the article I will return to it incidentally.

The mutations of societies, then, from generation to generation, are in the main due directly or indirectly to the acts or the example of individuals whose genius was so adapted to the receptivities of the moment or whose accidental position of authority was so critical that they became ferments, initiators of movement, setters of precedent or fashion, centers of corruption, or destroyers of other persons, whose gifts, had they had free play, would have led society in another direction.

We see this power of individual initiative exemplified on a small scale all about us, and on a large scale in the case of the leaders of history. It is only following the common-sense method of a Lyell, a Darwin, and a Whitney to interpret the unknown by the known, and reckon up cumulatively the only causes of social change we can directly observe. Societies of men are just like individuals in that both at any given moment offer ambiguous potentialities of development. Whether a young man enters business or the ministry may depend on a decision which has to be made before a certain day. He takes the place offered in the countinghouse, and is *committed*. Little by little, the habits, the knowledges, of the other career, which once lay so near, cease to be reckoned even among his possibilities. At first, he may sometimes doubt whether the self he murdered in that decisive hour might not have been the better of the two; but with the years such questions themselves expire, and the old alternative *ego*, once so vivid, fades into something less substantial than a dream. It is no otherwise with nations. They may be committed by kings and ministers to peace or war, by generals to victory or defeat, by prophets to this religion or to that, by various geniuses to fame in art, science, or industry. A war is a true point of bifurcation of future possibilities. Whether it fail or succeed, its declaration must be the starting point of new policies. Just so does a revolution, or any great civic precedent, become a deflecting influence, whose operations widen with the course of time. Communities obey their ideals; and an accidental success fixes an ideal, as an accidental failure blights it.

Would England have today the "imperial" ideal which she now has if a certain boy named Bob Clive had shot himself, as he tried to do, at Madras? Would she be the drifting raft she is now in European affairs if a Frederick the Great had inherited her throne instead of a Victoria, and if Messrs. Bentham, Mill, Cobden, and Bright had all been born in Prussia? England has, no doubt, today precisely the same intrinsic value relatively to the other nations that she ever had. There is no such fine accumulation of human material upon the globe. But in England the material has lost effective form, while in Germany it has found it. Leaders give the form. Would England be crying forward and backward at once, as she does now, "letting I will not wait upon I would," wishing to conquer but not to fight, if her ideal had in all these years been fixed by a succession of statesmen of supremely commanding personality, working in one direction? Certainly not. She would have espoused, for better or worse, either one course or another. Had Bismarck died in his cradle, the Germans would still be satisfied with appearing to themselves as a race of spectacled *Gelehrten* [scholars] and political herbivora, and to the French as *ces bons,* or *ces naifs, Allemands* [those good-hearted (or) those innocent Germans]. Bismarck's will showed them, to their own great astonishment, that they could play a far livelier game. The lesson will not be forgotten. Germany may have many vicissitudes, but they—

> will never do away, I ween,
> The marks of that which once hath been—

of Bismarck's initiative, namely, from 1860 to 1873.

The fermentative influence of geniuses must be admitted as, at any rate, one factor in the changes that constitute social evolution. The community *may* evolve in many ways. The accidental presence of this or that ferment decides in which way it *shall* evolve. Why, the very birds of the forest, the parrot, the myna, have the power of human speech, but never develop it of themselves; someone must be there to teach them. So with us individuals. Rembrandt must teach us to enjoy the struggle of light with darkness, Wagner to enjoy peculiar musical effects; Dickens gives a twist to our sentimentality, Artemus Ward to our humor; Emerson kindles a new moral light within us. But it is like Columbus' egg. "All can raise the flowers now, for all have got the seed." But if this be true of the individuals in the community, how can it be false of the community as a whole? If shown a certain way, a community may take it; if not, it will never find it. And the ways are to a large extent indeterminate in advance. A nation may obey either of many alternative impulses given by different men of genius and still live and be prosperous, just as a man may enter either of many businesses. Only, the prosperities may differ in their type.

But the indeterminism is not absolute. Not every "man" fits every "hour." Some incompatibilities there are. A given genius may come either too early or too late. Peter the Hermit would now be sent to a lunatic asylum. John Mill in the tenth century would have lived and died unknown. Cromwell and Napoleon need their revolutions, Grant his civil war. An Ajax gets no fame in the day of telescopic-sighted rifles; and, to express differently an instance which Spencer uses, what could a Watt have effected in a tribe which no precursive genius had taught to smelt iron or to turn a lathe?

Now, the important thing to notice is that what makes a certain genius now incompatible with his surroundings is usually the fact that some previous genius of a different strain has warped the community away from the sphere of his possible effectiveness. After Voltaire, no Peter the Hermit; after Charles IX and Louis XIV, no general protestantization of France; after a Manchester school, a Beaconsfield's success is transient; after a Philip II, a Castelar makes little headway; and so on. Each bifurcation cuts off certain sides of the field altogether, and limits the future possible angles of deflection. A community is a living thing, and in words which I can do no better than quote from Professor Clifford,[3] "It is the peculiarity of living things not merely that they change under the influence of surrounding circumstances, but that any change which takes place in them is not lost but retained, and as it were built into the organism to serve as the foundation for future actions. If you cause any distortion in the growth of a tree and make it crooked, whatever you may do afterwards to make the tree straight the mark of your distortion is there; it is absolutely indelible; it has become part of the tree's nature. . . . Suppose, however, that you take a lump of gold, melt it, and let it cool. . . . No one can tell by examining a piece of gold how often it has been melted and cooled in geologic ages, or even in the last year by the hand of man. Anyone who cuts down an oak can tell by the rings in its trunk how many times winter has frozen it into widowhood, and how many times summer has warmed it into life. A living being must always contain within itself the history, not merely of its own existence, but of all its ancestors."

Every painter can tell us how each added line deflects his picture in a certain sense. Whatever lines follow must be built on those first laid down. Every author who starts to rewrite a piece of work knows how impossible it becomes to use any of the first-written pages again. The new beginning has already excluded the possibility of those earlier phrases and transitions, while it has at the same time created the possibility of an indefinite set of new ones, no one of which, however, is completely determined in advance. Just so the social surroundings of the past and present hour exclude the possibility of accepting certain contributions from individuals; but they do not positively define what contributions

---

3. *Lectures and Essays,* i. 82.

shall be accepted, for in themselves they are powerless to fix what the nature of the individual offerings shall be.[4]

Thus social evolution is a resultant of the interaction of two wholly distinct factors—the individual, deriving his peculiar gifts from the play of physiological and infrasocial forces, but bearing all the power of initiative and origination in his hands; and, second, the social environment, with its power of adopting or rejecting both him and his gifts. Both factors are essential to change. The community stagnates without the impulse of the individual. The impulse dies away without the sympathy of the community.

All this seems nothing more than common sense. All who wish to see it developed by a man of genius should read that golden little work, Bagehot's *Physics and Politics*, in which (it seems to me) the complete sense of the way in which concrete things grow and change is as livingly present as the straining after a pseudo philosophy of evolution is livingly absent. But there are never wanting minds to whom such views seem personal and contracted, and allied to an anthropomorphism long exploded in other fields of knowledge. "The individual withers, and the world is more and more," to these writers; and in a Buckle, a Draper, and a Taine we all know how much the "world" has come to be almost synonymous with the *climate*. We all know, too, how the controversy has been kept up between the partisans of a "science of history" and those who deny the existence of anything like necessary "laws" where human societies are concerned. Mr. Spencer, at the opening of his Study of Sociology, makes an onslaught on the "great-man theory" of history, from which a few passages may be quoted:

> The genesis of societies by the action of great men may be comfortably believed so long as, resting in general notions, you do not ask for particulars. But now, if, dissatisfied with vagueness, we demand that our ideas shall be brought into focus and exactly defined, we discover the hypothesis to be utterly incoherent. If, not stopping at the explanation of social progress as due to the great man, we go back a step, and ask, Whence comes the great man? we find that the theory breaks down completely. The question has two conceivable answers: his origin is supernatural, or it is natural. Is his origin supernatural? Then he is a deputy god, and we have theocracy once removed—or, rather, not removed at all. . . . Is

---

4. Mr. Grant Allen himself, in an article from which I shall presently quote, admits that a set of people who, if they had been exposed ages ago to the geographical agencies of Timbuktu would have developed into Negroes might now, after a protracted exposure to the conditions of Hamburg, never become Negroes if transplanted to Timbuktu.

this an unacceptable solution? Then the origin of the great man is natural;
and immediately this is recognized, he must be classed with all other phenomena in the society that gave him birth as a product of its antecedents. Along with the whole generation of which he forms a minute part,
along with its institutions, language, knowledge, manners, and its multi-
tudinous arts and appliances, he is a *resultant*. . . . You must admit that
the genesis of the great man depends on the long series of complex influences which has produced the race in which he appears, and the social
state into which that race has slowly grown. . . . Before he can remake
his society, his society must make him. All those changes of which he is
the proximate initiator have their chief causes in the generations he descended from. If there is to be anything like a real explanation of those
changes, it must be sought in that aggregate of conditions out of which
both he and they have arisen.

Now, it seems to me that there is something which one might almost
call impudent in the attempt which Mr. Spencer makes, in the first
sentence of this extract, to pin the reproach of vagueness upon those who
believe in the power of initiative of the great man.

Suppose I say that the singular moderation which now distinguishes
social, political, and religious discussion in England, and contrasts so
strongly with the bigotry and dogmatism of sixty years ago, is largely due
to J. S. Mill's example. I may possibly be wrong about the facts; but I
am, at any rate, "asking for particulars," and not "resting in general notions." And if Mr. Spencer should tell me it started from no personal influence whatever, but from the "aggregate of conditions," the "generations," Mill and all his contemporaries "descended from," the whole past
order of nature in short, surely he, not I, would be the person "satisfied
with vagueness."

The fact is that Mr. Spencer's sociological method is identical with
that of one who would invoke the zodiac to account for the fall of the
sparrow, and the thirteen at table to explain the gentleman's death. It is
of little more scientific value than the oriental method of replying to
whatever question arises by the unimpeachable truism, "God is great."
Not to fall back on the gods, where a proximate principle may be
found, has with us Westerners long since become the sign of an efficient
as distinguished from an inefficient intellect.

To believe that the cause of everything is to be found in its antecedents
is the starting point, the initial postulate, not the goal and consummation,
of science. If she is simply to lead us out of the labyrinth by the same
hole we went in by three or four thousand years ago, it seems hardly
worthwhile to have followed her through the darkness at all. If anything

is humanly certain it is that the great man's society, properly so called, does *not* make him before he can remake it. Physiological forces, with which the social, political, geographical, and to a great extent anthropological conditions have just as much and just as little to do as the condition of the crater of Vesuvius has to do with the flickering of this gas by which I write, are what make him. Can it be that Mr. Spencer holds the convergence of sociological pressures to have so impinged on Stratford-upon-Avon about the 26th of April, 1564, that a W. Shakespeare, with all his mental peculiarities, had to be born there—as the pressure of water outside a certain boat will cause a stream of a certain form to ooze into a particular leak? And does he mean to say that if the aforesaid W. Shakespeare had died of cholera infantum, another mother at Stratford-upon-Avon would needs have engendered a duplicate copy of him to restore the sociologic equilibrium—just as the same stream of water will reappear, no matter how often you pass a sponge over the leak, so long as the outside level remains unchanged? Or might the substitute arise at "Stratford-atte-Bowe"? Here, as elsewhere, it is very hard, in the midst of Mr. Spencer's vagueness, to tell what he does mean at all.

We have, however, in his disciple, Mr. Grant Allen, one who leaves us in no doubt whatever of his precise meaning. This widely informed, suggestive, and brilliant writer published last year a couple of articles in the *Gentleman's Magazine,* in which he maintained that individuals have no initiative in determining social change.

> The differences between one nation and another, whether in intellect, commerce, art, morals, or general temperament, ultimately depend, not upon any mysterious properties of race, nationality, or any other unknown and unintelligible abstractions, but simply and solely upon the physical circumstances to which they are exposed. If it be a fact, as we know it to be, that the French nation differs recognizably from the Chinese, and the people of Hamburg differ recognizably from the people of Timbuktu, then the notorious and conspicuous differences between them are wholly due to the geographical position of the various races. If the people who went to Hamburg had gone to Timbuktu, they would now be indistinguishable from the semibarbarian Negroes who inhabit that central African metropolis; [5] and if the people who went to Timbuktu

---

5. No! not even though they were bodily brothers! The geographical factor utterly vanishes before the ancestral factor. The difference between Hamburg and Timbuktu as a cause of ultimate divergence of two races is as nothing to the difference of constitution of the ancestors of the two races, even though as in twin brothers, this difference might be invisible to the naked eye. No two couples of the most homogeneous race could possibly be found so identical as, if set in identical environments, to give rise to two identical lineages. The minute divergence at the start grows broader with each generation, and ends with entirely dissimilar breeds.

had gone to Hamburg, they would now have been white-skinned merchants driving a roaring trade in imitation sherry and indigestible port. . . . The differentiating agency must be sought in the great permanent geographical features of land and sea; . . . these have necessarily and inevitably molded the characters and histories of every nation upon the earth. . . . We cannot regard any nation as an active agent in differentiating itself. Only the surrounding circumstances can have any effect in such a direction. [These two sentences dogmatically deny the existence of the relatively independent physiological cycle of causation.] To suppose otherwise is to suppose that the mind of man is exempt from the universal law of causation. There is no caprice, no spontaneous impulse, in human endeavors. Even tastes and inclinations *must* themselves be the result of surrounding causes.

Elsewhere Mr. Allen, writing of the Greek culture, says:

It was absolutely and unreservedly the product of the geographical Hellas, acting upon the given factor of the undifferentiated Aryan brain. . . . To me it seems a self-evident proposition that nothing whatsoever can differentiate one body of men from another, except the physical conditions in which ·they are set—including, of course, under the term *physical conditions* the relations of place and time in which they stand with regard to other bodies of men. To suppose otherwise is to deny the primordial law of causation. To imagine that the mind can differentiate itself is to imagine that it can be differentiated without a cause.

This outcry about the law of universal causation being undone, the moment we refuse to invest in the kind of causation which is peddled round by a particular school, makes one impatient. These writers have no imagination of alternatives. With them there is no *tertium quid* between outward environment and miracle. *Aut Caesar, aut nullus* [Either Caesar or no one]! *Aut* Spencerism, *aut* catechism!

If by "physical conditions" Mr. Allen means what he does mean, the outward cycle of visible nature and man, his assertion is simply physiologically false. For a national mind differentiates "itself" whenever a genius is born in its midst by causes acting in the invisible and molecular cycle. But if Mr. Allen means by "physical conditions" the whole of nature, his assertion, though true, forms but the vague Asiatic profession of belief in an all-enveloping fate, which certainly need not plume itself on any specially advanced or scientific character.

And how can a thinker so clever as Mr. Allen fail to have distinguished in these matters between *necessary* conditions and *sufficient* conditions of a given result? The French say that to have an omelet we must break our eggs; that is, the breaking of eggs is a necessary condition of the omelet. But is it a sufficient condition? Does an omelet appear whenever three eggs are broken? So of the Greek mind. To get such versatile intelligence it may be that such commercial dealings with the world as the geographical Hellas afforded are a necessary condition. But if they are a sufficient condition, why did not the Phoenicians outstrip the Greeks in intelligence? No geographical environment can produce a given type of mind. It can only foster and further certain types fortuitously produced, and thwart and frustrate others. Once again, its function is simply selective, and determines what shall actually be only by destroying what is positively incompatible. An Arctic environment is incompatible with improvident habits in its denizens; but whether the inhabitants of such a region shall unite with their thrift the peacefulness of the Eskimo or the pugnacity of the Norseman is, so far as the climate is concerned, an accident. Evolutionists should not forget that we all have five fingers not because four or six would not do just as well, but merely because the first vertebrate above the fishes *happened* to have that number. He owed his prodigious success in founding a line of descent to some entirely other quality—we know not which—but the inessential five fingers were taken in tow and preserved to the present day. So of most social peculiarities. Which of them shall be taken in tow by the few qualities which the environment necessarily exacts is a matter of what physiological accidents shall happen among individuals. Mr. Allen promises to prove his thesis in detail by the examples of China, India, England, Rome, etc. I have not the smallest hesitation in predicting that he will do no more with these examples than he has done with Hellas. He will appear upon the scene after the fact, and show that the quality developed by each race was, naturally enough, not incompatible with its habitat. But he will utterly fail to show that the particular form of compatibility fallen into in each case was the one necessary and only possible form.

Naturalists know well enough how indeterminate the harmonies between a fauna and its environment are. An animal may better his chances of existence in either of many ways—growing aquatic, arboreal, or subterranean; small and swift, or massive and bulky; spiny, horny, slimy, or venomous; more timid or more pugnacious; more cunning or more fertile of offspring; more gregarious or more solitary; or in other ways besides—and any one of these ways may suit him to many widely different environments.

Readers of Mr. A. R. Wallace will well remember the striking illustrations of this in his *Malay Archipelago:*

Borneo closely resembles New Guinea not only in its vast size and its freedom from volcanoes, but in its variety of geological structure, its uniformity of climate, and the general aspect of the forest vegetation that clothes its surface; the Moluccas are the counterpart of the Philippines in their volcanic structure, their extreme fertility, their luxuriant forests, and their frequent earthquakes; and Bali, with the east end of Java, has a climate almost as dry and a soil almost as arid as that of Timor. Yet between these corresponding groups of islands, constructed, as it were, after the same pattern, subjected to the same climate, and bathed by the same oceans, there exists the greatest possible contrast when we compare their animal productions. Nowhere does the ancient doctrine that differences or similarities in the various forms of life that inhabit different countries are due to corresponding physical differences or similarities in the countries themselves meet with so direct and palpable a contradiction. Borneo and New Guinea, as alike physically as two distinct countries can be, are zoologically wide as the poles asunder; while Australia, with its dry winds, its open plains, its stony deserts, and its temperate climate, yet produces birds and quadrupeds which are closely related to those inhabiting the hot, damp, luxuriant forests which everywhere clothe the plains and mountains of New Guinea.

Here we have similar physical-geography environments harmonizing with widely differing animal lives, and similar animal lives harmonizing with widely differing geographical environments. A singularly accomplished writer, E. Gryzanovski, in the *North American Review*, uses the instances of Sardinia and Corsica in support of this thesis with great effect. He says:

These sister islands, lying in the very centre of the Mediterranean, at almost equal distances from the centres of Latin and Neo-Latin civilization, within easy reach of the Phoenician, the Greek, and the Saracen, with a coastline of more than a thousand miles, endowed with obvious and tempting advantages, and hiding untold sources of agricultural and mineral wealth, have nevertheless remained unknown, unheeded, and certainly uncared for during the thirty centuries of European history. . . . These islands have dialects, but no language; records of battles, but no history. They have customs, but no laws; the *vendetta*, but no justice. They have wants and wealth, but no commerce; timber and ports, but no shipping. They have legends, but no poetry; beauty, but no art; and twenty years ago it could still be said that they had universities, but no students. . . . That Sardinia, with all her emotional and picturesque barbarism, has never produced a single artist is almost as strange as her barbarism itself. . . . Near the focus of European civilization, in the very spot which an *à priori* geographer would point out as the most favorable

place for material and intellectual, commercial, and political development, these strange sister islands have slept their secular sleep, like *nodes*
on the sounding-board of history.

This writer then goes on to compare Sardinia and Sicily with some
detail. All the material advantages are in favor of Sardinia, "and the
Sardinian population, being of an ancestry more mixed than that of the
English race, would justify far higher expectations than that of Sicily."
Yet Sicily's past history has been brilliant in the extreme, and her commerce today is great. Dr. Gryzanovski has his own theory of the historic
torpor of these favored isles. He thinks they stagnated because they never
gained political autonomy, being always owned by some Continental
power. I will not dispute the theory; but I will ask, Why did they not
gain it? and answer immediately: Simply because no individuals were
born there with patriotism and ability enough to inflame their countrymen with national pride, ambition, and thirst for independent life.
Corsicans and Sardinians are probably as good stuff as any of their
neighbors. But the best woodpile will not blaze till a torch is applied, and
the appropriate torches seem to have been wanting.[6]

---

6. I am well aware that in much that follows (though in nothing that precedes) I
seem to be crossing the heavily shotted bows of Mr. Galton, for whose laborious
investigations into the heredity of genius I have the greatest respect. Mr. Galton
inclines to think that genius of intellect and passion is bound to express itself,
whatever the outward opportunity, and that within any given race an equal number of geniuses of each grade must needs be born in every equal period of time;
a subordinate race cannot possibly engender a large number of high-class geniuses,
etc. He would, I suspect, infer the suppositions I go on to make—of great men
fortuitously assembling around a given epoch and making it great, and of their
being fortuitously absent from certain places and times (from Sardinia, from
Boston now, etc.)—to be radically vicious. I hardly think, however, that he does
justice to the great complexity of the conditions of *effective* greatness, and to the
way in which the physiological averages of production may be masked entirely
during long periods, either by the accidental mortality of geniuses in infancy, or
by the fact that the particular geniuses born happened not to find tasks. I doubt
the truth of his assertion that *intellectual* genius, like murder, "will out." It is true
that certain types are irrepressible. Voltaire, Shelley, Carlyle can hardly be conceived leading a dumb and vegetative life in any epoch. But take Mr. Galton himself, take his cousin Mr. Darwin, and take Mr. Spencer: nothing is to me more
conceivable than that at another epoch all three of these men might have died
"with all their music in them," known only to their friends as persons of strong
and original character and judgment. What has started them on their career of
effective greatness is simply the accident of each stumbling upon a task vast,
brilliant, and congenial enough to call out the convergence of all his passions and
powers. I see no more reason why, in case they had not fallen in with their several
hobbies at propitious periods in their life, they need necessarily have hit upon
other hobbies, and made themselves equally great. Their case seems similar to that
of the Washingtons, Cromwells, and Grants, who simply rose to their occasions.
But apart from these causes of fallacy, I am strongly disposed to think that where
transcendent geniuses are concerned the numbers anyhow are so small that their

Sporadic great men come everywhere. But for a community to get vibrating through and through with intensely active life, many geniuses coming together and in rapid succession are required. This is why great epochs are so rare—why the sudden bloom of a Greece, an early Rome, a Renaissance is such a mystery. Blow must follow blow so fast that no cooling can occur in the intervals. Then the mass of the nation grows incandescent, and may continue to glow by pure inertia long after the originators of its internal movement have passed away. We often hear surprise expressed that in these high tides of human affairs not only the people should be filled with stronger life but that individual geniuses should seem so exceptionally abundant. This mystery is just about as deep as the time-honored conundrum as to why great rivers flow by great towns. It is true that great public fermentations awaken and adopt many geniuses who in more torpid times would have had no chance to work. But over and above this there must be an exceptional concourse of genius about a time to make the fermentation begin at all. The unlikeliness of the concourse is far greater than the unlikeliness of any particular genius; hence the rarity of these periods and the exceptional aspect which they always wear.

It is folly, then, to speak of the "laws of history" as of something inevitable, which science has only to discover, and whose consequences anyone can then foretell but do nothing to alter or avert. Why, the very laws of physics are conditional, and deal with *ifs*. The physicist does not say, "The water will boil anyhow;" he only says it will boil if a fire be kindled beneath it. And so the utmost the student of sociology can ever predict is that *if* a genius of a certain sort shows the way, society will be sure to follow. It might long ago have been predicted with great confidence that both Italy and Germany would reach a stable unity if someone could but succeed in starting the process. It could not have been predicted, however, that the *modus operandi* in each case would be subordination to a paramount state rather than federation, because no historian could have calculated the freaks of birth and fortune which gave at the same moment such positions of authority to three such peculiar individuals as Napoleon III, Bismarck, and Cavour. So of our own politics. It is certain now that the movement of the independents, reformers, or whatever one please to call them, will triumph. But whether it do so

---

appearance will not fit into any scheme of averages. That is, two or three might appear together, just as the two or three balls nearest the target center might be fired consecutively. Take longer epochs and more firing, and the great geniuses and near balls would on the whole be more spread out.

by converting the Republican party to its ends, or by rearing a new party on the ruins of both our present factions, the historian cannot say. There can be no doubt that the reform movement would make more progress in one year with an adequate personal leader than as now in ten without one. Were there a great citizen, splendid with every civic gift, to be its candidate, who can doubt that he would lead us to victory? But, at present, we, his environment, who sigh for him and would so gladly preserve and adopt him if he came, can neither move without him, nor yet do anything to bring him forth.[7]

To conclude: The evolutionary view of history, when it denies the vital importance of individual initiative, is, then, an utterly vague and unscientific conception, a lapse from modern scientific determinism into the most ancient oriental fatalism. The lesson of the analysis that we have made (even on the completely deterministic hypothesis with which we started) forms an appeal of the most stimulating sort to the energy of the individual. Even the dogged resistance of the reactionary conservative to changes which he cannot hope entirely to defeat is justified and shown to be effective. He retards the movement; deflects it a little by the concessions he extracts; gives it a resultant momentum, compounded of his inertia and his adversaries' speed; and keeps up, in short, a constant lateral pressure, which, to be sure, never heads it round about, but brings it up at last at a goal far to the right or left of that to which it would have drifted had he allowed it to drift alone.

I now pass to the last division of my subject, the function of the environment in *mental* evolution. After what I have already said, I may be quite concise. Here, if anywhere, it would seem at first sight as if that school must be right which makes the mind passively plastic, and the environment actively productive of the form and order of its conceptions; which, in a word, thinks that all mental progress must result from a series of adaptive changes, in the sense already defined of that word. We know what a vast part of our mental furniture consists of purely remembered, not reasoned, experience. The entire field of our habits and associations by contiguity belongs here. The entire field of those abstract conceptions which were taught us with the language into which we were born belongs here also. And, more than this, there is reason to think that the order of "outer relations" experienced by the individual may itself determine the order in which the general characters

---

7. Since this paper was written, President Cleveland has to a certain extent met the need. But who can doubt that if he had certain other qualities which he has not yet shown, his influence would have been still more decisive? (1896.)

imbedded therein shall be noticed and extracted by his mind.[8] The pleasures and benefits, moreover, which certain parts of the environment
yield, and the pains and hurts which other parts inflict, determine the
direction of our interest and our attention, and so decide at which points
the accumulation of mental experiences shall begin. It might, accordingly,
seem as if there were no room for any other agency than this; as if the
distinction we have found so useful between "spontaneous variation,"
as the producer of changed forms, and the environment, as their
preserver and destroyer, did not hold in the case of mental progress; as
if, in a word, the parallel with Darwinism might no longer obtain, and
Spencer might be quite right with his fundamental law of intelligence,
which says, "The cohesion between psychical states is proportionate to
the frequency with which the relation between the answering external
phenomena has been repeated in experience."

But, in spite of all these facts, I have no hesitation whatever in holding firm to the Darwinian distinction even here. I maintain that the facts
in question are all drawn from the lower strata of the mind, so to speak—
from the sphere of its least evolved functions, from the region of intelligence which man possesses in common with the brutes. And I can easily
show that throughout the whole extent of those mental departments
which are highest, which are most characteristically human, Spencer's
law is violated at every step; and that as a matter of fact the new conceptions, emotions, and active tendencies which evolve are originally
produced in the shape of random images, fancies, accidental outbirths of
spontaneous variation in the functional activity of the excessively instable
human brain, which the outer environment simply confirms or refutes,
adopts or rejects, preserves or destroys—selects, in short, just as it selects
morphological and social variations due to molecular accidents of an
analogous sort.

It is one of the tritest of truisms that human intelligences of a simple
order are very literal. They are slaves of habit, doing what they have been
taught without variation; dry, prosaic, and matter-of-fact in their remarks; devoid of humor, except of the coarse physical kind which re-
joices in a practical joke; taking the world for granted; and possessing in
their faithfulness and honesty the single gift by which they are sometimes able to warm us into admiration. But even this faithfulness seems
to have a sort of inorganic ring, and to remind us more of the im-

---

8. That is, if a certain general character be rapidly repeated in our outer experience
with a number of strongly contrasted concomitants, it will be sooner abstracted
than if its associates are invariable or monotonous.

mutable properties of a piece of inanimate matter than of the steadfastness of a human will capable of alternative choice. When we descend
to the brutes, all these peculiarities are intensified. No reader of
Schopenhauer can forget his frequent allusions to the *trockener ernst*
[dull earnestness] of dogs and horses, nor to their *ehrlichkeit* [honesty].
And every noticer of their ways must receive a deep impression of the
fatally literal character of the few, simple, and treadmill-like operations
of their minds.

But turn to the highest order of minds, and what a change! Instead
of thoughts of concrete things patiently following one another in a beaten
track of habitual suggestion, we have the most abrupt crosscuts and
transitions from one idea to another, the most rarefied abstractions and
discriminations, the most unheard-of combinations of elements, the
subtlest associations of analogy; in a word, we seem suddenly introduced
into a seething caldron of ideas, where everything is fizzling and bobbing
about in a state of bewildering activity, where partnerships can be
joined or loosened in an instant, treadmill routine is unknown, and the
unexpected seems the only law. According to the idiosyncrasy of the individual, the scintillations will have one character or another. They will
be sallies of wit and humor; they will be flashes of poetry and eloquence; they will be constructions of dramatic fiction or of mechanical
device, logical or philosophic abstractions, business projects, or scientific
hypotheses, with trains of experimental consequences based thereon;
they will be musical sounds, or images of plastic beauty or picturesque-
ness, or visions of moral harmony. But, whatever their differences may
be, they will all agree in this—that their genesis is sudden and, as it were,
spontaneous. That is to say, the same premises would not, in the mind
of another individual, have engendered just that conclusion; although,
when the conclusion is offered to the other individual, he may thoroughly
accept and enjoy it, and envy the brilliancy of him to whom it first occurred.

To Professor Jevons is due the great credit of having emphatically
pointed out how the genius of discovery depends altogether on the number of these random notions and guesses which visit the investigator's
mind. To be fertile in hypotheses is the first requisite, and to be willing
to throw them away the moment experience contradicts them is the next.
The Baconian method of collating tables of instances may be a useful aid
at certain times. But one might as well expect a chemist's notebook to
write down the name of the body analyzed, or a weather table to sum
itself up into a prediction of probabilities of its own accord, as to hope

that the mere fact of mental confrontation with a certain series of facts will be sufficient to make *any* brain conceive their law. The conceiving of the law is a spontaneous variation in the strictest sense of the term. It flashes out of one brain, and no other, because the instability of that brain is such as to tip and upset itself in just that particular direction. But the important thing to notice is that the good flashes and the bad flashes, the triumphant hypotheses and the absurd conceits, are on an exact equality in respect of their origin. Aristotle's absurd Physics and his immortal Logic flow from one source: the forces that produce the one produce the other. When walking along the street, thinking of the blue sky or the fine spring weather, I may either smile at some grotesque whim which occurs to me, or I may suddenly catch an intuition of the solution of a long-unsolved problem, which at that moment was far from my thoughts. Both notions are shaken out of the same reservoir—the reservoir of a brain in which the reproduction of images in the relations of their outward persistence or frequency has long ceased to be the dominant law. But to the thought, when it is once engendered, the consecration of agreement with outward relations may come. The conceit perishes in a moment, and is forgotten. The scientific hypothesis arouses in me a fever of desire for verification. I read, write, experiment, consult experts. Everything corroborates my notion, which being then published in a book spreads from review to review and from mouth to mouth, till at last there is no doubt I am enshrined in the Pantheon of the great diviners of nature's ways. The environment *preserves* the conception which it was unable to *produce* in any brain less idiosyncratic than my own.

Now, the spontaneous upsettings of brains this way and that at particular moments into particular ideas and combinations are matched by their equally spontaneous permanent tiltings or saggings towards determinate directions. The humorous bent is quite characteristic; the sentimental one equally so. And the personal tone of each mind, which makes it more alive to certain classes of experience than others, more attentive to certain impressions, more open to certain reasons, is equally the result of that invisible and unimaginable play of the forces of growth within the nervous system which, irresponsibly to the environment, makes the brain peculiarly apt to function in a certain way. Here again the selection goes on. The products of the mind with the determined aesthetic bent please or displease the community. We adopt Wordsworth, and grow unsentimental and serene. We are fascinated by Schopenhauer, and learn from him the true luxury of woe. The adopted bent becomes a ferment in the community, and alters its tone. The alteration may be a benefit or a misfortune, for it is (*pace* Mr. Allen) a differentiation from within, which has to run the gauntlet of the larger environment's selective power. Civilized Languedoc, taking the tone of its scholars, poets, princes, and theologians, fell a prey to its rude Catholic environment in the Albigensian crusade. France in 1792, taking the tone of its Saint-Justs and Marats, plunged into its long career of unstable outward relations. Prussia in 1806, taking the tone of its Humboldts and its Steins, proved itself in the most signal way "adjusted" to its environment in 1872.

Mr. Spencer, in one of the strangest chapters of his Psychology, tries to show the necessary order in which the development of conceptions in the human race occurs. No abstract conception can be developed, according to him, until the outward experiences have reached a certain degree of heterogeneity, definiteness, coherence, and so forth.

Thus the belief in an unchanging order, the belief in *law*, is a belief of which the primitive man is absolutely incapable. . . . Experiences such as he receives furnish but few data for the conception of uniformity, whether as displayed in things or in relations. . . . The daily impressions which the savage gets yield the notion very imperfectly, and in but few cases. Of all the objects around—trees, stones, hills, pieces of water, clouds, and so forth,—most differ widely, . . . and few approach complete likeness so nearly as to make discrimination difficult. Even between animals of the same species it rarely happens that, whether alive or dead, they are presented in just the same attitudes. . . . It is only along with a gradual development of the arts . . . that there come frequent experiences of perfectly straight lines admitting of complete apposition, bringing the perceptions of equality and inequality. Still more devoid is savage life of the experiences which generate the conception of the uniformity of succession. The sequences observed from hour to hour and day to day seem anything but uniform; difference is a far more conspicuous trait among them. . . . So that if we contemplate primitive human life as a whole, we see that multiformity of sequence, rather than uniformity, is the notion which it tends to generate. . . . Only as fast as the practice of the arts develops the idea of measure can the consciousness of uniformity become clear. . . . Those conditions furnished by advancing civilization which make possible the notion of uniformity simultaneously make possible the notion of *exactness*. . . . Hence the primitive man has little experience which cultivates the consciousness of what we call *truth*. How closely allied this is to the consciousness which the practice of the arts cultivates is implied even in language. We speak of a true surface as well as a true statement. Exactness describes perfection in a mechanical fit, as well as perfect agreement between the results of calculations.

The whole burden of Mr. Spencer's book is to show the fatal way in which the mind, supposed passive, is molded by its experiences of "outer relations." In this chapter the yardstick, the balance, the chronometer, and other machines and instruments come to figure among the "relations" external to the mind. Surely they are so after they have been manufactured, but only because of the preservative power of the social environment. Originally all these things and all other institutions were flashes of genius in an individual head, of which the outer environment showed no sign. Adopted by the race and become its heritage, they then supply instigations to new geniuses whom they environ to make new inventions and discoveries; and so the ball of progress rolls. But take out the geniuses, or alter their idiosyncrasies, and what increasing uniformities will the environment show? We defy Mr. Spencer or anyone else to reply.

The plain truth is that the "philosophy" of evolution (as distinguished from our special information about particular cases of change) is a metaphysical creed, and nothing else. It is a mood of contemplation, an emotional attitude, rather than a system of thought—a mood which is old as the world, and which no refutation of any one incarnation of it (such as the Spencerian philosophy) will dispel; the mood of fatalistic pantheism, with its intuition of the One and All, which was, and is, and ever shall be, and from whose womb each single thing proceeds. Far be it from us to speak slightingly here of so hoary and mighty a style of looking on the world as this. What we at present call scientific discoveries had nothing to do with bringing it to birth, nor can one easily conceive that they should ever give it its *quietus,* no matter how logically incompatible with its spirit the ultimate phenomenal distinctions which science accumulates should turn out to be. It can laugh at the phenomenal distinctions on which science is based, for it draws its vital breath from a region which— whether above or below—is at least altogether different from that in which science dwells. A critic, however, who cannot disprove the truth of the metaphysic creed, can at least raise his voice in protest against its disguising itself in "scientific" plumes. I think that all who have had the patience to follow me thus far will agree that the Spencerian "philosophy" of social and intellectual progress is an obsolete anachronism, reverting to a pre-darwinian type of thought, just as the Spencerian philosophy of "Force," effacing all the previous distinctions between actual and potential energy, momentum, work, force, mass, etc., which physicists have with so much agony achieved, carries us back to a pre-Galilean age.

Arthur Schopenhauer [1]

1788–1860

The controversy over education is almost as ancient as philosophy itself. It begins with Plato and Aristotle. Plato's most famous dialogue, *The Republic*,[2] is in large part an attempt to outline an ideal educational program. Book VIII of Aristotle's *Politics*[3] is a criticism of Plato's program and a presentation of Aristotle's own plan for education. From this beginning, the debate on education continues throughout the history of philosophy. It eventually involves (among many others) Montaigne, Descartes, Rousseau, Kant, Schopenhauer, and John Dewey.

Though the education controversy is centuries old, it has never before raged so fiercely as it has in the United States in the twentieth century. During this period, we have witnessed clashes between *progressivists* and *classicists*, between those who favor courses in social adjustment and those who think that all such courses should be eliminated, between those who think that children should learn "at their own pace" and those who want children to be "challenged," between those who favor indoctrination and those who think that children should be given complete intellectual freedom, and so on. A listing of all of the various grounds of dispute would require several pages.

Are Schopenhauer's views on education relevant to any of these controversies? Indeed they are, but partisans of either "traditional" or "modern" education will be disappointed to find that he cannot definitely be aligned on either side of the argument. When he says that "the branches of knowledge which are to be studied at any

---

[1] For a biography of Schopenhauer, see Vol. 5, pp. 120–122, in this set.
[2] See *Great Books of the Western World*, Vol. 7, pp. 295–441.
[3] See *Great Books of the Western World*, Vol. 9, pp. 542–548.

period of life should be such as the mind is equal to at that period and can perfectly understand," he might appear to be on the side of the modernist. But when he insists that "the memory should be specially taxed in youth," he approaches the traditionalist side.

Schopenhauer's main concern is that the method of education should be as *natural* as possible. In other words, the advance of education should be from the observation of particular facts to the formulation of general principles—not vice versa. If general principles are taught first, says Schopenhauer, they soon become *prejudices* which hinder the individual from seeing the world as it really is. When this occurs (and according to Schopenhauer, it usually does), the individual often must spend most of his adult life *unlearning* his childhood prejudices.

Schopenhauer is one of the most independent thinkers who ever lived. He is almost completely free of the illusions that we tend to associate with thought in the nineteenth century. Reading him today is like reading a contemporary. In fact, in parts of his essay *On Education*, Schopenhauer seems to be in advance of contemporary thinkers.

On Education

The human intellect is said to be so constituted that general ideas arise by abstraction from particular observations, and therefore come after them in point of time. If this is what actually occurs, as happens in the case of a man who has to depend solely upon his own experience for what he learns—who has no teacher and no book—such a man knows quite well which of his particular observations belong to and are represented by each of his general ideas. He has a perfect acquaintance with both sides of his experience, and accordingly he treats everything that comes in his way from a right standpoint. This might be called the natural method of education.

Contrarily, the artificial method is to hear what other people say, to learn and to read, and so to get your head crammed full of general ideas before you have any sort of extended acquaintance with the world as it is, and as you may see it for yourself. You will be told that the particular observations which go to make these general ideas will come to you later on in the course of experience; but until that time arrives you apply your general ideas wrongly, you judge men and things from a wrong standpoint, you see them in a wrong light, and treat them in a wrong way. So it is that education perverts the mind.

This explains why it so frequently happens that, after a long course of learning and reading, we enter upon the world in our youth, partly with an artless ignorance of things, partly with wrong notions about them; so that our demeanor savors at one moment of a nervous anxiety, at another of a mistaken confidence. The reason of this is simply that our head is full of general ideas which we are now trying to turn to some use, but which we hardly ever apply rightly. This is the result of acting in direct opposition to the natural development of the mind by obtaining general ideas first, and particular observations last: it is putting the cart before the horse. Instead of developing the child's own faculties of discernment, and teaching it to judge and think for itself, the teacher uses all his energies to stuff its head full of the ready-made thoughts of other people. The mistaken views of life, which spring from a false application of general ideas, have afterwards to be corrected by long years of experience; and it is seldom that they are wholly corrected. This is why so few men of learning are possessed of common sense, such as is often to be met with in people who have had no instruction at all.

To acquire a knowledge of the world might be defined as the aim of all education; and it follows from what I have said that special stress should be laid upon beginning to acquire this knowledge at the right end. As I have shown, this means, in the main, that the particular observation of a thing shall precede the general idea of it; further, that narrow and circumscribed ideas shall come before ideas of a wide range. It means, therefore, that the whole system of education shall follow in the steps that must have been taken by the ideas themselves in the course of their formation. But whenever any of these steps are skipped or left out the instruction is defective, and the ideas obtained are false; and finally a distorted view of the world arises, peculiar to the individual himself— a view such as almost everyone entertains for some time, and most men for as long as they live. No one can look into his own mind without seeing that it was only after reaching a very mature age, and in some cases when he least expected it, that he came to a right understanding or a clear view of many matters in his life that, after all, were not very difficult or complicated. Up till then they were points in his knowledge of the world which were still obscure, due to his having skipped some particular lesson in those early days of his education, whatever it may have been like—whether artificial and conventional, or of that natural kind which is based upon individual experience.

It follows that an attempt should be made to find out the strictly natural course of knowledge, so that education may proceed methodically by keeping to it; and that children may become acquainted with the ways of the world without getting wrong ideas into their heads, which very often cannot be got out again. If this plan were adopted, special care would have to be taken to prevent children from using words without clearly understanding their meaning and application. The fatal tendency to be satisfied with words instead of trying to understand things—to learn phrases by heart, so that they may prove a refuge in time of need —exists, as a rule, even in children; and the tendency lasts on into manhood, making the knowledge of many learned persons to consist in mere verbiage.

However, the main endeavor must always be to let particular observations precede general ideas, and not vice versa, as is usually and unfortunately the case; as though a child should come feet foremost into the world, or a verse be begun by writing down the rhyme! The ordinary method is to imprint ideas and opinions, in the strict sense of the world, prejudices, on the mind of the child before it has had any but a very few particular observations. It is thus that he afterwards comes to view the world and gather experience through the medium of those ready-made ideas, rather than to let his ideas be formed for him out of his own experience of life, as they ought to be.

A man sees a great many things when he looks at the world for himself, and he sees them from many sides; but this method of learning is not nearly so short or so quick as the method which employs abstract ideas and makes hasty generalizations about everything. Experience, therefore, will be a long time in correcting preconceived ideas, or perhaps never bring its task to an end; for, wherever a man finds that the aspect of things seems to contradict the general ideas he has formed, he will begin by rejecting the evidence it offers as partial and one sided; nay, he will shut his eyes to it altogether and deny that it stands in any contradiction at all with his preconceived notions, in order that he may thus preserve them uninjured. So it is that many a man carries about a burden of wrong notions all his life long—crotchets, whims, fancies, prejudices, which at last become fixed ideas. The fact is that he has never tried to form his fundamental ideas for himself out of his own experience of life, his own way of looking at the world, because he has taken over his ideas ready made from other people; and this it is that makes him— as it makes how many others!—so shallow and superficial.

Instead of that method of instruction care should be taken to educate children on the natural lines. No idea should ever be established in a child's mind otherwise than by what the child can see for itself, or at any rate it should be verified by the same means; and the result of this would be that the child's ideas, if few, would be well grounded and accurate. It would learn how to measure things by its own standard rather than by another's; and so it would escape a thousand strange fancies and prejudices, and not need to have them eradicated by the lessons it will subsequently be taught in the school of life. The child would, in this way, have its mind once for all habituated to clear views and thoroughgoing knowledge: it would use its own judgment and take an unbiased estimate of things.

And, in general, children should not form their notions of what life is like from the copy before they have learned it from the original, to whatever aspect of it their attention may be directed. Instead, therefore, of hastening to place books, and books alone, in their hands, let them be made acquainted, step by step, with things—with the actual circumstances of human life. And above all let care be taken to bring them to a clear and objective view of the world as it is, to educate them always to derive their ideas directly from real life, and to shape them in conformity with it—not to fetch them from other sources, such as books, fairy tales, or what people say, and then apply them ready made to real life. For this will mean that their heads are full of wrong notions, and that they will either see things in a false light or try in vain to remodel the world to suit their views, and so enter upon false paths; and that, too, whether they are only constructing theories of life or engaged in the actual business of it. It is incredible how much harm is done when the seeds of wrong notions are laid in the mind in those early years, later on to bear a crop of prejudice; for the subsequent lessons which are learned from real life in the world have to be devoted mainly to their extirpation. To unlearn the evil was the answer which, according to Diogenes Laërtius, Antisthenes gave when he was asked what branch of knowledge was most necessary; and we can see what he meant.

No child under the age of fifteen should receive instruction in subjects which may possibly be the vehicle of serious error, such as philosophy, religion, or any other branch of knowledge where it is necessary to take large views; because wrong notions imbibed early can seldom be rooted out, and of all the intellectual faculties judgment is the last to arrive at maturity. The child should give its attention either to subjects where no error is possible at all, such as mathematics, or to those in which there is no particular danger in making a mistake, such as languages, natural science, history, and so on. And in general, the branches of knowledge which are to be studied at any period of life should be such as the mind is equal to at that period and can perfectly understand. Childhood and youth form the time for collecting materials, for getting a special and thorough knowledge of individual and particular things. In those years it is too early to form views on a large scale; and ultimate explanations must be put off to a later date. The faculty of judgment, which cannot come into play without mature experience, should be left to itself; and care should be taken not to anticipate its action by inculcating prejudice, which will paralyze it forever.

On the other hand, the memory should be specially taxed in youth, since it is then that it is strongest and most tenacious. But in choosing

the things that should be committed to memory the utmost care and
forethought must be exercised, as lessons well learned in youth are never
forgotten. This precious soil must therefore be cultivated so as to bear as
much fruit as possible. If you think how deeply rooted in your memory
are those persons whom you knew in the first twelve years of your life,
how indelible the impression made upon you by the events of those
years, how clear your recollection of most of the things that happened
to you then, most of what was told or taught you, it will seem a natural
thing to take the susceptibility and tenacity of the mind at that period
as the groundwork of education. This may be done by a strict observance of method, and a systematic regulation of the impressions which
the mind is to receive.

But the years of youth allotted to man are short, and memory is, in
general, bound within narrow limits; still more so the memory of any one
individual. Since this is the case, it is all important to fill the memory
with what is essential and material in any branch of knowledge, to the
exclusion of everything else. The decision as to what is essential and material should rest with the masterminds in every department of thought;
their choice should be made after the most mature deliberation, and the
outcome of it fixed and determined. Such a choice would have to proceed
by shifting the things which it is necessary and important for a man to
know in general, and then necessary and important for him to know in
any particular business or calling. Knowledge of the first kind would have
to be classified, after an encyclopaedic fashion, in graduated courses,
adapted to the degree of general culture which a man may be expected
to have in the circumstances in which he is placed; beginning with a
course limited to the necessary requirements of primary education, and
extending upwards to the subjects treated of in all the branches of philosophical thought. The regulation of the second kind of knowledge
would be left to those who had shown genuine mastery in the several
departments into which it is divided; and the whole system would provide an elaborate rule or canon for intellectual education, which would,
of course, have to be revised every ten years. Some such arrangement
as this would employ the youthful power of the memory to best advantage, and supply excellent working material to the faculty of judgment,
when it made its appearance later on.

A man's knowledge may be said to be mature, in other words, to have
reached the most complete state of perfection to which he, as an individual, is capable of bringing it, when an exact correspondence is
established between the whole of his abstract ideas and the things he has

actually perceived for himself. This will mean that each of his abstract ideas rests, directly or indirectly, upon a basis of observation, which alone endows it with any real value; and also that he is able to place every observation he makes under the right abstract idea which belongs to it. Maturity is the work of experience alone; and therefore it requires time. The knowledge we derive from our own observation is usually distinct from that which we acquire through the medium of abstract ideas; the one coming to us in the natural way, the other by what people tell us, and the course of instruction we receive, whether it is good or bad. The result is that in youth there is generally very little agreement or correspondence between our abstract ideas, which are merely phrases fixed in the mind, and that real knowledge which we have obtained by our own observation. It is only later on that a gradual approach takes place between these two kinds of knowledge, accompanied by a mutual correction of error; and knowledge is not mature until this coalition is accomplished. This maturity or perfection of knowledge is something quite independent of another kind of perfection, which may be of a high or a low order—the perfection, I mean, to which a man may bring his own individual faculties; which is measured, not by any correspondence between the two kinds of knowledge, but by the degree of intensity which each kind attains.

For the practical man the most needful thing is to acquire an accurate and profound knowledge of the ways of the world. But this, though the most needful, is also the most wearisome of all studies, as a man may reach a great age without coming to the end of his task; whereas, in the domain of the sciences, he masters the more important facts when he is still young. In acquiring that knowledge of the world, it is while he is a novice, namely, in boyhood and in youth, that the first and hardest lessons are put before him; but it often happens that even in later years there is still a great deal to be learned.

The study is difficult enough in itself; but the difficulty is doubled by novels, which represent a state of things in life and the world such as, in fact, does not exist. Youth is credulous, and accepts these views of life, which then become part and parcel of the mind; so that, instead of a merely negative condition of ignorance, you have positive error—a whole tissue of false notions to start with; and at a later date these actually spoil the schooling of experience, and put a wrong construction on the lessons it teaches. If, before this, the youth had no light at all to guide him, he is now misled by a will-o'-the-wisp; still more often is this the case with a girl. They have both had a false view of things foisted onto them by reading novels; and expectations have been aroused which can never be fulfilled. This generally exercises a baneful influence on their whole life. In this respect those whose youth has allowed them no time or opportunity for reading novels—those who work with their hands and the like—are in a position of decided advantage. There are a few novels to which this reproach cannot be addressed—nay, which have an effect the contrary of bad. First and foremost, to give an example, *Gil Blas,* and the other works of Le Sage (or rather their Spanish originals); further, *The Vicar of Wakefield,* and, to some extent, Sir Walter Scott's novels. *Don Quixote* may be regarded as a satirical exhibition of the error to which I am referring.

The foregoing is from Schopenhauer's
STUDIES IN PESSIMISM.

Michael Faraday

1791–1867

$\mathbf{M}$ichael Faraday, one of the great men of science, was born in 1791 in a small village near London, England. His family was very poor, and it was necessary for him to begin working at an early age. When he was twelve, he became an errand boy for a bookseller and bookbinder. He made such an excellent impression upon his employer that a year later he was accepted as an apprentice bookbinder without fee.

Michael had little formal schooling, and the most important part of his early education was obtained from the books he came across in his work. He was particularly interested in works on chemistry and in the electrical treatises in *Encyclopædia Britannica*. When he was twenty, he attended a series of lectures on science by Sir Humphry Davy at the Royal Institution. He made careful notes of the lectures, bound them in a book, and sent them to Davy along with a request for employment at the Royal Institution. Davy at first attempted to discourage him from giving up the trade of bookbinding, but a few months later he offered Faraday the post of laboratory assistant. Faraday accepted, and from that time until his death he was closely associated with the Royal Institution.

As Davy's assistant, Faraday was engaged in many different types of scientific research, including studies of chlorine, glass, and the

Notes from the artist: "A design based on the equipment used in his experiments on the induction of currents forms the background for the portrait of Faraday. The pose was adapted from a portrait taken by C. L. Dodgson, better known as Lewis Carroll."

Michael
Faraday

liquefaction of gases. In 1821 he began work in the field in which he was to make his most important contributions: electromagnetism. The scientific world had been stirred the previous year by the researches of a Danish scientist, H. C. Oersted, which indicated a relationship between electricity and magnetism. Faraday was fascinated with the subject, but he was unable to turn his full attention to it for almost a decade. Then, through a series of experiments made in 1831, he discovered that an electric current could be induced in a coil of wire by the movement of a magnet in its vicinity. He also observed that the same effect could be achieved if the coil was moved while the magnet remained stationary. Later he discovered that an electric current in one wire caused induction in a neighboring wire. These fundamental discoveries led directly to the dynamo and the transformer, and they formed the basis of all subsequent developments in electricity.

Faraday continued his electrical research for many years, keeping a careful record of his observations. He published his findings under the general title *Experimental Researches in Electricity*.[1] The greatness of this work was quickly recognized, and it has long been considered a scientific classic. During his long life, Faraday received almost every important honor which could be bestowed upon a man of science. After a long period of ill health, he died in 1867.

At the time Faraday composed his lecture *Observations on Mental Education*, there was considerable clamor in England about "spiritualism." The air was filled with reports of seances, in which the dead communicated with the living. In a typical seance, a group of persons desiring to communicate with the dead sat around a heavy table in a dimly lit room. If the table moved, it indicated the presence of the dead. Many stories were told of tables rising several feet in the air or moving across a room unassisted.

Faraday was particularly interested in spiritualistic phenomena because many people had attempted to explain them in terms of electricity and magnetism. Always an open-minded man, he refused to pass judgment on such theories until he had personally observed a seance. His observations convinced him that the claims of the spiritualists were completely without substance. He was very dis-

---

[1] See *Great Books of the Western World*, Vol. 45.

turbed by what he learned about his fellow men through this experience. In a letter written to a friend at the time, he said, "What a weak, credulous, incredulous, unbelieving, superstitious, bold, frightened—what a ridiculous world ours is, as far as concerns the mind of men. How full of inconsistencies, contradictions, and absurdities it is!" He refers to his dealings with the table-movers several times in *Observations on Mental Education,* and the general theme of the lecture seems to have been directly inspired by them.

In his lecture Faraday argues that the greatest intellectual weakness of men is deficiency of judgment. By this he means primarily the tendency of men to draw sweeping conclusions from little or no evidence or to draw conclusions hastily without taking into account all the factors involved. Though he believes that the judgment can be partly trained through formal education, Faraday insists that it can be improved only if the individual is willing to make a strong personal effort. He describes in detail a series of steps by which the judgment can be self-educated.

Each of us is willing to admit that the judgments of others are often faulty, but we are inclined to assume that our own judgment is quite sound and dependable. Nevertheless, it is very unlikely that anyone can read *Observations on Mental Education* without discovering that he is guilty of one or more of the errors of judgment specified by Faraday. It is equally unlikely that the reader will fail to profit from Faraday's advice on how to improve his judgment.

The remarks at the beginning of this lecture are addressed to Prince Albert, who was present in the audience.

Observations
on Mental Education

I take courage, Sir, from your presence here this day, to speak boldly
that which is upon my mind. I feared that it might be unpleasant to some
of my audience, but as I know that your Royal Highness is a champion
for and desires the truth, I will believe that all here are united in the
same cause, and therefore will give utterance, without hesitation, to what
I have to say regarding the present condition of mental education.

If the term education may be understood in so large a sense as to
include all that belongs to the improvement of the mind, either by the
acquisition of the knowledge of others, or by increase of it through its
own exertions, then I may hope to be justified for bringing forward a few
desultory observations respecting the exercise of the mental powers in a
particular direction, which otherwise might seem out of place. The points
I have in view are general, but they are manifest in a striking manner,
among the physical matters which have occupied my life; and as the
latter afford a field for exercise in which cogitations and conclusions can
be subjected to the rigid tests of fact and experiment—as all classes
employ themselves more or less in the consideration of physical matters,
and may do so with great advantage, if inclined in the least degree to
profit by educational practices, so I hope that what I may say will find its
application in every condition of life.

Before entering upon the subject, I must take one distinction which,
however it may appear to others, is to me of the utmost importance. High
as man is placed above the creatures around him, there is a higher and
far more exalted position within his view; and the ways are infinite in
which he occupies his thoughts about the fears, or hopes, or expectations
of a future life. I believe that the truth of that future cannot be brought
to his knowledge by any exertion of his mental powers, however exalted

they may be; that it is made known to him by other teaching than his own, and is received through simple belief of the testimony given. Let no one suppose for a moment that the self-education I am about to commend in respect of the things of this life, extends to any considerations of the hope set before us, as if man by reasoning could find out God. It would be improper here to enter upon this subject further than to claim an absolute distinction between religious and ordinary belief. I shall be reproached with the weakness of refusing to apply those mental operations which I think good in respect of high things to the very highest. I am content to bear the reproach. Yet, even in earthly matters, I believe that the invisible things of Him from the creation of the world are clearly seen, being understood by the things that are made, even His eternal power and Godhead; and I have never seen anything incompatible between those things of man which can be known by the spirit of man which is within him, and those higher things concerning his future which he cannot know by that spirit.

Claiming, then, the use of the ordinary faculties of the mind in ordinary things, let me next endeavour to point out what appears to me to be a great deficiency in the exercise of the mental powers in every direction; three words will express this great want, deficiency of judgment. I do not wish to make any startling assertion, but I know that in physical matters multitudes are ready to draw conclusions who have little or no power of judgment in the cases; that the same is true of other departments of knowledge; and that, generally, mankind is willing to leave the faculties which relate to judgment almost entirely uneducated, and their decisions at the mercy of ignorance, prepossessions, the passions, or even accident.

Do not suppose, because I stand here and speak thus, making no exceptions, that I except myself. I have learned to know that I fall infinitely short of that efficacious exercise of the judgment which may be attained. There are exceptions to my general conclusion, numerous and high; but if we desire to know how far education is required, we do not consider the few who need it not, but the many who have it not; and in respect of judgment, the number of the latter is almost infinite. I am moreover persuaded, that the clear and powerful minds which have realized in some degree the intellectual preparation I am about to refer to, will admit its importance, and indeed its necessity; and that they will not except themselves, nor think that I have made my statement too extensive.

As I believe that a very large proportion of the errors we make in judgment is a simple and direct result of our perfectly unconscious state, and think that a demonstration of the liabilities we are subject to would aid greatly in providing a remedy, I will proceed first to a few illustrations of a physical nature. Nothing can better supply them than the intimations we derive from our senses; to them we trust directly; by them we become acquainted with external things, and gain the power of increasing and varying facts upon which we entirely depend. Our sense perceptions are wonderful. Even in the observant, but unreflective, infant they soon produce a result which looks like intuition because of its perfection. Coming to the mind as so many data, they are stored up and, without our being conscious of it, are ever after used in like circumstances in forming our judgment; and it is not wonderful that man is accustomed to trust them without examination. Nevertheless, the result is the effect of education: the mind has to be instructed with regard to the senses and their intimations through every step of life; and where the instruction is imperfect, it is astonishing how soon and how much their evidence fails us. Yet, in the latter years of life we do not consider this matter, but, having obtained the ordinary teaching sufficient for ordinary purposes, we venture to judge of things which are extraordinary for the time, and almost always with the more assurance as our powers of observation are less educated. Consider the following case of a physical impression, derived from the sense of touch, which can be examined and verified at pleasure: If the hands be brought towards each other so that the tips of the corresponding fingers touch, the end of any finger may be considered as an object to be felt by the opposed finger, thus the two middle fingers may for the present be so viewed. If the attention be directed to them, no difficulty will be experienced in moving each lightly in a circle round the tip of the other, so that they shall each feel the opposite, and the motion may be either in one direction or the other—looking at the fingers, or with eyes employed elsewhere—or with the remaining fingers touching quiescently, or moving in a like direction; all is easy, because each finger is employed in the ordinary or educated manner whilst obeying the will, and whilst communicating through the sentient organ with the brain. But turn the hands half way round, so that their backs shall be towards each other, and then, crossing them at the wrists, again bring the like fingers into contact at the tips. If it be now desired to move the extremities of the middle fingers round each other, or to follow the contour of one finger by the tip of the opposed one, all sorts of confusion in the motion will ensue; and as the finger of one hand tries, under the instruction of the will, to move in one course, the touched finger will convey an intimation that it is moving in another. If all the fingers move at once, all will be in confusion, the ease and simplicity of the first case having entirely disappeared. If, after some considerable trial, familiarity with the new circumstances have removed part of the uncertainty, then, crossing the hands at the opposite sides of the wrists will renew it. These contrary results are dependent not on any change in the nature of the sentient indication, or of the surfaces or substances which the sense has to deal with, but upon the trifling circumstance of a little variation from the direction in which the sentient organs of these parts are usually exerted, and they show to what an extraordinary extent our interpretations of the sense impressions depend upon the experience, *i.e.*, the education which they have previously received, and their great inability to aid us at once in circumstances which are entirely new.

At other times they fail us because we cannot keep a true remembrance of former impressions. Thus, on the evening of the eleventh of March last, I and many others were persuaded that at one period the moon had a real green colour, and though I knew that the prevailing red tints of the general sky were competent to produce an effect of such a kind, yet there was so little of that in the neighbourhood of the planet, that I was doubtful whether the green tint was not produced on the moon by some aërial medium spread before it, until, by holding up white cards in a proper position, and comparing them with our satellite, I had determined experimentally that the effect was only one of contrast. In the midst of the surrounding tints, my memory could not recall the true sentient impression which the white of the moon most surely had before made upon the eye.

At other times the failure is because one impression is overpowered by another; for as the morning star disappears when the sun is risen, though still above the horizon and shining brightly as ever, so do stronger phenomena obscure weaker, even when both are of the same kind; till an uninstructed person is apt to pass the weaker unobserved, and even deny their existence.

So, error results occasionally from believing our senses: it ought to be considered, rather, as an error of the judgment than of the sense, for the latter has performed its duty; the indication is always correct, and in harmony with the great truth of nature. Where, then, is the mistake? Almost entirely with our judgment. We have not had that sufficient instruction by the senses which would justify our making a conclusion; we have to contrive extra and special means, by which their first impressions shall be corrected, or rather enlarged; and it is because our procedure was hasty, our data too few, and our judgment untaught, that we fell into mistake; not because the data were wrong. How frequently may each one of us perceive, in our neighbours, at least, that a result like this derived from the observation of physical things, happens in the ordinary affairs of common life.

When I become convicted of such haste, which is not unfrequently the case, I look back upon the error as one of "presumptuous judgment." Under that form it is easily presentable to the mind, and has a useful corrective action. I do not think the expression too strong; for if we are led, either by simplicity or vanity, to give an opinion upon matters respecting which we are not instructed, either by the knowledge of others, or our own intimate observation; if we are induced to ascribe an effect to one force, or deny its relation to another, knowing little or nothing of the laws of the forces, or the necessary conditions of the effect to be considered; surely our judgment must be qualified as "presumptuous."

There are multitudes who think themselves competent to decide, after the most cursory observation, upon the cause of this or that event (and they may be really very acute and correct in things familiar to them)—a not unusual phrase with them is that "it stands to reason," that the effect they expect should result from the cause they assign to it, and yet it is very difficult, in numerous cases that appear plain, to show this reason, or to deduce the true and only rational relation of cause and effect. In matters connected with natural philosophy, we have wonderful aid in the progress and assurance in the character, of our final judgment, afforded us by the facts which supply our data, and the experience which multiplies their number and varies their testimony. A fundamental fact, like an elementary principle, never fails us, its evidence is always true; but, on the other hand, we frequently have to ask, "What is the fact?"—often fail in distinguishing it, often fail in the very statement of it, and mostly overpass or come short of its true recognition.

If we are subject to mistake in the interpretation of our mere sense impressions, we are much more liable to error when we proceed to deduce from these impressions (as supplied to us by our ordinary experience), the relation of cause and effect; and the accuracy of our judgment, consequently, is more endangered. Then our dependence should be upon carefully observed facts and the laws of nature; and I shall proceed to a further illustration of the mental deficiency I speak of, by a brief reference to one of these.

The laws of nature, as we understand them, are the foundation of our knowledge in natural things. So much as we know of them has been developed by the successive energies of the highest intellects, exerted through many ages. After a most rigid and scrutinizing examination upon principle and trial, a definite expression has been given to them; they have become, as it were, our belief or trust. From day to day we still examine and test our expressions of them. We have no interest in their retention if erroneous; on the contrary, the greatest discovery a man could make would be to prove that one of these accepted laws was erroneous, and his greatest honour would be the discovery. Neither would there be any desire to retain the former expression—for we know that the new or the amended law would be far more productive in results, would greatly increase our intellectual acquisitions, and would prove an abundant source of fresh delight to the mind.

These laws are numerous, and are more or less comprehensive. They are also precise; for a law may present an apparent exception, and yet not be less a law to us, when the exception is included in the expression. Thus, that elevation of temperature expands all bodies is a well-defined law, though there be an exception in water for a limited temperature; because we are careful, whilst stating the law, to state the exception and its limits. Pre-eminent among these laws, because of its simplicity, its universality, and its undeviating truth, stands that enunciated by Newton (commonly called the law of gravitation), that matter attracts matter with a force inversely as the square of the distance. Newton showed that, by this law, the general condition of things on the surface of the earth is governed; and the globe itself, with all upon it, kept together as a whole. He demonstrated that the motions of the planets round the sun, and of the satellites about the planets, were subject to it. During and since his time, certain variations in the movements of the planets, which were called irregularities, and might, for aught that was then known, be due to some cause other than the attraction of gravitation, were found to be its necessary consequences. By the close and scrutinizing attention of minds the most persevering and careful, it was ascertained that even the distant stars were subject to this law; and, at last, to place as it were the seal of assurance to its never-failing truth, it became, in the minds of Leverrier and Addams (1845), the foreteller and the discoverer of an orb rolling in the depths of space, so large as to equal nearly sixty earths, yet so far away as to be invisible to the unassisted eye. What truth, beneath that of revelation, can have an assurance stronger than this!

Yet this law is often cast aside as of no value or authority, because of the unconscious ignorance amidst which we dwell. You hear at the present day, that some persons can place their fingers on a table, and then elevating their hands, the table will rise up and follow them; that the piece of furniture, though heavy, will ascend, and that their hands bear no weight, or are not drawn down to the wood; you do not hear of this as a conjuring manoeuvre, to be shown for your amusement, but are expected seriously to believe it; and are told that it is an important fact, a great discovery amongst the truths of nature. Your neighbour, a well-meaning, conscientious person, believes it; and the assertion finds acceptance in every rank of society, and amongst classes which are esteemed to be educated. Now, what can this imply but that society, speaking generally, is not only ignorant as respects education of the judgment, but is also ignorant of its ignorance. The parties who are thus persuaded, and those who are inclined to think and to hope that they are right, throw up Newton's law at once, and that in a case which of all others is fitted to be tested by it; or if the law be erroneous, to test the law. I will not say they oppose the law, though I have heard the supposed fact quoted triumphantly against it; but as far as my observation has gone, they will not apply it. The law affords the simplest means of testing the fact, and if there be, indeed, anything in the latter new to our knowledge (and who shall say that new matter is not presented to us daily, passing away unrecognized), it also affords the means of placing that before us separately in its simplicity and truth. Then why not consent to apply the knowledge we have to that which is under development? Shall we educate ourselves in what is known, and then casting away all we have acquired, turn to our ignorance for aid to guide us among the unknown? If so, instruct a man to write, but employ one who is unacquainted with letters to read that which is written; the end will be just as unsatisfactory, though not so injurious, for the book of nature, which we have to read, is written by the finger of God. Why should not one who can thus lift a table, proceed to verify and simplify his fact, and bring it into relation with the law of Newton? Why should he not take the top of his table (it may be a small one), and placing it in a balance, or on a lever, proceed to ascertain how much weight he can raise by the draught of his fingers upwards; and of this weight, so ascertained, how much is unrepresented by any pull upon the fingers downward? He will then be able to investigate the further question, whether electricity, or any new force of matter, is made manifest in his operations; or whether action and reaction being unequal, he has at his command the source of a perpetual motion. Such a man, furnished with a nicely constructed carriage on a railway, ought to travel by the mere draught of his own fingers. A far less prize than this would gain him the attention of the whole scientific and commercial world; and he may rest assured, that if he can make the most delicate balance incline or decline by attraction, though it be only with the force of an ounce, or even a grain, he will not fail to gain universal respect and most honourable reward.

When we think of the laws of nature (which by continued observation have become known to us), as the proper tests to which any new fact or our theoretical representation of it should, in the first place, be subjected, let us contemplate their assured and large character. Let us go out into the field and look at the heavens with their solar, starry, and planetary glories; the sky with its clouds; the waters descending from above or wandering at our feet; the animals, the trees, the plants; and consider the permanency of their actions and conditions under the government of these laws. The most delicate flower, the tenderest insect, continues in its species through countless years; always varying, yet ever the same. When we think we have discovered a departure, as in the *Aphides*, *Medusae*, *Distomae*, etc.,[1] the law concerned is itself the best means of instituting an investigation, and hitherto we have always found the witness to return to its original testimony. These frail things are never ceasing, never changing, evidence of the law's immutability. It would be well for a man who has an anomalous case before him to contemplate a blade of grass, and when he has considered the numerous ceaseless, yet certain, actions there located, and his inability to change the character of the least among them, to recur to his new subject; and, in place of accepting unwatched and unchecked results, to search for a like certainty and recurrence in the appearances and actions which belong to it.

Perhaps it may be said, the delusion of table-moving is past, and need not be recalled before an audience like the present [2]—even granting this, let us endeavour to make the subject leave one useful result; let it serve for an example, not to pass into forgetfulness. It is so recent, and was received by the public in a manner so strange, as to justify a reference to it, in proof of the uneducated condition of the general mind. I do not object

---

1. See Claparède's *Account of Alternating Generation and the Metamorphoses of Inferior Animals.*
2. As an illustration of the present state of the subject, I will quote one letter from among many like it which I have received—M. F.

"April 5, 1854.

Sir,   I am one of the clergymen of this parish, and have had the subject of table-turning brought under my notice by some of my younger parishioners; I gave your solution of it as a sufficient answer to the mystery. The reply was made, that you had since seen reason to alter your opinion. Would you have the politeness to inform me if you have done so? With many apologies for troubling you,
I am, your obedient servant,
———."

to table-moving, for *itself;* for being once stated it becomes a fit, though a very unpromising subject for experiment; but I am opposed to the unwillingness of its advocates to investigate; their boldness to assert; the credulity of the lookers-on; their desire that the reserved and cautious objector should be in error; and I wish, by calling attention to these things, to make the general want of mental discipline and education manifest.

Having endeavoured to point out this great deficiency in the exercise of the intellect, I will offer a few remarks upon the means of subjecting it to the improving processes of instruction. Perhaps many who watch over the interests of the community, and are anxious for its welfare, will conclude that the development of the judgment cannot properly be included in the general idea of education; that as the education proposed must, to a very large degree, be of *self,* it is so far incommunicable; that the master and the scholar merge into one, and both disappear; that the instructor is no wiser than the one to be instructed, and thus the usual relations of the two lose their power. Still, I believe that the judgment may be educated to a very large extent, and might refer to the fine arts, as giving proof in the affirmative; and though, as respects the community and its improvement in relation to common things, any useful education must be of *self,* I think that society, as a body, may act powerfully in the cause. Or it may still be objected that my experience is imperfect, is chiefly derived from exercise of the mind within the precincts of natural philosophy, and has not that generality of application which can make it of any value to society at large. I can only repeat my conviction, that society occupies itself now-a-days about physical matters, and judges them as common things. Failing in relation to them, it is equally liable to carry such failures into other matters of life. The proof of deficient judgment in one department shows the habit of mind, and the general want, in relation to others. I am persuaded that all persons may find in natural things an admirable school for self-instruction, and a field for the necessary mental exercise; that they may easily apply their habits of thought, thus formed, to a social use; and that they ought to do this, as a duty to themselves and their generation.

Let me first try to illustrate the former part of the case, and at the same time state what I think a man may and ought to do for himself.

The *self-education* to which he should be stimulated by the desire to improve his judgment, requires no blind dependence upon the dogmas of others, but is commended to him by the suggestions and dictates of his own common sense. The first part of it is founded in mental discipline: happily it requires no unpleasant avowals; appearances are preserved, and vanity remains unhurt; but it is necessary that a man examine himself, and that not carelessly. On the contrary, as he advances, he should become more and more strict, till he ultimately prove a sharper critic to himself than any one else can be; and he ought to intend this, for, so far as he consciously falls short of it, he acknowledges that others may have reason on their side when they criticize him. A first result of this habit of mind will be an internal conviction of ignorance in many things respecting which his neighbours are taught, and, that his opinions and conclusions on such matters ought to be advanced with reservation. A mind so disciplined will be open to correction upon good grounds in all things, even in those it is best acquainted with; and should familiarize itself with the idea of such being the case: for though it sees no reason to suppose itself in error, yet the possibility exists. The mind is not enfeebled by this internal admission, but strengthened; for, if it cannot distinguish proportionately between the probable right and wrong of things known imperfectly, it will tend either to be rash or to hesitate; whilst that which admits the due amount of probability is likely to be justified in the end. It is right that we should stand by and act on our principles; but not right to hold them in obstinate blindness, or retain them when proved to be erroneous. I remember the time when I believed a spark was produced between voltaic metals as they approached to contact (and the reasons why it might be possible yet remain); but others doubted the fact and denied the proofs, and on re-examination I found reason to admit their corrections were well founded. Years ago I believed that electrolytes could conduct electricity by a conduction proper; that has also been denied by many through long time: though I believed myself right, yet circumstances have induced me to pay that respect to criticism as to reinvestigate the subject, and I have the pleasure of thinking that nature confirms my original conclusions. So though evidence may appear to preponderate extremely in favour of a certain decision, it is wise and proper to hear a counter-statement. You can have no idea how often and how much, under such an impression, I have desired that the marvellous descriptions which have reached me might prove, in some points, correct; and how frequently I have submitted myself to hot fires, to friction with magnets, to the passes of hands, etc., lest I should be shutting out discovery—encouraging the strong desire that something might be true, and that I might aid in the development of a new force of nature.

Among those points of self-education which take up the form of mental discipline, there is one of great importance, and, moreover, difficult to deal with, because it involves an internal conflict, and equally touches our vanity and our ease. It consists in the tendency to deceive ourselves regarding all we wish for, and the necessity of resistance to these desires. It is impossible for any one who has not been constrained, by the course of his occupation and thoughts, to a habit of continual self-correction to be aware of the amount of error in relation to judgment arising from this tendency. The force of the temptation which urges us to seek for such evidence and appearances as are in favour of our desires, and to disregard those which oppose them, is wonderfully great. In this respect we are all, more or less, active promoters of error. In place of practising wholesome self-abnegation, we ever make the wish the father to the thought: we receive as friendly that which agrees with, we resist with dislike that which opposes us; whereas the very reverse is required by every dictate of common sense. Let me illustrate my meaning by a case where the proof being easy, the rejection of it under the temptation is the more striking. In old times a ring or a button would be tied by a boy to one end of a long piece of thread, which he would then hold at the other end, letting the button hang within a glass, or over a piece of slate-pencil, or sealing-wax, or a nail; he would wait and observe whether the button swung, and whether in swinging it tapped the glass as many times as the clock struck last, or moved along or across the slate-pencil, or in a circle or oval. In late times parties in all ranks of life have renewed and repeated the boy's experiment. They have sought to ascertain a very simple fact—namely, whether the effect was as reported; but how many were unable to do this? They were sure they could keep their hands immovable —were sure they could do so whilst watching the result—were sure that accordance of swing with an expected direction was not the result of their desires or involuntary motions. How easily all these points could be put to the proof by not looking at the objects, yet how difficult for the experimenter to deny himself that privilege. I have rarely found one who would freely permit the substance experimented with to be screened from his sight, and then its position changed.

When engaged in the investigation of table-turning, I constructed a very simple apparatus, serving as an index, to show the unconscious motions of the hands upon the table. The results were either that the index moved before the table, or that neither index nor table moved; and in numerous cases all moving power was annihilated. A universal objection was made to it by the table-turners. It was said to paralyze the powers of the mind—but the experimenters need not see the index; they may leave their friends to watch that, and their minds may revel in any power that their expectation or their imagination can confer. So restrained, a *dislike* to the trial arises; but what is that except a proof that whilst they trust themselves they doubt themselves, and are not willing to proceed to the decision, lest the trust which they like should fail them, and the doubt which they dislike rise to the authority of truth.

Again, in respect of the action of magnets on the body, it is almost impossible for an uninstructed person to enter profitably upon such an inquiry. He may observe *any* symptom which his expectation has been accidentally directed to—yet be unconscious of any, if unaware of his subjection to the magnetic force or of the conditions and manner of its application.

As a proof of the extent of this influence, even on the minds of those well aware of its force, and desirous under every circumstance to escape from it, I will mention the practice of the chemist, who, dealing with the balance, that impartial decider which never fails in its indication but offers its evidence with all simplicity, durability, and truth, still remembers he should doubt himself; and, with the desire of rendering himself inaccessible to temptation, takes a counterpoised but unknown quantity of the substance for analysis, that he may remain ignorant of the proportions which he ought to obtain, and only at last compares the sum of his products with his counterpoise.

The inclination we exhibit in respect of any report or opinion that harmonizes with our preconceived notions, can only be compared in degree with the incredulity we entertain towards everything that opposes them; and these opposite and apparently incompatible, or at least inconsistent, conditions are accepted simultaneously in the most extraordinary manner. At one moment a departure from the laws of nature is admitted without the pretence of a careful examination of the proof; and at the next, the whole force of these laws, acting undeviatingly through all time, is denied, because the testimony they give is disliked.

It is my firm persuasion that no man can examine himself in the most common things, having any reference to him personally, or to any person, thought, or matter related to him, without being soon made aware of the temptation and the difficulty of opposing it. I could give you many illustrations personal to myself, about atmospheric magnetism, lines of force, attraction, repulsion, unity of power, nature of matter, etc.; or in things more general to our common nature, about likes and dislikes, wishes, hopes, and fears; but it would be unsuitable and also unnecessary, for each must be conscious of a large field sadly uncultivated in this respect. *I will simply express my strong belief that that point of self-education which consists in teaching the mind to resist its desires and inclinations, until they are proved to be right, is the most important of all, not only in things of natural philosophy, but in every department of daily life.*

There are numerous precepts resulting more or less from the principles of mental discipline already insisted on as essential, which are very useful in forming a judgment about matters of fact, whether among natural things or between man and man. Such a precept, and one that should recur to the mind early in every new case, is to know the conditions of the matter, respecting which we are called upon to make a judgment. To suppose that any would judge before they professed to know the conditions would seem to be absurd; on the other hand, to assume that the community does wait to know the conditions before it judges is an assumption so large that I cannot accept it. Very few search out the conditions; most are anxious to sink those which oppose their preconceptions; yet none can be left out if a right judgment is to be formed. It is true that many conditions must ever remain unknown to us even in regard to the simplest things in nature: thus as to the wonderful action of gravity, whose law never fails us, we cannot say whether the bodies are acting truly at a distance, or by a physical line of force as a connecting link between them. The great majority think the former is the case; Newton's judgment is for the latter. But of the conditions which are within our reach we should search out all; for in relation to those which remain unknown or unsuspected, we are in that very ignorance (regarding judgment) which it is our present object, first to make manifest, and then to remove.

One exercise of the mind, which largely influences the power and character of the judgment, is the habit of forming clear and precise ideas. If, after considering a subject in our ordinary manner, we return upon it with the special purpose of noticing the condition of our thoughts, we shall be astonished to find how little precise they remain. On recalling the phenomena relating to a matter of fact, the circumstances modifying them, the kind and amount of action presented, the real or probable result, we shall find that the first impressions are scarcely fit for the foundation of a judgment, and that the second thoughts will be best. For the acquirement of a good condition of mind in this respect, the thoughts should be trained to a habit of clear and precise formation, so that vivid and distinct impressions of the matter in hand, its circumstances and consequences, may remain.

Before we proceed to consider any question involving physical principles, we should set out with clear ideas of the naturally possible and impossible. There are many subjects uniting more or less of the most sure

and valuable investigations of science with the most imaginary and unprofitable speculation, that are continually passing through their various
phases of intellectual, experimental, or commercial development: some
to be established, some to disappear, and some to recur again and again,
like ill weeds that cannot be extirpated, yet can be cultivated to no result
as wholesome food for the mind. Such, for instance, in different degrees,
are the caloric engine, the electric light, the Pasilalinic sympathetic compass, mesmerism, homeopathy, odylism, the magneto-electric engine,
the perpetual motion, etc.: all hear and talk of these things; all use their
judgment more or less upon them, and all might do that effectively if
they were to instruct themselves to the extent which is within their reach.
I am persuaded that natural things offer an admirable school for self-
instruction, a most varied field for the necessary mental practice, and
that those who exercise themselves therein may easily apply the habits of
thought thus formed to a social use. As a first step in such practice, clear
ideas should be obtained of what is possible and what is impossible. Thus,
it is impossible to *create* force. We may employ it; we may evoke it in one
form by its consumption in another; we may hide it for a period; but we
can neither create nor destroy it. We may cast it away; but where we dismiss it, there it will do its work. If, therefore, we desire to consider a
proposition respecting the employment or evolution of power, let us carry
our judgment, educated on this point, with us. If the proposal include the
double use of a force with only one excitement, it implies a creation of
power, and that cannot be. If we could by the fingers draw a heavy piece
of wood or stone upward without effort, and then, letting it sink, could
produce by its gravity an effort equal to its weight, that would be a creation of power, and cannot be.

So again we cannot annihilate matter, nor can we create it. But if we
are satisfied to rest upon that dogma, what are we to think of table-
lifting? If we could make the table to cease from acting by gravity upon
the earth beneath it, or by reaction upon the hand supposed to draw it
upwards, we should annihilate it, in respect of that very property which
characterizes it as matter.

Considerations of this nature are very important aids to the judgment;
and when a statement is made claiming our assent, we should endeavour
to reduce it to some consequence which can be immediately compared
with, and tried by, these or like compact and never failing truths. If incompatibility appears, then we have reason to suspend our conclusion,
however attractive to the imagination the proposition may be, and pursue
the inquiry further, until accordance is obtained; it must be a most un-

educated and presumptuous mind that can at once consent to cast off the tried truth and accept in its place the mere loud assertion. We should endeavour to separate the points before us, and concentrate each, so as to evolve a clear type idea of the ruling fact and its consequences; looking at the matter on every side, with the great purpose of distinguishing the constituent reality, and recognizing it under every variety of aspect.

In like manner we should accustom ourselves to clear and definite language, especially in physical matters, giving to a word its true and full, but measured, meaning, that we may be able to convey our ideas clearly to the minds of others. Two persons cannot mutually impart their knowledge, or compare and rectify their conclusions, unless both attend to the true intent and force of language. If by such words as attraction, electricity, polarity, or atom, they imply different things, they may discuss facts, deny results, and doubt consequences for an indefinite time without any advantageous progress. I hold it as a great point in self-education that the student should be continually engaged in forming exact ideas, and in expressing them clearly by language. Such practice insensibly opposes any tendency to exaggeration or mistake, and increases the sense and love of truth in every part of life.

I should be sorry, however, if what I have said were understood as meaning that education for the improvement and strengthening of the judgment is to be altogether repressive of the imagination, or confine the exercise of the mind to processes of a mathematical or mechanical character. I believe that, in the pursuit of physical science, the imagination should be taught to present the subject investigated in all possible, and even in impossible views; to search for analogies of likeness and (if I may say so) of opposition—inverse or contrasted analogies; to present the fundamental idea in every form, proportion, and condition; to clothe it with suppositions and probabilities, that all cases may pass in review, and be touched, if needful, by the Ithuriel spear of experiment. But all this must be under government, and the result must not be given to society until the judgment, educated by the process itself, has been exercised upon it. Let us construct our hypotheses for an hour, or a day, or for years; they are of the utmost value in the elimination of truth, "which is evolved more freely from error than from confusion"; but, above all things, let us not cease to be aware of the temptation they offer, or, because they gradually become familiar to us, accept them as established. We could not reason about electricity without thinking of it as a fluid, or a vibration, or some other existent state or form. We should give up half our advantage in the consideration of heat if we refused to consider it as a principle, or a state of motion. We could scarcely touch such subjects by experiment, and we should make no progress in their practical application, without hypothesis; still it is absolutely necessary that we should learn to doubt the conditions we assume, and acknowledge we are uncertain, whether heat and electricity are vibrations or substances, or either.

When the different data required are in our possession, and we have succeeded in forming a clear idea of each, the mind should be instructed to balance them one against another, and not suffered carelessly to hasten to a conclusion. This reserve is most essential; and it is especially needful that the reasons which are adverse to our expectations or our desires should be carefully attended to. We often receive truth from unpleasant sources; we often have reason to accept unpalatable truths. We are never freely willing to admit information having this unpleasant character, and it requires much self-control in this respect, to preserve us even in a moderate degree from errors. I suppose there is scarcely one investigator in original research who has not felt the temptation to disregard the reasons and results which are against his views. I acknowledge that I have experienced it very often, and will not pretend to say that I have yet learned on all occasions to avoid the error. When a bar of bismuth or phosphorus is placed between the poles of a powerful magnet, it is drawn into a position across the line joining the poles; when only one pole is near the bar, the latter recedes; this and the former effect is due to repulsion, and is strikingly in contrast with the attraction shown by iron. To account for it, I at one time suggested the idea that a polarity was induced in the phosphorus or bismuth the reverse of the polarity induced in iron, and that opinion is still sustained by eminent philosophers. But observe a necessary result of such a supposition, which appears to follow when the phenomena are referred to elementary principles. Time is shown, by every result bearing on the subject, to be concerned in the coming on and passing away of the inductive condition produced by magnetic force, and the consequence, as Thomson pointed out, is, that if a ball of bismuth could be suspended between the poles of a magnet, so as to encounter no resistance from the surrounding medium, or from friction or torsion, and were once put in motion round a vertical axis, it would, because of the assumed polar state, go on for ever revolving, the parts which at any moment are axial moving like the bar, so as to become the next moment equatorial. Now, as we believe the mechanical forces of nature tend to bring things into a stable, and not into an unstable condition; as we believe that a perpetual motion is impossible; so because both these points are involved in the notion of the reverse polarity, which itself is not supposed to be dependant on any consumption of power, I feel bound to hold the judgment balanced, and therefore hesitate to accept a conclusion founded on such a notion of the physical action; the more especially as the peculiar test facts [3] which prove the polarity of iron are not reproduced in the case of diamagnetic bodies.

As a result of this wholesome mental condition, we should be able to form a proportionate judgment. The mind naturally desires to settle upon one thing or another; to rest upon an affirmative or a negative; and that with a degree of absolutism which is irrational and improper. In drawing a conclusion it is very difficult, but not the less necessary, to make it proportionate to the evidence: except where certainty exists (a case of rare occurrence), we should consider our decisions as probable only. The probability may appear very great, so that in affairs of the world we often accept such as certainty, and trust our welfare or our lives upon it. Still, only an uneducated mind will confound probability with certainty, especially when it encounters a contrary conclusion drawn by another from like data. This suspension in degree of judgment will not make a man less active in life, or his conclusions less certain as truths; on the contrary, I believe him to be the more ready for the right amount and direction of action on any emergency; and am sure his conclusions and statements will carry more weight in the world than those of the incautious man.

When I was young, I received from one well able to aid a learner in his endeavours toward self-improvement, a curious lesson in the mode of estimating the amount of belief one might be induced to attach to our conclusions. The person was Dr. Wollaston, who, upon a given point, was induced to offer me a wager of two to one on the affirmative. I rather impertinently quoted Butler's well-known lines [4] about the kind of persons who use wagers for argument, and he gently explained to me, that he considered such a wager not as a thoughtless thing, but as an expression of the amount of belief in the mind of the person offering it; combining this curious application of the wager, as a meter, with the necessity that ever existed of drawing conclusions, not absolute but proportionate to the evidence.

Occasionally and frequently the exercise of the judgment ought to end

---

3. *Experimental Researches in Electricity*, paragraphs 2657–2681. See *Great Books of the Western World*, Vol. 45, pp. 662–666.
4. "Quoth she, 'I've heard old cunning stagers,
   Say fools for arguments use wagers.'"

in absolute reservation. It may be very distasteful, and great fatigue, to suspend a conclusion, but as we are not infallible, so we ought to be cautious; we shall eventually find our advantage, for the man who rests in his position is not so far from right as he who, proceeding in a wrong direction, is ever increasing his distance. In the year 1824, Arago discovered that copper and other bodies placed in the vicinity of a magnet, and having no direct action of attraction or repulsion upon it, did affect it when moved, and was affected by it. A copper plate revolving near a magnet carried the magnet with it; or if the magnet revolved, and not the copper, it carried the copper with it. A magnetic needle vibrating freely over a disc of glass or wood, was exceedingly retarded in its motion when these were replaced by a disc of copper. Arago stated most clearly all the conditions, and resolved the forces into three directions, but not perceiving the physical cause of the action, exercised a most wise and instructive reservation as to his conclusion. Others, as Haldat, considered it as the proof of the universality of a magnetism of the ordinary kind, and held to that notion though it was contradicted by the further facts; and it was only at a future period that the true physical cause, namely, magneto-electric currents induced in the copper, became known to us. What an education Arago's mind must have received in relation to philosophical reservation; what an antithesis he forms with the mass of table-turners; and what a fine example he has left us of that condition of judgment to which we should strive to attain!

If I may give another illustration of the needful reservation of judgment, I will quote the case of oxygen and hydrogen gases, which, being mixed, will remain together uncombined for years in contact with glass, but in contact with spongy platinum combine at once. We have the same fact in many forms, and many suggestions have been made as to the mode of action, but as yet we do not know clearly how the result comes to pass. We cannot tell whether electricity acts or not. Then we should suspend our conclusions. Our knowledge of the fact itself, and the many varieties of it, is not the less abundant or sure; and when the truth shall hereafter emerge from the mist, we ought to have no opposing prejudice, but be prepared to receive it.

The education which I advocate will require patience and labour of thought in every exercise tending to improve the judgment. It matters not on what subject a person's mind is occupied, he should engage in it with the conviction that it will require mental labour. A powerful mind will be able to draw a conclusion more readily and more correctly than one of moderate character, but both will surpass themselves if they make an earnest, careful investigation, instead of a careless or prejudiced one; and education for this purpose is the more necessary for the latter, because the man of less ability may, through it, raise his rank and amend his position. I earnestly urge this point of self-education, for I believe it to be more or less in the power of every man greatly to improve his judgment. I do not think that one has the complete capacity for judgment which another is naturally without. I am of opinion that all may judge, and that we only need to declare on every side the conviction that mental education is wanting, and lead men to see that through it they hold, in a large degree, their welfare and their character in their own hands, to cause in future years an abundant development of right judgment in every class.

This education has for its first and its last step *humility*. It can commence only because of a conviction of deficiency; and if we are not disheartened under the growing revelations which it will make, that conviction will become stronger unto the end. But the humility will be founded, not on comparison of ourselves with the imperfect standards around us, but on the increase of that internal knowledge which alone can make us aware of our internal wants. The first step in correction is to learn our deficiencies, and having learned them, the next step is almost complete: for no man who has discovered that his judgment is hasty, or illogical, or imperfect would go on with the same degree of haste, or irrationality, or presumption as before. I do not mean that all would at once be cured of bad mental habits, but I think better of human nature than to believe, that a man in any rank of life, who has arrived at the consciousness of such a condition, would deny his common sense, and still judge and act as before. And though such self-schooling must continue to the end of life to supply an experience of deficiency rather than of attainment, still there is abundant stimulus to excite any man to perseverance. What he has lost are things imaginary, not real; what he gains are riches before unknown to him, yet invaluable; and though he may think more humbly of his own character, he will find himself at every step of his progress more sought for than before, more trusted with responsibility and held in pre-eminence by his equals, and more highly valued by those whom he himself will esteem worthy of approbation.

And now a few words upon the mutual relation of two classes, namely, those who decline to educate their judgments in regard to the matters on which they decide, and those who, by self-education, have endeavoured to improve themselves; and upon the remarkable and somewhat unreasonable manner in which the latter are called upon, and occasionally taunted, by the former. A man who makes assertions, or draws conclusions, regarding any given case, ought to be competent to investigate it. He has no right to throw the onus on others, declaring it their duty to prove him right or wrong. His duty is to demonstrate the truth of that which he asserts, or to cease from asserting. The men he calls upon to consider and judge have enough to do with themselves, in the examination, correction, or verification of their own views. The world little knows how many of the thoughts and theories which have passed through the mind of a scientific investigator have been crushed in silence and secrecy by his own severe criticism and adverse examination; that in the most successful instances, not a tenth of the suggestions, the hopes, the wishes, the preliminary conclusions have been realised. And is a man so occupied to be taken from his search after truth in the path he hopes may lead to its attainment, and occupied in vain upon nothing but a broad assertion?

Neither has the assertor of any new thing a right to claim an answer in the form of Yes or No; or think, because none is forthcoming, that he is to be considered as having established his assertion. So much is unknown to the wisest man, that he may often be without an answer: as frequently he is so, because the subject is in the region of hypothesis, and not of facts. In either case he has the right to refuse to speak. I cannot tell whether there are two fluids of electricity or any fluid at all. I am not bound to explain how a table tilts any more than to indicate how, under the conjurer's hands, a pudding appears in a hat. The means are not known to me. I am persuaded that the results, however strange they may appear, are in accordance with that which is truly known, and if carefully investigated would justify the well-tried laws of nature; but, as life is limited, I am not disposed to occupy the time it is made of in the investigation of matters which, in what is known to me of them, offer no reasonable prospect of any useful progress, or anything but negative results. We deny the right of those who call upon us to answer their speculations "if we can," whilst we have so many of our own to develop and correct; and claim the right for ourselves of withholding either our conclusions or the reasons for them, without in the least degree admitting that their affirmations are unanswerable. We are not even called upon to give an answer to the best of our belief: nor bound to admit a bold assertion because we do not know to the contrary. No one is justified in claiming our assent to the spontaneous generation of insects, because we cannot circumstantially explain how a mite or the egg of a mite has entered into a particular bottle. Let those who affirm the exception to the general law of nature, or those others who upon the affirmation accept the result, work out the experimental proof. It has been done in this case by Schulze, and is in the negative; but how few among the many who make, or repeat, the assertion, would have the requisite self-abnegation, the subjected judgment, the perseverance, and the precision which has been displayed in that research.

When men, more or less marked by their advance, are led by circumstances to give an opinion adverse to any popular notion, or to the assertions of any sanguine inventor, nothing is more usual than the attempt to neutralize the force of such an opinion by reference to the mistakes which like educated men have made; and their occasional misjudgments and erroneous conclusions are quoted, as if they were less competent than others to give an opinion, being even disabled from judging like matters to those which are included in their pursuits by the very exercise of their minds upon them. How frequently has the reported judgment of Davy, upon the impossibility of gas-lighting on a large scale, been quoted by speculators engaged in tempting monied men into companies, or in the pages of journals occupied with the popular fancies of the day; as if an argument were derivable from that in favour of some special object to be commended. Why should not men taught in the matter of judgment far beyond their neighbours, be expected to err sometimes, since the very education in which they are advanced can only terminate with their lives? What is there about them, derived from this education, which sets up the shadow of a pretence to perfection? Such men cannot learn all things, and may often be ignorant. The very progress which science makes amongst them as a body is a continual correction of ignorance—*i.e.*, of a state which is ignorance in relation to the future, though wisdom and knowledge in relation to the past. In 1823 Wollaston discovered that beautiful substance which he called titanium, believing it to be a simple metal: and it was so accepted by all philosophers. Yet this was a mistake, for Wöhler, in 1850, showed the substance was a very compound body. This is no reproach to Wollaston or to those who trusted in him; he made a step in metallurgy which advanced knowledge, and perhaps we may hereafter, through it, learn to know that metals are compound bodies. Who, then, has a right to quote his mistake as a reproach against him? Who could correct him but men intellectually educated as he himself was? Who does not feel that the investigation remains a bright gem in the circlet that memory offers to his honour?

If we are to estimate the utility of an educated judgment, do not let us hear merely of the errors of scientific men, which have been corrected by others taught in the same careful school; but let us see what, as a body, they have produced, compared with that supplied by their reproachers. Where are the established truths and triumphs of ring-swingers, table-turners, table-speakers? What one result in the numerous divisions of science or its applications can be traced to their exertions? Where is the investigation completed, so that, as in gas-lighting, all may admit that the principles are established and a good end obtained, without the shadow of a doubt?

If we look to electricity, it, in the hands of the careful investigator, has advanced to the most extraordinary results: it approaches at the motion of his hand; bursts from the metal; descends from the atmosphere; surrounds the globe: it talks, it writes, it records, it appears to him (cautious as he has learned to become) as a universal spirit in nature. If we look to photography, whose origin is of our own day, and see what it has become in the hands of its discoverers and their successors, how wonderful are the results! The light is made to yield impressions upon the dead silver or the coarse paper, beautiful as those it produced upon the living and sentient retina: its most transient impression is rendered durable for years; it is made to leave a visible or an invisible trace; to give a result to be seen now or a year hence; made to paint all natural forms and even colours; it serves the offices of war, of peace, of art, science, and economy: it replaces even the mind of the human being in some of its lower services; for a little camphine lamp is set down and left to itself, to perform the duty of watching the changes of magnetism, heat, and other forces of nature, and to record the results, in pictorial curves, which supply an enduring record of their most transitory actions.

What has clairvoyance, or mesmerism, or table-rapping done in comparison with results like these? What have the snails at Paris told us from the snails at New York? What have any of these intelligences done in aiding such developments? Why did they not inform us of the possibility of photography? Or when that became known, why did they not favour us with some instructions for its improvement? They all profess to deal with agencies far more exalted in character than an electric current or a ray of light: they also deal with mechanical forces; they employ both the bodily organs and the mental; they profess to lift a table, to turn a hat, to see into a box, or into the next room, or a town—why should they not move a balance, and so give us the element of a new mechanical power? Take cognizance of a bottle and its contents, and tell us how they will act upon those of a neighbouring bottle? Either see or feel into a crystal, and inform us of what it is composed? Why have they not added one metal to the fifty known to mankind, or one planet to the number daily increasing under the observant eye of the astronomer? Why have they not corrected one of the mistakes of the philosophers? There are no doubt very many that require it. There has been plenty of time for the development and maturation of some of the numerous public pretences that have risen up in connexion with these supposed agencies; how is it that not one new power has been added to the means of investigation employed by the philosophers, or one valuable utilitarian application presented to society?

In conclusion, I will freely acknowledge that all I have said regarding the great want of judgment manifested by society as a body, and the high value of any means which would tend to supply the deficiency, have been developed and declared on numerous occasions, by authority far above any I possess. The deficiency is known hypothetically, but I doubt if in reality; the individual acknowledges the state in respect of others, but is unconscious of it in regard to himself. As to the world at large, the condition is accepted as a necessary fact; and so it is left untouched, almost ignored. I think that education in a large sense should be applied to this state of the subject, and that society, though it can do little in the way of communicated experience, can do much, by a declaration of the evil that exists and of its remediable character; by keeping alive a sense of the deficiency to be supplied; and by directing the minds of men to the practice and enlargement of that self-education which every one pursues more or less, but which under conviction and method would produce a tenfold amount of good. I know that the multitude will always be behindhand in this education, and to a far greater extent than in respect of the education which is founded on book learning. Whatever advance books make, they retain; but each new being comes on to the stage of life, with the same average amount of conceit, desires, and passions, as his predecessors, and in respect of self-education has all to learn. Does the circumstance that we can do little more than proclaim the necessity of instruction justify the ignorance? Or our silence? Or make the plea for this education less strong? Should it not, on the contrary, gain its strength from the fact that all are wanting more or less? I desire we should admit that, as a body, we are universally deficient in judgment. I do not mean that we are utterly ignorant, but that we have advanced only a little way in the requisite education, compared with what is within our power.

If the necessity of the education of the judgment were a familiar and habitual idea with the public, it would often afford a sufficient answer to the statement of an ill-informed or incompetent person; if quoted to recall to his remembrance the necessity of a mind instructed in a matter, and accustomed to balance evidence, it might frequently be an answer to the individual himself. Adverse influence might, and would, arise from the careless, the confident, the presumptuous, the hasty, and the dilatory man, perhaps extreme opposition; but I believe that the mere acknowledgment and proclamation of the ignorance, by society at large, would, through its moral influence, destroy the opposition, and be a great means to the attainment of the good end desired: for if no more be done than to lead such to turn their thoughts inwards, a step in education is gained: if they are convinced in any degree, an important advance is made; if they learn only to suspend their judgment, the improvement will be one above price.

It is an extraordinary thing that man, with a mind so wonderful that there is nothing to compare with it elsewhere in the known creation, should leave it to run wild in respect of its highest elements and qualities. He has a power of comparison and judgment, by which his final resolves, and all those acts of his material system which distinguish him from the brutes, are guided—shall he omit to educate and improve them when education can do much? Is it towards the very principles and privileges that distinguish him above other creatures, he should feel indifference? Because the education is internal, it is not the less needful; nor is it more the duty of a man that he should cause his child to be taught than that he should teach himself. Indolence may tempt him to neglect the self-examination and experience which form his school, and weariness may induce the evasion of the necessary practices; but surely a thought of the prize should suffice to stimulate him to the requisite exertion: and to those who reflect upon the many hours and days, devoted by a lover of sweet sounds, to gain a moderate facility upon a mere mechanical instrument, it ought to bring a correcting blush of shame, if they feel convicted of neglecting the beautiful living instrument, wherein play all the powers of the mind.

I will conclude this subject—believe me when I say I have been speaking from self-conviction. I did not think this an occasion on which I ought to seek for flattering words regarding our common nature; if so, I should have felt unfaithful to the trust I had taken up; so I have spoken from experience. In thought I hear the voice, which judges me by the precepts I have uttered. I know that I fail frequently in that very exercise of judgment to which I call others; and have abundant reason to believe that much more frequently I stand manifest to those around me, as one who errs, without being corrected by knowing it. I would willingly have evaded appearing before you on this subject, for I shall probably do but little good, and may well think it was an error of judgment to consent: having consented, my thoughts would flow back amongst the events and reflections of my past life, until I found nothing present itself but an open declaration, almost a confession, as the means of performing the duty due to the subject and to you.

"Observations on Mental Education"
is from Faraday's
LECTURES ON EDUCATION.

Edmund Burke

1729–1797

Edmund Burke was born in Dublin. January 12, 1729, is the most probable date. His father, a well-to-do lawyer, was a Protestant, his mother a Roman Catholic. Burke took his B.A. at Trinity College, Dublin. In 1750 he began to read law at the Middle Temple, London. He soon turned to writing. His first two books appeared in 1756. The same year he married the daughter of a Dr. Nugent, of Bath.

In 1761 he went back to Dublin for a while in the household of the Secretary for Ireland. When Rockingham became British Prime Minister in 1765, he hired Burke as his secretary. Burke went into Parliament as a member for Wendover. Two speeches on the American problem made his reputation. About this time he joined "The Club," whose members, then or later, included Dr. Johnson, Gibbon, Adam Smith, Boswell, and Burke's father-in-law, Dr. Nugent.

Burke fought hard to get workable justice for the American Colonies. Out of this quarrel sprang such powerful arguments as his *Speech on Conciliation with America* and the *Letter to the Sheriffs of Bristol* (see below). Some of his most famous speeches were delivered during his fourteen-year prosecution of Warren Hastings for high crimes in India. Hastings was acquitted.

In 1790 Burke's *Reflections on the Revolution in France* became the manifesto of conservative Europe. George III and Catherine of Russia praised it. It ran through eleven editions in about a year. Thomas Paine replied to it in *The Rights of Man*. Most of the other Whig leaders favored the French Revolution at first. Thus Burke was thrust more and more outside his party's councils. In 1794 he resigned from Parliament. He was given a pension of £2,500. The Duke of Bedford and Lord Lauderdale objected to this. Burke replied with a last great flash of eloquence in *A Letter to a Noble Lord*. He died on July 9, 1797.

In the late twentieth century we have speeches and White House press conferences on the television networks. At the same moment a whole nation may see and listen to the President, a senator, or a candidate. Burke, like Lincoln and Washington, spoke to a few hundred people. His printed words might reach a few thousand more. He held no great offices, led no armies, put his name to no important treaties. So we find it hard to imagine how he gained his tremendous reputation.

Part of the answer lies in his concentration. He was a statesman—altogether that, and nothing but that. Everything he did was done in that light. Unlike Cicero, his model as a writer and a man, he was not an effective orator. He lacked the commanding voice and presence. Nor was he a great politician. His record, as a party strategist and at the polls, is dotted with errors. Moreover, he seems to have been—a little too often—the honorable champion of lost causes. But he comes down to us, formidable still, as the great framer of issues. He was the one man in his nation and time who could fasten on some political problem, spell it out in bold letters, and place it in relation to the general ideas that influence the life of mankind.

His talent is close to its best in a *Letter to the Sheriffs of Bristol*. Here his famous style—large, firm, bold—builds a solid house of argument. When the letter was written, he was a member of Parliament from Bristol, at that time the second largest city in England. It is a "letter" in format only—in fact, like all his writings, it is a speech. He is aware that he has been criticized for "steadily pursuing the pernicious maxim of not obeying the voice of his constituents." Here—to the sheriffs, who were important local officials, and through

Notes from the artist: "Burke is shown sitting under a quotation from Reflections on the Revolution in France. He had defended the American Revolution but attacked the French because of its excesses and what he considered to be crimes against humanity."

Because half a dozen grasshoppers under a fern make the field ring with their importunate chink, whilst thousands of great cattle, reposed beneath the shadow of the British oak, chew the cud and are silent, pray do not imagine that those who make the noise are the only inhabitants of the field; that, of course, they are many in number, or that, after all, they are other than the, little, shrivelled, meagre, hopping, though loud and troublesome *insects* of the hour.

them to the voters—Burke gives an account of his recent service in Parliament and of the motives that led him to act as he did.

But this is only the immediate pretext for his letter. He writes in the midst of the American Revolution. He knows that many of the voters in his district are anti-American. He lays out the full force of his logic in the hope that he can persuade them to his own views. Here his political intentions and his devotion to the ruling ideas of freedom and justice merge in one powerful argument. Thoroughness, as John Morley said, was one of his great virtues. He knows what he is talking about. He does not set Englishmen against Americans, as the war has done. He speaks of both as Englishmen, and argues that what hurts one hurts the other. The partial suspension of habeas corpus is as dangerous to English liberty as it is unjust to Americans. "Bodies," he writes, "tied together by so unnatural a bond of union as mutual hatred are only connected to their ruin." So he pleads for a quick ending to the war in "an honourable and liberal accommodation."

Few Englishmen listened. Burke and his friends could only wait for the muffled drums of Yorktown in 1781.

Letter to the
Sheriffs of Bristol

Gentlemen—I have the honour of sending you the two last acts which have been passed with regard to the troubles in America. These acts are similar to all the rest which have been made on the same subject. They operate by the same principle, and they are derived from the very same policy. I think they complete the number of this sort of statutes to nine. It affords no matter for very pleasing reflection to observe that our subjects diminish as our laws increase.

If I have the misfortune of differing with some of my fellow-citizens on this great and arduous subject, it is no small consolation to me that I do not differ from you. With you I am perfectly united. We are heartily agreed in our detestation of a civil war. We have ever expressed the most unqualified disapprobation of all the steps which have led to it, and of all those which tend to prolong it. And I have no doubt that we feel exactly the same emotions of grief and shame on all its miserable consequences, whether they appear, on the one side or the other, in the shape of victories or defeats, of captures made from the English on the continent or from the English in these islands, of legislative regulations which subvert the liberties of our brethren or which undermine our own.

Of the first of these statutes (that for the letter of marque) I shall say little. Exceptionable as it may be, and as I think it is in some particulars, it seems the natural, perhaps necessary, result of the measures we have taken and the situation we are in. The other (for a partial suspension of the *habeas corpus*) appears to me of a much deeper malignity. During its progress through the House of Commons, it has been amended, so as to express, more distinctly than at first it did, the avowed sentiments of those who framed it; and the main ground of my exception to it is, because it does express, and does carry into execution, purposes which appear to me so contradictory to all the principles, not only of the constitutional policy of Great Britain, but even of that species of hostile justice which no asperity of war wholly extinguishes in the minds of a civilized people.

It seems to have in view two capital objects: the first, to enable administration to confine, as long as it shall think proper, those whom that act is pleased to qualify by the name of *pirates.* Those so qualified I understand to be the commanders and mariners of such privateers and ships of war belonging to the colonies as in the course of this unhappy contest may fall into the hands of the crown. They are therefore to be detained in prison, under the criminal description of piracy, to a future trial and ignominious punishment, whenever circumstances shall make it convenient to execute vengeance on them, under the colour of that odious and infamous offence.

To this first purpose of the law I have no small dislike, because the act does not (as all laws and all equitable transactions ought to do) fairly describe its object. The persons who make a naval war upon us, in consequence of the present troubles, may be rebels; but to call and treat them as pirates is confounding not only the natural distinction of things, but the order of crimes—which, whether by putting them from a higher part of the scale to the lower or from the lower to the higher, is never done without dangerously disordering the whole frame of jurisprudence. Though piracy may be, in the eye of the law, a *less* offence than treason, yet, as both are, in effect, punished with the same death, the same forfeiture, and the same corruption of blood, I never would take from any fellow-creature whatever any sort of advantage which he may derive to his safety from the pity of mankind, or to his reputation from their general feelings, by degrading his offence, when I cannot soften his punishment. The general sense of mankind tells me that those offences which may possibly arise from mistaken virtue are not in the class of infamous actions. Lord Coke, the oracle of the English law, conforms to that general sense, where he says that "those things which are of the highest criminality may be of the least disgrace." The act prepares a sort of masked proceeding, not honourable to the justice of the kingdom, and by no means necessary for its safety. I cannot enter into it. If Lord Balmerino, in the last rebellion, had driven off the cattle of twenty clans, I should have thought it would have been a scandalous and low juggle, utterly unworthy of the manliness of an English judicature, to have tried him for felony as a stealer of cows.

Besides, I must honestly tell you that I could not vote for, or countenance in any way, a statute which stigmatizes with the crime of piracy these men whom an act of Parliament had previously put out of the protection of the law. When the legislature of this kingdom had ordered all their ships and goods, for the mere new-created offence of exercising trade, to be divided as a spoil among the seamen of the navy—to consider the necessary reprisal of an unhappy, proscribed, interdicted people, as the crime of piracy, would have appeared, in any other legislature than ours, a strain of the most insulting and most unnatural cruelty and injustice. I assure you I never remember to have heard of anything like it in any time or country.

The second professed purpose of the act is to detain in England for trial those who shall commit high treason in America.

That you may be enabled to enter into the true spirit of the present law, it is necessary, Gentlemen, to apprise you that there is an act, made so long ago as in the reign of Henry VIII, before the existence or thought of any English colonies in America, for the trial in this kingdom of treasons committed out of the realm. In the year 1769 Parliament thought proper to acquaint the crown with their construction of that act in a formal address, wherein they entreated his Majesty to cause persons charged with high treason in America to be brought into this kingdom for trial. By this act of Henry VIII, so construed and so applied, almost all that is substantial and beneficial in a trial by jury is taken away from the subject in the colonies. This is, however, saying too little; for to try a man under that act is, in effect, to condemn him unheard. A person is brought hither in the dungeon of a ship's hold; thence he is vomited into a dungeon on land, loaded with irons, unfurnished with money, unsupported by friends, three thousand miles from all means of calling upon or confronting evidence, where no one local circumstance that tends to detect perjury can possibly be judged of; such a person may be executed according to form, but he can never be tried according to justice.

I therefore could never reconcile myself to the bill I send you, which is expressly provided to remove all inconveniences from the establishment of a mode of trial which has ever appeared to me most unjust and most unconstitutional. Far from removing the difficulties which impede the execution of so mischievous a project, I would heap new difficulties upon it, if it were in my power. All the ancient, honest, juridical principles and institutions of England are so many clogs to check and retard the headlong course of violence and oppression. They were invented for this one good purpose, that what was not just should not be convenient. Convinced of this, I would leave things as I found them. The old, cool-headed, general law is as good as any deviation dictated by present heat.

I could see no fair, justifiable expedience pleaded to favour this new suspension of the liberty of the subject. If the English in the colonies can support the independency to which they have been unfortunately driven, I suppose nobody has such a fanatical zeal for the criminal justice of Henry VIII that he will contend for executions which must be retaliated tenfold on his own friends, or who has conceived so strange an idea of English dignity as to think the defeats in America compensated by the triumphs at Tyburn. If, on the contrary, the colonies are reduced to the obedience of the crown, there must be, under that authority, tribunals in the country itself fully competent to administer justice on all offenders. But if there are not, and that we must suppose a thing so humiliating to our government as that all this vast continent should unanimously concur in thinking that no ill fortune can convert resistance to the royal authority into a criminal act, we may call the effect of our victory peace, or obedience, or what we will, but the war is not ended; the hostile mind continues in full vigour, and it continues under a worse form. If your peace be nothing more than a sullen pause from arms, if their quiet be nothing but the meditation of revenge, where smitten pride smarting from its wounds festers into new rancour, neither the act of Henry VIII nor its handmaid of this reign will answer any wise end of policy or justice. For, if the bloody fields which they saw and felt are not sufficient to subdue the reason of America, (to use the expressive phrase of a great lord in office,) it is not the judicial slaughter which is made in another hemisphere against their universal sense of justice that will ever reconcile them to the British government.

I take it for granted, Gentlemen, that we sympathize in a proper horror of all punishment further than as it serves for an example. To whom, then, does the example of an execution in England for this American rebellion apply? Remember, you are told every day, that the present is a contest between the two countries, and that we in England are at war for our own dignity against our rebellious children. Is this true? If it be, it is surely among such rebellious children that examples for disobedience should be made, to be in any degree instructive: for who ever thought of teaching parents their duty by an example from the punishment of an undutiful son? As well might the execution of a fugitive Negro in the plantations be considered as a lesson to teach masters humanity to their slaves. Such executions may, indeed, satiate our revenge; they may harden our hearts, and puff us up with pride and arrogance. Alas! this is not instruction.

If anything can be drawn from such examples by a parity of the case, it is to show how deep their crime and how heavy their punishment will be, who shall at any time dare to resist a distant power actually disposing of their property without their voice or consent to the disposition, and overturning their franchises without charge or hearing. God forbid that England should ever read this lesson written in the blood of any of her offspring!

War is at present carried on between the king's natural and foreign troops, on one side, and the English in America, on the other, upon the usual footing of other wars; and accordingly an exchange of prisoners has been regularly made from the beginning. If, notwithstanding this hitherto equal procedure, upon some prospect of ending the war with success (which, however, may be delusive) administration prepares to act against those as traitors who remain in their hands at the end of the troubles, in my opinion we shall exhibit to the world as indecent a piece of injustice as ever civil fury has produced. If the prisoners who have been exchanged have not by that exchange been virtually pardoned, the cartel (whether avowed or understood) is a cruel fraud; for you have received the life of a man, and you ought to return a life for it, or there is no parity or fairness in the transaction.

If, on the other hand, we admit that they who are actually exchanged are pardoned, but contend that you may justly reserve for vengeance those who remain unexchanged, then this unpleasant and unhandsome consequence will follow: that you judge of the delinquency of men merely by the time of their guilt, and not by the heinousness of it; and you make fortune and accidents, and not the moral qualities of human action, the rule of your justice.

These strange incongruities must ever perplex those who confound the unhappiness of civil dissension with the crime of treason. Whenever a rebellion really and truly exists, which is as easily known in fact as it is difficult to define in words, government has not entered into such military conventions, but has ever declined all intermediate treaty which should put rebels in possession of the law of nations with regard to war. Commanders would receive no benefits at their hands, because they could make no return for them. Who has ever heard of capitulation, and parole of honour, and exchange of prisoners in the late rebellions in this kingdom? The answer to all demands of that sort was, "We can engage for nothing; you are at the king's pleasure." We ought to remember, that, if our present enemies be in reality and truth rebels, the king's generals have no right to release them upon any conditions whatsoever; and they are themselves answerable to the law, and as much in want of a pardon, for doing so, as the rebels whom they release.

Lawyers, I know, cannot make the distinction for which I contend; because they have their strict rule to go by. But legislators ought to do what lawyers cannot; for they have no other rules to bind them but the great principles of reason and equity and the general sense of mankind. These they are bound to obey and follow; and rather to enlarge and enlighten law by the liberality of legislative reason than to fetter and bind their higher capacity by the narrow constructions of subordinate, artificial justice. If we had adverted to this, we never could consider the convulsions of a great empire, not disturbed by a little disseminated faction, but divided by whole communities and provinces, and entire legal representatives of a people, as fit matter of discussion under a commission of Oyer and Terminer. It is as opposite to reason and prudence as it is to humanity and justice.

This act, proceeding on these principles, that is, preparing to end the present troubles by a trial of one sort of hostility under the name of piracy, and of another by the name of treason, and executing the act of Henry VIII according to a new and unconstitutional interpretation, I have thought evil and dangerous, even though the instruments of effecting such purposes had been merely of a neutral quality.

But it really appears to me, that the means which this act employs are, at least, as exceptionable as the end. Permit me to open myself a little upon this subject, because it is of importance to me, when I am obliged to submit to the power without acquiescing in the reason of an act of legislature, that I should justify my dissent by such arguments as may be supposed to have weight with a sober man.

The main operative regulation of the act is to suspend the common law, and the statute *habeas corpus* (the sole securities either for liberty or justice), with regard to all those who have been out of the realm, or on the high seas, within a given time. The rest of the people, as I understand, are to continue as they stood before.

I confess, Gentlemen, that this appears to me as bad in the principle, and far worse in its consequence, than a universal suspension of the *Habeas Corpus* Act; and the limiting qualification, instead of taking out the sting, does in my humble opinion sharpen and envenom it to a greater degree. Liberty, if I understand it at all, is a general principle, and the clear right of all the subjects within the realm or of none. Partial freedom seems to me a most invidious mode of slavery. But, unfortunately, it is the kind of slavery the most easily admitted in times of civil discord; for parties are but too apt to forget their own future safety in their desire of sacrificing their enemies. People without much difficulty admit the entrance of that injustice of which they are not to be the immediate victims.

In times of high proceeding it is never the faction of the predominant power that is in danger; for no tyranny chastises its own instruments. It is the obnoxious and the suspected who want the protection of law; and there is nothing to bridle the partial violence of state factions but this: "that whenever an act is made for a cessation of law and justice, the whole people should be universally subjected to the same suspension of their franchises." The alarm of such a proceeding would then be universal. It would operate as a sort of call of the nation. It would become every man's immediate and instant concern to be made very sensible of the absolute necessity of this total eclipse of liberty. They would more carefully advert to every renewal, and more powerfully resist it. These great determined measures are not commonly so dangerous to freedom. They are marked with too strong lines to slide into use. No plea, nor pretence, of inconvenience or evil example (which must in their nature be daily and ordinary incidents) can be admitted as a reason for such mighty operations. But the true danger is, when liberty is nibbled away, for expedients, and by parts. The *Habeas Corpus* Act supposes, contrary to the genius of most other laws, that the lawful magistrate may see particular men with a malignant eye, and it provides for that identical case. But when men, in particular descriptions, marked out by the magistrate himself, are delivered over by Parliament to this possible malignity, it is not the *habeas corpus* that is occasionally suspended, but its spirit that is mistaken, and its principle that is subverted. Indeed nothing is security to any individual but the common interest of all.

This act, therefore, has this distinguished evil in it, that it is the first *partial* suspension of the *habeas corpus* that has been made. The precedent, which is always of very great importance, is now established. For the first time a distinction is made among the people within this realm. Before this act, every man putting his foot on English ground, every stranger owing only a local and temporary allegiance, even Negro slaves who had been sold in the colonies and under an act of Parliament, became as free as every other man who breathed the same air with them. Now a line is drawn, which may be advanced farther and farther at pleasure on the same argument of mere expedience on which it was first described. There is no equality among us; we are not fellow-citizens, if the mariner who lands on the quay does not rest on as firm legal ground as the merchant who sits in his counting-house. Other laws may injure the community, this dissolves it. As things now stand, every man in the West Indies, every one inhabitant of three unoffending provinces on the continent, every person coming from the East Indies, every gentleman who has travelled for his health or education, every mariner who has navigated the seas, is, for no other offence, under a temporary proscription. Let any of these facts (now become presumptions of guilt) be proved against him, and the bare suspicion of the crown puts him out of the law. It is even by no means clear to me whether the negative proof does not lie upon the person apprehended on suspicion to the subversion of all justice.

I have not debated against this bill in its progress through the House, because it would have been vain to oppose and impossible to correct it. It is some time since I have been clearly convinced that in the present state of things all opposition to any measures proposed by ministers, where the name of America appears, is vain and frivolous. You may be sure that I do not speak of my opposition, which in all circumstances must be so, but that of men of the greatest wisdom and authority in the nation. Everything proposed against America is supposed of course to be in favour of Great Britain. Good and ill success are equally admitted as reasons for persevering in the present methods. Several very prudent and very well-intentioned persons were of opinion that during the prevalence of such dispositions, all struggle rather inflamed than lessened the distemper of the public councils. Finding such resistance to be considered as factious by most within doors, and by very many without, I cannot conscientiously support what is against my opinion, nor prudently contend with what I know is irresistible. Preserving my principles unshaken, I reserve my activity for rational endeavours; and I hope that my past conduct has given sufficient evidence that if I am a single day from my place, it is not owing to indolence or love of dissipation. The slightest hope of doing good is sufficient to recall me to what I quitted with regret. In declining for some time my usual strict attendance, I do not in the least condemn the spirit of those gentlemen who, with a just confidence in their abilities (in which I claim a sort of share from my love and admiration of them), were of opinion that their exertions in this desperate case might be of some service. They thought that by contracting the sphere of its application they might lessen the malignity of an evil principle. Perhaps they were in the right. But when my opinion was so very clearly to the contrary, for the reasons I have just stated, I am sure my attendance would have been ridiculous.

I must add in further explanation of my conduct that, far from softening the features of such a principle, and thereby removing any part of the popular odium or natural terrors attending it, I should be sorry that anything framed in contradiction to the spirit of our Constitution did not instantly produce, in fact, the grossest of the evils with which it was preg-nant in its nature. It is by lying dormant a long time, or being at first very rarely exercised, that arbitrary power steals upon a people. On the next unconstitutional act, all the fashionable world will be ready to say—Your prophecies are ridiculous, your fears are vain, you see how little of the mischiefs which you formerly foreboded are come to pass. Thus, by degrees, that artful softening of all arbitrary power, the alleged infre-quency or narrow extent of its operation, will be received as a sort of aphorism—and Mr. Hume will not be singular in telling us that the felicity of mankind is no more disturbed by it than by earthquakes or thunder or the other more unusual accidents of nature.

The act of which I speak is among the fruits of the American war; a war in my humble opinion productive of many mischiefs of a kind which distinguish it from all others. Not only our policy is deranged, and our empire distracted, but our laws and our legislative spirit appear to have been totally perverted by it. We have made war on our colonies, not by arms only, but by laws. As hostility and law are not very concordant ideas, every step we have taken in this business has been made by trampling on some maxim of justice, or some capital principle of wise government. What precedents were established, and what principles overturned (I will not say of English privilege, but of general justice), in the Boston Port, the Massachusetts Charter, the Military Bill, and all that long array of hostile acts of Parliament by which the war with America has been begun and supported! Had the principles of any of these acts been first exerted on English ground they would probably have expired as soon as they touched it. But by being removed from our persons they have rooted in our laws, and the latest posterity will taste the fruits of them.

Nor is it the worst effect of this unnatural contention that our laws are corrupted. Whilst manners remain entire, they will correct the vices of law, and soften it at length to their own temper. But we have to lament that in most of the late proceedings we see very few traces of that gener-osity, humanity, and dignity of mind which formerly characterized this nation. War suspends the rules of moral obligation, and what is long sus-pended is in danger of being totally abrogated. Civil wars strike deepest of all into the manners of the people. They vitiate their politics; they corrupt their morals; they pervert even the natural taste and relish of equity and justice. By teaching us to consider our fellow-citizens in a hostile light, the whole body of our nation becomes gradually less dear to us. The very names of affection and kindred, which were the bond of charity whilst we agreed, become new incentives to hatred and rage, when the communion of our country is dissolved. We may flatter ourselves that we shall not fall into this misfortune. But we have no charter of exemption, that I know of, from the ordinary frailties of our nature.

What but that blindness of heart which arises from the frenzy of civil contention could have made any persons conceive the present situation of the British affairs as an object of triumph to themselves, or of congratulation to their sovereign? Nothing surely could be more lamentable to those who remember the flourishing days of this kingdom than to see the insane joy of several unhappy people, amidst the sad spectacle which our affairs and conduct exhibit to the scorn of Europe. We behold (and it seems some people rejoice in beholding) our native land, which used to sit the envied arbiter of all her neighbours, reduced to a servile dependence on their mercy—acquiescing in assurances of friendship which she does not trust, complaining of hostilities which she dares not resent, deficient to her allies, lofty to her subjects, and submissive to her enemies—whilst the liberal government of this free nation is supported by the hireling sword of German boors and vassals, and three millions of the subjects of Great Britain are seeking for protection to English privileges in the arms of France!

These circumstances appear to me more like shocking prodigies than natural changes in human affairs. Men of firmer minds may see them without staggering or astonishment. Some may think them matters of congratulation and complimentary addresses; but I trust your candour will be so indulgent to my weakness as not to have the worse opinion of me for my declining to participate in this joy, and my rejecting all share whatsoever in such a triumph. I am too old, too stiff in my inveterate partialities, to be ready at all the fashionable evolutions of opinion. I scarcely know how to adapt my mind to the feelings with which the Court Gazettes mean to impress the people. It is not instantly that I can be brought to rejoice, when I hear of the slaughter and captivity of long lists of those names which have been familiar to my ears from my infancy, and to rejoice that they have fallen under the sword of strangers, whose barbarous appellations I scarcely know how to pronounce. The glory acquired at the White Plains by Colonel Rahl has no charms for me, and I fairly acknowledge that I have not yet learned to delight in finding Fort Kniphausen in the heart of the British dominions.

It might be some consolation for the loss of our old regards, if our reason were enlightened in proportion as our honest prejudices are removed. Wanting feelings for the honour of our country, we might then in cold blood be brought to think a little of our interests as individual citizens and our private conscience as moral agents.

Indeed, our affairs are in a bad condition. I do assure those gentlemen who have prayed for war, and obtained the blessing they have sought, that they are at this instant in very great straits. The abused wealth of this country continues a little longer to feed its distemper. As yet they, and their German allies of twenty hireling states, have contended only with the unprepared strength of our own infant colonies. But America is not subdued. Not one unattacked village which was originally adverse throughout that vast continent has yet submitted from love or terror. You have the ground you encamp on, and you have no more. The cantonments of your troops and your dominions are exactly of the same extent. You spread devastation, but you do not enlarge the sphere of authority.

The events of this war are of so much greater magnitude than those who either wished or feared it ever looked for, that this alone ought to fill every considerate mind with anxiety and diffidence. Wise men often tremble at the very things which fill the thoughtless with security. For many reasons I do not choose to expose to public view all the particulars of the state in which you stood with regard to foreign powers during the whole course of the last year. Whether you are yet wholly out of danger from them is more than I know, or than your rulers can divine. But even if I were certain of my safety, I could not easily forgive those who had brought me into the most dreadful perils, because by accidents, unforeseen by them or me, I have escaped.

Believe me, Gentlemen, the way still before you is intricate, dark, and full of perplexed and treacherous mazes. Those who think they have the clue may lead us out of this labyrinth. We may trust them as amply as we think proper; but as they have most certainly a call for all the reason which their stock can furnish, why should we think it proper to disturb its operation by inflaming their passions? I may be unable to lend a helping hand to those who direct the state; but I should be ashamed to make myself one of a noisy multitude to halloo and hearten them into doubtful and dangerous courses. A conscientious man would be cautious how he dealt in blood. He would feel some apprehension at being called to a tremendous account for engaging in so deep a play without any sort of knowledge of the game. It is no excuse for presumptuous ignorance, that it is directed by insolent passion. The poorest being that crawls on earth, contending to save itself from injustice and oppression, is an object respectable in the eyes of God and man. But I cannot conceive any existence under heaven (which in the depths of its wisdom tolerates all sorts of things) that is more truly odious and disgusting than an impotent, helpless creature, without civil wisdom or military skill, without a consciousness of any other qualification for power but his servility to it, bloated with pride and arrogance, calling for battles which he is not to fight, contending for a violent dominion which he can never exercise, and satisfied to be himself mean and miserable, in order to render others contemptible and wretched.

If you and I find our talents not of the great and ruling kind, our conduct, at least, is conformable to our faculties. No man's life pays the forfeit of our rashness. No desolate widow weeps tears of blood over our ignorance. Scrupulous and sober in a well-grounded distrust of ourselves, we would keep in the port of peace and security; and perhaps in recommending to others something of the same diffidence, we should show ourselves more charitable to their welfare than injurious to their abilities.

There are many circumstances in the zeal shown for civil war which seem to discover but little of real magnanimity. The addressers offer their own persons, and they are satisfied with hiring Germans. They promise their private fortunes, and they mortgage their country. They have all the merit of volunteers, without risk of person or charge of contribution; and when the unfeeling arm of a foreign soldiery pours out their kindred blood like water, they exult and triumph as if they themselves had performed some notable exploit. I am really ashamed of the fashionable language which has been held for some time past, which, to say the best of it, is full of levity. You know that I allude to the general cry against the cowardice of the Americans, as if we despised them for not making the king's soldiery purchase the advantage they have obtained at a dearer rate. It is not, Gentlemen, it is not to respect the dispensations of Providence, nor to provide any decent retreat in the mutability of human affairs. It leaves no medium between insolent victory and infamous defeat. It tends to alienate our minds further and further from our natural regards, and to make an eternal rent and schism in the British nation. Those who do not wish for such a separation would not dissolve that cement of reciprocal esteem and regard which can alone bind together the parts of this great fabric. It ought to be our wish, as it is our duty, not only to forbear this style of outrage ourselves, but to make every one as sensible as we can of the impropriety and unworthiness of the tempers which give rise to it, and which designing men are labouring with such malignant industry to diffuse amongst us. It is our business to counteract them, if possible—if possible, to awake our natural regards, and to revive the old partiality to the English name. Without something of this kind I do not see how it is ever practicable really to reconcile with those whose affection, after all, must be the surest hold of our government, and which is a thousand times more worth to us than the mercenary zeal of all the circles of Germany.

I can well conceive a country completely overrun, and miserably wasted, without approaching in the least to settlement. In my apprehension, as long as English government is attempted to be supported over Englishmen by the sword alone, things will thus continue. I anticipate in my mind the moment of the final triumph of foreign military force. When that hour arrives (for it may arrive), then it is that all this mass of weakness and violence will appear in its full light. If we should be expelled from America, the delusion of the partisans of military government might still continue. They might still feed their imaginations with the possible good consequences which might have attended success. Nobody could prove the contrary by facts. But in case the sword should do all that the sword can do, the success of their arms and the defeat of their policy will be one and the same thing. You will never see any revenue from America. Some increase of the means of corruption, without ease of the public burdens, is the very best that can happen. Is it for this that we are at war—and in such a war?

As to the difficulties of laying once more the foundations of that government which, for the sake of conquering what was our own, has been voluntarily and wantonly pulled down by a court faction here, I tremble to look at them. Has any of these gentlemen who are so eager to govern all mankind shown himself possessed of the first qualification towards government, some knowledge of the object, and of the difficulties which occur in the task they have undertaken?

I assure you, that, on the most prosperous issue of your arms, you will not be where you stood when you called in war to supply the defects of your political establishment. Nor would any disorder or disobedience to government which could arise from the most abject concession on our part ever equal those which will be felt after the most triumphant violence. You have got all the intermediate evils of war into the bargain.

I think I know America—if I do not, my ignorance is incurable, for I have spared no pains to understand it—and I do most solemnly assure those of my constituents who put any sort of confidence in my industry and integrity, that everything that has been done there has arisen from a total misconception of the object: that our means of originally holding America, that our means of reconciling with it after quarrel, of recovering it after separation, of keeping it after victory, did depend, and must depend, in their several stages and periods, upon a total renunciation of that unconditional submission which has taken such possession of the minds of violent men. The whole of those maxims upon which we have made and continued this war must be abandoned. Nothing, indeed (for I would not deceive you), can place us in our former situation. That hope must be laid aside. But there is a difference between bad and the worst of all. Terms relative to the cause of the war ought to be offered by the authority of Parliament. An arrangement at home promising some security for them ought to be made. By doing this, without the least impairing of our strength, we add to the credit of our moderation, which, in itself, is always strength more or less.

I know many have been taught to think that moderation in a case like this is a sort of treason, and that all arguments for it are sufficiently answered by railing at rebels and rebellion, and by charging all the present or future miseries which we may suffer on the resistance of our brethren. But I would wish them, in this grave matter, and if peace is not wholly removed from their hearts, to consider seriously, first, that to criminate and recriminate never yet was the road to reconciliation, in any difference amongst men. In the next place, it would be right to reflect that the American English (whom they may abuse, if they think it honourable to revile the absent) can, as things now stand, neither be provoked at our railing or bettered by our instruction. All communication is cut off between us. But this we know with certainty, that, though we cannot reclaim them, we may reform ourselves. If measures of peace are necessary, they must begin somewhere; and a conciliatory temper must precede and prepare every plan of reconciliation. Nor do I conceive that we suffer anything by thus regulating our own minds. We are not disarmed by being disencumbered of our passions. Declaiming on rebellion never added a bayonet or a charge of powder to your military force; but I am afraid that it has been the means of taking up many muskets against you.

This outrageous language, which has been encouraged and kept alive by every art, has already done incredible mischief. For a long time, even amidst the desolations of war, and the insults of hostile laws daily accumulated on one another, the American leaders seem to have had the greatest difficulty in bringing up their people to a declaration of total independence. But the Court Gazette accomplished what the abettors of independence had attempted in vain. When that disingenuous compilation and strange medley of railing and flattery was adduced as a proof of the united sentiments of the people of Great Britain, there was a great change throughout all America. The tide of popular affection, which had still set towards the parent country, began immediately to turn, and to flow with great rapidity in a contrary course. Far from concealing these wild declarations of enmity, the author of the celebrated pamphlet which prepared the minds of the people for independence [1] insists largely on the multitude and the spirit of these addresses; and he draws an argument from them, which, if the fact were as he supposes, must be irresistible. For I never knew a writer on the theory of government so partial to authority as not to allow that the hostile mind of the rulers to their people did fully justify a change of government; nor can any reason whatever be given why one people should voluntarily yield any degree of pre-eminence to another but on a supposition of great affection and benevolence towards them. Unfortunately, your rulers, trusting to other things, took no notice of this great principle of connection. From the beginning of this affair, they have done all they could to alienate your minds from your own kindred; and if they could excite hatred enough in one of the parties towards the other, they seemed to be of opinion that they had gone half the way towards reconciling the quarrel.

I know it is said, that your kindness is only alienated on account of their resistance, and therefore, if the colonies surrender at discretion, all sort of regard, and even much indulgence, is meant towards them in future. But can those who are partisans for continuing a war to enforce such a surrender be responsible (after all that has passed) for such a future use of a power that is bound by no compacts and restrained by no terror? Will they tell us what they call indulgences? Do they not at this instant call the present war and all its horrors a lenient and merciful proceeding?

No conqueror that I ever heard of has professed to make a cruel, harsh, and insolent use of his conquest. No! The man of the most declared pride scarcely dares to trust his own heart with this dreadful secret of ambition. But it will appear in its time; and no man who professes to reduce another to the insolent mercy of a foreign arm ever had any sort of goodwill towards him. The profession of kindness, with that sword in his hand, and that demand of surrender, is one of the most provoking acts of his hostility. I shall be told that all this is lenient as against rebellious adversaries. But are the leaders of their faction more lenient to those who submit? Lord Howe and General Howe have powers, under an act of

---

1. Burke refers to Thomas Paine's *Common Sense*.

Parliament, to restore to the king's peace and to free trade any men or district which shall submit. Is this done? We have been over and over informed by the authorized gazette, that the city of New York and the countries of Staten and Long Island have submitted voluntarily and cheerfully, and that many are very full of zeal to the cause of administration. Were they instantly restored to trade? Are they yet restored to it? Is not the benignity of two commissioners, naturally most humane and generous men, some way fettered by instructions, equally against their dispositions and the spirit of Parliamentary faith, when Mr. Tryon, vaunting of the fidelity of the city in which he is governor, is obliged to apply to ministry for leave to protect the king's loyal subjects, and to grant to them, not the disputed rights and privileges of freedom, but the common rights of men, by the name of *graces?* Why do not the commissioners restore them on the spot? Were they not named as commissioners for that express purpose? But we see well enough to what the whole leads. The trade of America is to be dealt out in private indulgences and graces, that is, in jobs to recompense the incendiaries of war. They will be informed of the proper time in which to send out their merchandise. From a national, the American trade is to be turned into a personal monopoly, and one set of merchants are to be rewarded for the pretended zeal of which another set are the dupes; and thus, between craft and credulity, the voice of reason is stifled, and all the misconduct, all the calamities of the war are covered and continued.

If I had not lived long enough to be little surprised at anything, I should have been in some degree astonished at the continued rage of several gentlemen, who, not satisfied with carrying fire and sword into America, are animated nearly with the same fury against those neighbours of theirs whose only crime it is, that they have charitably and humanely wished them to entertain more reasonable sentiments, and not always to sacrifice their interest to their passion. All this rage against unresisting dissent convinces me, that, at bottom, they are far from satisfied they are in the right. For what is it they would have? A war? They certainly have at this moment the blessing of something that is very like one; and if the war they enjoy at present be not sufficiently hot and extensive, they may shortly have it as warm and as spreading as their hearts can desire. Is it the force of the kingdom they call for? They have it already; and if they choose to fight their battles in their own person, nobody prevents their setting sail to America in the next transports. Do they think that the service is stinted for want of liberal supplies? Indeed they complain without reason. The table of the House of Commons will glut them, let their appetite for expense be never so keen. And I assure them further, that

those who think with them in the House of Commons are full as easy
in the control as they are liberal in the vote of these expenses. If this be
not supply or confidence sufficient, let them open their own private purse-
strings, and give, from what is left to them, as largely and with as little
care as they think proper.

Tolerated in their passions, let them learn not to persecute the moderation of their fellow-citizens. If all the world joined them in a full cry
against rebellion, and were as hotly inflamed against the whole theory
and enjoyment of freedom as those who are the most factious for servitude, it could not, in my opinion, answer any one end whatsoever in this
contest. The leaders of this war could not hire (to gratify their friends)
one German more than they do, or inspire him with less feeling for the
persons or less value for the privileges of their revolted brethren. If we
all adopted their sentiments to a man, their allies, the savage Indians,
could not be more ferocious than they are: they could not murder one
more helpless woman or child, or with more exquisite refinements of
cruelty torment to death one more of their English flesh and blood, than
they do already. The public money is given to purchase this alliance;
and they have their bargain.

They are continually boasting of unanimity, or calling for it. But before
this unanimity can be matter either of wish or congratulation, we ought
to be pretty sure that we are engaged in a rational pursuit. Frenzy does
not become a slighter distemper on account of the number of those who
may be infected with it. Delusion and weakness produce not one mischief the less because they are universal. I declare that I cannot discern
the least advantage which could accrue to us, if we were able to persuade
our colonies that they had not a single friend in Great Britain. On the
contrary, if the affections and opinions of mankind be not exploded as
principles of connection, I conceive it would be happy for us, if they
were taught to believe that there was even a formed American party in
England, to whom they could always look for support. Happy would it be
for us, if, in all tempers, they might turn their eyes to the parent state,
so that their very turbulence and sedition should find vent in no other
place than this! I believe there is not a man (except those who prefer
the interest of some paltry faction to the very being of their country) who
would not wish that the Americans should from time to time carry many
points, and even some of them not quite reasonable, by the aid of any
denomination of men here, rather than they should be driven to seek for
protection against the fury of foreign mercenaries and the waste of savages in the arms of France.

When any community is subordinately connected with another, the great danger of the connection is the extreme pride and self-complacency of the superior, which in all matters of controversy will probably decide in its own favour. It is a powerful corrective to such a very rational cause of fear, if the inferior body can be made to believe that the party inclination or political views of several in the principal state will induce them in some degree to counteract this blind and tyrannical partiality. There is no danger that any one acquiring consideration or power in the presiding state should carry this leaning to the inferior too far. The fault of human nature is not of that sort. Power, in whatever hands, is rarely guilty of too strict limitations on itself. But one great advantage to the support of authority attends such an amicable and protecting connection: that those who have conferred favours obtain influence, and from the foresight of future events can persuade men who have received obligations sometimes to return them. Thus, by the mediation of those healing principles (call them good or evil), troublesome discussions are brought to some sort of adjustment, and every hot controversy is not a civil war.

But, if the colonies (to bring the general matter home to us) could see that in Great Britain the mass of the people is melted into its government, and that every dispute with the ministry must of necessity be always a quarrel with the nation, they can stand no longer in the equal and friendly relation of fellow-citizens to the subjects of this kingdom. Humble as this relation may appear to some, when it is once broken, a strong tie is dissolved. Other sort of connections will be sought. For there are very few in the world who will not prefer a useful ally to an insolent master.

Such discord has been the effect of the unanimity into which so many have of late been seduced or bullied, or into the appearance of which they have sunk through mere despair. They have been told that their dissent from violent measures is an encouragement to rebellion. Men of great presumption and little knowledge will hold a language which is contradicted by the whole course of history. General rebellions and revolts of a whole people never were encouraged, now or at any time. They are always provoked. But if this unheard-of doctrine of the encouragement of rebellion were true, if it were true that an assurance of the friendship of numbers in this country towards the colonies could become an encouragement to them to break off all connection with it, what is the inference? Does anybody seriously maintain, that, charged with my share of the public councils, I am obliged not to resist projects which I think mischievous, lest men who suffer should be encouraged to resist? The very tendency of such projects to produce rebellion is one of the chief reasons against them. Shall that reason not be given? Is it, then, a rule, that no man in this nation shall open his mouth in favour of the colonies, shall defend their rights, or complain of their sufferings—or when war finally breaks out, no man shall express his desires of peace? Has this been the law of our past, or is it to be the terms of our future connection? Even looking no further than ourselves, can it be true loyalty to any government, or true patriotism towards any country, to degrade their solemn councils into servile drawing-rooms, to flatter their pride and passions rather than to enlighten their reason, and to prevent them from being cautioned against violence lest others should be encouraged to resistance? By such acquiescence great kings and mighty nations have been undone; and if any are at this day in a perilous situation from rejecting truth and listening to flattery, it would rather become them to reform the errors under which they suffer than to reproach those who forewarned them of their danger.

But the rebels looked for assistance from this country. They did so, in the beginning of this controversy, most certainly; and they sought it by earnest supplications to government, which dignity rejected, and by a suspension of commerce, which the wealth of this nation enabled you to despise. When they found that neither prayers nor menaces had any sort of weight, but that a firm resolution was taken to reduce them to unconditional obedience by a military force, they came to the last extremity. Despairing of us, they trusted in themselves. Not strong enough themselves, they sought succour in France. In proportion as all encouragement here lessened, their distance from this country increased. The encouragement is over; the alienation is complete.

In order to produce this favourite unanimity in delusion, and to prevent all possibility of a return to our ancient happy concord, arguments for our continuance in this course are drawn from the wretched situation itself into which we have been betrayed. It is said, that, being at war with the colonies, whatever our sentiments might have been before, all ties between us are now dissolved, and all the policy we have left is to strengthen the hands of government to reduce them. On the principle of this argument, the more mischiefs we suffer from any administration, the more our trust in it is to be confirmed. Let them but once get us into a war, and then their power is safe, and an act of oblivion passed for all their misconduct.

But is it really true that government is always to be strengthened with the instruments of war, but never furnished with the means of peace? In former times, ministers, I allow, have been sometimes driven by the popular voice to assert by arms the national honour against foreign powers. But the wisdom of the nation has been far more clear, when those ministers have been compelled to consult its interests by treaty. We all know that the sense of the nation obliged the court of Charles the Second to abandon the Dutch War: a war, next to the present, the most impolitic which we ever carried on. The good people of England considered Holland as a sort of dependency on this kingdom; they dreaded to drive it to the protection or subject it to the power of France by their own inconsiderate hostility. They paid but little respect to the court jargon of that day; nor were they inflamed by the pretended rivalship of the Dutch in trade—by the massacre at Amboyna, acted on the stage to provoke the public vengeance—nor by declamations against the ingratitude of the United Provinces for the benefits England had conferred upon them in their infant state. They were not moved from their evident interest by all these arts; nor was it enough to tell them, they were at war, that they must go through with it, and that the cause of the dispute was lost in the consequences. The people of England were then, as they are now, called upon to make government strong. They thought it a great deal better to make it wise and honest.

When I was amongst my constituents at the last summer assizes, I remember that men of all descriptions did then express a very strong desire for peace, and no slight hopes of attaining it from the commission sent out by my Lord Howe. And it is not a little remarkable, that, in proportion as every person showed a zeal for the court measures, he was then earnest in circulating an opinion of the extent of the supposed powers of that commission. When I told them that Lord Howe had no powers to treat, or to promise satisfaction on any point whatsoever of the controversy, I was hardly credited, so strong and general was the desire of terminating this war by the method of accommodation. As far as I could discover, this was the temper then prevalent through the kingdom. The king's forces, it must be observed, had at that time been obliged to evacuate Boston. The superiority of the former campaign rested wholly with the colonists. If such powers of treaty were to be wished whilst success was very doubtful, how came they to be less so, since his Majesty's arms have been crowned with many considerable advantages? Have these successes induced us to alter our mind, as thinking the season of victory not the time for treating with honour or advantage? Whatever changes have happened in the national character, it can scarcely be our wish that terms of accommodation never should be proposed to our enemy, except when they must be attributed solely to our fears. It has happened, let me say unfortunately, that we read of his Majesty's commission for making peace, and his troops evacuating his last town in the Thirteen Colonies, at the same hour and in the same gazette. It was still more unfortunate that no commission went to America to settle the troubles there, until several months after an act had been passed to put the colonies out of the protection of this government, and to divide their trading property, without a possibility of restitution, as spoil among the seamen of the navy. The most abject submission on the part of the colonies could not redeem them. There was no man on that whole continent, or within three thousand miles of it, qualified by law to follow allegiance with protection or submission with pardon. A proceeding of this kind has no example in history. Independency, and independency with an enmity (which, putting ourselves out of the question, would be called natural and much provoked), was the inevitable consequence. How this came to pass the nation may be one day in a humour to inquire.

All the attempts made this session to give fuller powers of peace to the commanders in America were stifled by the fatal confidence of victory and the wild hopes of unconditional submission. There was a moment favourable to the king's arms, when, if any powers of concession had existed on the other side of the Atlantic, even after all our errors, peace in all probability might have been restored. But calamity is unhappily the usual season of reflection; and the pride of men will not often suffer reason to have any scope, until it can be no longer of service.

I have always wished, that as the dispute had its apparent origin from things done in Parliament, and as the acts passed there had provoked the war, that the foundations of peace should be laid in Parliament also. I have been astonished to find that those whose zeal for the dignity of our body was so hot as to light up the flames of civil war should even publicly declare that these delicate points ought to be wholly left to the crown. Poorly as I may be thought affected to the authority of Parliament, I shall never admit that our constitutional rights can ever become a matter of ministerial negotiation.

I am charged with being an American. If warm affection towards those over whom I claim any share of authority be a crime, I am guilty of this charge. But I do assure you (and they who know me publicly and privately will bear witness to me) that if ever one man lived more zealous than another for the supremacy of Parliament and the rights of this imperial crown, it was myself. Many others, indeed, might be more knowing in the extent of the foundation of these rights. I do not pretend to be an antiquary, a lawyer, or qualified for the chair of professor in metaphysics. I never ventured to put your solid interests upon speculative grounds. My having constantly declined to do so has been attributed to my incapacity for such disquisitions; and I am inclined to believe it is partly the cause. I never shall be ashamed to confess, that, where I am ignorant, I am diffident. I am, indeed, not very solicitous to clear myself of this imputed incapacity; because men even less conversant than I am in this kind of subtleties, and placed in stations to which I ought not to aspire, have, by the mere force of civil discretion, often conducted the affairs of great nations with distinguished felicity and glory.

When I first came into a public trust, I found your Parliament in possession of an unlimited legislative power over the colonies. I could not open the statute-book without seeing the actual exercise of it, more or less, in all cases whatsoever. This possession passed with me for a title. It does so in all human affairs. No man examines into the defects of his title to his paternal estate or to his established government. Indeed, common sense taught me that a legislative authority not actually limited by the express terms of its foundation, or by its own subsequent acts, cannot have its powers parcelled out by argumentative distinctions, so as to enable us to say that here they can and there they cannot bind. Nobody was so obliging as to produce to me any record of such distinctions, by compact or otherwise, either at the successive formation of the several colonies or during the existence of any of them. If any gentlemen were able to see how one power could be given up (merely on abstract reasoning) without giving up the rest, I can only say that they saw further than I could. Nor did I ever presume to condemn any one for being clear-sighted when I was blind. I praise their penetration and learning, and hope that their practice has been correspondent to their theory.

I had, indeed, very earnest wishes to keep the whole body of this authority perfect and entire as I found it, and to keep it so, not for our advantage solely, but principally for the sake of those on whose account all just authority exists: I mean the people to be governed. For I thought I saw that many cases might well happen in which the exercise of every power comprehended in the broadest idea of legislature might become, in its time and circumstances, not a little expedient for the peace and union of the colonies amongst themselves, as well as for their perfect harmony with Great Britain. Thinking so (perhaps erroneously, but being honestly of that opinion), I was at the same time very sure that the authority of which I was so jealous could not, under the actual circumstances of our plantations, be at all preserved in any of its members, but by the greatest reserve in its application, particularly in those delicate points in which the feelings of mankind are the most irritable. They who

thought otherwise have found a few more difficulties in their work than
(I hope) they were thoroughly aware of, when they undertook the present business. I must beg leave to observe, that it is not only the invidious
branch of taxation that will be resisted, but that no other given part of
legislative rights can be exercised, without regard to the general opinion
of those who are to be governed. That general opinion is the vehicle and
organ of legislative omnipotence. Without this, it may be a theory to entertain the mind, but it is nothing in the direction of affairs. The completeness of the legislative authority of Parliament over this kingdom is
not questioned; and yet many things indubitably included in the abstract
idea of that power, and which carry no absolute injustice in themselves,
yet being contrary to the opinions and feelings of the people, can as little
be exercised as if Parliament in that case had been possessed of no right
at all. I see no abstract reason, which can be given, why the same power
which made and repealed the High Commission Court and the Star-
chamber might not revive them again; and these courts, warned by their
former fate, might possibly exercise their powers with some degree of justice. But the madness would be as unquestionable as the competence of
that Parliament which should attempt such things. If anything can be
supposed out of the power of human legislature, it is religion; I admit,
however, that the established religion of this country has been three or
four times altered by act of Parliament, and therefore that a statute binds
even in that case. But we may very safely affirm, that, notwithstanding
this apparent omnipotence, it would be now found as impossible for King
and Parliament to alter the established religion of this country as it was
to King James alone, when he attempted to make such an alteration without a Parliament. In effect, to follow, not to force, the public inclination,
to give a direction, a form, a technical dress, and a specific sanction, to
the general sense of the community, is the true end of legislature.

It is so with regard to the exercise of all the powers which our Constitution knows in any of its parts, and indeed to the substantial existence of
any of the parts themselves. The king's negative to bills is one of the most
indisputed of the royal prerogatives; and it extends to all cases whatsoever. I am far from certain, that if several laws, which I know, had fallen
under the stroke of that sceptre, that the public would have had a very
heavy loss. But it is not the propriety of the exercise which is in question.
The exercise itself is wisely forborne. Its repose may be the preservation
of its existence; and its existence may be the means of saving the Constitution itself, on an occasion worthy of bringing it forth.

As the disputants whose accurate and logical reasonings have brought us into our present condition think it absurd that powers or members of any constitution should exist, rarely, if ever, to be exercised, I hope I shall be excused in mentioning another instance that is material. We know that the Convocation of the Clergy had formerly been called, and sat with nearly as much regularity to business as Parliament itself. It is now called for form only. It sits for the purpose of making some polite ecclesiastical compliments to the king, and, when that grace is said, retires and is heard of no more. It is, however, a part of the Constitution, and may be called out into act and energy, whenever there is occasion, and whenever those who conjure up that spirit will choose to abide the consequences. It is wise to permit its legal existence: it is much wiser to continue it a legal existence only. So truly has prudence (constituted as the god of this lower world) the entire dominion over every exercise of power committed into its hands! And yet I have lived to see prudence and conformity to circumstances wholly set at nought in our late controversies, and treated as if they were the most contemptible and irrational of all things. I have heard it a hundred times very gravely alleged, that, in order to keep power in wind, it was necessary, by preference, to exert it in those very points in which it was most likely to be resisted and the least likely to be productive of any advantage.

These were the considerations, Gentlemen, which led me early to think, that, in the comprehensive dominion which the Divine Providence had put into our hands, instead of troubling our understandings with speculations concerning the unity of empire and the identity or distinction of legislative powers, and inflaming our passions with the heat and pride of controversy, it was our duty, in all soberness, to conform our government to the character and circumstances of the several people who composed this mighty and strangely diversified mass. I never was wild enough to conceive that one method would serve for the whole, that the natives of Hindostan and those of Virginia could be ordered in the same manner, or that the cutchery court and the grand jury of Salem could be regulated on a similar plan. I was persuaded that government was a practical thing, made for the happiness of mankind, and not to furnish out a spectacle of uniformity to gratify the schemes of visionary politicians. Our business was to rule, not to wrangle; and it would have been a poor compensation that we had triumphed in a dispute, whilst we lost an empire.

If there be one fact in the world perfectly clear, it is this, "that the disposition of the people of America is wholly averse to any other than a free government"; and this is indication enough to any honest statesman how he ought to adapt whatever power he finds in his hands to their case. If any ask me what a free government is, I answer, that, for any practical purpose, it is what the people think so, and that they, and not I, are the natural, lawful, and competent judges of this matter. If they practically allow me a greater degree of authority over them than is consistent with any correct ideas of perfect freedom, I ought to thank them for so great a trust, and not to endeavour to prove from thence that they have reasoned amiss, and that, having gone so far, by analogy they must hereafter have no enjoyment but by my pleasure.

If we had seen this done by any others, we should have concluded them far gone in madness. It is melancholy, as well as ridiculous, to observe the kind of reasoning with which the public has been amused, in order to divert our minds from the common sense of our American policy. There are people who have split and anatomized the doctrine of free government, as if it were an abstract question concerning metaphysical liberty and necessity, and not a matter of moral prudence and natural feeling. They have disputed whether liberty be a positive or a negative idea; whether it does not consist in being governed by laws, without considering what are the laws, or who are the makers; whether man has any rights by Nature; and whether all the property he enjoys be not the alms of his government, and his life itself their favour and indulgence. Others, corrupting religion as these have perverted philosophy, contend that Christians are redeemed into captivity, and the blood of the Saviour of mankind has been shed to make them the slaves of a few proud and insolent sinners. These shocking extremes provoking to extremes of another kind, speculations are let loose as destructive to all authority as the former are to all freedom; and every government is called tyranny and usurpation which is not formed on their fancies. In this manner the stirrers-up of this contention, not satisfied with distracting our dependencies and filling them with blood and slaughter, are corrupting our understandings: they are endeavouring to tear up, along with practical liberty, all the foundations of human society, all equity and justice, religion and order.

Civil freedom, Gentlemen, is not, as many have endeavoured to persuade you, a thing that lies hid in the depth of abstruse science. It is a blessing and a benefit, not an abstract speculation; and all the just reasoning that can be upon it is of so coarse a texture as perfectly to suit the ordinary capacities of those who are to enjoy, and of those who are to defend it. Far from any resemblance to those propositions in geometry and metaphysics which admit no medium, but must be true or false in all their latitude, social and civil freedom, like all other things in common life, are variously mixed and modified, enjoyed in very different degrees, and shaped into an infinite diversity of forms, according to the temper and circumstances of every community. The extreme of liberty (which is its abstract perfection, but its real fault) obtains nowhere, nor ought to obtain anywhere; because extremes, as we all know, in every point which relates either to our duties or satisfactions in life, are destructive both to virtue and enjoyment. Liberty, too, must be limited in order to be possessed. The degree of restraint it is impossible in any case to settle precisely. But it ought to be the constant aim of every wise public counsel to find out by cautious experiments, and rational, cool endeavours, with how little, not how much, of this restraint the community can subsist: for liberty is a good to be improved, and not an evil to be lessened. It is not only a private blessing of the first order, but the vital spring and energy of the state itself, which has just so much life and vigour as there is liberty in it. But whether liberty be advantageous or not (for I know it is a fashion to decry the very principle), none will dispute that peace is a blessing; and peace must, in the course of human affairs, be frequently bought by some indulgence and toleration at least to liberty: for, as the Sabbath (though of divine institution) was made for man, not man for the Sabbath, government, which can claim no higher origin or authority, in its exercise at least, ought to conform to the exigencies of the time, and the temper and character of the people with whom it is concerned, and not always to attempt violently to bend the people to their theories of subjection. The bulk of mankind, on their part, are not excessively curious concerning any theories whilst they are really happy; and one sure symptom of an ill-conducted state is the propensity of the people to resort to them.

But when subjects, by a long course of such ill conduct, are once thoroughly inflamed, and the state itself violently distempered, the people must have some satisfaction to their feelings more solid than a sophistical speculation on law and government. Such was our situation: and such a satisfaction was necessary to prevent recourse to arms; it was necessary towards laying them down; it will be necessary to prevent the taking them up again and again. Of what nature this satisfaction ought to be I wish it had been the disposition of Parliament seriously to consider. It was certainly a deliberation that called for the exertion of all their wisdom.

I am, and ever have been, deeply sensible of the difficulty of reconciling the strong presiding power, that is so useful towards the conservation of a vast, disconnected, infinitely diversified empire, with that liberty and safety of the provinces which they must enjoy (in opinion and practice at least), or they will not be provinces at all. I know, and have long felt, the difficulty of reconciling the unwieldy haughtiness of a great ruling nation, habituated to command, pampered by enormous wealth, and confident from a long course of prosperity and victory, to the high spirit of free dependencies, animated with the first glow and activity of juvenile heat, and assuming to themselves, as their birthright, some part of that very pride which oppresses them. They who perceive no difficulty in reconciling these tempers (which, however, to make peace, must some way or other be reconciled) are much above my capacity, or much below the magnitude of the business. Of one thing I am perfectly clear: that it is not by deciding the suit, but by compromising the difference, that peace can be restored or kept. They who would put an end to such quarrels by declaring roundly in favour of the whole demands of either party have mistaken, in my humble opinion, the office of a mediator.

The war is now of full two years' standing: the controversy of many more. In different periods of the dispute, different methods of reconciliation were to be pursued. I mean to trouble you with a short state of things at the most important of these periods, in order to give you a more distinct idea of our policy with regard to this most delicate of all objects. The colonies were from the beginning subject to the legislature of Great Britain on principles which they never examined; and we permitted to them many local privileges, without asking how they agreed with that legislative authority. Modes of administration were formed in an insensible and very unsystematic manner. But they gradually adapted themselves to the varying condition of things. What was first a single kingdom stretched into an empire; and an imperial superintendency, of some kind or other, became necessary. Parliament, from a mere representative of the people, and a guardian of popular privileges for its own immediate constituents, grew into a mighty sovereign. Instead of being a control on the crown on its own behalf, it communicated a sort of strength to the royal authority, which was wanted for the conservation of a new object, but which could not be safely trusted to the crown alone. On the other hand, the colonies, advancing by equal steps, and governed by the same necessity, had formed within themselves, either by royal instruction or royal charter, assemblies so exceedingly resembling a parliament, in all their forms, functions, and powers, that it was impossible they should not imbibe some opinion of a similar authority.

At the first designation of these assemblies, they were probably not intended for anything more (nor perhaps did they think themselves much higher) than the municipal corporations within this island, to which some at present love to compare them. But nothing in progression can rest on its original plan. We may as well think of rocking a grown man in the cradle of an infant. Therefore, as the colonies prospered and increased to a numerous and mighty people, spreading over a very great tract of the globe, it was natural that they should attribute to assemblies so respectable in their formal constitution some part of the dignity of the great nations which they represented. No longer tied to by-laws, these assemblies made acts of all sorts and in all cases whatsoever. They levied money, not for parochial purposes, but upon regular grants to the crown, following all the rules and principles of a parliament, to which they approached every day more and more nearly. Those who think themselves wiser than Providence and stronger than the course of Nature may complain of all this variation, on the one side or the other, as their several humours and prejudices may lead them. But things could not be otherwise; and English colonies must be had on these terms, or not had at all. In the mean time neither party felt any inconvenience from this double legislature, to which they had been formed by imperceptible habits, and old custom, the great support of all the governments in the world. Though these two legislatures were sometimes found perhaps performing the very same functions, they did not very grossly or systematically clash. In all likelihood this arose from mere neglect, possibly from the natural operation of things, which, left to themselves, generally fall into their proper order. But whatever was the cause, it is certain that a regular revenue, by the authority of Parliament, for the support of civil and military establishments, seems not to have been thought of until the colonies were too proud to submit, too strong to be forced, too enlightened not to see all the consequences which must arise from such a system.

If ever this scheme of taxation was to be pushed against the inclinations of the people, it was evident that discussions must arise, which would let loose all the elements that composed this double constitution, would show how much each of their members had departed from its original principles, and would discover contradictions in each legislature, as well to its own first principles as to its relation to the other, very difficult, if not absolutely impossible, to be reconciled.

Therefore, at the first fatal opening of this contest, the wisest course seemed to be to put an end as soon as possible to the immediate causes of the dispute, and to quiet a discussion, not easily settled upon clear principles, and arising from claims which pride would permit neither party to abandon, by resorting as nearly as possible to the old, successful course. A mere repeal of the obnoxious tax, with a declaration of the legislative authority of this kingdom, was then fully sufficient to procure peace to both sides. Man is a creature of habit, and, the first breach being of very short continuance, the colonies fell back exactly into their ancient state. The Congress has used an expression with regard to this pacification which appears to me truly significant. After the repeal of the Stamp Act, "the colonies fell," says this assembly, "into their ancient state of unsuspecting confidence in the mother country." This unsuspecting confidence is the true centre of gravity amongst mankind, about which all the parts are at rest. It is this unsuspecting confidence that removes all difficulties, and reconciles all the contradictions which occur in the complexity of all ancient puzzled political establishments. Happy are the rulers which have the secret of preserving it!

The whole empire has reason to remember with eternal gratitude the wisdom and temper of that man and his excellent associates, who, to recover this confidence, formed a plan of pacification in 1766. That plan, being built upon the nature of man, and the circumstances and habits of the two countries, and not on any visionary speculations, perfectly answered its end, as long as it was thought proper to adhere to it. Without giving a rude shock to the dignity (well or ill understood) of this Parliament, they gave perfect content to our dependencies. Had it not been for the mediatorial spirit and talents of that great man between such clashing pretensions and passions, we should then have rushed headlong (I know what I say) into the calamities of that civil war in which, by departing from his system, we are at length involved; and we should have been precipitated into that war at a time when circumstances both at home and abroad were far, very far, more unfavourable unto us than they were at the breaking out of the present troubles.

I had the happiness of giving my first votes in Parliament for that pacification. I was one of those almost unanimous members who, in the necessary concessions of Parliament, would as much as possible have preserved its authority and respected its honour. I could not at once tear from my heart prejudices which were dear to me, and which bore a resemblance to virtue. I had then, and I have still, my partialities. What Parliament gave up I wished to be given as of grace and favour and affection, and not as a restitution of stolen goods. High dignity relented as it was soothed; and a benignity from old acknowledged greatness had its full effect on our dependencies. Our unlimited declaration of legislative authority produced not a single murmur. If this undefined power has become odious since that time, and full of horror to the colonies, it is because the unsuspicious confidence is lost, and the parental affection, in the bosom of whose boundless authority they reposed their privileges, is become estranged and hostile.

It will be asked, if such was then my opinion of the mode of pacification, how I came to be the very person who moved, not only for a repeal of all the late coercive statutes, but for mutilating, by a positive law, the entireness of the legislative power of Parliament, and cutting off from it the whole right of taxation. I answer, Because a different state of things requires a different conduct. When the dispute had gone to these last extremities (which no man laboured more to prevent than I did), the concessions which had satisfied in the beginning could satisfy no longer; because the violation of tacit faith required explicit security. The same cause which has introduced all formal compacts and covenants among men made it necessary: I mean habits of soreness, jealousy, and distrust. I parted with it as with a limb, but as a limb to save the body: and I would have parted with more, if more had been necessary; anything rather than a fruitless, hopeless, unnatural civil war. This mode of yielding would, it is said, give way to independency without a war. I am persuaded, from the nature of things, and from every information, that it would have had a directly contrary effect. But if it had this effect, I confess that I should prefer independency without war to independency with it; and I have so much trust in the inclinations and prejudices of mankind, and so little in anything else, that I should expect ten times more benefit to this kingdom from the affection of America, though under a separate establishment, than from her perfect submission to the crown and Parliament, accompanied with her terror, disgust, and abhorrence. Bodies tied together by so unnatural a bond of union as mutual hatred are only connected to their ruin.

One hundred and ten respectable members of Parliament voted for that concession. Many not present when the motion was made were of the sentiments of those who voted. I knew it would then have made peace. I am not without hopes that it would do so at present, if it were adopted. No benefit, no revenue, could be lost by it; something might possibly be gained by its consequences. For be fully assured, that, of all the phantoms that ever deluded the fond hopes of a credulous world, a Parliamentary revenue in the colonies is the most perfectly chimerical. Your breaking them to any subjection, far from relieving your burdens (the pretext for this war), will never pay that military force which will be kept up to the destruction of their liberties and yours. I risk nothing in this prophecy.

Gentlemen, you have my opinions on the present state of public affairs. Mean as they may be in themselves, your partiality has made them of some importance. Without troubling myself to inquire whether I am under a formal obligation to it, I have a pleasure in accounting for my conduct to my constituents. I feel warmly on this subject, and I express myself as I feel. If I presume to blame any public proceeding, I cannot be supposed to be personal. Would to God I could be suspected of it! My fault might be greater, but the public calamity would be less extensive. If my conduct has not been able to make any impression on the warm part of that ancient and powerful party with whose support I was not honoured at my election, on my side, my respect, regard, and duty to them is not at all lessened. I owe the gentlemen who compose it my most humble service in everything. I hope that whenever any of them were pleased to command me, that they found me perfectly equal in my obedience. But flattery and friendship are very different things; and to mislead is not to serve them. I cannot purchase the favour of any man by concealing from him what I think his ruin.

By the favour of my fellow-citizens, I am the representative of an honest, well-ordered, virtuous city, of a people who preserve more of the original English simplicity and purity of manners than perhaps any other. You possess among you several men and magistrates of large and cultivated understandings, fit for any employment in any sphere. I do, to the best of my power, act so as to make myself worthy of so honourable a choice. If I were ready, on any call of my own vanity or interest, or to answer any election purpose, to forsake principles (whatever they are) which I had formed at a mature age, on full reflection, and which had been confirmed by long experience, I should forfeit the only thing which makes you pardon so many errors and imperfections in me.

Not that I think it fit for any one to rely too much on his own understanding, or to be filled with a presumption not becoming a Christian man in his own personal stability and rectitude. I hope I am far from that vain confidence which almost always fails in trial. I know my weakness in all respects, as much at least as any enemy I have; and I attempt to take security against it. The only method which has ever been found effectual to preserve any man against the corruption of nature and example is a habit of life and communication of councils with the most virtuous and public-spirited men of the age you live in. Such a society cannot be kept without advantage, or deserted without shame. For this rule of conduct I may be called in reproach a party man; but I am little affected with such aspersions. In the way which they call party I worship the Constitution of your fathers; and I shall never blush for my political company. All reverence to honour, all idea of what it is, will be lost out of the world, before it can be imputed as a fault to any man, that he has been closely connected with those incomparable persons, living and dead, with whom for eleven years I have constantly thought and acted. If I have wandered out of the paths of rectitude into those of interested faction, it was in company with the Saviles, the Dowdeswells, the Wentworths, the Bentincks; with the Lenoxes, the Manchesters, the Keppels, the Saunderses; with the temperate, permanent, hereditary virtue of the whole house of Cavendish: names, among which, some have extended your fame and empire in arms, and all have fought the battle of your liberties in fields not less glorious. These, and many more like these, grafting public principles on private honour, have redeemed the present age, and would have adorned the most splendid period in your history. Where could any man, conscious of his own inability to act alone, and willing to act as he ought to do, have arranged himself better? If any one thinks this kind of society to be taken up as the best method of gratifying low personal pride or ambitious interest, he is mistaken, and knows nothing of the world.

Preferring this connection, I do not mean to detract in the slightest degree from others. There are some of those whom I admire at something of a greater distance, with whom I have had the happiness also perfectly to agree, in almost all the particulars in which I have differed with some successive administrations; and they are such as it never can be reputable to any government to reckon among its enemies.

I hope there are none of you corrupted with the doctrine taught by wicked men for the worst purposes, and received by the malignant credulity of envy and ignorance, which is, that the men who act upon the public stage are all alike, all equally corrupt, all influenced by no other views than the sordid lure of salary and pension. The thing I know by experience to be false. Never expecting to find perfection in men, and not looking for divine attributes in created beings, in my commerce with my contemporaries I have found much human virtue. I have seen not a little public spirit, a real subordination of interest to duty, and a decent and regulated sensibility to honest fame and reputation. The age unquestionably produces (whether in a greater or less number than former times I know not) daring profligates and insidious hypocrites. What then? Am I not to avail myself of whatever good is to be found in the world, because of the mixture of evil that will always be in it? The smallness of the quantity in currency only heightens the value. They who raise suspicions on the good on account of the behaviour of ill men are of the party of the latter. The common cant is no justification for taking this party. I have been deceived, say they, by Titius and Maevius; I have been the dupe of this pretender or of that mountebank; and I can trust appearances no longer. But my credulity and want of discernment cannot, as I conceive, amount to a fair presumption against any man's integrity. A conscientious person would rather doubt his own judgment than condemn his species. He would say, "I have observed without attention, or judged upon erroneous maxims; I trusted to profession, when I ought to have attended to conduct." Such a man will grow wise, not malignant, by his acquaintance with the world. But he that accuses all mankind of corruption ought to remember that he is sure to convict only one. In truth, I should much rather admit those whom at any time I have disrelished the most to be patterns of perfection than seek a consolation to my own unworthiness in a general communion of depravity with all about me.

That this ill-natured doctrine should be preached by the missionaries of a court I do not wonder. It answers their purpose. But that it should be heard among those who pretend to be strong assertors of liberty is not only surprising, but hardly natural. This moral levelling is a servile principle. It leads to practical passive obedience far better than all the doctrines which the pliant accommodation of theology to power has ever produced. It cuts up by the roots, not only all idea of forcible resistance, but even of civil opposition. It disposes men to an abject submission, not by opinion, which may be shaken by argument or altered by passion, but by the strong ties of public and private interest. For, if all men who act in a public situation are equally selfish, corrupt, and venal, what reason can be given for desiring any sort of change, which, besides the evils which must attend all changes, can be productive of no possible advantage? The active men in the state are true samples of the mass. If they are universally depraved, the commonwealth itself is not sound. We may amuse ourselves with talking as much as we please of the virtue of middle or humble life; that is, we may place our confidence in the virtue of those who have never been tried. But if the persons who are continually emerging out of that sphere be no better than those whom birth has placed above it, what hopes are there in the remainder of the body which is to furnish the perpetual succession of the state? All who have ever written on government are unanimous, that among a people generally corrupt liberty cannot long exist. And, indeed, how is it possible, when those who are to make the laws, to guard, to enforce, or to obey them, are, by a tacit confederacy of manners, indisposed to the spirit of all generous and noble institutions?

I am aware that the age is not what we all wish. But I am sure that the only means of checking its precipitate degeneracy is heartily to concur with whatever is the best in our time, and to have some more correct standard of judging what that best is than the transient and uncertain favour of a court. If once we are able to find, and can prevail on ourselves to strengthen a union of such men, whatever accidentally becomes indisposed to ill-exercised power, even by the ordinary operation of human passions, must join with that society, and cannot long be joined without in some degree assimilating to it. Virtue will catch as well as vice by contact; and the public stock of honest, manly principle will daily accumulate. We are not too nicely to scrutinize motives as long as action is irreproachable. It is enough (and for a worthy man perhaps too much) to deal out its infamy to convicted guilt and declared apostasy.

This, Gentlemen, has been from the beginning the rule of my conduct; and I mean to continue it, as long as such a body as I have described can by any possibility be kept together; for I should think it the most dreadful of all offences, not only towards the present generation, but to all the future, if I were to do anything which could make the minutest breach in this great conservatory of free principles. Those who perhaps have the same intentions, but are separated by some little political animosities, will, I hope, discern at last how little conducive it is to any rational purpose to lower its reputation. For my part, Gentlemen, from much experience, from no little thinking, and from comparing a great variety of things, I am thoroughly persuaded that the last hopes of preserving the spirit of the English Constitution, or of reuniting the dissipated members of the English race upon a common plan of tranquillity and liberty, does entirely depend on their firm and lasting union, and above all on their keeping themselves from that despair which is so very apt to fall on those whom a violence of character and a mixture of ambitious views do not support through a long, painful, and unsuccessful struggle.

There never, Gentlemen, was a period in which the steadfastness of some men has been put to so sore a trial. It is not very difficult for well-formed minds to abandon their interest; but the separation of fame and virtue is a harsh divorce. Liberty is in danger of being made unpopular to Englishmen. Contending for an imaginary power, we begin to acquire the spirit of domination, and to lose the relish of honest equality. The principles of our forefathers become suspected to us, because we see them animating the present opposition of our children. The faults which grow out of the luxuriance of freedom appear much more shocking to us than the base vices which are generated from the rankness of servitude.

Accordingly, the least resistance to power appears more inexcusable in our eyes than the greatest abuses of authority. All dread of a standing military force is looked upon as a superstitious panic. All shame of calling in foreigners and savages in a civil contest is worn off. We grow indifferent to the consequences inevitable to ourselves from the plan of ruling half the empire by a mercenary sword. We are taught to believe that a desire of domineering over our countrymen is love to our country, that those who hate civil war abet rebellion, and that the amiable and conciliatory virtues of lenity, moderation, and tenderness to the privileges of those who depend on this kingdom are a sort of treason to the state.

It is impossible that we should remain long in a situation which breeds such notions and dispositions without some great alteration in the national character. Those ingenuous and feeling minds who are so fortified against all other things, and so unarmed to whatever approaches in the shape of disgrace, finding these principles, which they considered as sure means of honour, to be grown into disrepute, will retire disheartened and disgusted. Those of a more robust make, the bold, able, ambitious men, who pay some of their court to power through the people, and substitute the voice of transient opinion in the place of true glory, will give into the general mode; and those superior understandings which ought to correct vulgar prejudice will confirm and aggravate its errors. Many things have been long operating towards a gradual change in our principles; but this American war has done more in a very few years than all the other causes could have effected in a century. It is therefore not on its own separate account, but because of its attendant circumstances, that I consider its continuance, or its ending in any way but that of an honourable and liberal accommodation, as the greatest evils which can befall us. For that reason I have troubled you with this long letter. For that reason I entreat you, again and again, neither to be persuaded, shamed, or frighted out of the principles that have hitherto led so many of you to abhor the war, its cause, and its consequences. Let us not be amongst the first who renounce the maxims of our forefathers.

> *I have the honour to be,*
>
> *Gentlemen,*
>
> *Your most obedient and faithful humble servant,*
>
> EDMUND BURKE.

Beaconsfield, April 3, 1777.

P. S.   You may communicate this letter in any manner you think proper to my constituents.

John C. Calhoun

1782–1850

Few American statesmen have had so illustrious a career as John C. Calhoun. From 1807 to 1852 he was (in succession) a state legislator, a United States Congressman, Secretary of War, Vice-President, Senator, Presidential candidate, and Secretary of State. He was also an astute political thinker. Some of his speeches and essays are generally considered to be the classic statements of the political position of the South prior to the Civil War.

Calhoun was born in the Abbeville district of South Carolina in 1782. Because he had little opportunity for education there, he was sent to live with his brother-in-law, a Presbyterian minister. In 1802 he entered Yale College as a junior. After being graduated from Yale, he went to the Litchfield Law School, in Connecticut, and by 1807 was a licensed lawyer. In 1808 he became a member of the South Carolina legislature.

Calhoun's national political career began in 1811, when he was elected to the U.S. House of Representatives. At first he was a fervent nationalist, but as the years passed he became more and more concerned about preserving the institutions of the South. Though he always insisted that his primary aim was to save the Union, he gradually came to be thought of as a sectionalist.

Calhoun was Secretary of War from 1817 to 1825, and he served

---

Notes from the artist: ". . . a stern portrait of Calhoun
with a war hawk on his shoulder, symbolizing the militancy
of his position on states' rights. At the left, Andrew Jackson,
Calhoun's antagonist in the federal-state argument. Jackson once
admitted that his only regret was not having hanged Calhoun."

J C Calhoun

as Vice-President under two Presidents, John Quincy Adams and Andrew Jackson. He resigned the Vice-Presidency in 1832 (the only man ever to do so) because of his opposition to certain government policies, particularly tariff policies.

In 1824 and 1828 Congress had passed tariff laws which were designed to protect northern industries but which proved to be harmful to the South. Calhoun maintained that the southern states had the right to declare those laws unconstitutional. He argued that since the states had entered into the federal union to secure certain benefits, they had the right to "nullify" those federal laws which were harmful to their interests. In advancing this argument, he advocated the "strict construction" of the Constitution. (According to the strict constitution theory, the federal government has only those powers *explicitly* granted to it by the Constitution.)

Shortly after his resignation from the Vice-Presidency, Calhoun was elected to the Senate from South Carolina. There he engaged in a debate on nullification with Daniel Webster. Webster's views eventually triumphed, and the nullification theory was rejected. During the remainder of his Senate career, Calhoun did his best to defend states' rights and the slavery system, but the movement of history was against him. In the election of 1844 he was temporarily a presidential candidate. He withdrew from the race and was appointed Secretary of State. In 1845 he was re-elected to the Senate, where he remained until a few days before his death in 1850.

Since the appearance of John Stuart Mill's essay *On Liberty*,[1] the phrase "tyranny of the majority" has become part of the common language of political discussion. But Mill was by no means the first to realize that the majority in a society might use its power to oppress the minority. John C. Calhoun had recognized this danger almost a generation earlier, and he had offered his remedy for it in "The Concurrent Majority."

Calhoun begins by attempting to prove, through an analysis of human nature, the necessity of government. He maintains that each individual's feeling for himself is stronger than his feeling for others, and that each individual is ready to sacrifice the interests of others in order to further his own. Government is necessary, therefore, to protect men from exploitation and oppression by others.

---

[1] See *Great Books of the Western World*, Vol. 43, pp. 267–323.

Following this preliminary analysis, Calhoun turns to the central question of his essay: if men pursue their own interests at the expense of others, and if governments are composed of men, how can we guarantee that the men who control the government will not use their power to oppress the governed? Calhoun thinks that the answer is some form of representative government—that is, a government whose leaders are chosen by the governed. But, according to Calhoun, representative government based upon a simple *numerical* majority is not a sufficient guarantee against oppression.

It is true that the ultimate power of government has been transferred from the government itself to the people who are governed, and that a government which acts against the interests of the majority cannot long survive. But what is to prevent a majority of the people from using the government to oppress a minority? Calhoun insists that there is nothing to prevent it, and that it can be prevented only by introducing the principle of the *concurrent* majority.

Calhoun's thinking was undoubtedly influenced by his conviction that the interests of the South were slowly being undermined by a government controlled by the North and the West. The adoption of the principle of the concurrent majority, which in effect gives veto power to minorities, would have protected the South—at least temporarily. Whether such protection was desirable is still very much a disputed matter. But whatever our views concerning the Old South and its institutions, we must not underestimate the importance of the issue raised by Calhoun. How are we to prevent a representative democracy from turning into a "tyranny of the majority"? Perhaps, as Calhoun says, it can be prevented only by the application of some form of the principle of the concurrent majority.

The Concurrent Majority
from *A Disquisition on Government*

I n order to have a clear and just conception of the nature and object of government, it is indispensable to understand correctly what that constitution or law of our nature is in which government originates; or, to express it more fully and accurately, that law without which government would not, and with which it must necessarily, exist. Without this, it is as impossible to lay any solid foundation for the science of government as it would be to lay one for that of astronomy without a like understanding of that constitution or law of the material world according to which the several bodies composing the solar system mutually act on each other and by which they are kept in their respective spheres. The first question, accordingly, to be considered is: What is that constitution or law of our nature without which government would not exist and with which its existence is necessary?

In considering this, I assume, as an incontestable fact, that man is so constituted as to be a social being. His inclinations and wants, physical and moral, irresistibly impel him to associate with his kind; and he has, accordingly, never been found, in any age or country, in any state other than the social. In no other, indeed, could he exist; and in no other— were it possible for him to exist—could he attain to a full development of his moral and intellectual faculties or raise himself, in the scale of being, much above the level of the brute creation.

I next assume, also, as a fact not less incontestable, that, while man is so constituted as to make the social state necessary to his existence and the full development of his faculties, this state itself cannot exist without government. The assumption rests on universal experience. In no age or country has any society or community ever been found, whether enlightened or savage, without government of some description.

Having assumed these, as unquestionable phenomena of our nature, I shall, without further remark, proceed to the investigation of the primary and important question: What is that constitution of our nature which, while it impels man to associate with his kind, renders it impossible for society to exist without government?

The answer will be found in the fact (not less incontestable than either of the others) that, while man is created for the social state, and is accordingly so formed as to feel what affects others as well as what affects himself, he is, at the same time, so constituted as to feel more intensely what affects him directly than what affects him indirectly through others; or, to express it differently, he is so constituted that his direct or individual affections are stronger than his sympathetic or social feelings. I intentionally avoid the expression "*selfish* feelings" as applicable to the former, because, as commonly used, it implies an unusual excess of the individual over the social feelings in the person to whom it is applied, and, consequently, something depraved and vicious. My object is to exclude such inference and to restrict the inquiry exclusively to facts in their bearings on the subject under consideration, viewed as mere phenomena appertaining to our nature—constituted as it is—and which are as unquestionable as is that of gravitation or any other phenomenon of the material world.

In asserting that our individual are stronger than our social feelings, it is not intended to deny that there are instances, growing out of peculiar relations—as that of a mother and her infant—or resulting from the force of education and habit over peculiar constitutions, in which the latter have overpowered the former; but these instances are few and always regarded as something extraordinary. The deep impression they make, whenever they occur, is the strongest proof that they are regarded as exceptions to some general and well-understood law of our nature, just as some of the minor powers of the material world are apparently to gravitation.

I might go further and assert this to be a phenomenon, not of our nature only, but of all animated existence, throughout its entire range, so far as our knowledge extends. It would, indeed, seem to be essentially connected with the great law of self-preservation which pervades all that feels, from man down to the lowest and most insignificant reptile or insect. In none is it stronger than in man. His social feelings may, indeed, in a state of safety and abundance, combined with high intellectual and moral culture, acquire great expansion and force; but not so great as to overpower this all-pervading and essential law of animated existence.

But that constitution of our nature which makes us feel more intensely what affects us directly than what affects us indirectly through others necessarily leads to conflict between individuals. Each, in consequence, has a greater regard for his own safety or happiness than for the safety or happiness of others and, where these come in opposition, is ready to sacrifice the interests of others to his own. And, hence, the tendency to a universal state of conflict between individual and individual, accompanied by the connected passions of suspicion, jealousy, anger, and revenge —followed by insolence, fraud, and cruelty—and, if not prevented by some controlling power, ending in a state of universal discord and confusion, destructive of the social state and the ends for which it is ordained. This controlling power, wherever vested, or by whomsoever exercised, is GOVERNMENT.

It follows, then, that man is so constituted that government is necessary to the existence of society, and society to his existence and the perfection of his faculties. It follows, also, that government has its origin in this twofold constitution of his nature: the sympathetic or social feelings constituting the remote, and the individual or direct, the proximate, cause.

If man had been differently constituted in either particular—if, instead of being social in his nature, he had been created without sympathy for his kind, and independent of others for his safety and existence; or if, on the other hand, he had been so created as to feel more intensely what affected others than what affected himself (if that were possible), or, even, had this supposed interest been equal—it is manifest that, in either case, there would have been no necessity for government and that none would ever have existed. But, although society and government are thus intimately connected with and dependent on each other—of the two society is the greater. It is the first in the order of things and in the dignity of its object: that of society being primary, to preserve and perfect our race; and that of government secondary and subordinate, to preserve and perfect society. Both are, however, necessary to the existence and well-being of our race and equally of divine ordination.

I have said if it were possible for man to be so constituted as to feel what affects others more strongly than what affects himself or even as strongly, because it may be well doubted whether the stronger feeling or affection of individuals for themselves, combined with a feebler and subordinate feeling or affection for others, is not, in beings of limited reason and faculties, a constitution necessary to their preservation and existence. If reversed—if their feelings and affections were stronger for others than for themselves, or even as strong—the necessary result would seem to be that all individuality would be lost, and boundless and remediless disorder and confusion would ensue. For each, at the same moment, intensely participating in all the conflicting emotions of those around him, would, of course, forget himself and all that concerned him immediately, in his officious intermeddling with the affairs of all others; which, from his limited reason and faculties, he could neither properly understand nor manage. Such a state of things would, as far as we can see, lead to endless disorder and confusion, not less destructive to our race than a state of anarchy. It would, besides, be remediless, for government would be impossible; or, if it could by possibility exist, its object would be reversed. Selfishness would have to be encouraged and benevolence discouraged. Individuals would have to be encouraged, by rewards, to become more selfish and deterred, by punishments, from being too benevolent; and this, too, by a government administered by those who, on the supposition, would have the greatest aversion for selfishness, and the highest admiration for benevolence.

To the Infinite Being, the Creator of all, belongs exclusively the care and superintendence of the whole. He, in His infinite wisdom and goodness, has allotted to every class of animated beings its condition and appropriate functions and has endowed each with feelings, instincts, capacities, and faculties best adapted to its allotted condition. To man He has assigned the social and political state as best adapted to develop the great capacities and faculties, intellectual and moral, with which He has endowed him and has, accordingly, constituted him so as not only to impel him into the social state but to make government necessary for his preservation and well-being.

But government, although intended to protect and preserve society, has itself a strong tendency to disorder and abuse of its powers, as all experience and almost every page of history testify. The cause is to be found in the same constitution of our nature which makes government indispensable. The powers which it is necessary for government to possess, in order to repress violence and preserve order, cannot execute themselves. They must be administered by men in whom, like others, the individual are stronger than the social feelings. And, hence, the powers vested in them to prevent injustice and oppression on the part of others will, if left unguarded, be by them converted into instruments to oppress the rest of the community. That by which this is prevented, by whatever name called, is what is meant by CONSTITUTION, in its most comprehensive sense, when applied to GOVERNMENT.

Having its origin in the same principle of our nature, *constitution* stands to *government* as *government* stands to *society*, and as the end for which society is ordained would be defeated without government, so that for which government is ordained would, in a great measure, be defeated without constitution. But they differ in this striking particular: There is no difficulty in forming government. It is not even a matter of choice whether there shall be one or not. Like breathing, it is not permitted to depend on our volition. Necessity will force it on all communities in some one form or another. Very different is the case as to constitution. Instead of a matter of necessity, it is one of the most difficult tasks imposed on man to form a constitution worthy of the name; while to form a perfect one—one that would completely counteract the tendency of government to oppression and abuse and hold it strictly to the great ends for which it is ordained—has thus far exceeded human wisdom and possibly ever will. From this another striking difference results. Constitution is the contrivance of man, while government is of divine ordination. Man is left to perfect what the wisdom of the Infinite ordained as necessary to preserve the race.

With these remarks, I proceed to the consideration of the important and difficult question: How is this tendency of government to be counteracted? Or, to express it more fully: How can those who are invested with the powers of government be prevented from employing them as the means of aggrandizing themselves instead of using them to protect and preserve society? It cannot be done by instituting a higher power to control the government and those who administer it. This would be but to change the seat of authority and to make this higher power, in reality, the government; with the same tendency, on the part of those who might control its powers, to pervert them into instruments of aggrandizement. Nor can it be done by limiting the powers of government, so as to make it too feeble to be made an instrument of abuse; for, passing by the difficulty of so limiting its powers, without creating a power higher than the government itself to enforce the observance of the limitations, it is a sufficient objection that it would, if practicable, defeat the end for which government is ordained, by making it too feeble to protect and preserve society. The powers necessary for this purpose will ever prove sufficient to aggrandize those who control it, at the expense of the rest of the community. . . .

In answering the important question under consideration, it is not necessary to enter into an examination of the various contrivances adopted by these celebrated governments to counteract this tendency to disorder and abuse, nor to undertake to treat of constitution in its most comprehensive sense. What I propose is far more limited—to explain on what principles government must be formed in order to resist, by its own interior structure—or, to use a single term, *organism*—the tendency to abuse of power. This structure, or organism, is what is meant by constitution in its strict and more usual sense; and it is this which distinguishes what are called constitutional governments from absolute. It is in this strict and more usual sense that I propose to use the term hereafter.

How government, then, must be constructed in order to counteract, through its organism, this tendency on the part of those who make and execute the laws to oppress those subject to their operation is the next question which claims attention.

There is but one way in which this can possibly be done, and that is by such an organism as will furnish the ruled with the means of resisting successfully this tendency on the part of the rulers to oppression and abuse. Power can only be resisted by power—and tendency by tendency. Those who exercise power and those subject to its exercise—the rulers and the ruled—stand in antagonistic relations to each other. The same constitution of our nature which leads rulers to oppress the ruled— regardless of the object for which government is ordained—will, with equal strength, lead the ruled to resist when possessed of the means of making peaceable and effective resistance. Such an organism, then, as will furnish the means by which resistance may be systematically and peaceably made on the part of the ruled to oppression and abuse of power on the part of the rulers is the first and indispensable step toward *forming* a constitutional government. And as this can only be effected by or through the right of suffrage (the right on the part of the ruled to choose their rulers at proper intervals, and to hold them thereby responsible for their conduct) the responsibility of the rulers to the ruled, through the right of suffrage, is the indispensable and primary principle in the *foundation* of a constitutional government. When this right is properly guarded, and the people sufficiently enlightened to understand their own rights and the interests of the community, and duly to appreciate the motives and conduct of those appointed to make and execute the laws, it is all sufficient to give to those who elect effective control over those they have elected.

I call the right of suffrage the indispensable and primary principle, for it would be a great and dangerous mistake to suppose, as many do, that it is of itself sufficient to form constitutional governments. To this erroneous opinion may be traced one of the causes why so few attempts to form constitutional governments have succeeded; and why, of the few which have, so small a number have had durable existence. It has led, not only to mistakes in the attempts to form such governments, but to their overthrow, when they have, by some good fortune, been correctly formed. So far from being of itself sufficient—however well guarded it might be, and however enlightened the people—it would, unaided by other provisions, leave the government as absolute as it would be in the hands of irresponsible rulers; and with a tendency, at least as strong, toward oppression and abuse of its powers, as I shall next proceed to explain.

The right of suffrage of itself can do no more than give complete control to those who elect over the conduct of those they have elected. In doing this, it accomplishes all it possibly can accomplish. This is its aim —and, when this is attained, its end is fulfilled. It can do no more, however enlightened the people, or however widely extended or well guarded the right may be. The sum total, then, of its effects, when most successful, is to make those elected the true and faithful representatives of those who elected them—instead of irresponsible rulers—as they would be without it; and thus, by converting it into an agency, and the rulers into agents, to divest government of all claims to sovereignty and to retain it unimpaired to the community. But it is manifest that the right of suffrage, in making these changes, transfers, in reality, the actual control over the government from those who make and execute the laws to the body of the community and thereby places the powers of the government as fully in the mass of the community as they would be if they, in fact, had assembled, made, and executed the laws themselves without the intervention of representatives or agents. The more perfectly it does this, the more perfectly it accomplishes its ends; but, in doing so, it only changes the seat of authority, without counteracting, in the least, the tendency of the government to oppression and abuse of its powers.

If the whole community had the same interests, so that the interest of each and every portion would be so affected by the action of the government that the laws which oppressed or impoverished one portion would necessarily oppress and impoverish all others—or the reverse—then the right of suffrage of itself would be all-sufficient to counteract the tendency of the government to oppression and abuse of its powers and, of course, would form of itself a perfect constitutional government. The interest of all being the same, by supposition, as far as the action of the government was concerned, all would have like interests as to what laws should be made and how they should be executed. All strife and struggle would cease as to who should be elected to make and execute them. The only question would be who was most fit; who the wisest and most capable of understanding the common interest of the whole. This decided, the election would pass off quietly and without party discord, as no one portion could advance its own peculiar interest without regard to the rest by electing a favorite candidate.

But such is not the case. On the contrary, nothing is more difficult than to equalize the action of the government in reference to the various and diversified interests of the community; and nothing more easy than to pervert its powers into instruments to aggrandize and enrich one or more interests by oppressing and impoverishing the others; and this too under the operation of laws couched in general terms—and which, on their face, appear fair and equal. Nor is this the case in some particular communities only. It is so in all; the small and the great, the poor and the rich, irrespective of pursuits, productions, or degrees of civilization— with, however, this difference: that the more extensive and populous the country, the more diversified the condition and pursuits of its population; and the richer, more luxurious, and dissimilar the people, the more difficult is it to equalize the action of the government and the more easy for one portion of the community to pervert its powers to oppress and plunder the other.

Such being the case, it necessarily results that the right of suffrage, by placing the control of the government in the community, must, from the same constitution of our nature which makes government necessary to preserve society, lead to conflict among its different interests—each striving to obtain possession of its powers, as the means of protecting itself against the others, or of advancing its respective interests, regardless of the interests of others. For this struggle, a struggle will take place between the various interests to obtain a majority in order to control the government. If no one interest be strong enough of itself to obtain it, a combination will be formed between those whose interests are most alike —each conceding something to the others, until a sufficient number is obtained to make a majority. The process may be slow, and much time may be required before a compact, organized majority can be thus formed; but formed it will be in time, even without preconcert or design, by the sure workings of that principle or constitution of our nature in which government itself originates. When once formed, the community will be divided into two great parties—a major and minor—between which there will be incessant struggles on the one side to retain and on the other to obtain the majority—and, thereby, the control of the government and the advantages it confers. . . .

As, then, the right of suffrage, without some other provision, cannot

counteract this tendency of government, the next question for consideration is: What is that other provision? This demands the most serious consideration, for, of all the questions embraced in the science of government, it involves a principle the most important and the least understood,
and, when understood, the most difficult of application in practice. It is,
indeed, emphatically, that principle which *makes* the constitution, in its
strict and limited sense.

From what has been said it is manifest that this provision must be of a
character calculated to prevent any one interest, or combination of interests, from using the powers of government to aggrandize itself at the
expense of the others. Here lies the evil; and just in proportion as it shall
prevent, or fail to prevent it, in the same degree it will effect, or fail to
effect, the end intended to be accomplished. There is but one certain
mode in which this result can be secured, and that is by the adoption of
some restriction or limitation which shall so effectually prevent any one
interest, or combination of interests, from obtaining the exclusive control
of the government as to render hopeless all attempts directed to that end.
There is, again, but one mode in which this can be affected, and that is
by taking the sense of each interest or portion of the community, which
may be unequally and injuriously affected by the action of the government, separately, through its own majority, or in some other way by
which its voice may be fairly expressed; and to require the consent of
each interest either to put or to keep the government in action. This, too,
can be accomplished only in one way—and that is by such an organism of
the government—and, if necessary for the purpose, of the community
also—as will, by dividing and distributing the powers of government,
give to each division or interest, through its appropriate organ, either a
concurrent voice in making and executing the laws or a veto on their
execution. It is only by such an organism that the assent of each can be
made necessary to put the government in motion; or the power made
effectual to arrest its action when put in motion—and it is only by the
one or the other that the different interests, orders, classes, or portions
into which the community may be divided can be protected, and all
conflict and struggle between them prevented—by rendering it impossible to put or to keep it in action, without the concurrent consent of all.

Such an organism as this, combined with the right of suffrage, constitutes, in fact, the elements of constitutional government. The one, by
rendering those who make and execute the laws responsible to those on
whom they operate, prevents the rulers from oppressing the ruled; and
the other, by making it impossible for any one interest or combination of

interests or class, or order, or portion of the community to obtain exclusive control, prevents any one of them from oppressing the other. It is clear that oppression and abuse of power must come, if at all, from the one or the other quarter. From no other can they come. It follows that the two, suffrage and proper organism combined, are sufficient to counteract the tendency of government to oppression and abuse of power and to restrict it to the fulfilment of the great ends for which it is ordained. . . .

It may be readily inferred from what has been stated that the effect of organism is neither to supersede nor diminish the importance of the right of suffrage but to aid and perfect it. The object of the latter is to collect the sense of the community. The more fully and perfectly it accomplishes this, the more fully and perfectly it fulfils its end. But the most it can do, of itself, is to collect the sense of the greater number; that is, of the stronger interests, or combination of interests; and to assume this to be the sense of the community. It is only when aided by a proper organism that it can collect the sense of the entire community—of each and all its interests; of each, through its appropriate organ, and of the whole, through all of them united. This would truly be the sense of the entire community, for whatever diversity each interest might have within itself—as all would have the same interest in reference to the action of the government—the individuals composing each would be fully and truly represented by its own majority or appropriate organ, regarded in reference to the other interests. In brief, every individual of every interest might trust, with confidence, its majority or appropriate organ against that of every other interest.

It results, from what has been said, that there are two different modes in which the sense of the community may be taken: one, simply by the right of suffrage, unaided; the other, by the right through a proper organism. Each collects the sense of the majority. But one regards numbers only and considers the whole community as a unit, having but one common interest throughout, and collects the sense of the greater number of the whole as that of the community. The other, on the contrary, regards interests as well as numbers—considering the community as made up of different and conflicting interests as far as the action of the government is concerned—and takes the sense of each, through its majority or appropriate organ, and the united sense of all as the sense of the entire community. The former of these I shall call the numerical or absolute majority; and the latter, the concurrent or constitutional majority. I call it the constitutional majority, because it is an essential element in every constitutional government—be its form what it may. So great is the difference, politically speaking, between the two majorities that they cannot be confounded without leading to great and fatal errors; and yet the distinction between them has been so entirely overlooked that, when the term *majority* is used in political discussions, it is applied exclusively to designate the numerical—as if there were no other. Until this distinction is recognized, and better understood, there will continue to be great liability to error in properly constructing constitutional governments, especially of the popular form, and of preserving them when properly constructed. Until then, the latter will have a strong tendency to slide, first, into the government of the numerical majority and, finally, into absolute government of some other form. To show that such must be the case, and at the same time to mark more strongly the difference between the two, in order to guard against the danger of overlooking it, I propose to consider the subject more at length.

The first and leading error which naturally arises from overlooking the distinction referred to is to confound the numerical majority with the people, and this so completely as to regard them as identical. This is a consequence that necessarily results from considering the numerical as the only majority. All admit that a popular government, or democracy, is the government of the people, for the terms imply this. A perfect government of the kind would be one which would embrace the consent of every citizen or member of the community; but as this is impracticable, in the opinion of those who regard the numerical as the only majority, and who can perceive no other way by which the sense of the people can be taken, they are compelled to adopt this as the only true basis of popular government, in contradistinction to governments of the aristocratical or monarchical form. Being thus constrained, they are, in the next place, forced to regard the numerical majority as, in effect, the entire people; that is, the greater part as the whole; and the government of the greater part as the government of the whole. It is thus the two come to be confounded, and a part made identical with the whole. And it is thus, also, that all the rights, powers, and immunities of the whole people come to be attributed to the numerical majority; and, among others, the supreme, sovereign authority of establishing and abolishing governments at pleasure.

This radical error, the consequence of confounding the two, and of regarding the numerical as the only majority, has contributed more than any other cause to prevent the formation of popular constitutional governments—and to destroy them even when they have been formed. It leads to the conclusion that, in their formation and establishment, nothing more is necessary than the right of suffrage—and the allotment to each division of the community a representation in the government, in proportion to numbers. If the numerical majority were really the people, and if to take its sense truly were to take the sense of the people truly, a government so constituted would be a true and perfect model of a popular constitutional government; and every departure from it would detract from its excellence. But, as such is not the case—as the numerical majority, instead of being the people, is only a portion of them—such a government, instead of being a true and perfect model of the people's government, that is, a people self-governed, is but the government of a part over a part, the major over the minor portion. . . .

Nor would the division of government into separate and, as it regards each other, independent departments prevent this result. Such a division may do much to facilitate its operations and to secure to its administration greater caution and deliberation; but as each and all the departments—and, of course, the entire government—would be under the control of the numerical majority, it is too clear to require explanation that a mere distribution of its powers among its agents or representatives could do little or nothing to counteract its tendency to oppression and abuse of power. To effect this, it would be necessary to go one step further and make the several departments the organs of the distinct interests or portions of the community and to clothe each with a negative on the others. But the effect of this would be to change the government from the numerical into the concurrent majority.

Having now explained the reasons why it is so difficult to form and preserve popular constitutional government, so long as the distinction between the two majorities is overlooked, and the opinion prevails that a written constitution, with suitable restrictions and a proper division of its powers, is sufficient to counteract the tendency of the numerical majority to the abuse of its power, I shall next proceed to explain, more fully, why the concurrent majority is an indispensable element in forming constitutional governments and why the numerical majority, of itself, must, in all cases, make governments absolute.

The necessary consequence of taking the sense of the community by the concurrent majority is, as has been explained, to give to each interest or portion of the community a negative on the others. It is this mutual negative among its various conflicting interests which invests each with the power of protecting itself—and places the rights and safety of each, where only they can be securely placed, under its own guardianship.

Without this there can be no systematic, peaceful, or effective resistance to the natural tendency of each to come into conflict with the others; and without this there can be no constitution. It is this negative power—the power of preventing or arresting the action of the government—be it called by what term it may, veto, interposition, nullification, check, or balance of power—which, in fact, forms the constitution. They are all but different names for the negative power. In all its forms, and under all its names, it results from the concurrent majority. Without this there can be no negative and, without a negative, no constitution. The assertion is true in reference to all constitutional governments, be their forms what they may. It is, indeed, the negative power which makes the constitution —and the positive which makes the government. The one is the power of acting—and the other the power of preventing or arresting action. The two, combined, make constitutional governments.

But, as there can be no constitution without the negative power, and no negative power without the concurrent majority, it follows, necessarily, that where the numerical majority has the sole control of the government, there can be no constitution, as constitution implies limitation or restriction—and, of course, is inconsistent with the idea of sole or exclusive power. And hence, the numerical, unmixed with the concurrent majority, necessarily forms, in all cases, absolute government. . . .

Liberty, indeed, though among the greatest of blessings, is not so great as that of protection; inasmuch as the end of the former is the progress and improvement of the race—while that of the latter is its preservation and perpetuation. And hence, when the two come into conflict, liberty must, and ever ought, to yield to protection, as the existence of the race is of greater moment than its improvement.

It follows, from what has been stated, that it is a great and dangerous error to suppose that all people are equally entitled to liberty. It is a reward to be earned, not a blessing to be gratuitously lavished on all alike—a reward reserved for the intelligent, the patriotic, the virtuous and deserving—and not a boon to be bestowed on a people too ignorant, degraded, and vicious to be capable either of appreciating or of enjoying it. Nor is it any disparagement to liberty that such is and ought to be the case. On the contrary, its greatest praise, its proudest distinction, is that an all-wise Providence has reserved it as the noblest and highest reward for the development of our faculties, moral and intellectual. A reward more appropriate than liberty could not be conferred on the deserving, nor a punishment inflicted on the undeserving more just than to be subject to lawless and despotic rule. This dispensation seems to be the result of some fixed law—and every effort to disturb or defeat it, by attempting to elevate a people in the scale of liberty above the point to which they are entitled to rise, must ever prove abortive and end in disappointment. The progress of a people rising from a lower to a higher point in the scale of liberty is necessarily slow—and, by attempting to precipitate, we either retard or permanently defeat it.

There is another error, not less great and dangerous, usually associated with the one which has just been considered. I refer to the opinion that liberty and equality are so intimately united that liberty cannot be perfect without perfect equality.

That they are united to a certain extent and that equality of citizens, in the eyes of the law, is essential to liberty in a popular government are conceded. But to go further and make equality of *condition* essential to liberty would be to destroy both liberty and progress. The reason is that inequality of condition, while it is a necessary consequence of liberty, is, at the same time, indispensable to progress. In order to understand why this is so, it is necessary to bear in mind that the mainspring to progress is the desire of individuals to better their condition and that the strongest impulse which can be given to it is to leave individuals free to exert themselves in the manner they may deem best for that purpose, as far at least as it can be done consistently with the ends for which government is ordained—and to secure to all the fruits of their exertions. Now, as individuals differ greatly from each other, in intelligence, sagacity, energy, perseverance, skill, habits of industry and economy, physical power, position, and opportunity, the necessary effect of leaving all free to exert themselves to better their condition must be a corresponding inequality between those who may possess these qualities and advantages in a high degree and those who may be deficient in them. The only means by which this result can be prevented are either to impose such restrictions on the exertions of those who may possess them in a high degree as will place them on a level with those who do not or to deprive them of the fruits of their exertions. But to impose such restrictions on them would be destructive of liberty, while to deprive them of the fruits of their exertions would be to destroy the desire of bettering their condition. It is, indeed, this inequality of condition between the front and rear ranks, in the march of progress, which gives so strong an impulse to the former to maintain their position and to the latter to press forward into their files. This gives to progress its greatest impulse. To force the front rank back to the rear, or attempt to push forward the rear into line with the front, by the interposition of the government, would put an end to the impulse and effectually arrest the march of progress.

These great and dangerous errors have their origin in the prevalent opinion that all men are born free and equal—than which nothing can be more unfounded and false. It rests upon the assumption of a fact which is contrary to universal observation in whatever light it may be regarded. It is, indeed, difficult to explain how an opinion so destitute of all sound reason ever could have been so extensively entertained, unless we regard it as being confounded with another, which has some semblance of truth—but which, when properly understood, is not less false and dangerous. I refer to the assertion that all men are equal in the state of nature, meaning, by a state of nature, a state of individuality, supposed to have existed prior to the social and political state and in which men lived apart and independent of each other. If such a state ever did exist, all men would have been, indeed, free and equal in it; that is, free to do as they please and exempt from the authority or control of others— as, by supposition, it existed anterior to society and government. But such a state is purely hypothetical. It never did nor can exist, as it is inconsistent with the preservation and perpetuation of the race. It is, therefore, a great misnomer to call it *the state of nature*. Instead of being the natural state of man, it is, of all conceivable states, the most opposed to his nature, most repugnant to his feelings, and most incompatible with his wants. His natural state is the social and political—the one for which his Creator made him, and the only one in which he can preserve and perfect his race. As, then, there never was such a state as the so-called state of nature, and never can be, it follows that men, instead of being born in it, are born in the social and political state and, of course, instead of being born free and equal, are born subject not only to parental authority but to the laws and institutions of the country where born and under whose protection they draw their first breath. . . .

---

*The foregoing is taken
from Calhoun's* A DISQUISITION ON GOVERNMENT.

Thomas Babington Macaulay

1800–1859

Thomas Babington Macaulay was born on October 25, 1800, at Rothley Temple, Leicestershire, England. His father, Zachary, was a noted reformer strongly opposed to the slave trade, and a leading layman of the Evangelical party of the Church of England.

Thomas was a child prodigy, who learned to read when he was three years old and talked in a bookish manner at the age when most youngsters are still learning to speak sentences. When a servant spilled hot coffee on the four-year-old boy's legs, he said to his apologetic hostess, "Thank you, Madam, the agony is abated."

In 1812 Macaulay was sent to a private school run by an Evangelical minister. When he was eighteen he went to Cambridge, where he was a brilliant student in all subjects except mathematics. He twice won the medal for English verse, and gained a reputation as an accomplished debater.

Macaulay was admitted to the bar in 1826, but his career as a writer had already begun, and he never actively practiced law. In 1825 his essay on Milton had appeared in the *Edinburgh Review*. This was the first of a series of essays that brought fame to both Macaulay and the *Review* for twenty years.

Elected to Parliament in 1830, Macaulay championed reform legislation and worked for a bill to abolish slavery in the English colonies. In 1834 Macaulay accepted a seat in the Supreme Council of India. Until 1838 he stayed in India, where he prepared a new penal code and worked to increase the education of the natives.

Macaulay spent the rest of his life serving in Parliament and writing. He won many honors for both activities, including a degree of Doctor of Civil Law at Oxford. In 1857 he was made Baron Macaulay of Rothley.

The book on which he spent most of his time was the ambitious *The History of England from the Accession of James II.* It was probably the most popular history ever written. Macaulay used the techniques of the historical novel—reconstructing incidents and giving social background—to make his history interesting and lively. As popular as his essays and history was a group of long narrative poems, *Lays of Ancient Rome,* which includes the once widely memorized "Horatius at the Bridge."

Macaulay had completed four volumes and part of a fifth of his ambitious history when he died on December 28, 1859. He was buried in the Poets' Corner of Westminster Abbey.

M acaulay, in this essay, endeavors to prove that Machiavelli was not the devil incarnate, but a brilliant, sagacious, enlightened, and patriotic man of his time. The time was the Italian Renaissance, the greatest flowering season of the arts, literature, and science in modern history, but also the period of the most destructive invasions and internal dissensions. The then life expectancy on the Italian peninsula, incomparably rich in treasures, art and genius, has been estimated at sixteen years.

The evils that afflicted Italy, like those of ancient Greece, might be remedied if only the country could be unified under a strong ruler. But how could this be accomplished? In *The Prince,* Machiavelli defines the wise but ruthless course the prince must take. He must not shrink from any useful treachery or bloodshed. Men and principles alike must be considered as means to the supreme ends of power, order, and peace.

Such immoralism, says Macaulay, was not an invention of Machiavelli. He simply expressed in lucid language and for long-range patriotic ends maxims commonly accepted at the time and employed

---

Notes from the artist: "Macaulay and some of the subjects of his essays: Clive, Cromwell, and Charles I; Hastings and a soldier of the East India Company; Milton."

for narrow selfish goals. The mercenaries whom his countrymen relied on to defend their lands—their women and children and treasures—were useless against the warlike, rapacious conquerors from the North. Italy, the repository and seedbed of culture, was at their mercy. Machiavelli tried to strengthen the defense by organizing a militia in Florence, but it came too late. He realized that only a great prince like Cesare Borgia, coldly calculating and remorseless, could create a power sufficient to resist them.

It is easy to condemn. Macaulay seeks to understand Machiavelli as a historical product and makes brilliant forays back and forth in history to present the Florentine historian, political analyst, dramatist, and statesman in his proper colors. Is it true that "to understand all is to forgive all"? Macaulay's criticism of Machiavelli may seem to you too mild. He considers means more than ends, Macaulay says, and he does not sufficiently recognize that society and laws are justified only if they promote "the sum of private happiness." The idea that there is a good of the state distinct from the good of its members, he points out, is a widespread and dangerous error.

Macaulay adds, however, that these are errors which Machiavelli, situated as he was, "could scarcely avoid." Do you agree with him? If not, what advice should Machiavelli have given the prince at the time?

Machiavelli

Those who have attended to the practice of our literary tribunal are well aware that, by means of certain legal fictions similar to those of Westminster Hall, we are frequently enabled to take cognizance of cases lying beyond the sphere of our original jurisdiction. We need hardly say, therefore, that in the present instance M. [J. V.] Périer [translator of Machiavelli's works] is merely a Richard Roe, who will not be mentioned in any subsequent stage of the proceedings, and whose name is used for the sole purpose of bringing Machiavelli into court.

We doubt whether any name in literary history be so generally odious as that of the man whose character and writings we now propose to consider. The terms in which he is commonly described would seem to import that he was the Tempter, the Evil Principle, the discoverer of ambition and revenge, the original inventor of perjury, and that, before the publication of his fatal *Prince,* there had never been a hypocrite, a tyrant, or a traitor, a simulated virtue, or a convenient crime. One writer gravely assures us that Maurice of Saxony learned all his fraudulent policy from that execrable volume. Another remarks that since it was translated into Turkish, the sultans have been more addicted than formerly to the custom of strangling their brothers. Lord Lyttelton charges the poor Florentine with the manifold treasons of the house of Guise, and with the massacre of St. Bartholomew. Several authors have hinted that the Gunpowder Plot is to be primarily attributed to his doctrines, and seem to think that his effigy ought to be substituted for that of Guy Fawkes, in those processions by which the ingenious youth of England annually commemorate the preservation of the Three Estates. The Church of Rome has pronounced his works accursed things. Nor have our own countrymen been backward in testifying their opinion of his merits. Out of his surname they have coined an epithet for a knave, and out of his Christian name a synonym for the Devil.[1]

It is indeed scarcely possible for any person, not well acquainted with the history and literature of Italy, to read without horror and amazement the celebrated treatise which has brought so much obloquy on the name of Machiavelli. Such a display of wickedness, naked yet not ashamed, such cool, judicious, scientific atrocity, seemed rather to belong to a fiend than to the most depraved of men. Principles which the most hardened ruffian would scarcely hint to his most trusted accomplice, or avow, without the disguise of some palliating sophism, even to his own mind, are professed without the slightest circumlocution, and assumed as the fundamental axioms of all political science.

It is not strange that ordinary readers should regard the author of such a book as the most depraved and shameless of human beings. Wise men, however, have always been inclined to look with great suspicion on the angels and demons of the multitude: and in the present instance, several circumstances have led even superficial observers to question the justice of the vulgar decision. It is notorious that Machiavelli was, through life, a zealous republican. In the same year in which he composed his manual of king-craft, he suffered imprisonment and torture in the cause of public liberty. It seems inconceivable that the martyr of freedom should have designedly acted as the apostle of tyranny. Several eminent writers have, therefore, endeavoured to detect in this unfortunate performance some concealed meaning, more consistent with the character and conduct of the author than that which appears at the first glance.

One hypothesis is that Machiavelli intended to practise on the young Lorenzo de' Medici a fraud similar to that which Sunderland is said to have employed against our James the Second, and that he urged his pupil to violent and perfidious measures, as the surest means of accelerating the moment of deliverance and revenge. Another supposition which Lord Bacon seems to countenance, is that the treatise was merely a piece of grave irony, intended to warn nations against the arts of ambitious men. It would be easy to show that neither of these solutions is consistent with many passages in *The Prince* itself. But the most decisive refutation is that which is furnished by the other works of Machiavelli. In all the writings which he gave to the public, and in all those which the research of editors has, in the course of three centuries, discovered, in his come-

---

1. Nick Machiavel had ne'er a trick,
   Tho' he gave his name to our old Nick.
   Hudibras, Part III, Canto I.
   But, we believe, there is a schism on this subject among the antiquarians.

dies, designed for the entertainment of the multitude, in his comments on Livy, intended for the perusal of the most enthusiastic patriots of Florence, in his *History*, inscribed to one of the most amiable and estimable of the Popes, in his public despatches, in his private memoranda, the same obliquity of moral principle for which *The Prince* is so severely censured is more or less discernible. We doubt whether it would be possible to find, in all the many volumes of his compositions, a single expression indicating that dissimulation and treachery had ever struck him as discreditable.

After this, it may seem ridiculous to say that we are acquainted with few writings which exhibit so much elevation of sentiment, so pure and warm a zeal for the public good, or so just a view of the duties and rights of citizens, as those of Machiavelli. Yet so it is. And even from *The Prince* itself we could select many passages in support of this remark. To a reader of our age and country this inconsistency is, at first, perfectly bewildering. The whole man seems to be an enigma, a grotesque assemblage of incongruous qualities, selfishness and generosity, cruelty and benevolence, craft and simplicity, abject villainy and romantic heroism. One sentence is such as a veteran diplomatist would scarcely write in cipher for the direction of his most confidential spy; the next seems to be extracted from a theme composed by an ardent schoolboy on the death of Leonidas. An act of dexterous perfidy, and an act of patriotic self-devotion, call forth the same kind and the same degree of respectful admiration. The moral sensibility of the writer seems at once to be morbidly obtuse and morbidly acute. Two characters altogether dissimilar are united in him. They are not merely joined, but interwoven. They are the warp and the woof of his mind; and their combination, like that of the variegated threads in shot silk, gives to the whole texture a glancing and ever changing appearance. The explanation might have been easy, if he had been a very weak or a very affected man. But he was evidently neither the one nor the other. His works prove, beyond all contradiction, that his understanding was strong, his taste pure, and his sense of the ridiculous exquisitely keen.

This is strange: and yet the strangest is behind. There is no reason whatever to think that those amongst whom he lived saw anything shocking or incongruous in his writings. Abundant proofs remain of the high estimation in which both his works and his person were held by the most respectable among his contemporaries. Clement the Seventh patronized the publication of those very books which the Council of Trent, in the following generation, pronounced unfit for the perusal of Christians. Some members of the democratical party censured the Secretary for dedicating *The Prince* to a patron who bore the unpopular name of Medici. But to those immoral doctrines which have since called forth such severe reprehensions no exception appears to have been taken. The cry against them was first raised beyond the Alps, and seems to have been heard with amazement in Italy. The earliest assailant, as far as we are aware, was a countryman of our own, Cardinal Pole. The author of the Anti-Machiavelli was a French Protestant.

It is, therefore, in the state of moral feeling among the Italians of those times that we must seek for the real explanation of what seems most mysterious in the life and writings of this remarkable man. As this is a subject which suggests many interesting considerations, both political and metaphysical, we shall make no apology for discussing it at some length.

During the gloomy and disastrous centuries which followed the downfall of the Roman Empire, Italy had preserved, in a far greater degree than any other part of Western Europe, the traces of ancient civilization. The night which descended upon her was the night of an Arctic summer. The dawn began to reappear before the last reflection of the preceding sunset had faded from the horizon. It was in the time of the French Merovingians and of the Saxon Heptarchy that ignorance and ferocity seemed to have done their worst. Yet even then the Neapolitan provinces, recognizing the authority of the Eastern Empire, preserved something of Eastern knowledge and refinement. Rome, protected by the sacred character of her Pontiffs, enjoyed at least comparative security and repose. Even in those regions where the sanguinary Lombards had fixed their monarchy, there was incomparably more of wealth, of information, of physical comfort, and of social order than could be found in Gaul, Britain, or Germany.

That which most distinguished Italy from the neighbouring countries was the importance which the population of the towns, at a very early period, began to acquire. Some cities had been founded in wild and remote situations, by fugitives who had escaped from the rage of the barbarians. Such were Venice and Genoa, which preserved their freedom by their obscurity, till they became able to preserve it by their power. Other cities seem to have retained, under all the changing dynasties of invaders, under Odoacer and Theodoric, Narses and Alboin, the municipal institutions which had been conferred on them by the liberal policy of the Great Republic. In provinces which the central government was too feeble either to protect or to oppress, these institutions gradually acquired stability and vigour. The citizens, defended by their walls, and governed by their own magistrates and their own by-laws, enjoyed a considerable share of republican independence. Thus a strong democratic spirit was called into action. The Carlovingian sovereigns were too imbecile to subdue it. The generous policy of Otho encouraged it. It might perhaps have been suppressed by a close coalition between the Church and the Empire. It was fostered and invigorated by their disputes. In the twelfth century it attained its full vigour, and, after a long and doubtful conflict, triumphed over the abilities and courage of the Swabian princes.

The assistance of the Ecclesiastical power had greatly contributed to the success of the Guelphs. That success would, however, have been a doubtful good, if its only effect had been to substitute a moral for a political servitude, and to exalt the Popes at the expense of the Caesars. Happily the public mind of Italy had long contained the seeds of free opinions, which were now rapidly developed by the genial influence of free institutions. The people of that country had observed the whole machinery of the Church, its saints and its miracles, its lofty pretensions and its splendid ceremonial, its worthless blessings and its harmless curses, too long and too closely to be duped. They stood behind the scenes on which others were gazing with childish awe and interest. They witnessed the arrangement of the pulleys, and the manufacture of the thunders. They saw the natural faces and heard the natural voices of the actors. Distant nations looked on the Pope as the Vicegerent of the Almighty, the oracle of the All-wise, the umpire from whose decisions, in the disputes either of theologians or of kings, no Christian ought to appeal. The Italians were acquainted with all the follies of his youth, and with all the dishonest arts by which he had attained power. They knew how often he had employed the keys of the Church to release himself from the most sacred engagements, and its wealth to pamper his mistresses and nephews. The doctrines and rites of the established religion they treated with decent reverence. But though they still called themselves Catholics, they had ceased to be Papists. Those spiritual arms which carried terror into the palaces and camps of the proudest sovereigns excited only contempt in the immediate neighbourhood of the Vatican. Alexander, when he commanded our Henry the Second to submit to the lash before the tomb of a rebellious subject, was himself an exile. The Romans, apprehending that he entertained designs against their liberties, had driven him from their city; and though he solemnly promised to confine himself for the future to his spiritual functions, they still refused to readmit him.

In every other part of Europe, a large and powerful privileged class trampled on the people and defied the government. But in the most flourishing parts of Italy, the feudal nobles were reduced to comparative insignificance. In some districts they took shelter under the protection of the powerful commonwealths which they were unable to oppose, and gradually sank into the mass of burghers. In other places they possessed great influence; but it was an influence widely different from that which was exercised by the aristocracy of any transalpine kingdom. They were not petty princes, but eminent citizens. Instead of strengthening their fastnesses among the mountains, they embellished their palaces in the market-place. The state of society in the Neapolitan dominions, and in some parts of the Ecclesiastical State, more nearly resembled that which existed in the great monarchies of Europe. But the governments of Lombardy and Tuscany, through all their revolutions, preserved a different character. A people, when assembled in a town, is far more formidable to its rulers than when dispersed over a wide extent of country. The most arbitrary of the Caesars found it necessary to feed and divert the inhabitants of their unwieldy capital at the expense of the provinces. The citizens of Madrid have more than once besieged their sovereign in his own palace, and extorted from him the most humiliating concessions. The sultans have often been compelled to propitiate the furious rabble of Constantinople with the head of an unpopular vizier. From the same cause there was a certain tinge of democracy in the monarchies and aristocracies of Northern Italy.

Thus liberty, partially indeed and transiently, revisited Italy; and with liberty came commerce and empire, science and taste, all the comforts and all the ornaments of life. The Crusades, from which the inhabitants of other countries gained nothing but relics and wounds, brought to the rising commonwealths of the Adriatic and Tyrrhene seas a large increase of wealth, dominion, and knowledge. The moral and geographical position of those commonwealths enabled them to profit alike by the barbarism of the West and by the civilization of the East. Italian ships covered every sea. Italian factories rose on every shore. The tables of Italian money-changers were set in every city. Manufactures flourished. Banks were established. The operations of the commercial machine were facilitated by many useful and beautiful inventions. We doubt whether any country of Europe, our own excepted, have at the present time reached so high a point of wealth and civilization as some parts of Italy had attained four hundred years ago. Historians rarely descend to those details from which alone the real state of a community can be collected. Hence posterity is too often deceived by the vague hyperboles of poets and rhetoricians, who mistake the splendour of a court for the happiness of a people. Fortunately, John Villani has given us an ample and precise account of the state of Florence in the early part of the fourteenth century. The revenue of the Republic amounted to three hundred thousand florins; a sum which, allowing for the depreciation of the precious metals, was at least equivalent to six hundred thousand pounds sterling; a larger sum than England and Ireland, two centuries ago, yielded annually to Elizabeth. The manufacture of wool alone employed two hundred factories and thirty thousand workmen. The cloth annually produced sold, at an average, for twelve hundred thousand florins; a sum fully equal in exchangeable value to two millions and a half of our money. Four hundred thousand florins were annually coined. Eighty banks conducted the commercial operations, not of Florence only but of all Europe. The transactions of these establishments were sometimes of a magnitude which may surprise even the contemporaries of the Barings and the Rothschilds. Two houses advanced to Edward the Third of England upwards of three hundred thousand marks, at a time when the mark contained more silver than fifty shillings of the present day, and when the value of silver was more than quadruple of what it now is. The city and its environs contained a hundred and seventy thousand inhabitants. In the various schools about ten thousand children were taught to read; twelve hundred studied arithmetic; six hundred received a learned education.

The progress of elegant literature and of the fine arts was proportioned to that of the public prosperity. Under the despotic successors of Augustus, all the fields of intellect had been turned into arid wastes, still marked out by formal boundaries, still retaining the traces of old cultivation, but yielding neither flowers nor fruit. The deluge of barbarism came. It swept away all the landmarks. It obliterated all the signs of former tillage. But it fertilized while it devastated. When it receded, the wilderness was as the garden of God, rejoicing on every side, laughing, clapping its hands, pouring forth, in spontaneous abundance, everything brilliant, or fragrant, or nourishing. A new language, characterized by simple sweetness and simple energy, had attained perfection. No tongue ever furnished more gorgeous and vivid tints to poetry; nor was it long before a poet appeared who knew how to employ them. Early in the fourteenth century came forth the *Divine Comedy*, beyond comparison the greatest work of imagination which had appeared since the poems of Homer. The following generation produced indeed no second Dante: but it was eminently distinguished by general intellectual activity. The study of the Latin writers had never been wholly neglected in Italy. But

Petrarch introduced a more profound, liberal, and elegant scholarship, and communicated to his countrymen that enthusiasm for the literature, the history, and the antiquities of Rome, which divided his own heart with a frigid mistress and a more frigid Muse. Boccaccio turned their attention to the more sublime and graceful models of Greece.

From this time, the admiration of learning and genius became almost an idolatry among the people of Italy. Kings and republics, cardinals and doges, vied with each other in honouring and flattering Petrarch. Embassies from rival states solicited the honour of his instructions. His coronation agitated the Court of Naples and the people of Rome as much as the most important political transaction could have done. To collect books and antiques, to found professorships, to patronize men of learning, became almost universal fashions among the great. The spirit of literary research allied itself to that of commercial enterprise. Every place to which the merchant princes of Florence extended their gigantic traffic, from the bazaars of the Tigris to the monasteries of the Clyde, was ransacked for medals and manuscripts. Architecture, painting, and sculpture were munificently encouraged. Indeed it would be difficult to name an Italian of eminence, during the period of which we speak, who, whatever may have been his general character, did not at least affect a love of letters and of the arts.

Knowledge and public prosperity continued to advance together. Both attained their meridian in the age of Lorenzo the Magnificent. We cannot refrain from quoting the splendid passage, in which the Tuscan Thucydides describes the state of Italy at that period. *Ridotta tutta in somma pace e tranquillità, coltivata non meno ne' luoghi più montuosi e più sterili che nelle pianure e regioni più fertili, nè sottoposta ad altro imperio che de' suoi medesimi, non solo era abbondantissima d' abitatori e di ricchezze; ma illustrata sommamente dalla magnificenza di molti principi, dallo splendore di molte nobilissime e bellissime città, dalla sedia e maestà della religione, fioriva d' uomini prestantissimi nell' amministrazione delle cose pubbliche, e d' ingegni molto nobili in tutte le scienze, ed in qualunque arte preclara ed industriosa.* [The whole country basked in sublime peace and tranquillity, cultivated not less in the more mountainous and barren spots than in the plains and more fertile areas. Subject to no other authority than its own, it not only overflowed with inhabitants and wealth but was most especially famous for the magnificence of many princes, for the splendour of many noble and fair cities, for the seat and majesty of religion. It abounded in men who excelled in the administration of public activities and in the highest genius in all sciences, as well as in every illustrious and useful art.] When we peruse this just and splendid description, we can scarcely persuade ourselves that we are reading of times in which the annals of England and France present us only with a frightful spectacle of poverty, barbarity, and ignorance. From the oppressions of illiterate masters, and the sufferings of a degraded peasantry, it is delightful to turn to the opulent and enlightened States of Italy, to the vast and magnificent cities, the ports, the arsenals, the villas, the museums, the libraries, the marts filled with every article of comfort or luxury, the factories swarming with artisans, the Apennines covered with rich cultivation up to their very summits, the Po wafting the harvests of Lombardy to the granaries of Venice, and carrying back the silks of Bengal and the furs of Siberia to the palaces of Milan. With peculiar pleasure, every cultivated mind must repose on the fair, the happy, the glorious Florence, the halls which rang with the mirth of Pulci, the cell where twinkled the midnight lamp of Politian, the statues on which the young eye of Michael Angelo glared with the frenzy of a kindred inspiration, the gardens in which Lorenzo meditated some sparkling song for the May-day dance of the Etrurian virgins. Alas for the beautiful city! Alas for the wit and the learning, the genius and the love:

> Le donne, e i cavalier, gli affanni, e gli agi,
> Che ne 'nvogliava amore e cortesia
> Là dove i cuor son fatti sì malvagi.
> [The ladies and the knights, the toils and the sports
> To which love and courtesy inspired us,
> There where hearts have become so wicked.]

A time was at hand, when all the seven vials of the Apocalypse were to be poured forth and shaken out over those pleasant countries, a time of slaughter, famine, beggary, infamy, slavery, despair.

In the Italian States, as in many natural bodies, untimely decrepitude was the penalty of precocious maturity. Their early greatness, and their early decline, are principally to be attributed to the same cause, the preponderance which the towns acquired in the political system.

In a community of hunters or of shepherds, every man easily and necessarily becomes a soldier. His ordinary avocations are perfectly compatible with all the duties of military service. However remote may be the expedition on which he is bound, he finds it easy to transport with him the stock from which he derives his subsistence. The whole people is an army; the whole year a march. Such was the state of society which facilitated the gigantic conquests of Attila and Tamerlane.

But a people which subsists by the cultivation of the earth is in a very different situation. The husbandman is bound to the soil on which he labours. A long campaign would be ruinous to him. Still his pursuits are such as give to his frame both the active and the passive strength necessary to a soldier. Nor do they, at least in the infancy of agricultural science, demand his uninterrupted attention. At particular times of the year he is almost wholly unemployed, and can, without injury to himself, afford the time necessary for a short expedition. Thus the legions of Rome were supplied during its earlier wars. The season during which the fields did not require the presence of the cultivators sufficed for a short inroad and a battle. These operations, too frequently interrupted to produce decisive results, yet served to keep up among the people a degree of discipline and courage which rendered them not only secure but formidable. The archers and billmen of the Middle Ages, who, with provisions for forty days at their backs, left the fields for the camp, were troops of the same description.

But when commerce and manufactures begin to flourish a great change takes place. The sedentary habits of the desk and the loom render the exertions and hardships of war insupportable. The business of traders and artisans requires their constant presence and attention. In such a community there is little superfluous time; but there is generally much superfluous money. Some members of the society are, therefore, hired to relieve the rest from a task inconsistent with their habits and engagements.

The history of Greece is, in this, as in many other respects, the best commentary on the history of Italy. Five hundred years before the Christian era, the citizens of the republics round the Aegean Sea formed perhaps the finest militia that ever existed. As wealth and refinement advanced, the system underwent a gradual alteration. The Ionian States were the first in which commerce and the arts were cultivated, and the first in which the ancient discipline decayed. Within eighty years after the battle of Plataea, mercenary troops were everywhere plying for battles and sieges. In the time of Demosthenes, it was scarcely possible to persuade or compel the Athenians to enlist for foreign service. The laws of Lycurgus prohibited trade and manufactures. The Spartans, therefore, continued to form a national force long after their neighbours had begun to hire soldiers. But their military spirit declined with their singular institutions. In the second century before Christ, Greece contained only one nation of warriors, the savage highlanders of Aetolia, who were some generations behind their countrymen in civilization and intelligence.

All the causes which produced these effects among the Greeks acted still more strongly on the modern Italians. Instead of a power like Sparta, in its nature warlike, they had amongst them an ecclesiastical state, in its nature pacific. Where there are numerous slaves, every freeman is induced by the strongest motives to familiarize himself with the use of arms. The commonwealths of Italy did not, like those of Greece, swarm with thousands of these household enemies. Lastly, the mode in which military operations were conducted during the prosperous times of Italy was peculiarly unfavourable to the formation of an efficient militia. Men covered with iron from head to foot, armed with ponderous lances, and mounted on horses of the largest breed, were considered as composing the strength of an army. The infantry was regarded as comparatively worthless, and was neglected till it became really so. These tactics maintained their ground for centuries in most parts of Europe. That foot-soldiers could withstand the charge of heavy cavalry was thought utterly impossible till, towards the close of the fifteenth century, the rude mountaineers of Switzerland dissolved the spell, and astounded the most experienced generals by receiving the dreaded shock on an impenetrable forest of pikes.

The use of the Grecian spear, the Roman sword, or the modern bayonet, might be acquired with comparative ease. But nothing short of the daily exercise of years could train the man-at-arms to support his ponderous panoply, and manage his unwieldy weapon. Throughout Europe this most important branch of war became a separate profession. Beyond the Alps, indeed, though a profession, it was not generally a trade. It was the duty and the amusement of a large class of country gentlemen. It was the service by which they held their lands, and the diversion by which, in the absence of mental resources, they beguiled their leisure. But in the Northern States of Italy, as we have already remarked, the growing power of the cities, where it had not exterminated this order of men, had completely changed their habits. Here, therefore, the practice of employing mercenaries became universal, at a time when it was almost unknown in other countries.

When war becomes the trade of a separate class, the least dangerous course left to a government is to force that class into a standing army. It is scarcely possible that men can pass their lives in the service of one state without feeling some interest in its greatness. Its victories are their victories. Its defeats are their defeats. The contract loses something of its mercantile character. The services of the soldier are considered as the effects of patriotic zeal, his pay as the tribute of national gratitude. To betray the power which employs him, to be even remiss in its service, are in his eyes the most atrocious and degrading of crimes.

When the princes and commonwealths of Italy began to use hired troops, their wisest course would have been to form separate military establishments. Unhappily this was not done. The mercenary warriors of the Peninsula, instead of being attached to the service of different powers, were regarded as the common property of all. The connection between the state and its defenders was reduced to the most simple and naked traffic. The adventurer brought his horse, his weapons, his strength, and his experience into the market. Whether the King of Naples or the Duke of Milan, the Pope or the Signory of Florence struck the bargain was to him a matter of perfect indifference. He was for the highest wages and the longest term. When the campaign for which he had contracted was finished, there was neither law nor punctilio to prevent him from instantly turning his arms against his late masters. The soldier was altogether disjoined from the citizen and from the subject.

The natural consequences followed. Left to the conduct of men who neither loved those whom they defended, nor hated those whom they opposed, who were often bound by stronger ties to the army against which they fought than to the state which they served, who lost by the termination of the conflict, and gained by its prolongation, war completely changed its character. Every man came into the field of battle impressed with the knowledge that, in a few days, he might be taking the pay of the power against which he was then employed, and fighting by the side of his enemies against his associates. The strongest interests and the strongest feelings concurred to mitigate the hostility of those who had lately been brethren in arms, and who might soon be brethren in arms once more. Their common profession was a bond of union not to be forgotten even when they were engaged in the service of contending parties. Hence it was that operations, languid and indecisive beyond any recorded in history, marches and countermarches, pillaging expeditions and blockades, bloodless capitulations and equally bloodless combats make up the military history of Italy during the course of nearly two centuries. Mighty armies fight from sunrise to sunset. A great victory is won. Thousands of prisoners are taken; and hardly a life is lost. A pitched battle seems to have been really less dangerous than an ordinary civil tumult.

Courage was now no longer necessary even to the military character. Men grew old in camps, and acquired the highest renown by their warlike achievements, without being once required to face serious danger. The political consequences are too well known. The richest and most enlightened part of the world was left undefended to the assaults of every barbarous invader, to the brutality of Switzerland, the insolence of France, and the fierce rapacity of Aragon. The moral effects which followed from this state of things were still more remarkable.

Among the rude nations which lay beyond the Alps, valour was absolutely indispensable. Without it none could be eminent; few could be secure. Cowardice was, therefore, naturally considered as the foulest reproach. Among the polished Italians, enriched by commerce, governed by law, and passionately attached to literature, everything was done by superiority and intelligence. Their very wars, more pacific than the peace of their neighbours, required rather civil than military qualifications. Hence, while courage was the point of honour in other countries, ingenuity became the point of honour in Italy.

From these principles were deduced, by processes strictly analogous, two opposite systems of fashionable morality. Through the greater part of Europe, the vices which peculiarly belong to timid dispositions, and which are the natural defence of weakness, fraud, and hypocrisy, have always been most disreputable. On the other hand, the excesses of haughty and daring spirits have been treated with indulgence, and even with respect. The Italians regarded with corresponding lenity those crimes which require self-command, address, quick observation, fertile invention, and profound knowledge of human nature.

Such a prince as our Henry the Fifth would have been the idol of the North. The follies of his youth, the selfish ambition of his manhood, the Lollards roasted at slow fires, the prisoners massacred on the field of battle, the expiring lease of priestcraft renewed for another century, the dreadful legacy of a causeless and hopeless war bequeathed to a people who had no interest in its event—everything is forgotten but the victory of Agincourt. Francis Sforza, on the other hand, was the model of Italian heroes. He made his employers and his rivals alike his tools. He first overpowered his open enemies by the help of faithless allies; he then armed himself against his allies with the spoils taken from his enemies. By his incomparable dexterity, he raised himself from the precarious and dependent situation of a military adventurer to the first throne of Italy. To such a man much was forgiven, hollow friendship, ungenerous enmity, violated faith. Such are the opposite errors which men commit, when their morality is not a science but a taste, when they abandon eternal principles for accidental associations.

We have illustrated our meaning by an instance taken from history. We will select another from fiction. Othello murders his wife; he gives orders for the murder of his lieutenant; he ends by murdering himself. Yet he never loses the esteem and affection of Northern readers. His intrepid and ardent spirit redeems everything. The unsuspecting confidence with which he listens to his adviser, the agony with which he shrinks from the thought of shame, the tempest of passion with which he commits his crimes, and the haughty fearlessness with which he avows them give an extraordinary interest to his character. Iago, on the contrary, is the object of universal loathing. Many are inclined to suspect that Shakespeare has been seduced into an exaggeration unusual with him, and has drawn a monster who has no archetype in human nature. Now we suspect that an Italian audience in the fifteenth century would have felt very differently. Othello would have inspired nothing but detestation and contempt. The folly with which he trusts the friendly professions of a man whose promotion he had obstructed, the credulity with which he takes unsupported assertions, and trivial circumstances, for unanswerable proofs, the violence with which he silences the exculpation till the exculpation can only aggravate his misery would have excited the abhorrence and disgust of the spectators. The conduct of Iago they would assuredly have condemned; but they would have condemned it as we condemn that of his victim. Something of interest and respect would have mingled with their disapprobation. The readiness of the traitor's wit, the clearness of his judgment, the skill with which he penetrates the dispositions of others and conceals his own would have ensured to him a certain portion of their esteem.

So wide was the difference between the Italians and their neighbours. A similar difference existed between the Greeks of the second century before Christ, and their masters the Romans. The conquerors, brave and resolute, faithful to their engagements, and strongly influenced by religious feelings, were, at the same time, ignorant, arbitrary, and cruel. With the vanquished people were deposited all the art, the science, and the literature of the Western world. In poetry, in philosophy, in painting, in architecture, in sculpture, they had no rivals. Their manners were polished, their perceptions acute, their invention ready; they were tolerant, affable, humane; but of courage and sincerity they were almost utterly destitute. Every rude centurion consoled himself for his intellectual inferiority, by remarking that knowledge and taste seemed only to make men atheists, cowards, and slaves. The distinction long continued to be strongly marked, and furnished an admirable subject for the fierce sarcasms of Juvenal.

The citizen of an Italian commonwealth was the Greek of the time of Juvenal and the Greek of the time of Pericles, joined in one. Like the former, he was timid and pliable, artful and mean. But, like the latter, he had a country. Its independence and prosperity were dear to him. If his character were degraded by some base crimes, it was, on the other hand, ennobled by public spirit and by an honourable ambition.

A vice sanctioned by the general opinion is merely a vice. The evil terminates in itself. A vice condemned by the general opinion produces a pernicious effect on the whole character. The former is a local malady, the latter a constitutional taint. When the reputation of the offender is lost, he too often flings the remains of his virtue after it in despair. The Highland gentleman who, a century ago, lived by taking blackmail from his neighbours, committed the same crime for which Wild was accompanied to Tyburn by the huzzas of two hundred thousand people. But there can be no doubt that he was a much less depraved man than Wild. The deed for which Mrs. Brownrigg was hanged sinks into nothing, when compared with the conduct of the Roman who treated the public to a hundred pair of gladiators. Yet we should greatly wrong such a Roman if we supposed that his disposition was as cruel as that of Mrs. Brownrigg. In our own country, a woman forfeits her place in society by what, in a man, is too commonly considered as an honourable distinction, and, at worst, as a venial error. The consequence is notorious. The moral principle of a woman is frequently more impaired by a single lapse from virtue than that of a man by twenty years of intrigues. Classical antiquity would furnish us with instances stronger, if possible, than those to which we have referred.

We must apply this principle to the case before us. Habits of dissimulation and falsehood, no doubt, mark a man of our age and country as utterly worthless and abandoned. But it by no means follows that a similar judgment would be just in the case of an Italian of the middle ages. On the contrary, we frequently find those faults which we are accustomed to consider as certain indications of a mind altogether depraved, in company with great and good qualities, with generosity, with benevolence, with disinterestedness. From such a state of society, Palamedes, in the admirable dialogue of Hume, might have drawn illustrations of his theory as striking as any of those with which Fourli furnished him. These are not, we well know, the lessons which historians are generally most careful to teach, or readers most willing to learn. But they are not therefore useless. How Philip disposed his troops at Chaeronea, where Hannibal crossed the Alps, whether Mary blew up Darnley, or Siquier shot Charles the Twelfth, and ten thousand other questions of the same description are in themselves unimportant. The inquiry may amuse us, but the decision leaves us no wiser. He alone reads history aright who, observing how powerfully circumstances influence the feelings and opinions of men, how often vices pass into virtues and paradoxes into axioms, learns to distinguish what is accidental and transitory in human nature from what is essential and immutable.

In this respect no history suggests more important reflections than that of the Tuscan and Lombard commonwealths. The character of the Italian statesman seems, at first sight, a collection of contradictions, a phantom as monstrous as the portress of hell in Milton, half divinity, half snake, majestic and beautiful above, grovelling and poisonous below. We see a man whose thoughts and words have no connection with each other, who never hesitates at an oath when he wishes to seduce, who never wants a pretext when he is inclined to betray. His cruelties spring not from the heat of blood or the insanity of uncontrolled power but from deep and cool meditation. His passions, like well-trained troops, are impetuous by rule, and in their most headstrong fury never forget the discipline to which they have been accustomed. His whole soul is occupied with vast and complicated schemes of ambition: yet his aspect and language exhibit nothing but philosophical moderation. Hatred and revenge eat into his heart: yet every look is a cordial smile, every gesture a familiar caress. He never excites the suspicion of his adversaries by petty provocations. His purpose is disclosed only when it is accomplished. His face is unruffled, his speech is courteous, till vigilance is laid asleep, till a vital point is exposed, till a sure aim is taken; and then he strikes for the first and last time. Military courage, the boast of the sottish German, of the frivolous and prating Frenchman, of the romantic and arrogant Spaniard, he neither possesses nor values. He shuns danger, not because he is insensible to shame, but because, in the society in which he lives, timidity has ceased to be shameful. To do an injury openly is, in his estimation, as wicked as to do it secretly, and far less profitable. With him the most honourable means are those which are the surest, the speediest, and the darkest. He cannot comprehend how a man should scruple to deceive those whom he does not scruple to destroy. He would think it madness to declare open hostilities against rivals whom he might stab in a friendly embrace, or poison in a consecrated wafer.

Yet this man, black with the vices which we consider as most loathsome, traitor, hypocrite, coward, assassin, was by no means destitute even
of those virtues which we generally consider as indicating superior elevation of character. In civil courage, in perseverance, in presence of mind,
those barbarous warriors, who were foremost in the battle or the breach,
were far his inferiors. Even the dangers which he avoided with a caution
almost pusillanimous never confused his perceptions, never paralysed his
inventive faculties, never wrung out one secret from his smooth tongue,
and his inscrutable brow. Though a dangerous enemy, and a still more
dangerous accomplice, he could be a just and beneficent ruler. With so
much unfairness in his policy, there was an extraordinary degree of fairness in his intellect. Indifferent to truth in the transactions of life, he was
honestly devoted to truth in the researches of speculation. Wanton cruelty
was not in his nature. On the contrary, where no political object was at
stake, his disposition was soft and humane. The susceptibility of his
nerves and the activity of his imagination inclined him to sympathize with
the feelings of others, and to delight in the charities and courtesies of social life. Perpetually descending to actions which might seem to mark a
mind diseased through all its faculties, he had nevertheless an exquisite
sensibility, both for the natural and the moral sublime, for every graceful
and every lofty conception. Habits of petty intrigue and dissimulation
might have rendered him incapable of great general views, but that the
expanding effect of his philosophical studies counteracted the narrowing
tendency. He had the keenest enjoyment of wit, eloquence, and poetry.
The fine arts profited alike by the severity of his judgment, and by the liberality of his patronage. The portraits of some of the remarkable Italians
of those times are perfectly in harmony with this description. Ample and
majestic foreheads, brows strong and dark, but not frowning, eyes of
which the calm full gaze, while it expresses nothing, seems to discern
everything, cheeks pale with thought and sedentary habits, lips formed
with feminine delicacy, but compressed with more than masculine decision, mark out men at once enterprising and timid, men equally skilled in
detecting the purposes of others, and in concealing their own, men who
must have been formidable enemies and unsafe allies, but men, at the
same time, whose tempers were mild and equable, and who possessed an
amplitude and subtlety of intellect which would have rendered them eminent either in active or in contemplative life, and fitted them either to
govern or to instruct mankind.

Every age and every nation has certain characteristic vices, which prevail almost universally, which scarcely any person scruples to avow, and

which even rigid moralists but faintly censure. Succeeding generations change the fashion of their morals, with the fashion of their hats and their coaches; take some other kind of wickedness under their patronage, and wonder at the depravity of their ancestors. Nor is this all. Posterity, that high court of appeal which is never tired of eulogizing its own justice and discernment, acts on such occasions like a Roman dictator after a general mutiny. Finding the delinquents too numerous to be all punished, it selects some of them at hazard, to bear the whole penalty of an offence in which they are not more deeply implicated than those who escape. Whether decimation be a convenient mode of military execution, we know not; but we solemnly protest against the introduction of such a principle into the philosophy of history.

In the present instance, the lot has fallen on Machiavelli, a man whose public conduct was upright and honourable, whose views of morality, where they differed from those of the persons around him, seemed to have differed for the better, and whose only fault was that, having adopted some of the maxims then generally received, he arranged them more luminously, and expressed them more forcibly, than any other writer.

Having now, we hope, in some degree cleared the personal character of Machiavelli, we come to the consideration of his works. As a poet he is not entitled to a high place; but his comedies deserve attention.

The *Mandragola*, in particular, is superior to the best of Goldoni, and inferior only to the best of Molière. It is the work of a man who, if he had devoted himself to the drama, would probably have attained the highest eminence, and produced a permanent and salutary effect on the national taste. This we infer, not so much from the degree, as from the kind of its excellence. There are compositions which indicate still greater talent, and which are perused with still greater delight, from which we should have drawn very different conclusions. Books quite worthless are quite harmless. The sure sign of the general decline of an art is the frequent occurrence, not of deformity, but of misplaced beauty. In general, Tragedy is corrupted by eloquence, and Comedy by wit.

The real object of the drama is the exhibition of human character. This, we conceive, is no arbitrary canon, originating in local and temporary associations, like those canons which regulate the number of acts in a play, or of syllables in a line. To this fundamental law every other regulation is subordinate. The situations which most signally develop character form the best plot. The mother tongue of the passions is the best style.

This principle, rightly understood, does not debar the poet from any grace of composition. There is no style in which some man may not under some circumstances express himself. There is therefore no style which the drama rejects, none which it does not occasionally require. It is in the discernment of place, of time, and of person that the inferior artists fail. The fantastic rhapsody of Mercutio, the elaborate declamation of Antony, are, where Shakespeare has placed them, natural and pleasing. But Dryden would have made Mercutio challenge Tybalt in hyperboles as fanciful as those in which he describes the chariot of Mab. Corneille would have represented Antony as scolding and coaxing Cleopatra with all the measured rhetoric of a funeral oration.

No writers have injured the Comedy of England so deeply as Congreve and Sheridan. Both were men of splendid wit and polished taste. Unhappily, they made all their characters in their own likeness. Their works bear the same relation to the legitimate drama which a transparency bears to a painting. There are no delicate touches, no hues imperceptibly fading into each other: the whole is lighted up with an universal glare. Outlines and tints are forgotten in the common blaze which illuminates all. The flowers and fruits of the intellect abound; but it is the abundance of a jungle, not of a garden, unwholesome, bewildering, unprofitable from its very plenty, rank from its very fragrance. Every fop, every boor, every valet is a man of wit. The very butts and dupes, Tattle, Witwould, Puff, Acres, outshine the whole Hôtel of Rambouillet. To prove the whole system of this school erroneous, it is only necessary to apply the test which dissolved the enchanted Florimel, to place the true by the false Thalia, to contrast the most celebrated characters which have been drawn by the writers of whom we speak with the Bastard in *King John* or the Nurse in *Romeo and Juliet*. It was not surely from want of wit that Shakespeare adopted so different a manner. Benedick and Beatrice throw Mirabel and Millamant into the shade. All the good sayings of the facetious houses of Absolute and Surface might have been clipped from the single character of Falstaff, without being missed. It would have been easy for that fertile mind to have given Bardolph and Shallow as much wit as Prince Hal, and to have made Dogberry and Verges retort on each other in sparkling epigrams. But he knew that such indiscriminate prodigality was, to use his own admirable language, "from the purpose of playing, whose end, both at the first and now, was and is, to hold, as 'twere, the mirror up to Nature."

This digression will enable our readers to understand what we mean when we say that in the *Mandragola*, Machiavelli has proved that he completely understood the nature of the dramatic art, and possessed talents which would have enabled him to excel in it. By the correct and vigorous delineation of human nature, it produces interest without a pleasing or skilful plot, and laughter without the least ambition of wit. The lover, not a very delicate or generous lover, and his adviser, the parasite, are drawn with spirit. The hypocritical confessor is an admirable portrait. He is, if we mistake not, the original of Father Dominic, the best comic character of Dryden. But old Nicias is the glory of the piece. We cannot call to mind anything that resembles him. The follies which Molière ridicules are those of affection, not those of fatuity. Coxcombs and pedants, not absolute simpletons, are his game. Shakespeare has indeed a vast assortment of fools; but the precise species of which we speak is not, if we remember right, to be found there. Shallow is a fool. But his animal spirits supply, to a certain degree, the place of cleverness. His talk is to that of Sir John what soda-water is to champagne. It has the effervescence though not the body or the flavour. Slender and Sir Andrew Aguecheek are fools, troubled with an uneasy consciousness of their folly, which in the latter produces meekness and docility, and in the former, awkwardness, obstinacy, and confusion. Cloten is an arrogant fool, Osric a foppish fool, Ajax a savage fool; but Nicias is, as Thersites says of Patroclus, a fool positive. His mind is occupied by no strong feeling; it takes every character, and retains none; its aspect is diversified, not by passions, but by faint and transitory semblances of passion, a mock joy, a mock fear, a mock love, a mock pride, which chase each other like shadows over its surface, and vanish as soon as they appear. He is just idiot enough to be an object, not of pity or horror, but of ridicule. He bears some resemblance to poor Calandrino, whose mishaps, as recounted by Boccaccio, have made all Europe merry for more than four centuries. He perhaps resembles still more closely Simon da Villa, to whom Bruno and Buffalmacco promised the love of the Countess Civillari. Nicias is, like Simon, of a learned profession; and the dignity with which he wears the doctoral fur renders his absurdities infinitely more grotesque. The old Tuscan is the very language for such a being. Its peculiar simplicity gives even to the most forcible reasoning and the most brilliant wit an infantine air, generally delightful, but to a foreign reader sometimes a little ludicrous. Heroes and statesmen seem to lisp when they use it. It becomes Nicias incomparably, and renders all his silliness infinitely more silly.

We may add that the verses with which the *Mandragola* is interspersed appear to us to be the most spirited and correct of all that Machiavelli has written in metre. He seems to have entertained the same opinion, for he has introduced some of them in other places. The contemporaries of the author were not blind to the merits of this striking piece. It was acted at Florence with the greatest success. Leo the Tenth was among its admirers, and by his order it was represented at Rome.[2]

The *Clizia* is an imitation of the *Casina* of Plautus, which is itself an imitation of the lost *kleroumenoi* [appointed ones] of Diphilus. Plautus was, unquestionably, one of the best Latin writers; but the *Casina* is by no means one of his best plays; nor is it one which offers great facilities to an imitator. The story is as alien from modern habits of life as the manner in which it is developed from the modern fashion of composition. The lover remains in the country and the heroine in her chamber during the whole action, leaving their fate to be decided by a foolish father, a cunning mother, and two knavish servants. Machiavelli has executed his task with judgment and taste. He has accommodated the plot to a different state of society, and has very dexterously connected it with the history of his own times. The relation of the trick put on the doting old lover is exquisitely humorous. It is far superior to the corresponding passage in the Latin comedy, and scarcely yields to the account which Falstaff gives of his ducking.

Two other comedies without titles, the one in prose, the other in verse, appear among the works of Machiavelli. The former is very short, lively enough, but of no great value. The latter we can scarcely believe to be genuine. Neither its merits nor its defects remind us of the reputed author. It was first printed in 1796, from a manuscript discovered in the celebrated library of the Strozzi. Its genuineness, if we have been rightly informed, is established solely by the comparison of hands. Our suspicions are strengthened by the circumstance that the same manuscript contained a description of the plague of 1527, which has also, in consequence, been added to the works of Machiavelli. Of this last composition the strongest external evidence would scarcely induce us to believe him guilty. Nothing was ever written more detestable in matter and manner. The narrations, the reflections, the jokes, the lamentations, are all the very worst of their respective kinds, at once trite and affected, threadbare tinsel from the Rag Fairs and Monmouth Streets of literature. A foolish schoolboy might write such a piece, and, after he had written it, think it much finer than the incomparable introduction of the *Decameron*. But that a shrewd statesman, whose earliest works are characterized by

---

2. Nothing can be more evident than that Paulus Jovius designates the *Mandragola* under the name of the *Nicias*. We should not have noticed what is so perfectly obvious, were it not that this natural and palpable misnomer has led the sagacious and industrious Bayle into a gross error.

manliness of thought and language, should, at near sixty years of age, descend to such puerility, is utterly inconceivable.

The little novel of *Belphegor* is pleasantly conceived and pleasantly told. But the extravagance of the satire in some measure injures its effect. Machiavelli was unhappily married; and his wish to avenge his own cause, and that of his brethren in misfortune, carried him beyond even the licence of fiction. Jonson seems to have combined some hints taken from this tale, with others from Boccaccio, in the plot of *The Devil Is an Ass*, a play which, though not the most highly finished of his compositions, is perhaps that which exhibits the strongest proofs of genius.

The political correspondence of Machiavelli, first published in 1767, is unquestionably genuine, and highly valuable. The unhappy circumstances in which his country was placed during the greater part of his public life gave extraordinary encouragement to diplomatic talents. From the moment that Charles the Eighth descended from the Alps, the whole character of Italian politics was changed. The governments of the Peninsula ceased to form an independent system. Drawn from their old orbit by the attraction of the larger bodies which now approached them, they became mere satellites of France and Spain. All their disputes, internal and external, were decided by foreign influence. The contests of opposite factions were carried on, not as formerly in the senate-house or in the market-place, but in the antechambers of Louis and Ferdinand. Under these circumstances, the prosperity of the Italian States depended far more on the ability of their foreign agents, than on the conduct of those who were entrusted with the domestic administration. The ambassador had to discharge functions far more delicate than transmitting orders of knighthood, introducing tourists, or presenting his brethren with the homage of his high consideration. He was an advocate to whose management the dearest interests of his clients were entrusted, a spy clothed with an inviolable character. Instead of consulting, by a reserved manner and ambiguous style, the dignity of those whom he represented, he was to plunge into all the intrigues of the Court at which he resided, to discover and flatter every weakness of the prince, and of the favourite who governed the prince, and of the lackey who governed the favourite. He was to compliment the mistress and bribe the confessor, to panegyrize or supplicate, to laugh or weep, to accommodate himself to every caprice, to lull every suspicion, to treasure every hint, to be everything, to observe everything, to endure everything. High as the art of political intrigue had been carried in Italy, these were times which required it all.

On these arduous errands Machiavelli was frequently employed. He was sent to treat with the King of the Romans and with the Duke of Valentinois. He was twice ambassador of the Court of Rome, and thrice at that of France. In these missions, and in several others of inferior importance, he acquitted himself with great dexterity. His despatches form one of the most amusing and instructive collections extant. The narratives are clear and agreeably written; the remarks on men and things clever and judicious. The conversations are reported in a spirited and characteristic manner. We find ourselves introduced into the presence of the men who, during twenty eventful years, swayed the destinies of Europe. Their wit and their folly, their fretfulness and their merriment, are exposed to us. We are admitted to overhear their chat, and to watch their familiar gestures. It is interesting and curious to recognize, in circumstances which elude the notice of historians, the feeble violence and shallow cunning of Louis the Twelfth; the bustling insignificance of Maximilian, cursed with an impotent pruriency for renown, rash yet timid, obstinate yet fickle, always in a hurry, yet always too late; the fierce and haughty energy which gave dignity to the eccentricities of Julius; the soft and graceful manners which masked the insatiable ambition and the implacable hatred of Cesare Borgia.

We have mentioned Cesare Borgia. It is impossible not to pause for a moment on the name of a man in whom the political morality of Italy was so strongly personified, partially blended with the sterner lineaments of the Spanish character. On two important occasions Machiavelli was admitted to his society; once, at the moment when Cesare's splendid villainy achieved its most signal triumph, when he caught in one snare and crushed at one blow all his most formidable rivals; and again when, exhausted by disease and overwhelmed by misfortunes, which no human prudence could have averted, he was the prisoner of the deadliest enemy of his house. These interviews between the greatest speculative and the greatest practical statesman of the age are fully described in the *Correspondence,* and form perhaps the most interesting part of it. From some passages in *The Prince,* and perhaps also from some indistinct traditions, several writers have supposed a connection between those remarkable men much closer than ever existed. The Envoy has even been accused of prompting the crimes of the artful and merciless tyrant. But from the official documents it is clear that their intercourse, though ostensibly amicable, was in reality hostile. It cannot be doubted, however, that the imagination of Machiavelli was strongly impressed, and his speculations on government coloured, by the observations which he made on the singular character and equally singular fortunes of a man who under such disadvantages had achieved such exploits; who, when sensuality, varied through innumerable forms, could no longer stimulate his sated mind, found a more powerful and durable excitement in the intense thirst of empire and revenge; who emerged from the sloth and luxury of the Roman purple the first prince and general of the age; who, trained in an unwarlike profession, formed a gallant army out of the dregs of an unwarlike people; who, after acquiring sovereignty by destroying his enemies, acquired popularity by destroying his tools; who had begun to employ for the most salutary ends the power which he had attained by the most atrocious means; who tolerated within the sphere of his iron despotism no plunderer or oppressor but himself; and who fell at last amidst the mingled curses and regrets of a people of whom his genius had been the wonder, and might have been the salvation. Some of those crimes of Borgia which to us appear the most odious would not, from causes which we have already considered, have struck an Italian of the fifteenth century with equal horror. Patriotic feeling also might induce Machiavelli to look with some indulgence and regret on the memory of the only leader who could have defended the independence of Italy against the confederate spoilers of Cambrai.

On this subject Machiavelli felt most strongly. Indeed the expulsion of the foreign tyrants, and the restoration of that golden age which had preceded the irruption of Charles the Eighth, were projects which, at that time, fascinated all the master-spirits of Italy. The magnificent vision delighted the great but ill-regulated mind of Julius. It divided, with manuscripts and sauces, painters, and falcons, the attention of the frivolous Leo. It prompted the generous treason of Morone. It imparted a transient energy to the feeble mind and body of the last Sforza. It excited for one moment an honest ambition in the false heart of Pescara. Ferocity and insolence were not among the vices of the national character. To the discriminating cruelties of politicians, committed for great ends on select victims, the moral code of the Italians was too indulgent. But though they might have recourse to barbarity as an expedient, they did not require it as a stimulant. They turned with loathing from the atrocity of the strangers who seemed to love blood for its own sake, who, not content with subjugating, were impatient to destroy, who found a fiendish pleasure in razing magnificent cities, cutting the throats of enemies who cried for quarter, or suffocating an unarmed population by thousands in the caverns to which it had fled for safety. Such were the cruelties which daily excited the terror and disgust of a people among whom, till lately, the worst that a soldier had to fear in a pitched battle was the loss of his horse and the expense of his ransom. The swinish intemperance of Switzerland, the wolfish avarice of Spain, the gross licentiousness of the French, indulged in violation of hospitality, of decency, of love itself, the wanton inhumanity which was common to all the invaders had made them objects of deadly hatred to the inhabitants of the Peninsula. The wealth which had been accumulated during centuries of prosperity and repose was rapidly melting away. The intellectual superiority of the oppressed people only rendered them more keenly sensible of their political degradation. Literature and taste, indeed, still disguised with a flush of hectic loveliness and brilliancy the ravages of an incurable decay. The iron had not yet entered into the soul. The time was not yet come when eloquence was to be gagged, and reason to be hoodwinked, when the harp of the poet was to be hung on the willows of Arno, and the right hand of the painter to forget its cunning. Yet a discerning eye might even then have seen that genius and learning would not long survive the state of things from which they had sprung, and that the great men whose talents gave lustre to that melancholy period had been formed under the influence of happier days, and would leave no successors behind them. The times which shine with the greatest splendour in literary history are not always those to which the human mind is most indebted. Of this we may be convinced, by comparing the generation which follows them with that which had preceded them. The first fruits which are reaped under a bad system often spring from seed sown under a good one. Thus it was, in some measure, with the Augustan age. Thus it was with the age of Raphael and Ariosto, of Aldus and Vida.

Machiavelli deeply regretted the misfortunes of his country, and clearly discerned the cause and the remedy. It was the military system of the Italian people which had extinguished their value and discipline, and left their wealth an easy prey to every foreign plunderer. The Secretary projected a scheme alike honourable to his heart and to his intellect, for abolishing the use of mercenary troops, and for organizing a national militia.

The exertions which he made to effect this great object ought alone to rescue his name from obloquy. Though his situation and his habits were pacific, he studied with intense assiduity the theory of war. He made himself master of all its details. The Florentine government entered into his views. A council of war was appointed. Levies were decreed. The indefatigable minister flew from place to place in order to superintend the execution of his design. The times were, in some respects, favourable to the experiment. The system of military tactics had undergone a great revolution. The cavalry was no longer considered as forming the strength of an army. The hours which a citizen could spare from his ordinary employments, though by no means sufficient to familiarize him with the exercise of a man-at-arms, might render him an useful foot-soldier. The dread of a foreign yoke, of plunder, massacre, and conflagration, might have conquered that repugnance to military pursuits which both the industry and the idleness of great towns commonly generate. For a time the scheme promised well. The new troops acquitted themselves respectably in the field. Machiavelli looked with parental rapture on the success of his plan, and began to hope that the arms of Italy might once more be formidable to the barbarians of the Tagus and the Rhine. But the tide of misfortune came on before the barriers which should have withstood it were prepared. For a time, indeed, Florence might be considered as peculiarly fortunate. Famine and sword and pestilence had devastated the fertile plains and the stately cities of the Po. All the curses denounced of old against Tyre seemed to have fallen on Venice. Her merchants already stood afar off, lamenting for their great city. The time seemed near when the seaweed should overgrow her silent Rialto, and the fisherman wash his nets in her deserted arsenal. Naples had been four times conquered and reconquered by tyrants equally indifferent to its welfare, and equally greedy for its spoils. Florence, as yet, had only to endure degradation and extortion, to submit to the mandates of foreign powers, to buy over and over again, at an enormous price, what was already justly her own, to return thanks for being wronged, and to ask pardon for being in the right. She was at length deprived of the blessings even of this infamous and servile repose. Her military and political institutions were swept away together. The Medici returned, in the train of foreign invaders, from their long exile. The policy of Machiavelli was abandoned; and his public services were requited with poverty, imprisonment, and torture.

The fallen statesman still clung to his project with unabated ardour. With the view of vindicating it from some popular objections and of refuting some prevailing errors on the subject of military science, he wrote his seven books on *The Art of War*. This excellent work is in the form of a dialogue. The opinions of the writer are put into the mouth of Fabrizio Colonna, a powerful nobleman of the Ecclesiastical State, and an officer of distinguished merit in the service of the King of Spain. Colonna visits Florence on his way from Lombardy to his own domains. He is invited to meet some friends at the house of Cosimo Rucellai, an amiable and accomplished young man, whose early death Machiavelli

feelingly deplores. After partaking of an elegant entertainment, they retire from the heat into the most shady recesses of the garden. Fabrizio is
struck by the sight of some uncommon plants. Cosimo says that, though
rare in modern days, they are frequently mentioned by the classical
authors, and that his grandfather, like many other Italians, amused himself with practising the ancient methods of gardening. Fabrizio expresses
his regret that those who, in later times, affected the manners of the old
Romans should select for imitation the most trifling pursuits. This leads
to a conversation on the decline of military discipline and on the best
means of restoring it. The institution of the Florentine militia is ably
defended; and several improvements are suggested in the details.

The Swiss and the Spaniards were, at that time, regarded as the best
soldiers in Europe. The Swiss battalion consisted of pikemen, and bore a
close resemblance to the Greek phalanx. The Spaniards, like the soldiers
of Rome, were armed with the sword and the shield. The victories of
Flamininus and Aemilius over the Macedonian kings seem to prove the
superiority of the weapons used by the legions. The same experiment had
been recently tried with the same result at the battle of Ravenna, one of
those tremendous days into which human folly and wickedness com-
press the whole devastation of a famine or a plague. In that memorable
conflict, the infantry of Aragon, the old companions of Gonsalvo, deserted by all their allies, hewed a passage through the thickest of the
imperial pikes, and effected an unbroken retreat, in the face of the
gendarmerie of De Foix, and the renowned artillery of Este. Fabrizio,
or rather Machiavelli, proposes to combine the two systems, to arm the
foremost lines with the pike for the purpose of repulsing cavalry, and
those in the rear with the sword, as being a weapon better adapted for
every other purpose. Throughout the work, the author expresses the
highest admiration of the military science of the ancient Romans, and the
greatest contempt for the maxims which had been in vogue amongst the
Italian commanders of the preceding generation. He prefers infantry to
cavalry, and fortified camps to fortified towns. He is inclined to substitute
rapid movements and decisive engagements for the languid and dilatory
operations of his countrymen. He attaches very little importance to the
invention of gunpowder. Indeed he seems to think that it ought scarcely
to produce any change in the mode of arming or of disposing troops. The
general testimony of historians, it must be allowed, seems to prove that
the ill-constructed and ill-served artillery of those times, though useful in
a siege, was of little value on the field of battle.

Of the tactics of Machiavelli we will not venture to give an opinion:

but we are certain that his book is most able and interesting. As a commentary on the history of his times, it is invaluable. The ingenuity, the grace, and the perspicuity of the style, and the eloquence and animation of particular passages must give pleasure even to readers who take no interest in the subject.

The Prince and the *Discourses on Livy* were written after the fall of the Republican government. The former was dedicated to the Young Lorenzo de' Medici. This circumstance seems to have disgusted the contemporaries of the writer far more than the doctrines which have rendered the name of the work odious in later times. It was considered as an indication of political apostasy. The fact however seems to have been that Machiavelli, despairing of the liberty of Florence, was inclined to support any government which might preserve her independence. The interval which separated a democracy and a despotism, Soderini and Lorenzo, seemed to vanish when compared with the difference between the former and the present state of Italy, between the security, the opulence, and the repose which she had enjoyed under her native rulers, and the misery in which she had been plunged since the fatal year in which the first foreign tyrant had descended from the Alps. The noble and pathetic exhortation with which *The Prince* concludes shows how strongly the writer felt upon this subject.

The Prince traces the progress of an ambitious man, the *Discourses* the progress of an ambitious people. The same principles on which, in the former work, the elevation of an individual is explained are applied in the latter to the longer duration and more complex interest of a society. To a modern statesman the form of the *Discourses* may appear to be puerile. In truth Livy is not an historian on whom implicit reliance can be placed, even in cases where he must have possessed considerable means of information. And the first Decade, to which Machiavelli has confined himself, is scarcely entitled to more credit than our Chronicle of British Kings who reigned before the Roman invasion. But the commentator is indebted to Livy for little more than a few texts which he might as easily have extracted from the *Vulgate* or the *Decameron*. The whole train of thought is original.

On the peculiar immorality which has rendered *The Prince* unpopular, and which is almost equally discernible in the *Discourses,* we have already given our opinion at length. We have attempted to show that it belonged rather to the age than to the man, that it was a partial taint, and by no means implied general depravity. We cannot, however, deny that it is a great blemish, and that it considerably diminishes the pleasure which, in other respects, those works must afford to every intelligent mind.

It is, indeed, impossible to conceive a more healthful and vigorous constitution of the understanding than that which these works indicate. The qualities of the active and the contemplative statesman appear to have been blended in the mind of the writer into a rare and exquisite harmony. His skill in the details of business had not been acquired at the expense of his general powers. It had not rendered his mind less comprehensive; but it had served to correct his speculations and to impart to them that vivid and practical character which so widely distinguishes them from the vague theories of most political philosophers.

Every man who has seen the world knows that nothing is so useless as a general maxim. If it be very moral and very true, it may serve for a copy to a charity-boy. If, like those of Rochefoucauld, it be sparkling and whimsical, it may make an excellent motto for an essay. But few indeed of the many wise apophthegms which have been uttered, from the time of the Seven Sages of Greece to that of Poor Richard, have prevented a single foolish action. We give the highest and the most peculiar praise to the precepts of Machiavelli when we say that they may frequently be of real use in regulating conduct, not so much because they are more just or more profound than those which might be culled from other authors, as because they can be more readily applied to the problems of real life.

There are errors in these works. But they are errors which a writer, situated like Machiavelli, could scarcely avoid. They arise, for the most part, from a single defect which appears to us to pervade his whole system. In his political scheme, the means had been more deeply considered than the ends. The great principle, that societies and laws exist only for the purpose of increasing the sum of private happiness, is not recognized with sufficient clearness. The good of the body, distinct from the good of the members, and sometimes hardly compatible with the good of the members, seems to be the object which he proposes to himself. Of all political fallacies, this has perhaps had the widest and the most mischievous operation. The state of society in the little commonwealths of Greece, the close connection and mutual dependence of the citizens, and the severity of the laws of war tended to encourage an opinion which, under such circumstances, could hardly be called erroneous. The interests of every individual were inseparably bound up with those of the State. An invasion destroyed his cornfields and vineyards, drove him from his home, and compelled him to encounter all the hardships of a military life. A treaty of peace restored him to security and comfort. A victory doubled the number of his slaves. A defeat perhaps made him a slave himself. When Pericles, in the Peloponnesian War, told the Athenians that, if their country triumphed, their private losses would speedily be repaired, but that, if their arms failed of success, every individual amongst them would probably be ruined, he spoke no more than the truth. He spoke to men whom the tribute of vanquished cities supplied with food and clothing, with the luxury of the bath and the amusements of the theatre, on whom the greatness of their country conferred rank, and before whom the members of less prosperous communities trembled; to men who, in case of a change in the public fortunes, would, at least, be deprived of every comfort and every distinction which they enjoyed. To be butchered on the smoking ruins of their city, to be dragged in chains to a slave-market, to see one child torn from them to dig in the quarries of Sicily, and another to guard the harems of Persepolis, these were the frequent and probable consequences of national calamities. Hence, among the Greeks, patriotism became a governing principle, or rather an ungovernable passion. Their legislators and their philosophers took it for granted that, in providing for the strength and greatness of the state, they sufficiently provided for the happiness of the people. The writers of the Roman empire lived under despots, into whose dominion a hundred nations were melted down, and whose gardens would have covered the little commonwealths of Phlius and Plataea. Yet they continued to employ the same language, and to cant about the duty of sacrificing everything to a country to which they owed nothing.

Causes similar to those which had influenced the disposition of the Greeks operated powerfully on the less vigorous and daring character of the Italians. The Italians, like the Greeks, were members of small communities. Every man was deeply interested in the welfare of the society to which he belonged, a partaker in its wealth and its poverty, in its glory and its shame. In the age of Machiavelli this was peculiarly the case. Public events had produced an immense sum of misery to private citizens. The Northern invaders had brought want to their boards, infamy to their beds, fire to their roofs, and the knife to their throats. It was natural that a man who lived in times like these should overrate the importance of those measures by which a nation is rendered formidable to its neighbours, and undervalue those which make it prosperous within itself.

Nothing is more remarkable in the political treatises of Machiavelli than the fairness of mind which they indicate. It appears where the author is in the wrong, almost as strongly as where he is in the right.

He never advances a false opinion because it is new or splendid, because he can clothe it in a happy phrase, or defend it by an ingenious sophism. His errors are at once explained by a reference to the circumstances in which he was placed. They evidently were not sought out; they lay in his way, and could scarcely be avoided. Such mistakes must necessarily be committed by early speculators in every science.

In this respect it is amusing to compare *The Prince* and the *Discourses* with the *Spirit of Laws*. Montesquieu enjoys, perhaps, a wider celebrity than any political writer of modern Europe. Something he doubtless owes to his merit, but much more to his fortune. He had the good luck of a Valentine. He caught the eye of the French nation, at the moment when it was waking from the long sleep of political and religious bigotry; and, in consequence, he became a favourite. The English, at that time, considered a Frenchman who talked about constitutional checks and fundamental laws as a prodigy not less astonishing than the learned pig or the musical infant. Specious but shallow, studious of effect, indifferent to truth, eager to build a system, but careless of collecting those materials out of which alone a sound and durable system can be built, the lively President constructed theories as rapidly and as slightly as card-houses, no sooner projected than completed, no sooner completed than blown away, no sooner blown away than forgotten. Machiavelli errs only because his experience, acquired in a very peculiar state of society, could not always enable him to calculate the effect of institutions differing from those of which he had observed the operation. Montesquieu errs, because he has a fine thing to say, and is resolved to say it. If the phenomena which lie before him will not suit his purpose, all history must be ransacked. If nothing established by authentic testimony can be racked or chipped to suit his Procrustean hypothesis, he puts up with some monstrous fable about Siam, or Bantam, or Japan, told by writers compared with whom Lucian and Gulliver were veracious, liars by a double right, as travellers and as Jesuits.

Propriety of thought, and propriety of diction, are commonly found together. Obscurity and affectation are the two greatest faults of style. Obscurity of expression generally springs from confusion of ideas; and the same wish to dazzle at any cost, which produces affectation in the manner of a writer, is likely to produce sophistry in his reasonings. The judicious and candid mind of Machiavelli shows itself in his luminous, manly, and polished language. The style of Montesquieu, on the other hand, indicates in every page a lively and ingenious, but an unsound, mind. Every trick of expression, from the mysterious conciseness of an oracle to the flippancy of a Parisian coxcomb, is employed to disguise the fallacy of some positions, and the triteness of others. Absurdities are brightened into epigrams; truisms are darkened into enigmas. It is with difficulty that the strongest eye can sustain the glare with which some parts are illuminated, or penetrate the shade in which others are concealed.

The political works of Machiavelli derive a peculiar interest from the mournful earnestness which he manifests whenever he touches on topics connected with the calamities of his native land. It is difficult to conceive any situation more painful than that of a great man, condemned to watch the lingering agony of an exhausted country, to tend it during the alternate fits of stupefaction and raving which precede its dissolution, and to see the symptoms of vitality disappear one by one, till nothing is left but coldness, darkness, and corruption. To this joyless and thankless duty was Machiavelli called. In the energetic language of the prophet, he was "mad for the sight of his eyes which he saw," disunion in the council, effeminacy in the camp, liberty extinguished, commerce decaying, national honour sullied, an enlightened and flourishing people given over to the ferocity of ignorant savages. Though his opinions had not escaped the contagion of that political immorality which was common among his countrymen, his natural disposition seems to have been rather stern and impetuous than pliant and artful. When the misery and degradation of Florence and the foul outrage which he had himself sustained recur to his mind, the smooth craft of his profession and his nation is exchanged for the honest bitterness of scorn and anger. He speaks like one sick of the calamitous times and abject people among whom his lot is cast. He pines for the strength and glory of ancient Rome, for the fasces of Brutus, and the sword of Scipio, the gravity of the curule chair, and the bloody pomp of the triumphal sacrifice. He seems to be transported back to the days when eight hundred thousand Italian warriors sprung to arms at the rumour of a Gallic invasion. He breathes all the spirit of those intrepid and haughty senators who forgot the dearest ties of nature in the claims of public duty, who looked with disdain on the elephants and on the gold of Pyrrhus, and listened with unaltered composure to the tremendous tidings of Cannae. Like an ancient temple deformed by the barbarous architecture of a later age, his character acquires an interest from the very circumstances which debase it. The original proportions are rendered more striking by the contrast which they present to the mean and incongruous additions.

The influence of the sentiments which we have described was not apparent in his writings alone. His enthusiasm, barred from the career which it would have selected for itself, seems to have found a vent in desperate levity. He enjoyed a vindictive pleasure in outraging the opinions of a society which he despised. He became careless of the decencies which were expected from a man so highly distinguished in the literary and political world. The sarcastic bitterness of his conversation disgusted those who were more inclined to accuse his licentiousness than their own degeneracy, and who were unable to conceive the strength of those emotions which are concealed by the jests of the wretched, and by the follies of the wise.

The historical works of Machiavelli still remain to be considered. The *Life of Castruccio Castracani* will occupy us for a very short time, and would scarcely have demanded our notice, had it not attracted a much greater share of public attention than it deserves. Few books, indeed, could be more interesting than a careful and judicious account, from such a pen, of the illustrious Prince of Lucca, the most eminent of those Italian chiefs who, like Pisistratus and Gelon, acquired a power felt rather than seen, and resting, not on law or on prescription, but on the public favour and on their great personal qualities. Such a work would exhibit to us the real nature of that species of sovereignty, so singular and so often misunderstood, which the Greeks denominated tyranny, and which, modified in some degree by the feudal system, reappeared in the commonwealths of Lombardy and Tuscany. But this little composition of Machiavelli is in no sense a history. It has no pretensions to fidelity. It is a trifle, and not a very successful trifle. It is scarcely more authentic than the novel of *Belphegor*, and is very much duller.

The last great work of this illustrious man was the history of his native city. It was written by command of the Pope, who, as chief of the house of Medici, was at that time sovereign of Florence. The characters of Cosimo, of Piero, and of Lorenzo are, however, treated with a freedom and impartiality equally honourable to the writer and to the patron. The miseries and humiliations of dependence, the bread which is more bitter than every other food, the stairs which are more painful than every other ascent, had not broken the spirit of Machiavelli. The most corrupting post in a corrupting profession had not depraved the generous heart of Clement.

The *History* does not appear to be the fruit of much industry or research. It is unquestionably inaccurate. But it is elegant, lively, and picturesque, beyond any other in the Italian language. The reader, we believe, carries away from it a more vivid and a more faithful impression of the national character and manners than from more correct accounts. The truth is that the book belongs rather to ancient than to modern literature. It is in the style, not of Davila and Clarendon, but of Herodotus and Tacitus. The classical histories may almost be called romances founded in fact. The relation is, no doubt, in all its principal points, strictly true. But the numerous little incidents which heighten the interest, the words, the gestures, the looks are evidently furnished by the imagination of the author. The fashion of later times is different. A more exact narrative is given by the writer. It may be doubted whether more exact notions are conveyed to the reader. The best portraits are perhaps those in which there is a slight mixture of caricature, and we are not certain that the best histories are not those in which a little of the exaggeration of fictitious narrative is judiciously employed. Something is lost in accuracy; but much is gained in effect. The fainter lines are neglected; but the great characteristic features are imprinted on the mind for ever.

The *History* terminates with the death of Lorenzo de' Medici. Machiavelli had, it seems, intended to continue his narrative to a later period. But his death prevented the execution of his design; and the melancholy task of recording the desolation and shame of Italy devolved on Guicciardini.

Machiavelli lived long enough to see the commencement of the last struggle for Florentine liberty. Soon after his death monarchy was finally established, not such a monarchy as that of which Cosimo had laid the foundations deep in the institutions and feelings of his countryman, and which Lorenzo had embellished with the trophies of every science and every art; but a loathsome tyranny, proud and mean, cruel and feeble, bigoted and lascivious. The character of Machiavelli was hateful to the new masters of Italy; and those parts of his theory which were in strict accordance with their own daily practice afforded a pretext for blackening his memory. His works were misrepresented by the learned, misconstrued by the ignorant, censured by the Church, abused with all the rancour of simulated virtue by the tools of a base government, and the priests of a baser superstition. The name of the man whose genius had illuminated all the dark places of policy, and to whose patriotic wisdom an oppressed people had owed their last chance of emancipation and revenge, passed into a proverb of infamy. For more than two hundred years his bones lay undistinguished. At length, an English nobleman paid the last honours to the greatest statesman of Florence. In the church of Santa Croce a monument was erected to his memory, which is contemplated with reverence by all who can distinguish the virtues of a great mind through the corruptions of a degenerate age, and which will be approached with still deeper homage when the object to which his public life was devoted shall be attained, when the foreign yoke shall be broken, when a second Procida shall avenge the wrongs of Naples, when a happier Rienzi shall restore the good estate of Rome, when the streets of Florence and Bologna shall again resound with their ancient war-cry, *Popolo; popolo; muoiano i tiranni* [The people; the people; May tyrants die]!

"Machiavelli" is from a collection
of Macaulay's essays
entitled CRITICAL AND HISTORICAL ESSAYS.

Voltaire [1]

1694-1778

The years of exile which Voltaire spent in England, from 1726 to 1729, were the crucial ones of his life. They made him serious. Until then he had been a talented littérateur with a faculty for criticizing and infuriating the orthodoxies of his day. He was welcomed in England as an exile from French illiberality. Accepted in all the leading literary circles, he also moved in the highest ranks of society. Of more significance, he found a subject to study and to write about. The first results appeared in 1733 after he had returned to France. They consisted, as originally entitled, of *Philosophical Letters on the English.*

Voltaire claims that "a Frenchman who arrives in London will find philosophy, like everything else, very much changed there." The center and source of the change he traces to the empirical science and philosophy which had Sir Isaac Newton as its idol. In these letters Voltaire set himself the task, among others, of expounding this new philosophy. Those dealing with Bacon, Newton, and Locke serve in fact as popular introductions to the major work of these authors. He even attempts the far from easy task of simplifying and popularizing Newton's theory of gravitational attraction, of the decomposition of light, and of the calculus, or the theory of fluxions as it was then known.

Voltaire in fact became so interested in the physics of Newton that he set up a laboratory for conducting experiments in the château at Cirey, where he lived on returning to France. The Marquise du Châtelet, to whom the château belonged, was an accomplished mathematician and physicist. She collaborated with Voltaire on a

---

[1] For a biography of Voltaire, see Vol. 2, pp. 237–239, in this set.

long treatise on the Newtonian system. In addition to writing another treatise on physics, she also made the first French translation of Newton's great work.

Voltaire rarely wrote anything that was entirely without a political purpose. The *Letters* pretend to be a report on conditions in England. At the time that Voltaire was there, England was still thought of as a land of political unrest, even of revolution, since memory of the Civil War of the seventeenth century was still fresh. Yet under the guise of a panegyric on English ways, the *Letters* constitute an attack on all the authorities then reigning in France. Praise of the new empirical philosophy is turned into criticism of the philosophy and physics of Descartes, then dominant in France. The account of liberty in England is made an attack upon the despotism of the French church and state. The *Letters* were originally published with certain "remarks" upon Pascal which were found so offensive to orthodoxy that the book was condemned and burned.

Reason and its triumphs is a theme that runs throughout the *Letters* as well as the *Philosophical Dictionary* [2] and the science-fiction story *Micromégas.* [3] In this Voltaire well illustrates what is usually referred to as the rationalism of the French Enlightenment. It shows the climate of opinion, which Voltaire himself helped to form, that resulted in the French Revolution and the downfall of the ancient regime.

---

[2] See Vol. 10, pp. 453–474, in this set.
[3] See Vol. 2, pp. 241–256, in this set.

English Men and Ideas

from *Letters on the English*

ON THE PARLIAMENT

The members of the English Parliament are fond of comparing themselves to the old Romans.

Not long since Mr. Shippen opened a speech in the House of Commons with these words, "The majesty of the people of England would be wounded." The singularity of the expression occasioned a loud laugh; but this gentleman, so far from being disconcerted, repeated the same words with a resolute tone of voice, and the laugh ceased. In my opinion, the majesty of the people of England has nothing in common with that of the people of Rome, much less is there any affinity between their governments. There is in London a senate, some of the members whereof are accused (doubtless very unjustly) of selling their voices on certain occasions, as was done in Rome; this is the only resemblance. Besides, the two nations appear to me quite opposite in character, with regard both to good and evil. The Romans never knew the dreadful folly of religious wars, an abomination reserved for devout preachers of patience and humility. Marious and Sylla, Caesar and Pompey, Anthony and Augustus, did not draw their swords and set the world in a blaze merely to determine whether the flamen should wear his shirt over his robe, or his robe over his shirt, or whether the sacred chickens should eat and drink, or eat only, in order to take the augury. The English have hanged one another by law, and cut one another to pieces in pitched battles, for quarrels of as trifling nature. The sects of the Episcopalians and Presbyterians quite distracted these very serious heads for a time. But I fancy they will hardly ever be so silly again, they seeming to be grown wiser at their own expense; and I do not perceive the least inclination in them to murder one another merely about syllogisms, as some zealots among them once did.

But here follows a more essential difference between Rome and England, which gives the advantage entirely to the latter—viz., that the civil wars of Rome ended in slavery, and those of the English in liberty. The English are the only people upon earth who have been able to prescribe limits to the power of kings by resisting them; and who, by a series of struggles, have at last established that wise government where the prince is all powerful to do good, and, at the same time, is restrained from committing evil; where the nobles are great without insolence, though there are no vassals; and where the people share in the government without confusion.

The House of Lords and that of the Commons divide the legislative power under the King, but the Romans had no such balance. The patricians and plebeians in Rome were perpetually at variance, and there was no intermediate power to reconcile them. The Roman senate, who were so unjustly, so criminally proud as not to suffer the plebeians to share with them in anything, could find no other artifice to keep the latter out of the administration than by employing them in foreign wars. They considered the plebeians as a wild beast, whom it behoved them to let loose upon their neighbours, for fear they should devour their masters. Thus the greatest defect in the government of the Romans raised them to be conquerors. By being unhappy at home, they triumphed over and possessed themselves of the world, till at last their divisions sunk them to slavery.

The government of England will never rise to so exalted a pitch of glory, nor will its end be so fatal. The English are not fired with the splendid folly of making conquests, but would only prevent their neighbours from conquering. They are not only jealous of their own liberty, but even of that of other nations. The English were exasperated against Louis XIV for no other reason but because he was ambitious, and declared war against him merely out of levity, not from any interested motives.

The English have doubtless purchased their liberties at a very high price, and waded through seas of blood to drown the idol of arbitrary power. Other nations have been involved in as great calamities, and have shed as much blood; but then the blood they spilt in defence of their liberties only enslaved them the more.

That which rises to a revolution in England is no more than a sedition in other countries. A city in Spain, in Barbary, or in Turkey takes up arms in defence of its privileges, when immediately it is stormed by mercenary troops, it is punished by executioners, and the rest of the nation kiss the chains they are loaded with. The French are of opinion that the government of this island is more tempestuous than the sea which surrounds it, which indeed is true; but then it is never so but when the King raises the storm—when he attempts to seize the ship of which he is only the chief pilot. The civil wars of France lasted longer, were more cruel, and productive of greater evils than those of England; but none of these civil wars had a wise and prudent liberty for their object.

In the detestable reigns of Charles IX and Henry III the whole affair was only whether the people should be slaves to the Guises. With regard to the last war of Paris, it deserves only to be hooted at. Methinks I see a crowd of schoolboys rising up in arms against their master, and afterwards whipped for it. Cardinal de Retz, who was witty and brave (but to no purpose), rebellious without a cause, factious without design, and head of a defenceless party, caballed for caballing's sake, and seemed to foment the civil war merely out of diversion. The parliament did not know what he intended, nor what he did not intend. He levied troops by act of Parliament, and the next moment cashiered them. He threatened, he begged pardon; he set a price upon Cardinal Mazarin's head, and afterwards congratulated him in a public manner. Our civil wars under Charles VI were bloody and cruel, those of the League execrable, and that of the Frondeurs ridiculous.

That for which the French chiefly reproach the English nation is the murder of King Charles I, whom his subjects treated exactly as he would have treated them had his reign been prosperous. After all, consider on one side Charles I, defeated in a pitched battle, imprisoned, tried, sentenced to die in Westminster Hall, and then beheaded. And on the other, the Emperor Henry VII, poisoned by his chaplain at his receiving the Sacrament; Henry III stabbed by a monk; thirty assassinations projected against Henry IV, several of them put in execution, and the last bereaving that great monarch of his life. Weigh, I say, all these wicked attempts and then judge.

ON THE GOVERNMENT

That mixture in the English government, that harmony between King, Lords, and Commons, did not always subsist. England was enslaved for a long series of years by the Romans, the Saxons, the Danes, and the French successively. William the Conqueror particularly, ruled them with a rod of iron. He disposed as absolutely of the lives and fortunes of his conquered subjects as an eastern monarch; and forbade, upon pain of death, the English either fire or candle in their houses after eight o'clock; whether he did this to prevent their nocturnal meetings, or only to try, by this odd and whimsical prohibition, how far it was possible for one man to extend his power over his fellow-creatures. It is true, indeed, that the English had parliaments before and after William the Conqueror, and they boast of them, as though these assemblies then called parliaments, composed of ecclesiastical tyrants and of plunderers entitled barons, had been the guardians of the public liberty and happiness.

The barbarians who came from the shores of the Baltic, and settled in the rest of Europe, brought with them the form of government called states or parliaments, about which so much noise is made, and which are so little understood. Kings, indeed, were not absolute in those days; but then the people were more wretched upon that very account, and more completely enslaved. The chiefs of these savages, who had laid waste France, Italy, Spain, and England, made themselves monarchs. Their generals divided among themselves the several countries they had conquered, whence sprung those margraves, those peers, those barons, those petty tyrants, who often contested with their sovereigns for the spoils of whole nations. These were birds of prey fighting with an eagle for doves whose blood the victorious was to suck. Every nation, instead of being governed by one master, was trampled upon by a hundred tyrants. The priests soon played a part among them. Before this it had been the fate of the Gauls, the Germans, and the Britons to be always governed by their Druids and the chiefs of their villages, an ancient kind of barons, not so tyrannical as their successors. These Druids pretended to be mediators between God and man. They enacted laws, they fulminated their excommunications, and sentenced to death. The bishops succeeded, by insensible degrees, to their temporal authority in the Goth and Vandal government. The popes set themselves at their head, and armed with their briefs, their bulls, and reinforced by monks, they made even kings tremble, deposed and assassinated them at pleasure, and employed every artifice to draw into their own purses moneys from all parts of Europe. The weak Ina, one of the tyrants of the Saxon Heptarchy in England, was the first monarch who submitted, in his pilgrimage to Rome, to pay St. Peter's penny (equivalent very near to a French crown) for every house in his dominions. The whole island soon followed his example; England became insensibly one of the Pope's provinces, and the Holy Father used to send from time to time his legates thither to levy exorbitant taxes. At last King John delivered up by a public instrument the kingdom of England to the Pope, who had excommunicated him; but the barons, not finding their account in this resignation, dethroned the wretched King John and seated Louis, father to St. Louis, King of France, in his place. However, they were soon weary of their new monarch, and accordingly obliged him to return to France.

Whilst that the barons, the bishops, and the popes, all laid waste England, where all were for ruling; the most numerous, the most useful, even the most virtuous, and consequently the most venerable part of mankind, consisting of those who study the laws and the sciences, of traders, of artificers, in a word, of all who were not tyrants—that is, those who are called the people: these, I say, were by them looked upon as so many animals beneath the dignity of the human species. The Commons in those ages were far from sharing in the government, they being villains or peasants, whose labour, whose blood, were the property of their masters who entitled themselves the nobility. The major part of men in Europe were at that time what they are to this day in several parts of the world—they were villains or bondsmen of lords—that is, a kind of cattle bought and sold with the land. Many ages passed away before justice could be done to human nature—before mankind were conscious that it was abominable for many to sow and but few reap. And was not France very happy when the power and authority of those petty robbers was abolished by the lawful authority of kings and of the people?

Happily, in the violent shocks which the divisions between kings and the nobles gave to empires, the chains of nations were more or less heavy. Liberty in England sprang from the quarrels of tyrants. The barons forced King John and King Henry III to grant the famous Magna Carta, the chief design of which was indeed to make kings dependent on the Lords; but then the rest of the nation were a little favoured in it, in order that they might join on proper occasions with their pretended masters. This great charter, which is considered as the sacred origin of the English liberties, shows in itself how little liberty was known.

The title alone proves that the king thought he had a just right to be absolute; and that the barons, and even the clergy, forced him to give up the pretended right, for no other reason but because they were the most powerful.

Magna Carta begins in this style: "We grant, of our own free will, the following privileges to the archbishops, bishops, priors, and barons of our kingdom," etc.

The House of Commons is not once mentioned in the articles of this charter—a proof that it did not yet exist, or that it existed without power. Mention is therein made, by name, of the freemen of England—a melancholy proof that some were not so. It appears, by Article XXXII, that these pretended freemen owed service to their lords. Such a liberty as this was not many removes from slavery.

By Article XXI, the king ordains that his officers shall not henceforward seize upon, unless they pay for them, the horses and carts of freemen. The people considered this ordinance as a real liberty, though it was a greater tyranny. Henry VII, that happy usurper and great politician, who pretended to love the barons, though he in reality hated and feared them, got their lands alienated. By this means the villains, afterwards acquiring riches by their industry, purchased the estates and country seats of the illustrious peers who had ruined themselves by their folly and extravagance, and all the lands got by insensible degrees into other hands.

The power of the House of Commons increased every day. The families of the ancient peers were at last extinct; and as peers only are properly noble in England, there would be no such thing in strictness of law as nobility in that island, had not the kings created new barons from time to time, and preserved the body of peers, once a terror to them, to oppose them to the Commons, since become so formidable.

All these new peers who compose the higher house receive nothing but their titles from the king, and very few of them have estates in those places whence they take their titles. One shall be Duke of D——, though he has not a foot of land in Dorsetshire; and another is Earl of a village, though he scarce knows where it is situated. The peers have power, but it is only in the parliament house.

There is no such thing here as *haute, moyenne,* and *basse justice* [high, middle, and low justice]—that is, a power to judge in all matters civil and criminal; nor a right or privilege of hunting in the grounds of a citizen, who at the same time is not permitted to fire a gun in his own field.

No one is exempted in this country from paying certain taxes because he is a nobleman or a priest. All duties and taxes are settled by the House of Commons, whose power is greater than that of the Peers, though inferior to it in dignity. The spiritual as well as temporal Lords have the liberty to reject a money bill brought in by the Commons; but they are not allowed to alter anything in it, and must either pass or throw it out without restriction. When the bill has passed the Lords and is signed by the King, then the whole nation pays, every man in proportion to his revenue or estate, not according to his title, which would be absurd. There is no such thing as an arbitrary subsidy or poll-tax, but a real tax on the lands, of all which an estimate was made in the reign of the famous King William III.

The land-tax continues still upon the same foot, though the revenue of the lands is increased. Thus no one is tyrannized over, and every one is easy. The feet of the peasants are not bruised by wooden shoes; they eat white bread, are well clothed, and are not afraid of increasing their stock of cattle, nor of tiling their houses, from any apprehension that their taxes will be raised the year following. The annual income of the estates of a great many commoners in England amounts to two hundred thousand livres, and yet these do not think it beneath them to plough the lands which enrich them, and on which they enjoy their liberty.

ON TRADE

As trade enriched the citizens in England, so it contributed to their freedom, and this freedom on the other side extended their commerce, whence arose the grandeur of the state. Trade raised by insensible degrees the naval power, which gives the English a superiority over the seas, and they now are masters of very near two hundred ships of war. Posterity will very probably be surprised to hear that an island whose only produce is a little lead, tin, fuller's-earth, and coarse wool should become so powerful by its commerce as to be able to send, in 1723, three fleets at the same time to three different and far distanced parts of the globe. One before Gibraltar, conquered and still possessed by the English; a second to Porto Bello, to dispossess the King of Spain of the treasures of the West Indies; and a third into the Baltic, to prevent the Northern Powers from coming to an engagement.

At the time when Louis XIV made all Italy tremble, and that his armies, which had already possessed themselves of Savoy and Piedmont, were upon the point of taking Turin, Prince Eugene was obliged to march from the middle of Germany in order to succour Savoy. Having no money, without which cities cannot be either taken or defended, he addressed himself to some English merchants. These, at an hour and a half's warning, lent him five millions, whereby he was enabled to deliver Turin, and to beat the French; after which he wrote the following short letter to the persons who had disbursed him the above-mentioned sums: "Gentlemen, I received your money, and flatter myself that I have laid it out to your satisfaction." Such a circumstance as this raises a just pride in an English merchant, and makes him presume (not without some reason) to compare himself to a Roman citizen; and, indeed, a peer's brother does not think traffic beneath him. When the Lord Townshend was Minister of

State, a brother of his was content to be a city merchant; and at the time that the Earl of Oxford governed Great Britain, his younger brother was no more than a factor in Aleppo, where he chose to live, and where he died. This custom, which begins, however, to be laid aside, appears monstrous to Germans, vainly puffed up with their extraction. These think it morally impossible that the son of an English peer should be no more than a rich and powerful citizen, for all are princes in Germany. There have been thirty highnesses of the same name, all whose patrimony consisted only in their escutcheons and their pride.

In France the title of marquis is given gratis to any one who will accept of it; and whosoever arrives at Paris from the midst of the most remote provinces with money in his purse, and a name terminating in *ac* or *ille*, may strut about and cry, "Such a man as I! A man of my rank and figure!" and may look down upon a trader with sovereign contempt; whilst the trader on the other side, by thus often hearing his profession treated so disdainfully, is fool enough to blush at it. However, I need not say which is most useful to a nation; a lord, powdered in the tip of the mode, who knows exactly at what o'clock the king rises and goes to bed, and who gives himself airs of grandeur and state, at the same time that he is acting the slave in the ante-chamber of a prime minister; or a merchant, who enriches his country, dispatches orders from his counting-house to Surat and Grand Cairo, and contributes to the felicity of the world.

ON INOCULATION

It is inadvertently affirmed in the Christian countries of Europe that the English are fools and madmen. Fools, because they give their children the smallpox to prevent their catching it; and madmen, because they wantonly communicate a certain and dreadful distemper to their children, merely to prevent an uncertain evil. The English, on the other side, call the rest of the Europeans cowardly and unnatural. Cowardly, because they are afraid of putting their children to a little pain; unnatural, because they expose them to die one time or other of the smallpox. But that the reader may be able to judge whether the English or those who differ from them in opinion are in the right, here follows the history of the famed inoculation, which is mentioned with so much dread in France.

The Circassian women have, from time immemorial, communicated the smallpox to their children when not above six months old by making an incision in the arm, and by putting into this incision a pustule, taken carefully from the body of another child. This pustule produces the same effect in the arm it is laid in as yeast in a piece of dough; it ferments, and diffuses through the whole mass of blood the qualities with which it is impregnated. The pustules of the child in whom the artificial smallpox has been thus inoculated are employed to communicate the same distemper to others. There is an almost perpetual circulation of it in Circassia; and when unhappily the smallpox has quite left the country, the inhabitants of it are in as great trouble and perplexity as other nations when their harvest has fallen short.

The circumstance that introduced a custom in Circassia, which appears so singular to others, is nevertheless a cause common to all nations—I mean maternal tenderness and interest.

The Circassians are poor, and their daughters are beautiful, and indeed, it is in them they chiefly trade. They furnish with beauties the seraglios of the Turkish Sultan, of the Persian Sophy, and of all those who are wealthy enough to purchase and maintain such precious merchandise. These maidens are very honourably and virtuously instructed to fondle and caress men; are taught dances of a very polite and effeminate kind; and how to heighten by the most voluptuous artifices the pleasures of their disdainful masters for whom they are designed. These unhappy creatures repeat their lesson to their mothers, in the same manner as little girls among us repeat their catechism without understanding one word they say.

Now it often happened that, after a father and mother had taken the utmost care of the education of their children, they were frustrated of all their hopes in an instant. The smallpox getting into the family, one daughter died of it, another lost an eye, a third had a great nose at her recovery, and the unhappy parents were completely ruined. Even, frequently, when the smallpox became epidemical, trade was suspended for several years, which thinned very considerably the seraglios of Persia and Turkey.

A trading nation is always watchful over its own interests, and grasps at every discovery that may be of advantage to its commerce. The Circassians observed that scarce one person in a thousand was ever attacked by a smallpox of a violent kind. That some, indeed, had this distemper very favourably three or four times, but never twice so as to prove fatal; in a word, that no one ever had it in a violent degree twice in his life. They observed further, that when the smallpox is of the milder sort, and the pustules have only a tender, delicate skin to break through, they never leave the least scar in the face. From these natural observations they concluded that in case an infant of six months or a year old should have a milder sort of smallpox, he would not die of it, would not be marked, nor be ever afflicted with it again.

In order, therefore, to preserve the life and beauty of their children, the only thing remaining was to give them the smallpox in their infant years. This they did by inoculating in the body of a child a pustule taken from the most regular and at the same time the most favourable sort of smallpox that could be procured.

The experiment could not possibly fail. The Turks, who are people of good sense, soon adopted this custom, insomuch that at this time there is not a bassa in Constantinople but communicates the smallpox to his children of both sexes immediately upon their being weaned.

Some pretend that the Circassians borrowed this custom anciently from the Arabians; but we shall leave the clearing up of this point of history to some learned Benedictine, who will not fail to compile a great many folios on this subject, with the several proofs or authorities. All I have to say upon it is that, in the beginning of the reign of King George I, the Lady Wortley Montagu, a woman of as fine a genius, and endued with as great a strength of mind, as any of her sex in the British Kingdoms, being with her husband, who was ambassador at the Porte, made no scruple to communicate the smallpox to an infant of which she was delivered in Constantinople.

The chaplain represented to his lady, but to no purpose, that this was an un-Christian operation, and therefore that it could succeed with none but infidels. However, it had the most happy effect upon the son of the Lady Wortley Montagu, who, at her return to England, communicated the experiment to the Princess of Wales, now Queen of England. It must be confessed that this princess, abstracted from her crown and titles, was born to encourage the whole circle of arts, and to do good to mankind. She appears as an amiable philosopher on the throne, having never let slip one opportunity of improving the great talents she received from Nature, nor of exerting her beneficence. It is she who, being informed that a daughter of Milton was living, but in miserable circumstances, immediately sent her a considerable present. It is she who protects the learned Father Courayer. It is she who condescended to attempt a reconciliation between Dr. Clark and Mr. Leibnitz. The moment this princess heard of inoculation, she caused an experiment of it to be made on four criminals sentenced to die, and by that means preserved their lives doubly; for she not only saved them from the gallows, but by means of this artificial smallpox prevented their ever having that distemper in a natural way, with which they would very probably have been attacked one time or other, and might have died of in a more advanced age.

The princess being assured of the usefulness of this operation, caused her own children to be inoculated. A great part of the kingdom followed her example, and since that time ten thousand children, at least, of persons of condition owe in this manner their lives to her Majesty and to the Lady Wortley Montagu; and as many of the fair sex are obliged to them for their beauty.

Upon a general calculation, threescore persons in every hundred have the smallpox. Of these threescore, twenty die of it in the most favourable season of life, and as many more wear the disagreeable remains of it in their faces so long as they live. Thus, a fifth part of mankind either die or are disfigured by this distemper. But it does not prove fatal to so much as one among those who are inoculated in Turkey or in England, unless the patient be infirm, or would have died had not the experiment been made upon him. Besides, no one is disfigured, no one has the smallpox a second time, if the inoculation was perfect. It is therefore certain that had the lady of some French ambassador brought this secret from Constantinople to Paris, the nation would have been for ever obliged to her. Then the Duke de Villequier, father to the Duke d'Aumont, who enjoys the most vigorous constitution, and is the healthiest man in France, would not have been cut off in the flower of his age.

The Prince of Soubise, happy in the finest flush of health, would not have been snatched away at five-and-twenty, nor the Dauphin, grandfather to Louis XV, have been laid in his grave in his fiftieth year. Twenty thousand persons whom the smallpox swept away at Paris in 1723 would have been alive at this time. But are not the French fond of life, and is beauty so inconsiderable an advantage as to be disregarded by the ladies? It must be confessed that we are an odd kind of people. Perhaps our nation will imitate ten years hence this practice of the English, if the clergy and the physicians will but give them leave to do it; or possibly our countrymen may introduce inoculation three months hence in France out of mere whim, in case the English should discontinue it through fickleness.

I am informed that the Chinese have practised inoculation these hundred years, a circumstance that argues very much in its favour, since they are thought to be the wisest and best governed people in the world. The Chinese, indeed, do not communicate this distemper by inoculation, but at the nose, in the same manner as we take snuff. This is a more agreeable way, but then it produces the like effects; and proves at the same time that had inoculation been practised in France it would have saved the lives of thousands.

ON THE LORD BACON

Not long since the trite and frivolous question following was debated in a very polite and learned company, viz., Who was the greatest man, Caesar, Alexander, Tamerlane, Cromwell, etc.?

Somebody answered that Sir Isaac Newton excelled them all. The gentleman's assertion was very just; for if true greatness consists in having received from heaven a mighty genius, and in having employed it to enlighten our own mind and that of others, a man like Sir Isaac Newton, whose equal is hardly found in a thousand years, is the truly great man. And those politicians and conquerors (and all ages produce some) were generally so many illustrious wicked men. That man claims our respect who commands over the minds of the rest of the world by the force of truth, not those who enslave their fellow-creatures: he who is acquainted with the universe, not they who deface it.

Since, therefore, you desire me to give you an account of the famous personages whom England has given birth to, I shall begin with Lord Bacon, Mr. Locke, Sir Isaac Newton, etc. Afterwards the warriors and ministers of state shall come in their order.

I must begin with the celebrated Viscount Verulam, known in Europe by the name of Bacon, which was that of his family. His father had been Lord Keeper, and himself was a great many years Lord Chancellor under King James I. Nevertheless, amidst the intrigues of a court, and the affairs of his exalted employment, which alone were enough to engross his whole time, he yet found so much leisure for study as to make himself a great philosopher, a good historian, and an elegant writer; and a still more surprising circumstance is that he lived in an age in which the art of writing justly and elegantly was little known, much less true philosophy. Lord Bacon, as is the fate of man, was more esteemed after his death than in his lifetime. His enemies were in the British court, and his admirers were foreigners.

When the Marquis d'Effiat attended in England upon the Princess Henrietta Maria, daughter to Henry IV, whom King Charles I had married, that minister went and visited the Lord Bacon, who, being at that time sick in his bed, received him with the curtains shut close. "You resemble the angels," said the Marquis to him; "we hear those beings spoken of perpetually, and we believe them superior to men, but are never allowed the consolation to see them."

You know that this great man was accused of a crime very unbecoming a philosopher: I mean bribery and extortion. You know that he was sentenced by the House of Lords to pay a fine of about four hundred thousand French livres, to lose his peerage and his dignity of Chancellor; but in the present age the English revere his memory to such a degree, that they will scarce allow him to have been guilty. In case you should ask what are my thoughts on this head, I shall answer you in the words which I heard the Lord Bolingbroke use on another occasion. Several gentlemen were speaking, in his company, of the avarice with which the late Duke of Marlborough had been charged, some examples whereof being given, the Lord Bolingbroke was appealed to (who, having been in the opposite party, might perhaps, without the imputation of indecency, have been allowed to clear up that matter): "He was so great a man," replied his lordship, "that I have forgot his vices."

I shall therefore confine myself to those things which so justly gained Lord Bacon the esteem of all Europe.

The most singular and the best of all his pieces is that which, at this time, is the most useless and the least read I mean his *Novum Scientiarum Organum*. This is the scaffold with which the new philosophy was raised; and when the edifice was built, part of it at least, the scaffold was no longer of service.

The Lord Bacon was not yet acquainted with nature, but then he knew, and pointed out, the several paths that lead to it. He had despised in his younger years the thing called philosophy in the universities, and did all that lay in his power to prevent those societies of men instituted to improve human reason from depraving it by their quiddities, their horrors of the vacuum, their substantial forms, and all those impertinent terms which not only ignorance had rendered venerable, but which had been made sacred by their being ridiculously blended with religion.

He is the father of experimental philosophy. It must, indeed, be confessed that very surprising secrets had been found out before his time —the sea-compass, printing, engraving on copper plates, oil-painting, looking-glasses; the art of restoring, in some measure, old men to their sight by spectacles; gunpowder, etc., had been discovered. A new world has been sought for, found, and conquered. Would not one suppose that these sublime discoveries had been made by the greatest philosophers, and in ages much more enlightened than the present? But it was far otherwise; all these great changes happened in the most stupid and barbarous times. Chance only gave birth to most of those inventions; and it is very probable that what is called chance contributed very much to the discovery of America; at least, it has been always thought that Christopher Columbus undertook his voyage merely on the relation of a captain of a ship which a storm had driven as far westward as the Caribbean Islands. Be this as it will, men had sailed round the world, and could destroy cities by an artificial thunder more dreadful than the real one; but, then, they were not acquainted with the circulation of the blood, the weight of the air, the laws of motion, light, the number of our planets, etc. And a man who maintained a thesis on Aristotle's "Categories," on the universals *a parte rei* [from the material side], or such-like nonsense, was looked upon as a prodigy.

The most astonishing, the most useful inventions, are not those which reflect the greatest honour on the human mind. It is to a mechanical instinct, which is found in many men, and not to true philosophy, that most arts owe their origin.

The discovery of fire, the art of making bread, of melting and preparing metals, of building houses, and the invention of the shuttle, are infinitely more beneficial to mankind than printing or the sea-compass: and yet these arts were invented by uncultivated, savage men.

What a prodigious use the Greeks and Romans made afterwards of mechanics! Nevertheless, they believed that there were crystal heavens, that the stars were small lamps which sometimes fell into the sea, and one of their greatest philosophers, after long researches, found that the stars were so many flints which had been detached from the earth.

In a word, no one before the Lord Bacon was acquainted with experimental philosophy, nor with the several physical experiments which have been made since his time. Scarce one of them but is hinted at in his work, and he himself had made several. He made a kind of pneumatic engine, by which he guessed the elasticity of the air. He approached, on all sides as it were, to the discovery of its weight, and had very near attained it, but some time after Torricelli seized upon this truth. In a little time experimental philosophy began to be cultivated on a sudden in most parts of Europe. It was a hidden treasure which the Lord Bacon had some notion of, and which all the philosophers, encouraged by his promises, endeavoured to dig up.

But that which surprised me most was to read in his work, in express terms, the new attraction, the invention of which is ascribed to Sir Isaac Newton.

We must search, says Lord Bacon, whether there may not be a kind of magnetic power which operates between the earth and heavy bodies, between the moon and the ocean, between the planets, etc. In another place he says either heavy bodies must be carried towards the centre of the earth, or must be reciprocally attracted by it; and in the latter case it is evident that the nearer bodies, in their falling, draw towards the earth, the stronger they will attract one another. We must, says he, make an experiment to see whether the same clock will go faster on the top of a mountain or at the bottom of a mine; whether the strength of the weights decreases on the mountain and increases in the mine. It is probable that the earth has a true attractive power.

This forerunner in philosophy was also an elegant writer, an historian, and a wit.

His moral essays are greatly esteemed, but they were drawn up in the view of instructing rather than of pleasing; and, as they are not a satire upon mankind, like La Rochefoucauld's *Maxims,* nor written upon a sceptical plan, like Montaigne's *Essays,* they are not so much read as those two ingenious authors.

His *History of Henry VII* was looked upon as a masterpiece, but how is it possible that some persons can presume to compare so little a work with the history of our illustrious Thuanus?

Speaking about the famous impostor Perkin, son to a converted Jew, who assumed boldly the name and title of Richard IV, King of England, at the instigation of the Duchess of Burgundy, and who disputed the crown with Henry VII, the Lord Bacon writes as follows:

> At this time the King began again to be haunted with sprites, by the magic and curious arts of the Lady Margaret, who raised up the ghost of Richard, Duke of York, second son to King Edward IV, to walk and vex the King.
>
> After such time as she (Margaret of Burgundy) thought he (Perkin Warbeck) was perfect in his lesson, she began to cast with herself from what coast this blazing star should first appear, and at what time it must be upon the horizon of Ireland; for there had the like meteor strong influence before.

Methinks our sagacious Thuanus does not give in to such fustian, which formerly was looked upon as sublime, but in this age is justly called nonsense.

ON MR. LOCKE

Perhaps no man ever had a more judicious or more methodical genius, or was a more acute logician than Mr. Locke, and yet he was not deeply skilled in the mathematics. This great man could never subject himself to the tedious fatigue of calculations, nor to the dry pursuit of mathematical truths, which do not at first present any sensible objects to the mind; and no one has given better proofs than he that it is possible for a man to have a geometrical head without the assistance of geometry. Before his time, several great philosophers had declared, in the most positive terms, what the soul of man is; but as these absolutely knew nothing about it, they might very well be allowed to differ entirely in opinion from one another.

In Greece, the infant seat of arts and of errors, and where the grandeur as well as folly of the human mind went such prodigious lengths, the people used to reason about the soul in the very same manner as we do.

The divine Anaxagoras, in whose honour an altar was erected for his having taught mankind that the sun was greater than Peloponnesus, that snow was black, and that the heavens were of stone, affirmed that the soul was an aerial spirit, but at the same time immortal. Diogenes (not he who was a cynical philosopher after having coined base money) declared that the soul was a portion of the substance of God: an idea which we must confess was very sublime. Epicurus maintained that it was composed of parts in the same manner as the body.

Aristotle, who has been explained a thousand ways, because he is unintelligible, was of opinion, according to some of his disciples, that the understanding in all men is one and the same substance.

The divine Plato, master of the divine Aristotle—and the divine Socrates, master of the divine Plato—used to say that the soul was corporeal and eternal. No doubt but the demon of Socrates had instructed him in the nature of it. Some people, indeed, pretend that a man who boasted his being attended by a familiar genius must infallibly be either a knave or a madman, but this kind of people are seldom satisfied with any-thing but reason.

With regard to the Fathers of the Church, several in the primitive ages believed that the soul was human, and the angels and God corporeal. Men naturally improve upon every system. St. Bernard, as Father Mabillon confesses, taught that the soul after death does not see God in the celestial regions, but converses with Christ's human nature only. However, he was not believed this time on his bare word; the adventure of the crusade having a little sunk the credit of his oracles. Afterwards a thou-sand schoolmen arose, such as the Irrefragable Doctor, the Subtile Doctor, the Angelic Doctor, the Seraphic Doctor, and the Cherubic Doctor, who were all sure that they had a very clear and distinct idea of the soul, and yet wrote in such a manner that one would conclude they were resolved no one should understand a word in their writings. Our Descartes, born to discover the errors of antiquity, and at the same time to substitute his own; and hurried away by that systematic spirit which throws a cloud over the minds of the greatest men, thought he had demonstrated that the soul is the same thing as thought, in the same manner as matter, in his opinion, is the same as extension. He asserted that man thinks eternally, and that the soul, at its coming into the body, is informed with the whole series of metaphysical notions: knowing God, infinite space, possessing all abstract ideas—in a word, completely endued with the most sublime lights, which it unhappily forgets at its issuing from the womb.

Father Malebranche, in his sublime illusions, not only admitted innate ideas, but did not doubt of our living wholly in God, and that God is, as it were, our soul.

Such a multitude of reasoners having written the romance of the soul, a sage at last arose, who gave, with an air of the greatest modesty, the history of it. Mr. Locke has displayed the human soul in the same manner as an excellent anatomist explains the springs of the human body. He everywhere takes the light of physics for his guide. He sometimes presumes to speak affirmatively, but then he presumes also to doubt. Instead of concluding at once what we know not, he examines gradually what we would know. He takes an infant at the instant of his birth; he traces, step by step, the progress of his understanding; examines what things he has in common with beasts, and what he possesses above them. Above all, he consults himself: the being conscious that he himself thinks.

"I shall leave," says he, "to those who know more of this matter than myself, the examining whether the soul exists before or after the organization of our bodies. But I confess that it is my lot to be animated with one of those heavy souls which do not think always; and I am even so unhappy as not to conceive that it is more necessary the soul should think perpetually than that bodies should be for ever in motion."

With regard to myself, I shall boast that I have the honour to be as stupid in this particular as Mr. Locke. No one shall ever make me believe that I think always; and I am as little inclined as he could be to fancy that some weeks after I was conceived I was a very learned soul, knowing at that time a thousand things which I forgot at my birth, and possessing when in the womb (though to no manner of purpose) knowledge which I lost the instant I had occasion for it, and which I have never since been able to recover perfectly.

Mr. Locke, after having destroyed innate ideas, after having fully renounced the vanity of believing that we think always, after having laid down—from the most solid principles—that ideas enter the mind through the senses, having examined our simple and complex ideas, having traced the human mind through its several operations, having shown that all the languages in the world are imperfect, and the great abuse that is made of words every moment, he at last comes to consider the extent or rather the narrow limits of human knowledge. It was in this chapter he presumed to advance, but very modestly, the following words: "We shall, perhaps, never be capable of knowing whether a being, purely material, thinks or not." This sage assertion was, by more divines than one, looked upon as a scandalous declaration that the soul is material and mortal. Some Englishmen, devout after their way, sounded an alarm. The superstitious are the same in society as cowards in an army; they themselves are seized with a panic fear, and communicate it to others. It was loudly exclaimed that Mr. Locke intended to destroy religion; nevertheless, religion had nothing to do in the affair, it being a question purely philosophical, altogether independent of faith and revelation. Mr. Locke's opponents needed but to examine, calmly and impartially, whether the declaring that matter can think implies a contradiction, and whether God is able to communicate thought to matter. But divines are too apt to begin their declarations with saying that God is offended when people differ from them in opinion; in which they too much resemble the bad poets, who used to declare publicly that Boileau spoke irreverently of Louis XIV, because he ridiculed their stupid productions. Bishop Stillingfleet got the reputation of a calm and unprejudiced divine because he did not expressly make use of injurious terms in his dispute with Mr. Locke. That divine entered the lists against him, but was defeated; for he argued as a schoolman, and Locke as a philosopher, who was perfectly acquainted with the strong as well as the weak side of the human mind, and who fought with weapons whose temper he knew. If I might presume to give my opinion on so delicate a subject after Mr. Locke, I would say that men have long disputed on the nature and the immortality of the soul. With regard to its immortality, it is impossible to give a demonstration of it, since its nature is still the subject of controversy; which, however, must be thoroughly understood before a person can be able to determine whether it be immortal or not. Human reason is so little able, merely by its own strength, to demonstrate the immortality of the soul that it was absolutely necessary religion should reveal it to us. It is of advantage to society in general that mankind should believe the soul to be immortal; faith commands us to do this; nothing more is required, and the matter is cleared up at once. But it is otherwise with respect to its nature; it is of little importance to religion, which only requires the soul to be virtuous, whatever substance it may be made of. It is a clock which is given us to regulate, but the artist has not told us of what materials the spring of this clock is composed.

I am a body, and, I think, that's all I know of the matter. Shall I ascribe to an unknown cause what I can so easily impute to the only second cause I am acquainted with? Here all the school philosophers interrupt me with their arguments, and declare that there is only extension and solidity in bodies, and that there they can have nothing but motion and figure. Now motion, figure, extension and solidity cannot form a thought, and consequently the soul cannot be matter. All this so often repeated mighty series of reasoning amounts to no more than this: I am absolutely ignorant what matter is; I guess, but imperfectly, some properties of it; now I absolutely cannot tell whether these properties may be joined to thought. As I therefore know nothing, I maintain positively that matter cannot think. In this manner do the schools reason.

Mr. Locke addressed these gentlemen in the candid, sincere manner following: At least confess yourselves to be as ignorant as I. Neither your imaginations nor mine are able to comprehend in what manner a body is susceptible of ideas; and do you conceive better in what manner a substance, of what kind soever, is susceptible of them? As you cannot comprehend either matter or spirit, why will you presume to assert anything?

The superstitious man comes afterwards and declares that all those must be burned for the good of their souls who so much as suspect that it is possible for the body to think without any foreign assistance. But what would these people say should they themselves be proved irreligious? And indeed, what man can presume to assert, without being guilty at the same time of the greatest impiety, that it is impossible for the Creator to form matter with thought and sensation? Consider only, I beg you, what a dilemma you bring yourselves into, you who confine in this manner the power of the Creator. Beasts have the same organs, the same sensations, the same perceptions as we; they have memory, and combine certain ideas. In case it was not in the power of God to animate matter, and inform it with sensation, the consequence would be either that beasts are mere machines or that they have a spiritual soul.

Methinks it is clearly evident that beasts cannot be mere machines, which I prove thus. God has given to them the very same organs of sensation as to us: if therefore they have no sensation, God has created a useless thing; now according to your own confession God does nothing in vain; He therefore did not create so many organs of sensation, merely for them to be uninformed with this faculty; consequently beasts are not mere machines. Beasts, according to your assertion, cannot be animated with a spiritual soul; you will, therefore, in spite of yourself, be reduced to this only assertion, viz., that God has endued the organs of beasts, who are mere matter, with the faculties of sensation and perception, which you call instinct in them. But why may not God, if He pleases, communicate to our more delicate organs that faculty of feeling, perceiving, and thinking which we call human reason? To whatever side you turn, you are forced to acknowledge your own ignorance, and the boundless power of the Creator. Exclaim therefore no more against the sage, the modest philosophy of Mr. Locke, which so far from interfering with religion, would be of use to demonstrate the truth of it, in case religion wanted any such support. For what philosophy can be of a more religious nature than that, which affirming nothing but what it conceives clearly, and conscious of its own weakness, declares that we must always have recourse to God in our examining of the first principles?

Besides, we must not be apprehensive that any philosophical opinion will ever prejudice the religion of a country. Though our demonstrations clash directly with our mysteries, that is nothing to the purpose, for the latter are not less revered upon that account by our Christian philosophers, who know very well that the objects of reason and those of faith are of a very different nature. Philosophers will never form a religious sect, the reason of which is their writings are not calculated for the vulgar, and they themselves are free from enthusiasm. If we divide mankind into twenty parts, it will be found that nineteen of these consist of persons employed in manual labour, who will never know that such a man as Mr. Locke existed. In the remaining twentieth part how few are readers? And among such as are so, twenty amuse themselves with romances to one who studies philosophy. The thinking part of mankind is confined to a very small number, and these will never disturb the peace and tranquillity of the world.

Neither Montaigne, Locke, Bayle, Spinoza, Hobbes, the Lord Shaftesbury, Collins, nor Toland lighted up the firebrand of discord in their countries; this has generally been the work of divines, who being at first puffed up with the ambition of becoming chiefs of a sect, soon grew very desirous of being at the head of a party. But what do I say? All the works of the modern philosophers put together will never make so much noise as even the dispute which arose among the Franciscans, merely about the fashion of their sleeves and of their cowls.

ON DESCARTES AND SIR ISAAC NEWTON

A Frenchman who arrives in London will find philosophy, like everything else, very much changed there. He had left the world a plenum, and he now finds it a vacuum. At Paris the universe is seen composed of vortices of subtile matter; but nothing like it is seen in London. In France it is the pressure of the moon that causes the tides; but in England it is the sea that gravitates towards the moon; so that when you think that the moon should make it flood with us, those gentlemen fancy it should be ebb, which very unluckily cannot be proved. For to be able to do this, it is necessary the moon and the tides should have been inquired into at the very instant of the creation.

You will observe further that the sun, which in France is said to have nothing to do in the affair, comes in here for very near a quarter of its assistance. According to your Cartesians, everything is performed by an impulsion, of which we have very little notion; and according to Sir Isaac Newton, it is by an attraction, the cause of which is as much unknown to us. At Paris you imagine that the earth is shaped like a melon, or of an oblique figure; at London it has an oblate one. A Cartesian declares that light exists in the air; but a Newtonian asserts that it comes from the sun in six minutes and a half. The several operations of your chemistry are performed by acids, alkalies and subtile matter; but attraction prevails even in chemistry among the English.

The very essence of things is totally changed. You neither are agreed upon the definition of the soul, nor on that of matter. Descartes, as I observed in my last, maintains that the soul is the same thing with thought, and Mr. Locke has given a pretty good proof of the contrary.

Descartes asserts further that extension alone constitutes matter, but Sir Isaac adds solidity to it.

How furiously contradictory are these opinions!

> *Non nostrum inter vos tantas componere lites.*
>
> Virgil, Eclog. III.

'Tis not for us to end such great disputes.

This famous Newton, this destroyer of the Cartesian system, died in March, *anno* 1727. His countrymen honoured him in his lifetime, and interred him as though he had been a king who had made his people happy.

The English read with the highest satisfaction, and translated into their tongue, the eulogium of Sir Isaac Newton, which M. de Fontenelle spoke in the Academy of Sciences. M. de Fontenelle presides as judge over philosophers; and the English expected his decision, as a solemn declaration of the superiority of the English philosophy over that of the French. But when it was found that this gentleman had compared Descartes to Sir Isaac, the whole Royal Society in London rose up in arms. So far from acquiescing with M. Fontenelle's judgment, they criticized his discourse. And even several (who, however, were not the ablest philosophers in that body) were offended at the comparison, and for no other reason but because Descartes was a Frenchman.

It must be confessed that these two great men differed very much in conduct, in fortune, and in philosophy.

Nature had indulged Descartes with a shining and strong imagination, whence he became a very singular person both in private life and in his manner of reasoning. This imagination could not conceal itself even in his philosophical works, which are everywhere adorned with very shining, ingenious metaphors and figures. Nature had almost made him a poet; and indeed he wrote a piece of poetry for the entertainment of Christina, Queen of Sweden, which however was suppressed in honour to his memory.

He embraced a military life for some time, and afterwards becoming a complete philosopher, he did not think the passion of love derogatory to his character. He had by his mistress a daughter called Froncine, who died young, and was very much regretted by him. Thus he experienced every passion incident to mankind.

He was a long time of opinion that it would be necessary for him to fly from the society of his fellow creatures, and especially from his native country, in order to enjoy the happiness of cultivating his philosophical studies in full liberty.

Descartes was very right, for his contemporaries were not knowing enough to improve and enlighten his understanding, and were capable of little else than of giving him uneasiness.

He left France purely to go in search of truth, which was then persecuted by the wretched philosophy of the schools. However, he found that reason was as much disguised and depraved in the universities of Holland, into which he withdrew, as in his own country. For at the time that the French condemned the only propositions of his philosophy which were true, he was persecuted by the pretended philosophers of Holland, who understood him no better; and who, having a nearer view of his glory, hated his person the more, so that he was obliged to leave Utrecht.

Descartes was injuriously accused of being an atheist, the last refuge of religious scandal: and he who had employed all the sagacity and penetration of his genius in searching for new proofs of the existence of a God was suspected to believe there was no such Being.

Such a persecution from all sides must necessarily suppose a most exalted merit as well as a very distinguished reputation, and indeed he possessed both. Reason at that time darted a ray upon the world through the gloom of the schools, and the prejudices of popular superstition. At last his name spread so universally that the French were desirous of bringing him back into his native country by rewards, and accordingly offered him an annual pension of a thousand crowns. Upon these hopes Descartes returned to France; paid the fees of his patent, which was sold at that time, but no pension was settled upon him. Thus disappointed, he returned to his solitude in North Holland, where he again pursued the study of philosophy, whilst the great Galileo, at fourscore years of age, was groaning in the prisons of the Inquisition, only for having demonstrated the earth's motion.

At last Descartes was snatched from the world in the flower of his age at Stockholm. His death was owing to a bad regimen, and he expired in the midst of some literati who were his enemies, and under the hands of a physician to whom he was odious.

The progress of Sir Isaac Newton's life was quite different. He lived happy, and very much honoured in his native country, to the age of fourscore and five years.

It was his peculiar felicity, not only to be born in a country of liberty, but in an age when all scholastic impertinences were banished from the world. Reason alone was cultivated, and mankind could only be his pupil, not his enemy.

One very singular difference in the lives of these two great men is that Sir Isaac, during the long course of years he enjoyed, was never sensible to any passion, was not subject to the common frailties of mankind, nor ever had any commerce with women—a circumstance which was assured me by the physician and surgeon who attended him in his last moments.

We may admire Sir Isaac Newton on this occasion, but then we must not censure Descartes.

The opinion that generally prevails in England with regard to these new philosophers is that the latter was a dreamer, and the former a sage.

Very few people in England read Descartes, whose works indeed are now useless. On the other side, but a small number peruse those of Sir Isaac, because to do this the student must be deeply skilled in the mathematics, otherwise those works will be unintelligible to him. But notwithstanding this, these great men are the subject of everyone's discourse. Sir Isaac Newton is allowed every advantage, whilst Descartes is not indulged a single one. According to some, it is to the former that we owe the discovery of a vacuum, that the air is a heavy body, and the invention of telescopes. In a word, Sir Isaac Newton is here as the Hercules of fabulous story, to whom the ignorant ascribed all the feats of ancient heroes.

In a critique that was made in London on M. de Fontenelle's discourse, the writer presumed to assert that Descartes was not a great geometrician. Those who make such a declaration may justly be reproached with flying in their master's face. Descartes extended the limits of geometry as far beyond the place where he found them as Sir Isaac did after him. The former first taught the method of expressing curves by equations. This geometry which, thanks to him for it, is now grown common was so abstruse in his time that not so much as one professor would undertake to explain it; and Schotten in Holland, and Format in France, were the only men who understood it.

He applied this geometrical and inventive genius to dioptrics, which, when treated of by him, became a new art. And if he was mistaken in some things, the reason of that is a man who discovers a new tract of land cannot at once know all the properties of the soil. Those who come after him, and make these lands fruitful, are at least obliged to him for the discovery. I will not deny but that there are innumerable errors in the rest of Descartes' works.

Geometry was a guide he himself had in some measure fashioned, which would have conducted him safely through the several paths of natural philosophy. Nevertheless, he at last abandoned this guide, and gave entirely into the humour of forming hypotheses; and then philosophy was no more than an ingenious romance, fit only to amuse the ignorant. He was mistaken in the nature of the soul, in the proofs of the existence of a God, in matter, in the laws of motion, and in the nature of light. He admitted innate ideas, he invented new elements, he created a world; he made man according to his own fancy; and it is justly said that the man of Descartes is, in fact, that of Descartes only, very different from the real one.

He pushed his metaphysical errors so far as to declare that two and two make four for no other reason but because God would have it so. However, it will not be making him too great a compliment if we affirm that he was valuable even in his mistakes. He deceived himself, but then it was at least in a methodical way. He destroyed all the absurd chimeras with which youth had been infatuated for two thousand years. He taught his contemporaries how to reason, and enabled them to employ his own weapons against himself. If Descartes did not pay in good money, he however did great service in crying down that of a base alloy.

I indeed believe that very few will presume to compare his philosophy in any respect with that of Sir Isaac Newton. The former is an essay, the latter a masterpiece. But then the man who first brought us to the path of truth was perhaps as great a genius as he who afterwards conducted us through it.

Descartes gave sight to the blind. These saw the errors of antiquity and of the sciences. The path he struck out is since become boundless. Robault's little work was, during some years, a complete system of physics; but now all the Transactions of the several academies in Europe put together do not form so much as the beginning of a system. In fathoming this abyss no bottom has been found. We are now to examine what discoveries Sir Isaac Newton has made in it.

ON ATTRACTION

The discoveries which gained Sir Isaac Newton so universal a reputation relate to the system of the world, to light, to geometrical infinities, and lastly, to chronology, with which he used to amuse himself after the fatigue of his severer studies.

I will now acquaint you (without prolixity if possible) with the few things I have been able to comprehend of all these sublime ideas. With regard to the system of our world, disputes were a long time maintained on the cause that turns the planets and keeps them in their orbits, and on those causes which make all bodies here below descend towards the surface of the earth.

The system of Descartes, explained and improved since his time, seemed to give a plausible reason for all those phenomena; and this reason seemed more just, as it is simple and intelligible to all capacities. But in philosophy, a student ought to doubt of the things he fancies he understands too easily, as much as of those he does not understand.

Gravity, the falling of accelerated bodies on the earth, the revolution of the planets in their orbits, their rotations round their axis, all this is mere motion. Now motion cannot perhaps be conceived any otherwise than by impulsion; therefore all those bodies must be impelled. But by what are they impelled? All space is full, it therefore is filled with a very subtile matter, since this is imperceptible to us; this matter goes from west to east, since all the planets are carried from west to east. Thus from hypothesis to hypothesis, from one appearance to another, philosophers have imagined a vast whirlpool of subtile matter, in which the planets are carried round the sun; they also have created another particular vortex which floats in the great one, and which turns daily round the planets. When all this is done, it is pretended that gravity depends on this diurnal motion; for, say these, the velocity of the subtile matter that turns round our little vortex must be seventeen times more rapid than that of the earth; or, in case its velocity is seventeen times greater than that of the earth, its centrifugal force must be vastly greater, and consequently impel all bodies towards the earth. This is the cause of gravity, according to the Cartesian system. But the theorist, before he calculated the centrifugal force and velocity of the subtile matter, should first have been certain that it existed.

Sir Isaac Newton seems to have destroyed all these great and little vortices, both that which carries the planets round the sun, as well as the other which supposes every planet to turn on its own axis.

First, with regard to the pretended little vortex of the earth, it is demonstrated that it must lose its motion by insensible degrees; it is demonstrated that if the earth swims in a fluid its density must be equal to that of the earth; and in case its density be the same, all the bodies we endeavour to move must meet with an insuperable resistance.

With regard to the great vortices, they are still more chimerical, and it is impossible to make them agree with Kepler's law, the truth of which has been demonstrated. Sir Isaac shows that the revolution of the fluid in which Jupiter is supposed to be carried is not the same with regard to the revolution of the fluid of the earth as the revolution of Jupiter with respect to that of the earth. He proves that as the planets make their revolutions in ellipses, and consequently being at a much greater distance one from the other in their aphelia and a little nearer in their perihelia, the earth's velocity, for instance, ought to be greater when it is nearer Venus and Mars, because the fluid that carries it along, being then more pressed, ought to have a greater motion; and yet it is even then that the earth's motion is slower.

He proves that there is no such thing as a celestial matter which goes from west to east, since the comets traverse those spaces, sometimes from east to west, and at other times from north to south.

In fine, the better to resolve, if possible, every difficulty, he proves, and even by experiments, that it is impossible there should be a plenum, and brings back the vacuum, which Aristotle and Descartes had banished from the world.

Having by these and several other arguments destroyed the Cartesian vortices, he despaired of ever being able to discover whether there is a secret principle in nature which, at the same time, is the cause of the motion of all celestial bodies, and that of gravity on the earth. But being retired in 1666, upon account of the Plague, to a solitude near Cambridge, as he was walking one day in his garden and saw some fruits fall from a tree, he fell into a profound meditation on that gravity, the cause of which had so long been sought, but in vain, by all the philosophers, whilst the vulgar think there is nothing mysterious in it. He said to himself that from what height soever in our hemisphere those bodies might descend, their fall would certainly be in the progression discovered by Galileo; and the spaces they run through would be as the square of the times. Why may not this power which causes heavy bodies to descend, and is the same without any sensible diminution at the remotest distance from the centre of the earth, or on the summits of the highest mountains, why, said Sir Isaac, may not this power extend as high as the moon? And in case its influence reaches so far, is it not very probable that this power retains it in its orbit, and determines its motion? But in case the moon obeys this principle (whatever it be) may we not conclude very naturally that the rest of the planets are equally subject to it? In case this power exists (which besides is proved) it must increase in an inverse ratio of the squares of the distances. All, therefore, that remains is to examine how far a heavy body which should fall upon the earth from a moderate height would go, and how far in the same time a body which should fall from the orbit of the moon would descend. To find this, nothing is wanted but the measure of the earth, and the distance of the moon from it.

Thus Sir Isaac Newton reasoned. But at that time the English had but a very imperfect measure of our globe, and depended on the uncertain supposition of mariners, who computed a degree to contain but sixty English miles, whereas it consists in reality of near seventy. As this false computation did not agree with the conclusions which Sir Isaac intended to draw from them, he laid aside this pursuit. A half-learned philosopher, remarkable only for his vanity, would have made the measure of the earth agree, anyhow, with his system. Sir Isaac, however, chose rather to quit the researches he was then engaged in. But after Mr. Picard had measured the earth exactly, by tracing that meridian which redounds so much to the honour of the French, Sir Isaac Newton resumed his former reflections, and found his account in Mr. Picard's calculation.

A circumstance which has always appeared wonderful to me is that such sublime discoveries should have been made by the sole assistance of a quadrant and a little arithmetic.

The circumference of the earth is 123,249,600 feet. This, among other things, is necessary to prove the system of attraction.

The instant we know the earth's circumference, and the distance of the moon, we know that of the moon's orbit, and the diameter of this orbit. The moon performs its revolution in that orbit in twenty-seven days, seven hours, forty-three minutes. It is demonstrated that the moon in its mean motion makes a hundred and fourscore and seven thousand nine hundred and sixty feet (of Paris) in a minute. It is likewise demonstrated, by a known theorem, that the central force which should make a body fall from the height of the moon would make its velocity no more than fifteen Paris feet in a minute of time. Now if the law by which bodies gravitate and attract one another in an inverse ratio to the squares of the distances be true, if the same power acts according to that law throughout all nature, it is evident that as the earth is sixty semi-diameters distant from the moon, a heavy body must necessarily fall (on the earth) fifteen feet in the first second, and fifty-four thousand feet in the first minute.

Now a heavy body falls, in reality, fifteen feet in the first second, and goes in the first minute fifty-four thousand feet, which number is the square of sixty multiplied by fifteen. Bodies, therefore, gravitate in an inverse ratio of the squares of the distances; consequently, what causes gravity on earth, and keeps the moon in its orbit, is one and the same power; it being demonstrated that the moon gravitates on the earth, which is the centre of its particular motion, it is demonstrated that the earth and the moon gravitate on the sun which is the centre of their annual motion.

The rest of the planets must be subject to this general law; and if this law exists, these planets must follow the laws which Kepler discovered. All these laws, all these relations are indeed observed by the planets with the utmost exactness; therefore, the power of attraction causes all the planets to gravitate towards the sun, in like manner as the moon gravitates towards our globe.

Finally as in all bodies reaction is equal to action, it is certain that the earth gravitates also towards the moon, and that the sun gravitates towards both. That every one of the satellites of Saturn gravitates towards the other four, and the other four towards it; all five towards Saturn, and Saturn towards all. That it is the same with regard to Jupiter; and that all these globes are attracted by the sun, which is reciprocally attracted by them.

This power of gravitation acts proportionably to the quantity of matter in bodies, a truth which Sir Isaac has demonstrated by experiments. This new discovery has been of use to show that the sun (the centre of the planetary system) attracts them all in a direct ratio of their quantity of matter combined with their nearness. From hence Sir Isaac, rising by degrees to discoveries which seemed not to be formed for the human mind, is bold enough to compute the quantity of matter contained in the sun and in every planet; and in this manner shows, from the simple laws of mechanics, that every celestial globe ought necessarily to be where it is placed.

His bare principle of the laws of gravitation accounts for all the apparent inequalities in the course of the celestial globes. The variations of the moon are a necessary consequence of those laws. Moreover, the reason is evidently seen why the nodes of the moon perform their revolutions in nineteen years, and those of the earth in about twenty-six thousand. The several appearances observed in the tides are also a very simple effect of this attraction. The proximity of the moon, when at the full, and when it is new, and its distance in the quadratures or quarters, combined with the action of the sun, exhibit a sensible reason why the ocean swells and sinks.

After having shown by his sublime theory the course and inequalities of the planets, he subjects comets to the same law. The orbit of these fires (unknown for so great a series of years), which was the terror of mankind and the rock against which philosophy split, placed by Aristotle below the moon, and sent back by Descartes above the sphere of Saturn, is at last placed in its proper seat by Sir Isaac Newton.

He proves that comets are solid bodies which move in the sphere of the sun's activity, and that they describe an ellipsis so very eccentric, and so near to parabolas, that certain comets must take up above five hundred years in their revolution.

The learned Dr. Halley is of opinion that the comet seen in 1680 is the same which appeared in Julius Caesar's time. This shows more than any other that comets are hard, opaque bodies; for it descended so near to the sun as to come within a sixth part of the diameter of this planet from it, and consequently might have contracted a degree of heat two thousand times stronger than that of red-hot iron; and would have been soon dispersed in vapour, had it not been a firm, dense body. The guessing the course of comets began then to be very much in vogue. The celebrated Bernoulli concluded by his system that the famous comet of 1680 would appear again the 17th of May, 1719. Not a single astronomer in Europe went to bed that night. However, they needed not to have broken their rest, for the famous comet never appeared. There is at least more cunning, if not more certainty, in fixing its return to so remote a distance as five hundred and seventy-five years. As to Mr. Whiston, he affirmed very seriously that in the time of the Deluge a comet overflowed the terrestrial globe. And he was so unreasonable as to wonder that people laughed at him for making such an assertion. The ancients were almost in the same way of thinking with Mr. Whiston, and fancied that comets were always the forerunners of some great calamity which was to befall mankind. Sir Isaac Newton, on the contrary, suspected that they are very beneficent, and that vapours exhale from them merely to nourish and vivify the planets, which imbibe in their course the several particles the sun has detached from the comets, an opinion which, at least, is more probable than the former. But this is not all. If this power of gravitation or attraction acts on all the celestial globes, it acts undoubtedly on the several parts of these globes. For in case bodies attract one another in proportion to the quantity of matter contained in them, it can only be in proportion to the quantity of their parts; and if this power is found in the whole, it is undoubtedly in the half, in the quarter, in the eighth part, and so on *in infinitum*.

This is attraction, the great spring by which all Nature is moved. Sir Isaac Newton, after having demonstrated the existence of this principle, plainly foresaw that its very name would offend; and, therefore, this philosopher, in more places than one of his books, gives the reader some caution about it. He bids him beware of confounding this name with what the ancients called occult qualities, but to be satisfied with knowing that there is in all bodies a central force, which acts to the utmost limits of the universe, according to the invariable laws of mechanics.

It is surprising, after the solemn protestations Sir Isaac made, that such eminent men as Mr. Sorin and M. de Fontenelle should have imputed to this great philosopher the verbal and chimerical way of reasoning of the Aristotelians; Mr. Sorin in the Memoirs of the Academy of 1709, and M. de Fontenelle in the very eulogium of Sir Isaac Newton.

Most of the French (the learned and others) have repeated this reproach. These are for ever crying out, "Why did he not employ the word *impulsion*, which is so well understood, rather than that of *attraction*, which is unintelligible?"

Sir Isaac might have answered these critics thus: "First, you have as imperfect an idea of the word impulsion as of that of attraction; and in case you cannot conceive how one body tends towards the centre of another body, neither can you conceive by what power one body can impel another.

"Secondly, I could not admit of impulsion; for to do this I must have known that a celestial matter was the agent. But so far from knowing that there is any such matter, I have proved it to be merely imaginary.

"Thirdly, I use the word attraction for no other reason but to express an effect which I discovered in Nature—a certain and indisputable effect of an unknown principle—a quality inherent in matter, the cause of which persons of greater abilities than I can pretend to may, if they can, find out."

"What have you, then, taught us?" will these people say further; "and to what purpose are so many calculations to tell us what you yourself do not comprehend?"

"I have taught you," may Sir Isaac rejoin, "that all bodies gravitate towards one another in proportion to their quantity of matter; that these central forces alone keep the planets and comets in their orbits, and cause them to move in the proportion before set down. I demonstrate to you that it is impossible there should be any other cause which keeps the planets in their orbits than that general phenomenon of gravity. For heavy bodies fall on the earth according to the proportion demonstrated of central forces; and the planets finishing their course according to these same proportions, in case there were another power that acted upon all those bodies, it would either increase their velocity or change their direction. Now, not one of those bodies ever has a single degree of motion or velocity, or has any direction but what is demonstrated to be the effect of the central forces. Consequently it is impossible there should be any other principle."

Give me leave once more to introduce Sir Isaac speaking. Shall he not be allowed to say: "My case and that of the ancients is very different. These saw, for instance, water ascend in pumps, and said, 'the water rises because it abhors a vacuum.' But with regard to myself, I am in the case of a man who should have first observed that water ascends in pumps, but should leave others to explain the cause of this effect. The anatomist, who first declared that the motion of the arm is owing to the contraction of the muscles, taught mankind an indisputable truth. But are they less obliged to him because he did not know the reason why the muscles contract? The cause of the elasticity of the air is unknown, but he who first discovered this spring performed a very signal service to natural philosophy. The spring that I discovered was more hidden and more universal, and for that very reason mankind ought to thank me the more. I have discovered a new property of matter—one of the secrets of the Creator—and have calculated and discovered the effects of it. After this, shall people quarrel with me about the name I give it?"

Vortices may be called an occult quality because their existence was never proved. Attraction, on the contrary, is a real thing because its effects are demonstrated, and the proportions of it are calculated. The cause of this cause is among the *Arcana* of the Almighty.

Procedes huc, et non amplius.
[Thus far shalt thou go, and no farther.]

ON SIR ISAAC NEWTON'S OPTICS

The philosophers of the last age found out a new universe; and a circumstance which made its discovery more difficult was that no one had so much as suspected its existence. The most sage and judicious were of opinion that it was a frantic rashness to dare so much as to imagine that it was possible to guess the laws by which the celestial bodies move and the manner how light acts. Galileo, by his astronomical discoveries, Kepler, by his calculation, Descartes (at least, in his dioptrics), and Sir Isaac Newton, in all his works, severally saw the mechanism of the springs of the world. The geometricians have subjected infinity to the laws of calculation. The circulation of the blood in animals, and of the sap in vegetables, have changed the face of Nature with regard to us. A new kind of existence has been given to bodies in the air-pump. By the assistance of telescopes bodies have been brought nearer to one another. Finally, the several discoveries which Sir Isaac Newton has made on light are equal to the boldest things which the curiosity of man could expect after so many philosophical novelties.

Till Antonio de Dominis the rainbow was considered as an inexplicable miracle. This philosopher guessed that it was a necessary effect of the sun and rain. Descartes gained immortal fame by his mathematical explication of this so natural a phenomenon. He calculated the reflections and refractions of light in drops of rain. And his sagacity on this occasion was at that time looked upon as next to divine.

But what would he have said had it been proved to him that he was mistaken in the nature of light; that he had not the least reason to maintain that it is a globular body? That it is false to assert that this matter, spreading itself through the whole, waits only to be projected forward by the sun, in order to be put in action, in like manner as a long staff acts at one end when pushed forward by the other. That light is certainly darted by the sun; in fine, that light is transmitted from the sun to the earth in about seven minutes, though a cannon-ball, which were not to lose any of its velocity, could not go that distance in less than twenty-five years. How great would have been his astonishment had he been told that light does not reflect directly by impinging against the solid parts of bodies, that bodies are not transparent when they have large pores, and that a man should arise who would demonstrate all these paradoxes, and anatomize a single ray of light with more dexterity than the ablest artist dissects a human body. This man is come. Sir Isaac Newton has demonstrated to the eye, by the bare assistance of the prism, that light is a composition of coloured rays, which, being united, form white colour. A single ray is by him divided into seven, which all fall upon a piece of linen, or a sheet of white paper, in their order, one above the other, and at unequal distances. The first is red, the second orange, the third yellow, the fourth green, the fifth blue, the sixth indigo, the seventh a violet-purple. Each of these rays, transmitted afterwards by a hundred other prisms, will never change the colour it bears; in like manner, as gold, when completely purged from its dross, will never change afterwards in the crucible. As a super-abundant proof that each of these elementary rays has inherently in itself that which forms its colour to the eye, take a small piece of yellow wood, for instance, and set it in the ray of a red colour; this wood will instantly be tinged red. But set it in the ray of a green colour, it assumes a green colour, and so of all the rest.

From what cause, therefore, do colours arise in Nature? It is nothing but the disposition of bodies to reflect the rays of a certain order and to absorb all the rest.

What, then, is this secret disposition? Sir Isaac Newton demonstrates that it is nothing more than the density of the small constituent particles of which a body is composed. And how is this reflection performed? It was supposed to arise from the rebounding of the rays, in the same manner as a ball on the surface of a solid body. But this is a mistake, for Sir Isaac taught the astonished philosophers that bodies are opaque for no other reason but because their pores are large, that light reflects on our eyes from the very bosom of those pores, that the smaller the pores of a body are the more such a body is transparent. Thus paper, which reflects the light when dry, transmits it when oiled, because the oil, by filling its pores, makes them much smaller.

It is there that examining the vast porosity of bodies, every particle having its pores, and every particle of those particles having its own, he shows we are not certain that there is a cubic inch of solid matter in the universe, so far are we from conceiving what matter is. Having thus divided, as it were, light into its elements, and carried the sagacity of his discoveries so far as to prove the method of distinguishing compound colours from such as are primitive, he shows that these elementary rays, separated by the prism, are ranged in their order for no other reason but because they are refracted in that very order; and it is this property (unknown till he discovered it) of breaking or splitting in this proportion; it is this unequal refraction of rays, this power of refracting the red less than the orange colour, etc., which he calls the different refrangibility. The most reflexible rays are the most refrangible, and from hence he evinces that the same power is the cause both of the reflection and refraction of light.

But all these wonders are merely but the opening of his discoveries. He found out the secret to see the vibrations or fits of light which come and go incessantly, and which either transmit light or reflect it, according to the density of the parts they meet with. He has presumed to calculate the density of the particles of air necessary between two glasses, the one flat, the other convex on one side, set one upon the other, in order to operate such a transmission or reflection, or to form such and such a colour.

From all these combinations he discovers the proportion in which light acts on bodies and bodies act on light.

He saw light so perfectly that he has determined to what degree of perfection the art of increasing it, and of assisting our eyes by telescopes, can be carried.

Descartes, from a noble confidence that was very excusable, considering how strongly he was fired at the first discoveries he made in an art which he almost first found out; Descartes, I say, hoped to discover in the stars, by the assistance of telescopes, objects as small as those we discern upon the earth.

But Sir Isaac has shown that dioptric telescopes cannot be brought to a greater perfection, because of that refraction, and of that very refrangibility, which at the same time that they bring objects nearer to us, scatter too much the elementary rays. He has calculated in these glasses the proportion of the scattering of the red and of the blue rays; and proceeding so far as to demonstrate things which were not supposed even to exist, he examines the inequalities which arise from the shape or figure of the glass, and that which arises from the refrangibility. He finds that the object glass of the telescope being convex on one side and flat on the other, in case the flat side be turned towards the object, the error which arises from the construction and position of the glass is above five thousand times less than the error which arises from the refrangibility; and, therefore, that the shape or figure of the glasses is not the cause why telescopes cannot be carried to a greater perfection, but arises wholly from the nature of light.

For this reason he invented a telescope which discovers objects by reflection, and not by refraction. Telescopes of this new kind are very hard to make, and their use is not easy; but, according to the English, a reflective telescope of but five feet has the same effect as another of a hundred feet in length.

ON INFINITES IN GEOMETRY, AND SIR ISAAC NEWTON'S CHRONOLOGY

The labyrinth and abyss of infinity is also a new course Sir Isaac Newton has gone through, and we are obliged to him for the clue, by whose assistance we are enabled to trace its various windings.

Descartes got the start of him also in this astonishing invention. He advanced with mighty steps in his geometry, and was arrived at the very borders of infinity, but went no farther. Dr. Wallis, about the middle of the last century, was the first who reduced a fraction by a perpetual division to an infinite series.

The Lord Brouncker employed this series to square the hyperbola.

Mercator published a demonstration of this quadrature; much about which time Sir Isaac Newton, being then twenty-three years of age, had invented a general method to perform on all geometrical curves what had just before been tried on the hyperbola.

It is to this method of subjecting everywhere infinity to algebraical calculations that the name is given of differential calculations or of fluxions and integral calculation. It is the art of numbering and measuring exactly a thing whose existence cannot be conceived.

And, indeed, would you not imagine that a man laughed at you who should declare that there are lines infinitely great which form an angle infinitely little?

That a right line, which is a right line so long as it is finite, by changing infinitely little its direction, becomes an infinite curve; and that a curve may become infinitely less than another curve?

That there are infinite squares, infinite cubes, and infinites of infinites, all greater than one another, and the last but one of which is nothing in comparison of the last?

All these things, which at first appear to be the utmost excess of frenzy, are in reality an effort of the subtlety and extent of the human mind, and the art of finding truths which till then had been unknown.

This so bold edifice is even founded on simple ideas. The business is to measure the diagonal of a square, to give the area of a curve, to find the square root of a number, which has none in common arithmetic. After all, the imagination ought not to be startled any more at so many orders of infinites than at the so well-known proposition, viz., that curve lines may always be made to pass between a circle and a tangent, or at that other, namely, that matter is divisible *in infinitum*. These two truths have been demonstrated many years, and are no less incomprehensible than the things we have been speaking of.

For many years the invention of this famous calculation was denied to Sir Isaac Newton. In Germany Mr. Leibnitz was considered as the inventor of the differences or moments, called fluxions, and Mr. Bernoulli claimed the integral calculus. However, Sir Isaac is now thought to have first made the discovery, and the other two have the glory of having once made the world doubt whether it was to be ascribed to him or them. Thus some contested with Dr. Harvey the invention of the circulation of the blood, as others disputed with Mr. Perrault that of the circulation of the sap.

Hartsocher and Leuwenhoek disputed with each other the honour of having first seen the *vermiculi* of which mankind are formed. This Hartsocher also contested with Huygens the invention of a new method of calculating the distance of a fixed star. It is not yet known to what philosopher we owe the invention of the cycloid.

Be this as it will, it is by the help of this geometry of infinites that Sir Isaac Newton attained to the most sublime discoveries. I am now to speak of another work, which, though more adapted to the capacity of the human mind, does nevertheless display some marks of that creative genius with which Sir Isaac Newton was informed in all his researches. The work I mean is a chronology of a new kind, for what province soever he undertook he was sure to change the ideas and opinions received by the rest of men.

Accustomed to unravel and disentangle chaos, he was resolved to convey at least some light into that of the fables of antiquity which are blended and confounded with history, and fix an uncertain chronology. It is true that there is no family, city, or nation, but endeavours to remove its original as far backward as possible. Besides, the first historians were the most negligent in setting down the eras: books were infinitely less common than they are at this time, and, consequently, authors being not so obnoxious to censure, they therefore imposed upon the world with greater impunity; and, as it is evident that these have related a great number of fictitious particulars, it is probable enough that they also gave us several false eras.

It appeared in general to Sir Isaac that the world was five hundred years younger than chronologers declare it to be. He grounds his opinion on the ordinary course of nature, and on the observations which astronomers have made.

By the course of nature we here understand the time that every generation of men lives upon the earth. The Egyptians first employed this vague and uncertain method of calculating when they began to write the beginning of their history. These computed three hundred and forty-one generations from Menes to Sethon; and, having no fixed era, they supposed three generations to consist of a hundred years. In this manner they computed eleven thousand three hundred and forty years from Menes's reign to that of Sethon.

The Greeks before they counted by Olympiads followed the method of the Egyptians, and even gave a little more extent to generations, making each to consist of forty years.

Now, here, both the Egyptians and the Greeks made an erroneous computation. It is true, indeed, that, according to the usual course of nature, three generations last about a hundred and twenty years; but three reigns are far from taking up so many. It is very evident that mankind in general live longer than kings are found to reign, so that an author who should write a history in which there were no dates fixed, and should know that nine kings had reigned over a nation; such a historian would commit a great error should he allow three hundred years to these nine monarchs. Every generation takes about thirty-six years; every reign is, one with the other, about twenty. Thirty kings of England have swayed the sceptre from William the Conqueror to George I, the years of whose reigns added together amount to six hundred and forty-eight years; which, being divided equally among the thirty kings, give to every one a reign of twenty-one years and a half very near. Sixty-three kings of France have sat upon the throne; these have, one with another, reigned about twenty years each. This is the usual course of nature. The ancients, therefore, were mistaken when they supposed the durations in general of reigns to equal that of generations. They, therefore, allowed too great a number of years, and consequently some years must be subtracted from their computation.

Astronomical observations seem to have lent a still greater assistance to our philosopher. He appears to us stronger when he fights upon his own ground.

You know that the earth, besides its annual motion which carries it round the sun from west to east in the space of a year, has also a singular revolution which was quite unknown till within these late years. Its poles have a very slow retrograde motion from east to west, whence it happens that their position every day does not correspond exactly with the same point of the heavens. This difference, which is so insensible in a year, becomes pretty considerable in time; and in threescore and twelve years the difference is found to be of one degree, that is to say, the three hundred and sixtieth part of the circumference of the whole heaven. Thus after seventy-two years the colure of the vernal equinox which passed through a fixed star corresponds with another fixed star. Hence it is that the sun, instead of being in that part of the heavens in which the Ram was situated in the time of Hipparchus, is found to correspond with that part of the heavens in which the Bull was situated; and the Twins are placed where the Bull then stood. All the signs have changed their situation, and yet we still retain the same manner of speaking as the ancients did. In this age we say that the sun is in the Ram in the spring from the same principle of condescension that we say that the sun turns round.

Hipparchus was the first among the Greeks who observed some change in the constellations with regard to the equinoxes, or rather who learnt it from the Egyptians. Philosophers ascribed this motion to the stars; for in those ages people were far from imagining such a revolution in the earth, which was supposed to be immovable in every respect. They therefore created a heaven in which they fixed the several stars, and gave this heaven a particular motion by which it was carried towards the east, whilst that all the stars seemed to perform their diurnal revolution from east to west. To this error they added a second of much greater consequence, by imagining that the pretended heaven of the fixed stars advanced one degree eastward every hundred years. In this manner they were no less mistaken in their astronomical calculation than in their system of natural philosophy. As for instance, an astronomer in that age would have said that the vernal equinox was in the time of such and such an observation, in such a sign, and in such a star. It has advanced two degrees of each since the time that observation was made to the present. Now two degrees are equivalent to two hundred years; consequently the astronomer who made that observation lived just so many years before me. It is certain that an astronomer who had argued in this manner would have mistook just fifty-four years; hence it is that the ancients, who were doubly deceived, made their great year of the world, that is, the revolution of the whole heavens, to consist of thirty-six thousand years. But the moderns are sensible that this imaginary revolution of the heaven of the stars is nothing else than the revolution of the poles of the earth, which is performed in twenty-five thousand nine hundred years. It may be proper to observe transiently in this place that Sir Isaac, by determining the figure of the earth, has very happily explained the cause of this revolution.

All this being laid down, the only thing remaining to settle chronology is to see through what star the colure of the equinoxes passes, and where it intersects at this time the ecliptic in the spring; and to discover whether some ancient writer does not tell us in what point the ecliptic was intersected in his time, by the same colure of the equinoxes.

Clemens Alexandrinus informs us that Chiron, who went with the Argonauts, observed the constellations at the time of that famous expedition, and fixed the vernal equinox to the middle of the Ram; the autumnal equinox to the middle of Libra; our summer solstice to the middle of Cancer, and our winter solstice to the middle of Capricorn.

A long time after the expedition of the Argonauts, and a year before the Peloponnesian War, Methon observed that the point of the summer solstice passed through the eighth degree of Cancer.

Now every sign of the zodiac contains thirty degrees. In Chiron's time, the solstice was arrived at the middle of the sign, that is to say to the fifteenth degree. A year before the Peloponnesian War it was at the eighth, and therefore it had retarded seven degrees. A degree is equivalent to seventy-two years; consequently, from the beginning of the Peloponnesian War to the expedition of the Argonauts, there is no more than an interval of seven times seventy-two years, which make five hundred and four years, and not seven hundred years, as the Greeks computed. Thus in comparing the position of the heavens at this time with their position in that age, we find that the expedition of the Argonauts ought to be placed about nine hundred years before Christ, and not about fourteen hundred; and consequently that the world is not so old by five hundred years as it was generally supposed to be. By this calculation all the eras are drawn nearer, and the several events are found to have happened later than is computed. I don't know whether this ingenious system will be favourably received; and whether these notions will prevail so far with the learned as to prompt them to reform the chronology of the world. Perhaps these gentlemen would think it too great a condescension to allow one and the same man the glory of having improved natural philosophy, geometry, and history. This would be a kind of universal monarchy, with which the principle of self-love that is in man will scarce suffer him to indulge his fellow-creature; and, indeed, at the same time that some very great philosophers attacked Sir Isaac Newton's attractive principle, others fell upon his chronological system. Time, that should discover to which of these the victory is due, may perhaps only leave the dispute still more undetermined.

ON THE REGARD THAT OUGHT TO BE SHOWN TO MEN OF LETTERS

Neither the English nor any other people have foundations established in favour of the polite arts like those in France. There are universities in most countries, but it is in France only that we meet with so beneficial an encouragement for astronomy and all parts of the mathematics, for physic, for researches into antiquity, for painting, sculpture, and architecture. Louis XIV has immortalized his name by these several foundations, and this immortality did not cost him two hundred thousand livres a year.

I must confess that one of the things I very much wonder at is that, as the Parliament of Great Britain have promised a reward of £20,000 sterling to any person who may discover the longitude, they should never have once thought to imitate Louis XIV in his munificence with regard to the arts and sciences.

Merit, indeed, meets in England with rewards of another kind, which redound more to the honour of the nation. The English have so great a veneration for exalted talents that a man of merit in their country is always sure of making his fortune. Mr. Addison in France would have been elected a member of one of the academies, and, by the credit of some women, might have obtained a yearly pension of twelve hundred livres, or else might have been imprisoned in the Bastille, upon pretence that certain strokes in his tragedy of *Cato* had been discovered which glanced at the porter of some man in power. Mr. Addison was raised to the post of Secretary of State in England. Sir Isaac Newton was made Warden of the Royal Mint. Mr. Congreve had a considerable employment. Mr. Prior was Plenipotentiary. Dr. Swift is Dean of St. Patrick in Dublin, and is more revered in Ireland than the Primate himself. The religion which Mr. Pope professes excludes him, indeed, from preferments of every kind, but then it did not prevent his gaining two hundred thousand livres by his excellent translation of Homer. I myself saw a long time in France the author of *Rhadamistus* ready to perish for hunger. And the son of one of the greatest men our country ever gave birth to, and who was beginning to run the noble career which his father had set him, would have been reduced to the extremes of misery had he not been patronized by Monsieur Fagon.

But the circumstance which mostly encourages the arts in England is the great veneration which is paid them. The picture of the Prime Minister hangs over the chimney of his own closet, but I have seen that of Mr. Pope in twenty noblemen's houses. Sir Isaac Newton was revered in his lifetime, and had a due respect paid to him after his death; the greatest men in the nation disputing who should have the honour of holding up his pall. Go into Westminster Abbey, and you will find that what raises the admiration of the spectator is not the mausoleums of the English kings, but the monuments which the gratitude of the nation has erected to perpetuate the memory of those illustrious men who contributed to its glory. We view their statues in that abbey in the same manner as those of Sophocles, Plato, and other immortal personages were viewed in Athens; and I am persuaded that the bare sight of those glorious monuments has fired more than one breast, and been the occasion of their becoming great men.

The English have even been reproached with paying too extravagant honours to mere merit, and censured for interring the celebrated actress Mrs. Oldfield in Westminster Abbey, with almost the same pomp as Sir Isaac Newton. Some pretend that the English had paid her these great funeral honours, purposely to make us more strongly sensible of the barbarity and injustice which they object to in us, for having buried Mademoiselle Le Couvreur ignominiously in the fields.

But be assured from me that the English were prompted by no other principle in burying Mrs. Oldfield in Westminster Abbey than their good sense. They are far from being so ridiculous as to brand with infamy an art which has immortalized a Euripides and a Sophocles; or to exclude from the body of their citizens a set of people whose business is to set off with the utmost grace of speech and action those pieces which the nation is proud of.

Under the reign of Charles I and in the beginning of the civil wars raised by a number of rigid fanatics, who at last were the victims to it, a great many pieces were published against theatrical and other shows, which were attacked with the greater virulence because that monarch and his queen, daughter to Henry IV of France, were passionately fond of them.

One Mr. Prynne, a man of most furiously scrupulous principles, who would have thought himself damned had he worn a cassock instead of a short cloak, and have been glad to see one-half of mankind cut the other to pieces for the glory of God, and the *Propaganda Fide,* took it into his head to write a most wretched satire against some pretty good comedies, which were exhibited very innocently every night before their majesties. He quoted the authority of the Rabbis, and some passages from St. Bonaventure, to prove that the Oedipus of Sophocles was the work of the evil spirit; that Terence was excommunicated *ipso facto;* and added that doubtless Brutus, who was a very severe Jansenist, assassinated Julius Caesar for no other reason but because he, who was Pontifex Maximus, presumed to write a tragedy the subject of which was Oedipus. Lastly, he declared that all who frequented the theatre were excommunicated, as they thereby renounced their baptism. This was casting the highest insult on the king and all the royal family; and as the English loved their prince at that time, they could not bear to hear a writer talk of excommunicating him, though they themselves afterwards cut his head off. Prynne was summoned to appear before the Star Chamber; his wonderful book, from which Father Le Brun stole his, was sentenced to be burnt by the common hangman, and himself to lose his ears. His trial is now extant.

The Italians are far from attempting to cast a blemish on the opera, or to excommunicate Signor Senesino or Signora Cuzzoni. With regard to myself, I could presume to wish that the magistrates would suppress I know not what contemptible pieces written against the stage. For when the English and Italians hear that we brand with the greatest mark of infamy an art in which we excel; that we excommunicate persons who receive salaries from the king; that we condemn as impious a spectacle exhibited in convents and monasteries; that we dishonour sports in which Louis XIV and Louis XV performed as actors; that we give the title of the devil's works to pieces which are received by magistrates of the most severe character, and represented before a virtuous queen; when, I say, foreigners are told of this insolent conduct, this contempt for the royal authority, and this Gothic rusticity which some presume to call Christian severity, what an idea must they entertain of our nation? And how will it be possible for them to conceive, either that our laws give a sanction to an art which is declared infamous, or that some persons dare to stamp with infamy an art which receives a sanction from the laws, is rewarded by kings, cultivated and encouraged by the greatest men, and admired by whole nations? And that Father Le Brun's impertinent libel against the stage is seen in a bookseller's shop, standing the very next to the immortal labours of Racine, of Corneille, of Molière, etc.

ON THE ROYAL SOCIETY AND OTHER ACADEMIES

The English had an Academy of Sciences many years before us, but then it is not under such prudent regulations as ours, the only reason of which very possibly is because it was founded before the Academy of Paris; for had it been founded after, it would very probably have adopted some of the sage laws of the former and improved upon others.

Two things, and those the most essential to man, are wanting in the Royal Society of London, I mean rewards and laws. A seat in the Academy at Paris is a small but secure fortune to a geometrician or a chemist; but this is so far from being the case at London, that the several members of the Royal Society are at a continual, though indeed small expense. Any man in England who declares himself a lover of the mathematics and natural philosophy, and expresses an inclination to be a member of the Royal Society, is immediately elected into it. But in France it is not enough that a man who aspires to the honour of being a member of the Academy, and of receiving the royal stipend, has a love for the sciences; he must at the same time be deeply skilled in them; and is obliged to dispute the seat with competitors who are so much the more formidable as they are fired by a principle of glory, by interest, by the difficulty itself, and by that inflexibility of mind which is generally found in those who devote themselves to that pertinacious study, the mathematics.

The Academy of Sciences is prudently confined to the study of nature, and, indeed, this is a field spacious enough for fifty or three-score persons to range in. That of London mixes indiscriminately literature with physics; but methinks the founding an academy merely for the polite arts is more judicious, as it prevents confusion, and the joining, in some measure, of heterogeneals, such as a dissertation on the head-dresses of the Roman ladies with a hundred or more new curves.

As there is very little order and regularity in the Royal Society, and not the least encouragement, and that the Academy of Paris is on a quite different foot, it is no wonder that our transactions are drawn up in a more just and beautiful manner than those of the English. Soldiers who are under a regular discipline, and besides well paid, must necessarily at last perform more glorious achievements than others who are mere volunteers. It must indeed be confessed that the Royal Society boast their Newton, but then he did not owe his knowledge and discoveries to that body; so far from it that the latter were intelligible to very few of his fellow members. A genius like that of Sir Isaac belonged to all the academies in the world, because all had a thousand things to learn of him.

The celebrated Dean Swift formed a design, in the latter end of the late Queen's reign, to found an academy for the English tongue upon the model of that of the French. This project was promoted by the late Earl of Oxford, Lord High Treasurer, and much more by the Lord Bolingbroke, Secretary of State, who had the happy talent of speaking without premeditation in the Parliament House with as much purity as Dean Swift wrote in his closet, and who would have been the ornament and protector of that academy. Those only would have been chosen members of it whose works will last as long as the English tongue, such as Dean Swift, Mr. Prior, whom we saw here invested with a public character, and whose fame in England is equal to that of La Fontaine in France, Mr. Pope, the English Boileau, Mr. Congreve, who may be called their Molière, and several other eminent persons whose names I have forgot; all these would have raised the glory of that body to a great height even in its infancy. But Queen Anne being snatched suddenly from the world, the Whigs were resolved to ruin the protectors of the intended academy, a circumstance that was of the most fatal consequence to polite literature. The members of this academy would have had a very great advantage over those who first formed that of the French, for Swift, Prior, Congreve, Dryden, Pope, Addison, etc., had fixed the English tongue by their writings; whereas Chapelain, Colletet, Cassaigne, Faret, Perrin, Cotin, our first academicians, were a disgrace to their country; and so much ridicule is now attached to their very names, that if an author of some genius in this age had the misfortune to be called Chapelain or Cotin, he would be under a necessity of changing his name.

One circumstance, to which the English Academy should especially have attended, is to have prescribed to themselves occupations of a quite different kind from those with which our academicians amuse themselves. A wit of this country asked me for the memoirs of the French Academy. I answered, they have no memoirs, but have printed threescore or fourscore volumes in quarto of compliments. The gentleman perused one or two of them, but without being able to understand the style in which they were written; though he understood all our good authors perfectly. "All," says he, "I see in these elegant discourses is, that the member elect having assured the audience that his predecessor was a great man, that Cardinal Richelieu was a very great man, that the Chancellor Seguier was a pretty great man, that Louis XIV was a more than great man, the director answers in the very same strain, and adds, that the member elect may also be a sort of great man, and that himself, in quality of director, must also have some share in this greatness."

The cause why all these academical discourses have unhappily done so little honour to this body is evident enough. *Vitium est temporis potiùs quam hominis* (the fault is owing to the age rather than to particular persons). It grew up insensibly into a custom for every academician to repeat these eulogiums at his reception; it was laid down as a kind of law that the public should be indulged from time to time in the sullen satisfaction of yawning over these productions. If the reason should afterwards be sought why the greatest geniuses who have been incorporated into that body have sometimes made the worst speeches, I answer that it is wholly owing to a strong propension, the gentlemen in question had to shine, and to display a thread-bare, worn-out subject in a new and uncommon light. The necessity of saying something, the perplexity of having nothing to say, and a desire of being witty, are three circumstances which alone are capable of making even the greatest writer ridiculous. These gentlemen, not being able to strike out any new thoughts, hunted after a new play of words, and delivered themselves without thinking at all: in like manner as people who should seem to chew with great eagerness, and make as though they were eating, at the same time that they were just starved.

It is a law in the French Academy to publish all those discourses by which only they are known, but they should rather make a law never to print any of them.

But the Academy of the *Belles Lettres* have a more prudent and more useful object, which is, to present the public with a collection of transactions that abound with curious researches and critiques. These transactions are already esteemed by foreigners; and it were only to be wished that some subjects in them had been more thoroughly examined, and that others had not been treated at all. As, for instance, we should have been very well satisfied had they omitted I know not what dissertation on the prerogative of the right hand over the left; and some others, which, though not published under so ridiculous a title, are yet written on subjects that are almost as frivolous and silly.

The Academy of Sciences, in such of their researches as are of a more difficult kind and a more sensible use, embrace the knowledge of nature and the improvements of the arts. We may presume that such profound, such uninterrupted pursuits as these, such exact calculations, such refined discoveries, such extensive and exalted views, will, at last, produce something that may prove of advantage to the universe. Hitherto, as we have observed together, the most useful discoveries have been made in the most barbarous times. One would conclude that the business of the most enlightened ages and the most learned bodies is to argue and debate on things which were invented by ignorant people. We know exactly the angle which the sail of a ship is to make with the keel in order to make its sailing better, and yet Columbus discovered America without having the least idea of the property of this angle; however, I am far from inferring from hence that we are to confine ourselves merely to a blind practice, but happy it were would naturalists and geometricians unite, as much as possible, the practice with the theory.

Strange, but so it is, that those things which reflect the greatest honour on the human mind are frequently of the least benefit to it! A man who understands the four fundamental rules of arithmetic, aided by a little good sense, shall amass prodigious wealth in trade, shall become a Sir Peter Delmé, a Sir Richard Hopkins, a Sir Gilbert Heathcote, whilst a poor algebraist spends his whole life in searching for astonishing properties and relations in numbers, which at the same time are of no manner of use, and will not acquaint him with the nature of exchanges. This is very nearly the case with most of the arts: there is a certain point beyond which all researches serve to no other purpose than merely to delight an inquisitive mind. Those ingenious and useless truths may be compared to stars which, by being placed at too great a distance, cannot afford us the least light.

With regard to the French Academy, how great a service would they do to literature, to the language, and the nation, if, instead of publishing a set of compliments annually, they would give us new editions of the valuable works written in the age of Louis XIV, purged from the several errors of diction which are crept into them. There are many of these errors in Corneille and Molière, but those in La Fontaine are very numerous. Such as could not be corrected might at least be pointed out. By this means, as all the Europeans read those works, they would teach them our language in its utmost purity—which, by that means, would be fixed to a lasting standard; and valuable French books being then printed at the King's expense would prove one of the most glorious monuments the nation could boast. I have been told that Boileau formerly made this proposal, and that it has since been revived by a gentleman eminent for his genius, his fine sense, and just taste for criticism; but this thought has met with the fate of many other useful projects, of being applauded and neglected.

---

*The foregoing consists
of Letters* VIII, IX, X, XI, XII, XIII,
XIV, XV, XVI, XVII, XXIII *and* XXIV
of Voltaire's LETTERS ON THE ENGLISH.

Dante Alighieri

1265–1321

Dante was born at Florence, Italy, of an ancient family, in 1265. His early life is obscure, though he was obviously well educated, both in the ancient writers—notably Aristotle—and in the literature of his own day. The event of his youth, however, and in a sense of his life, was his meeting with Beatrice Portinari, a Florentine girl whom he was to know only slightly, but with whom nevertheless he fell in love. She may never have been much aware of him. The story of his passion he told in his *Vita Nuova* (*New Life*), which relates how Beatrice became for him the personification of divine grace and beauty.

Certainly she is that in Dante's later and greatest work, the *Divine Comedy*, a long poem in three parts—*Inferno, Purgatorio*, and *Paradiso*—describing the course of man's salvation. It is the Roman poet Virgil, representing philosophy, who guides Dante through Hell and Purgatory in the poem, but it is Beatrice, signifying revelation, who takes him at last to Heaven.

Dante's greatest concern, apart from poetry, was politics. He was much involved in the affairs of his beloved Florence, which in his time was torn by faction and civil discord. The contending parties were on the one hand the Ghibellines, who stood against the centralized authority of the papacy and the Holy Roman Empire, and on the other hand the Guelphs, who upheld that authority. Dante was born into a noble Guelph family, but his later sentiments were partly Ghibelline, too, since he came to feel that Italy would destroy itself unless it were united. This was a middle position impossible to hold among the violent feelings of the day. Caught in the midst of these, Dante was exiled from Florence in 1302 and never afterward saw it again. For the rest of his life, he lived elsewhere in Italy under the protection of various patrons who honored his increasing fame. He died in 1321 at Ravenna, where his bones still lie.

Any reader who considers the following selection from Dante's treatise on world government (*De Monarchia*), written around 1310, might do well to look at Clausewitz' *What Is War?* [1] The best way, perhaps, to comprehend a man whose interest is in universal peace is to read one whose concern is with the lack of it—who assumes, as Clausewitz does, that war is natural among nations. Clausewitz assumes this for the excellent reason that he finds no authority in the world beyond the several authorities of competing states. Within each of these there is a set of laws, but as all the states are equal with respect to each other, there are no laws governing their relation to one another.

War is the natural result of this condition, Clausewitz is saying, and if we understand that, we are well on the way to understanding Dante. For the central idea of the first book of *De Monarchia* is the same, only it is stated in opposite terms. The idea is that government is the condition of peace, and without government there is no peace. From this it follows that if there is to be peace among nations, there must be an authority greater than that of any nation: there must be, in other words, a government of the world.

No world government existed in Dante's time, any more than it did in Clausewitz' time, or does in ours. Yet one once did exist, Dante tells us, during the reign of the Roman emperor Augustus, who in the time of Jesus Christ extended his authority over the known world. The example is important, for it means that Dante, quite as much as Clausewitz, is talking about what he considers a real possibility. Both writers base their arguments on what they believe to be the facts of history, but their conclusions are exactly

---

[1] See Vol. 7, pp. 479–497, in this set.

opposed. Thus where Clausewitz implies that war and anarchy are natural to men, Dante very clearly says that peace and government are natural.

The answer to this apparent contradiction lies in the "higher nature" to which Dante refers in the first line of his treatise. By this he means the part of man that is divine—that partakes of the nature of the Creator. It is the rule of God in the universe, Dante says, that men emulate, so far as they imperfectly can, when they seek to rule themselves. Through the aspiration of reason, they tend toward the unity and perfect peace of the eternal world.

Whether they will listen to their reason—their higher nature—is admittedly another matter. Men are free to choose, Dante says, and there is another part of their nature that compels them powerfully to selfishness and strife. Hence the search for world government, or universal peace, must be a struggle. Men's intellects must be persuaded of the goodness of this goal. The form of Dante's book is therefore that of an argument designed to overcome the doubts and faulty understanding that keep men from their proper end. That end, finally, is to be with God, and the means to it is through the realization, so far as may be possible on earth, of God's unity and order.

It is important to note that peace is a *means*, rather than an end in itself. It is a means, as Dante says, to the fullest realization of the potentialities of the human mind. It is, therefore, an indispensable condition for achieving the earthly goal toward which the progress of mankind is directed.

On World Government

from *De Monarchia*

1

The knowledge of a single temporal government over mankind is most important and least explored.

All men whose higher nature has endowed them with a love of truth obviously have the greatest interest in working for posterity, so that in return for the patrimony provided for them by their predecessors' labors they may make provision for the patrimony of future generations. Certainly a man who has received public instruction would be far from performing his duty if he showed no concern for the public weal, for he would not be a "tree by the streams of waters, bearing his fruit in due season," but rather an erosive whirlpool always sucking in and never returning what it devours. Therefore, as I have often reminded myself of these things and wish not to be charged with burying my talent, I endeavor not only to grow in public usefulness but also to bear fruit by publishing truths that have not been attempted by others. For what fruit is there in proving once more a theorem in Euclid, or in trying to show man his true happiness, which Aristotle has already shown, or in defending old age as Cicero did? Fruitless and positively tiresome are such superfluous works.

Among the truths that remain hidden, though useful, the knowledge of the temporal government of the world is most useful and most unknown, but since this knowledge is not directly gainful it has been neglected by all. I therefore propose to drag it from its hiding place, in order that my alertness may be useful to the world and may bring me the glory of being the first to win this great prize. It is a difficult task I attempt and beyond my powers, but I rely not on my own ability; I trust in that giver of light who gives abundantly to all and reproaches none.

2

Since this theory is a practical science, its first principle is the goal of human civilization, which must be one and the same for all particular civilizations.

First, we must see what is meant by the temporal government of the world, both its kind and its aim. By the temporal government of the world or universal empire we mean a single government over all men in time, that is, over and in all things which can be measured by time. On this subject there are three chief questions to be examined: first, we must ask and inquire whether such a government is necessary for the good of the world; secondly, whether the Roman people has a right to assume such an office; and thirdly, whether the authority of this government comes directly from God or through some servant or vicar of God.

Since any truth which is not itself a principle is demonstrated as following from the truth of some principle, it is necessary in any inquiry to make clear from what principle the certainty of the subordinate propositions may be analytically derived. And since this treatise is an inquiry, we must first of all look for the principle on whose validity the derived propositions rest.

Now it is important to remember that there are some things entirely beyond our control, about which we can reason but do nothing, such as mathematics, physics, and theology, and there are others within our control not only for reasoning but for practice. In the latter case, action is not for the sake of thought, but thought for the sake of action, since in such matters the aim is action. Since our present concern is with politics, with the very source and principle of all right politics, and since all political matters are in our control, it is clear that our present concern is not aimed primarily at thought but at action. And furthermore, since in matters of action the final goal is the principle and cause of all, for by it the agent is first moved, it follows that any reasons for actions directed to this goal must be themselves derived from it. For example, the way to cut wood for building a house is different from the way to cut wood for a ship. Whatever, then, is the universal goal of human civilization, if there be such a goal, will serve as a first principle and will make sufficiently clear all the derivative propositions that follow. Now it would be foolish to admit that one civilization may have one goal, and another, another, and not to admit one goal for all.

3

This goal is proved to be the realization of man's ability to grow in intelligence.

Accordingly, we must now see what the whole of human civilization aims at; with this aim before us more than half our work is done, as the Philosopher says in his *Nicomachean Ethics*.[1] And as evidence for what we seek we ought to note that just as nature makes the thumb for one purpose, the whole hand for another, the arm for still another, and the whole man for a purpose different from all these, so an individual man has one purpose, a family another, a neighborhood another, a city another, a state another, and finally there is another for all of mankind, established by the Eternal God's art, which is nature. This goal it is that we are now seeking as the guiding principle of our inquiry. We should know, in this connection, that God and nature make nothing in vain, and that whatever is produced serves some function. For the intention of any act of creation, if it is really creative, is not merely to produce the existence of something but to produce the proper functioning of that existence. Hence a proper functioning does not exist for the sake of the being which functions, but rather the being exists for the sake of its function. There is therefore some proper function for the whole of mankind as an organized multitude which cannot be achieved by any single man, or family, or neighborhood, or city, or state. What that may be would be plain if we could see what the basic capacity of the whole of humanity is. Now I would say that no capacity which several different species have in common can be the basic power of any one of them. For in that case the basic capacity which characterizes a species would be the same for several species, which is impossible. Accordingly, man's basic power is not mere being, for he shares being with the elements; nor is it to be compounded, for this is found in minerals, too; nor is it to be alive, for so are plants; nor is it to be sensitive, for other animals share this power; but it is to be sensitive to intellectual growth, for this trait is not found in beings either above or below man. For though there are angelic beings that share intellect with man, they do not have intellectual growth, since their very

---

1. The "Philosopher" for Dante is Aristotle. Aristotle's *Nicomachean Ethics* is in *Great Books of the Western World*, Vol. 9, pp. 339–436 [Ed.].

being is to be intellect and nothing else and hence they are intellectual continuously, otherwise they would not be changeless. Therefore, it is clear that man's basic capacity is to have a potentiality or power for being intellectual. And since this power cannot be completely actualized in a single man or in any of the particular communities of men above mentioned, there must be a multitude in mankind through whom this whole power can be actualized; just as there must be a multitude of created beings to manifest adequately the whole power of prime matter, otherwise there would have to be a power distinct from prime matter, which is impossible. With this judgment Averroes agrees in his commentary on *De anima*. This intellectual power of which I am speaking is directed not only toward universals or species, but also by a sort of extension toward particulars. Hence it is commonly said that the speculative intellect becomes practical by extension, and acquires thus the aims of action and production. I distinguish between matters of action which are governed by political prudence, and matters of production which are governed by the arts; but all of them are extensions of theoretical intellect, which is the best function for which the Primal Goodness brought mankind into being. Now we have already thrown light on that saying in the *Politics* —that the intellectually vigorous naturally govern others.

4

The best means toward this end is universal peace.

I have now made clear enough that the proper work of mankind taken as a whole is to exercise continually its entire capacity for intellectual growth, first, in theoretical matters, and, secondarily, as an extension of theory in practice. And since the part is a sample of the whole, and since individual men find that they grow in prudence and wisdom when they can sit quietly, it is evident that mankind, too, is most free and easy to carry on its work when it enjoys the quiet and tranquillity of peace. Man's work is almost divine ("Thou hast made him a little lower than the angels"), and it is clear that of all the things that have been ordained for our happiness, the greatest is universal peace. Hence there rang out to the shepherds from on high the good news, not of riches, nor pleasures, nor honors, nor long life, nor health, nor strength, nor beauty, but peace. For the heavenly host proclaimed "glory to God in the highest and on earth peace to men of good will." Hence, too, "Peace be with you" was the salutation of Him who is the Salvation of men; for it was fitting that the Supreme Savior should give voice to the supreme salutation. His disciples took care to make this salutation customary, and so did Paul in his salutations, as must be evident to all.

What I have now said makes clear what is that better, that best, way by following which mankind may achieve its proper work, and consequently it is also clear what way we must directly take to attain that final goal set for all our work, which is universal peace. Let this, then, be our principle underlying all our subsequent arguments, as I said, and let it serve as a standard set before us by which to test the truth of whatever we shall try to prove.

5

To achieve this state of universal well-being a single world government is necessary.

There are three chief questions, as I said in the beginning, which must be raised and discussed concerning the temporal government of the world, more commonly called empire, and these three I propose, as I said, to take up in order. And so the first question is whether a single temporal world government is necessary for the world's well-being. There exists no weight of argument or of authority against this necessity and there are very strong and clear arguments for it. The first argument, which enjoys the authority of the Philosopher, is in his *Politics*,[2] where this venerable authority states that whenever several things are united into one thing, one of them must regulate and rule, the others must be regulated and ruled. This seems credible not only on the strength of the glorious name of its author, but also for inductive reasons. Consider, for example, an individual man; we see this truth exhibited in him, for while all his energies are directed toward happiness, he could not attain it did not his intellectual power rule and guide the others. Or consider a household whose aim it is to prepare the members of the family to live well; one alone must regulate and rule, whom we call father of the family, or else there is someone who takes his place. So says our Philosopher: "Every home is ruled by the eldest." It is his duty, as Homer says, to govern all and give laws to others. Hence the proverbial curse: "May you have an equal in your home!" Or consider a neighborhood whose aim is to provide mutual aid in persons and things. Someone must govern the others, either someone appointed by the others or some outstanding member whom the others consent to follow, otherwise the community will not only fail to

---

2. Aristotle's *Politics* is in *Great Books of the Western World*, Vol. 9, pp. 445–548 [Ed.].

furnish the mutual aid for which it exists, but, as sometimes happens when several strive for pre-eminence, the whole neighborhood is destroyed. Likewise a city, whose aim is to live well and self sufficiently, must have a single government, whether the city have a just or corrupt constitution. Otherwise not only does civil life fail to reach its goal, but the city ceases to be what it was. Or take finally a state or kingdom, whose aim is the same as that of a city, save that it takes more responsibility for peace—there must be a single government which both rules and governs; otherwise the end of the state is lost sight of, or the state itself falls to pieces, according to the infallible truth: "Every kingdom directed against itself shall be laid waste." If, therefore, these things are true among individuals and particular communities which have a unified goal, what we proposed above must be true. Since it appears that the whole of mankind is ordained to one end, as we proved above, it should therefore have a single rule and government, and this power should be called the Monarch or Emperor. And thus it is plain that for the well-being of the world there must be a single world rule or empire.

6

Since any particular institution needs unity of direction, mankind as a whole must also need it.

Whatever relation a part bears to its whole the structure of that part must bear to the total structure. But a part is related to the whole as to its end or greatest good. Hence we must conclude that the goodness of the partial structure cannot exceed the goodness of the total structure, rather the contrary. Now since there is a double structure among things—namely, the structure which relates part to part, and the structure which relates parts to a whole that is not itself a part, as in any army soldiers are related to each other and also to their commander—it follows the structure which makes a unity out of parts is better than the other structure, for it *is* what the other aims at. Therefore the relations among parts exist for the sake of the unifying structure, not vice versa. Hence, if the form of this structure is found among the partial associations of men, much more should it be found in the society of men as a totality, on the strength of the preceding syllogism, since the total structure or its form is the greater good. But, as we have seen sufficiently clearly in the preceding chapter, this unifying structure is found in all parts of human society; therefore it is found or should be found in mankind as a whole; and as those societies that are partial in a state and the state itself, as we saw, should be composed of a structure unified by a governor or government, so there must be a single world ruler or world government.

7

Human government is but a part of that single world administration which has its unity in God.

Furthermore, human society is a totality in relation to its parts, but is itself a part of another totality. For it is the totality of particular states and peoples, as we have seen, but it is obviously a mere part of the whole universe. Therefore, as through it the lower parts of human society are well ordered, so it, too, should fit into the order of the universe as a whole. But its parts are well ordered only on the basis of a single principle (this follows from all we have said), and hence it too must be well ordered on the basis of a single principle, namely, through its governor, God, who is the absolute world government. Hence we conclude that a single world government is necessary for the well-being of the world.

8

Man is by nature in God's likeness and therefore should, like God, be one.

Things are at their best when they go according to the intention of their original mover, who is God. And this is self-evident to all except those who deny that the divine goodness achieves the highest perfection. In the intention of God every creature exists to represent the divine likeness in so far as its nature makes this possible. According to what is said: "Let us make man after our image and likeness." Though we cannot speak of the divine "image" as being in things lower than man, we can speak of anything as being in His "likeness," since the whole universe is nothing but a kind of imprint of the divine goodness. Therefore, mankind exists at its best when it resembles God as much as it can. But mankind resembles God most when it is most unified, for the true ground of unity exists in Him alone, as is written: "Hear, O Israel, the Lord thy God is one." But mankind is then most one when it is unified into a single whole; which is possible only when it submits wholly to a single government, as is self-evident. Therefore mankind in submitting to a single government most resembles God and most nearly exists according to the divine intention, which is the same as enjoying well-being, as was proved at the beginning of this chapter.

9

The heavens are ruled by a single mover, God, and man is at his best when he follows the pattern of the heavens and the Heavenly Father.

So also a person is a good or perfect child when he follows, as far as nature permits, in the footsteps of a perfect father. But mankind is the son of heaven, which is most perfect in all its works; for "man is generated of man and sun," according to the author of *The Physics*.[3] Hence mankind is best when it follows in the footsteps of heaven as far as its nature permits. And as the whole heaven is governed in all its parts, motions, and movers by a single motion, the *primum mobile*, and by a single mover, God, as is very evident to a philosophizing reason if it syllogizes truly, it follows that mankind is then at its best when in all its movers and movements it is governed by a single mover or government and by a single motion or law. Thus it seems necessary that for the well-being of the world there be world government, that is, a single power, called Empire. This reasoning inspired Boëthius[4] when he said:

> O happy race of men,
> If like heaven your hearts
> Were ruled by love!

10

Human governments are imperfect as long as they are not subordinate to a supreme tribunal.

Wherever there can be contention, there judgment should exist; otherwise things would exist imperfectly, without their own means of adjustment or correction, which is impossible, since in things necessary God or nature is not defective. Between any two governments, neither of which is in any way subordinate to the other, contention can arise either through their own fault or that of their subjects. This is evident. Therefore there should be judication between them. And since neither can know the affairs of the other, not being subordinated (for among equals there is no authority), there must be a third and wider power which can rule both

---

3. See *Great Books of the Western World*, Vol. 9, Book II, Ch. 2, p. 271 [Ed.].
4. Author of *On the Consolation of Philosophy*, from which the following verse is taken [Ed.].

within its own jurisdiction. This third power is either the world government or it is not. If it is, we have reached our conclusion; if it is not, it
must in turn have its equal outside its jurisdiction, and then it will need a
third party as judge, and so ad infinitum, which is impossible. So we must
arrive at a first and supreme judge for whom all contentions are judiciable
either directly or indirectly; and this will be our world governor or
emperor. Therefore, world government is necessary for the world. The
Philosopher saw this argument when he said, "Things hate to be in
disorder, but a plurality of authorities is disorder; therefore, authority is
single." [5]

11

The world government is apt to be least greedy and most just.

Moreover, the world is best ordered when justice is its greatest power.
Thus Virgil, seeking to praise an age which seemed to be arising in his
day, sang in his *Bucolics:*

Iam redit et Virgo, redeunt Saturnia regna.[6]

By "Virgo" he meant justice, sometimes called "the starry." By "Saturnia
regna" he meant the best ages, sometimes called "the golden." Justice has
greatest power under a unitary government; therefore the best order of
the world demands world government or empire. The minor premise will
become evident if we recall that justice is by its nature a kind of rightness
or straight rule without deviation, and therefore, like whiteness, justice in
the abstract is not susceptible of degrees. For certain forms are of this
kind, entering into various compounds but each being in itself single and
invariable, as the author of the *Book of the Six Principles* rightly says.
However, when they are qualified by "more or less," they owe this qualification to the things with which they are mixed and which contain a mixture of qualities more or less incompatible. Hence wherever justice exists
with the least mixture of what is incompatible with it, either in *disposition*
or in *action,* there justice is most powerful. And then what the Philosopher
says can truly be said of her: "She is fairer than the morning or the evening
star." For then she resembles Phoebe in the glow and calm of dawn
facing her brother. As to its *disposition,* justice is often obscured by
volition, for when the will is not entirely freed of greed before justice is

---

5. This statement comes from Homer's *Iliad,* Book II, l. 204 (*Great Books of the
Western World,* Vol. 4, p. 12). It is quoted by Aristotle in his *Metaphysics,* Book
XI, Chapter 10 (*Great Books of the Western World,* Vol. 8, p. 595) [Ed.].
6. "At last the Virgin and the Saturnian Kingdoms are returning."

introduced, its justice lacks the brightness of purity, for it is mixed, however slightly, with something foreign to it; hence it is well that those be condemned who try to influence the sentiments of a judge. And as to its *action*, justice suffers from the limitations of human ability; for since justice is a virtue affecting others, how can a person act justly when he lacks the ability of giving to each his due? Whence it follows that the more powerful a just man is, the more adequate can justice be in its action.

And so, on the basis of this proposition, we may argue as follows: justice is most powerful in the world when it resides in the most willing and able being; the only being of this nature is the world governor. Therefore, justice is the most powerful in the world when it resides solely in the world governor. This compound syllogism is in the second figure necessarily negative, thus:

All B is A		All B is A
Only C is A	or	No non-C is A
Only C is B		No non-C is B

The major premise is evident from the foregoing. The minor is justified as follows: first, respecting *volition*, then, respecting *ability*. As evidence for the first we must note that greed is the extreme opposite of justice, as Aristotle says in the Fifth Book of his *Nicomachean Ethics*. Take away greed completely and nothing opposed to justice remains in the will. Hence the opinion of the Philosopher that whatever can be decided by law should not be left to a judge is based on the fear of greed, which readily twists the minds of men. Now where there is nothing left to desire, greed is impossible, for passions cannot exist when their objects are destroyed. But a universal ruler has nothing that he still desires, for his jurisdiction is bounded only by the ocean, which is true of no other ruler whose realm is bounded by those of others, as, for example, the King of Castile's is bounded by the King of Aragon's. Hence it follows that the world ruler is the purest among mortal wills in which justice may reside. Moreover, as greed, however slight, obscures the habits of justice, so charity or joy in righteousness refines and enlightens it. Whoever, therefore, is most disposed to find joy in righteousness can give to justice the greatest pre-eminence. Such is the world ruler, and if he exist, justice is or can be most powerful. That righteous joy does what I have claimed for it can be proved as follows: greed ignores man himself and seeks other things, but charity ignores all other things and seeks God and man, and consequently man's good.

And since of all human goods the greatest is to live in peace, as we said above, and since justice is its chief and most powerful promoter, charity is the chief promoter of justice—the greater charity, the more justice. And that of all men the world ruler should most enjoy righteousness can be made clear thus: if we love a thing, we love it more the closer it is to us; but men are closer to the world ruler than to other rulers; therefore he loves them most or should love them most. The major premise is evident to anyone who considers the nature of being passive and being active; the minor follows from the fact that men are close to other rulers only in part, but to the world ruler totally. Also, men approach other rulers through the ruler of all, not vice versa, and thus all men are the primary and immediate objects of concern for the world ruler, whereas other rulers care for them only through him from whose supreme care their own is derived. Besides, the more universal a cause is, the more genuinely it is a cause, for lower causes operate through the higher, as is explained in the book *De causis,* and the more a cause is a cause, the more it loves its effect, since such a love makes a cause what it is. Therefore, since the world ruler is among mortals the most universal cause of well-being, other rulers being so through him, as I have explained, it follows that he has the greatest love for human welfare.

Secondly, concerning the ability (rather than the will) to do justice, who could doubt such an ability in the world ruler, if he understands the meaning of the term? For since he governs all, he can have no enemies. The minor premise is now evident enough, and the conclusion seems certain—namely, that the world needs for its well-being a universal government.

12

Human freedom consists in being ruled by reason and in living for the goal of mankind. Such freedom is possible only under world government.

Mankind is at its best when it is most free. This will be clear if we grasp the principle of liberty. We must realize that the basic principle of our freedom is freedom to choose, which saying many have on their lips but few in their minds. For they go only so far as to say freedom of choice is freedom of will in judging. This is true, but they do not understand its import. They talk as our logicians do, who for their exercises in logic constantly use certain propositions, such as "A triangle has three angles equal to two right angles." And so I must explain that judgment lies between apprehension and appetition; for, first a thing is apprehended, then, being apprehended, is judged to be good or bad, and lastly, being judged, is either sought or rejected. Therefore, if the judgment completely dominates the appetite and is in no way prejudiced by appetite, it is free; but if the appetite somehow antecedes the judgment and influences it, the judgment cannot be free, since it does not move itself, but is led captive by another. For this reason, the lower animals cannot have free judgment, since their appetites always get ahead of their judgments. This also explains why intellectual beings whose wills are immutable and those spirits who have departed this life in grace do not lose their freedom of judgment, though their wills are fixed, but retain and exercise it perfectly.

If we grasp this principle, we can again appreciate why this liberty, the principle of all our liberty, is God's greatest gift to human nature (as I said in the "Paradiso"), for in this life it makes us happy as men, and in another it makes us happy as gods. If all this is true, who can deny that mankind lives best when it makes the most use of this principle?

But to live under a world ruler is to be most free. To understand this, we must know that to be free means to exist for one's own sake, not for another's, as the Philosopher puts it in his *De simpliciter ente*.[7] For whatever exists for the sake of another is under a necessity derived from that for which it exists, as a road is necessarily determined by its goal. Now it is only under the reign of a world ruler that mankind exists for itself and not for another, since then only is there a check on perverted forms of government such as democracies, oligarchies, and tyrannies, which carry mankind into slavery, as anyone can see who runs down the list of them all, whereas those only govern who are kings, aristocrats (called "the best"), and champions of the people's liberty. Hence the world ruler, who has the greatest love for men, as I have explained, desires that all men be made good, which is impossible among perverted politicians. Thus the Philosopher says in his *Politics* that "under a perverted form of government a good man is a bad citizen, while under a right form a good man and a good citizen are identical." In this way right forms of government aim at liberty, that is, men live for their own sake. For citizens do not live for their representatives nor peoples for their kings, but, on the contrary, representatives exist for citizens and kings for peoples. As a social order is established not for the sake of the

---

7. See Aristotle's *Metaphysics*, Book I, Chapter II (*Great Books of the Western World*, Vol. 8, p. 501) [Ed.].

laws, but the laws for its sake, so they who live according to law are ordered not for the sake of the legislator but rather he for them. This is the way the Philosopher puts it in his books on this subject that have come down to us. Hence it is clear that though in matters of policy representatives and kings are the rulers of others, in matters of aims they are the servants of others, and most of all the world ruler, who should be regarded as the servant of all. Hence we must be well aware that world government is itself governed by a pre-established end in establishing its laws. Therefore mankind lives best when it lives under a single ruler; and it follows that a single world government is necessary for the world's well-being.

13

The universal government is most apt to be reasonable.

Another argument: Whoever is himself best disposed to rule can best dispose others. For in any action what is primarily intended by the agent, either because his nature demands it or because he does it purposely, is to make manifest his own image; hence an agent is delighted when he is thus active, for as all things desire their own being, and as an agent in acting unfolds his own being, a state of delight naturally arises, for a thing desired always brings delight. An agent acts, therefore, only because he already is the kind of thing which what he acts on is supposed to become. On this subject the Philosopher says in *De simpliciter ente:* "Whatever is changed from potentiality into act is changed by something which actually exists in the form to which it is changed; if an agent tried to act otherwise, he would act in vain." And thus we can overcome the error of those who speak well but do ill and who nevertheless believe that they can improve the life and ways of others; they forget that Jacob's hands were more persuasive than his words, even though his words were true and his hands false. Hence the Philosopher says in his *Nicomachean Ethics:* "In matters of passion and action, words are less persuasive than deeds." Hence also Heaven spoke to David when he sinned, saying: "Wherefore dost thou tell of my righteousness?"—as much as to say: "Your speech is in vain when you are not as you speak." From all this we gather that whoever wishes to order others well should himself be well ordered. But it is the world ruler alone who is best constituted for ruling. The proof is as follows: A thing is most easily and perfectly adapted to a given course of action when it contains in itself few obstacles to this action. Thus those who have never heard of philosophizing truly are more easily and perfectly taught the habit [of it] than those who heard of it long ago and are full of false opinions. On this subject Galen well says: "It takes such persons double time to acquire science." Now since the world ruler can have no occasion for greed, or at least has much less than other mortals, as we explained above, and since this does not apply to other rulers, and since greed is itself the great corrupter of judgment and impediment to justice, it follows that the world ruler is wholly or to the greatest possible degree well constituted for ruling, since he above all others can let judgment and justice hold sway. These are the two chief qualities that legislators and administrators of law should have, as that most holy king testified when he asked God to give him what a king and a king's son should have: "God give thy judgment to the king, and thy justice to the king's son." Therefore, our minor premise is sound, in which we say that the world ruler alone has the best qualifications for ruling. Therefore, the world ruler can best govern others. Hence it follows that for the best state of the world a world government is necessary.

14

The universal government can best guide particular governments by establishing the laws which lead all men in common toward peace.

It is better that what can be done by one should be done by one, not by many. The demonstration of this proposition is: Let A be able to do something; let A and B be several who could also do it. Now if A can do what A and B do, B is useless, for his addition makes no difference to what A alone did. Such useless additions are superfluous and otiose, displeasing to God and Nature, and whatever is displeasing to God and Nature is evil (which is self-evident); it follows not only that it is better that one rather than many should do this work, but that it is good for one to do it and evil for several to do it.

Another proof: A thing is said to be better the nearer it is to the best. Now the end for which a deed is done is the standard of its goodness. But when it is done by one it is nearer the end. Therefore, it is better so. To prove that when it is done by one, it is nearer the end, let C be the end, let A be the deed of one, and let A and B be the deed of several. It is clear that the way from A direct to C is shorter than via B. Now mankind can be ruled by a single supreme ruler or world governor. In this connection it should be clearly understood that not every little regulation for every city could come directly from the world government, for even municipal regulations are sometimes defective and need amendment, as the Philosopher makes clear in his praise of equity in the *Nicomachean Ethics*. Thus nations, states, and cities have their own internal concerns which require special laws. For law is a rule to guide our lives. The Scythians must rule their lives in one way, living as they do beyond the seventh clime, suffering great inequalities of days and nights and being harried by an almost intolerable, freezing cold, whereas the Garamantes must do otherwise, living below the equinoctial circle, where daylight and dark of night are always balanced, and where the excessive heat makes clothes unendurable. World government, on the other hand, must be understood in the sense that it governs mankind on the basis of what all have in common and that by a common law it leads all toward peace. This common norm or law should be received by local governments in the same way that practical intelligence in action receives its major premises from the speculative intellect. To these it adds its own particular minor premises and then draws particular conclusions for the sake of its action. These basic norms not only can come from a single source, but must do so in order to avoid confusion among universal principles. Moses himself followed this pattern in the law which he composed, for, having chosen the chiefs of the several tribes, he left them the lesser judgments, reserving to himself alone the higher and more general. These common norms were then used by the tribal chiefs according to their special needs. Therefore, it is better for mankind to be governed by one, not by many; and hence by a single governor, the world ruler; and if it is better, it is pleasing to God, since He always wills the better. And when there are only two alternatives—the better is also the best, and is consequently not only pleasing to God, but the choice of "one" rather than "many" is what most pleases Him. Hence it follows that mankind lives best under a single government, and therefore that such a government is necessary for the well-being of the world.

15

Unity is basic to both "being" and "good."

Now I must explain that "being," "unity," and "good" have an order of precedence in the fifth sense of "precedence," namely, priority. For by its nature being is prior to unity and unity prior to the good, because whatever is in the fullest sense a being is most unified, and when most unified it is most good. Hence the less a thing has complete being, the less unity it has, and consequently it is less good. For this reason it is true in all matters whatsoever that the most unified is the best; so the Philosopher maintains in *De simpliciter ente*. Thus we see that at the root of what it means to be good is being one; and the root of what it means to be evil is being many. For this reason, as is explained in *De simpliciter ente*, Pythagoras in his system of relations places unity on the side of good and plurality on the side of evil. Thus we can see what sin is: it is to scorn unity and hence to proceed toward plurality. The Psalmist saw this very well when he said: "They are multiplied in the fruit of corn and wine and oil." It is therefore certain that whatever is good is good because it is unified. And since concord is essentially a good, it is clear that at its root there must be some kind of unity; what this root is will become evident if we examine the nature and ground of concord. Now concord is a uniform movement of many wills; in this definition we see that the uniform movement is due to the union of wills, and that this union is the root and very being of concord. For example, we would say that a number of clods of earth would all agree in falling toward the center and that they fell "in concord," if they did so voluntarily, and similarly flames would agree in rising to the circumference. So we speak of a number of men as being in concord when in moving together toward a single goal their wills are formally united, that is, the form of unity is in their wills, just as the quality of gravity is formally in the clods, and levity in the flames. For the ability to will is a kind of power, but the form of the will is the idea of an apprehended good. This form, like any other form (such as soul or number) is in itself a unity, but is multiplied in the various things with which it is compounded.

With this in mind we can now proceed to our argument in behalf of our proposition, as follows: All concord depends on a unity in wills; the best state of mankind is a kind of concord, for as a man is in excellent health when he enjoys concord in soul and body, and similarly a family, city, or state, so mankind as a whole. Therefore the well-being of mankind depends on the unity of its wills. But this is possible only if there is a single, dominant will which directs all others toward unity, for the wills of mortals need direction because they are subject to the captivating delights of youth (so teaches the Philosopher at the end of his *Nicomachean Ethics*). And this will cannot be if there be not a single governor of all whose will can be dominant and directive for all others. Now, if all the above arguments are true, and they are, it is necessary for the best state of mankind that there be in the world a single governor, and consequently world government is necessary for the well-being of the world.

16

The incarnation of Christ during the Augustan Empire when there prevailed a maximum of world peace bears witness that these principles are divine, and the miseries which have overtaken man since he departed from that golden age likewise bear witness.

Memorable experience confirms the above rational arguments. I refer to the state of things among mortals at the time when the Son of God took on human form for man's salvation, a state of things which He either awaited or arranged according to His will. For if we recall all the ages and conditions of men since the fall of our first parent, when the whole course of our wanderings began, we shall find that not until the time of Divus Augustus was there a complete and single world government which pacified the world. That in his time mankind enjoyed the blessing of universal peace and tranquillity is the testimony of all historians, of the illustrious poets, and even of the evangelist of Christ's gentleness [St. Luke]; and lastly this happiest of ages was called by Paul the "fullness of time." Truly the time was full and all things temporal so ordered that for every service toward our happiness there was a servant.

But the condition of the world since the day when the nail of greed tore that seamless garment is something we can all read about, if only we did not have to see it, too! O race of men, how many storms and misfortunes must thou endure, and how many shipwrecks, because thou, beast of many heads, strugglest in many directions! Thou art sick at heart and sick in mind, both theoretical and practical! No irrefutable arguments appeal to thy theoretical reason, and no amount of experience to thy practical intelligence, and even thine emotions are not moved by the sweet, divine persuasiveness which sounds to thee from the trumpet of the Holy Spirit: "Behold how good and how pleasant it is for brethren to dwell together in unity. Why have the nations raged, and the people devised vain things? The kings of the earth stood up and the princes met together against the Lord, and against his Christ. Let us break their bonds asunder: and let us cast away their yoke from us." [8]

---

8. Psalm 2:1–3.

The foregoing consists of Book I of Dante's DE MONARCHIA.

Jean Jacques Rousseau

1712–1778

Rousseau was born at Geneva in 1712, the son of a Protestant watchmaker whose family had left France a century earlier to avoid religious persecution. The boy's mother died shortly after giving birth to him, and he was brought up by his father, who taught him to read but provided no regular schooling. His books for several years were the romances which his mother had left—a library, as Rousseau later said, that inspired in him an "uninterrupted self-consciousness" and what he called his "odd, romantic notions of human life." At the same time, and as a sort of corrective, he read Plutarch, to whom he attributed his "free and republican spirit."

Rousseau's youth was fitful and unsettled, full of false starts and wanderings. He lived with his uncle, and from 1722 to 1724 was in Boissy, France. He then became an apprentice to an engraver, who treated Rousseau so brutally that he finally made his escape. At the age of sixteen, he left Geneva and took to the road, penniless, but happy in the countryside he always loved. At Annecy, in Savoy, he encountered Mme de Warens, who took him under her protection, arranging for his education at a Catholic seminary in Turin. Rousseau became a convert, but reluctantly, and later renounced Catholicism vigorously. For a time he became a teacher of music, though, as he later confessed, he knew little about the subject. Then he was back

Notes from the artist: ". . . an interpretation of Rousseau based on a picture made during his lifetime. The quote, "Man is born free, and everywhere he is in chains," is from the Social Contract. The other figures depict Marie Antoinette on her way to the guillotine —a victim of the new social order in part foreseen by Rousseau; and David Hume, an admirer of Rousseau, shaking hands with him."

L'homme est né libre, et
partout il est dans les fers.

Rousseau

with Mme de Warens, who for the next ten years was to be his mother and protector but also his mistress.

In 1740 Rousseau left Mme Warens. He lived variously in Italy, in Paris, and in the French countryside. He was successively a copyist of music, a tutor, and secretary to the French ambassador at Venice. While in Paris in the 1740's, he cultivated literary circles. His own career as a writer began in 1749 with an essay on the corruption of civilization. It won a prize at the Academy of Dijon. Thereafter he wrote steadily. Within a dozen years he had produced most of his major works, including the *Discourse on the Origin of Inequality* (1755), *Émile, or Education* (1762), and *The Social Contract* (1762).[1] The famous *Confessions* appeared later, in 1766–70.

Religious views expressed in *Émile* outraged the authorities, and the book was burned in both Paris and Geneva. Rousseau escaped from France in 1762, living for a time in Switzerland and then for a short time in England, on the invitation of David Hume. Back in France, Rousseau at last married Thérèse le Vasseur, his humble companion of many years. On his return to Paris in 1770, the now celebrated author lived in a garret, copying music for a living. Foreigners flocked to see the brilliant, enigmatic man, undismayed by the abuse they met. He died at Ermenonville in 1778.

The problem of world peace has become in our time the first problem of humanity; if a solution is not found, it will have been the last. Rousseau's interest had been aroused by the Abbé de Saint-Pierre's *Project for Perpetual Peace,* which had appeared in 1713. Although Rousseau acclaimed the motives and goal of this book, he believed that its method—that of appealing to the virtues of sovereigns and their desire for a fair reputation—had proved ineffective. He himself preferred to appeal to their interests alone and endeavored to demonstrate that the sovereigns of Europe have everything to gain, and little to lose, by binding themselves in a Federation which excludes the possibility of war.

In the following essay, Rousseau argues that any program of peace among nations must satisfy the interests of the participating mon-

---

[1] For these and other writings by Rousseau see *Great Books of the Western World,* Vol. 38.

archs. Henry IV of Navarre almost succeeded in uniting the whole of Europe against the Habsburgs of Austria and Spain. Had he not been assassinated, the peace of Europe might have been preserved, perhaps indefinitely. But what was it, Rousseau asks, that set all these monarchs into prodigious motion in the same direction? "Was it the public interest, which is never the interest of anyone? The Abbé de Saint-Pierre might have supposed so. But the truth is that each of them was working for his own private interest, which Henry had been clever enough to display to all of them in the most attractive light."

Most programs of world peace since Rousseau have assumed the position he takes: the peculiar interests of participating sovereigns must be satisfied. But how can this be done? Peace may be to the advantage of small weak nations, but is it always so for strong aggressors? Rousseau can easily point to the ruins of great empires which have been destroyed from within or without, and which perished by their own aggressions. Large empires and alliances do not thrive on war but rather on peace. If *they* can maintain the peace internally, Rousseau argues, then there is no good reason why Europe—already bound together by many ties of unity—cannot do the same. All that is required is that the sovereigns see their true interest.

The Federation which Rousseau invokes to outlaw war will "guarantee to each of its members the possession and government of all the dominions which he holds at the moment of the treaty." It will provide also that any member nation which attacks another will be "proscribed as a public enemy," and will find the whole Federation up in arms against it. Since no nation can possibly be strong enough to prevail against the united forces of the rest of Europe, no sovereign will be tempted, by any imagined advantage, to break the peace. Freed from the enormous costs of war, the several sovereigns will be content to replenish their treasuries and enrich their peoples.

The importance of the subject prompts us to sift Rousseau's proposals with care. Shall every monarch be guaranteed his hereditary office, no matter how oppressive, autocratic, and unjust his rule may be? Shall the Federation take up arms against republicans who wish to change the form of government? Similarly, will the large powers be content to have no more voice in the Diet of the Federation than the smallest ones have? What is to prevent them from utilizing the arms of the Federation for their own advantage and against that of the weak nations? Does Rousseau provide against such contingencies?

Rousseau, you will note, does provide that the Diet of the Federation of Europe shall agree upon regulations which are to the interest of all member nations. He does not profess to say what these will be. The majorities which he stipulates for such legislation are interesting. For the initial framing of the charter a bare majority will suffice, while for subsequent provisions, after five years, a three-quarters majority is required. What is the reason for this difference of required majorities? Is it a wise provision?

Two outstanding questions the reader will want to examine are: (1) Would Rousseau's Federation exclude the possibility of war? and (2) Could it be expected to satisfy the basic interests of European sovereigns?

A Lasting Peace
through the Federation of Europe

STATEMENT OF
SAINT-PIERRE'S PROJECT

Never did the mind of man conceive a scheme nobler, more beautiful, or more useful than that of a lasting peace between all the peoples of Europe. Never did a writer better deserve a respectful hearing than he who suggests means for putting that scheme in practice. What man, if he has a spark of goodness, but must feel his heart glow within him at so fair a prospect? Who would not prefer the illusions of a generous spirit, which overleaps all obstacles, to that dry, repulsive reason whose indifference to the welfare of mankind is ever the chief obstacle to all schemes for its attainment?

I doubt not that many readers will forearm themselves with scepticism, as the best defence against the pleasure of yielding to conviction. I pity the melancholy mood which makes them take obstinacy for wisdom. On the other hand, I trust that every generous spirit will share the thrill of emotion with which I take up the pen on a subject which concerns mankind so closely. I see in my mind's eye all men joined in the bonds of love. I call before my thoughts a gentle and peaceful brotherhood, all living in unbroken harmony, all guided by the same principles, all finding their happiness in the happiness of all. And, as I dwell upon this touching picture, the idea of an imaginary happiness will cheat me for a few moments into the enjoyment of a real one.

In these opening words, I could not refrain from giving way to the feelings which filled my heart. Now let us do our best to reason coolly. Resolved as I am to assert nothing which I cannot prove, I have the right to ask the reader in his turn to deny nothing which he is unable to refute. It is not so much the reasoners I am afraid of as those who, without yielding to my proofs, steadily refuse to bring any arguments against them.

No man can have thought long upon the means of bringing any government to perfection without realizing a host of difficulties and obstacles which flow less from its inherent nature than from its relation to its neighbours. The result of this is that the care which ought to be given to its internal welfare has to be largely spent upon its outward security; and we are compelled to think more of providing for its defence against others than of making it as good as may be in itself. If the social order were really, as is pretended, the work not of passion but of reason, should we have been so slow to see that, in the shaping of it, either too much, or too little, has been done for our happiness? that, each one of us being in the civil state as regards our fellow citizens, but in the state of nature as regards the rest of the world, we have taken all kinds of precautions against private wars only to kindle national wars a thousand times more terrible? and that, in joining a particular group of men, we have really declared ourselves the enemies of the whole race?

If there is any way of reconciling these dangerous contradictions, it is to be found only in such a form of federal government as shall unite nations by bonds similar to those which already unite their individual members, and place the one no less than the other under the authority of the law. Even apart from this, such a form of government seems to carry the day over all others; because it combines the advantages of the small and the large state, because it is powerful enough to hold its neighbours in awe, because it upholds the supremacy of the law, because it is the only force capable of holding the subject, the ruler, the foreigner equally in check.

Such a form of government is to some extent a novelty, and its principles have been fully understood only by the moderns. But it was not unknown among the ancients. The Greeks had their Amphictyons and the Etruscans their Lucumonies; the Latins had their *feriae* [public holidays] and the Gauls their city-leagues; the Achaean League gave lustre to the death-struggles of Greece. But not one of these federations was built up with half the wisdom which has gone to the making of the Germanic Body, of the Helvetic League, or of the States General. And if these bodies are still so scarce and so far from the perfection which we feel they might attain, that is because the realization of the good invariably falls short of the ideal; because, in politics as in morals, the more we enlarge our knowledge, the more we are forced to recognize the extent of our misery.

In addition to these formal confederations, it is possible to frame others, less visible but none the less real, which are silently cemented by community of interests, by conformity of habits and customs, by the acceptance of common principles, by other ties which establish mutual relations between nations politically divided. Thus the powers of Europe constitute a kind of whole, united by identity of religion, of moral standard, of international law; by letters, by commerce, and finally by a species of balance which is the inevitable result of all these ties and, however little any man may strive consciously to maintain it, is not to be destroyed so easily as many men imagine.

This concert of Europe has not always existed; and the special causes which produced it are still working to preserve it. The truth is that, before the conquests of the Romans, the nations of this continent, all sunk in barbarism and each utterly unknown to the others, had nothing in common beyond the character which belonged to them as men: a character which, degraded by the practice of slavery, differed little enough in their eyes from that which constitutes the brute. Accordingly the Greeks, vain and disputatious, divided mankind, it may almost be said, into two distinct races: the one—their own, of course—made to rule; the other—the entire rest of the world—created solely to be slaves. From this principle it followed that a Gaul or a Spaniard was no more to a Greek than a Kaffir or Red Indian; and the barbarians themselves were as deeply divided from each other as the Greeks from all of them.

But when these men, born to rule, had been conquered by their slaves the Romans, when half of the known universe had passed beneath the same yoke, a common bond of laws and government was established, and all found themselves members of the same empire. This bond was still further tightened by the recognized principle, either supremely wise or supremely foolish, of imparting to the conquered all the rights of the conqueror: above all, by the famous decree of Claudius, which placed all the subjects of Rome on the roll of her citizens.

Thus all members of the empire were united in one body politic. They were further united by laws and civil institutions which reinforced the political bond by defining equitably, clearly and precisely, so far as this was possible in so vast an empire, the mutual rights and duties of the ruler and the subject, of one citizen as against another. The Code of Theodosius and the later legislation of Justinian constituted a new bond of justice and reason, which came in to replace the sovereign power at the very moment when it showed unmistakable signs of slackening. This did more than anything else to stave off the break-up of the empire and to maintain its authority even over the barbarians who ravaged it.

A third and yet stronger bond was furnished by religion; and it cannot be denied that Europe, even now, is indebted more to Christianity than to any other influence for the union, however imperfect, which survives among her members. So true is this that the one nation which has refused to accept Christianity has always remained an alien among the rest. Christianity, so despised in its infancy, ended by serving as a sanctuary to its slanderers. And the Roman Empire, which had persecuted it for centuries with fruitless cruelty, drew from it a power which she could no longer find in her own strength. The missionaries did more for her than any victory; she dispatched bishops to redeem the mistake of her generals and triumphed by the aid of the priest when her soldiers were defeated. It is thus that the Franks, the Goths, the Burgundians, the Lombards, the Avars and many others ended by recognizing the authority of the empire which they had mastered, by admitting, at least in appearance, not only the law of the Gospel, but also that of the Prince at whose command it had been preached to them.

Such was the respect which this august body inspired even in its death-throes that, to the very end, its conquerors felt themselves honoured by the acceptance of its titles. The very generals who had humbled the empire became its ministers and officials; the proudest kings welcomed, nay even canvassed for, the patriciate, the prefecture, the consulate; and, like the lion who fawns upon the man he could easily devour, these terrible conquerors did homage to the imperial throne which they might at any moment have cast down.

Thus the priesthood and the empire wove a bond between various nations which, without any real community of interests, of rights, or of mutual dependence, found a tie in common principles and beliefs, the influence of which still survives even after its foundation is withdrawn. The venerable phantom of the Roman Empire has never ceased to unite the nations which once formed part of it; and as, after the fall of the empire, Rome still asserted her authority under another form,[1] Europe, the home of the temporal and spiritual powers, still retains a sense of fellowship far closer than is to be found elsewhere. The nations of the

---

1. Respect for the Roman Empire has so completely survived her power that many jurists have questioned whether the emperor of Germany is not the natural sovereign of the world; and Bartholus carried this doctrine so far as to treat anyone who dared to deny it as a heretic. The writings of the canonists are full of the corresponding doctrine of the temporal supremacy of the Roman Church.

other continents are too scattered for mutual intercourse; and they lack any other point of union such as Europe has enjoyed.

There are other, and more special, causes for this difference. Europe is more evenly populated, more uniformly fertile; it is easier to pass from one part of her to another. The interests of her princes are united by ties of blood, by commerce, arts and colonies. Communication is made easy by countless rivers winding from one country to another. An inbred love of change impels her inhabitants to constant travel, which frequently leads them to foreign lands. The invention of printing and the general love of letters has given them a basis of common knowledge and common intellectual pursuits. Finally, the number and smallness of her states, the cravings of luxury and the large diversity of climates which Europe offers for their satisfaction, make them all necessary to each other. All these causes combine to make of Europe not, like Asia and Africa, a purely imaginary assemblage of peoples with nothing in common save the name, but a real community with a religion and a moral code, with customs and even laws of its own, which none of the component nations can renounce without causing a shock to the whole frame.

Now look at the other side of the picture. Observe the perpetual quarrels, the robberies, the usurpations, the revolts, the wars, the murders, which bring daily desolation to this venerable home of philosophy, this brilliant sanctuary of art and science. Consider our fair speeches and our abominable acts, the boundless humanity of our maxims and the boundless cruelty of our deeds; our religion so merciful and our intolerance so ferocious; our policy so mild in our text-books and so harsh in our acts; our rulers so beneficent and our people so wretched; our governments so temperate and our wars so savage: and then tell me how to reconcile these glaring contradictions; tell me if this alleged brotherhood of the nations of Europe is anything more than a bitter irony to denote their mutual hatred.

But, in truth, what else was to be expected? Every community without laws and without rulers, every union formed and maintained by nothing better than chance, must inevitably fall into quarrels and dissensions at the first change that comes about. The historic union of the nations of Europe has entangled their rights and interests in a thousand complications; they touch each other at so many points that no one of them can move without giving a jar to all the rest; their variances are all the more deadly, as their ties are more closely woven; their frequent quarrels are almost savage as civil wars.

Let us admit then that the powers of Europe stand to each other strictly in a state of war, and that all the separate treaties between them are in the nature rather of a temporary truce than a real peace: whether because such treaties are seldom guaranteed by any except the contracting parties; or because the respective rights of those parties are never thoroughly determined and are therefore bound—they, or the claims which pass for rights in the eyes of powers who recognize no earthly superior—to give rise to fresh wars as soon as a change of circumstances shall have given fresh strength to the claimants.

More than this: the public law of Europe has never been passed or sanctioned by common agreement; it is not based upon any general principles; it varies incessantly from time to time and from place to place; it is therefore a mass of contradictory rules which nothing but the right of the stronger can reduce to order: so that, in the absence of any sure clue to guide her, reason is bound, in every case of doubt, to obey the promptings of self-interest—which, in itself, would make war inevitable, even if all parties desired to be just. With the best intentions in the world, all that can be done is to appeal to arms, or put the question to rest for the moment by a treaty. But the old quarrel soon comes to life again, complicated by others which have arisen in the interval; all is confusion and bewilderment; the truth is obscured so hopelessly that usurpation passes for right and weakness for wrong. In this general welter, all bearings have been so utterly lost that, if we could get back to the solid ground of primitive right, few would be the sovereigns in Europe who would not have to surrender all that they possess.

Another source of war, less obvious but not less real, is that things often change their spirit without any corresponding change of form; that states, hereditary in fact, remain elective in appearance; that we find parliaments or states general in monarchies and hereditary rulers in republics; that a power, in fact dependent on another, often retains the semblance of autonomy; that all the provinces ruled by the same sovereign are not always governed by the same laws; that the laws of succession differ in different dominions of the same sovereign; finally, that the tendency of every government to degenerate is a process which no human power can possibly arrest. Such are the causes, general and special, which unite us only to work our ruin. Such are the reasons which condemn us to write our high-sounding theories of fellowship with hands ever dyed afresh in blood.

The causes of the disease, once known, suffice to indicate the remedy, if indeed there is one to be found. Every one can see that what unites any form of society is community of interests, and what disintegrates is their conflict; that either tendency may be changed or modified by a thousand accidents; and therefore that, as soon as a society is founded, some coercive power must be provided to co-ordinate the actions of its members and give to their common interests and mutual obligations that firmness and consistency which they could never acquire of themselves.

It would, indeed, be a great mistake to suppose that the reign of violence, described above, could ever be remedied by the mere force of circumstances, or without the aid of human wisdom. The present balance of Europe is just firm enough to remain in perpetual oscillation without losing itself altogether; and, if our troubles cannot increase, still less can we put an end to them, seeing that any sweeping revolution is henceforth an impossibility.

In proof of this conclusion, let us begin by glancing at the present condition of Europe. The lie of the mountains, seas and rivers, which serve as frontiers for the various nations who people it, seems to have fixed for ever their number and their size. We may fairly say that the political order of the continent is, in some sense, the work of nature.

In truth, we must not suppose that this much vaunted balance is the work of any man, or that any man has deliberately done anything to maintain it. It is there; and men who do not feel themselves strong enough to break it conceal the selfishness of their designs under the pretext of preserving it. But, whether we are aware of it or no, the balance continues to support itself without the aid of any special intervention; if it were to break for a moment on one side, it would soon restore itself on another; so that, if the princes who are accused of aiming at universal monarchy were in reality guilty of any such project, they gave more proof of ambition than of genius. How could any man look such a project in the face without instantly perceiving its absurdity, without realizing that there is not a single potentate in Europe so much stronger than the others as ever to have a chance of making himself their master? No conqueror has ever changed the face of the world unless, appearing suddenly with an army of unexpected strength, or with foreign troops hardened to war in other service, he fell upon nations who were either disarmed, or divided, or undisciplined. But where is a European prince to find an army of unexpected strength sufficient to crush all the others, when the most powerful of them has only a fraction of the strength belonging to the whole body and all the rest are watching so carefully to prevent him? Will he have a larger army than all of them put together? It is impossible; or he will only ruin himself the sooner; or his troops will be less good, just because they are more numerous. Will his troops be better trained? They will be proportionally fewer; not to mention that discipline is now everywhere the same, or will have become so before long. Will he have more money? Its sources are open to all, and no great conquest was ever made by money. Will he fall upon his enemies suddenly? Famine, or fortresses, will bar his way at every step. Will he strive to win his way inch by inch? Then he will give his enemies time to unite their forces to resist him; time, money and men will all be bound to fail him. Will he try to divide the other powers and conquer them one by one? The traditional maxims of Europe make such a policy impossible; the very most stupid of princes would never fall into such a trap as that. In a word, as all the sources of power are equally open to them all, the resistance is in the long run as strong as the attack; and time soon repairs the sudden accidents of fortune, if not for each prince individually, at least for the general balance of the whole.

Now let us take the supposition that two or three potentates league themselves together to conquer all the rest. Those three potentates, take them where you please, will not together have behind them as much as half of Europe. The other half will, quite certainly, make common cause against them. They will therefore have to conquer an enemy stronger than themselves. I may add that their interests are too contradictory and their mutual jealousies too great to allow of such a project ever being formed. I may add further that, even if it were formed, even if it were put in act, even if it had some measure of success, that very success would sow the seeds of discord among our victorious allies. It is beyond the bounds of possibility that the prizes of victory should be so equally divided, that each will be equally satisfied with his share. The least fortunate will soon set himself to resist the further progress of his rivals, who in their turn, for the same reason, will speedily fall out with one another. I doubt whether, since the beginning of the world, there has been a single case in which three, or even two, powers have joined forces for the conquest of others, without quarrelling over their contingents, or over the division of the spoil, and without, in consequence of this disagreement, promptly giving new strength to their common enemy. From all this it appears improbable that, under any supposition, either a king, or a league of kings, is in a position to bring about any serious or permanent change in the established order of Europe.

This does not mean that the Alps, the Rhine, the sea and the Pyrenees are in themselves a barrier which no ambition can surmount; but that these barriers are supported by others which either block the path of the enemy, or serve to restore the old frontiers directly the first on-slaught has spent its force. The real strength of the existing order is, in truth, to be found partly in the play of conflicting policies which, in nine cases out of ten, keep each other mutually in check. But there is another bulwark more formidable yet. This is the Germanic Body, which lies almost in the centre of Europe and holds all the other parts in their place, serving still more perhaps for the protection of its neighbours than for that of its own members: a body formidable to all by its size and by the number and valour of its component peoples; but of service to all by its constitution which, depriving it both of the means and the will to conquer, makes it the rock on which all schemes of conquest are doomed infallibly to break. In spite of all its defects, it is certain that, so long as that constitution endures, the balance of Europe will never be broken; that no potentate need fear to be cast from his throne by any of his rivals; and that the Treaty of Westphalia will perhaps for ever remain the foundation of our international sys-tem. Accordingly, the system of public right, which the Germans study so diligently, is even more important than they suppose. It is the public right not only of Germany, but even, in many ways, of Europe as a whole.

But the established order, if indestructible, is for that very reason the more liable to constant storms. Between the powers of Europe there is a constant action and reaction which, without overthrowing them altogether, keeps them in continual agitation. Ineffectual as they are, these shocks perpetually renew themselves, like the waves which for ever trouble the surface of the sea without ever altering its level. The nations are incessantly ravaged, without any appreciable advantage to the sovereigns.

It would be easy for me to draw the same lesson from a study of the special interests of all the courts of Europe; to show that those interests are so cunningly interwoven as to hold their respective forces mutually in check. But current theories of commerce and money have bred a political bigotry which works such rapid changes in the apparent interests of princes that it is impossible to arrive at any firm conclusion as to their real interests, seeing that everything now depends upon the economic systems, for the most part thoroughly crazy, which chance to flit through a minister's brain. For all that, commerce tends more and more to establish a balance between state and state; and by depriving certain powers of the exclusive advantages they once drew from it, deprives them at the same time of one of the chief weapons they once employed for imposing their will upon the rest.[2]

If I have dwelt upon the equal distribution of forces which springs from the present constitution of Europe, it was in order to draw from it a conclusion of the highest importance to the project for establishing a general league among her peoples. For, if we are to form a solid and lasting federation, we must have put all the members of it in a state of such mutual dependence that no one of them is singly in a position to overbear all the others, and that separate leagues, capable of thwarting the general league, shall meet with obstacles formidable enough to hinder their formation. Failing this, the general league will be nothing but an empty name; and under an appearance of subjection, every member of it will in reality be independent. But, if those obstacles are such as I have described at the present moment—a moment when all the powers are entirely free to form separate leagues and offensive alliances —judge what they would become if there were a general league, fully armed and ready at any moment to forestall those who should conceive the design of destroying or resisting it. That in itself is enough to show that such a federation, so far from ending in mere vain discussions to be set at defiance with impunity, would on the contrary give birth to an effective power, capable of forcing any ambitious ruler to observe the terms of the general league which he has joined with others to set up.

From the above survey three certain conclusions may be drawn: the first that, Turkey excepted, there already exists among the nations of Europe a bond, imperfect indeed but still closer than the loose and general ties which exist between man and man in the state of nature; the second, that the imperfections of this association make the state of those who belong to it worse than it would be if they formed no community at all; the third, that these rudimentary ties, which make such an association injurious, make it at the same time readily capable of improvement, that all its members might easily find their happiness in what actually makes their misery, that from the state of war which now reigns among them they might perfectly well draw an abiding peace.

---

2. There has been a great change since I wrote these words (1756); but my principle will always remain true. It is easy enough to foresee, for instance, that England, with all her glory, will be ruined within twenty years, and, moreover, will have lost what remains of her freedom. All the world asserts that agriculture flourishes in that island. I would wager anything that it is dying fast. London grows every day; therefore the kingdom is being depleted. The English have set their minds on being conquerors; therefore they are hastening to be slaves.

Let us now consider the means by which this great work, begun by chance, may be completed by wisdom. Let us ask how the free and voluntary association which now unites the states of Europe may be converted, by taking to itself the strength and firmness of a genuine body politic, into an authentic federation. There is no doubt that such a federation, by giving to the existing bond the completeness which it now lacks, will increase all its advantages and compel all the parts to unite for the benefit of the whole body. But, before this result can be brought about, the federation must embrace all the important powers in its membership; it must have a legislative body, with powers to pass laws and ordinances binding upon all its members; it must have a coercive force capable of compelling every state to obey its common resolves whether in the way of command or of prohibition; finally, it must be strong and firm enough to make it impossible for any member to withdraw at his own pleasure the moment he conceives his private interest to clash with that of the whole body. Those are the sure signs by which the world may satisfy itself of the wisdom, usefulness and solidity of our structure. It only remains now to carry our speculation a stage further: to discover by analysis what are the practical consequences which should flow from it, what the means best fitted to realize it, and whether there is any reasonable hope of putting it in execution.

From time to time there are convoked in Europe certain general assemblies called congresses, to which deputies from every state repair solemnly, to return in the same way; where men assemble to say nothing; where all the affairs of Europe are overhauled in detail; where men lay their heads together to deliberate whether the table they sit at shall be square or round; whether the hall shall have six doors or five; whether one plenipotentiary shall sit with his face or his back to the window, whether another shall come two inches further, or less far, into the room on a visit of ceremony: in fine, on a thousand questions of equal importance which have been discussed without any settlement for the last three centuries and are assuredly very fit to engross the statesmen of our own.

It is possible that the members of one of these assemblies may, once in a way, be blessed with common sense. It is even not impossible that they may have a sincere desire for the general good. For reasons to be assigned shortly, it is further conceivable that, after smoothing away a thousand difficulties, they will receive orders from their sovereigns to sign the constitution of the Federation of Europe, which I suppose to have been summarily drafted in the five following articles.

By the first, the contracting sovereigns shall enter into a perpetual and irrevocable alliance, and shall appoint plenipotentiaries to hold, in a specified place, a permanent diet or congress, at which all questions at issue between the contracting parties shall be settled and terminated by way of arbitration or judicial pronouncement.

By the second shall be specified the number of the sovereigns whose plenipotentiaries shall have a vote in the Diet; those who shall be invited to accede to the treaty; the order, date and method by which the presidency shall pass, at equal intervals, from one to another; finally the quota of their respective contributions and the method of raising them for the defrayal of the common expenses.

By the third, the Federation shall guarantee to each of its members the possession and government of all the dominions which he holds at the moment of the treaty, as well as the manner of succession to them, elective or hereditary, as established by the fundamental laws of each province. Further, with a view to suppressing at a single stroke and at the source those incessant disputes which arise between them, it shall be agreed to take as basis of the respective rights of the contracting parties the possession of the moment, as settled in each case by the last treaty concluded, with a general renunciation on all sides of every anterior claim: exception being made for all disputed successions and other claims to fall due in the future, all which shall be determined by arbitration of the Diet, to the absolute exclusion of all attempts to settle the matter by force or to take arms against each other under any pretext whatsoever.

By the fourth shall be specified the conditions under which any confederate who may break this treaty shall be put to the ban of Europe and proscribed as a public enemy: namely, if he shall have refused to execute the decisions of the grand alliance, if he shall have made preparations for war, if he shall have made a treaty hostile to the ends of the Federation, if he shall have taken up arms to resist it or to attack any one of the confederates.

By the same article, it shall be agreed that all the confederates shall arm and take the offensive, conjointly and at the common expense, against any state put to the ban of Europe, and that they shall not desist until the moment when he shall have laid down his arms, carried out the decisions and orders of the Diet, made amends for his offence, paid all the costs and atoned even for such warlike preparations as he may have made in defiance of the treaty.

Finally, by the fifth article, the plenipotentiaries of the Federation of

Europe shall receive standing powers to frame—provisionally by a bare majority, definitively (after an interval of five years) by a majority of three-quarters—those measures which, on the instruction of their courts, they shall consider expedient with a view to the greatest possible advantage of the commonwealth of Europe and of its members, all and single. In none of the above five articles, however, shall any change ever be made except with the unanimous consent of the confederates.

These five articles, thus summarized and reduced to the most general form, are, I am aware, exposed to countless petty objections, several of which would call for lengthy explanations. But petty objections are easily removed in case of need; and, in an enterprise of this importance, they are beside the point. When the policy of the Congress comes to be considered, a thousand obstacles will present themselves and ten thousand ways of removing them. It is *our* business to ask whether, in the nature of the case, the enterprise is possible or no. We should lose ourselves in volumes of trifles if we had to foresee all and find an answer to all. Confining ourselves, as we do, to incontestable principles, we have no call to satisfy every reader, nor to solve every objection, nor to say how every detail will be settled. It is enough to show that a settlement is possible.

In judging of this scheme, then, what are the questions that have to be considered? Two only; for I will not insult the reader by proving to him the general proposition that the state of peace is a better thing than the state of war.

The first question is whether the Federation suggested would be certain to answer its purpose and give a solid and abiding peace to Europe. The second, whether it is for the interest of the various sovereigns to establish such a Federation and to pay the price I have mentioned to obtain a lasting peace.

When we have thus proved our scheme to be for the advantage both of Europe as a whole and of all the states composing her, what obstacle is left, we ask, that can possibly prevent the execution of a design which, after all, depends solely upon the will of those concerned?

In discussing the first article, for instance, let us apply what has been said above of the general order now established in Europe and of the common resolve which confines each power practically within its traditional limits and does not allow it wholly to crush any of the others. In order to make my argument clear, I give here a list of the nineteen powers here assumed to constitute the commonwealth of Europe, to each of which I give an equal voice, making altogether nineteen votes, in the deliberations of the Diet: the Emperor of the Romans; [3] the Emperor of Russia; the King of France; the King of Spain; the King of England; the States General,[4] the King of Denmark; Sweden; Poland; the King of Portugal; the Sovereign of Rome;[5] the King of Prussia; the Elector of Bavaria and his associates; the Elector Palatine and his associates; the Swiss and their associates; the ecclesiastical Electors and their associates; the Republic of Venice and her associates; the King of Naples; the King of Sardinia.

Several minor sovereigns—for instance, the Republic of Genoa, the dukes of Parma and Modena, and others—are omitted from the list. They will be associated with one or other of the less powerful states, with whom they will share a vote, after the fashion of the joint vote (*votum curiatum*) of the counts of the empire. It is useless to make the list more precise because, at any moment before the scheme is put in force, things may happen which, without affecting the principle of the measure, may call for alterations of detail.

A glance at the list will be enough to prove conclusively that it is impossible either for any single power to resist the united action of all the others, or for any partial league to be formed capable of defying the Federation as a whole.

How, indeed, could such a league be formed? Between the more powerful of the confederates? We have already proved that such a league could never last; and with the list before us, it is easy enough to see that it could never be reconciled with the traditional policy of any of the great powers, or with the interests inherent in their respective positions. Between a large state and a number of small ones? Then the other large states, with the Federation behind them, will crush such a league in no time; and it is clear that the Grand Alliance, being perpetually armed and concerted for action, will find no difficulty in forestalling and crushing in advance any partial and seditious alliance, likely to trouble the peace and the public order of Europe. Look at the cohesion of the Germanic Body: and that, in spite of its defective discipline and the glaring inequality of its members. Is there a single prince, not even excepting the most powerful, who would dare to expose himself to the ban of the empire by openly defying its laws, unless indeed he had good reason to suppose that the empire would

---

3. The potentate commonly, but incorrectly, called the Emperor of Germany.
4. The Dutch Netherlands.
5. The Pope.

never have the courage to take action against the culprit in good earnest?

That is why I regard it as proved that the Diet of Europe, once established, will have no rebellion to fear and that no abuses which may creep in are ever likely to defeat the aims with which it was founded. It remains to ask whether those aims are really secured by the proposed Federation.

With a view to answering this question, let us consider the motives by which princes are commonly led to take up arms. These motives are: either to make conquests, or to protect themselves from aggression, or to weaken a too powerful neighbour, or to maintain their rights against attack, or to settle a difference which has defied friendly negotiation, or, lastly, to fulfil some treaty obligation. There is no cause or pretext of war which cannot be brought under one or other of these six heads; and it is manifest that not one of the six is left standing under the new order which I propose.

As for the first, the thought of conquests will have to be given up from the absolute impossibility of making them. The aggressor is sure to find his way barred by forces stronger than his own; he is powerless to gain anything, and he risks the loss of all he has. At present, an ambitious prince, who wishes to extend his dominions in Europe, relies upon two weapons; he begins by securing strong allies, and then seeks to catch his enemy unawares. But, under the new conditions, no special alliance could stand for a moment before the General Alliance, which is stronger and subsists permanently; and as there is no longer any pretext for arming, no prince can do so without being at once detected, stopped and punished by the Federation always under arms.

Again, the very thing which destroys all hope of conquest relieves him at the same time from all fear of being attacked. And, under the guarantee of all Europe, not only are his territories as strongly assured to him as the possessions of any citizen in a well-ordered community, but they are even more so than they were when he was their sole and only defender; in exactly the same proportion as the whole of Europe is stronger than any one of her princes taken singly.

Thirdly, having no more reason to fear his neighbour, neither has he any more reason for desiring to weaken him; and having no hope of success in such an enterprise, he is under no temptation to attempt it.

As for the maintenance of his rights, I begin by remarking that a whole host of pettifogging claims and obscure pretensions will be swept away at one stroke by the third article of Federation, which settles for ever all the conflicting rights of the allied princes, on the basis of what they actually hold. By the same article, we have a clear principle for settling all claims and pretensions which may be raised in the future: each will be decided in the Diet, as it arises. It may be added that, if my rights are attacked, I am bound to defend them by the weapon used against me. They cannot be attacked by force of arms without bringing the ban of the Diet upon the assailant. It is not by arms then that I shall have to defend them. The same may be said of injuries, wrongs and claims for damage—in short, of all the unforeseen differences which may arise between two sovereigns. The same power which is bound to maintain their rights is bound also to redress their grievances.

As for the last head, the question settles itself. It is clear at a glance that, having no longer any assailant to fear, I have no longer any use for treaties of defence; and that, as no treaty can be so strong or so trustworthy as that guaranteed by the Grand Federation, any other treaty would be useless, illegitimate and consequently null and void.

For all these reasons it is impossible that the Federation, once established, can leave any seed of war between its members; impossible that our object, an abiding peace, should not be absolutely attained by the proposed system, if it were once set on foot.

It now remains to settle the other question: that relating to the interests of the several parties concerned. For everyone knows that the general interest is powerless to silence that of the individual. To prove that peace, as a general principle, is a better thing than war is to say nothing to the man who has private reasons for preferring war to peace; to show him the means for securing a lasting peace is only to encourage him to work against them.

In truth, we shall be told: "You are taking from sovereigns the right of doing themselves justice; that is to say, the precious right of being unjust when they please. You are taking from them the power of making themselves great at the expense of their neighbours. You are forcing them to renounce those antiquated claims whose value depends on their obscurity and which grow with every fresh growth in power; that parade of might and terror with which they love to awe the world; that pride of conquest which is the chief source of their glory. In one word, you are forcing them to be equitable and peaceful. What amends do you propose to make them for all these cruel privations?"

I do not venture to answer, with the Abbé de Saint-Pierre, that the true glory of princes lies in serving the good of the community and the happiness of their subjects, that their highest interest is to win a good name, and that such a name is awarded by the wise in exact proportion to the good which the ruler has done in the world; that the scheme of founding a lasting peace is the most lofty ever conceived and the most certain, if executed, to cover its author with undying glory; that such a scheme would not only do a greater service than any other to the people but also confer higher honour upon the sovereign; that this is the only ideal not stained with blood, rapine, curses and tears; in a word, that the surest way for a sovereign to raise himself above the common herd of kings is to labour for the good of the community. Let such language, which has covered the author and his projects with ridicule in all the council-chambers of Europe, be left to irresponsible declaimers. But let us never join in the cry against the arguments it embodies; and, whatever may be the truth as to the virtues of princes, let us confine ourselves to their interests.

All the powers of Europe have rights, or claims, as against each other. These rights are, from the nature of the case, incapable of ever being finally adjusted, because there is no common and unvarying standard for judging of their merits and because they are often based upon facts which are either disputed or of doubtful interpretation. Nor are the quarrels which spring from them any more capable of being settled beyond appeal, whether in default of any recognized umpire, or because, when the chance offers, every prince goes back shamelessly upon the cessions which have been forcibly torn from him by a stronger power through treaties, or after an unsuccessful war. It is therefore a mistake to think only of the claims we have on others, and to forget those they have on us, when in reality there is no more justice on one side than the other and both are equally capable of acquiring the means for enforcing their demands. Directly fortune is taken for arbiter, actual possession acquires a value which no wise man will stake against a possible gain in the future, even where chances are equal on both sides; and the rich man who, in the hope of doubling his fortune, ventures to risk it all upon one throw is blamed by the whole world. We have shown, however, that in schemes of self-aggrandizement the chances are never equal and that, even in the present order of things, the aggressor is always bound to find his enemy stronger than himself. The inevitable conclusion is that, the more powerful having no motive for staking his possessions and the weaker no hope of gaining on the throw, both will find their advantage in renouncing what they would like to win, in order to secure what they possess.

Think of the waste of men, of money, of strength in every form; think of the exhaustion in which any state is plunged by the most successful war; compare these ravages with the profit which results: and we shall find that we commonly lose where we suppose ourselves to gain; that the conqueror, always enfeebled by the war, can only console himself with the thought that the conquered is still more enfeebled than himself. And even this advantage is more in appearance than reality; for the strength which has been gained upon our opponent has been lost against the neutrals who, without changing themselves, are nevertheless stronger relatively to us by all the strength that we have lost.

If all kings have not yet thrown off the folly of conquests, it would seem that the wiser of them at any rate are beginning to realize that they sometimes cost more than they are worth. Without going into a thousand distinctions which would only distract us from our purpose, we may say broadly that a prince who, in extending his frontiers, loses as many of his old subjects as he gains new ones in the process only weakens himself by his aggrandizement; because, with a larger territory to defend, he has no more soldiers to defend it. Everyone knows, however, that, as war is waged nowadays, the smallest part of the resultant loss of life is due to losses in the field. Certainly, that is the loss which everyone sees and feels. But all the time there is taking place through the whole kingdom a loss far more serious and more irreparable than that of those who die: a loss due to those who are not born, to the increase of taxes, to the interruption of trade, to the desertion of the fields, to the neglect of their cultivation. This evil, which no one sees at first, makes itself felt cruelly in the end. And then the king is astonished to find himself so weak, as the result of making himself so strong.

There is another thing which makes conquests even less profitable than they used to be. It is that kings have at last learned the secret of doubling or trebling their power not only without enlarging their territory but even, it may be, by contracting it, after the wise example of Hadrian. The secret is that the strength of kings lies only in that of their subjects; and it follows from what I have just said that, given two states supporting an equal number of inhabitants, that which covers the smaller extent of territory is in reality the more powerful. It is then by good laws, by a wise discipline, by large views on economic policy that a sagacious sovereign is sure of increasing his power without incurring any hazard. It is in carrying out works more useful than his neighbours' that he makes conquests—the only true conquests—at their expense; and every subject born to him in excess of theirs is another enemy killed.

It may be objected that I prove too much and that, if the matter were as I put it, everyone being manifestly interested in avoiding war and the public interest combining with that of individuals for the preservation of peace, that peace ought to come of itself and of itself last for ever without any need of federation. Given the present state of things, however, that would be to reason very ill. It is quite true that it would be much better for all men to remain always at peace. But so long as there is no security for this, everyone, having no guarantee that he can avoid war, is anxious to begin it at the moment which suits his own interest and so forestall a neighbour, who would not fail to forestall the attack in his turn at any moment favourable to himself, so that many wars, even offensive wars, are rather in the nature of unjust precautions for the protection of the assailant's own possessions than a device for seizing those of others. However salutary it may be in theory to obey the dictates of public spirit, it is certain that, politically and even morally, those dictates are liable to prove fatal to the man who persists in observing them with all the world when no one thinks of observing them towards him.

I have nothing to say on the question of military parade because, when supported by no solid foundation either of hope or fear, such parade is mere child's play, and kings have no business to keep dolls. I am equally silent as to the glory of conquest because, if there really were men who would break their hearts at the thought of having no one to massacre, our duty would be not to reason with such monsters but to deprive them of all means for putting their murderous frenzy into act. All solid grounds of war being swept away by the third article, no king can have any motive for kindling its horrors against a rival which would not furnish that rival with equally strong grounds for kindling them against him. And it is a great gain to be delivered from a danger in which each finds himself alone against the world.

As for the dependence of all upon the Tribunal of Europe, it is abundantly clear by the same article that the rights of sovereignty, so far from being weakened, will, on the contrary, be strengthened and confirmed. For that article guarantees to each sovereign not only that his dominions shall be protected against foreign invasion, but also that his authority shall be upheld against the rebellion of his subjects. The prince accordingly will be none the less absolute, and his crown will be more fully assured. By submitting to the decision of the Diet in all disputes with his equals, and by surrendering the perilous right of seizing other men's possessions, he is, in fact, doing nothing more than securing his real rights and renouncing those which are purely fictitious. Besides, there is all the difference in the world between dependence upon a rival and dependence upon a body of which he is himself a member and of which each member in turn becomes the head. In the latter case, the pledges that are given him are really the security for his freedom: it would be forfeited, if lodged with a superior; it is confirmed, when lodged with equals. In support of this, I appeal to the example of the Germanic Body. It is quite true that the constitution of this is such as to trench in many ways upon the sovereignty of its members. It is quite true that their position is consequently less favourable than it would be in the Federation of Europe. But, in spite of those drawbacks, there is not one of them, however jealous he may be of his dignity, who would choose, even if he had the power, to win absolute independence at the cost of severance from the empire.

Observe further that the head of the Germanic Body, being permanent, is bound to usurp ceaselessly upon the rights of the other members. In the Diet of Europe, where the presidency passes from one to another without any regard to disparities of power, no such danger is to be feared.

There is yet another consideration which is likely to weigh even more with men so greedy of money as princes always are. Not only will an unbroken peace give them, as well as their subjects, every means of amassing abundant riches; they will also be spared vast expenses by the reduction of their military budget, of those innumerable fortresses, of those enormous armies, which swallow up their revenue and become daily more and more of a burden to their subjects and themselves. I know that it will not suit all sovereigns to suppress their army bodily and leave themselves with no force in hand to crush an unexpected revolt or repel a sudden invasion. I know also that they will have their contingent to furnish to the Federation with a view both to guarding the frontiers of Europe and to maintaining the federal army whose duty it will be, in case of need, to carry out the decrees of the Diet. But, when all these charges are met and, at the same time, the extraordinary expenses of war suppressed for ever, there will still be a saving of more than half the ordinary military budget; and that saving can be divided between the relief of the subject and the coffers of the prince. The result will be that the people will have to pay much less; that the prince, being much better off, will be in a position to encourage commerce, agriculture and the arts and to create useful foundations which will still further increase his subjects' riches and his own; and, over and above all this, that the state will enjoy a security far greater than it now draws from all its armies and from all that warlike parade which drains its strength in the very bosom of peace.

It will be said perhaps that the frontier countries of Europe will then be relatively worse off, since they will still have to face the chance of war either with the Turk, or the African Corsairs, or the Tartars.

The answer to this is (1) that those countries are under the same necessity at present, from which it follows that they will not be put to any positive disadvantage, but will only have an advantage the less; and this, in fact, is an inevitable consequence of their geographical position; (2) that, being freed from all anxiety on the side of Europe, they will be much more capable of resisting attacks from other quarters; (3) that the suppression of all fortresses in the inner parts of Europe and of all expenses needed for their maintenance would enable the Federation to build a large number on the eastern frontiers without bringing any fresh charge upon its members; (4) that these fortresses, built, maintained and garrisoned at the common charge, will mean so many fresh guarantees, and so much expense saved to the frontier powers for whose benefit they are built; (5) that the troops of the Federation, posted on the frontiers of Europe, will stand permanently ready to drive back the invader; (6) and finally, that a body so formidable as the commonwealth of Europe will make the foreigner think twice before attacking any of its members: just as the Germanic Body, though infinitely less powerful, is still strong enough to command the respect of its neighbours and offer valuable protection to all the princes who compose it.

It may be further objected that, when the nations of Europe have ceased to war among themselves, the art of war will be gradually forgotten, that her armies will lose their courage and discipline, that there will be no more soldiers or generals, and that Europe will lie at the mercy of the first comer.

My answer is that one of two things will happen. Either the neighbours of Europe will attack her and wage war against her; or they will be afraid of the Federation and leave her in peace.

In the former case, there will be plenty of opportunities for training military genius and talent, for practising and hardening our troops. The armies of the Federation will, in this way, be the school of Europe. Men will go to the frontiers to learn war, while in the heart of Europe there will reign the blessings of peace. The advantages of war and peace will be combined. Does anyone believe that no nation can become warlike without perpetual civil war? And are the French the less brave because Anjou and Touraine are not constantly fighting with each other?

In the latter case, it is true that there can be no more hardening for war. But neither will there be any more need for it. Of what use would it be to train for war, when you have no intention of ever making it? And which is the better course—to cultivate a pernicious art, or to destroy the need of it for ever? If the secret of perpetual health were discovered, would there be any sense in rejecting it, on the ground that doctors must not be deprived of the chance of gaining experience? And in making this parallel we have still to ask which of the two arts is the more beneficent in itself and the more deserving of encouragement.

Let no one threaten us with a sudden invasion. It is perfectly obvious that Europe has no invader to fear, and that the "first comer" will never come. The day of those barbarian irruptions, which seemed to fall from the clouds, is gone for ever. Now that the whole surface of the earth lies bare to our scrutiny, no danger can reach us which we have not foreseen for years. There is no power in the world now capable of threatening all Europe; and if one ever appears, Europe will either have time to make ready or, at the worst, will be much more capable of resisting him when she is united in one corporate body than she is now, when she would have to put a sudden end to all her quarrels and league herself in haste against the common invader.

We have thus seen that all the alleged evils of federation, when duly weighed, come to nothing. I now ask whether anyone in the world would dare to say as much of those which flow from the recognized method of settling disputes between one prince and another—the appeal to the sword: a method inseparable from the state of anarchy and war, which necessarily springs from the absolute independence conceded to all sovereigns under the imperfect conditions now prevailing in Europe. In order to put the reader in a better position to estimate these evils, I will give a short summary of them and leave him to judge of their significance.

(1) The existence of no solid right, except that of the stronger. (2) The perpetual and inevitable shifting of the balance from nation to nation, which makes it impossible for any one of them to keep in its grasp the power it holds at any moment. (3) The absence of complete security for any nation, so long as its neighbours are not subdued or annihilated. (4) The impossibility of annihilating them, in view of the fact that, directly one is conquered, another springs up in its place. (5) The necessity of endless precautions and expenses to keep guard against possible enemies. (6) Weakness, and consequent exposure to attack, during minorities or revolts; for, when the state is divided, who can support one faction against the other? (7) The absence of any guaran-

tee for international agreements. (8) The impossibility of obtaining justice from others without enormous cost and loss, which even so do not always obtain it, while the object in dispute is seldom worth the price. (9) The invariable risk of the prince's possessions, and sometimes of his life, in the quest of his rights. (10) The necessity of taking part against his will in the quarrels of his neighbours and of engaging in war at the moment when he would least have chosen it. (11) The stoppage of trade and revenue at the moment when they are most indispensable. (12) The perpetual dangers threatened by a powerful neighbour, if the prince is weak, and by an armed alliance, if he is strong. (13) Finally, the uselessness of prudence, when everything is left to chance; the perpetual impoverishment of nations; the enfeeblement of the state alike in victory and defeat; and the total inability of the prince ever to establish good government, ever to count upon his own possessions, ever to secure happiness either for himself or for his subjects.

In the same way, let us sum up the advantages which the arbitration of Europe would confer upon the princes who agree to it.

1. Absolute certainty that all their disputes, present and future, will always be settled without war: a certainty incomparably more useful to princes than total immunity from lawsuits to the individual.

2. The abolition, either total or nearly so, of matters of dispute, thanks to the extinction of all existing claims—a boon which, in itself, will make up for all the prince renounces and secure what he possesses.

3. An absolute and indefeasible guarantee not only for the persons of the prince and his family, but also for his dominions and the law of succession recognized by the custom of each province: and this, not only against the ambition of unjust and grasping claimants, but also against the rebellion of his subjects.

4. Absolute security for the execution of all engagements between princes, under the guarantee of the commonwealth of Europe.

5. Perfect freedom of trade for all time whether between state and state, or between any of them and the more distant regions of the earth.

6. The total suppression for all time of the extraordinary military expenses incurred by land and sea in time of war, and a considerable reduction of the corresponding ordinary expenses in time of peace.

7. A notable increase of population and agriculture, of the public wealth and the revenues of the prince.

8. An open door for all useful foundations, calculated to increase the power and glory of the sovereign, the public wealth and the happiness of the subject.

As I have already said, I leave it to the reader to weigh all these points and to make his own comparison between the state of peace which results from federation and the state of war which follows from the present anarchy of Europe.

If our reasoning has been sound in the exposition of this project, it has been proved: firstly, that the establishment of a lasting peace depends solely upon the consent of the sovereigns concerned and offers no obstacle except what may be expected from their opposition; secondly, that the establishment of such a peace would be profitable to them in all manner of ways, and that, even from their point of view, there is no comparison between its drawbacks and advantages; thirdly, that it is reasonable to expect their decision in this matter will coincide with their plain interest; and lastly, that such a peace, once established on the proposed basis, will be solid and lasting and will completely fulfil the purpose with which it was concluded.

This is not, of course, to say that the sovereigns will adopt this project —who can answer for the reason of another?—but only that they would adopt it, if they took counsel of their true interest. It must be observed that we have not assumed men such as they ought to be, good, generous, disinterested and devoted to the public good from motives of pure humanity; but such as they are, unjust, grasping and setting their own interest above all things. All that I do assume in them is understanding enough to see their own interest, and courage enough to act for their own happiness. If, in spite of all this, the project remains unrealized, that is not because it is utopian; it is because men are crazy, and because to be sane in a world of madmen is in itself a kind of madness.

ROUSSEAU'S CRITICISM OF SAINT-PIERRE'S PROJECT

The scheme of a lasting peace was of all others the most worthy to fascinate a man of high principle. Of all those which engaged the Abbé de Saint-Pierre, it was therefore that over which he brooded the longest and followed up with the greatest obstinacy. It is indeed hard to give any other name to the missionary zeal which never failed him in this enterprise: and that, in spite of the manifest impossibility of success, the ridicule which he brought upon himself day by day and the rebuffs which he had continually to endure. It would seem that his well-balanced spirit, intent solely on the public good, led him to measure his devotion to a cause purely by its utility, never letting himself be daunted by difficulties, never thinking of his own personal interest.

If ever moral truth were demonstrated, I should say it is the utility, national no less than international, of this project. The advantages which its realization would bring to each prince, to each nation, to the whole of Europe, are immense, manifest, incontestable; and nothing could be more solid or more precise than the arguments which the author employs to prove them. Realize his commonwealth of Europe for a single day, and you may be sure it will last for ever; so fully would experience convince men that their own gain is to be found in the good of all. For all that, the very princes who would defend it with all their might, if it once existed, would resist with all their might any proposal for its creation; they will as infallibly throw obstacles in the way of its establishment as they would in the way of its abolition. Accordingly Saint-Pierre's book on A Lasting Peace seems to be ineffectual for founding it and unnecessary for maintaining it. "It is then an empty dream," will be the verdict of the impatient reader. No: it is a work of solid judgment, and it is of the last importance for us to possess it.

Let us begin by examining the criticisms of those who judge of reasons not by reason, but by the event, and who have no objection to bring against the scheme except that it has never been put in practice. Well, such men will doubtless say, if its advantages are so certain, why is it that the sovereigns of Europe have never adopted it? Why do they ignore their own interest, if that interest is demonstrated so clearly? Do we see them reject any other means of increasing their revenue and their power? And, if this means were as efficacious as you pretend, is it conceivable that they should be less eager to try it than any of the schemes they have pursued for all these centuries? that they should prefer a thousand delusive expedients to so evident an advantage?

Yes, without doubt, that is conceivable; unless it be assumed that their wisdom is equal to their ambition, and that the more keenly they desire their own interest, the more clearly do they see it. The truth is that the severest penalty of excessive self-love is that it always defeats itself, that the keener the passion the more certain it is to be cheated of its goal. Let us distinguish them, in politics as in morals, between real and apparent interest. The former would be secured by an abiding peace; that is demonstrated in the Project. The latter is to be found in the state of absolute independence which frees sovereigns from the reign of law only to put them under that of chance. They are, in fact, like a madcap pilot who, to show off his idle skill and his power over his sailors, would rather toss to and fro among the rocks in a storm than moor his vessel at anchor in safety.

The whole life of kings, or of those on whom they shuffle off their duties, is devoted solely to two objects: to extend their rule beyond their frontiers and to make it more absolute within them. Any other purpose they may have is either subservient to one of these aims, or merely a pretext for attaining them. Such pretexts are "the good of the community," "the happiness of their subjects," or "the glory of the nation": phrases for ever banished from the council chamber, and employed so clumsily in proclamations that they are always taken as warnings of coming misery and that the people groans with apprehension when its masters speak to it of their "fatherly solicitude."

From these two fundamental maxims we can easily judge of the spirit in which princes are likely to receive a proposal which runs directly counter to the one and is hardly more favourable to the other. Anyone can see that the establishment of the Diet of Europe will fix the constitution of each state as inexorably as its frontiers; that it is impossible to guarantee the prince against the rebellion of his subjects without at the same time securing the subjects against the tyranny of the prince; and that, without this, the Federation could not possibly endure. And I ask whether there is in the whole world a single sovereign who, finding himself thus bridled for ever in his most cherished designs, would endure without indignation the very thought of seeing himself forced to be just not only with the foreigner, but even with his own subjects?

Again, anyone can understand that war and conquest without and the encroachments of despotism within give each other mutual support; that money and men are habitually taken at pleasure from a people of slaves, to bring others beneath the same yoke; and that conversely war furnishes a pretext for exactions of money and another, no less plausible, for keeping large armies constantly on foot, to hold the people in awe. In a word, anyone can see that aggressive princes wage war at least as much on their subjects as on their enemies, and that the conquering nation is left no better off than the conquered. "I have beaten the Romans," so Hannibal used to write to Carthage, "send me more troops. I have exacted an indemnity from Italy, send me more money." That is the real meaning of the *Te Deums*, the bonfires and rejoicings with which the people hail the triumphs of their masters.

As for disputes between prince and prince, is it reasonable to hope that we can force before a higher tribunal men who boast that they hold their power only by the sword, and who bring in the name of God solely because He "is in heaven"? Will sovereigns ever submit their quarrels to legal arbitration, when all the rigour of the laws has never succeeded in forcing private individuals to admit the principle in theirs? A private gentleman with a grievance is too proud to carry his case before the Court of the Marshals of France; and you expect a king to carry his claims before the Diet of Europe? Not to mention that the former offends against the laws, so risking his life twice over, while the latter seldom risks anything but the life of his subjects; and that, in taking up arms, he avails himself of a right recognized by all the world—a right for the use of which he claims to be accountable to God alone.

A prince who stakes his cause on the hazards of war knows well enough that he is running risks. But he is less struck with the risks than with the gains on which he reckons, because he is much less afraid of fortune than he is confident in his own wisdom. If he is strong, he counts upon his armies; if weak, upon his allies. Sometimes he finds it useful to purge ill humours, to weaken restive subjects, even to sustain reverses; and the wily statesman knows how to draw profit even from his own defeats. I trust it will be remembered that it is not I who reason in this fashion, but the court sophist, who would rather have a large territory with few subjects, poor and submissive, than that unshaken rule over the hearts of a happy and prosperous people, which is the reward of a prince who observes justice and obeys the laws.

It is on the same principle that he meets in his own mind the argument drawn from the interruption of commerce, from the loss of life, from the financial confusion and the real loss which result from an unprofitable conquest. It is a great miscalculation always to estimate the losses and gains of princes in terms of money; the degree of power they aim at is not to be reckoned by the millions in their coffers. The prince always makes his schemes rotate: he seeks to command in order to enrich himself, and to enrich himself in order to command. He is ready by turns to sacrifice the one aim to the other, with a view to obtaining which-ever of the two is most wanting at the moment. But it is only in the hope of winning them both in the long run that he pursues each of them apart. If he is to be master both of men and things, he must have empire and money at the same time.

Let us add finally that, though the advantages resulting to commerce from a general and lasting peace are in themselves certain and indis-putable, still, being common to all states, they will be appreciated by none. For such advantages make themselves felt only by contrast, and he who wishes to increase his relative power is bound to seek only such gains as are exclusive.

So it is that, ceaselessly deluded by appearances, princes would have nothing to do with peace on these terms, even if they calculated their interests for themselves. How will it be, when the calculation is made for them by their ministers, whose interests are always opposed to those of the people and almost always to the prince's? Ministers are in perpetual need of war, as a means of making themselves indispensable to their master, of throwing him into difficulties from which he cannot escape without their aid, of ruining the state, if things come to the worst, as the price of keeping their own office. They are in need of it, as a means of oppressing the people on the plea of national necessity, of finding places for their creatures, of rigging the market and setting up a thousand odious monopolies. They are in need of it, as a means of gratifying their passions and driving their rivals out of favour. They are in need of it, as a means of controlling the prince and withdrawing him from court whenever a dangerous plot is formed against their power. With a lasting peace, all these resources would be gone. And the world still persists in asking why, if such a scheme is practicable, these men have not adopted it. Is it not obvious that there is nothing impracticable about it, except its adoption by these men? What then will they do to oppose it? What they have always done: they will turn it into ridicule.

Again, even given the good will that we shall never find either in princes or their ministers, we are not to assume, with the Abbé de Saint-Pierre, that it would be easy to find the right moment for putting the project into act. For this, it would be essential that all the private interests concerned, taken together, should not be stronger than the general interest, and that everyone should believe himself to see in the good of all the highest good to which he can aspire for himself. But this requires a concurrence of wisdom in so many heads, a fortuitous concourse of so many interests, such as chance can hardly be expected ever to bring about. But, in default of such spontaneous agreement, the one thing left is force; and then the question is no longer to persuade but to compel, not to write books but to raise armies.

Accordingly, though the scheme in itself was wise enough, the means proposed for its execution betray the simplicity of the author. He fairly supposed that nothing was needed but to convoke a congress and lay the articles before it; that they would be signed directly and all be over on the spot. It must be admitted that, in all his projects, this good man saw clearly enough how things would work, when once set going, but that he judged like a child of the means for setting them in motion.

To prove that the project of the Christian Commonwealth is not utopian, I need do no more than name its original author. For no one will say that Henry IV was a madman, or Sully a dreamer. The Abbé de Saint-Pierre took refuge behind these great names, to revive their policy. But what a difference in the time, the circumstances, the scheme itself, the manner of bringing it forward and, above all, in its author!

To judge of this, let us glance at the state of Europe as it was at the moment which Henry chose for the execution of his project.

The power of Charles V, who reigned over one half of the world and struck awe into the other, had led him to aspire to universal empire, with great chances of success and great talents for making use of them. His son, more rich and less powerful, never ceased to nurse a design which he was incapable of carrying out, and throughout his reign kept Europe in a state of perpetual alarm. In truth, the House of Austria had acquired such an ascendancy over the other powers that no prince was safe upon his throne, unless he stood well with the Habsburgs. Philip III, with even fewer talents, inherited all his father's pretensions. Europe was still held in awe by the power of Spain, which continued to dominate the others rather by long habit of commanding than from any power to make herself obeyed. In truth, the revolt of the low countries, the struggle against England, the long drain of the civil wars in France had exhausted the strength of Spain and the riches of the Indies. The House of Austria, now divided into two branches, had ceased to act with the same unity; and the Emperor, although he strained every nerve to maintain or recover the authority of Charles V, only succeeded in affronting the lesser princes and provoking conspiracies which speedily broke out and came near to costing him his throne. Such were the slow stages which prepared the fall of the House of Austria and the new birth of the liberties of Europe. No one, however, had the courage to be the first to risk throwing off the yoke and exposing himself alone to the dangers of war; the example of Henry himself, who had come so ill out of the enterprise, damped the courage of all the rest. Moreover, if we except the Duke of Savoy, who was too weak and too much under the curb to move a step, there was not among all the sovereigns of the time a single one of ability enough to form and carry through such an enterprise; each one of them waited on time and circumstances for the moment to break his chains. Such, in rough outline, was the state of things at the time when Henry formed the plan of the Christian Commonwealth and prepared to put it in act. The project was vast indeed and, in itself, quite beyond praise. I have no wish to dim its glory. But, prompted as it was by the secret hope of

humbling a formidable enemy, it took from this urgent motive an impulse which could hardly have come from humanity alone.

Let us now see what were the means employed by this great man
to pave the way for so lofty an undertaking. In the front rank of these I
should be disposed to put that he had clearly recognized all the
difficulties of the task; so that, having formed the project in his youth,
he brooded over it all his life and reserved its accomplishment for
his old age. This proves in the first place that ardent and sustained
passion by which alone great obstacles can be overcome; and secondly,
that patient and considerate wisdom which smoothes the way in advance by forethought and calculation. For there is a great difference between an enforced undertaking, in which prudence itself counsels to
leave something to chance, and one which is to be justified only by
success; seeing that, being under no compulsion to engage in it,
we ought never to have attempted it unless that success were beyond
doubt. Again, the deep secrecy which he maintained all his life, until
the very moment of action, was as essential as it was difficult in so vast
an enterprise, where the concurrence of so many men was a necessity
and which so many men were interested in thwarting. It would seem
that, though he had drawn the greater part of Europe to his side and
was in league with her chief potentates, there was only one man to
whom he had confided the full extent of his design; and, by a boon
granted by heaven only to the best of kings, that one man was an
honest minister. But, though nothing was allowed to transpire of these
high aims, everything was silently moving towards their execution.
Twice over did Sully make the journey to London: James I was a party
to the plan, and the King of Sweden had fallen in with it. A league was
made with the Protestants of Germany; even the princes of Italy had
been secured. All were ready to join in the great purpose, though none
could say what it was; just as workmen are employed in making the
separate parts of a new machine, of whose shape and use they know
nothing. What was it then that set all these springs in motion? Was it
the craving for a lasting peace, which was foreseen by no one and
with which few would have troubled their heads? Was it the public
interest, which is never the interest of anyone? The Abbé de Saint-Pierre
might have supposed so. But the truth is that each of them was working for his own private interest which Henry had been clever enough
to display to all of them in the most attractive light. The King of England
was glad to deliver himself from the perpetual conspiracies of his Catholic
subjects, all of them fomented by Spain. He found a further advantage
in the liberation of the United Provinces, in whose support he was spend-

ing large sums, while every moment he was placed on the brink of a war which he dreaded, or in which he preferred to join once for all with the whole of Europe and then be quit of it for ever. The King of Sweden was anxious to make sure of Pomerania and so win a footing in Germany. The Elector Palatine, at that time a Protestant and head of the Lutheran Confession, had designs on Bohemia and shared all the plans of the King of England. The princes of Germany aimed at checking the encroachments of the House of Austria. The Duke of Savoy was to receive Milan and the crown of Lombardy which he passionately coveted. The Pope himself, weary of the Spanish tyranny, was in the league, bribed by the promise of the kingdom of Naples. The Dutch, better paid than all the rest, gained the assurance of their freedom. In a word, quite apart from the common interest of humbling a haughty power which was striving to tyrannize over all of them, each state had a private interest all the more keenly felt because it was not countered by the fear of exchanging one tyrant for another. It was agreed that the conquests should be distributed among all the Allies to the exclusion of France and England, who were bound to keep nothing for themselves. This was enough to quiet the most suspicious as to the ambitions of Henry. But that wise prince was well aware that in keeping nothing for himself by this treaty, he gained more than all the rest. Without adding a yard to his own patrimony, it was enough to partition that of the only man who excelled him in power, and he became the most powerful himself. And it is perfectly clear that, in taking all the precautions which would assure the success of his enterprise, he in no wise neglected those which were sure to give him the first place in the body he was creating.

More than that: he did not confine himself to forming formidable leagues beyond his frontiers, to making alliances with his own neighbours and the neighbours of his enemy. While engaging all these nations in the abasement of the first power in Europe, he did not forget to put himself in the way of securing the coveted position for himself. He spent fifteen years of peace in preparations worthy of the enterprise he had in mind. He filled his coffers with money, his arsenals with artillery, arms and munitions. He amassed resources of all kinds against unforeseen demands. But he did more than all, we may be very sure, by governing his people wisely, by silently removing all seeds of division, by putting his finances in such order as to meet all possible needs without any vexation of his subjects. So it was that, at peace within and formidable abroad, he saw himself in a position to arm and maintain sixty thousand men and twenty vessels of war, to quit his kingdom without leaving behind him the smallest germ of disorder and to carry on war for six years without touching his ordinary revenue or laying on a penny of new taxes.

To all these preparations must be added the assurance that the enterprise would be carried out, both by his minister and himself, with the same energy and prudence that had conceived and framed it. And, finally, the knowledge that all the military operations would be directed by a captain of his skill, while the enemy had none left to put against him. From all this it may be judged if any element which could promise success was wanting to his prospects. Without having fathomed his designs, all Europe was watching his preparations with a kind of awe. The great revolution was about to be launched on a slight pretext. A war, destined to be the end of all wars, was about to usher in eternal peace, when a deed, the horror of which is only increased by its mystery, came to quench for ever the last hope of the world. The blow which cut short the days of this good king also plunged Europe back into ceaseless wars, of which she can now never hope to see the end.

Such were the means prepared by Henry IV for founding the Federation which the Abbé de Saint-Pierre proposed to set up by a book.

Let us not say, then, that, if his system has not been adopted, that is because it was not good. Let us rather say that it was too good to be adopted. Evils and abuses, by which so many men profit, come in of themselves. Things of public utility, on the other hand, are seldom brought in but by force, for the simple reason that private interests are almost always ranged against them. Beyond doubt, a lasting peace is, under present circumstances, a project ridiculous enough. But give us back Henry IV and Sully, and it will become once more a reasonable proposal. Or rather, while we admire so fair a project, let us console ourselves for its failure by the thought that it could only have been carried out by violent means from which humanity must needs shrink.

No federation could ever be established except by a revolution. That being so, which of us would dare to say whether the League of Europe is a thing more to be desired or feared? It would perhaps do more harm in a moment than it would guard against for ages.

Translated by C. E. Vaughan.

Immanuel Kant

1724–1804

Born in Königsberg in 1724, the son of a saddler of Scottish ancestry, Immanuel Kant remained in this bleak Baltic city throughout his long life. There he went to school, acquiring a fine command of classical languages, in an atmosphere of gentle but inflexible pietism, which may have added to the austerity of his attitude toward life. At the University of Königsberg, from the age of sixteen to twenty-two, he studied Newton's physics and Wolff's philosophy —an offshoot of Leibniz' system. To make ends meet, he tutored sons of the nobility.

In 1755 he became an unsalaried lecturer at the University and remained in this humble post for fifteen years. He was made Professor of Logic and Metaphysics in 1770. By this time he was already famed for his publications. In one of these he had propounded the nebular theory of the origin of the solar system, maintaining against Newton that the solar system could have arisen from a spiral nebula. He had also advanced original ideas on the proofs of the existence of God. Still more important were his meditations on the writings of David Hume, for these were destined to change the whole course of his thought and to direct the history of philosophy into a new channel.

Kant is best known for his three "Critiques." [1] In the first and greatest of these, *The Critique of Pure Reason* (1781), he undertook to vindicate the rigor and certainty of mathematics and mathematical physics, which had been upset by the skeptical arguments of Hume. In the second, *The Critique of Practical Reason* (1788), he attempted to vindicate religious beliefs and to demonstrate the ra-

---

[1] For these and other writings by Kant, see *Great Books of the Western World*, Vol. 42.

tional certainty and universality of the moral law. The latter theme had also been developed in *Fundamental Principles of the Metaphysic of Morals* (1785). In *The Critique of Judgement,* in turn, he showed how mechanics and purpose could be reconciled, and developed a very original and important theory of beauty.

Kant's life is summed up in his writings, and there is little else to tell. He remained a bachelor and lived mostly in seclusion. Although cold, formal, austere, and often pedantic, he nevertheless reached sublime heights in his respect for universal law and the worth of the individual. One of his lasting insights was that we must not permit ourselves any act which we would condemn in another.

When the Holy Roman Empire gradually fell apart, modern nations arose which recognized no higher authority. The need for some new community or covenant of nations, capable of settling disputes peacefully, was keenly felt. In the sixteenth century, Erasmus addressed himself to the subject and was followed by Hugo Grotius, William Penn, Abbé de Sainte-Pierre, Rousseau, and Bentham. Kant's *Perpetual Peace,* written in 1795, when he was seventy-one years old, shows the impact of his predecessors, especially Rousseau, but adds a great deal that is novel in shrewdness, logical acumen, and broad perspective.

Since the subject of international peace is now becoming more crucial every year, it behooves us to take a good look at some of the provisions which Kant thought necessary to this end. His first preliminary article for perpetual peace condemns all treaties which tacitly reserve, or gloss over, issues that may lead to future war. A sovereign who makes such a treaty intends to honor it only so long as it serves his purpose. Kant might not mind calling such an agreement a "truce," but to call it a "treaty of peace" is rank deception, destroying that mutual trust which is the only foundation of peace. "Honesty is the best policy" is the deepest strand in Kant's thought.

Notes from the artist: "In a sidewalk pattern from the game of 'sky blue,' or hopscotch, Kant leaps on one foot from square to square toward 'Perpetual Peace'—Zum ewigen Frieden. Each square is a stage in Kant's philosophical development."

Though the whole world should go up in smoke, honesty must be maintained. He lays down the following "transcendent formula of public right": ". . . all the actions relative to the right of another whose maxim is not susceptible to publicity are unjust." It follows at once, he says, that revolution is never justified, even if its object is to overthrow a usurping tyrant. Why? Because the insurgent people would not dare to publish their design of revolt in advance. We can better understand this extreme position if we remember that in 1793 Louis XVI was executed, and that by 1795, when Kant published *Perpetual Peace,* French revolutionary armies, successful everywhere, threatened to topple monarchs all over Europe.

Treaties of peace, to anticipate Woodrow Wilson's language, must be "open" and "openly arrived at." There must be no hidden clauses except one. Kant insists that philosophers must be consulted about the provisions of treaties yet concedes that it would be humiliating for the monarch to confess in public that he depends on the wisdom of mere subjects. But would Kant have also insisted on full publicity of the stages of protracted negotiations between nations? That delicate negotiations are crippled by day-to-day reporting has been argued, in our own time, by Walter Lippmann.

Another requirement for perpetual peace is that the participating governments be republican in form. This will provide that the assent of each citizen shall be required for a declaration of war. It is not likely that the people themselves, who suffer all the calamities of war, will give their assent. Here Kant's position seems very strong. It is not as strong as it looks, however, for "republicanism" is not democracy; it thrives best, in fact, under monarchy. It is the people's representatives who decide on war, not the people, nor yet the monarch. Kant distrusted the people. But would they be fooled about the necessity or advantages of war as often as their representatives are?

The quality of Kant's essay is keen and challenging, sometimes warning of dangers, remote then, but real today. If hostile nations are prepared to employ any means, however infernal, so long as the enemy is subdued, all hope of peace may be extinguished, Kant argues. A war might then "cause the destruction of both parties at once, together with the annihilation of every right, [and] would permit the conclusion of a perpetual peace only upon the vast burial ground of the human species."

Perpetual Peace

W̲hether this satirical inscription on a Dutch innkeeper's sign upon which a churchyard was painted has for its object mankind in general, or in particular the governors of states who are insatiable of war, or whether it points merely towards those philosophers who indulge the sweet dream of a perpetual peace, it is impossible to decide. Be this as it may, the author of this essay publishes it on the following conditions.

The practical politician is accustomed to testify as much disdain towards the theorist as he has complaisance for himself. In his eyes the latter appears a mere pedant whose chimerical ideas can never be prejudicial to a state, which requires principles deduced from experience; a trifler, whom he suffers to play his game without taking measures against him. The application is easy: let the statesman condescend to be rational, and if, perchance, he discovers in this essay ideas opposite to his own, let him not imagine dangers to the state from opinions hazarded without ambition and published with freedom; by this *clausula salvatoria* [closing remark] the author expects to have secured himself from every malignant interpretation.

SECTION I

Containing the Preliminary Articles
for a Perpetual Peace
among States

I. *No treaty of peace shall be esteemed valid on which is tacitly reserved matter for future war.*

A treaty of this sort would be only a truce, a suspension, not a complete cessation of hostilities. To call such a peace perpetual would be a suspicious pleonasm. By a treaty of peace, every subject (at the time perhaps unthought of by the contracting parties) for renewing war becomes

441

annihilated, even should it, by the most refined cunning, be dug out from the dusty documents of archives. The reservation (*reservatio mentalis*) of ancient pretensions to be declared hereafter, of which neither party makes mention at the time, both being too much exhausted to carry on the war, together with the bad design of carrying them into effect at the first favorable opportunity, belongs to the casuistry of a Jesuit; estimated in itself, it is beneath the dignity of a sovereign, as the readiness of making deductions of this kind is beneath the dignity of a minister.

But if in consequence of enlightened principles of politics, the glory of the state is placed in its continual aggrandizement, by whatever means, my reasoning will then appear mere scholastic pedantry.

II. *Any state, of whatever extent, shall never pass under the dominion of another state, whether by inheritance, exchange, purchase, or donation.*

A state is not, like the soil upon which it is situate, a patrimony. It consists of a society of men over whom the state alone has a right to command and dispose. It is a trunk which has its own roots. But, like a graft, to incorporate it with another state would be to reduce it from a moral person to the condition of a thing, which contradicts the idea of a social compact, without which one cannot conceive of a right over a people.[1]

Everyone knows to what dangers Europe, the only part of the world where this abuse has existed, has been exposed, even down to our time, by this mercantile precedent, that states may espouse one another, a new kind of contrivance, which obtains, by means of family alliances, and without any expense of forces, excess of power or an immoderate increase of domain.

By a consequence of the same principle, it is forbidden to every state to let troops to another state, against an enemy not common to both; for this is making use of the subjects as things to be disposed of at pleasure.

III. *Standing armies* (miles perpetuus) *shall in time be totally abolished.*

For being ever ready for action, they incessantly menace other states, and excite them to increase without end the number of armed men. This rivalship, a source of inexhaustible expense, renders peace even more

---

1. An hereditary kingdom is not a state which can be transferred to another state, but whose right of administration may be inherited by another physical person. The state then acquires a chief; but this chief, as chief or master of another kingdom, acquires not the state.

burdensome than a short war, and frequently causes hostilities to be commenced with the mere view of being delivered thereby from so oppressive a load. Add to this that to be paid for killing or to be killed is to serve as an instrument or machine in the hands of another (the state), which is incompatible with the right which nature has given to everyone over his own person.[2]

Very different from this are the military exercises voluntarily undertaken and at stated times by the citizens in order to secure themselves and their country against foreign aggressions.

Treasure, a means of military power more efficacious perhaps than that of armies or alliances, would produce the same effect as standing armies, and would excite other states to war by menacing them with it, were it less difficult to become acquainted with the extent of the treasure.

IV. *National debts shall not be contracted with a view of maintaining the interests of the state abroad.*

Money borrowed, either in the interior of a state or of a foreign nation, would be a resource by no means suspicious if the sums thus obtained were destined to the economy of the country, such as the repairing of highways, new colonies, the establishment of magazines against unfruitful years, etc. But what can we think of a system of credit, the ingenious invention of a commercial people of this century, by means of which debts are accumulated without end, and yet cause no embarrassment in their reimbursements, since the creditors never make their demands all at one time. Considered as a political engine, it is a dangerous means of monied power, a treasure for war, superior to that of all other states collectively, and which cannot be exhausted except by a default in the taxes (an exhaustion eventually certain, but long kept off by the favorable reaction credit has upon commerce and industry). This facility of carrying on war, united with the natural inclination men have for it as soon as they possess the power, is an invincible obstacle to a perpetual peace. The abolition of the funding system must therefore be a preliminary article; the more so as sooner or later a national bankruptcy will take place by which other states would innocently be involved and find themselves openly aggrieved. They are therefore justifiable in joining in a confederacy against a state which adopts such obnoxious measures.

---

2. This is the meaning of the answer which a prince of Bulgaria returned to an emperor of the East who, wishing to spare the blood of his subjects, proposed to terminate their difference by single combat: "Will a blacksmith," he replied, "who possesses a pair of pincers take the hot iron from the fire with his hands?"

V. *No state shall by force interfere with either the constitution or government of another state.*

What is there that can authorize such a step? Perhaps the offense given to the subjects of another state; but the example of anarchy may, on the contrary, warn them of the danger they run by exposing themselves to it. Moreover, the bad example one free being gives to another is an offense taken (*scandalum acceptum*) and not a lesion of their rights. Very different would it be if a revolution should divide a state into two parts, each of which should pretend to the whole. To lend assistance to one of the parties cannot then be esteemed an interference with the government, it being then in a state of anarchy; but so long as these internal dissentions are not come to that point, the interference of a foreign power would be a violation of the rights of an independent nation struggling with internal evils; it is then an offense given that would render the autonomy of all states uncertain.

VI. *A state shall not, during war, admit of hostilities of a nature that would render reciprocal confidence in a succeeding peace impossible: such as employing assassins* (percussores), *poisoners* (venefici), *violation of capitulations, secret instigation to rebellion* (perduellio), *etc.*

These are dishonorable stratagems. Confidence in the principles of an enemy must remain even during war, otherwise a peace could never be concluded; and hostilities would degenerate into a war of extermination (*bellum internecinum*), since war in fact is but the sad resource employed in a state of nature in defense of rights, force standing there in lieu of juridical tribunals. Neither of the two parties can be accused of injustice, since for that purpose a juridical decision would be necessary. But here the event of a battle (as formerly the judgments of God) determines the justice of either party, since between states there cannot be a war of punishment (*bellum punitivum*), no subordination existing between them. A war *ad internae-cionem,* therefore, which might cause the destruction of both parties at once, together with the annihilation of every right, would permit the conclusion of a perpetual peace only upon the vast burial ground of the human species. This kind of war must therefore be absolutely interdicted, as well as the means that lead thereto; but that the above mentioned means will unavoidably lead thereto may be deduced from the following: that those infernal arts, infamous in themselves when once in use, will not cease with the war, like the use of spies, where one profits by the infamy of another only (an indignity the human species will never be totally purged from), but will remain in use even after a peace, which thereby is rendered completely abortive.

Although the laws pointed out here objectively considered, and such as they ought to be in the intention of those in power, are all prohibitary laws (*leges prohibitivae*), there are some of them of that rigorous kind that demand a prompt and absolute execution; such are No. 1, 5, 6. Others again, like No. 2, 3, 4, without making exception to the rule of right, are less rigorous (*leges latae*) as to the subjective possibility of their observance. These include the permission of delaying their execution, without however losing the end in view. Delay ought not to defer, for instance, the re-establishment of liberty in such states as have been deprived of it, *ad calendas Graecas* [at the Greek calends; *i.e.*, never], to make use of an expression of Augustus; for this would be to annul the law which ordains it; but this delay itself is only permitted to prevent a precipitation which might injure the aim proposed. The prohibition contained in the article 2 has for its object solely the manner of future acquisition, and not the actual possession, which, without being stamped with the title of a right, has nevertheless been esteemed lawful by all other states, according to the opinion in fashion at the time of its putative acquisition.[3]

3. It is not without cause that it has hitherto been uncertain whether, besides the command (*leges praeceptivae*) and the prohibition (*leges prohibitivae*), there are also laws of permission. For laws, in general, include the principle of objective practical necessity; a permission, on the contrary, the principle of a practical casualty of certain actions; a law of permission would compel then to an action to which no one can be obliged; which would imply a contradiction if the object of the law were the same under one and the other relation. Now in the law of permission, which is the question here, the prohibition has relation only to the mode of future acquisition (*i.e.* by succession); but the permission, which annuls this prohibition, regards only the actual possession. In the passage from the state of nature to the civil state, this putative possession, though illegal, may nevertheless be maintained as just, in virtue of a permission of a natural right. But its illegality ought not to be recognized, for from the moment when in the state of nature, a putative possession, and in the civil state, a like acquisition, are acknowledged as unjust, they could no longer exist, because they would then become an infringement of rights.

I have only wished to fix, by the way, the attention of the teachers of natural right upon the idea of the laws of permission, which presents itself to every systematic mind; principally, because it is of such frequent use in the civil law, though with this difference: the prohibition is there express and absolute, and the permission is not inserted as a respective condition, which it ought to be, but is found among the exceptions. We forbid this or that, it is there said, excepting No. 1, 2, 3, and so forth, without end. The exceptions are not joined to the law from a fixed principle, but by chance, and blindly applied to the various cases that occur; for otherwise the restrictions would be always inserted in the formula of prohibition, which would thereby become permissive law. It is likewise very much to be regretted that the question proposed by Count de Windischgraetz has been so soon relinquished. This profound sage had precisely insisted upon the point now under discussion in his ingenious problem, which still remains to be solved. Indeed we shall have no reason to promise ourselves an immutable and permanent legislation till the possibility of a mathematical formula shall be demonstrated which may serve as a foundation to laws. Without this we shall have general laws, which may be applied to a great number of cases, but no universal laws, applicable to all cases, as the idea of a law seems to require.

SECTION II

Containing the Definitive Articles
for a Perpetual Peace
among States

With men the state of nature (*status naturalis*) is not a state of peace, but of war; though not of open war, at least, ever ready to break out. A state of peace must therefore be established; for, in order to be sheltered against every act of hostility, it is not sufficient that none is committed; one neighbor must guarantee to another his personal security, which cannot take place except in a state of legislation; without which one may treat another as an enemy, after having in vain demanded this protection.[4]

FIRST DEFINITIVE ARTICLE FOR

A PERPETUAL PEACE

The civil constitution of every state ought to be republican.

The only constitution resulting from the idea of the social compact, upon which every good legislation of a nation ought to be founded, is a

---

4. The common opinion is that one dares act hostilely only against an aggressor; and this is true when both live in a state of civil legislation. For, on entering into it, they reciprocally guarantee to themselves the requisite security by the common obedience which they pay to the sovereign. But the man, or the nation, that lives in a state of nature deprives me of that security and attacks me without being an aggressor by the mere circumstance of living contiguous to me in a state of anarchy and without laws; menaced perpetually by him with hostilities, against which I have no protection, I have a right to compel him either to associate with me under the dominion of common laws or to quit my neighborhood.

Here is a principle then upon which all the subsequent articles are established: All men who have a mutual influence over one another ought to have a civil constitution. Now every legitimate constitution considered in respect of the persons who are the object of it is

I. Either conformable to the *civil right*, and is limited to a people (*jus civitatis*).

II. Or to the *rights of nations*, and regulates the relations of nations among each other (*jus gentium*).

III. Or to the *cosmopolitical right*, as far as men or states are considered as influencing one another, in quality of constituent parts of the great state of the human race (*jus cosmopoliticum*).

This division is not arbitrary, but necessary in respect of the idea of a perpetual peace. For if two nations under one of these three relations were in a state of nature, and having reciprocal physical influence upon each other, the state of war would be immediately revived, to be freed from which is the present end in view.

republican constitution.[5] It is the only one established upon principles compatible with, first, the liberty of all the members of a society in the quality of men; second, with the submission of all to a common legislation, as subjects; and third, with the right of equality, which all share as members of a state. This then is the only constitution which in respect of right serves for a primitive basis to all civil constitutions; it remains now to be shown whether it also is the only one that can lead to a perpetual peace. By examining the nature of this constitution, it will be found that besides the purity of its origin, which derives from the idea itself of right, it also promises the most happy effect, namely, a perpetual peace, in the following manner.

According to the form of this constitution, the assent of every citizen is necessary to decide the question, Whether war shall be declared or not. But to decree war would be to the citizens to decree against themselves all the calamities of war, such as fighting in person, furnishing from their

---

5. Legal (and together with it) exterior liberty is not, as it is ordinarily defined, the faculty of doing whatever one wishes to do provided he injures not another. It consists in rendering obedience to those laws alone to which I have been able to give my assent. In the same manner, legal equality in a state is the relation of the citizens to one another according to which one cannot compel another juridically without subjecting himself also to the law by which in his turn he may also be compelled in the same manner. The principle of submission to laws, being already comprised in the idea of a constitution in general, needs not a particular explanation. The inviolability of these innate and imprescriptible rights of man manifests itself still more gloriously when we represent to ourselves man in relation with beings of a superior nature, as citizen of a world of intelligences. For, to begin with my liberty, even the laws of God can be binding upon me only so far as I have been able to concur in their formation, since I attain to the knowledge of the will of God only by the law which my own reason imposes on my liberty in elevating me above the necessity of the laws of nature. As to the principle of equality, however exalted the nature of a being may be, were he even the next in rank after God (as the Great Aeon of the Gnostics), if I do my duty in the post assigned me, as he in his, there is no reason why the duty of obeying should rest on me alone, and in him the right of commanding. What renders the principle of equality inapplicable to our relations with God is that, of all beings, it is He alone who cannot be represented as subject to duty. But as to the right of equality common to all citizens in quality of subjects, in order to decide if a hereditary nobility can be tolerated it will be sufficient to ask whether the pre-eminence of rank granted by the state ought to be anterior to merit or whether merit ought to precede rank. Now it is evident if dignity is attached to birth, merit will be uncertain, and, consequently, it would be the same thing to give command to a favorite without any merit; which would never be decreed by the general will of a people in the social pact, the only foundation of all rights. For if birth gives nobility, it does not at the same time bestow nobleness of the mind and heart. It is quite otherwise with the nobility or dignity attached to magistracies, which merit alone can obtain. In this case rank depends not on the person, but on the post; and this kind of nobility alters not the equality, because on quitting the office one renounces the rank it confers, in order to re-enter into the class of the people.

own means towards the expense of the war; painfully to repair the devastations it occasions; and, to fill up the measure of evils, load upon themselves the weight of a national debt that would embitter even peace itself and which, on account of constant new wars, can never be liquidated. They will certainly beware of plunging into an enterprise so hazardous. Whereas, in a constitution wherein the subjects are not citizens of the state, that is to say, a constitution not republican, a declaration of war is a most easy matter to resolve upon, as it does not require of the chief, proprietor and not member of the state, the least sacrifice of his pleasures, either of the table, the chase, the country, or the court, etc. He may therefore resolve on war as on a party of pleasure, for reasons the most frivolous, and with perfect indifference leave the justification of the same, which decency requires, to the diplomatic corps, who are ever ready to undertake it.

In order not to confound (as is frequently done) a republican constitution with a democracy, the following observations should be made.

The forms of a state may be divided either according to the persons who enjoy the sovereign power or according to the mode of administration exercised by the chief, under whatever title, over a people. The first is called form of sovereignty (*forma imperii*), of which there can be but three: autocracy, where one alone possesses supreme power; aristocracy, when divided between a few; democracy, when exercised by all the members of society.

The second is the form of government (*forma regiminis*); this is the constitutional mode according to which the general will of the people has decided that its power shall be exercised; and in this relation it is either republican or despotic. Republicanism is the political principle according to which the executive power (the government) is separated from the legislative. Despotism is where the legislator executes his own laws; consequently, where the private will of the chief is substituted to the will of the public. Democracy is necessarily despotism, as it establishes an executive power contrary to the general will; all being able to decide against one whose opinion may differ; the will of all is therefore not that of all: which is contradictory and opposite to liberty.

Every form of government that is not representative is, properly, formless; the legislator being as little capable of being united in the same person with the executor of his will as in a syllogism the universal of the major is capable of serving as the particular of the minor. Although an aristocracy and autocracy are defective, inasmuch as they are susceptible of the vice here mentioned, they nevertheless contain the possibility of representative administration, so far at least as Frederic II insinuated when he declared himself the first servant of the state; [6] whereas a democracy renders the representative system impossible, every one striving to be master. It may therefore be affirmed that the smaller the number of governors, and the more extensive the representation, the nearer the constitution approaches to republicanism, and may even arrive at it by successive reforms.

This then shows why it is more difficult to arrive at this form of government, the only one that perfectly corresponds with the rights of man, in an aristocracy than in a monarchy; and in a democratic state it is even impossible to arrive at it, except by violent revolutions.

The form of government is, however, of far greater importance to a people than the form of sovereignty; [7] though the greater or lesser relation of this latter with the aim proposed is nothing less than trivial. However, to be fully conformable to the principle of right, the form of government must be representative. This is the only one that permits republicanism, without which the government is arbitrary and despotic, whatever the constitution may be. Of all the ancient pretended republics, not one of them knew this system; they consequently all terminated in despotism, though the least insupportable of all, that of one alone.

---

6. The lofty epithets of "the Lord's anointed," "the executor of 'the divine will,'" "the representative of God," which have been lavished on sovereigns, have been frequently censured as gross and intoxicating flatteries; but I think without reason. So far from inspiring a monarch with pride, these surnames ought to render him humble if he possesses understanding (which ought to be supposed) and if he reflects that he is charged with an employment superior to the powers of a man, namely, to protect what is the most sacred to God upon earth, the *rights of man*, and that he ought to be in perpetual fear of having injured this beloved pledge of the divinity.

7. Mallet du Pan, in his pompous but senseless language, pretends to have at length attained to a conviction, after long experience, of the truth of this well-known saying of Pope's:

> For forms of government let fools contest:
> The state that's best administer'd is best.

If this means that the state the best administered is the best administered, he has, to make use of an expression of Swift's, "cracked a nut to come at a maggot." But if this saying is to signify that in the state the best administered, the government is the best, as to its constitution, then nothing is more false, for a good administration proves nothing in favor of the government. Who has reigned better than Titus and Marcus Aurelius? And yet one had for his successor a Domitian, and the other a Commodus; which could never have happened in a good constitution, their inaptitude to this post having been soon enough known, and the power of the sovereign being sufficient to exclude them.

SECOND DEFINITIVE ARTICLE FOR

A PERPETUAL PEACE

The public right ought to be founded upon a federation of free states.
Nations, as states, like individuals, if they live in a state of nature and without laws, by their vicinity alone commit an act of lesion. One may, in order to secure its own safety, require of another to establish within it a constitution which should guarantee to all their rights. This would be a federation of nations, without the people however forming one and the same state, the idea of a state supposing the relation of a sovereign to the people, of a superior to his inferior. Now several nations united into one state would no longer form but one; which contradicts the supposition, the question here being of the reciprocal rights of nations, inasmuch as they compose a multitude of different states which ought not to be incorporated into one and the same state.

But when we see savages in their anarchy prefer the perpetual combats of licentious liberty to a reasonable liberty, founded upon constitutional order, can we refrain to look down with the most profound contempt on this animal degradation of humanity? Must we not blush at the contempt to which the want of civilization reduces men? And would one not rather be led to think that civilized nations, each of which form a constituted state, would hasten to extricate themselves from an order of things so ignominious? But what, on the contrary, do we behold? Every state placing its majesty (for it is absurd to talk of the majesty of the people) precisely in this independence of every constraint of any external legislation whatever.

The sovereign places his glory in the power of disposing at his pleasure (without much exposing himself) of many millions of men ever ready to sacrifice themselves for an object that does not concern them. The only difference between the savages of America and those of Europe is that the former have eaten up many a hostile tribe, whereas the latter have known how to make a better use of their enemies; they preserve them to augment the number of their subjects, that is to say, of instruments destined to more extensive conquests. When we consider the perverseness of human nature, which shows itself unveiled and unrestrained in the relations of nations with each other, where it is not checked, as in a state of civilization, by the coercive power of the law, one may well be astonished that the word right has not yet been totally abolished from war politics as a pedantic word, and that a state has not yet been found bold enough openly to profess this doctrine. For hitherto Grotius, Pufendorf,

Vattel, and other useless and impotent defenders of the rights of nations have been constantly cited in justification of war; though their code, purely philosophic or diplomatic, has never had the force of law, and cannot obtain it, states not being as yet subjected to any coercive power. There is no instance where their reasonings, supported by such respectable authorities, have induced a state to desist from its pretensions. However this homage which all states render to the principle of right, if even consisting only in words, is a proof of a moral disposition which, though still slumbering, tends nevertheless vigorously to subdue in man that evil principle of which he cannot entirely divest himself. For otherwise states would never pronounce the word right when going to war with each other; it were then ironically, as a Gallic prince interpreted it. "It is," said he, "the prerogative nature has given to the stronger to make himself obeyed by the weaker."

However, the field of battle is the only tribunal before which states plead their cause; but victory, by gaining the suit, does not decide in favor of their cause. Though the treaty of peace puts an end to the present war, it does not abolish a state of war (a state where continually new pretenses for war are found); which one cannot affirm to be unjust, since being their own judges, they have no other means of terminating their differences. The law of nations cannot even force them, as the law of nature obliges individuals to get free from this state of war, since having already a legal constitution, as states, they are secure against every foreign compulsion which might tend to establish among them a more extended constitutional order.

Since, however, from her highest tribunal of moral legislation, reason without exception condemns war as a mean of right, and makes a state of peace an absolute duty; and since this peace cannot be effected or be guaranteed without a compact among nations, they must form an alliance of a peculiar kind, which might be called a pacific alliance (*foedus pacificum*), different from a treaty of peace (*pactum pacis*) inasmuch as it would forever terminate all wars, whereas the latter only finishes one. This alliance does not tend to any dominion over a state, but solely to the certain maintenance of the liberty of each particular state partaking of this association, without being therefore obliged to submit, like men in a state of nature, to the legal constraint of public force. It can be proved that the idea of a federation, which should insensibly extend to all states and thus lead them to a perpetual peace, may be realized. For if fortune should so direct that a people as powerful as enlightened should constitute itself into a republic (a government which in its nature inclines to a perpetual peace), from that time there would be a center for this federative association; other states might adhere thereto in order to guarantee their liberty according to the principles of public right; and this alliance might insensibly be extended.

That a people should say, "There shall not be war among us: we will form ourselves into a state; that is to say, we will ourselves establish a legislative, executive, and judiciary power to decide our differences" can be conceived.

But if this state should say, "There shall not be war between us and other states, although we do not acknowledge a supreme power that guarantees our reciprocal rights," upon what then can this confidence in one's rights be founded, except it is upon this free federation, this supplement of the social compact, which reason necessarily associates with the idea of public right.

The expression of public right, taken in a sense of right of war, presents properly no idea to the mind; since thereby is understood a power of deciding right, not according to universal laws, which restrain within the same limits all individuals, but according to partial maxims, namely, by force. Except one would wish to insinuate by this expression that it is right that men who admit such principles should destroy each other, and thus find perpetual peace only in the vast grave that swallows them and their iniquities.

At the tribunal of reason there is but one mean of extricating states from this turbulent situation, in which they are constantly menaced with war; namely, to renounce, like individuals, the anarchic liberty of savages, in order to submit themselves to coercive laws, and thus form a society of nations (*civitas gentium*) which would insensibly embrace all the nations of the earth. But as the ideas which they have of public right absolutely prevent the realization of this plan, and make them reject in practice what is true in theory, there can only be substituted, to the positive idea of a universal republic (if all is not to be lost), the negative supplement of a permanent alliance which prevents war, insensibly spreads, and stops the torrent of those unjust and inhuman passions which always threaten to break down this fence.[8]

Furor impius intus fremit horridus ore cruento.
[Bristling with gore, unholy madness roars within.]

VIRGIL.

---

8. It would not ill become a people that has just terminated a war to order, besides their thanksgiving day, a solemn fast in order to ask forgiveness of God for the crime the nation has just committed, and which the human race still goes on to perpetrate, for refusing to live with other nations in legal order; to which, jealous of a proud independence, it prefers the barbarous means of war, without being

THIRD DEFINITIVE ARTICLE FOR

A PERPETUAL PEACE

The cosmopolitical right shall be limited to conditions of universal hospitality.

In this article, as well as in the preceding ones, it is a question of right, not of philanthropy. Hospitality there signifies solely the right every stranger has of not being treated as an enemy in the country in which he arrives. One may refuse to receive him if it can be done without endangering his existence; but dares not act hostilely towards him so long as he does not offend anyone. The question is not about the right of being received and admitted into the house of an individual: this benevolent custom demanding particular conventions. One speaks here only of the right all men have of demanding of others to be admitted into their society; a right founded upon that of the common possession of the surface of the earth, whose spherical form obliges them to suffer others to subsist contiguous to them, because they cannot disperse themselves to an indefinite distance, and because originally one has not a greater right to a country than another. The sea and uninhabitable deserts divide the surface of the globe; but the ship and the camel, that vessel of the desert, reestablish the communication and facilitate the right which the human species all possess of profiting in common by its surface. The inhospitality of the inhabitants of the coasts (for instance of the coast of Barbary), their custom of taking the vessels in the neighboring seas, or that of reducing to slavery the unhappy wretches shipwrecked on their shores; the barbarous practice which in their sandy deserts the Bedouin Arabs exercise of pillaging all those who approach their wandering tribes; all these customs then are contrary to the right of nature, which, nevertheless, in ordaining hospitality, was contented with fixing the conditions on which one may endeavor to form connections with the inhabitants of a country. In this manner distant regions may contract amicable relations with each other, sanctioned in the end by public laws, and thus insensibly mankind may approach towards a cosmopolitical constitution.

At how great a distance from this perfection are the civilized nations, and especially the commercial nations of Europe? At what an excess of

---

able to obtain thereby what it desires, the secure enjoyment of its rights. The thanksgivings which are rendered during the war, the hymns that are chanted by us, like true Israelites, to the God of hosts, are glaringly inconsistent with the moral idea of the Father of men; they announce a culpable indifference for the principles which nations ought to observe in the defense of their rights, and express an infernal joy at having slain a multitude of men or annihilated their happiness.

injustice do we not behold them arrive when they discover strange countries and nations? (Which with them is the same thing as to conquer.) America, the countries inhabited by the Negroes, the Spice Islands, the Cape, etc., were to them countries without proprietors, for the inhabitants they counted as nothing. Under pretext of establishing factories in Hindostan, they carried thither foreign troops and by their means oppressed the natives, excited wars among the different states of that vast country, spread famine, rebellion, perfidy, and the whole deluge of evils that afflict mankind, among them.

The Chinese and Japanese, whom experience has taught to know the Europeans, wisely refuse their entry into the country, though the former permit their approach, which the latter grant to one European nation only, the Dutch; still, however, excluding them like captives from every communication with the inhabitants. The worst, or, to speak with the moralist, the best, of the matter is that all these outrages are to no purpose; that all the commercial companies guilty of them touch upon the instant of their ruin; that the sugar islands, that den of slavery the most refined and cruel, produce no real revenue, and are profitable only indirectly, serving views not very laudable, namely, to form sailors for the navies, consequently to carry on war in Europe; which service they render to powers who boast the most of piety, and who, while they drink iniquity like water, pretend to equal the elect in point of orthodoxy.

The connections, more or less near, which have taken place among the nations of the earth having been carried to that point that a violation of rights committed in one place is felt throughout the whole, the idea of a cosmopolitical right can no longer pass for a fantastic exaggeration of right; but is the last step of perfection necessary to the tacit code of civil and public right, these systems at length conducting towards a public right of men in general, and towards a perpetual peace, but to which one cannot hope continually to advance except by means of the conditions here indicated.

SUPPLEMENT

SUPPLEMENT THE FIRST

Of the Guarantee
for a Perpetual Peace

The guarantee of this treaty is nothing less than the great and ingenious artist, nature (*natura daedala rerum*). Her mechanical march evidently announces the grand aim of producing among men, against their intention, harmony from the very bosom of their discords. Hence it is that we call it destiny, viewing it as a cause absolute in its effects but unknown as to the laws of its operations. But the regular order which we observe in the course of the events of this world makes us call it Providence, inasmuch as we discern in her the profound wisdom of a superior cause which predetermines the course of fate and makes it tend to the final purpose of human existence. It is true, we do not discover this providence in the methodical arrangements of nature, nor can we by reasonings deduce it therefrom; we can only suppose it, which we do, as often as we refer the modes of things to some end. We stand even in need of this supposition to form to ourselves an idea of the possibility of an order of nature analogous to the operations of human art. The idea of a relation of this mechanism to the moral end which reason immediately prescribes, though rash in theory, is a well-founded truth in practice; for instance, by making this physical order of nature serve towards the realization of the duty of a perpetual peace. Since reason cannot apply the relations of causes and effects to any other objects than such as experience has made known to us, it is more modest and conformable to the limits of the human understanding to employ the word *nature*, when theory and not religion is the question, preferably to that of *Providence*, which intimates a pretended knowledge of its mysteries, and a flight as temerarious as that of Icarus towards the sanctuary of its impenetrable designs.

Before we determine the manner in which nature guarantees a perpetual peace, it will be necessary to examine the situation in which she places the beings that figure upon this vast stage, and the measures she has taken to render this peace necessary to them.

These are her preparatory arrangements:

I. She has in every climate provided for the existence of man.

II. She has by means of war dispersed them in order to populate the most inhospitable regions.

III. She has, by the same means, compelled them to contract relations more or less legal.

That in the vast plains which border the icy sea, the moss however grows, which the reindeer digs from beneath the snow in order to make itself subservient to the nourishment or to the conveyance of the Ostyak or the Samoyed; that the saline sandy deserts should contain the camel, which appears created for the very purpose of traversing them, is already wonderful. Still more clearly marked does this end appear in the care nature has taken to place on the shores of the icy sea, besides the animals covered with furs, seals and whales, whose flesh serves as food and whose fat as firing to the inhabitants. But the maternal providence of nature is most wonderfully manifested by the singular manner in which she furnishes (in a manner not well known) those countries destitute of vegetation with wood, without which the inhabitants could have neither canoes, weapons, or huts, being, besides, so occupied with defending themselves against the wild beasts that they live in peace with each other. But probably it was war alone which carried them into these climates. The first instrument of war was without doubt the horse, being tamed and trained up for combat when the earth began to be peopled with inhabitants. The elephant served in later times to the luxury of states already formed. As also the culture of diverse sorts of corn, originally herbs now unknown; and the increase and improvement of fruit trees, by transplanting and ingrafting them, since primeval Europe produced only wild apple and pear trees; these operations then could only take place after an established constitution secured to every proprietor the enjoyment of his possessions. But before this could take place, it was necessary that men who at first subsisted in a state of anarchic liberty, either by the chase or the fishery, should have passed from the pastoral life to a life of agriculture; that salt and iron should be discovered (probably the two first objects of commerce between different nations) to produce among them pacific relations, and to contract, even with the most distant, some relations of convention and society.

Now as nature has provided an existence for men in every part of the earth, she insists upon their living in every part; and so despotic is this her will that they obey it even against their inclination, and without being forced to it by any moral law. War is the only means she employs to obtain this end. By this means she has separated people whose identity of language proclaims that of their origin. We find the Samoyeds on the coasts of the icy sea speak the Mongol language of the inhabitants of the Altai Mountains, situated two hundred miles from them; between these two we find a Mongol nation of horsemen, and of course warlike; is it not probable that the latter should have driven the former into these inhospitable icy lands, into which they would certainly not have penetrated from inclination? It is the same with the Finlanders, who, in the northern extremity of Europe, are called Laplanders. They have been separated by the Goths and Sarmatians from the Hungarians, whose language is the same with theirs. What can have carried into the north of America the Eskimos, that race of men so entirely different from all other nations of the New World, descended perhaps from some European adventurers; and into the south the Pescherais as far as Tierra del Fuego, if it was not war, which nature uses to people all the earth?

As to war itself, it requires no particular motive; it appears ingrafted on human nature; it passes even for an act of greatness, to which the love of glory alone, without any other motive, impels. Thus, among the savages of America, as among the Europeans in the times of chivalry, military valor obtained great honors, not only during war, which would be just, but also when in order to signalize itself it undertakes war; so that a kind of dignity is attached to war itself, and that philosophers are found who commend it as a noble prerogative of humanity, forgetting this sentence of a Greek: "War is an evil inasmuch as it produces more wicked men than it takes off."

Enough has been said of the measures nature takes to lead mankind, considering them as they compose a class of animals, to the end she has proposed to herself.

We have now to examine what is most essential relatively to a perpetual peace, that is to say, what nature has done with regard to it; how she favors the moral views of man, and guarantees the execution of the laws reason prescribes to him; so that whatever man should do freely, according to the civil, public, and cosmopolitical right, if he neglects it, he shall be forced to do it, by a constraint of nature, without prejudice to his liberty.

When I say nature wills that this or that arrive, this does not mean that she makes it a duty to us; it is practical reason alone that can prescribe laws to free beings without constraining them; but it means that nature does it herself, whether we will or no.

Fata volentem ducunt, nolentem trahunt.
[Fate leads us when we are willing, drags us when we are not.]

I. If even intestine discords were not to force a people to submit to the constraint of laws, they would be compelled thereto by the external means of war, nature having placed, as has already been seen, by the side of each people another neighboring people which presses upon it, and obliges it to form itself into a state in order to form a power capable of opposing the enterprises of the other. Now as a republican constitution is the only one that is entirely conformable to the rights of man, it is also the most difficult to establish and to maintain; so much so that it has been said it required angels, and not men under the dominion of interested inclinations, to realize a form of government so sublime. But nature employs these interested inclinations themselves to give to the general will, with the respect due to reason, upon which it is founded, the efficacious practice it stands in need of. The question is only so to organize a state (and this is certainly not beyond the power of mortals) that the action and reaction of these various inclinations either annihilate or moderate their injurious effect, and by rendering it null to reason, force man to be, if not a good moral being, at least a good citizen.

The problem of a constitution is solvable even to a nation of devils (I shall be forgiven what is offensive in the expression) if this people is but endowed with understanding. "A multitude of reasonable beings desire for their preservation universal laws, though every one among them has a secret inclination to exempt himself from the observance of them. A constitution must therefore be given them that so confines their individual passions, one by means of the other, that in their public conduct their effect becomes as inconsiderable as if they had not these hostile dispositions." A problem like this must be solvable. It does not require that one should obtain the desired effect of a moral reform in man. It only demands that one should derive advantage from the mechanism of nature in order so to direct the opposition of personal interests that all the individuals who compose a nation should constrain one another to range themselves beneath the coercive power of a legislation, and thus introduce a pacific state of legislation.

However imperfect the organization of the existing states may be, they nevertheless give us a proof of what has been advanced. They approach in some degree to what the idea of right exacts in their external conduct, though the intrinsic principles of morality do certainly not contribute towards it, nor can they contribute towards it, as it is not for morality to lead to a good constitution, but for this latter to produce the moral reform in man. The example here cited sufficiently shows that the mechanism of nature, according to which the interested propensities ought to defeat each other even in their effects, may serve reason as the means of procuring to the principle of right the sovereignty to which it tends, and to the state the establishment and sure maintenance of an external and even internal peace.

Here nature in an absolute manner wills that right should at length obtain the victory. What one neglects to do she does herself, though by very unpleasant means.

> *Vous pliez d'un roseau le fragile soutien;*
> *Courbez trop, il rompra. Qui veut trop, ne veut rien,*

[Bend the tender stem of a reed;
Bend it too much and it breaks.
He who attempts too much attempts nothing.]
                                        Bouterweck.

II. The idea of the law of nations supposes the reciprocal independence of several neighboring and separate states; and although this situation is in itself a state of war, if a federative union prevents not hostilities, reason yet prefers this coexistence of states to their union under one superior power to the rest, which would at length end in a universal monarchy. For the laws always lose in energy what the government gains in extent; and a despotism, which, destroying the minds, stifles the germs of every good, and sooner or later degenerates into anarchy.

However, there is no state the chief of which does not desire to secure to himself a constant state of peace by the conquest of the whole universe if it were possible. But nature opposes this; she employs two means in order to prevent nations from mixing one with another: a diversity of language and religion.[9]

It is true this variety contains the germ of reciprocal hatred, and furnishes even frequently a pretext for war: but in proportion as men come nearer in their principles, in consequence of progress in their civilization, the difference of language and of religions leads to and secures a well-founded peace, not, like that of despotism, upon the grave of liberty and by means of the extinction of all power, but by the equilibrium they maintain with each other in spite of the contest resulting from their diversity.

If nature wisely separates nations, which every state would seek to combine by artifice or force, and even according to the principles of the law of nations, who, on the other hand, through the interested spirit of all nations, produces a union between them, which the idea of the cosmopolitical right alone would not have sufficiently secured from war and violence? It is the spirit of commerce that sooner or later takes hold of every nation, and is incompatible with war: the power of money being that which of all others gives the greatest spring to states, they find themselves obliged to labor at the noble work of peace, though without any

---

9. Diversity of religion: a very singular expression! It is precisely as if one spoke of a diversity of morals. There may be different kinds of historical faith attached to relative events, not to religion, but to its establishment, and which appertain to the jurisdiction of the learned; there may likewise be different books of religion (the Zendavesta, the Veda, the Koran, etc.), but there is only one religion true for all men and all times. These can therefore be only accidental means, which serve as a vehicle to religion, and change according to times and places.

moral view; and instantly seek to stifle, by mediations, war, in whatever part it may break out, as if for this purpose they had contracted a perpetual alliance; great associations in a war are naturally rare, and less frequently still successful. It is in this manner that nature, by means of the human propensities, guarantees a perpetual peace; and though the assurance which she gives us thereof is not sufficient to predict theoretically, yet it prevents us from regarding it as a chimerical aim, and makes it thereby a duty in us to contribute towards it.

SUPPLEMENT THE SECOND

Secret Article

for a Perpetual Peace

It would be contradictory to enter into the procedures of public right, a secret article as to its object; though it may well contain secrets subjectively as to the quality of the persons who dictate them, these perhaps fearing to expose their dignity if openly they should declare themselves the authors. The only article of that kind is the following: *The maxims of philosophers on the conditions which render a perpetual peace possible shall be consulted by those states armed for war.*

But it appears humiliating for the legislative authority of a state, to whom naturally the greatest wisdom is attributed, to be informed of the rules to be observed in the relations with other states, by the philosophers, its subjects. Nevertheless, it is necessary to consult them. The state, therefore, tacitly invites them to give their opinion; namely, by keeping secret the intention of following them, it permits their freely publishing the general maxims respecting peace and war, for they will not fail to speak if silence is not imposed upon them. Nor does it require to agree on this point a particular convention of states, since the obligation which thereby is imposed is derived from the universal principles of legislative reason.

However, it is not claimed that the state should give the preference to the principles of the philosopher over the decisions of the lawyer, the representative of the sovereign; it is only asked that he may be heard. The lawyer, who for his symbol has chosen, besides the balance of right, the sword of justice, does not always employ this latter solely for the purpose of removing from the former all foreign influence; but if one of the scales leans not to his mind, he adds the sword (*vae victis!*), a temptation to which the lawyer often finds himself exposed because he is not always philosopher enough, even morally so. His vocation leads him to apply positive laws, and not to examine whether they stand in need of reform. And though his functions are by this very circumstance evidently inferior, nevertheless, as the faculty of right is invested with power, like that of theology and medicine, the lawyer assigns one of the first ranks to his. The faculty of philosophers is by these coalesced powers forced to be content with a much inferior place. Philosophy, they say, is but the servant of theology, and the other faculties say as much. But one takes great care not to examine whether she precedes her mistress, with the flambeau in her hand, or whether she bears her train.

That kings should become philosophers, or philosophers kings, can scarce be expected; nor is it to be wished, since the enjoyment of power inevitably corrupts the judgment of reason, and perverts its liberty. But kings or people-kings, that is to say, the people who govern themselves by laws of equality, should not suffer that the class of philosophers be reduced to disappear, or to maintain silence, but, on the contrary, should permit them to be freely heard. This is what the well administration of a government exacts; which can never be sufficiently enlightened. Besides, the class of philosophers, incapable by its nature to betray truth, or to be instrumental to the interested views of leaders and clubbists, runs not the risk of being suspected of propagandism.

APPENDIX

PART I

On the Opposition Which Exists
Between Morality and Politics
with Respect to the Subject
of a Perpetual Peace

Morality has already in itself a practical object, it being the sum of the absolute laws according to which we ought to act. It is absurd to grant to the idea of duty all its authority, and yet pretend that it cannot be fulfilled, which would annihilate the very idea of duty (*ultra posse, nemo obligatur* [no one is obligated beyond the possible]). Politics, inasmuch as it is a practical jurisprudence, cannot therefore be in contradiction to morality, considered as the theory of right (that is to say, there is no opposition between the theory and the practice); unless by morality were meant the sum of the rules of prudence, or the theory of the most proper means to accomplish the views of self-interest; *i.e.*, except every idea of morality were entirely rejected.

Policy says, "Be wise as serpents"; morality adds thereto the restriction: "and harmless (without falsehood) as doves." If the one is incompatible with the other in the same precept, policy is really in opposition to morality; but if these two qualities ought absolutely to be united, the idea of contrariety is absurd, and the question of how politics are to be reconciled with morality can no longer be proposed as problematical. Though this proposition, *honesty is the best policy*, announces a theory too frequently, alas! contradicted by experience; yet no objection will ever overthrow this: *honesty is better than all policy*, and is even an essential condition of it. The tutelary divinity of morality yields not to Jupiter; this god of power is also subject to destiny: *i.e.*, reason is not sufficiently enlightened to embrace the entire series of predetermining causes; the knowledge of which would alone enable it to foresee with certainty the happy or unhappy effects which, according to the mechanism of nature, must result from human actions (though we know enough to hope that they will be conformable to our wishes). But what we have to do in order to remain faithful to duty, and to observe the rules of wisdom, which is the end of reason, she furnishes us all with sufficient instruction to discern.

Now the statesman, to whom morality is mere theory, although he acknowledges the duty and the possibility of its execution, nevertheless cruelly aims to ravish from us the consoling hope of its realization; such is the nature of man, he says, that he will never desire what would be necessary to effect a perpetual peace.

It is doubtless not enough in order to accomplish it that each individual should desire to live according to the principles of liberty in a legal constitution, or to make use of scholastic terms; that there be distributive unity of the will of all, it is likewise necessary that there be collective unity of the will of all in behalf of this condition. Not the dispersed individual but the organs by which they co-operate as a body form the civil society into a whole. Not the sum or balance of the volitions of the several monads constitute the general will, but those volitions alone taken by the concert of all. It is necessary then that a cause of union assemble the individual wills of all for there to be a general will. Now, no individual being able to effect this union, since he possesses only one particular will, there will remain no other mean of realizing in practice the idea of a constitutional state than force, upon which the public right is afterwards founded. Though one cannot but expect very striking contrasts between the execution of this idea and the theory, since one can scarcely hope to find in the legislator morality enough to induce him to commit to the general will the establishment of a constitution after having formed a nation of a horde of savages. It will then be said he who has the power in his own hands will not suffer the people to prescribe laws for him. A state once arrived at independence will not submit to the decision of other states the manner in which it ought to maintain its rights against them. One part of the world that feels itself superior to another will not neglect to increase its power by subduing its inferior in strength; and thus vanish all the delightful plans of civil, public, and cosmopolitical right in chimerical theories: whereas a practice founded upon principles deduced from a knowledge of human nature, and which blushes not to borrow its maxims from the usages of the world, can alone hope to place the structure of its politics upon a firm basis.

It must be confessed that if there is neither liberty nor moral law deriving from it, if all that happens and may happen is but a simple mechanism of nature, all practical science may be reduced to politics, i.e., to the art of employing this mechanism for the governing of men: the idea of duty will then be only a chimera. But if, on the contrary, to combine this idea with politics appears indispensable, even as a necessary condition of it, the possibility of their combination must be confessed. Now I can very easily represent to myself a moral politician, i.e., a statesman, who might only act according to the principles avowed by morality; whereas I cannot conceive the idea of a political moralist, who adapts morality to the interests of the statesman.

The principle of the moral politician will be that if defects have slipped either into the constitution of a state, or into the relations of states with one another, it is principally the duty of chiefs to make instantly such amendments as are conformable to the natural right founded on reason; were they even to sacrifice their own interests to these changes. This does not imply that they should violently tear the bonds of society, civil and cosmopolitical, even before they have a better form to substitute to the old one; an operation no less rude than disapproved of by morality as well as politics: but we may demand of governors to have constantly in view the duty of bringing about these reforms, and by continual advancements to lead towards the best possible constitution. A state may have a republican government even then, when a despotic power is still suffered to exist, till the nation at length yields to the influence of the authority of law alone, as to any physical power, and becomes capable of being its own lawgiver, as its primitive rights demand. Even when a violent revolution, necessitated by a defective government, has introduced, by unjust means, a better order of things, it would no longer be permitted to lead the people back towards their ancient constitution, though every one of those who, during the revolution, openly or secretly have shared in it have justly incurred the chastisement due to rebellion. As to the external relations of states, it cannot be pretended that a nation should renounce its constitution (were it even despotic, and consequently most formidable to foreign enemies) so long as it is exposed to the danger of being swallowed up by other states. This reform must then be deferred till a more favorable epoch.[10]

It may be that the despotic moralists violate more than once the political rules in the measures they adopt or propose with too great precipitation; however, experience will soon lead them back to nature. Whereas, political moralists, by questioning the faculty of human nature to obey moral reason, favor state maxims contrary to right, and in reality strive to render all reform impossible, and to perpetuate the violation of right.

So far from possessing this practical science which they boast of, these expert politicians have only the cunning of business; solely occupied in flattering the ruling power, because their personal interest is benefited by it; they sacrifice the nation, and would (if they were able) subvert the whole world. This is what happens to all lawyers by profession who are not occupied in legislation. Without reasoning upon the laws, they are obliged to execute them; the last which appear then are always the best to them, and nothing can induce them to deviate from the mechanical order to which they are accustomed. Nevertheless, the facility which they have acquired of adapting themselves to all circumstances inspires them with the vanity of believing that they can likewise judge of the universal principles of right and of government.

The multiplicity of their connections causes them to acquire the knowledge of a great number of men, and they take this knowledge for that of man, though it is very different, and though, to obtain the latter, it is necessary to contemplate man and his faculties in a more elevated point of view. Proud of their spirit of observation, do they aspire to civil and pub-

---

10. These are the permissive laws given by reason. The abolition of an unjust right may be delayed, till every thing becomes of itself ripe for a reform, or till maturity has been produced by peaceable means. A constitution, however imperfect, is yet preferable to the state of anarchy that would infallibly result from a precipitate reform. Political wisdom will therefore make it a duty to reform the actual state of things upon the ideas of public right; but it will not *employ* revolutions, which the nature of things brings on to authorize an oppression still more tyrannical; on the contrary, it will profit by them to establish, by solid reforms and upon principles of freedom, a legal constitution, the only one durable.

lic right? They will be able to carry thither only the spirit of chicane; they will apply their mechanical mode of proceeding even there where despotic laws have no existence, and where reason tolerates no other constraint than that of a legal liberty, the sole and only foundation of a constitution which can guarantee right. Upon this the practitioner in the law reflects very little; he fancies himself able to fetch his notions from experience; and, without having need of principles of reason, he applies to the constitutions which have hitherto passed for the best, though they are almost all contrary to right, to obtain the idea of the best possible constitution.

These are some of the maxims of a sophist which he implicitly follows, and to which may be reduced almost all his skill.

I. *Fac et excusa* [First do and then excuse]. Seize every favorable opportunity of usurping a right over thy own state, or a neighboring state. After the action, its justification may be made with greater ease and elegance (especially in the first case, where the supreme power is at the same time the legislator, whose will must be implicitly obeyed). It is far more convenient to commit an act of violence, and afterwards excuse it, than laboriously to consider of convincing arguments, and losing time in listening to objections. This very boldness itself indicates a sort of conviction of the legitimacy of the action, and the God of success (*Bonus Eventus*) is afterwards the best advocate.

II. *Si fecisti nega.* Deny whatever thou hast committed. For instance, if thou hast reduced thy people to despair, and thus to rebellion, do not confess it was through thy fault. Place all to the account of the stubbornness of thy subjects. If thou hast taken possession of a neighboring state, maintain that the fault lies in the nature of man, who, if he is not anticipated, will certainly seize upon the fortunes of another.

III. *Divide et impera* [Divide and govern]. If there exists among a people certain privileged chiefs who have conferred upon thee sovereign power (*primus inter pares*), set them at variance with each other, embroil them with the people. Favor the latter, and promise them more liberty, and all will soon depend on thy will. Or if thy views extend to foreign states, excite discord among them; and, under pretense of always assisting the weaker, thou wilt soon subject them all, one after the other.

No one, it is true, is now the dupe of these maxims; they are too universally known still to impose. Nor are they blushed at, as if their injustice was too glaring. Great powers blush only at the judgment of other great powers, and not at that of the vulgar. Moreover, their being all on a par as to the morality of their maxims, they blush not when they are imputed to them, but when they employ them without success. Political honor still remains to them which cannot be disputed, namely, the aggrandizement of their power, in whatever manner it may have been effected.[11]

All these windings in which an immoral policy engages to conduct men from a state of war, which is that of nature, to a pacific situation prove, at least, that in their personal affinity, or in their public relation, men cannot reject the idea of right; that they do not venture to found politics upon simple prudential artifices, and consequently do not withdraw themselves from the idea of universal right; that, on the contrary, they pay every possible regard to it, especially in public rights, even at a time they are inventing numberless pretenses and palliatives to escape therefrom in practice; and that, in fact, they by a gross error attribute the origin and maintenance of right to force, assisted by deceit. Let us put an end, if not to injustice itself, at least to the sophisms used to veil it; let us force the perfidious representatives of power to confess that their pleadings are not in favor of right, but of force, which is discovered in their imperious tone, as if their power extended even to a command of truth.

To obtain this, let us unveil the imposture which deceives the mind; let us ascend towards the principle that necessitates a perpetual peace; and let us show that the evil which is an obstacle to its proceeds from this that the political moralist begins where the moral politician would properly end; and thus, by rendering the principles subordinate to the end (which

---

11. If we still doubt of the stock of perverseness which appears rooted in men who live in a state of society; if even we impute, with some probability, the immoral phenomenons we now and then perceive in them to a want of civilization; this malignity is evidently manifested in the external relations of states. In the interior of a state, it is veiled by the restraint of civil law; the propensity towards reciprocal acts of violence is with the citizen fettered by the superior power of government. This it is which not only casts over the whole of society an appearance of morality but really facilitates the development of moral faculties by placing a barrier to the effervescence of unlawful inclinations, and thus prepares men to respect right on their own account. For everyone imagines that he could well respect the sacred idea of right if he were sure that others would not violate it with regard to him. Now the government, which partly gives this certainty to everyone, opens thereby the path to morality; and though it produces not respect for the very idea of right, it nevertheless conducts to that immediate and disinterested respect which renders duty observed without hopes of a return. It is true that with the good opinion everyone has of himself, he always supposes his neighbor guilty of a malicious disposition. From thence arise the continual condemnations of one another, declaring that in fact none of them are worth much. We shall not here examine from what this general depravation results; the nature of man who is free cannot be accused of it. We shall only say that as the idea of right, to which no one can refuse respect, solemnly sanctions the theory which supposes the possibility of realizing this idea, everyone perceives that he must conform to it, without troubling himself about what others may do.

is called placing the cart before the horse), he hurts his own cause, and himself prevents the agreement of politics with morality.

Let us begin with deciding a general question, from which depends the uniformity which ought to reign in practical philosophy. In order to solve the problem proposed to practical reason, we must begin with examining the material end proposed (such as the advantage and happiness that would result from the action, and which is the object of the will); or shall we, not regarding these perceptible relations, simply attend to the formal principle, namely, to the condition under which liberty may be exercised outwardly? a principle expressed by this law: act in such a manner that thou mayest desire that the maxim according to which thou determinest may become a general law (let the end thou aimest at be whatever it may).

We must undoubtedly begin with the formal principle; since in quality of a principle of right it contains an absolute necessity; whereas the material principle obliges only conditionally, and under the sole supposition that one wishes to attain the end in view; and when this end is itself a duty (as for instance perpetual peace) it must however have been deduced from the formal principle of free actions.

But here the problem of a civil, public, and cosmopolitical right is to the political moralist only a technical problem, whereas it becomes a moral problem to the moral politician. Each will have a very different track to follow for the establishment of perpetual peace, considered by the one as a simple physical good, but by the other as a situation rendered necessary by duty.

The first stands in need of a very extensive acquaintance with nature, so as to render its mechanism useful to his political end; notwithstanding the result of all his prudence will still leave a perpetual peace in uncertainty. To be convinced of this, take a view of the three species of public right. What is the most proper means of maintaining a people in obedience and prosperity; severity, or the charms of distinctions flattering to vanity; the power of one only, or that of several chiefs united; a nobility, or the power of the people? Nothing is more uncertain. History furnishes us with instances of the contrary in all forms of government (excepting that which is truly republican, and which can alone enter the mind of the moral politician). Still greater uncertainty exists in this pretended public right, founded upon ministerial ordinances: an expression void of sense, marking only conventional acts, concluded with a mental restriction of their violation.

Very different is the problem of the moral politician. The solution here, in some measure, offers itself to the mind; everyone owns its evidence. It makes the politician blush at the inutility of his maneuvres. It immediately conducts to the aim, though by an insensible progress, and without forcing it by violent precipitation.

It is there said, "Seek first the reign of pure practical reason and its justice, and your end (the blessing of perpetual peace) will necessarily follow." This is the prerogative of morality, especially in its principles of public right, consequently in its politics a priori. The less it aims in its conduct to the end proposed, that is to say, the physical or moral advantage in view, the more, nevertheless, it leads to it. For it is the general will regulated a priori which determines the right, whether of one people or of nations among each other. Now, provided it is consistently put in practice, this union of the will of all may at the same time, through the mechanism of nature, produce the desired effect, and contribute towards the realization of the idea of right.

It is, for instance, a principle in moral politics that a people shall constitute itself into a state only according to the ideas of a right of liberty and equality; and this principle is not founded upon prudence but duty. Let the political moralists oppose it as much as they please; let them exhaust themselves with arguments on the inefficacy of these principles against the natural affections of the members of society; let them even allege, in order to strengthen their objections, the example of ancient and modern constitutions, all badly organized (as that of democracies without the representative system), all their arguments do not merit any attention; especially since they themselves occasion perhaps this vicious morality, whose existence they suppose, by their fatal theory, which confounds man in one and the same class with other living machines, and which, in order to render him the most wretched of all beings, has only to take from him the consciousness of liberty.

The sentence somewhat free, but true, *fiat justitia, pereat mundus, i.e.,* let justice reign, should all the rascals of the universe perish: this sentence, which has become a proverb, is an energetic principle of right, and courageously cuts asunder the whole tissue of artifice or of force. But it is necessary that it be well understood. It does not authorize one to enforce his rights with all possible rigour; morality opposes this. It only enjoins the powerful neither to refuse nor to extenuate to anyone his right from aversion or commiseration for others; this is what is required, on the one hand, by an interior constitution founded upon the principles of right, and on the other, by a convention with other states analogous to a cosmopolitical constitution, and tending to regulate their differences legally. This sentence only imports that political maxims ought not to be founded upon the prosperity which may be expected to result from them to the state; that in their establishment attention ought not to be paid to the material aim, the object of the will of each state, and which cannot serve for a first principle to politics, only when it derives its maxims from experience; that state maxims ought to be deduced from the pure idea of duty, whatever may be the physical consequences thereof. And certainly, the universe would not totter if there were fewer wicked men in it. Such is the essential nature of moral evil that even the opposition of the views of its partisans insensibly destroys it, and that, annihilating itself, it by degrees gives place to the principle of moral good.

Objectively, or in the theory, there is no opposition between morality and politics. But it will always exist subjectively, *i.e.*, in consequence of the selfish propensity of man (I would say in the practice if this term did not imply a conduct founded upon the maxims of reason). And, in reality, this struggle is conducive to the exercise of virtue.

Tu ne cede malis, sed contra audentior ito.
[Do not withdraw from evils but go more boldly against them.]

But the most courageous exertion of virtue consists less in this case in defying the evils inseparable from this combat than in detecting and vanquishing within us the bad principle, whose crafty illusion and treacherous sophisms tend incessantly to persuade us that human frailty justifies every crime.

The political moralist may in reality say: If the prince and the people, or the people among themselves, employ fraud or force in order to go to war, they do no injustice to one another, though they are guilty of injustice in refusing all respect to the idea of right, which alone could serve as the basis to a perpetual peace. For the one failing in his duty towards the other, to the full as ill-disposed in his regard, it is in order that they destroy one another; unhappily there still remains enough of this race to occasion this game to continue to the remotest ages, and to furnish to posterity a terrible lesson. Providence, which regulates the course of the world, is sufficiently justified by the maintenance of moral principle, which is never extinct in man; for, on the contrary, the continual advances of the human mind progressively develop reason, and render it more adapted to realize the idea of right, conformable to moral principle, as they render more culpable those who violate it. There is only the existence and even the creation of this depraved race which seems incapable of being justified by any theodicy, if we admit that the human race can never be meliorated. But we are not permitted to elevate ourselves, in our theoretical judgments, beyond our sphere; and infinite power is too incomprehensible for us to presume to apply to it our ideas of wisdom.

Such are the afflicting consequences resulting from a system in which the principles of right are affirmed to be impracticable. It is necessary then to admit their objective reality; it is upon them that the people of each state must regulate their conduct, and the states their reciprocal relations, however specious the objections may be which policy deduces from experience.

Thus true politics can never take a step without having previously rendered homage to morality; united with this, it is no longer a difficult or complicated art; morality cuts the knot which politics is incapable of untying, whenever they are in opposition to each other. The rights of man ought to be religiously respected should sovereigns in rendering it make the greatest sacrifices. One cannot compromise here between right and utility; politics must bend the knee before morality; but by this means it may also expect insensibly to attain to an eminence, where it will shine with an immortal glory.

PART II

Of the Harmony
Which the Transcendent Idea of Right Establishes
between Politics and Morality

When I represent to myself, according to the usage of the lawyers, the public right in all its habitudes with the relations of the individuals of a state, and of states among themselves; if I then make an abstraction of all the material of right, there still remains to me a form, which is essential to it, that of publicity. Without it there is no justice, for one cannot conceive of it only as being able to be rendered public: there would be then no longer right, since it is founded only on justice. Each juridical claim ought to be capable of being made public; and as it is very easy to judge in each case if the principles of him who acts would bear publicity, this possibility itself may commodiously serve as a criterion purely intellectual in order to discover by reason alone the injustice of a juridical pretension.

I understand by the material of civil and public right all what experience alone can make us add to its idea (such is, for instance, the pretended wickedness of human nature, which necessarily requires constraint). Let us make an abstraction of all that we then shall have a transcendent formula of public right; here it is:

"All the actions relative to the right of another whose maxim is not susceptible of publicity are unjust."

This principle is not only moral and essential to the doctrine of virtue; it is likewise juridical and equally respects the right of men. For a maxim which I dare not divulge without defeating my own ends, which absolutely requires secrecy in order to succeed, and which I cannot publicly avow without arming all others against my projects, such a maxim can only owe to the injustice with which it menaces them this infallible and universal opposition, of which reason foresees the absolute necessity.

Besides, this principle is purely negative; it is only subservient to the detection of what is repugnant to the right of others. There is evidence and certitude of axioms, and one may easily make application of them. Some examples drawn from public right go to prove it.

I. In civil right a question occurs, considered as of very difficult solution, and which the transcendent principle of publicity immediately decides; *i.e.*, if a people act consistently with right in shaking off by rebellion the yoke of a tyrant (*non titulo, sed exercitio talis* [tyrant in fact and practice, though not in title]). The rights of the people are violated; but no wrong is done to the tyrant by dethroning him; that is beyond a doubt. It is not less true that the subjects are in the highest degree wrong in pursuing their right in this manner, and that they cannot complain of injustice if, subdued in the struggle, they afterwards suffer in consequence thereof the severest punishments.

If one wishes to decide the question by a dogmatical deduction of rights, one will argue a long time for and against; but our transcendent principle of public right frees us from all these difficulties.

According to this principle, a nation would ask itself prior to the institution of the social contract whether on a given occasion it dare publish the design it might entertain of revolting. It is manifest that if, in founding a constitution, a nation reserved to itself the condition of being able, in a supposed case, to employ force against its chief, it would assume a legitimate power over him; but then the chief would cease to be so; or if it was wished to make this condition a clause of the constitution, this would be impossible, and the nation would fail of its end. The injustice of rebellion then is manifest inasmuch as publicity would render the maxim impracticable which permits it; by consequence it would be necessary to keep it secret. Now, it would not be thus with the chief of the state; he can boldly declare that he will inflict the punishment of death upon every author of revolt, even when the conspirators might imagine that the chief has first violated the fundamental law of the civil constitution; the chief must enjoy an irresistible and inviolable power, since he could not have the right to command each if he had not the power to protect each against the others. For feeling himself invested with this power, he has no longer to fear acting hostilely to his own views in making his maxims public. A consequence not less evident of this principle is that if the nation succeed in its revolt, the chief, re-entering into the class of subjects, dares neither renew the rebellion in order to reascend the throne nor be summoned to render an account of his preceding administration.

II. The right of nations supposes a juridical state; for being a public right, it includes already in its notion the declaration of rights which the general will assigns to each. This juridical state ought to result from an antecedent pact founded not upon the laws of constraint, like the civil pact, but upon a free and permanent association, such as the federation of states which has been treated of above.

In the state of nature, and without a sort of juridical state, which might unite among themselves the divers physical and moral persons, there can exist only individual right. Now, it is equally evident that here exists between politics and morality, which have respect to right, an opposition just as easy to be removed if one apply thereto the principle of publicity of maxims. I suppose, however, that the federation of nations will have for its object only the maintenance of peace, and not of conquests. The following are the problems in which politics are at variance with morality, and their solution.

1. When one state has promised to another succors, the cession of some province, or subsidies, etc., it is demanded whether it can retract its promise, in case the safety of the state be exposed, by pretending to consider it under a double point of view: sometimes as sovereign, free from all responsibility towards the state; sometimes as first public functionary, accountable to its fellow citizens: so that it may retract in this last quality engagements entered into in the first.

But if a state, or its chief, rendered this maxim public, all others would naturally avoid treating therewith, or would associate with one another in order to resist its pretensions; which proves that politics, with all its address, would of itself, in practicing sincerity, defeat its object; and consequently the maxim in question must be unjust.

2. If a power is become formidable by its acquisitions, dare it be admitted that it will, because it can, oppress others; and have the powers of the second order a right to attack it conjointly without their having been injured by it? A state which should openly declare this maxim would only augment the evil instead of extinguishing it. For the superior power would anticipate the less, and the association of others is only a feeble reed, incapable of resisting any one who well understands the *divide et impera*. This maxim of politics, rendered notorious, necessarily annihilates of itself its effect, and consequently it is unjust.

3. When a small state is so situate as to intercept, between the parts of a great state, the communication necessary to its preservation, is not the greater authorized to subject the other, or to incorporate it with itself?

It is easy to perceive that it ought well to guard against suffering this maxim to transpire before the execution; for either the small states would form betimes defensive alliances or other great powers would dispute the prey. Publicity then would render this maxim impracticable; a certain mark that it is unjust. It may likewise be unjust in a very high degree. For however small the object of an injustice may be, the injustice itself may be very great.

III. I pass in silence the cosmopolitical right, because it is very easy to form and to appreciate its maxims on account of its analogy to the right of nations.

Here is then a character by which we are able to recognize the non-conformity of a maxim of politics to the morality which has relation to right; *i.e.*, the incompatibility of maxims of public right with publicity. It concerns us now to know the conditions under which these maxims accord with the right of nations. For it cannot be inferred from the notoriety of a maxim that it is just, since one has no need of concealing his plans when he possesses a decided superiority of power.

The first condition necessary to render the public right possible is in general the existence of a juridical order. Now we have seen above that there is no other juridical state compatible with the liberty of states than their federative association for the sole maintenance of peace. The agreement of politics with morality then can take place only by means of a similar association, founded upon intellectual principles of right, and which is consequently requisite. All politics is founded upon this legal federalism; otherwise it is only a refinement of injustice. The jesuitical casuists have not more of subtilities than has this false policy. It has, first, mental restrictions, ambiguities which it knows how adroitly to slip into public treaties in order to be able afterwards to explain them to its advantage; as, for instance, the distinction between the states *quo de fait et de droit* [in fact and in right]; the *probabilismus* [probability]: merely to forge hostile intentions, and to attribute them to others; to imagine a probable superiority of power, and to make of it a right, for the sake of which peaceable states may be undermined; lastly, the *peccatum philosophicum* (*peccatillum bagatelle*) [philosophical sin (the trivial fault)] in order to be able to regard as a very pardonable fault, and perhaps even as a blessing to mankind, that great states should swallow up the lesser ones.[12]

Morality itself is the specious pretext of all these maxims, whose various branches political duplicity knows how to employ to its own ends. Benevolence is a duty as well as respect for the rights of man; but it is only a conditional duty; this is absolute and necessary. One must be sure of having never wounded this last, in order to be able to give one's self up to the sweet sentiment of benevolence. Politics easily accords with morality, inasmuch as this regulates the manners, in order to be able to abandon the rights of men to their superiors; but as to morality, inasmuch as it establishes the rights of man, instead of prostrating itself before it, as it ought, politics finds it convenient to combat it and dispute with it all reality, confining itself to reduce all duties to benevolence. Now this artifice of gloomy politics would be soon unmasked by the publicity of its maxims, which philosophers would give to open day, if it possessed but the courage to allow them the publication of their principles.

In this view, I propose another transcendent and affirmative principle of public right, whose formula should be:

"All maxims which, in order to have their effect, stand in need of publicity agree with politics and morality combined."

For if they cannot produce their effect only as far as they are notorious, they must accord with the general end of the public, with happiness; consequently they are reconcilable with politics, which is occupied in con-

---

12. The examples of the application of all these maxims may be seen in Counselor Garve's "Dissertation on the Union of Politics with Morality," 1788. This respectable learned man confesses himself, from the beginning, unable completely to solve this problem. But to approve of this union without thinking one's self able to refute all the objections that are made to it, is it not granting more than ought to be to those who are but too well disposed to abuse such a facility?

ceiving a state of things with which each may be satisfied. And if this end can be attained only by the publicity of maxims which are proposed, *i.e.*, in removing from them all subject of distrust, they must be moreover conformable to the rights of the public: the only point of union at which the particular ends of all can be made to meet. I shall defer till another occasion the development of this principle. I only add that it is transcendent, since its formula includes nothing material, nothing which relates to the doctrine of happiness, and that it must be drawn from experience; it aims only at the form of universality which gives the force of laws to maxims.

If it is a duty, if the hope can even be conceived, of realizing, though by an endless progress, the reign of public right—perpetual peace, which will succeed to the suspensions of hostilities, hitherto named treaties of peace, is not then a chimera, but a problem of which time, probably abridged by the uniformity of the progress of the human mind, promises us the solution.

Karl von Clausewitz

1780–1831

Karl von Clausewitz, army general and theorist of war, was
among the Prussian military figures—including General Gerhard
von Scharnhorst (1755–1813) and Field Marshal Count Neithardt
von Gneisenau (1760–1831)—who during the wars against Napoleon
organized a military system for their country that strongly influenced
its national character. They were inspired to do this by the Battle of
Jena (1806), where Napoleon destroyed the Prussian forces, which,
since Frederick the Great (1712–1786), had been thought to be the
finest in the world. That disaster showed the superiority of an
inspired national army over professional legions of the sort created
by Frederick. The lesson taught Prussia—and Europe—the effectiveness of a kind of war that was later to be called total.

Clausewitz himself, who was only thirty-five when Napoleon at
last surrendered, missed the chance to achieve first distinction as a
field officer. Yet his career began so early that he rose to higher rank
than most men of his age. He was born near Magdeburg, Saxony,
of parents too poor to educate their children. At twelve he entered
the army. By the time he was fourteen, he was a veteran who had
received a commission. He was captured by the French at Prenzlau.
Subsequently, he returned to Prussia to help Scharnhorst re-establish
the army, went afterward with many of his fellow officers to help the
Russians resist and defeat Napoleon's invasion of 1812, and was
chief of staff to one of the Prussian generals at the Battle of Waterloo
(1815).

Meanwhile he had managed to educate himself. His talents as a
theorist of military affairs were recognized before he was twenty-
five. During interludes of peace he served as an administrator and
teacher of military organization. When the long war with France

was finished he became director, in 1818, of the Prussian Allgemeine Kriegsschule (War College), where he carried on the work that Scharnhorst had begun. In 1830 he was transferred to active duty near the Polish border, becoming chief of staff to Gneisenau, with whom he had served in Russia. He died at Breslau the next year of cholera, a disease which in the same year also killed his commander.

Clausewitz' writings were collected and published after his death. Besides lives of Scharnhorst and Gneisenau, they include histories of the Napoleonic campaigns and studies of various military leaders. But the work for which their author has become famous is the treatise *Vom Kriege* (*On War*). The selection that follows is the first chapter of that work.

What is war? It is a kind of duel, Clausewitz says, in which the aim is to disarm your enemy so that you may impose your will upon him. It is not, in other words, a polite exercise of the sort sometimes undertaken by eighteenth-century kings and generals. In theory, war is without limits, save for those "restrictions, hardly worth mentioning, which it imposes on itself under the name of international law and usage."

In practice, however, Clausewitz suggests, war is limited by political considerations. War as he conceives it is really a means to the political objects of competing states, and from these objects it cannot, or should not, be separated. The implication is that in time of war a well-ordered state and its army are the same thing, while even in time of peace the proper national spirit is a militant one.

Such reflections have often been opposed in two different ways. In the first place, with respect to Clausewitz' book as a whole, it can be said—as Homer seems to and as Tolstoy certainly does say—that war is not a philosophical subject. War cannot be reduced to a system of which there can be a science. Even if it is admitted that war can be systematized, it must also be said that it is not civilized. War, as such, is not a legitimate social enterprise. It can be maintained, as Virgil seems to do, that war constitutes a failure of civilization rather than a practice of it. It has been doubted whether any national object exists, apart from survival, which war can justifiably serve. One might hesitate to admit that such a thing as war can be "a real political instrument, a continuation of political intercourse, a carrying out of the same by other means."

Those who oppose Clausewitz' view on these or other grounds cannot deny his fierce realism. "War is an act of force," he says, "and to the application of that force there is no limit." These words were written to refute certain eighteenth-century theorists who considered war a game—"a sort of algebra of action," as Clausewitz scornfully puts it. War in itself has no intrinsic restraints. Clausewitz did not fear an unlimited war, since he supposed that extrinsic political objectives would always exist to limit it. But it is the opinion of some modern writers that war has become unrestrainable. We may wonder whether Clausewitz would maintain that any political objectives whatever could limit a conflict between two opponents armed with nuclear weapons.

What Is War?

1. INTRODUCTION

We propose to consider, first, the several elements of our subject, then its several parts or divisions, and, finally, the whole in its internal connection. Thus we proceed from the simple to the complex. But in this subject more than in any other it is necessary to begin with a glance at the nature of the whole, because here more than elsewhere the part and the whole must always be considered together.

2. DEFINITION

We shall not begin here with a clumsy, pedantic definition of war, but confine ourselves to its essence, the duel. War is nothing but a duel on a larger scale. If we would combine into one conception the countless separate duels of which it consists, we would do well to think of two wrestlers. Each tries by physical force to compel the other to do his will; his immediate object is to overthrow his adversary and thereby make him incapable of any further resistance.

War is thus an act of force to compel our adversary to do our will.

Force, to meet force, arms itself with the inventions of art and science. It is accompanied by insignificant restrictions, hardly worth mentioning, which it imposes on itself under the name of international law and usage, but which do not really weaken its power. Force, that is to say, physical force (for no moral force exists apart from the conception of a state and law), is thus the *means;* to impose our will upon the enemy is the *object*. To achieve this object with certainty we must disarm the enemy, and this disarming is by definition the proper aim of military action. It takes the place of the object and in a certain sense pushes it aside as something not belonging to war itself.

3. THE USE OF FORCE
THEORETICALLY WITHOUT LIMITS

Now philanthropic souls might easily imagine that there was an artistic way of disarming or overthrowing our adversary without too much bloodshed and that this was what the art of war should seek to achieve. However agreeable this may sound, it is a false idea which must be demolished. In affairs so dangerous as war, false ideas proceeding from kindness of heart are precisely the worst. As the most extensive use of physical force by no means excludes the co-operation of intelligence, he who uses this force ruthlessly, shrinking from no amount of bloodshed, must gain an advantage if his adversary does not do the same. Thereby he forces his adversary's hand, and thus each pushes the other to extremities to which the only limitation is the strength of resistance on the other side.

This is how the matter must be regarded, and it is a waste—and worse than a waste—of effort to ignore the element of brutality because of the repugnance it excites.

If the wars of civilized nations are far less cruel and destructive than those of the uncivilized, the reason lies in the social condition of the states, both in themselves and in their relations to one another. From this condition, with its attendant circumstances, war arises and is shaped, limited and modified. But these things do not themselves belong to war; they already exist. Never in the philosophy of war itself can we introduce a modifying principle without committing an absurdity.

Conflict between men really consists of two different elements: hostile feeling and hostile intention. We have chosen the latter of these two elements as the distinguishing mark of our definition because it is the more general. We cannot conceive the most savage, almost instinctive, passion of hatred as existing without hostile intention, whereas there are many hostile intentions accompanied by absolutely no hostility, or, at all events, no predominant hostility, of feeling. Among savages intentions inspired by emotion prevail; among civilized peoples those prescribed by intelligence. But this difference lies not in the intrinsic nature of savagery and civilization, but in their accompanying circumstances, institutions, and so forth. It does not necessarily, therefore, exist in every case, but only prevails in the majority of cases. In a word, even the most civilized nations can be passionately inflamed against one another.

From this we see how far from the truth we should be if we ascribed

war among civilized men to a purely rational act of the governments and
conceived it as continually freeing itself more and more from all passion,
so that at last there was no longer need of the physical existence of
armies, but only of the theoretical relations between them—a sort
of algebra of action.

Theory was already beginning to move in this direction when the
events of the last war [1] taught us better. If war is an act of force, the
emotions are also necessarily involved in it. If war does not originate
from them, it still more or less reacts upon them, and the degree of this
depends not upon the stage of civilization, but upon the importance and
duration of the hostile interests.

If, therefore, we find that civilized peoples do not put prisoners to
death or sack cities and lay countries waste, this is because intelligence
plays a greater part in their conduct of war and has taught them more
effective ways of applying force than these crude manifestations of
instinct.

The invention of gunpowder and the advances continually being made
in the development of firearms in themselves show clearly enough that
the demand for the destruction of the enemy, inherent in the theoretical conception of war, has been in no way actually weakened or diverted
by the advance of civilization.

So we repeat our statement: War is an act of force, and to the application of that force there is no limit. Each of the adversaries forces the
hand of the other, and a reciprocal action results which in theory can
have no limit. This is the first reciprocal action that we meet and the first
extreme.

(*First reciprocal action*)

4. THE AIM IS TO DISARM THE ENEMY

We have said that the disarming of the enemy is the aim of military
action, and we shall now show that, theoretically, at all events, this is
necessarily so.

If our opponent is to do our will, we must put him in a position more
disadvantageous to him than the sacrifice would be that we demand.
The disadvantages of his position should naturally, however, not be
transitory, or, at least, should not appear to be so, or our opponent would
wait for a more favorable moment and refuse to yield. Every change
in his position that will result from the continuance of military activity

1. The war with Napoleon.

must thus, at all events in theory, lead to a position still less advantageous. The worst position in which a belligerent can be placed is that of being completely disarmed. If, therefore, our opponent is to be forced by military action to do our will, we must either actually disarm him or put him in such a condition that he is threatened with the probability of our doing so. From this it follows that the disarming or the overthrow of the enemy—whichever we choose to call it—must always be the aim of military action.

Now war is not the action of a live force upon a dead mass—absolute nonresistance would be no sort of war at all—but always the collision of two live forces with each other, and what we have said of the ultimate aim of military action must be assumed to apply to both sides. Here, then, is again reciprocal action. So long as I have not overthrown my adversary I must fear that he may overthrow me. I am no longer my own master, but he forces my hand as I force his. This is the second reciprocal action, which leads to the second extreme.

(*Second reciprocal action*)

5. UTMOST EXERTION OF FORCES

If we want to overthrow our opponent, we must proportion our effort to his power of resistance. This power is expressed as a product of two inseparable factors: *the extent of the means at his disposal* and *the strength of his will.* The extent of the means at his disposal would be capable of estimation, as it rests (though not entirely) on figures, but the strength of the will is much less so and only approximately to be measured by the strength of the motive behind it. Assuming that in this way we have got a reasonably probable estimate of our opponent's power of resistance, we can proportion our efforts accordingly and increase them so as to secure a preponderance or, if our means do not suffice for this, as much as we can. But our opponent does the same; and thus a fresh competition arises between us which in pure theory once more involves pushing to an extreme. This is the third reciprocal action we meet and a third extreme.

(*Third reciprocal action*)

6. MODIFICATIONS IN PRACTICE

In the abstract realm of pure conceptions the reflective mind nowhere finds rest till it has reached the extreme, because it is with an extreme that it has to do—a conflict of powers left to themselves and obeying no law but their own. If, therefore, we wanted from the mere theoretical conception of war to deduce an absolute aim which we are to set before ourselves and the means we are to employ, these continuous reciprocal actions would land us in extremes which would be nothing but a play of fancies produced by a scarcely visible train of logical hairsplitting. If, adhering closely to the absolute, we proposed to get round all difficulties with a stroke of the pen and insist with logical strictness that on every occasion we must be prepared for the extreme of resistance and meet it with the extreme of effort, such a stroke of the pen would be a mere paper law with no application to the real world.

Assuming, too, that this extreme of effort were an absolute quantity that could easily be discovered, we must nevertheless admit that the human mind would hardly submit to be ruled by such logical fantasies. In many cases the result would be a futile expenditure of strength which would be bound to find a restriction in other principles of statesmanship. An effort of will would be required disproportionate to the object in view and impossible to call forth. For the will of man never derives its strength from logical hairsplitting.

Everything, however, assumes a different shape if we pass from the abstract world to that of reality. In the former everything had to remain subject to optimism and we had to conceive both one side and the other as not merely striving toward perfection but also attaining it. Will this ever be so in practice? It would if:

1. war were a wholly isolated act, which arose quite suddenly and had no connection with the previous course of events,

2. if it consisted of a single decision or of several simultaneous decisions,

3. if its decision were complete in itself and the ensuing political situation were not already being taken into account and reacting upon it.

7. WAR IS NEVER AN ISOLATED ACT

With reference to the first of these three points we must remember that neither of the two opponents is for the other an abstract person, even as regards that factor in the power of resistance which does not depend on external things, namely, the will. This will is no wholly unknown quantity: what it has been today tells us what it will be tomorrow. War never breaks out quite suddenly, and its spreading is not the work of a moment. Each of the two opponents can thus to a great extent form an opinion of the other from what he actually is and does, not from what, theoretically, he should be and should do. With his imperfect organization, however, man always remains below the level of the absolute best, and thus these deficiencies, operative on both sides, become a modifying influence.

8. WAR DOES NOT CONSIST
OF ONE BLOW WITHOUT DURATION

The second of the three points gives occasion for the following observations:

If the issue in war depended on a single decision or several simultaneous decisions, the preparations for that decision or those several decisions would naturally have to be carried to the last extreme. A lost opportunity could never be recalled; the only standard the real world could give us for the preparations we must make would, at best, be those of our adversary, so far as they are known to us, and everything else would once more be relegated to the realm of abstraction. But if the decision consists of several successive acts, each of these with all its attendant circumstances can provide a measure for those which follow, and thus here, too, the real world takes the place of the abstract, and modifies, accordingly, the trend to the extreme.

Every war, however, would necessarily be confined to a single decision or several simultaneous decisions if the means available for the conflict were all brought into operation together or could be so brought into operation. For an adverse decision necessarily diminishes these means, and if they have all been used up in the first decision, a second really becomes unthinkable. All acts of war which could follow would be essentially part of the first and really only constitute its duration.

But we have seen that in the preparations for war the real world has already taken the place of the mere abstract idea, and an actual standard that of a hypothetical extreme. Each of the two opponents, if for no other reason, will therefore in their reciprocal action stop short of the extreme effort, and their resources will thus not all be called up together.

But the very nature of these resources and of their employment makes it impossible to put them all into operation at one and the same moment. They consist of *the military forces proper, the country* with its superficial extent and its population, and *the allies.*

The country with its superficial extent and its population, as well as being the source of all military forces proper, is also in itself an integral part of the factors operative in war, if only with that part which provides the theatre of war or has a marked influence upon it.

Now all movable military resources can very well be put into operation simultaneously, but not all the fortresses, rivers, mountains, inhabitants, and so forth—in a word, the whole country, unless it is so small as to be wholly embraced by the first act of war. Furthermore, the cooperation of the allies does not depend upon the will of the belligerents, and from the very nature of political relations, it frequently does not come into effect or become active till later, for the purpose of restoring a balance of forces that has been upset.

That this part of the means of resistance, which cannot be brought into operation all at once, in many cases is a much larger part of the whole than at first sight we should think, and that consequently it is capable of restoring the balance of forces even when the first decision has been made with great violence and that balance has thus been seriously disturbed, will be more fully explained later. At this point it is enough to show that to make all our resources available at one and the same moment is contrary to the nature of war. Now in itself this could furnish no ground for relaxing the intensity of our efforts for the first decision, because an unfavorable issue is always a disadvantage to which no one will purposely expose himself, because even if the first decision is followed by others, the more decisive it has been, the greater will be its influence upon them. But the possibility of a subsequent decision is something in which man's shrinking from excessive effort causes him to seek refuge, and thus for the first decision his resources are not concentrated and strained to the same degree as they would otherwise have been. What either of the two opponents omits from weakness becomes for the other a real, objective ground for relaxing his own efforts, and thus, through this reciprocal action, the trend to the extreme is once more reduced to a limited measure of effort.

9. THE RESULT OF A WAR IS NEVER ABSOLUTE

Lastly, the final decision of a whole war is not always to be regarded as an absolute one. The defeated state often sees in it only a transitory evil, for which a remedy can yet be found in the political circumstances of a later day. How greatly this also must modify the violence of the strain and the intensity of the effort is obvious.

10. THE PROBABILITIES OF REAL LIFE TAKE THE PLACE
OF THE EXTREME AND ABSOLUTE DEMANDED BY THEORY

In this way the whole field of war ceases to be subject to the strict law of forces pushed to the extreme. If the extreme is no longer shunned and no longer sought, it is left to the judgment to determine the limits of effort, and this can only be done by deduction according to the *laws of probability* from the data supplied by the phenomena of the real world. If the two adversaries are no longer mere abstractions but individual states and governments, if the course of events is no longer theoretical but one that is determined according to its own laws, then the actual situation supplies the data for ascertaining what is to be expected, the unknown that has to be discovered.

From the character, the institutions, the situation and the circumstances of the adversary, each side will draw its conclusions, in accordance with the laws of probability, as to what the action of the other will be and determine its own accordingly.

11. THE POLITICAL OBJECT
NOW COMES FORWARD AGAIN

At this point a subject, which in Section 2 we had dismissed, now once more insists on claiming our consideration: namely, *the political object of the war.* The law of the extreme, the intention of disarming the enemy and overthrowing him, had up to now, so to speak, more or less swallowed it up. As this law loses its force, and this intention falls short of its aim, the political object of the war once more comes to the front. If all we have to consider is a calculation of probabilities starting from definite persons and circumstances, the political object as the original motive must be an essential factor in this process. The smaller the sacrifice we demand from our adversary, the slighter we may expect his efforts to be to refuse it to us. The slighter, however, his effort, the smaller need our own be. Furthermore, the less important our political object, the less will be the value we attach to it and the readier we shall be to abandon it. For this reason also our own efforts will be the slighter.

Thus the political object as the original motive of the war will be the standard alike for the aim to be attained by military action and for the efforts required for this purpose. It cannot be in itself an absolute standard, but, as we are dealing with real things and not with mere ideas, it will be the standard relative to the two contending states. One and the same political object can in different nations, and even in one and the same nation at different times, produce different reactions. We can therefore allow the political object to serve as a standard only in so far as we bear in mind its influence on the masses which it is to affect. So the character of these masses must be considered. It is easy to see that the result may be quite different, according as the action is strengthened or weakened by the feeling of the masses. In two nations and states such tensions, and such a mass of hostile feelings, may exist that a motive for war, very trifling in itself, still can produce a wholly disproportionate effect—a positive explosion.

This holds good for the efforts which the political object can call forth in the two states, and for the aim it can assign to military action. Sometimes it can itself become this aim, for example, if it is the conquest of a certain province. Sometimes the political object will not itself be suited to provide the aim for military action, and in such cases one must be chosen of such a kind as will serve as an equivalent for it and can take its place in the conclusion of peace. But in this case also due consideration for the character of the states concerned is always presupposed. There are circumstances in which the equivalent must be much more considerable than the political object, if the latter is to be attained by it. The greater the indifference of the masses and the less serious the tensions that on other grounds also exist in the two states and their relations, the more dominant as a standard, and decisive in itself, will the political object be. There are cases in which it is, almost by itself, the deciding factor.

Now if the aim of the military action is an equivalent for the political object, that action will in general diminish as the political object diminishes. The more this object comes to the front, the more will this be so. This explains how, without self-contradiction, there can be wars of all degrees of importance and energy, from a war of extermination down to a mere state of armed observation. But this leads us to a question of another kind, which we have still to analyze and answer.

12. A SUSPENSION OF MILITARY ACTION
NOT EXPLAINED BY ANYTHING YET SAID

However insignificant the political claims made on either side, however weak the means employed and however trifling the aim to which military action is directed, can this action ever for a moment be suspended? This is a question that goes deep into the essence of the matter.

Every action requires for its accomplishment a certain time, which we call its duration. This may be longer or shorter, according as the person acting is more or less quick in his movements.

About this we shall not here trouble ourselves. Everyone does his business in his own fashion; but the slow person does not do it more slowly because he wants to spend more time on it but because by his nature he needs more time, and if he were to make greater haste, he would do it less well. This time, therefore, depends on subjective causes and belongs to the actual duration of the action.

If we now allow to every action in war its duration, we must admit, at all events at first sight, that every expenditure of time in excess of this duration, that is to say, every suspension of military action, seems to be absurd. In this connection we must always remember that the question is not of the progress of one or other of the two opponents, but of the progress of the military action as a whole.

13. THERE IS ONLY ONE CAUSE THAT CAN SUSPEND ACTION, AND THIS SEEMS ALWAYS TO BE POSSIBLE ON ONE SIDE ONLY

If two parties have armed themselves for the conflict, a hostile motive must have caused them to do so. So long then as they remain under arms, so long, that is, as they do not make peace, this motive must be present and can only cease to act with either of the two opponents for one sole reason, namely, *that he wants to wait for a more favorable moment for action.* Now, it is obvious that this reason can only be present on one of the two sides, because by its very nature it becomes the opposite on the other. If it is to the interest of the one commander to act, it must be to the interest of the other to wait.

A complete equilibrium of forces can never produce a suspension of action, for in such a suspension he who has the positive aim—that is, the assailant—would necessarily retain the initiative.

But if we chose to conceive the equilibrium as such that he who has the positive aim, and therefore the stronger motive, has at the same time the smaller forces at his disposition, so that the equation would arise from the product of motives and forces, we should still have to say that if no change in this condition of equilibrium is to be foreseen, both sides must make peace. But if a change is to be foreseen, it will be in favor of one side only, and for that reason the other will necessarily be moved to action. We see that the idea of an equilibrium cannot explain a suspension of hostilities, but all it amounts to is the waiting for a more favorable moment. Let us assume, therefore, that of two states one has a positive aim, the conquest, for instance, of one of the adversary's provinces to be used as a counter in the settlement of peace. After this conquest his political object is attained, the need for action ceases and he can take rest. If his adversary is prepared to acquiesce in this result, he must make peace; if not, he must act. If it is thought now that in four weeks' time he will be in a better condition to do so, then he has sufficient grounds for postponing his action.

But from that moment the duty of action seems to fall logically upon his opponent, in order that no time be allowed to the vanquished to prepare for action. In all this, it is, of course, assumed that each side has a complete knowledge of the circumstances.

14. THUS A CONTINUITY WOULD BE INTRODUCED INTO MILITARY ACTION FORCING EVERYTHING AGAIN TO A CLIMAX

If this continuity of military action actually existed, everything would again be driven by it to the extreme. For apart from the fact that such ceaseless activity would give a greater bitterness to the feelings and impart to the whole a higher degree of passion and a greater elemental force, there would also arise through the continuity of action a more inevitable sequence of events and a less disturbed causal connection between them. Each action would in consequence become more important and thus more dangerous.

But we know that military action seldom or never has this continuity, and that there are many wars in which action fills by far the smallest part of the time occupied, and inaction all the rest. This cannot possibly be always an anomaly. Suspension of military action must be possible, that is to say, not a contradiction in itself. That this is so, and why, we will now show.

15. HERE, THEREFORE, A PRINCIPLE OF POLARITY IS BROUGHT INTO EVIDENCE

By supposing the interests of the one commander to be always diametrically opposed to those of the other, we have assumed a true *polarity*. We propose later on to devote a special chapter to this principle, but for the present must make one observation upon it.

The principle of polarity only holds good if it is conceived in one and the same thing, in which the positive and its opposite, the negative, exactly destroy one another. In a battle each of the two parties wishes to win; that is true polarity, for the victory of the one destroys that of the other. But if we are speaking of two different things which have a common relation external to themselves, it is not the things but their relations that have the polarity.

16. ATTACK AND DEFENSE ARE THINGS DIFFERENT IN KIND AND OF UNEQUAL FORCE. POLARITY THEREFORE IS NOT APPLICABLE TO THEM

If there were only one form of war, namely, the attack of the enemy, therefore no defense; in other words if the attack were distinguished from the defense merely by the positive motive, which the one has and the other has not, but the methods of the fight were always one and the same, in such a fight every advantage to the one side would be an equal disadvantage to the other and true polarity would exist.

But military activity takes two separate forms, attack and defense, which, as we shall later on explain in detail, are very different and of unequal strength. Polarity lies therefore in that to which they both bear a relation, namely, the decision, but not in attack or defense itself. If one commander wishes to postpone the decision, the other must wish to hasten it, but, of course, only in the same form of conflict. If it is to A's interest not to attack his opponent at once but four weeks hence, it is to B's interest to be attacked by him at once and not four weeks hence. Here is a direct opposition; but it does not follow therefrom that it is to B's interest to attack A at once. That is obviously something quite different.

17. THE EFFECT OF POLARITY IS OFTEN DESTROYED BY THE SUPERIORITY OF THE DEFENSE TO THE ATTACK. THIS EXPLAINS THE SUSPENSION OF MILITARY ACTION

If the form of defense, as we shall hereafter show, is stronger than that of attack, the question arises whether the advantage of a deferred decision is as great for the one side as that of the defense is for the other. When it is not, it cannot by means of its opposite outweigh the latter and so influence the course of military action. We thus see that the impulsive force which lies in the polarity of interests may be lost in the difference between the strength of the attack and that of the defense, and thereby becomes ineffectual.

If, therefore, the side for which the present is favorable is too weak to be able to dispense with the advantage of the defensive, it must resign itself to facing a less favorable future. For it may still be better to fight a defensive battle in the unfavorable future than an offensive one in the present, or than to make peace. Now as we are convinced that the superiority of the defense (rightly understood) is very great and much greater than may appear at first sight, a very large proportion of the periods of suspended action which occur in war are thereby explained, without our being necessarily involved in a contradiction. The weaker the motives to action are, the more they will be swallowed up and neutralized by this difference between attack and defense. The more frequently, therefore, will military action be brought to a standstill, as, indeed, experience teaches.

18. A SECOND CAUSE LIES IN THE IMPERFECT KNOWLEDGE OF THE SITUATION

But there is still another cause that can stop military action, and that is imperfect knowledge of the situation. No commander has accurate personal knowledge of any position but his own; that of his adversary is only known to him by uncertain reports. He can make a mistake in his judgment of them and in consequence of this mistake believe that the initiative lies with his opponent when it really lies with himself. This want of knowledge could, it is true, just as often occasion untimely action as untimely inaction and would in itself no more contribute to delay than to hasten military action. Still it must always be regarded as one of the natural causes that, without involving an internal contradiction, may bring military action to a standstill. If, however, we reflect how much more we are inclined and induced to estimate the strength of our opponent too high rather than too low, because it lies in human nature to do so, we must also admit that imperfect knowledge of the situation must in general greatly contribute to putting a stop to military action and modifying the principles on which it is conducted.

The possibility of a standstill introduces into military action a new modification by diluting it, so to speak, with the element of time, halting danger in its stride and increasing the means for restoring a lost balance of forces. The greater the tensions out of which the war has sprung and the greater in consequence the energy with which it is waged, the shorter will be these periods of inaction; the weaker the hostile feeling, the longer will they be. For stronger motives increase the power of the will, and this, as we know, is always a factor in the product of our forces.

19. FREQUENT PERIODS OF INACTION REMOVE WAR
STILL FURTHER FROM THE REALM OF EXACT THEORY
AND MAKE IT STILL MORE A CALCULATION OF PROBABILITIES

But the more slowly military action proceeds and the longer and more frequent the periods of inaction, so much the more readily can a mistake be repaired, the bolder the commander will thus become in his assumptions, and the more readily will he at the same time remain below the extreme demanded by theory and build everything upon probability and conjecture. So the more or less leisurely course of military action allows more or less time for what the nature of the concrete situation in itself already demands, namely, a calculation of probabilities in accordance with the given circumstances.

20. SO ONLY THE ELEMENT OF CHANCE IS NOW LACKING
TO MAKE OF WAR A GAMBLE, AND IN THIS
ELEMENT IT IS LEAST OF ALL DEFICIENT

We see from the foregoing how much the objective nature of war makes it a calculation of probabilities. It now needs but one single element more to make of it a gamble, and that element it certainly does not lack—the element of *chance*. There is no human activity that stands in such constant and universal contact with chance as does war. Thus together with chance, the accidental and, with it, good luck play a great part in war.

21. THROUGH ITS SUBJECTIVE AS WELL AS THROUGH
ITS OBJECTIVE NATURE WAR BECOMES A GAMBLE

If we now glance at the *subjective nature* of war, that is, at those qualities with which it must be carried on, it must strike us as still more like a gamble. The element in which the activity of war moves is danger; but, in danger, which is the most superior of all moral qualities? It is *courage*. Now courage is certainly quite compatible with prudent calculation, but courage and calculation are nevertheless things different in kind and belonging to different parts of the mind. On the other hand, daring, reliance on good fortune, boldness and foolhardiness are only manifestations of courage, and all these efforts of the spirit seek the accidental because it is their proper element.

We thus see that from the very first the absolute, the so-called theoretical, faculty finds nowhere a sure basis in the calculations of the art of war. From the outset there is a play of possibilities and probabilities, of good and bad luck, which permeates every thread, great or small, of its web and makes war, of all branches of human activity, the most like a game of cards.

22. HOW THIS BEST ACCORDS
WITH THE HUMAN MIND IN GENERAL

Although our intellect always feels itself urged toward clarity and certainty, our mind still often feels itself attracted by uncertainty. Instead of threading its way with the intellect along the narrow path of philosophical investigation and logical deduction, in order, almost unconsciously, to arrive in spaces where it finds itself a stranger and where all familiar objects seem to abandon it, it prefers to linger with imagination in the realm of chance and luck. Instead of being confined, as in the first instance, to meager necessity, it revels here in the wealth of possibilities. Enraptured thereby, courage takes to itself wings, and thus daring and danger become the element into which it flings itself as a fearless swimmer flings himself into the stream.

Shall theory leave it here and move on, self-satisfied, to absolute conclusions and rules? In that case it is of no practical use. Theory must also take into account the human element and accord a place to courage and boldness and even to foolhardiness. The art of war has to do with living and with moral forces; from this it follows that it can nowhere attain the absolute and certain; there remains always a margin for the accidental just as much with the greatest things as with the smallest. As on the one side stands this accidental element, so on the other courage and self-confidence must step forward and fill up the gap. The greater the courage and self-confidence, the larger the margin that may be left for the accidental. Courage and self-confidence are thus principles absolutely essential for war. Consequently theory must only lay down such rules as allow free scope for these necessary and noblest of military virtues in all their degrees and variations. Even in daring there is still wisdom and prudence as well, only they are estimated by a different standard of value.

23. YET WAR STILL REMAINS A SERIOUS MEANS FOR A
SERIOUS OBJECT. MORE PARTICULAR DEFINITIONS OF IT

Such is war, such the commander who conducts it, and such the theory that rules it. But war is no pastime, no mere passion for daring and winning, no work of a free enthusiasm; it is a serious means to a serious end. All that it displays of that glamour of fortune, all that it assimilates of the thrills of passion and courage, of imagination and enthusiasm, are only particular properties of this means.

The war of a community—of whole nations and particularly of civilized nations—always arises from a political condition and is called forth by a political motive. It is, therefore, a political act. Now if it were an act complete in itself and undisturbed, an absolute manifestation of violence, as we had to deduce it from its mere conception, it would, from the moment it was called forth by policy, step into the place of policy and, as something quite independent of it, set it aside and follow only its own laws, just as a mine, when it is going off, can no longer be guided into any other direction than that given it by previous adjustments. This is how the thing has hitherto been regarded even in practice, whenever a lack of harmony between policy and the conduct of war has led to theoretical distinctions of this kind. But it is not so, and this idea is radically false. War in the real world, as we have seen, is no such extreme thing releasing its tension in a single discharge; it is the operation of forces which do not in every case develop in exactly the same way and the same proportion but which at one moment rise to a pitch sufficient to overcome the resistance which inertia and friction oppose to them, while at another, they are too weak to produce any effect. War is, therefore, so to speak, a regular pulsation of violence, more or less vehement and consequently more or less quick in relaxing tensions and exhausting forces—in other words, more or less quickly leading to its goal. But it always lasts long enough to exert, in its course, an influence upon that goal, so that its direction can be changed in this way or that—in short, long enough to remain subject to the will of a guiding intelligence. Now if we reflect that war has its origin in a political object, we see that this first motive, which called it into existence, naturally remains the first and highest consideration to be regarded in its conduct. But the political object is not on that account a despotic lawgiver; it must adapt itself to the nature of the means at its disposal and is often thereby completely changed, but it must always be the first thing to be considered. Policy, therefore, will permeate the whole action of war and exercise a continual influence upon it, so far as the nature of the explosive forces in it allow.

24. WAR IS A MERE CONTINUATION OF POLICY BY OTHER MEANS

We see, therefore, that war is not merely a political act but a real political instrument, a continuation of political intercourse, a carrying out of the same by other means. What now still remains peculiar to war relates merely to the peculiar character of the means it uses. The art of war in general and the commander in each particular case can demand that the tendencies and designs of policy shall be not incompatible with these means, and the claim is certainly no trifling one. But however powerfully it may react on political designs in particular cases, still it must always be regarded as only a modification of them; for the political design is the object, while war is the means, and the means can never be thought of apart from the object.

25. DIVERSITY IN THE NATURE OF WARS

The greater and the more powerful the motives for war, the more they affect the whole existence of the nations involved, and the more violent the tension which precedes war, so much the more closely will war conform to its abstract conception. The more it will be concerned with the destruction of the enemy, the more closely the military aim and the political object coincide, and the more purely military, and the less political, war seems to be. But the weaker the motives and the tensions, the less will the natural tendency of the military element, the tendency to violence, coincide with the directives of policy; the more, therefore, must war be diverted from its natural tendency, the greater is the difference between the political object and the aim of an ideal war, and the more does war seem to become political.

But that the reader may not form false conceptions, we must here remark that by this natural tendency of war we only mean the philosophical, the strictly logical, tendency, and by no means that of the forces actually engaged in conflict, to the point where, for instance, all emotions and passions of the combatants should be reckoned as included. These too, it is true, might in many cases be excited to such a pitch that they could with difficulty be kept confined to the political road; but in most cases such a contradiction will not arise, because the existence of such strong emotions will imply the existence also of a great plan in harmony with them. If the plan is directed only to a trifling object, the emotional excitement of the masses will be so slight that they will always be rather in need of being pushed on than of being held back.

26. ALL WARS MAY BE REGARDED
AS POLITICAL ACTS

To return to our main subject: Though it is true that in one kind of war policy seems entirely to disappear, while in another it very definitely comes to the front, we can nevertheless maintain that the one kind is as political as the other. For if we regard policy as the intelligence of the personified state; we must include among the combinations of circumstances which its calculations have to take into account that in which the nature of all the circumstances postulates a war of the first kind. It is only if we understand the term policy not as a comprehensive knowledge of the situation but the conventional idea of a cautious, crafty, even dishonest cunning, averse to violence, that the latter kind of war could belong to it more than does the former.

27. CONSEQUENCES OF THIS VIEW FOR THE UNDERSTANDING OF MILITARY HISTORY AND FOR THE FOUNDATIONS OF THEORY

We see, therefore, in the first place that in all circumstances we have to think of war not as an independent thing, but as a political instrument. And only by taking this point of view can we avoid falling into contradiction with the whole of military history. This alone opens the great book to intelligent appreciation. In the second place, this same point of view shows us how wars must differ according to the nature of their motives and of the circumstances out of which they arise.

Now the first, the greatest and the most decisive act of the judgment which a statesman and commander performs is that of correctly recognizing in this respect the kind of war he is undertaking, of not taking it for, or wishing to make it, something which by the nature of the circumstances it cannot be. This is, therefore, the first and most comprehensive of all strategic questions. Later on, in the chapter on the plan of a war, we shall examine it more closely.

For the moment we content ourselves with having brought our subject to this point and thereby fixed the main point of view from which war and the theory of war must be regarded.

28. RESULT FOR THEORY

War is, therefore, not only a veritable chameleon, because in each concrete case it changes somewhat its character, but it is also, when regarded as a whole, in relation to the tendencies predominating in it, a strange trinity, composed of the original violence of its essence, the hate and enmity which are to be regarded as a blind, natural impulse, of the play of probabilities and chance, which make it a free activity of the emotions, and of the subordinate character of a political tool, through which it belongs to the province of pure intelligence.

The first of these three sides is more particularly the concern of the people, the second that of the commander and his army, the third that of the government. The passions which are to blaze up in war must be already present in the peoples concerned; the scope that the play of courage and talent will get in the realm of the probabilities of chance depends on the character of the commander and the army; the political objects, however, are the concern of the government alone.

These three tendencies, which appear as so many lawgivers, lie deep in the nature of the subject and at the same time vary in magnitude. A theory which insisted on leaving one of them out of account, or on fixing an arbitrary relation between them, would immediately fall into such contradiction with reality that through this alone it would forthwith necessarily be regarded as destroyed.

The problem, therefore, is that of keeping the theory poised between these three tendencies as between three centers of attraction.

How this difficult problem can be solved in the most satisfactory way, we propose to investigate in the book dealing with the theory of war. In any case this definition of the conception of war becomes for us the first ray of light that falls upon the foundations of theory, and will for the first time separate its main features and enable us to distinguish them.

The foregoing is Chapter I
of von Clausewitz' ON WAR.

Thomas Robert Malthus

1766–1834

Thomas Malthus was born in Surrey, England, in 1766. He was educated at home until he went to Jesus College, Cambridge, where he was elected to a fellowship in 1793. He took orders in 1797 and was appointed curate at Albury, in Surrey.

Soon afterward, Malthus' famous essay on population was published. It grew out of an argument between the young man and his father, a man of liberal opinions who had been a friend of Rousseau. Daniel Malthus believed with Rousseau, William Godwin, Condorcet, and other proponents of the "perfectibility of man" that man was essentially good and capable of creating an ideal society. Young Malthus argued, on the contrary, that even if man were essentially good and capable of creating such a society, it would contain within it the seeds of its own destruction. An "ideal" society would bring about population growth beyond any conceivable means of feeding it. His father persuaded him to publish his ideas and in 1798 appeared *An Essay on the Principle of Population as It Affects the Future Improvement of Society with Remarks on the Speculations of Mr. Godwin, M. Condorcet and Other Writers.*

In 1803 Malthus published an enlarged and considerably altered version of his essay, heavily larded with facts and figures to prove his thesis. Other editions appeared, the sixth and last being published in 1826. In 1805 Malthus, who had married and thus been forced to

---

Notes from the artist: "Malthus and illustrations based upon the quotation from An Essay on the Principle of Population. *. . . Above, subsistence: peasants of the fifteenth century harvesting and milling grain; below, the population 'explosion': the infamous Dorothie, who was believed in the thirteenth century to have given birth to thirty-five children!"*

Population, when unchecked, increases in a geometrical ratio. Subsistence only increases in an arithmetical ratio.

malthus

give up his Cambridge fellowship, was made Professor of Modern History and Political Economy at East India College, Haileybury. There he remained for the rest of his life, teaching and writing books in economic history and theory. Among them were: *Observations of the Effect of the Corn Laws, An Inquiry into the Nature and Progress of Rent*, and *Principles of Political Economy*. He died on December 23, 1834.

The publication of Malthus' first essay on population, from which the following selection is taken, raised a storm in England. Godwin, Coleridge, and Hazlitt, in particular, wrote blistering attacks on his theory. But the Prime Minister, William Pitt, was so affected by Malthus' argument that he dropped a proposed Poor Law Bill that would have allowed relief to be paid to families in proportion to their size, since this would obviously stimulate the growth of population.

The question of the growth of population was not new in Malthus' time, any more than it is in our own. Plato and Aristotle had long before warned of overpopulated states. In the eighteenth century Hume, Adam Smith, and Benjamin Franklin had all written about the dangers of surplus population. Why then did Malthus' book produce such a sensation? Malthus developed the idea and made spectacular applications. Pitt's Poor Law, he said, possessed the "great and radical defect of all systems of the kind, that of tending to increase population without increasing the means for its support." That the young parson went on to recommend that parish support for the destitute be withdrawn altogether was shocking. Were the many thousands who then lived at the expense of the parishes to be left to starve?

Malthus argued that population tends to increase in the geometric ratio of 1, 2, 4, 8, 16, etc., whereas the food supply increases, at best, only in the arithmetic ratio of 1, 2, 3, 4, 5, etc. The attraction between the sexes, he pointed out, is universal. Almost any man will raise a family if he can and so will his children. Thus in new countries such as the United States (of 1798), where the food supply is ample and there is a big frontier, population had doubled itself in twenty-five years. Malthus admitted that this increase was partly due to immigration. Yet he insisted that prosperity itself would bring a glut of population, which no improvement of agriculture could ever accommodate. In later editions of his *Essay*, he amassed population statistics and attempted to prove his point inductively, but he no longer insisted on his arbitrary ratios.

The inevitable increase of population, Malthus held, can be countered in two ways. It can be eliminated by wars, famine, and disease, or prevented by vice and moral restraint, *i.e.*, late marriages and abstinence. Since Malthus was opposed to "vice," *i.e.*, birth control, and had little faith in self-restraint, his outlook tended to be pessimistic. The main curb on population would continue to be wars, famine, and disease.

If we consider the "population explosion" today, it would seem that Malthus was right. The population of the world is now estimated at over three billion, and it is said to be increasing at a rate of nearly two per cent yearly. In some parts of the world, the increase is even greater. It is approaching the rate which Malthus predicted when he said that population, under ideal conditions, would double every twenty-five years. The overproduction of human beings has thus become a crucial problem. Even Malthus' most ardent opponents admit that something must be done to cope with the teeming new millions.

The opponents of Malthus advance two remedies. First, they contend that the food resources of the earth are far from being exhausted, and that technology is in its infancy. Vast areas of the earth are not cultivated at present, and many plants rich in food values are neglected. Famines have occurred in the midst of plenty —plenty of plants which, like common grass and seaweed, are highly nutritious, requiring only proper processing. And if the resources of the earth should fail, there are an infinite number of meals to be extracted from the air.

The second remedy advocated is birth control. That this method is feasible has been demonstrated in a number of highly civilized nations. For twenty-five years (1841–66), the population of France remained practically the same, though the standard of living was on the upgrade.

Though few agree with Malthus' reluctant remedy of wars, famine, and disease, he certainly set us all to thinking. And the thinking is not always easy. For example, should people in rich countries urge family limitation in poor overcrowded countries, but not in their own? Another question raised by Malthus is whether progress in agriculture and technology can go on indefinitely or whether there is something in the human situation which prevents it. These are questions which we cannot ignore today.

The Principle of Population
from *Population: The First Essay*

CHAPTER I

The great and unlooked for discoveries that have taken place of late years in natural philosophy, the increasing diffusion of general knowledge from the extension of the art of printing, the ardent and unshackled spirit of inquiry that prevails throughout the lettered and even unlettered world, the new and extraordinary lights that have been thrown on political subjects, which dazzle and astonish the understanding, and particularly that tremendous phenomenon in the political horizon, the French revolution, which, like a blazing comet, seems destined either to inspire with fresh life and vigour or to scorch up and destroy the shrinking inhabitants of the earth, have all concurred to lead many able men into the opinion that we were touching on a period big with the most important changes, changes that would in some measure be decisive of the future fate of mankind.

It has been said that the great question is now at issue, whether man shall henceforth start forwards with accelerated velocity towards illimitable and hitherto unconceived improvement, or be condemned to a perpetual oscillation between happiness and misery, and after every effort remain still at an immeasurable distance from the wished-for goal.

Yet, anxiously as every friend of mankind must look forwards to the termination of this painful suspense, and eagerly as the inquiring mind would hail every ray of light that might assist its view into futurity, it is much to be lamented that the writers on each side of this momentous question still keep far aloof from each other. Their mutual arguments do not meet with a candid examination. The question is not brought to rest on fewer points, and even in theory scarcely seems to be approaching to a decision.

The advocate for the present order of things is apt to treat the sect of speculative philosophers either as a set of artful and designing knaves who preach up ardent benevolence and draw captivating pictures of a happier state of society only the better to enable them to destroy the present establishments and to forward their own deep-laid schemes of ambition, or as wild and mad-headed enthusiasts whose silly speculations and absurd paradoxes are not worthy the attention of any reasonable man.

The advocate for the perfectibility of man, and of society, retorts on the defender of establishments a more than equal contempt. He brands him as the slave of the most miserable and narrow prejudices, or as the defender of the abuses of civil society, only because he profits by them. He paints him either as a character who prostitutes his understanding to his interest, or as one whose powers of mind are not of a size to grasp anything great and noble, who cannot see above five yards before him, and who must therefore be utterly unable to take in the views of the enlightened benefactor of mankind.

In this unamicable contest the cause of truth cannot but suffer. The really good arguments on each side of the question are not allowed to have their proper weight. Each pursues his own theory, little solicitous to correct or improve it by an attention to what is advanced by his opponents.

The friend of the present order of things condemns all political speculations in the gross. He will not even condescend to examine the grounds from which the perfectibility of society is inferred. Much less will he give himself the trouble in a fair and candid manner to attempt an exposition of their fallacy.

The speculative philosopher equally offends against the cause of truth. With eyes fixed on a happier state of society, the blessings of which he paints in the most captivating colours, he allows himself to indulge in the most bitter invectives against every present establishment, without applying his talents to consider the best and safest means of removing abuses and without seeming to be aware of the tremendous obstacles that threaten, even in theory, to oppose the progress of man towards perfection.

It is an acknowledged truth in philosophy that a just theory will always be confirmed by experiment. Yet so much friction and so many minute circumstances occur in practice, which it is next to impossible for the most enlarged and penetrating mind to foresee, that on few subjects can any theory be pronounced just that has not stood the test of experience. But an untried theory cannot fairly be advanced as probable, much less as just till all the arguments against it have been maturely weighed and clearly and consistently refuted.

I have read some of the speculations on the perfectibility of man and of society with great pleasure. I have been warmed and delighted with the enchanting picture which they hold forth. I ardently wish for such happy improvements. But I see great, and, to my understanding, unconquerable difficulties in the way to them. These difficulties it is my present purpose to state, declaring, at the same time, that so far from exulting in them, as a cause of triumph over the friends of innovation, nothing would give me greater pleasure than to see them completely removed.

The most important argument that I shall adduce is certainly not new. The principles on which it depends have been explained in part by Hume, and more at large by Dr. Adam Smith. It has been advanced and applied to the present subject, though not with its proper weight, or in the most forcible point of view, by Mr. Wallace, and it may probably have been stated by many writers that I have never met with. I should certainly therefore not think of advancing it again, though I mean to place it in a point of view in some degree different from any that I have hitherto seen, if it had ever been fairly and satisfactorily answered.

The cause of this neglect on the part of the advocates for the perfectibility of mankind is not easily accounted for. I cannot doubt the talents of such men as Godwin and Condorcet. I am unwilling to doubt their candour. To my understanding, and probably to that of most others, the difficulty appears insurmountable. Yet these men of acknowledged ability and penetration scarcely deign to notice it, and hold on their course in such speculations, with unabated ardour and undiminished confidence. I have certainly no right to say that they purposely shut their eyes to such arguments. I ought rather to doubt the validity of them, when neglected by such men, however forcibly their truth may strike my own mind. Yet in this respect it must be acknowledged that we are all of us too prone to err. If I saw a glass of wine repeatedly presented to a man, and he took no notice of it, I should be apt to think that he was blind or uncivil. A juster philosophy might teach me rather to think that my eyes deceived me and that the offer was not really what I conceived it to be.

In entering upon the argument I must premise that I put out of the question, at present, all mere conjectures, that is, all suppositions, the probable realization of which cannot be inferred upon any just philosophical grounds. A writer may tell me that he thinks man will ultimately become an ostrich. I cannot properly contradict him. But before he can expect to bring any reasonable person over to his opinion, he ought to show that the necks of mankind have been gradually elongating, that the lips have grown harder and more prominent, that the legs and feet are daily altering their shape, and that the hair is beginning to change into stubs of feathers. And till the probability of so wonderful a conversion can be shown, it is surely lost time and lost eloquence to expatiate on the happiness of man in such a state; to describe his powers, both of running and flying, to paint him in a condition where all narrow luxuries would be contemned, where he would be employed only in collecting the necessaries of life, and where, consequently, each man's share of labour would be light, and his portion of leisure ample.

I think I may fairly make two postulata.

First, that food is necessary to the existence of man.

Secondly, that the passion between the sexes is necessary and will remain nearly in its present state.

These two laws, ever since we have had any knowledge of mankind, appear to have been fixed laws of our nature, and, as we have not hitherto seen any alteration in them, we have no right to conclude that they will ever cease to be what they now are without an immediate act of power in that Being who first arranged the system of the universe, and for the advantage of his creatures, still executes, according to fixed laws, all its various operations.

I do not know that any writer has supposed that on this earth man will ultimately be able to live without food. But Mr. Godwin has conjectured that the passion between the sexes may in time be extinguished. As, however, he calls this part of his work a deviation into the land of conjecture, I will not dwell longer upon it at present than to say that the best arguments for the perfectibility of man are drawn from a contemplation of the great progress that he has already made from the savage state and the difficulty of saying where he is to stop. But towards the extinction of the passion between the sexes, no progress whatever has hitherto been made. It appears to exist in as much force at present as it did two thousand or four thousand years ago. There are individual exceptions now as there always have been. But, as these exceptions do not appear to increase in number, it would surely be a very unphilosophical mode of arguing to infer merely from the existence of an exception that the exception would, in time, become the rule, and the rule the exception.

Assuming then, my postulata as granted, I say that the power of population is indefinitely greater than the power in the earth to produce subsistence for man.

Population, when unchecked, increases in a geometrical ratio. Subsistence increases only in an arithmetical ratio. A slight acquaintance with numbers will show the immensity of the first power in comparison of the second.

By that law of our nature which makes food necessary to the life of man, the effects of these two unequal powers must be kept equal.

This implies a strong and constantly operating check on population from the difficulty of subsistence. This difficulty must fall somewhere and must necessarily be severely felt by a large portion of mankind.

Through the animal and vegetable kingdoms, nature has scattered the seeds of life abroad with the most profuse and liberal hand. She has been comparatively sparing in the room and the nourishment necessary to rear them. The germs of existence contained in this spot of earth, with ample food, and ample room to expand in, would fill millions of worlds in the course of a few thousand years. Necessity, that imperious all-pervading law of nature, restrains them within the prescribed bounds. The race of plants and the race of animals shrink under this great restrictive law. And the race of man cannot, by any efforts of reason, escape from it. Among plants and animals its effects are waste of seed, sickness, and premature death; among mankind, misery and vice. The former, misery, is an absolutely necessary consequence of it. Vice is a highly probable consequence, and we therefore see it abundantly prevail, but it ought not, perhaps, to be called an absolutely necessary consequence. The ordeal of virtue is to resist all temptation to evil.

This natural inequality of the two powers of population and of production in the earth and that great law of our nature which must constantly keep their effects equal form the great difficulty that to me appears insurmountable in the way to the perfectibility of society. All other arguments are of slight and subordinate consideration in comparison of this. I see no way by which man can escape from the weight of this law, which pervades all animated nature. No fancied equality, no agrarian regulations in their utmost extent, could remove the pressure of it even for a single century. And it appears, therefore, to be decisive against the possible existence of a society all the members of which should live in ease, happiness, and comparative leisure, and feel no anxiety about providing the means of subsistence for themselves and families.

Consequently, if the premises are just, the argument is conclusive against the perfectibility of the mass of mankind.

I have thus sketched the general outline of the argument, but I will examine it more particularly, and I think it will be found that experience, the true source and foundation of all knowledge, invariably confirms its truth.

CHAPTER II

I said that population, when unchecked, increased in a geometrical ratio, and subsistence for man in an arithmetical ratio.

Let us examine whether this position be just.

I think it will be allowed that no state has hitherto existed (at least that we have any account of) where the manners were so pure and simple, and the means of subsistence so abundant, that no check whatever has existed to early marriages among the lower classes, from a fear of not providing well for their families, or among the higher classes, from a fear of lowering their condition in life. Consequently, in no state that we have yet known has the power of population been left to exert itself with perfect freedom.

Whether the law of marriage be instituted or not, the dictate of nature and virtue seems to be an early attachment to one woman. Supposing a liberty of changing in the case of an unfortunate choice, this liberty would not affect population till it arose to a height greatly vicious; and we are now supposing the existence of a society where vice is scarcely known.

In a state therefore of great equality and virtue, where pure and simple manners prevailed, and where the means of subsistence were so abundant that no part of the society could have any fears about providing amply for a family, the power of population being left to exert itself unchecked, the increase of the human species would evidently be much greater than any increase that has been hitherto known.

In the United States of America, where the means of subsistence have been more ample, the manners of the people more pure, and consequently the checks to early marriages fewer than in any of the modern states of Europe, the population has been found to double itself in twenty-five years.

This ratio of increase, though short of the utmost power of population, yet as the result of actual experience, we will take as our rule, and say that population, when unchecked, goes on doubling itself every twenty-five years or increases in a geometrical ratio.

Let us now take any spot of earth, this Island for instance, and see in what ratio the subsistence it affords can be supposed to increase. We will begin with it under its present state of cultivation.

If I allow that by the best possible policy, by breaking up more land and by great encouragements to agriculture, the produce of this Island may be doubled in the first twenty-five years, I think it will be allowing as much as any person can well demand.

In the next twenty-five years, it is impossible to suppose that the produce could be quadrupled. It would be contrary to all our knowledge of the qualities of land. The very utmost that we can conceive is that the increase in the second twenty-five years might equal the present produce. Let us then take this for our rule, though certainly far beyond the truth, and allow that by great exertion the whole produce of the Island might be increased every twenty-five years by a quantity of subsistence equal to what it at present produces. The most enthusiastic speculator cannot suppose a greater increase than this. In a few centuries it would make every acre of land in the Island like a garden.

Yet this ratio of increase is evidently arithmetical.

It may be fairly said, therefore, that the means of subsistence increase in an arithmetical ratio. Let us now bring the effects of these two ratios together.

The population of the Island is computed to be about seven millions, and we will suppose the present produce equal to the support of such a number. In the first twenty-five years the population would be fourteen millions, and the food being also doubled, the means of subsistence would be equal to this increase. In the next twenty-five years the population would be twenty-eight millions, and the means of subsistence only equal to the support of twenty-one millions. In the next period, the population would be fifty-six millions, and the means of subsistence just sufficient for half that number. And at the conclusion of the first century the population would be one hundred and twelve millions and the means of subsistence only equal to the support of thirty-five millions, which would leave a population of seventy-seven millions totally unprovided for.

A great emigration necessarily implies unhappiness of some kind or other in the country that is deserted. For few persons will leave their families, connections, friends, and native land to seek a settlement in untried foreign climes without some strong subsisting causes of uneasiness where they are, or the hope of some great advantages in the place to which they are going.

But to make the argument more general and less interrupted by the partial views of emigration, let us take the whole earth, instead of one spot, and suppose that the restraints to population were universally removed. If the subsistence for man that the earth affords was to be increased every twenty-five years by a quantity equal to what the whole world at present produces, this would allow the power of production in the earth to be absolutely unlimited, and its ratio of increase much greater than we can conceive that any possible exertions of mankind could make it.

Taking the population of the world at any number, a thousand millions, for instance, the human species would increase in the ratio of—1, 2, 4, 8, 16, 32, 64, 128, 256, 512, etc., and subsistence as—1, 2, 3, 4, 5, 6, 7, 8, 9, 10, etc. In two centuries and a quarter, the population would be to the means of subsistence as 512 to 10: in three centuries as 4096 to 13, and in two thousand years the difference would be almost incalculable, though the produce in that time would have increased to an immense extent.

No limits whatever are placed to the productions of the earth; they may increase forever and be greater than any assignable quantity; yet still the power of population being a power of a superior order, the increase of the human species can only be kept commensurate to the increase of the means of subsistence by the constant operation of the strong law of necessity acting as a check upon the greater power.

The effects of this check remain now to be considered.

Among plants and animals the view of the subject is simple. They are all impelled by a powerful instinct to the increase of their species, and this instinct is interrupted by no reasoning or doubts about providing for their offspring. Wherever therefore there is liberty, the power of increase is exerted, and the superabundant effects are repressed afterwards by want of room and nourishment, which is common to animals and plants, and among animals, by becoming the prey of others.

The effects of this check on man are more complicated. Impelled to the increase of his species by an equally powerful instinct, reason interrupts his career and asks him whether he may not bring beings into the world, for whom he cannot provide the means of subsistence. In a state of equality, this would be the simple question. In the present state of society, other considerations occur. Will he not lower his rank in life? Will he not subject himself to greater difficulties than he at present feels? Will he not be obliged to labour harder? and if he has a large family, will his utmost exertions enable him to support them? May he not see his offspring in rags and misery, and clamouring for bread that he cannot give them? And may he not be reduced to the grating necessity of forfeiting his independence, and of being obliged to the sparing hand of charity for support?

These considerations are calculated to prevent, and certainly do prevent, a very great number in all civilized nations from pursuing the dictate of nature in an early attachment to one woman. And this restraint almost necessarily, though not absolutely so, produces vice. Yet in all societies, even those that are most vicious, the tendency to a virtuous attachment is so strong that there is a constant effort towards an increase of population. This constant effort as constantly tends to subject the lower classes of the society to distress and to prevent any great permanent amelioration of their condition.

The way in which these effects are produced seems to be this.

We will suppose the means of subsistence in any country just equal to the easy support of its inhabitants. The constant effort towards population, which is found to act even in the most vicious societies, increases the number of people before the means of subsistence are increased. The food therefore which before supported seven millions must now be divided among seven millions and a half or eight millions. The poor consequently must live much worse, and many of them be reduced to severe distress. The number of labourers also being above the proportion of the work in the market, the price of labour must tend toward a decrease, while the price of provisions would at the same time tend to rise. The labourer therefore must work harder to earn the same as he did before. During this season of distress, the discouragements to marriage and the difficulty of rearing a family are so great that population is at a stand. In the mean time the cheapness of labour, the plenty of labourers, and the necessity of an increased industry amongst them encourage cultivators to employ more labour upon their land, to turn up fresh soil, and to manure and improve more completely what is already in tillage, till ultimately the means of subsistence become in the same proportion to the population as at the period from which we set out. The situation of the labourer being then again tolerably comfortable, the restraints to population are in some degree loosened, and the same retrograde and progressive movements with respect to happiness are repeated.

This sort of oscillation will not be remarked by superficial observers, and it may be difficult even for the most penetrating mind to calculate its periods. Yet that in all old states some such vibration does exist, though from various transverse causes, in a much less marked, and in a much more irregular manner than I have described it, no reflecting man who considers the subject deeply can well doubt.

Many reasons occur why this oscillation has been less obvious, and less decidedly confirmed by experience, than might naturally be expected.

One principal reason is that the histories of mankind that we possess are histories only of the higher classes. We have but few accounts that can be depended upon of the manners and customs of that part of mankind where these retrograde and progressive movements chiefly take place. A satisfactory history of this kind, of one people, and of one period, would require the constant and minute attention of an observing mind during a long life. Some of the objects of inquiry would be, in what proportion to the number of adults was the number of marriages, to what extent vicious customs prevailed in consequence of the restraints upon matrimony, what was the comparative mortality among the children of the most distressed part of the community and those who lived rather more at their ease, what were the variations in the real price of labour, and what were the observable differences in the state of the lower classes of society with respect to ease and happiness, at different times during a certain period.

Such a history would tend greatly to elucidate the manner in which the constant check upon population acts and would probably prove the existence of the retrograde and progressive movements that have been mentioned, though the times of their vibration must necessarily be rendered irregular from the operation of many interrupting causes, such as the introduction or failure of certain manufactures, a greater or less prevalent spirit of agricultural enterprise, years of plenty, or years of scarcity, wars and pestilence, poor-laws, the invention of processes for shortening labour without the proportional extension of the market for the commodity, and, particularly, the difference between the nominal and real price of labour, a circumstance which has perhaps more than any other contributed to conceal this oscillation from common view.

It very rarely happens that the nominal price of labour universally falls, but we well know that it frequently remains the same, while the nominal price of provisions has been gradually increasing. This is, in effect, a real fall in the price of labour, and during this period the condition of the lower orders of the community must gradually grow worse and worse. But the farmers and capitalists are growing rich from the real cheapness of labour. Their increased capitals enable them to employ a greater number of men. Work therefore may be plentiful, and the price of labour would consequently rise. But the want of freedom in the market of labour, which occurs more or less in all communities, either from parish laws or the more general cause of the facility of combination among the rich, and its difficulty among the poor, operates to prevent the price of labour from rising at the natural period, and keeps it down some time longer; perhaps, till a year of scarcity, when the clamour is too loud, and the necessity too apparent to be resisted.

The true cause of the advance in the price of labour is thus concealed, and the rich affect to grant it as an act of compassion and favour to the poor in consideration of a year of scarcity, and, when plenty returns, indulge themselves in the most unreasonable of all complaints, that the price does not again fall, when a little reflection would show them that it must have risen long before but from an unjust conspiracy of their own.

But though the rich by unfair combinations contribute frequently to prolong a season of distress among the poor, yet no possible form of society could prevent the almost constant action of misery upon a great part of mankind, if in a state of inequality, and upon all, if all were equal.

The theory on which the truth of this position depends appears to me so extremely clear that I feel at a loss to conjecture what part of it can be denied.

That population cannot increase without the means of subsistence is a proposition so evident that it needs no illustration.

That population does invariably increase where there are the means of subsistence, the history of every people that have ever existed will abundantly prove.

And that the superior power of population cannot be checked without producing misery or vice, the ample portion of these too bitter ingredients in the cup of human life and the continuance of the physical causes that seem to have produced them bear too convincing a testimony.

But in order more fully to ascertain the validity of these three propositions, let us examine the different states in which mankind have been known to exist. Even a cursory review will, I think, be sufficient to convince us that these propositions are incontrovertible truths.

CHAPTER III

In the rudest state of mankind, in which hunting is the principal occupation, and the only mode of acquiring food, the means of subsistence being scattered over a large extent of territory, the comparative population must necessarily be thin. It is said that the passion between the sexes is less ardent among the North American Indians than among any other race of men. Yet notwithstanding this apathy, the effort towards population, even in this people, seems to be always greater than the means to support it. This appears from the comparatively rapid population that takes place whenever any of the tribes happen to settle in some fertile spot and to draw nourishment from more fruitful sources than that of hunting, and it has been frequently remarked that when an Indian family has taken up its abode near any European settlement and adopted a more easy and civilized mode of life, that one woman has reared five or six or more children, though in the savage state it rarely happens that above one or two in a family grow up to maturity. The same observation has been made with regard to the Hottentots near the Cape. These facts prove the superior power of population to the means of subsistence in nations of hunters, and that this power always shows itself the moment it is left to act with freedom.

It remains to inquire whether this power can be checked, and its effects kept equal to the means of subsistence, without vice or misery.

The North American Indians, considered as a people, cannot justly be called free and equal. In all the accounts we have of them, and, indeed, of most other savage nations, the women are represented as much more completely in a state of slavery to the men than the poor are to the rich in civilized countries. One half the nation appears to act as Helots to the other half, and the misery that checks population falls chiefly, as it always must do, upon that part whose condition is lowest in the scale of society. The infancy of man in the simplest state requires considerable attention, but this necessary attention the women cannot give, condemned as they are to the inconveniences and hardships of frequent change of place and to the constant and unremitting drudgery of preparing every thing for the reception of their tyrannic lords. These exertions, sometimes during pregnancy or with children at their backs, must occasion frequent miscarriages, and prevent any but the most robust infants from growing to maturity. Add to these hardships of the women, the constant war that prevails among savages, and the necessity which they frequently labour under of exposing their aged and helpless parents, and of thus violating the first feelings of nature, and the picture will not appear very free from the blot of misery. In estimating the happiness of a savage nation, we must not fix our eyes only on the warrior in the prime of life: he is one of a hundred: he is the gentleman, the man of fortune, the chances have been in his favour; and many efforts have failed ere this fortunate being was produced, whose guardian genius should preserve him through the numberless dangers with which he would be surrounded from infancy to manhood. The true points of comparison between two nations seem to be the ranks in each which appear nearest to answer to each other. And in this view, I should compare the warriors in the prime of life with the gentlemen, and the women, children, and aged, with the lower classes of the community in civilized states.

May we not then fairly infer from this short review, or rather, from the accounts that may be referred to of nations of hunters, that their population is thin from the scarcity of food, that it would immediately increase if food was in greater plenty, and that, putting vice out of the question among savages, misery is the check that represses the superior power of population and keeps its effects equal to the means of subsistence. Actual observation and experience tell us that this check, with a few local and temporary exceptions, is constantly acting now upon all savage nations, and the theory indicates that it probably acted with nearly equal strength a thousand years ago, and it may not be much greater a thousand years hence.

Of the manners and habits that prevail among nations of shepherds, the next state of mankind, we are even more ignorant than of the savage state. But that these nations could not escape the general lot of misery arising from the want of subsistence, Europe, and all the fairest countries in the world, bear ample testimony. Want was the goad that drove the Scythian shepherds from their native haunts, like so many famished wolves in search of prey. Set in motion by this all powerful cause, clouds of Barbarians seemed to collect from all points of the northern hemisphere. Gathering fresh darkness and terror as they rolled on, the congregated bodies at length obscured the sun of Italy and sank the whole world in universal night. These tremendous effects, so long and so deeply felt throughout the fairest portions of the earth, may be traced to the simple cause of the superior power of population, to the means of subsistence.

It is well known that a country in pasture cannot support so many inhabitants as a country in tillage, but what renders nations of shepherds so formidable is the power which they possess of moving all together and the necessity they frequently feel of exerting this power in search of fresh pasture for their herds. A tribe that was rich in cattle had an immediate plenty of food. Even the parent stock might be devoured in a case of absolute necessity. The women lived in greater ease than among nations of hunters. The men bold in their united strength and confiding in their power of procuring pasture for their cattle by change of place, felt, probably, but few fears about providing for a family. These combined causes soon produced their natural and invariable effect on extended population. A more frequent and rapid change of place became then necessary. A wider and more extensive territory was successively occupied. A broader desolation extended all around them. Want pinched the less fortunate members of the society, and, at length, the impossibility of supporting such a number together became too evident to be resisted. Young scions were then pushed out from the parent-stock and instructed to explore fresh regions and to gain happier seats for themselves by their swords. "The world was all before them where to chuse." Restless from present distress, flushed with the hope of fairer prospects, and animated with the spirit of hardy enterprise, these daring adventurers were likely to become formidable adversaries to all who opposed them. The peaceful inhabitants of the countries on which they rushed could not long withstand the energy of men acting under such powerful motives of exertion. And when they fell in with any tribes like their own, the contest was a struggle for existence, and they fought with a desperate courage, inspired by the reflection that death was the punishment of defeat and life the prize of victory.

In these savage contests many tribes must have been utterly exterminated. Some, probably, perished by hardship and famine. Others, whose leading star had given them a happier direction, became great and powerful tribes, and, in their turns, sent off fresh adventurers in search of still more fertile seats. The prodigious waste of human life occasioned by this perpetual struggle for room and food was more than supplied by the mighty power of population, acting, in some degree, unshackled from the constant habit of emigration. The tribes that migrated towards the South, though they won these more fruitful regions by continual battles, rapidly increased in number and power from the increased means of subsistence. Till at length, the whole territory, from the confines of China to the shores of the Baltic, was peopled by a various race of Barbarians, brave, robust, and enterprising, inured to hardship, and delighting in war. Some tribes maintained their independence. Others ranged themselves under the standard of some barbaric chieftain who led them to victory after victory, and, what was of more importance, to regions abounding in corn, wine, and oil, the long wished-for consummation, and great reward of their labours. An Alaric, an Attila, or a Genghis Khan, and the chiefs around them, might fight for glory, for the fame of extensive conquests, but the true cause that set in motion the great tide of northern emigration, and that continued to propel it till it rolled at different periods against China, Persia, Italy, and even Egypt, was a scarcity of food, a population extended beyond the means of supporting it.

The absolute population at any one period, in proportion to the extent of territory, could never be great, on account of the unproductive nature of some of the regions occupied; but there appears to have been a most rapid succession of human beings, and as fast as some were mowed down by the scythe of war or of famine, others rose in increased numbers to supply their place. Among these bold and improvident Barbarians, population was probably but little checked, as in modern states, from a fear of future difficulties. A prevailing hope of bettering their condition by change of place, a constant expectation of plunder, a power, even if distressed, of selling their children as slaves, added to the natural careless-ness of the barbaric character, all conspired to raise a population which remained to be repressed afterwards by famine or war.

Where there is any inequality of conditions, and among nations of shepherds this soon takes place, the distress arising from a scarcity of pro-visions must fall hardest upon the least fortunate members of the society. This distress also must frequently have been felt by the women, exposed to casual plunder in the absence of their husbands, and subject to con-tinual disappointments in their expected return.

But without knowing enough of the minute and intimate history of these people to point out precisely on what part the distress for want of food chiefly fell, and to what extent it was generally felt, I think we may fairly say, from all the accounts that we have of nations of shepherds, that population invariably increased among them whenever, by emigration or any other cause, the means of subsistence were increased, and that a further population was checked and the actual population kept equal to the means of subsistence by misery and vice.

For, independently of any vicious customs that might have prevailed amongst them with regard to women, which always operate as checks to population, it must be acknowledged I think, that the commission of war is vice, and the effect of it misery, and none can doubt the misery of want of food.

CHAPTER IV

In examining the next state of mankind with relation to the question before us, the state of mixed pasture and tillage, in which with some variation in the proportions the most civilized nations must always re-main, we shall be assisted in our review by what we daily see around us, by actual experience, by facts that come within the scope of every man's observation.

Notwithstanding the exaggerations of some old historians, there can remain no doubt in the mind of any thinking man that the population of the principal countries of Europe, France, England, Germany, Russia, Poland, Sweden, and Denmark is much greater than ever it was in former times. The obvious reason of these exaggerations is the formidable aspect that even a thinly peopled nation must have, when collected together and moving all at once in search of fresh seats. If to this tremendous appearance be added a succession at certain intervals of similar emigrations, we shall not be much surprised that the fears of the timid nations of the South represented the North as a region absolutely swarming with human beings. A nearer and juster view of the subject at present enables us to see that the inference was as absurd as if a man in this country, who was continually meeting on the road drove of cattle from Wales and the North, was immediately to conclude that these countries were the most productive of all the parts of the kingdom.

The reason that the greater part of Europe is more populous now than it was in former times is that the industry of the inhabitants has made these countries produce a greater quantity of human subsistence. For I conceive that it may be laid down as a position not to be controverted that, taking a sufficient extent of territory to include within it exportation and importation, and allowing some variation for the prevalence of luxury, or of frugal habits, that population constantly bears a regular proportion to the food that the earth is made to produce. In the controversy concerning the populousness of ancient and modern nations, could it be clearly ascertained that the average produce of the countries in question, taken altogether, is greater now than it was in the times of Julius Caesar, the dispute would be at once determined.

When we are assured that China is the most fertile country in the world, that almost all the land is in tillage, and that a great part of it bears two crops every year, and further, that the people live very frugally, we may infer with certainty that the population must be immense, without busying ourselves in inquiries into the manners and habits of the lower classes and the encouragements to early marriages. But these inquiries are of the utmost importance, and a minute history of the customs of the lower Chinese would be of the greatest use in ascertaining in what manner the checks to a further population operate; what are the vices, and what are the distresses that prevent an increase of numbers beyond the ability of the country to support.

Hume, in his essay on the populousness of ancient and modern nations, when he intermingles, as he says, an inquiry concerning causes with that concerning facts, does not seem to see with his usual penetration how very little some of the causes he alludes to could enable him to form any judgment of the actual population of ancient nations. If any inference can be drawn from them, perhaps it should be directly the reverse of what Hume draws, though I certainly ought to speak with great diffidence in dissenting from a man who of all others on such subjects was the least likely to be deceived by first appearances. If I find that at a certain period in ancient history the encouragements to have a family were great, that early marriages were consequently very prevalent, and that few persons remained single, I should infer with certainty that population was rapidly increasing, but by no means that it was then actually very great; rather, indeed, the contrary, that it was then thin and that there was room and food for a much greater number. On the other hand, if I find that at this period the difficulties attending a family were very great, that, consequently, few early marriages took place, and that a great number of both sexes remained single, I infer with certainty that population was at a stand, and, probably, because the actual population was very great in proportion to the fertility of the land and that there was scarcely room and food for more. The number of footmen, housemaids, and other persons remaining unmarried in modern states Hume allows to be rather an argument against their population. I should rather draw a contrary inference and consider it an argument of their fullness, though this inference is not certain, because there are many thinly inhabited states that are yet stationary in their population. To speak, therefore, correctly, perhaps it may be said that the number of unmarried persons in proportion to the whole number existing at different periods in the same or different states will enable us to judge whether population at these periods was increasing, stationary, or decreasing, but will form no criterion by which we can determine the actual population.

There is, however, a circumstance taken notice of in most of the accounts we have of China that it seems difficult to reconcile with this reasoning. It is said that early marriages very generally prevail through all the ranks of the Chinese. Yet Dr. Adam Smith supposes that population in China is stationary. These two circumstances appear to be irreconcilable. It certainly seems very little probable that the population of China is fast increasing. Every acre of land has been so long in cultivation that we can hardly conceive there is any great yearly addition to the average produce. The fact, perhaps, of the universality of early marriages may not be sufficiently ascertained. If it be supposed true, the only way of accounting for the difficulty, with our present knowledge of the subject, appears to be that the redundant population, necessarily occasioned by the prevalence of early marriages, must be repressed by occasional famines, and by the custom of exposing children, which, in times of distress, is probably more frequent than is ever acknowledged to Europeans. Relative to this barbarous practice, it is difficult to avoid remarking that there cannot be a stronger proof of the distresses that have been felt by mankind for want of food than the existence of a custom that thus violates the most natural principle of the human heart. It appears to have been very general among ancient nations, and certainly tended rather to increase population.

In examining the principal states of modern Europe, we shall find that though they have increased very considerably in population since they were nations of shepherds, yet that at present their progress is but slow, and instead of doubling their numbers every twenty-five years they require three or four hundred years or more for that purpose. Some, indeed, may be absolutely stationary, and others even retrograde. The cause of this slow progress in population cannot be traced to a decay of the passion between the sexes. We have sufficient reason to think that this natural propensity exists still in undiminished vigour. Why then do not its effects appear in a rapid increase of the human species? An intimate view of the state of society in any one country in Europe, which may serve equally for all, will enable us to answer this question, and to say that a foresight of the difficulties attending the rearing of a family acts as a preventive check, and the actual distresses of some of the lower classes, by which they are disabled from giving the proper food and attention to their children, acts as a positive check to the natural increase of population.

England, as one of the most flourishing states of Europe, may be fairly taken for an example, and the observations made will apply with but little variation to any other country where the population increases slowly.

The preventive check appears to operate in some degree through all the ranks of society in England. There are some men, even in the highest rank, who are prevented from marrying by the idea of the expenses that they must retrench, and the fancied pleasures that they must deprive themselves of, on the supposition of having a family. These considerations are certainly trivial, but a preventive foresight of this kind has objects of much greater weight for its contemplation as we go lower.

A man of liberal education, but with an income only just sufficient to enable him to associate in the rank of gentlemen, must feel absolutely certain that if he marries and has a family he shall be obliged, if he mixes at all in society, to rank himself with moderate farmers and the lower class of tradesmen. The woman that a man of education would naturally make the object of his choice would be one brought up in the same tastes and sentiments with himself and used to the familiar intercourse of a society totally different from that to which she must be reduced by marriage. Can a man consent to place the object of his affection in a situation so discordant, probably, to her tastes and inclinations? Two or three steps of descent in society, particularly at this round of the ladder, where education ends and ignorance begins, will not be considered by the generality of people as a fancied and chimerical, but a real and essential evil. If society be held desirable, it surely must be free, equal, and reciprocal society, where benefits are conferred as well as received, and not such as the dependent finds with his patron or the poor with the rich.

These considerations undoubtedly prevent a great number in this rank of life from following the bent of their inclinations in an early attachment. Others, guided either by a stronger passion, or a weaker judgment, break through these restraints, and it would be hard indeed, if the gratification of so delightful a passion as virtuous love, did not, sometimes, more than counterbalance all its attendant evils. But I fear it must be owned that the more general consequences of such marriages are rather calculated to justify than to repress the forebodings of the prudent.

The sons of tradesmen and farmers are exhorted not to marry, and generally find it necessary to pursue this advice till they are settled in some business or farm that may enable them to support a family. These events may not, perhaps, occur till they are far advanced in life. The scarcity of farms is a very general complaint in England. And the competition in every kind of business is so great that it is not possible that all should be successful.

The labourer who earns eighteen pence a day and lives with some degree of comfort as a single man will hesitate a little before he divides that pittance among four or five, which seems to be but just sufficient for one. Harder fare and harder labour he would submit to for the sake of living with the woman that he loves, but he must feel conscious, if he thinks at all, that should he have a large family, and any ill luck whatever, no degree of frugality, no possible exertion of his manual strength could preserve him from the heart-rending sensation of seeing his children starve, or of forfeiting his independence, and being obliged to the parish for their support. The love of independence is a sentiment that surely none would wish to be erased from the breast of man, though the parish law of England, it must be confessed, is a system of all others the most calculated gradually to weaken this sentiment, and in the end may eradicate it completely.

The servants who live in gentlemen's families have restraints that are yet stronger to break through in venturing upon marriage. They possess the necessaries, and even the comforts of life, almost in as great plenty as their masters. Their work is easy and their food luxurious compared with the class of labourers. And their sense of dependence is weakened by the conscious power of changing their masters if they feel themselves offended. Thus comfortably situated at present, what are their prospects in marrying? Without knowledge or capital, either for business or farming, and unused and therefore unable to earn a subsistence by daily labour, their only refuge seems to be a miserable ale-house, which certainly offers no very enchanting prospect of a happy ending to their lives. By much the greater part, therefore, deterred by this uninviting view of their future situation, content themselves with remaining single where they are.

If this sketch of the state of society in England be near the truth, and I do not conceive that it is exaggerated, it will be allowed that the preventive check to population in this country operates, though with varied force, through all the classes of the community. The same observation will hold true with regard to all old states. The effects, indeed, of these restraints upon marriage are but too conspicuous in the consequent vices that are produced in almost every part of the world, vices that are continually involving both sexes in inextricable unhappiness.

CHAPTER V

The positive check to population, by which I mean the check that represses an increase which is already begun, is confined chiefly, though not perhaps solely, to the lowest orders of society. This check is not so obvious to common view as the other I have mentioned, and to prove distinctly the force and extent of its operation would require, perhaps, more data than we are in possession of. But I believe it has been very generally remarked by those who have attended to bills of mortality that of the number of children who die annually, much too great a proportion belongs to those who may be supposed unable to give their offspring proper food and attention, exposed as they are occasionally to severe distress and confined, perhaps, to unwholesome habitations and hard labour. This mortality among the children of the poor has been constantly taken notice of in all towns. It certainly does not prevail in an equal degree in the country, but the subject has not hitherto received sufficient attention to enable any one to say that there are not more deaths in proportion among the children of the poor, even in the country, than among those of the middling and higher classes. Indeed, it seems difficult to suppose that a labourer's wife who has six children, and who is sometimes in absolute want of bread, should be able always to give them the food and attention necessary to support life. The sons and daughters of peasants will not be found such rosy cherubs in real life as they are described to be in romances. It cannot fail to be remarked by those who live much in the country that the sons of labourers are very apt to be stunted in their growth, and are a long while arriving at maturity. Boys that you would guess to be fourteen or fifteen are, upon inquiry, frequently found to be eighteen or nineteen. And the lads who drive plough, which must certainly be a healthy exercise, are very rarely seen with any appearance of calves to their legs, a circumstance which can only be attributed to a want either of proper or of sufficient nourishment.

To remedy the frequent distresses of the common people, the poor-laws of England have been instituted; but it is to be feared that though they may have alleviated a little the intensity of individual misfortune, they have spread the general evil over a much larger surface. It is a subject often started in conversation and mentioned always as a matter of great surprise that notwithstanding the immense sum that is annually collected for the poor in England, there is still so much distress among them. Some think that the money must be embezzled, others that the church-wardens and overseers consume the greater part of it in dinners. All agree that somehow or other it must be very ill managed. In short, the fact that nearly three millions are collected annually for the poor and yet that their distresses are not removed is the subject of continual astonishment. But a man who sees a little below the surface of things would be very much more astonished if the fact were otherwise than it is observed to be, or even if a collection universally of eighteen shillings in the pound instead of four were materially to alter it. I will state a case which I hope will elucidate my meaning.

Suppose that by a subscription of the rich the eighteen pence a day which men earn now was made up five shillings; it might be imagined, perhaps, that they would then be able to live comfortably and have a piece of meat every day for their dinners. But this would be a very false conclusion. The transfer of three shillings and sixpence a day to every labourer would not increase the quantity of meat in the country. There is not at present enough for all to have a decent share. What would then be the consequence? The competition among the buyers in the market of meat would rapidly raise the price from six pence or seven pence, to two or three shillings in the pound, and the commodity would not be divided among many more than it is at present. When an article is scarce, and cannot be distributed to all, he that can show the most valid patent, that is, he that offers most money, becomes the possessor. If we can suppose the competition among the buyers of meat to continue long enough for a greater number of cattle to be reared annually, this could only be done at the expense of the corn, which would be a very disadvantageous exchange, for it is well known that the country could not then support the same population, and when subsistence is scarce in proportion to the number of people, it is of little consequence whether the lowest members of the society possess eighteen pence or five shillings. They must at all events be reduced to live upon the hardest fare and in the smallest quantity.

It will be said, perhaps, that the increased number of purchasers in every article would give a spur to productive industry and that the whole produce of the island would be increased. This might in some degree be the case. But the spur that these fancied riches would give to population would more than counterbalance it, and the increased produce would be to be divided among a more than proportionably increased number of people. All this time I am supposing that the same quantity of work would be done as before. But this would not really take place. The receipt of five shillings a day, instead of eighteen pence, would make every man fancy himself comparatively rich and able to indulge himself in many hours or days of leisure. This would give a strong and immediate check to productive industry, and in a short time, not only the nation would be poorer, but the lower classes themselves would be much more distressed than when they received only eighteen pence a day.

A collection from the rich of eighteen shillings in the pound, even if distributed in the most judicious manner, would have a little the same effect as that resulting from the supposition I have just made, and no possible contributions of sacrifices of the rich, particularly in money, could for any time prevent the recurrence of distress among the lower members of society whoever they were. Great changes might, indeed, be made. The rich might become poor, and some of the poor rich, but a part of the society must necessarily feel a difficulty of living, and this difficulty will naturally fall on the least fortunate members.

It may at first appear strange, but I believe it is true, that I cannot by means of money raise a poor man and enable him to live much better than he did before, without proportionably depressing others in the same class. If I retrench the quantity of food consumed in my house, and give him what I have cut off, I then benefit him, without depressing any but myself and family, who, perhaps, may be well able to bear it. If I turn up a piece of uncultivated land and give him the produce, I then benefit both him and all the members of the society, because what he before consumed is thrown into the common stock, and probably some of the new produce with it. But if I only give him money, supposing the produce of the country to remain the same, I give him a title to a larger share of that produce than formerly, which share he cannot receive without diminishing the shares of others. It is evident that this effect, in individual instances, must be so small as to be totally imperceptible; but still it must exist, as many other effects do, which like some of the insects that people the air, elude our grosser perceptions.

Supposing the quantity of food in any country to remain the same for many years together, it is evident that this food must be divided according to the value of each man's patent,[1] or the sum of money that he can afford to spend in this commodity so universally in request. It is a demonstrative truth, therefore, that the patents of one set of men could not be increased in value without diminishing the value of the patents of some other set of men. If the rich were to subscribe and give five shillings a day to five hundred thousand men without retrenching their own tables, no doubt can exist, that as these men would naturally live more at their ease and consume a greater quantity of provisions, there would be less food remaining to divide among the rest, and consequently each man's patent would be diminished in value or the same number of pieces of silver would purchase a smaller quantity of subsistence.

An increase of population without a proportional increase of food will evidently have the same effect in lowering the value of each man's patent. The food must necessarily be distributed in smaller quantities, and consequently a day's labour will purchase a smaller quantity of provisions. An increase in the price of provisions would arise either from an increase of population faster than the means of subsistence, or from a different distribution of the money of the society. The food of a country that has been long occupied, if it be increasing, increases slowly and regularly and cannot be made to answer any sudden demands, but variations in the distribution of the money of a society are not unfrequently occurring, and are undoubtedly among the causes that occasion

---

1. Mr. Godwin calls the wealth that a man receives from his ancestors a mouldy patent. It may, I think, very properly be termed a patent, but I hardly see the propriety of calling it a mouldy one, as it is an article in such constant use.

the continual variations which we observe in the price of provisions.

The poor-laws of England tend to depress the general condition of the poor in these two ways. Their first obvious tendency is to increase population without increasing the food for its support. A poor man may marry with little or no prospect of being able to support a family in independence. They may be said therefore in some measure to create the poor which they maintain, and as the provisions of the country must, in consequence of the increased population, be distributed to every man in smaller proportions, it is evident that the labour of those who are not supported by parish assistance will purchase a smaller quantity of provisions than before and consequently more of them must be driven to ask for support.

Secondly, the quantity of provisions consumed in workhouses upon a part of the society that cannot in general be considered as the most valuable part diminishes the shares that would otherwise belong to more industrious and more worthy members, and thus in the same manner forces more to become dependent. If the poor in the workhouses were to live better than they now do, this new distribution of the money of the society would tend more conspicuously to depress the condition of those out of the workhouses by occasioning a rise in the price of provisions.

Fortunately for England, a spirit of independence still remains among the peasantry. The poor-laws are strongly calculated to eradicate this spirit. They have succeeded in part, but had they succeeded as completely as might have been expected their pernicious tendency would not have been so long concealed.

Hard as it may appear in individual instances, dependent poverty ought to be held disgraceful. Such a stimulus seems to be absolutely necessary to promote the happiness of the great mass of mankind, and every general attempt to weaken this stimulus, however benevolent its apparent intention, will always defeat its own purpose. If men are induced to marry from a prospect of parish provision, with little or no chance of maintaining their families in independence, they are not only unjustly tempted to bring unhappiness and dependence upon themselves and children, but they are tempted, without knowing it, to injure all in the same class with themselves. A labourer who marries without being able to support a family may in some respects be considered as an enemy to all his fellow-labourers.

I feel no doubt whatever that the parish laws of England have contributed to raise the price of provisions and to lower the real price of labour. They have therefore contributed to impoverish that class of people whose only possession is their labour. It is also difficult to suppose that they have not powerfully contributed to generate that carelessness and want of frugality observable among the poor, so contrary to the disposition frequently to be remarked among petty tradesmen and small farmers. The labouring poor, to use a vulgar expression, seem always to live from hand to mouth. Their present wants employ their whole attention, and they seldom think of the future. Even when they have an opportunity of saving they seldom exercise it, but all that is beyond their present necessities goes, generally speaking, to the ale-house. The poor-laws of England may therefore be said to diminish both the power and the will to save among the common people, and thus to weaken one of the strongest incentives to sobriety and industry, and consequently to happiness.

It is a general complaint among master manufacturers that high wages ruin all their workmen, but it is difficult to conceive that these men would not save a part of their high wages for the future support of their families, instead of spending it in drunkenness and dissipation, if they did not rely on parish assistance for support in case of accidents. And that the poor employed in manufactures consider this assistance as a reason why they may spend all the wages they earn and enjoy themselves while they can appears to be evident from the number of families that, upon the failure of any great manufactory, immediately fall upon the parish, when perhaps the wages earned in this manufactory while it flourished were sufficiently above the price of common country labour to have allowed them to save enough for their support till they could find some other channel for their industry.

A man who might not be deterred from going to the ale-house from the consideration that on his death, or sickness, he should leave his wife and family upon the parish might yet hesitate in thus dissipating his earnings if he were assured that, in either of these cases, his family must starve or be left to the support of casual bounty. In China, where the real as well as nominal price of labour is very low, sons are yet obliged by law to support their aged and helpless parents. Whether such a law would be advisable in this country I will not pretend to determine. But it seems at any rate highly improper, by positive institutions, which render dependent poverty so general, to weaken that disgrace, which for the best and most humane reasons ought to attach to it.

The mass of happiness among the common people cannot but be diminished, when one of the strongest checks to idleness and dissipation is thus removed, and when men are thus allured to marry with little or no prospect of being able to maintain a family in independence. Every obstacle in the way of marriage must undoubtedly be considered as a species of unhappiness. But as from the laws of our nature some check to population must exist, it is better that it should be checked from a foresight of the difficulties attending a family and the fear of dependent poverty than that it should be encouraged, only to be repressed afterwards by want and sickness.

It should be remembered always that there is an essential difference between food and those wrought commodities, the raw materials of which are in great plenty. A demand for these last will not fail to create them in as great a quantity as they are wanted. The demand for food has by no means the same creative power. In a country where all the fertile spots have been seized, high offers are necessary to encourage the farmer to lay his dressing on land from which he cannot expect a profitable return for some years. And before the prospect of advantage is sufficiently great to encourage this sort of agricultural enterprise, and while the new produce is rising, great distresses may be suffered from the want of it. The demand for an increased quantity of subsistence is, with few exceptions, constant everywhere, yet we see how slowly it is answered in all those countries that have been long occupied.

The poor-laws of England were undoubtedly instituted for the most benevolent purpose, but there is great reason to think that they have not succeeded in their intention. They certainly mitigate some cases of very severe distress which might otherwise occur, yet the state of the poor who are supported by parishes, considered in all its circumstances, is very far from being free from misery. But one of the principal objections to them is that for this assistance which some of the poor receive, in itself almost a doubtful blessing, the whole class of the common people of England is subjected to a set of grating, inconvenient, and tyrannical laws, totally inconsistent with the genuine spirit of the constitution. The whole business of settlements, even in its present amended state, is utterly contradictory to all ideas of freedom. The parish persecution of men whose families are likely to become chargeable, and of poor women who are near lying-in, is a most disgraceful and disgusting tyranny. And the obstructions continually occasioned in the market of labour by these laws have a constant tendency to add to the difficulties of those who are struggling to support themselves without assistance.

These evils attendant on the poor-laws are in some degree irremediable. If assistance be to be distributed to a certain class of people, a power must be given somewhere of discriminating the proper objects and of managing the concerns of the institutions that are necessary, but any great interference with the affairs of other people is a species of tyranny, and in the common course of things the exercise of this power may be expected to become grating to those who are driven to ask for support. The tyranny of justices, churchwardens, and overseers is a common complaint among the poor, but the fault does not lie so much in these persons, who probably before they were in power were not worse than other people, but in the nature of all such institutions.

The evil is perhaps gone too far to be remedied, but I feel little doubt in my own mind that if the poor-laws had never existed, though there might have been a few more instances of very severe distress, yet that the aggregate mass of happiness among the common people would have been much greater than it is at present.

Mr. Pitt's Poor-bill has the appearance of being framed with benevolent intentions, and the clamour raised against it was in many respects ill directed, and unreasonable. But it must be confessed that it possesses in a high degree the great and radical defect of all systems of the kind, that of tending to increase population without increasing the means for its support, and thus to depress the condition of those that are not supported by parishes, and, consequently, to create more poor.

To remove the wants of the lower classes of society is indeed an arduous task. The truth is that the pressure of distress on this part of a community is an evil so deeply seated that no human ingenuity can reach it. Were I to propose a palliative, and palliatives are all that the nature of the case will admit, it should be, in the first place, the total abolition of all the present parish laws. This would at any rate give liberty and freedom of action to the peasantry of England, which they can hardly be said to possess at present. They would then be able to settle without interruption wherever there was a prospect of a greater plenty of work and a higher price for labour. The market of labour would then be free, and those obstacles removed which, as things are now, often for a considerable time prevent the price from rising according to the demand.

Secondly, premiums might be given for turning up fresh land, and all possible encouragements held out to agriculture above manufactures, and to tillage above grazing. Every endeavour should be used to weaken and destroy all those institutions relating to corporations, apprenticeships, etc., which cause the labours of agriculture to be worse paid than the labours of trade and manufactures. For a country can never produce its proper quantity of food while these distinctions remain in favour of artisans.

Such encouragements to agriculture would tend to furnish the market with an increasing quantity of healthy work, and at the same time, by augmenting the produce of the country, would raise the comparative price of labour and ameliorate the condition of the labourer. Being now in better circumstances, and seeing no prospect of parish assistance, he would be more able, as well as more inclined, to enter into associations for providing against the sickness of himself or family.

Lastly, for cases of extreme distress, county workhouses might be established, supported by rates upon the whole kingdom, and free for persons of all counties, and indeed of all nations. The fare should be hard, and those that were able obliged to work. It would be desirable that they should not be considered as comfortable asylums in all difficulties, but merely as places where severe distress might find some alleviation. A part of these houses might be separated, or others built for a most beneficial purpose, which has not been unfrequently taken notice of, that of providing a place where any person, whether native or foreigner, might do a day's work at all times and receive the market price for it. Many cases would undoubtedly be left for the exertion of individual benevolence.

A plan of this kind, the preliminary of which should be an abolition of all the present parish laws, seems to be the best calculated to increase the mass of happiness among the common people of England. To prevent the recurrence of misery, is, alas! beyond the power of man. In the vain endeavour to attain what in the nature of things is impossible, we now sacrifice not only possible but certain benefits. We tell the common people that if they will submit to a code of tyrannical regulations, they shall never be in want. They do submit to these regulations. They perform their part of the contract, but we do not, nay cannot, perform ours, and thus the poor sacrifice the valuable blessing of liberty and receive nothing that can be called an equivalent in return.

Notwithstanding then the institution of the poor-laws in England, I think it will be allowed that considering the state of the lower classes altogether, both in the towns and in the country, the distresses which they suffer from the want of proper and sufficient food, from hard labour and unwholesome habitations, must operate as a constant check to incipient population.

To these two great checks to population in all long-occupied countries, which I have called the preventive and the positive checks, may be added vicious customs with respect to women, great cities, unwholesome manufactures, luxury, pestilence, and war.

All these checks may be fairly resolved into misery and vice. And that these are the true causes of the slow increase of population in all the states of modern Europe will appear sufficiently evident from the comparatively rapid increase that has invariably taken place whenever these causes have been in any considerable degree removed.

The foregoing consists
of Chapters I–V
of Malthus' POPULATION: THE FIRST ESSAY